ST/ESA/SER.R/126

Department for Economic and Social Information and Policy Analysis
Population Division

International Migration Policies and the Status of Female Migrants

Proceedings of the United Nations
Expert Group Meeting
on International Migration Policies
and the Status of Female Migrants
San Miniato, Italy, 28-31 March 1990

United Nations
New York, 1995

NOTE

The designations employed and the presentation of the material in the present publication do not imply the expression of any opinion whatsoever on the part of the Secretariat of the United Nations concerning the legal status of any country, territory, city or area or of its authorities, or concerning the delimitation of its frontiers or boundaries.

The term "country" as used in the text and tables also refers, as appropriate, to territories or areas.

In some tables, the designations "developed" and "developing" economies are intended for statistical convenience and do not necessarily express a judgement about the stage reached by a particular country or area in the development process.

The views expressed in the report are those of the individual authors and do not imply the expression of any opinion on the part of the United Nations Secretariat.

Papers have been edited and consolidated in accordance with United Nations practice and requirements.

ST/ESA/SER.R/126

UNITED NATIONS PUBLICATION

Sales No. E.95.XIII.10

ISBN 92-1-151281-6

PREFACE

Women are as likely as men to be international migrants and yet their roles and status as such have failed to attract the attention that they deserve from those interested in the evolution of international migration and its implications. In an increasingly interconnected world, where women are becoming better able to make decisions and act upon them, growing numbers are likely to opt for international migration as a means of improving their life chances. It is therefore particularly appropriate to consider how the international migration of women affects and is affected by changes in their status and how international migration policies condition the migration options open to women. In order to address those issues, the Population Division of the Department of International and Economic and Social Affairs,[*] in collaboration with the Facoltà di Economia e Commercio of the University of Pisa and with the financial support of the United Nations Population Fund (UNFPA), convened an Expert Group Meeting on International Migration Policies and the Status of Female Migrants. The Meeting was held in San Miniato, Italy, from 27 to 30 March 1990. Contained in this volume are the report and recommendations of the Meeting as well as a selection of the papers presented to it.

The United Nations acknowledges with appreciation the support provided by Alberto Bonaguidi, Director of the Dipartimento di Statistica e Matematica Applicata all'Economia, Facoltà di Economia e Commercio of the University of Pisa and of Laura Lecchini, Researcher at the Dipartimento di Statistica e Matematica Applicata all'Economia, who coordinated the local organizational aspects of the Meeting and greatly contributed to its success. In addition, full recognition is due to the experts who prepared invited papers and who graciously made the necessary revisions of those papers, as well as to other participants in the Meeting, who contributed significantly and constructively to the deliberations. Lastly, the financial support of UNFPA, which made this publication possible, is gratefully acknowledged.

---

[*]Now the Department for Economic and Social Information and Policy Analysis.

CONTENTS

PART ONE. REPORT AND RECOMMENDATIONS OF THE MEETING

ANNEXES

PART TWO. EXTENT OF FEMALE INTERNATIONAL MIGRATION AND GENERAL DISCUSSION OF ITS IMPACT ON FEMALE STATUS

PART THREE. FEMALE MIGRANTS IN DEVELOPED COUNTRIES

TABLES

No.

Figures

Explanatory notes

Symbols of United Nations documents are composed of capital letters combined with figures.

The following symbols have been used in the tables throughout this report:

Two dots (..) indicate that data are not available or are not separately reported.
An em dash (—) indicates that the amount is nil or negligible.
A hyphen (-) indicates that the item is not applicable.
A minus sign (–) before a number indicates a decrease.
A point (.) is used to indicate decimals.
A slash (/) indicates a crop year or financial year, e.g., 1988/89.
Use of a hyphen (-) between dates representing years (e.g., 1985-1989), signifies the full period involved, including the beginning and end years.

Details and percentages in table do not necessarily add to totals because of rounding.

Reference to "dollars" ($) indicates United States dollars, unless otherwise stated.

The term "billion" signifies a thousand million.

The following abbreviations have been used in this report:

ABS	Australian Bureau of Statistics
BMS	Business migration programme (Australia)
CBS	Centraal Bureau voor de Statistiek (Netherlands)
CNRS	Centre national pour la recherche sociale
CRSS	Community Refugee Resettlement Scheme (Australia)
DFS	Dutch Fertility Survey
DHS	Demographic and Health Survey
DIEA	Department of Immigration and Ethnic Affairs (Australia)
DILGEA	Department of Immigration, Local Government and Ethnic Affairs (Australia)
ECA	Economic Commission for Africa
EC	European Community
ECE	Economic Commission for Europe
ENS	Employer nomination scheme (Australia)
ESCAP	Economic and Social Commission for Asia and the Pacific
FAO	Food and Agriculture Organization of the United Nations
GCC	Gulf Cooperation Council
ICM	Intergovernmental Committee for Migration
IFS	Immigrant Fertility Survey (Netherlands)
ILO	International Labour Organisation
INED	Institut national d'études démographiques (Paris)
INSEE	Institut national de la statistique et des études économiques
IOM	International Organization for Migration
IRCA	Immigration Reform and Control Act (United States of America)
IUD	intrauterine device
IUSSP	International Union for the Scientific Study of Population
MFS	Moroccan Fertility Survey
NCBS	Netherlands Central Bureau of Statistics

NIDI	Netherlands Interuniversity Demographic Institute
OECD	Organisation for Economic Co-operation and Development
OSS	Occupational share scheme (Australia)
RCMW	Reintegration Center for Migrant Workers (Greece)
SMR	standard mortality ratio
SAW	special agricultural workers (United States of America)
SOPEMI	Continuous Reporting System on Migration
TFS	Turkish Fertility Survey
UNESCO	United Nations Educational, Scientific and Cultural Organization
UNFPA	United Nations Population Fund
UNHCR	United Nations High Commissioner for Refugees
UNIDO	United Nations Industrial Development Organization
UNRWA	United Nations Relief and Works Agency for Palestine Refugees in the Near East
WENAE	Women from Ethnic Minorities and Education (Australia)
WFS	World Fertility Survey

THE INTERNATIONAL MIGRATION OF WOMEN: AN OVERVIEW

United Nations Secretariat*

During the twentieth century, international migration has been a means of improving the life chances of millions of people. Because countries experiencing labour shortages have often used migrant workers to meet their labour demand, international migration has traditionally been viewed as a mechanism allowing the redistribution of labour and its economic aspects have been stressed. As a result, international migrants have generally been equated with migrant workers and the analysis of migration, its causes and consequences, has either implicitly or explicitly been based on the view that most, if not all, migrant workers are men. If the migration of women has been acknowledged at all, it has usually been relegated to the consideration of the international movement of "dependants" and more attention has been given to the "women left behind" than to those who have migrated in the company of their husbands or other relatives.

Although efforts to redress the balance in favour of research focusing on women who migrate internationally have been more numerous since 1980, much remains to be done to eliminate the invisibility of women in the international migration field. One such effort was undertaken by the Population Division of the Department of International Economic and Social Affairs of the United Nations Secretariat, which, in collaboration with the Facoltà di Economia e Commercio of the University of Pisa, organized an Expert Group Meeting on International Migration Policies and the Status of Female Migrants, held in San Miniato, Italy, from 27 to 30 March 1990. The Meeting brought together a number of scholars who addressed various issues regarding the impact of international migration policies and the migration process in general on the status of international female migrants. Women were found to participate

in every type of international migration flow, although international migration policies and the status of women in the countries of origin conditioned the sex selectivity of migration. The policies of receiving countries played an important role in determining the position of migrant women in the host society, and their impact on the adaptation and eventual integration of migrant women to the host society was significant. However, migrant women themselves were important agents of change, devising strategies to make the transition between the norms and values of their societies of origin and those of the society of destination. Indeed, in all the cases considered, migrant women were key actors in the migration process, a finding that belies the widespread view that they are mere adjuncts to migrant men. As this overview will show, there are many considerations that make the international migration of women relevant in its own right.

A. INTERNATIONAL FEMALE MIGRANTS: THE INVISIBLE HALF

The invisibility of migrant women often starts and is reinforced by the statistics on international migration commonly available. Indeed, if data on overall international migration are scarce, those relative to the migration of women are even less abundant. So pervasive is the idea that international migrants are mostly men that the sex of migrants is often not recorded at all or, if recorded, the information is not used in preparing tabulations for publication. Consequently, the sex of migrants has to be inferred from the category in which they are admitted, assuming, for instance, that spouses are mostly women or that women constitute most of the migrants in certain occupations, such as nursing, domestic service or entertainment. Lack of information is hardly conducive to a more realistic assessment of women's participation in international migration or of their roles as migrants.

*Population Division of the Department of International Economic and Social Affairs (now the Department for Economic and Social Information and Policy Analysis).

For many countries, censuses represent the main source of information on international migration by sex (United Nations Secretariat, chapter IV in this volume). By defining international migrants as persons born outside the country of enumeration, censuses permit an assessment of the participation of women in lifetime migration. Census information dating from the 1970s and early 1980s indicates that women accounted then for about half of all international migrants in the world or, to be precise, their share of lifetime international migration was 48 per cent. Thus, although the evidence confirms that women are major participants in international migration, it nevertheless indicates also that they are somewhat underrepresented among the international migrant stock. Furthermore, there is considerable variation in the share of women among international migrants enumerated in particular countries. Thus, the percentage of women among the international migrant stock ranged from 24.5 per cent in Bahrain to 69.4 per cent in Nepal (United Nations Secretariat, chapter IV). In three quarters of the countries with information available, women accounted for 51 per cent or less of all international migrants and there was a tendency for women to be better represented among international migrants in developed countries than among those in developing countries. That is, women accounted for slightly over half of all international migrants in developed countries whereas their share among international migrants in developing countries was a low 45.4 per cent.

Among countries that have or have had explicit policies allowing the admission of large numbers of international migrants, women have tended to be underrepresented in those countries that have relied on foreign labour, especially if structured recruitment systems have been used to secure the workers needed. In Europe, for instance, the share of women among the foreign population of countries such as France, Germany or Switzerland has generally remained below 45 per cent. In the labour-importing countries of Western Asia, women also account for very low percentages of the foreign population, even though their participation in labour migration has been increasing. In the Republic of South Africa, a country that has a long history as a labour importer, women accounted for a low 35 per cent of all international migrants in 1985. Since the recruit-

ment efforts of countries admitting migrant workers have mostly targeted men and restrictions have generally been imposed on the admission of immediate relatives of the foreign workers involved, women have had fewer opportunities to migrate legally to labour-importing countries than men. Yet the numbers of female migrants in those countries have been far from trivial and, be it because of the relaxation of family reunification regulations or because increasing numbers of women are being admitted as migrant workers in their own right, their share of the migrant population in those countries has been increasing and will likely continue to do so.

Women have tended to be better represented in countries favouring migration for resettlement. Thus, around 1980 women outnumbered men among the foreign-born populations present in countries such as Canada, Israel or the United States of America. In immigration countries, the sex distribution of immigrants by category of admission indicates that women tend to predominate among immigrants admitted under the various family reunion categories (United Nations Secretariat, chapter IV). One interpretation of such a tendency is that women are more likely than men to be "secondary" migrants, following or joining other migrants rather than initiating migration by themselves. Another is that women, just as men, respond to the opportunities for migration open to them and, to the extent that those opportunities are shaped by prevailing norms and values determining what is appropriate female behaviour within the family or in society at large, their outcome will be mostly a reflection of those norms and values rather than an accurate depiction of individual motivation.

When international migration statistics are derived from administrative records gathered for the purpose of controlling migration, their interpretation regarding the participation of women in different types of migration flows faces similar quandaries. Those gathering information on migration assume that migrant women admitted as spouses of other migrants or of citizens are dependants and that, consequently, there is little need to find more about their socio-economic background, their educational attainment or their labour force participation. The common practice of lumping together women and children in the category of "dependants" is indicative of the lack of consideration that migrant women receive. Unfortunately, all too often, that attitude is shared by researchers and by those in charge of policy formulation.

The growing participation of women in labour migration, though serving to dispel the myth that all migrant workers are men, has not contributed to produce a more realistic or balanced image of migrant women. Indeed, because the evidence available tends to be partial, incomplete or downright biased, it suggests that women who participate in labour migration tend to be selected from the lower rungs of the socio-economic scale, that they usually undertake the most menial or otherwise unappealing jobs, and that, if they migrate at all, it is because of the dire needs of their families. In reality, a more comprehensive assessment of female labour migration would likely show that women from all types of backgrounds and a variety of occupations are involved. Although the data to carry out such an assessment are lacking, it is important to avoid creating yet another misleading stereotype of who migrant women really are. Indeed, the 48 million female international migrants enumerated by censuses are unlikely to be characterized by a single image and especially not by one that stresses their vulnerability or dependency.

As this discussion makes clear, there is much that is unknown about "the other half", that is, about the women who are international migrants. Even establishing the extent of women's participation in international migration is a major step forward, but much remains to be done to characterize female international migrants in all their diversity. A first and necessary step in that direction is to promote the gathering and publication of international migration statistics by sex. As long as statistics keep on hiding women or presenting them in guises that are not far removed from common stereotypes, the true position of women as international migrants will remain misunderstood.

B. THE ROLE OF INTERNATIONAL MIGRATION POLICIES

Through their policies, nation States are major actors in the international migration process. Thus,

any person wishing to become an international migrant must deal with the conditions for entry and stay imposed by potential countries of destination and, in many instances, must also consider those concerning departure from the country of origin. In the case of women, the relevant conditions are often coloured by implicit or explicit assumptions about the status and roles of women both within the family and in society. In labour-exporting countries, for instance, conditions that effectively prevent women from engaging in labour migration have been imposed, ostensibly to protect women from possible exploitation (Abella, chapter XIV; Lim, chapter III). The implicit views underlying such policies are that women are essentially vulnerable and that their respectability is likely to be compromised by the mere fact that they migrate on their own. Thus, some countries only allow women to become migrant workers if they have completed most of their child-bearing life and are thus presumably less likely to suffer from the stigma attached to women working abroad on their own. Press reports about migrant women who are raped or forced into prostitution do little to dispel the view that women must remain at home to be protected by "their" men. There is no denying that the sexual abuse and exploitation of women is a major problem that should be combated in all fronts, but it should not be treated as if it were a problem affecting primarily international female migrants. Furthermore, it must be recognized that women's vulnerability is largely a social construct that is intimately related to the low status of women as reflected by their limited access to resources, their legally dependent position within the family, and their occupational segregation in low-paying jobs that command little prestige.

International migration policies may reinforce some of the factors responsible for the social vulnerability of migrant women. Thus, fearing the loss of market share, the labour-exporting countries in Asia have contributed to the further institutionalization of low wages for "female" jobs by establishing that the minimum standard wages overseas employers must pay may be lower for migrant women than for migrant men. Labour-importing countries, particularly those in which native women are still far from having legal or economic equality with men, have few incentives to promote the legal or economic independence of international female migrants. Consequently, the migration regulations of those countries tend to emphasize the responsibilities of migrants rather than those of the State, and their record regarding the protection of migrants' rights is generally poor. In particular, the dependence of migrant women on their employers is exacerbated by regulations that do not allow foreign workers to change employers or that establish the immediate deportation of those who do not fulfil their contracts (Russell, chapter XV).

In the former labour-importing countries of Europe, women admitted as dependants of the migrant workers who were allowed to stay are generally subject to a number of restrictions. As Boyd (chapter V) points out, the separation of residence and work permits gives rise to situations where a migrant can be a legal resident but an illegal worker. That is often the situation of migrant women, whose status as dependants of their migrant husbands or fathers prevents them from having legal access to the labour market for a certain period (often lasting several years). Such provisions reinforce the economic dependence of women within the family and, if they work illegally, makes them more vulnerable to exploitation by unscrupulous employers.

Even in the traditional countries of immigration—Australia, Canada and the United States—women tend to be disproportionately represented in the category of immigrants admitted as dependants of other immigrants or citizens (United Nations Secretariat, chapter IV). Although women who secure permanent residence rights in those countries on the basis of their family ties to other persons are treated as if they had acquired those rights on their own merits, their assumed dependence on others makes them ineligible for government assistance during some period following migration and may lead therefore to their de facto dependence (Boyd, chapter V).

Although a careful analysis of the rules and regulations governing migration in most countries would yield few examples of direct or overt discrimination on the basis of sex, covert or indirect discrimination may arise from their application in ways that produce different outcomes for men and women. Usually, sex-selective outcomes result from norms regarding acceptable gender roles as well as from stereotypical images about the place of women in society. Even in societies where the status of women is high by current standards, the treatment of female international migrants is still coloured by traditional views about family structure and the position of women within the family that provide a rationale for the subordinate nature of women's roles as migrants. Those views, however, may have some positive implications for female migration, since they suggest that women are less threatening than men as economic actors and, consequently, countries concerned about the impact of international migration on the labour force may be less inclined to stop the migration of women and children as dependants than to prevent the admission of economically active men. In the former labour-importing countries of Europe, for instance, calls to restrict family reunification have grown as the children of the original migrant workers have begun to marry foreigners and request their admission. The fact that a high proportion of the foreign spouses involved are men has been interpreted to mean that family reunification is being used as a covert means of labour migration. That such interpretation is never questioned reveals how far we are still from achieving a gender-neutral view of family ties and economic roles.

C. WOMEN AS MIGRANTS AND WORKERS

In most of the world, the term "migrant worker" conjures the image of a young, able-bodied man. The prevalence of such a stereotype owes much to the low visibility of women as both migrants and workers. Just as the participation of women in international migration has been downplayed, so have their economic roles been underrated, partly because much of women's work goes unrecognized. As Waring (1988) notes, many of the activities in which women play a dominant role are not considered work because they do not produce a monetary income. In the case of international female migrants, there is the added issue of whether and to what extent their migrant status allows them free access to the labour market of the receiving State. In labour-importing countries, for instance, women admitted as dependants of male migrant workers may be prohibited from exercising an economic activity

4

and women admitted as migrant workers in their own right may not be allowed to change jobs (Boyd, chapter V; Russell, chapter XV).

Yet, despite the constraints that they face, many women who migrate internationally become economically active in their place of destination. Indeed, for many migrant women, being able to secure salaried employment outside the home is one of the incentives prompting migration. In the United States, migrant women were among the first to work outside the home, long before their American-born counterparts began joining the labour force in large numbers (Asis, chapter XIII). Even today, certain groups of female migrants display higher labour force participation rates than their non-migrant counterparts. In Canada, for instance, the age standardized labour force participation rate of foreign-born women was 55 per cent in 1981, compared to 51 per cent among native women (OECD, 1991). In 1987, women residing in Western Germany who were citizens of other member States of the European Community had a higher age-standardized economic activity rate than women who were German citizens: 42.1 per cent versus 40.6 per cent (OECD, 1991). In Australia, the labour force participation of native women has tended to be lower than that of women born in other countries of Oceania or in the United Kingdom of Great Britain and Northern Ireland (Ware and Lucas, chapter XI).

As with women in general, international female migrants display a wide range of labour force participation rates. In the United States, for instance, 52 per cent of all foreign-born women were economically active according to the 1990 census (U.S. Department of Commerce, 1993). In Europe, in contrast, data for six of the main receiving countries show that economic activity rates among foreign women tended to be lower than in the United States, particularly when standardized by age. Thus, in 1987, such rates varied from 23 per cent in the Netherlands to 41 per cent in the United Kingdom, being of the order of 33 and 36 per cent, respectively, in France and Western Germany (OECD, 1991). Labour force participation rates were particularly low among foreign women who were not citizens of European Community countries partly because their participation in an economic activity was subject to greater legal constraints.

Evidence from the overseas countries of immigration suggests that migrant women tend to have higher economic activity rates the longer they have lived in the receiving country and that they are more likely to be economically active if they have a good command of the local language. Their marital status does not seem to affect their labour force participation. Indeed, married migrant women often display higher labour force participation rates than all foreign women taken together (OECD, 1991). Such findings are consistent with those reported by Asis regarding Filipino and Korean married women who immigrated to the United States. When those women were interviewed in their home countries prior to migration, a high proportion expected to join the labour force in the United States, even though considerably lower proportions had been economically active before departure (Asis, chapter XIII). Such intentions reveal that, even among married women migrating in the company of their families, individual economic motivations are not absent from the rational calculus involved in opting for migration. Asis further shows that, on the whole, Filipino women have been more successful than Korean women in meeting their employment expectations once established in the United States. Such difference is explained, at least partly, by the fact that Filipino immigrants have a better command of English.

The importance of having adequate language skills is stressed in a variety of other contexts. Ware and Lucas (chapter XI) note that women from non-English speaking countries have greater difficulties in adapting to Australian society and securing employment than other migrant women. Migrant women lacking English skills are more likely to work in ethnic enclaves or do piecework at home, thus being caught in a vicious circle where their economic and social isolation from mainstream Australian society prevents them from improving their language skills and, consequently, their economic prospects. Barsotti and Lecchini (chapter IX) argue that Filipino female migrants in Italy are largely constrained to work in domestic service because they lack language skills which, given their relatively high levels of educational attainment and their previous working experience, would probably allow them to find better types of employment in the service sector.

Yet language and legal barriers are only part of the explanation of why women from different countries of origin display such varied tendencies to join the labour force in the country of destination. In France, for instance, women of European origin have substantially higher economic activity rates than women from Northern Africa or Turkey. Although such differences stem in part from different lengths of stay for the various nationality groups, as Tapinos (chapter VI) notes, special traits associated with the society of origin are also at work. Thus, the high labour force participation rates of Yugoslav migrant women in every European country where their numbers are significant is associated with similarly high labour force participation rates of women in the former Yugoslavia, particularly in those areas from which most migrants originate. Similarly, low labour force participation rates are observed among both women in Northern African countries and their migrant counterparts in various European countries. Cultural factors and the extent to which women are socialized to work outside the home have an effect. Thus, in the Netherlands, the relatively few Moroccan women who work are highly selected among those with an urban background (Schoorl, chapter VIII). Among migrant Turkish women, those who migrated at a young age, who have lived several years in the Netherlands, have few children at home and a good command of Dutch are the most likely to be employed (Schoorl, chapter VIII).

The need for income is the most important reason compelling migrant women to work. Yet there is considerable evidence indicating that, on average, migrant women are the group receiving the lowest salaries. In France, for instance, average wages are highest for French men, followed by foreign men, then by French women and lastly by foreign women (Tapinos, chapter VI). Although such differences may be related to differences in seniority, educational attainment and type of occupation, discriminatory practices cannot be ruled out. In the case of Kuwait, working women in general earn about half as much as working men, despite the fact that the

average educational attainment of working women is somewhat higher than that of men. In addition, the salaries of Kuwaiti working women are, on average, 46 per cent higher than those of Jordanian or Palestinian women who have similar educational levels and occupations (Russell, chapter XV). The fact that migrant women are generally concentrated in "female" occupations is a major cause of such salary differentials. Indeed, it is common the world over for women's work to be undervalued simply because it is performed by women.

The occupational segregation of international female migrants tends to be most marked in labour-importing countries where foreign women can be admitted as workers only if they are employed in certain occupations. Such practices are not new. Corti (1993) remarks that they were well established in nineteenth century Europe when Italian women migrated to France, Switzerland or even further afield to work in various types of factories or as domestic workers in private homes. Indeed, according to the 1900 census of France, 619,000 Italian women worked in French industry, 220,000 of whom were under 18 years of age. Many others worked for families, often as wet nurses. Discussions of Italian emigration at the time focused on the negative effects of the "mercenary" breast-feeding that wet nurses performed in foreign lands and on the generally pernicious consequences that the migration of single women could have on their sexual conduct (Corti, 1993, pp. 118-119). Similar concerns are common in the sending countries of today.

Domestic service continues to be an important occupation for unskilled women all over the world. In most countries, domestic workers are subject to working conditions that can be considered exploitative, involving, as they do, long working hours, very low wages, no benefits, a high dependence on the employer for food and housing, limited freedom of movement, and restricted access to the means of communication. Such conditions prevail irrespective of the migration status of the women concerned. During the past 20 years, a growing number of women have migrated specifically to become domestic workers abroad, particularly within Asia. Studies on the situation of those migrant women have generally concluded that not only are their working conditions unlikely to result in improvements of their status but that, in addition, the contribution that they make to family income is often short-lived (see, for instance, Eelens, chapter XVI). Because many of the women concerned are married and belong to the lower socio-economic strata of the countries of origin, their migration is seen as a family strategy to secure needed income. That is, women opt to work abroad under trying conditions for the good of the family group, aware that they themselves may gain little from the experience. Although this interpretation of women's international labour migration is widely accepted, not enough has been done to explore how the decision to migrate is actually made or whether the family and especially the women concerned could opt for any other income-earning opportunities in the home country. If the choice facing women is that between poorly paid domestic work in the home country and better paying domestic work abroad, it is not surprising that, despite the costs, risks and uncertainties involved, many opt for the second. The issue, therefore, is not whether women's status is improved by their engaging in domestic service abroad but rather the lack of attractive employment opportunities for women in the country of origin.

In Latin America, women have traditionally migrated within their countries to become domestic workers in urban centres. In some cases, such migration involves the crossing of international borders. According to the 1980 census of Argentina, for instance, over half the economically active female migrants from Chile and Paraguay worked in personal services and nearly 43 per cent of those originating in Bolivia did so (Balán, chapter XVII). The low level of educational attainment of the migrant women involved conditions the economic opportunities open to them in the country of destination. Thus, an analysis of the characteristics of migrants to Neuquén, a medium-sized city in Argentina, indicates that in 1980 the percentage of women working in domestic service was considerably higher among international migrants (60 per cent) and among migrant women originating in the provinces close to Neuquén (38 per cent) than among migrant women originating in other parts of Argentina (less than 11 per cent). Not surprisingly, some 80 per cent of the women in the first two groups had at most reached intermediate levels of educational attainment. In contrast, over 40 per cent of the migrant women originating in the rest of Argentina had reached higher levels of educational attainment and were thus able to work in a wider variety of occupations (Lattes and Mychaszula, 1993).

In most countries, the occupational segregation to which women are subject tends to relegate most of them to low-status, poorly paid occupations. However, as growing numbers of women join the labour force, an increasing proportion of them is gaining access to the higher end of the occupational scale. International female migrants are no exception, even though they often face greater obstacles than native women to obtain well-paid jobs. In Australia, for instance, nearly 24 per cent of the economically active foreign-born women occupied managerial, administrative, professional or para-professional positions, compared to 28 per cent of their native counterparts (Hugo, chapter XII). Even among Asian-born women in Australia, one in five worked as administrators, professionals and para-professionals.

In France, about 12 per cent of the economically active foreign women work as professionals, teachers, managers or in the education and health sectors. The equivalent proportion among French women is 41 per cent, indicating that foreign women still have a long way to go to attain parity with nationals (Tapinos, chapter VI). That is likely to be the situation in other former and current labour-importing countries. Yet, despite existing disparities, the point worth stressing is that international female migrants are well represented at both ends of the occupational scale and that, given the chance, they are eager to take advantage of the economic opportunities open to them. Especially in the case of women, the very fact of engaging in international migration corroborates their dynamism and willingness to face challenges. Thus, even upon their return to the home country, migrant women constitute a special group, being more likely than non-migrants to be economically active and to work in professional and technical occupations, as the case of Greece illustrates (Emke-Poulopoulos, chapter X). Just as women in general, migrant women are increasingly being recognized as important economic actors in their own right and there are many instances in which international migration has contributed to the improvement of their economic status. A hundred years ago, migrant lace-makers and wet-nurses contributed to laying the ground for the eventual entry into the labour force of women from all walks of life. Today, migrant women are still breaking ground, spearheading change and bearing the brunt of its implications. The entreprise is not without risk but its potential rewards are worthwhile. Most migrant women have proved to have the courage and determination to pursue and attain their goals.

D. MIGRANT WOMEN AS AGENTS OF CHANGE

Within the family, women are usually in charge of the socialization of children. Women who are international migrants have generally the added task of ensuring that the family maintains some degree of continuity with the culture, norms and values of the society of origin while at the same time embarking in a process of adaptation to the host society. Evidence about the ways in which migrant women negotiate the transition between the two societies is scarce. As Tribalat (1991) notes, an analysis of the adaptation process of migrant communities to the host society presupposes that there are significant differences between the behaviour of migrants and that of natives, and that adaptation depends on the convergence, over time, of the behaviour of migrants to that of natives. However, such convergence need not entail a consistent reduction of differences as time elapses. Under certain circumstances, the path towards eventual adaptation may lead at first to an exacerbation of the differences between migrants and natives. That is the case, for instance, when an increase in the tendency of migrant women to join the labour force leads to a short-term increase in their unemployment rather than to higher employment. In addition, migrants are usually a heterogeneous group whose average behaviour is not necessarily representative of the various subgroups involved. Thus, an analysis of fertility behaviour among migrant and non-migrant groups in France indicates that couples where the two spouses are foreigners have tended to have higher fertility than those where both spouses have become French citizens by naturalization and the latter group has higher

fertility than either the group of all French couples or that of all mixed couples, defined as those in which only one of the spouses is French by birth (Tribalat, 1991). Indeed, mixed couples tend to have the lowest fertility, indicating that migrant men or women who marry natives represent a selected group that has completed the adaptation to the host society.

In general, the fertility levels of migrant women in France are converging to those of French women, but the degree and pace of convergence varies considerably by country of origin. Algerian migrant women, for instance, have experienced a fertility decline that parallels the one recorded in Algeria itself, but at lower levels. Increasing age at marriage and a moderate reduction of completed family size are the main factors explaining such a decline. In contrast, the rapid fertility reductions observed among Portuguese women in France have occurred in conjunction with lower ages at marriage and a decisive limitation of births within marriage, in a process similar to that observed in Portugal (Tribalat, 1991). These findings suggest that migrant women are prone to maintain behavioural patterns similar to those of the society of origin, even as they adapt to that of destination. In fact, full adaptation may only be achieved by the second generation. In France, the daughters of North African women are already showing signs of adopting local mores regarding the entry into marriage (Boulahbel-Villac, chapter VII). Thus, whereas 70 per cent of the North African migrant women interviewed in 1982 who had a daughter born in 1961 had married before the age of 20, only 15 per cent of their daughters had married by that age (Tribalat, 1991). According to detailed interviews with Algerian migrants in France, the nature of marriage in the expatriate Algerian community is changing, with more women entering marriages arranged on the basis of mutual agreement between the partners. In fact, influenced by local norms, few of the migrant couples interviewed admitted that their marriages had been contracted without their consent (Boulahbel-Villac, chapter VII).

Another example of how migrant women manage to maintain a certain continuity of behaviour in the face of transformation is provided by their engaging in informal economic activities that are an extension of the ones that they performed in the country of origin. Thus, Algerian migrant women in France engage in small-scale trade and commerce, selling traditional wares to other Algerian migrants in France or transporting to Algeria those French goods that are in demand, so as to sell them to friends and relatives. Through such activities, migrant women manage to accumulate some savings and thus acquire some degree of independence (Boulahbel-Villac, chapter VII).

In Latin America, Bolivian women migrating to Argentina also tend to engage in informal economic activities similar to those that were traditional for them in the home country. However, many of those activities find no market in the urban areas of Argentina where the migrants settle. Consequently, migrant women experience a certain erosion of their income-earning capacity unless they become employees instead of own-account workers, thus losing some of their independence of action (Balán, chapter XVII).

In western Africa, it is also common for international female migrants to engage in petty trade and commerce, thereby securing the income that boosts their status within the family. Detailed interviews with migrant women in Nigeria indicate that they perceive as a positive consequence of migration the opportunity of getting to know another culture (Iyun and United Nations Secretariat, chapter XVIII). In that context, as in many others, the importance of learning the local language and being able to interact with the native population is essential for the successful adaptation of migrants. In many receiving countries, migrant women are handicapped from initiating social change by their relative isolation from the host society, which is largely attributable to their inadequate language skills. Providing access to adequate language training is therefore one of the most important steps that a receiving country can take to facilitate the adaptation of migrant women and their families.

E. CONCLUSION

It is increasingly recognized that women are too valuable a resource to waste. Women who migrate internationally are no exception. Being almost as numerous as their male counterparts, they deserve to be considered in their own right as economic and social actors. The very act of migrating demonstrates that women have agency and are willing to take risks in order to improve their status and that of their families. The fact that most women migrate as part of a family unit should not be used as an excuse to downplay their role as migrants or to ignore that, as in many other enterprises, their collaboration with men is essential to ensure social and economic progress.

The papers in the present volume document the many facets of women's participation in international migration. The picture that emerges is one of variety and dynamism. Women, just as men, choose to migrate for multiple reasons and must negotiate admission by the receiving countries on the terms set by the latter. In many instances, the socially sanctioned "dependent" position of women increases their opportunities for admission. Dependency, however, is not the most desirable basis on which to start a new life in new surroundings. Yet, despite such handicaps, migrant women evince considerable resilience and manage to make the most of the opportunities that migration opens to them.

In studying female migration, it is common to emphasize that the problems faced by migrant women are compounded by their being both women and migrants. True, most societies are still far from being gender neutral and the status of women in general is not yet equivalent to that of men. In addition, particularly in the post-Cold War era characterized by growing political instability and economic recession, international migrants in many countries are being viewed as liabilities rather than assets. Yet, migration is essential to human development and has always involved individuals of both sexes. Consequently, even under less than ideal conditions, women will continue to migrate and, just as men, they will continue to engage actively in effecting change. Acknowledging their capacity to do so and understanding the strategies that they and their families devise to achieve their goals is a first and necessary step to develop measures that increase the effectiveness of those strategies. After all, the vulnerability of migrant women is a social construct that can and must be "deconstructed".

REFERENCES

Abella, Manolo I. (1995). Sex selectivity of migration regulations governing international migration in Southern and South-eastern Asia. Chapter XIV in the present volume.

Asis, Maruja M. (1995). Labour force experience of migrant women: Filipino and Korean women in transition. Chapter XIII in the present volume.

Balán, Jorge (1995). Household economy and gender in international migration: the case of Bolivians in Argentina. Chapter XVII in the present volume.

Barsotti, Odo, and Laura Lecchini (1995). The experience of Filipino female migrants in Italy. Chapter IX in the present volume.

Boulahbel-Villac, Yeza (1995). The integration of Algerian women in France: a compromise between tradition and modernity. Chapter VII in the present volume.

Boyd, Monica (1995). Migration regulations and sex selective outcomes in developed countries. Chapter V in the present volume.

Corti, Paola (1993). Sociétés sans hommes et intégrations des femmes à l'étranger: mouvements migratoires et rôles féminins. Le cas de l'Italie. *Revue européenne des migrations internationales* (Poitiers, France), vol. 9, No. 2, pp. 113-123.

Eelens, Frank (1995). Migration of Sri Lankan women to Western Asia. Chapter XVI in the present volume.

Emke-Poulopoulos, Ira (1995). Analysis of changes in the status of female returnees in Greece. Chapter X in the present volume.

Hugo, Graeme J. (1995). Migration of Asian women to Australia. Chapter XII in the present volume.

Iyun, Folasade, and United Nations Secretariat (1995). Female migration in sub-Saharan Africa: the case of Nigeria. Chapter XVIII in the present volume.

Lattes, Zulma, and Sonia María Mychaszula (1993). Female migration and labour force participation in a medium-sized city of a highly urbanized country. In *Internal Migration of Women in Developing Countries*. Sales No. E.94.XIII.3. New York: United Nations.

Lim, Lin Lean (1995). The status of women and international migration. Chapter III in the present volume.

Organisation for Economic Co-operation and Development (OECD) (1991). *Continuous Reporting System on Migration. SOPEMI 1990.* Paris: OECD.

Russell, Sharon Stanton (1995). Policy dimensions of female migration to the Arab countries of Western Asia. Chapter XV in the present volume.

Schoorl, Jeannette J. (1995). Comparing the position of Moroccan and Turkish women in the Netherlands and in the countries of origin. Chapter VIII in the present volume.

Tapinos, Georges P. (1995). Female migration and the status of foreign women in France. Chapter VI in the present volume.

Tribalat, Michèle, ed. (1991). *Cent ans d'immigration, étrangers d'hier, Français d'aujourd'hui.* Travaux et Documents. Cahiers No. 131. Paris: Institut national d'études démographiques.

United Nations Secretariat (1995). Measuring the extent of female international migration. Chapter IV in the present volume.

United States Department of Commerce (1993). *1990 Census of Population. The Foreign-born Population in the United States.* Washington, D.C.: Government Printing Office.

Ware, Helen, and David Lucas (1995). The new Sheilas: European immigrant women in Australia, their status and adaptation. Chapter XI in the present volume.

Waring, Marilyn (1988). *If Women Counted: A New Feminist Economics.* San Francisco, California: Harper Collins.

Part One

REPORT AND RECOMMENDATIONS OF THE MEETING

I. REPORT OF THE MEETING

Nearly one out of every two international migrants in the world is a woman. That fact alone justifies devoting greater attention to the migration experience of women, especially in relation to the changing status of female migrants. Such was the task undertaken by the participants in the United Nations Expert Group Meeting on International Migration Policies and the Status of Female Migrants organized by the Population Division of the United Nations Secretariat in collaboration with the Facoltà di Economia e Commercio of the University of Pisa. About 45 international experts attended the Meeting, including representatives from several international organizations, including, the United Nations High Commissioner for Refugees (UNHCR), the United Nations Population Fund (UNFPA), the International Labour Organization (ILO), the Food and Agriculture Organization of the United Nations (FAO), the United Nations Educational, Scientific and Cultural Organization (UNESCO) and the International Organization for Migration (IOM). Representatives of the Economic Commission for Africa (ECA) and the Economic Commission for Europe (ECE) were also present. This activity was carried out as part of a larger project on women and demographic processes funded by UNFPA.

The Meeting was opened by the Honourable Laura Balbo, member of the Italian Chamber of Deputies, who underscored the need to bring migrant women into the political agenda. United Nations representatives noted that issues related to the status of migrant women and measures for its improvement would be one of the topics considered during the forthcoming session of the Commission on the Status of Women and that both the status of women and international migration were issues slated to receive particular attention in planning the 1994 International Conference on Population and Development.

The Meeting started by noting that, despite the difficulties inherent in measuring the extent of female migration worldwide, the available evidence indicated that women constituted 48 per cent of all persons enumerated outside their country of birth at some point during 1970-1987. In terms of flows, until the early 1980s women had predominated over men among permanent immigrants admitted by the United States of America and had constituted substantial proportions of those admitted by other countries of permanent settlement. In Europe, the proportion of women among the foreign population had tended to increase since the mid-1970s as a result of the cessation of labour recruitment and the promotion of family reunion. Even with respect to flows of temporary migrant workers, female participation was becoming more visible, especially among South and South-eastern Asian migrants going to the Middle East.

A. MIGRATION POLICIES AND THE STATUS OF FEMALE MIGRANTS

Participants noted that international migration generally involved a move from one system of gender stratification to another and thus constituted a demographic process having important implications for the status of women. In addition, migration policies and regulations had a differential impact on male and female migrants. In considering the implications of policy on female migration and the status of female migrants, participants underscored the importance of taking the following points into account: (*a*) the various contexts influencing the status of female migrants so as to distinguish those that were amenable to direct policy intervention from those that were not; (*b*) the interplay of political, economic, institutional and social forces that might lead to conflicting policy objectives and thus complicate efforts to address the needs of international female migrants; (*c*) the explicit or implicit nature of migration policies, whether by countries of origin or those of destination; (*d*) the need for affirmative-action measures to deal with particularly vulnerable groups of female migrants; and (*e*) the heterogeneity of migrant women, especially in terms of their stage in the life cycle.

In considering the sex selectivity of international migration flows, experts concluded that it was generally determined by the interplay of migration regulations, country-specific ideologies and systems of sex stratification. Although regulations tended not to be explicitly discriminatory on the basis of sex, their implementation was often influenced by stereotypical images of the roles men and women played in the societies of origin or destination, images that reinforced gender inequality and resulted in differential migration outcomes by sex. Thus, women were largely admitted as dependants in both traditional countries of immigration and European countries, whereas men tended to predominate in migrant categories of an economic nature.

It was noted that in European countries, where the right to residence had generally been divorced from the right to employment, migrant women admitted as dependants were generally not allowed to work, at least during a certain period following admission. Such restrictions were considered to reinforce the de facto economic dependence of migrant women on other family members or on their employers when they engaged in clandestine work. Even in traditional countries of immigration, where migrant women admitted as dependants were not restricted from participation in the labour force, the linkage of their migrant status with that of a sponsor was judged to reinforce dependency, if only because it generally restricted the migrant women's access to welfare services. The fact that economically active migrant women generally earned less than their male counterparts was highlighted as a constraint on their ability to sponsor the migration of other close relatives.

Participants noted that, in considering the equity of migration regulations with respect to sex, it was necessary to determine what constituted discrimination. Two possible approaches to gauge discrimination were mentioned: an assessment of biases operating at the individual level, on a case-by-case basis; and comparisons of outcomes at the aggregate level. When discrimination at the aggregate level was found to exist, unequal outcomes had to be redressed irrespective of the processes leading to them. Use of the aggregate approach was said to demand adequate indices of comparison. In the case of migrant women,

comparisons might be carried out between them and migrant men or between them and native women. Both types of comparisons were judged relevant in establishing the existence of discrimination. To fight discrimination, measures ranging from consciousness-raising to affirmative action in regard to vulnerable groups of female migrants were mentioned.

In considering the possibility of adopting measures of reverse discrimination to facilitate the admission of women on an equal footing with men, the concerns of receiving countries were highlighted. Women were judged to be more likely to be admitted as migrants if they were not seen as economic actors. Restrictions on the admission of fiancées or fiancés were justified in terms of preventing migrants from using such relationships to circumvent migration regulations. Granting migrants immediate access to welfare entitlements was said to be considered as a threat by the welfare State.

Several methodological issues arising from the assessment of female status in relation to migration were identified. First, since the citizenship of migrants was usually the basis for their differential treatment in regard to the law, it was judged necessary to focus attention on the different foreign groups in a country. Second, the need to distinguish between discrimination due to the status of women *vis-à-vis* men and that deriving from the migration process was underscored. Ideally, the selectivity of migration should be controlled for in attempts to identify which differences arise from migration or female status and which from particular characteristics of the various foreign groups (including those stemming from a distinctive age distribution, differential educational attainment, skills etc.). In France, for instance, the foreign population would not be representative of all migrants since naturalization was common.

The growing participation of women in international migration flows originating in countries of Southern and South-eastern Asia was documented to the extent possible. Asian women were reported to be working temporarily in the Middle East, Hong Kong, Singapore and Japan, generally as housemaids or entertainers. The efforts made by countries of origin to control and direct the flow of female migrant workers were reviewed and it was found that the degree of control exercised by Governments had no effect on the extent of clandestine outflows experienced by the different countries of origin. In most countries, economic needs had counterbalanced the cultural and religious factors that traditionally restricted the mobility of women.

It was noted that measures adopted by Asian countries to control the exit of temporary female migrants had to take account of economic realities in order to be enforceable. The case of Sri Lanka, where authorities had set unrealistic limits on recruitment fees and thus forced recruiters into illegality, was cited. Lacking the possibility of providing viable economic alternatives locally, countries of origin had been unable to control labour migration effectively. Difficult economic conditions propelled migrants, especially women, to seek opportunities abroad, irrespective of the risks or constraints they faced. It was stressed that most women decided to work abroad in order to ensure the basic survival of their families.

Receiving countries were found to be more successful in enforcing migration policies. Analysis of the case of Kuwait revealed that approximately 40 policy instruments had been in operation at different times during 1959-1985. A fair degree of association between the policies in force and the levels and characteristics of migrant inflows was found. Since 1965 the presence of women in migrant inflows increased, first through the family reunification of Arab migrants and later through the arrival of female Asian workers. Restrictions on the labour force participation of dependants were found to have affected women mostly. Asian women working as domestic servants were usually subject to restrictions regarding length of stay and type of employment.

B. THE IMPACT OF FEMALE STATUS ON MIGRATION SELECTIVITY

The analysis of the impact of female status on migration selectivity was judged to be hampered by lack of adequate data, since migrants tended to be studied once the move had taken place and their reports on the reasons for moving were likely to be rationalized in retrospect. Emphasis was put on the need to analyse how gender considerations operated within the household or family so as to understand how male and female migrants were mobilized, especially when associational migration was involved. Differential labour-market opportunities for men and women in the society of destination were judged to be especially relevant when migration was of an autonomous/individual type.

Reports from a survey carried out in a village in Cochabamba, Bolivia, revealed that a high degree of complementarity existed between the roles of men and women at origin, especially in the economic sphere. Men were engaged in agriculture while women dealt in crafts and trade. With land fragmentation resulting from overpopulation, men were pressured to find wage employment abroad, while women were able to continue their traditional activities. Thus, specific sex roles had a direct impact on the sex selectivity of migration. When women migrated, they normally did so to follow husbands or fathers and were usually handicapped to enter the labour market in the country of destination (Argentina). Their loss of economic independence after migration led to a reduction of their leverage in household decision-making and contributed to their maladjustment to the host society. Thus, migration did not contribute to improving their status with respect to the one they had in Bolivia.

The cases of Filipino and Sri Lankan women were different in that their decision to migrate was explicitly based on economic reasons, their main objective for migrating being to improve the economic situation of the families they had left behind. Both Filipino and Sri Lankan women tended to engage in domestic work while abroad. Filipino women in Italy were generally young and educated, and most of them had held a job in the Philippines before migrating. According to the migrants themselves, their experiences in Italy were usually positive, since wages were much higher than in the Philippines and savings could be accrued.

Most Sri Lankan women in the Middle East also engaged in domestic service to provide the support needed by their families at home. The relatively late entry of Sri Lanka into the regional labour market implied that the domestic service sector was the largest open to its citizens. The relatively low recruitment fees characterizing that sector had contributed to the mobilization of women rather than men. Foreign domestic workers were reported to lack legal protection and be dependent on employers for food, clothing, housing and even the possibility of contacting other people. Such situations undermined their position and left them prone to exploitation. The high incidence of premature returns among women migrating to the Middle East was interpreted as indicative of the stressful nature of their situation.

These cases were used to show that migration did not necessarily entail an improvement of status or upward mobility. Filipino and Sri Lankan women moved for the benefit of others, generally their families, a fact that underscored the need to consider the decision-making process at the family level. It also raised the issue of determining an appropriate standard for comparison: should migrant women be compared to migrant men, native women or non-migrant women in the country of origin? Or was the appropriate standard the position that migrant women and their immediate families had before the move? Whatever the standard, it was stressed that assessments of status should take account of "cultural relativism" and of the possibility that certain dimensions of status might not be measurable in an ordered unilinear scale. To avoid gross misinterpretations of discrimination, it was suggested that the views that migrant women themselves had about migration and its outcomes should be taken into account.

The crucial role played by intermediaries was highlighted in discussing the cases of both Filipino and Sri Lankan migrants. Two types of intermediaries were distinguished: informal networks revolving around kinship ties and commercial recruitment agencies. The latter, by operating on the basis of profit, made explicit the direct costs of migration. Less was known about the operation of the former, though they might also involve costs to the migrant, perhaps in terms of social obligations. Intermediaries were judged to influence the selectivity of migration and to be an equilibrating mechanism linking national and international labour markets. By raising the costs of emigration, intermediaries dissuaded some potential migrants from seeking employment abroad.

C. IMPACT OF ADAPTATION ON THE ROLES AND STATUS OF MIGRANT WOMEN

The heterogeneity characterizing migrant inflows was singled out as a factor preventing useful generalizations about the impact of adaptation on the status of migrant women. Not only did the different national origins of migrants give rise to heterogeneity, it was also detected among migrants having a common origin. Changes in the composition of flows through time appeared to be the rule. In Australia, for instance, European immigrants, which predominated until 1970, had given way to those from Asia. Among the latter, the proportion of women had increased substantially during the 1980s.

Significant differences were reported regarding the adaptation strategies of the various ethnic groups. The Vietnamese, for instance, tended to live in ethnic enclaves which were judged to have beneficial impacts on the adjustment of migrant women over the short run. In the long term, however, enclaves tended to isolate migrants from the community at large, prevented them from acquiring needed language skills, reduced their access to better employment opportunities and perpetuated traditional gender stratification systems.

European migration to Australia was by no means homogeneous. In studying the adaptation process of these migrants care was taken not to equate "Western" or "modern" values with a higher status for women. Migration was found to involve both gains and losses in status. It was suggested that the ultimate effects of migration on female status should be assessed with respect to the second generation. Although consideration of factors such as educational attainment, labour force participation or occupation was judged to be enlightening, the need to take into account changing social relations and the relative power of men and women was stressed. The importance of language proficiency in reducing the barriers faced by female migrants during the adaptation process was also emphasized.

In analysing the adaptation of Algerian women to France, it was pointed out that, for them, migration represented a conscious choice leading to greater opportunities in both the social and economic spheres.

Marriage was often a vehicle leading to migration. Algerian women marrying migrant men were reported to be considerably younger than their husbands, to come from an urban environment and have a higher socio-economic status than the husband's family of origin. Algerian migrant women were portrayed as social actors devising strategies to forge their future and that of their children. Their status within the host society was depicted as arising from a negotiated compromise between tradition and modernity. Thus, their relatively low labour force participation was justified in terms of the innovative strategies they used to create their own employment in the informal sector, a type of employment that satisfied the constraints set by tradition.

It was noted that, to the extent that migration policies incorporated criteria to select those most likely to adapt, such criteria were generally applied to men rather than women, since the latter were usually admitted as dependants. Hence, selectivity for adaptation was largely self-induced, as migrants, especially women, made conscious choices regarding strategies to qualify for admission. Even among refugees, those admitted for resettlement were most likely to be men, since the criteria used for their selection were the same as those applied to immigrants. It was therefore necessary to call for special programmes that, based on humanitarian considerations, would permit the admission of women in vulnerable situations, particularly female refugees. Because migrant women admitted as dependants were likely to face greater adjustment problems than principal migrants, programmes to facilitate their adaptation were judged to be necessary.

D. STATUS OF FEMALE MIGRANTS AS COMPARED TO THAT OF WOMEN IN THE SOCIETIES OF ORIGIN AND DESTINATION

Data from a longitudinal survey of Filipino and Korean migrants to the United States were used to assess changes in the status of women before and after migration. The survey results served to combat the widespread perception that women admitted as dependants, particularly married women, were not involved in economic activity. Information on the economic activity of married Filipino and Korean women before and two years after migration re-

vealed that their expectations regarding labour force participation after migration were largely realized. Those expectations, however, involved in most cases a decline of occupational status in relation to educational attainment and previous job experience. Yet, because of the recency of the migration experience being analysed, such results were not considered definitive. It was suggested that the crucial role that women played in facilitating the social adaptation of their families might delay their entry into the labour force or retard their advancement. The need for language training programmes was emphasized, since language proficiency proved to be an important determinant of labour force participation.

Information regarding Moroccan and Turkish migrants in the Netherlands showed that the independence of women who had migrated long after their husbands had peaked while they were alone in the country of origin having sole responsibility for raising the children. The majority of migrant women reported that they wanted to move at the time migration took place, and older women tended to play a more important role in the decision-making process than younger women. When migrant and non-migrant women having the same origin were compared, the former tended to be better educated, to have lower labour-force participation rates and lower fertility. Yet, with respect to participation rates, the results were difficult to interpret without controlling for age.

It was noted that an assessment of status on the basis of labour force participation had to take into account prior skills and the value, in terms of status, that was attached to women's work (in some societies the need for women to work was considered to lower their status). It was also important to assess the labour force participation of wives in terms of the position of husbands in the labour market. Three strategies used by migrant women to insert themselves into the labour market of the host society were identified: (a) by meeting the demands arising in the formal sector; (b) by creating their own employment opportunities through the informal sector; and (c) by satisfying a potential demand for services which would otherwise have been met through unpaid family work. In general, the last two strategies were judged unlikely to bring about a significant rise in status.

E. RETURNING FEMALE MIGRANTS

Return migration was considered important because, for a large proportion of migrants, it was said to represent the last stage of the migration process and the attainment of the ultimate migration goal. Information on migrants returning to the metropolitan area of Barcelona who were heads of household indicated that the migration of most women was conditioned by family considerations, while that of men was prompted by economic motivations. Women showed greater inertia, tending to stay longer in any given place. Their labour force participation upon return was lower than that of males. However, lack of control for age or for the different stages of the life cycle in which returning migrants found themselves made interpretation of these results difficult.

Most female migrants returning to Greece were also found to do so because of family considerations. However, while upon emigration men had usually preceded women, upon return, women were more likely to migrate first. Heterogeneity among Greek returnees was found to be associated with the different destinations they were returning from. A number of measures aimed at aiding returnees were discussed. It was suggested that legal advice in family matters be provided, especially for women who, having married foreigners, returned after a divorce and needed to secure family allowances. Mention was made of the need to reduce bureaucratic and financial barriers to resettlement, to facilitate currency transfers at a fair rate of exchange and to aid returnees in validating studies or other training obtained abroad. It was recognized that special services for returnees would be difficult to implement without causing resentment among the non-migrant population.

Interviews with female returnees living in Ibadan and Oubokosho, Nigeria, showed that most of them had migrated in connection with other family members, mainly their husbands. Their principal destinations were Ghana or Europe. Migration had gener-

ally occurred several years before interview and women varied in their assessment of the benefits derived from it. A few had worked to help their husbands study abroad and had been deserted upon return. Female returnees felt that their status had been reduced drastically upon return. This assessment was ascribed to the re-adaptation problems they faced after having acquired new norms and attitudes abroad.

F. CONCLUSION

A set of recommendations to guide government action regarding migrant women was adopted by the Meeting. Governments were urged to make an assessment of the effects on migrant women of current migration policies, legislation and regulations, and to modify those that were found to produce negative outcomes for female migrants. The recommendations also highlighted the needs of migrant women belonging to especially vulnerable groups, including the elderly, those involved in domestic service and refugees. Measures to ensure the equal access of legally admitted migrant women to the labour market and to welfare and social services were recommended. Special attention was given to the needs of women engaging in temporary worker migration. In addition, Governments of receiving countries were urged to ensure that regularization drives offer equal opportunities for legalization to male and female undocumented migrants.

The Meeting was concluded by underscoring the need to keep in sight the positive aspects of migration. Even in cases where the status of migrant women could not be said to improve in an objective manner, at the subjective level women often assessed their experience as positive. Furthermore, in most instances migrant women proved to be active agents of change and adaptation, rather than passive victims of circumstances. Being intent on improving their own standing and that of their families, migrant women deserved recognition for the important roles they played in the migration process.

II. RECOMMENDATIONS TO IMPROVE THE STATUS OF INTERNATIONAL FEMALE MIGRANTS

Given that women constitute nearly half of the international migrants worldwide and that, as migrants and women, they are often subject to overt or covert discrimination, measures to meet their needs are necessary if they are to receive a fair and equal treatment. Taking account of the principles and objectives of the Universal Declaration of Human Rights (General Assembly resolution 217 A(III)), the International Covenants on Human Rights (resolution 2200 A (XXI), annex), the Declaration on the Elimination of Discrimination against Women (resolution 2263 (XXII)), the Convention on the Elimination of All Forms of Discrimination against Women (resolution 34/180, annex), the Declaration on the Participation of Women in Promoting International Peace and Co-operation (resolution 37/63, annex) and other international instruments and plans of action[1] aimed at improving the situation of women and ensuring their full integration into society on an equal basis with men, the following recommendations suggest strategies to achieve that goal with respect to international female migrants.

A. GENERAL MEASURES

Recommendation 1. Governments are encouraged to review periodically and, where necessary, to revise their migration policies and legislation as well as their implementation so as to avoid discriminatory practices against women, taking into account international conventions and recommendations on equal treatment and non-discrimination.

Recommendation 2. Governments should simplify procedures to secure travel documents and clearance for the exit and return of their female and male citizens.

Recommendation 3. Governments of countries of origin are encouraged to provide information, especially to emigrant women or those who are about to emigrate, on consular services available to their nationals in countries of destination.

Recommendation 4. Governments should take appropriate steps to provide adequate support services for elderly migrant women, including elderly returnees, who often find themselves isolated and deprived of traditional sources of support.

Recommendation 5. Governments should take appropriate steps to protect the rights of vulnerable groups of migrant women, for example, those in domestic service, those engaging in out-work, those who are victims of trafficking and involuntary prostitution, and any others in potentially exploitable circumstances, including mail-order brides.

Recommendation 6. Governments are encouraged to provide equal access to welfare and social services to women and men who are temporary migrant workers during their period of stay in the country.

B. TOOLS FOR ADAPTATION TO THE RECEIVING SOCIETY

Recommendation 7. Governments of receiving countries should ensure that all migrants, but especially women, are provided information about their legal rights and obligations in their own languages. Measures could include the provision of counselling services and legal advice to female migrants, especially in regard to the acquisition and maintenance of legal status, marriage and divorce, domestic violence, labour laws, legislation on sex discrimination, and welfare and other social entitlements including family planning.

Recommendation 8. Governments of receiving countries are urged to facilitate the creation of associations by and for migrant women. Such associations should, among other things, promote the dissemination of information among migrants, provide counselling and other social and legal services, identify problems and make them known to decision makers.

Recommendation 9. Governments of receiving countries should take measures to ensure that training in the language of the host country is available and accessible to female migrants. In planning language training programmes, account should be taken of the special needs and circumstances of migrant women.

Recommendation 10. Governments should assure children of migrants equal access to education and child-care facilities.

C. ECONOMIC ROLES OF FEMALE MIGRANTS

Recommendation 11. Governments should ensure that migrant women have equal access to training programmes for employment and entry into the labour force.

Recommendation 12. Governments are urged to extend the right to economic activity to migrants admitted as dependants.

Recommendation 13. Governments should make efforts for the effective enforcement of recruitment regulations covering temporary migrant workers, including sanctions against recruitment agents who violate those regulations.

D. RETURNING FEMALE MIGRANTS

Recommendation 14. Governments of countries of origin should take measures to facilitate the reintegration of migrants upon return, including those of the second generation.

Recommendation 15. Governments of receiving countries and countries of origin are urged to conduct bilateral negotiations with a view to ensuring the transferability and maintenance of social security entitlements accrued by migrant women and men.

E. FEMALE REFUGEES

Recommendation 16. The international community should cooperate with UNHCR, other appropri-

ate bodies and specialized agencies by providing urgent and adequate protection and assistance to all refugee women and taking into account their special situation in formulating national refugee policies. Countries of asylum should ensure the right of female refugees to physical safety and facilitate their access to counselling and health services, material assistance, education and employment. Countries of resettlement are urged to emphasize in immigration legislation the humanitarian elements required to ensure the equal opportunity of refugee women to be resettled, bearing in mind the special needs of women-at-risk.

F. UNDOCUMENTED MIGRATION

Recommendation 17. In devising regularization drives, Governments of receiving countries are urged to take measures to ensure that female migrants in an irregular situation have the same opportunities as male migrants in an irregular situation to qualify for regularization.

G. DATA IMPROVEMENT

Recommendation 18. Given that more comparable and detailed information on the extent and characteristics of female migration is sorely needed, Governments are urged to facilitate the collection and dissemination of adequate information on that topic by, *inter alia*, (*a*) collecting and publishing available data on major categories of migrants classified by sex, including return migrants; (*b*) making available to researchers detailed information on the characteristics of migrants by sex; (*c*) providing, as appropriate, information by sex on the number and type of cases processed in administrative procedures, such as applications for admission, changes of status, applications for work permits, asylum requests, naturalization etc., including rejected applications by type and reason; (*d*) carrying out censuses and surveys (including longitudinal surveys) that throw needed light on important dimensions of the migration process and, especially, those relevant for the assessment of the changing status of female migrants.

Recommendation 19. Given the importance of understanding the dynamics of migration and its interactions with the status of female migrants, the preparation of country case-studies and further research is recommended. Such studies should aim at elucidating those aspects of the migration process that, being amenable to policy intervention, are likely to foster positive changes in the various dimensions of female status.

NOTE

[1]Especially the World Plan of Action for the Implementation of the Objectives of the International Woman's Year, adopted at Mexico City in 1975 and endorsed by the General Assembly in its resolution 3520 (XXX); the Programme of Action for the Second Half of the United Nations Decade for Women, adopted in 1980 at the Copenhagen World Conference and endorsed by the General Assembly in its resolution 35/136; and the Nairobi Forward-looking Strategies for the Advancement of Women endorsed by the General Assembly in its resolution 40/108.

ANNEXES

ANNEX I

Agenda

1. Opening of the meeting.

2. Adoption of the agenda and other organization matters.

3. The extent of female international migration and general discussion of its impact on female status:

   (a) Measuring the extent of female international migration;

   (b) The status of women and international migration.

4. International migration policies and regulations controlling entry or exit as determinants of the sex selectivity of international migration flows:

   (a) Migration regulations and sex selective outcomes in settlement and European countries;

   (b) The sex selectivity of exit regulations governing international migration in Southern and South-eastern Asia.

5. The effect on the status of female migrants of measures adopted by Governments to control the stay and exercise of economic activity of aliens:

   (a) Policy dimensions of female migration to the Arab Gulf;

   (b) Female migration and the status of foreign women in France.

6. The impact of female status on migration selectivity:

   (a) Gender, household economy and females in international migration: a case study of Bolivians in Argentina;

   (b) A comparison of male and female migration strategies: the cases of African and Filipino migrants in Italy;

   (c) Sri Lankan women in the Middle East.

7. The impact that the processes of adaptation or integration have on the roles and status of migrant women:

   (a) The adaptation of Asian migrants to Australia;

   (b) New Sheilas: female European migrants to Australia—status and adaptation;

   (c) Algerian women in France: a negotiated status as a paradoxical form of integration.

8. Examination of the status of female migrants with respect to the general status of women in selected sending and receiving countries:

   (a) International migration and the changing labour force experience of women;

   (b) Some aspects of the position of Turkish and Moroccan women in the Netherlands, compared with that of women in Turkey and Morocco.

9. Return migration and its relationships to female status:

   (a) Female migration and life histories: the return from other European countries;

   (b) The interrelations of international migration and the status of migrant women in sub-Saharan Africa;

   (c) The analysis of changes in the status of female returnees in Greece.

10. Recommendations to improve the status of female international migrants.

11. Closing statements.

ANNEX II

List of participants

EXPERTS

Manolo I. Abella, Regional Adviser on Migrant Workers, Regional Office for Asia and the Pacific, International Labour Organisation, Bangkok

Maruja M. Asis, East-West Center, Population Institute, Honolulu, Hawaii, United States of America

Jorge Balán, Centro de Estudios de Estado y Sociedad, Buenos Aires

Laura Balbo, Gruppo Indipendente, Camera dei Deputati, Rome

Odo Barsotti, Istituto di Sociologia, Facoltà di Scienze Politiche, Pisa, Italy

Alberto Bonaguidi, Facoltà di Economia e Commercio, Università di Pisa, Pisa, Italy

Yeza Boulahbel-Villac, Université Tolliac, Paris

Monica Boyd, Department of Sociology and Anthropology, Carleton University, Ottawa

Frank Eelens, Central Bureau voor de Statistiek, San Nicolas, Aruba

Ira Emke-Poulopoulos, Institute for the Study of Greek Economy, Athens

Graeme J. Hugo, School of Social Sciences, Flinders University of South Australia, Adelaide

Folasade Iyun, Department of Geography, University of Ibadan, Nigeria

Mary Kritz, Department of Rural Sociology, Cornell University, Ithaca, New York, United States of America

Laura Lecchini, Facoltà di Economia e Commercio, Università di Pisa, Pisa, Italy

Lin Lean Lim, Regional Adviser on Women Workers' Questions, Regional Office for Asia and the Pacific, International Labour Organisation, Bangkok

Massimo Livi-Bacci, Dipartimento Statistico, Università degli Studi di Firenze, Firenze, Italy

Angels Pascual de Sans, Department of Geography, Autonomous University of Barcelona, Barcelona, Spain

Sharon Stanton Russell, Research Scholar, Center for International Studies, Massachusetts Institute of Technology, Cambridge, Massachusetts, United States of America

Jeannette J. Schoorl, Nederlands Interdisciplinair Demografisch Instituut (NIDI), AR Den Haag, The Netherlands

Georges P. Tapinos, Institut national d'études démographiques (INED), Paris

Helen Ware, High Commissioner, Australian High Commission, Lusaka, Zambia

UNITED NATIONS SECRETARIAT

Population Division of the Department of International Economic and Social Affairs
Donald Heisel, Associate Director
Birgitta Bucht, Chief, Population Trends and Structure Section
Hania Zlotnik, Population Affairs Officer
Marco Breschi, Junior Professional Officer
Bela Hovy, Junior Professional Officer

Centre for Social Development and Humanitarian Affairs
John Mathiason, Deputy Director, Division for the Advancement of Women

United Nations Population Fund
Catherine Pierce, Chief, Special Unit for Women, Population and Development

Economic Commission for Africa
Toma Makanna, Demographer, Population Division

Economic Commission for Europe
John Kelly, Statistical Division

United Nations High Commissioner for Refugees
Mary Petevi, Senior Resettlement Officer
Ruven Menikdiwela, Associate Legal Adviser

SPECIALIZED AGENCIES

International Labour Organisation
Patricia Weinert, Associate Expert, Employment and Development Department

Food and Agriculture Organization of the United Nations
Marie-Jane Mermillod, Women in Agricultural Production and Rural Development Service

United Nations Educational, Scientific and Cultural Organization
Serim Timur, Population and Human Settlements Division, Sector of Social and Human Sciences

INTER-GOVERNMENTAL ORGANIZATION

International Organization for Migration
Martha Lapeyriere, Chief, Division for Technical Cooperation

OBSERVERS

Italy

Ana Maria Birindelli
Carla Collicelli
Simonetta di Cori
Nora Federici
Guiseppe Gesano
Antonio Golini

Carlo Maccheroni
Dionisia Maffioli
Eros Moretti
Silvana Salvini
Graziano Tassello

ANNEX III

List of documents

Document No.	Agenda item	Title and author
IESA/P/AC.31/1	2	Provisional agenda
IESA/P/AC.31/2	3	Measuring the extent of female international migration United Nations Secretariat
IESA/P/AC.31/3	3	The status of women and international migration Lin Lean Lim
IESA/P/AC.31/4	4	The sex selectivity of exit regulations governing international migration in South and South-east Asia Manolo I. Abella
IESA/P/AC.31/5	4	Migration regulations and sex selective outcomes in settlement and European countries Monica Boyd
IESA/P/AC.31/6	5	Policy dimensions of female migration to the Arab Gulf Sharon Stanton Russell
IESA/P/AC.31/7	5	Female migration and the status of foreign women in France Georges P. Tapinos
IESA/P/AC.31/8	6	Gender, household economy and females in international migration: a case-study of Bolivians in Argentina Jorge Balán
IESA/P/AC.31/9	6	A comparison of male and female migration strategies: the case of African and Filipino migrants to Italy Odo Barsotti and Laura Lecchini
IESA/P/AC.31/10	7	Algerian women in France: a negotiated status as a paradoxical form of integration Yeza Boulahbel-Villac
IESA/P/AC.31/11	7	The adaptation of Asian migrants to Australia Graeme J. Hugo
IESA/P/AC.31/12	9	The interrelations of international migration and the status of migrant women in sub-Saharan Africa Folasade Iyun

Document No.	Agenda item	Title and author
IESA/P/AC.31/13	7	New Sheilas: female European migrants to Australia - status and adaptation Helen Ware and David Lucas
IESA/P/AC.31/14	8	International migration and the changing labour force experience of women Maruja M. Asis
IESA/P/AC.31/15	8	Some aspects of the position of Turkish and Moroccan women in the Netherlands, compared with that of women in Turkey and Morocco Jeannette J. Schoorl
IESA/P/AC.31/16	6	Sri Lankan women in the Middle East Frank Eelens
IESA/P/AC.31/17	9	Female migration and life histories: the return from other European countries Jordi Cardelus and Angels Pascual de Sans
IESA/P/AC.31/18	9	The analysis of changes in the status of female returnees in Greece Ira Emke-Poulopoulos
IESA/P/AC.31/19	10	Recommendations to improve the status of female international migrants
IESA/P/AC.31/INF.1	-	Provisional list of participants
IESA/P/AC.31/INF.2/Rev.1	-	Provisional list of documents
IESA/P/AC.31/INF.3	-	Assistance to migrant women: programmes and services of the International Organization for Migration International Organization for Migration
IESA/P/AC.31/INF.4	-	The extent, causes and consequences of the participation of women in international migration in the Economic Commission for Africa member States Economic Commission for Africa
IESA/P/AC.31/INF.5	-	The special situation and the needs of refugee women United Nations High Commissioner for Refugees
IESA/P/AC.31/INF.6	-	Provisional organization of work of the Meeting

Part Two

EXTENT OF FEMALE INTERNATIONAL MIGRATION
AND GENERAL DISCUSSION OF ITS IMPACT
ON FEMALE STATUS

III. THE STATUS OF WOMEN AND INTERNATIONAL MIGRATION

Lin Lean Lim*

In response to the international community's call for work leading to a better understanding of the interrelations between demographic phenomena and the roles and status of women, the focus of research has been mainly on fertility and mortality, rather than on migration. Even where available, information on female migration deals mainly with movements within countries. While some of the issues associated with female internal migration emerge also in relation to the mobility of women across international borders, the situation of female international migrants is more complex and has been relatively neglected in the realms of both research and policy formulation. This neglect needs to be redressed, not just because women account for a sizeable proportion of international migrants but, more importantly, because the policy context which is so crucial in international migration tends to affect men and women differentially; because the mobility of women and their subsequent adaptation or integration to the host society, especially their participation in the labour force, are more intimately linked than those of men to the structure of the family and the social forces defining the sexual division of labour both in countries of origin and of destination; and because international migration, more than internal migration, involves a shift in socio-cultural contexts coterminous with a change in gender stratification systems, which could improve, erode or leave unaffected women's position relative to men. In so far as women's status is a socially constructed rather than a biologically dictated concept (Caldwell, 1982; Mason, 1984; Smith, 1986; Benería and Roldán, 1987; Cleland and Wilson, 1987; Nagaraj and Lim, 1988a; Tienda and Booth, 1988), international migration, more than any other demographic phenomenon, has major implications for changing women's status, since migrant women move from one social context

to another. From another perspective, the interactions of forces generated by markets, nation States and social networks, all of which shape international migration flows (Lim, 1992), are of special relevance for the study of female migration.

Both gender and migration issues are important in analysing the roles and status of women as determinants and consequences of international migration. These issues can be briefly identified in terms of:

(*a*) Implications of sex selectivity, that is, what the distribution of migrants by sex, or by sex and other variables such as age, marital status or country of origin, reflects of the political, economic and socio-cultural contexts in which the status of women is embedded;

(*b*) Influence of gender relations on the motives and potential for the international migration of women;

(*c*) Similarities or differences between the determinants of international migration for men and women and their causes;

(*d*) Extent to which and manner in which laws and regulations controlling international migration are not gender-neutral;

(*e*) Selective impact by sex of labour market dynamics in both countries of origin and destination;

(*f*) Relative importance of international migration *per se* as a mechanism generating or restructuring gender asymmetries given the change in social environment that migration usually entails;

(*g*) Relative vulnerability of migrant women, that is, whether being female and foreign in an alien environment leads to the "double discrimination" and "threefold or fourfold oppression" of migrant women.[1]

*Regional Adviser on Women Workers' Questions, Regional Office for Asia and the Pacific, International Labour Organization, Bangkok, Thailand.

This paper attempts to stimulate thinking and research on those issues most relevant for the sound formulation of policy regarding female migrants. It is not intended to be a comprehensive review of present knowledge. It will first introduce some basic concepts drawn from the literature and research on women's status and on international migration. The concepts discussed emphasize the dynamic character of the phenomena at hand and operate at different levels, the society or economy as a whole, the family, the individual. The implications of women's status for their participation in international migration are examined next, focusing on whether, how and under what circumstances the move across international borders affects the position of migrant women in relation to migrant men and other groups of women. Suggestions are made for possible research approaches that may facilitate policy formulation, evaluation and the identification of data needs.

The lack of reliable and adequate data is a major drawback. Aside from the limited international migration statistics by sex published by the United Nations (1979 and 1988), *SOPEMI* (OECD, 1988) and the OECD Monitoring Panel on Migrant Women (Boyd, 1988a), and information on the migrant stock by sex as enumerated by national population censuses, relevant data on migrants are often not available by sex and other essential characteristics, such as age, marital status, country of origin and labour force participation. At the country level, national recording systems tend to throw a veil of invisibility over migrant women mostly because whatever data are gathered on international migrants tend not to be published, or otherwise disseminated, classified by sex. Researchers must therefore rely very often on less than ideal information, often obtained from participant observation and focused biographies which may offer depth but not breadth of coverage and usually lack representativity.

Different definitions of what constitutes an international migrant, the complications brought about by illegal or undocumented migration and a general lack of consensus on the types of statistics that ought to be produced exacerbate the problem, which is largely attributable to policy neglect and misperceptions concerning female migrants. The data avail- able reflect concepts underlying national policies that are rarely formulated in order to satisfy data needs (Tapinos, 1983; Kritz, 1987). Yet the improvement of information on female migrants is necessary to facilitate the formulation and evaluation of policy.

A. DEVELOPING A CONCEPT OF WOMEN'S STATUS RELEVANT TO INTERNATIONAL MIGRATION

Since a major stumbling block in understanding the interrelations of the "status of women" with international migration is the vagueness of the concept itself, it is useful to clarify the multidimensional and context-dependent facets of women's status that can be operationalized in empirical research and linked to international migration.

The status of women refers to women's position relative to men and to each other over the course of a lifetime within a particular socio-economic, cultural and politico-legal context. Although gender inequality is the focus of our concern, international migration policies, even if gender neutral, may differentiate between migrants on the basis of ethnicity or country of origin and thus have an impact on the status of certain female migrants. In addition, the general position of migrant women versus that of non-migrant women is of fundamental interest.

Focusing on gender inequality, the position of women relative to men can be viewed as a composite of different dimensions in terms of women's situational advantages or disadvantages, their freedom or lack of it from men's control, and their rights and obligations as compared to those of men. To characterize and measure gender inequality, the main referents are:

(a) *Economic indicators of status*, that is, possession of and control over resources, including knowledge, time, money and material goods;

(b) *Political indicators of status*, that is, the ability or power to make decisions, such as the decision to migrate, to participate in the labour force or to control the disbursement of income from work, and the ability to exercise control over other people as, for instance, being the mobilizing force behind the migration of family members;

(c) *Social indicators of status* including the prestige, respect or esteem accorded to women (these indicators reflect differences in socio-cultural norms and attitudes between the country of origin and that of destination).

These indicators of women's status permit the calibration of women's relative position before and after migration. Since they do not necessarily reinforce each other during the migration process, they may reflect contradictory migration outcomes whereby the status of migrant women improves in some respects, while being eroded in others. That happens when, for instance, migrant women secure paid employment for the first time in the country of destination but fail to achieve control over their earnings. Similarly, women encouraged to become temporary labour migrants by the changing international structure of opportunities (often as domestic servants or in the entertainment industry) may fail to earn social respect either in the country of origin or that of destination.

It is easier to assess women's relative control over resources, power and prestige if these are thought of as closely linked to or accruing from the roles that women play within their families or as members of a community within the society of origin or that of destination. The roles of women refer to their actual or expected patterns of behaviour or to their concrete activities, a fundamental assumption being that women act in a certain manner partly because of the treatment or reactions expected from those with respect to whom they play a particular role. For each role that a woman plays in a certain socio-cultural context, there is a reciprocal role played by men. Women have been identified as having seven major roles in society: (a) producers or members of the paid or unpaid labour force; (b) wives; (c) mothers; (d) housewives; (e) kin; (f) community members; and (g) individuals (Oppong, 1980; Oppong and Abu, 1985). In each of these roles, women may be exposed to different mobility influences. For example, migration policies may favour particular roles, such as the conjugal role of women migrating under

family reunification schemes or their economic role when they move as migrant workers. By relating women's status to role behaviour and expectations, a more systematic and comprehensive picture can be obtained of the resources, rewards and satisfactions that women derive from (or conversely, the conflicts or constraints that they face in) what they do and of the contexts in which migration decisions are made (whether by the women themselves or by someone else).

A theoretical distinction between the behaviours and expectations related to different roles is useful for purposes of data collection and statistical analysis. As distinct from role behaviours, role expectations can be classified according to whether they express what ought to be (norms), what is preferred (preferences or values), or what is thought to exist (perceptions) (Oppong, 1980, p. 9). The normative dimension of expectations or perceptions is important because it draws attention to how women perceive, understand, accept, condemn or fight against their subjugation both within the family and in society (Morokvasic, 1988, p. 161). The normative dimension is emphasized in the fourfold oppression models of migrant women. For instance, if migrant women perceive that their low status as workers is due to their status as foreigners rather than to their class affiliation or sex they may feel a sense of solidarity with migrant men instead of viewing them as a source of oppression.

It should be underscored that the various dimensions of women's status are context-dependent or location-specific. Gender interactions take place and women's status is determined in different spheres, locations or "social fields" (Epstein, 1986, p. 2): the family; the community or kin group; and the broader society. Women's status has therefore micro- and macro-dimensions that need to be integrated in research. Consideration of different contexts is relevant both for the understanding of international migration and of the various dimensions of the status of women, since such status may improve in society at large without changing the relative position of women within the family. That is the case when the social context in the place of destination is characterized by flexible sex hierarchies that facilitate the labour force participation of migrant women whose position within the family may nevertheless remain subordinate. Another perspective, offered by Tienda and Booth (1988), is that economic exchanges based on market rules, which may be gender-neutral (and which can be directly influenced by government policies), are different from social exchanges which involve allocation principles within the family that institute unequal access to resources for male and female family members.

Various studies emphasize the importance of the family setting to understand female status (and female migration). It is usually within the family that women's subordination to male authority is clearer and most crucial (in terms of its influence on women's lives). Curtis (1986), for example, concludes that the family is the primary unit generating gender inequality, that the roots of patriarchal authority are familial rather than sexual, and that the authority exercised by men as fathers or husbands over women as daughters or wives can extend to control over the non-familial roles that women play. Hence, to understand women's status and migration it is particularly useful to focus on women as family members with their assigned or expected roles, enjoying certain rights and subject to certain familial obligations, and to consider the interdependence and synchronization of the life histories of male and female family members. Such an approach demands consideration of a woman's stage in the life cycle (age or duration of marriage may be used as proxies for it) and of her position within the family (as daughter, mother, sibling, daughter-in-law, mother-in-law, head of household, widow etc.) prior to and following migration. The family and marital status of a woman is likely to influence her propensity to migrate, while the impact of migration on her relative position is also likely to depend on her family status prior to moving. The position of a woman's family in the class structure of the sending and the receiving society must also be considered. Women from lower social classes or poor families may be less constrained by social norms discouraging the independent migration of women because of their need to work and contribute to family survival. Behavioural changes may occur, however, if migration leads to upward social mobility.

The social context is significant because gender is widely recognized as a "socially constructed rather than biologically dictated category" (Benería and Roldán, 1987, p. 12). It is only by taking into account the embeddedness of gender in a structure of culturally, socially and politically circumscribed obligations and expectations, that the implications of the actions and achievements of individual women can be understood (Granovetter, 1985; Curtis, 1986). For research purposes, it is necessary to consider individual women within gender stratification systems that can be identified along the lines of culture, ethnicity, nationality or political systems. Thus, it is membership in a particular cultural or ethnic group or residence in a particular country that exposes a woman to specific cultural orientations, normative controls and systematic institutional socialization concerning her normally subordinate position in relation to men. It is from such a perspective that the micro- and macro-aspects of women's status as well as the situation of women as "in between" or "torn between" cultures should be considered.

Migration can be viewed as a move between gender stratification systems, but whether such move improves or erodes women's position will have to be examined empirically on the basis of concrete situations. The research challenge is to identify what aspects of the gender stratification system are similar or different between countries of origin and destination and, more importantly, which of them impinge directly on the status of female migrants. Migrants can be viewed as embodying the interactions between the norms and attitudes determining female status in sending and receiving countries. Such interactions are dynamic, meaning that the status of female migrants is subject to change. The longer their residence in the country of destination and the more successful their integration, the more likely that their status (or the status of their daughters) may reflect the social norms of the host society.

At its widest, the social context should be considered in connection with the emerging global economy where countries are increasingly linked by the flows of commodities, capital, technology and people. This broad and dynamic perspective is recommended because, in line with current literature on international migration, it allows attention to be focused on the political, economic, institutional and social processes that shape migration flows between countries and that bring about changes in the roles and status of female migrants. Such an approach would permit consideration of how global developments, such as the pervasiveness of international capital flows and technology transfers, affect female migrants. It would also shed light on the gender selectivity of intermediaries, such as recruitment agents, or the influence exercised by social networks on the migration of women.

B. FEMALE ASPECTS OF INTERNATIONAL MIGRATION PROCESSES

Just as there are macro- and micro-aspects to women's status, so too the general literature on international migration emphasizes that research should focus not only on motivations at the individual level but also on the broad processes that link sending and receiving countries within a global system. The parallels between the study of women's status and international migration become evident: both emphasize the need to understand individual-level phenomena first within the context of the family or the community, and then within the broader context of the social, economic and political settings.

This section focuses on those processes shaping international migration at the macro-level which—by design or in actual occurrence—may not be gender neutral or which are likely to have special implications for female migrants. Current research on international migration strongly supports a systems approach focusing upon the "relational dynamics" linking sending and receiving countries in an increasingly interdependent world (Zolberg, 1981; Petras, 1981; Bach, 1985; Weiner, 1985; OECD, 1987; Lim, 1987 and 1989; Portes and Böröcz, 1989). Relational dynamics are shaped by the interactions between economic, political, institutional and social processes that determine the composition, magnitude, directionality and impact of international migration flows as well as other linkages between countries. Those processes can be thought of as generating opportunities and constraints for international mobility that may affect men and women differently. Their implications for international migration and the status of female migrants are discussed below and some suggestions to guide empirical research are made.

Economic processes

The economic processes of exchange underlying international migration can be understood in terms of differential supply and demand conditions for the factors of production in sending and receiving countries (Lim, 1992). A country faced with labour shortages, high and inflexible wages and a falling comparative advantage in international markets can resort to trade protectionism, shift to production technologies or a product mix requiring less labour, import foreign workers to ease supply bottlenecks and contribute to wage moderation, or export capital to countries with cheap labour. The last two options are particularly likely to impinge on women and should therefore be the subject of study.

One may ask, for instance, if a country resorting to "insertion" policies in order to obtain cheap and easily controllable labour or to fill marginalized jobs no longer desired by nationals may consider migrant women as a more attractive source of labour supply. According to theories of labour market segmentation or dualism (Berger and Piore, 1980; Piore, 1983), the research issue would be to determine whether the demand for female migrant labour in countries of destination arises at the lowest rungs of the occupational hierarchy in sex segregated markets[2] and the extent to which demand is predicated on correlates of women's sex roles—cheapness of labour, docility and obedience (Sassen-Koob, 1984).

Research on the economic processes underlying female labour migration could focus on: (a) the growth of foreign investment in export-oriented manufacturing industries in developing countries (Marshall, 1979; Pang and Lim, 1982; Hancock, 1983; Lim, 1988b); (b) reasons for the growing demand for migrant women in large cities of developed countries, including the general shift to a service economy, the downgrading of manufacturing, the direct and indirect demand for low-wage labour, and the tendency to move jobs to the informal sector in various sectors of the economy (Sassen-Koob, 1984, pp. 1161-1162); (c) the recent reduction in the demand for male migrant labour that has occurred simultaneously with a rise in demand in certain traditionally feminized occupations such as domestic service, nursing, teaching etc. (Lim, 1988b); and (d) the increasing dependence of certain countries, such as Sri Lanka and the Philippines, on the foreign exchange earnings obtained from remittances from their relatively large number of migrant women, a means of extracting the most from the "comparative advantage of women's disadvantages" (Charlton, 1984).

With respect to the implications of the strategy whereby countries export capital instead of importing labour, the research issue is to what extent such "new international division of labour" (Froebel, Heinrichs and Kreye, 1980; Nash and Fernandez-Kelly, 1983; Sassen-Koob, 1983) is based on the "exploitation" of female workers (Hancock, 1983; Eisold, 1984; Lim, 1988b). Is it the availability of a ready supply of cheap, docile and malleable female workers that attracts international capital and technology to developing countries (UNIDO, 1980)? While the exploitation of women in the context of the new international division of labour is an increasingly well-developed theme, it is less clear how the international flows of capital affect the international mobility of women. Does the relocation of capital to developing countries reduce the incentives (or the need) for women to migrate abroad in search of jobs or does that relocation contribute to the increase of the volume and diversity of international labour movements as some authors have suggested (Portes, 1983; Sassen-Koob, 1983; Pastor, 1985)?

Similar issues could be examined in relation to the impact of technology flows. For instance, does the growing importance of technology in interactions between countries affect the sex selectivity of migration? One may speculate on how the use of more capital-intensive techniques is likely to affect migration opportunities for female labour. As both countries sending and receiving capital flows increasingly emphasize the importance of new technology in gaining a competitive edge in international markets, it has been predicted that specialists will increase in future international labour flows (Laroque, 1987). The implications of such trends for female migration remain to be elucidated.

Institutional processes

The role of institutional processes in shaping international migration has only recently been recog-
nized. The institutions of relevance are mainly those that can be described as playing an "intermediary" role in migration. They cover the full spectrum ranging from legal recruitment agents to underground syndicates operating illegally in either the country of origin or that of destination, or in both. Documenting their activities and modes of operation is particularly relevant to enhance our understanding of female migration, especially because intermediaries operating illegally are prone to exploit the disadvantaged position of women. There is a need to evaluate the extent to which intermediaries either provide a necessary service that improves the opportunities for migration or increase the constraints and costs of migration. It has been noted that some intermediaries charge such high recruitment fees that they condemn migrant women and their families to indebtedness even after the benefits of migration have accrued (Go, Postrado and Jimenez, 1983a; Abella, 1992). Welfare organizations, church groups and the media have drawn attention to the plight of large numbers of young women who, lured by attractive offers of work in the "entertainment industry", have found themselves forced into prostitution far from their home countries (*Asia Magazine*, 6 September 1987).

Another example of an institutional process shaping migration is the role of transnational corporations in moving their employees internationally (Salt, 1988). The numerical significance of those movements is difficult to assess, but they raise interesting questions about the nature of female migration. For instance, to what extent do highly qualified women participate in international migration? Are women equally well represented at the higher end of the skill spectrum in migration streams as at the lower end? Do institutions involved in promoting the migration of highly skilled personnel provide equal opportunities to men and women?

Political processes

The policies adopted by both countries of origin and destination are widely recognized as crucial determinants of the characteristics of migration flows. Thus, migration policies and the regulations adopted to implement them largely determine the legal or illegal nature of a flow, whether legal admissions are constituted mainly by workers or dependants, and whether close family ties with persons resident in a country are a sufficient basis for admission. The implications of such policies and regulations for the intended or unintended sex selectivity of migration need to be explored. In addition, it is important to assess whether the regulations adopted by receiving countries to control the entry, stay or exercise of economic activity of migrants provide equal opportunities to men and women.

Just as some admission policies have been overtly discriminatory by region or country of origin, others have been so on the basis of sex. Thus, colonial Governments generally prohibited women from living in newly developed towns, mining camps and plantations. Roussel (1975) attributed the preponderance of males in the migration streams to Ghana and Côte d'Ivoire in the late 1950s to the nature of work to be done and the colonial prejudices about "suitable" work for women. In the case of Peninsular Malaysia the sex ratio of migrants improved after 1933 when the British colonial Government imposed quotas on the entry of men but encouraged the free admission of migrant women, mostly from China (Sidhu and Jones, 1981, p. 31).

More recently, admission policies have tended to be less blatantly discriminatory along gender lines. However, even gender-neutral policies may be applied in a discriminatory fashion. The task of unveiling covert discrimination is crucial to understand the conditions under which women accede to migration opportunities. When a supposedly gender-neutral policy establishes de facto distinctions between the entry status of male and female migrants, the potentially disadvantaged position of the latter may become a reality. Thus, migrant women admitted as "dependants" may, by that very fact, be cast on a legally dependent position in relation to men. A systematic analysis of the circumstances under which covert discrimination detrimental to women arises and its implications is urgently needed.

Studying the situation in Canada, Boyd (1987b, p. 22) has noted that the question is whether and how "rules and regulations, which inherently do not discriminate by sex or immigrant status, in practice and in combination with other rules and regulations produce inequitable outcomes which operate to the disadvantage of some immigrant women". More gen-

erally, one can ask whether the terms of admission make sufficient allowance for the typical position of women in society and, more specifically, in the societies of origin. For instance, though many countries allow migration for the purpose of family reunification, the definition of family they adopt may be rather restrictive. It is important, therefore, to examine the definitions of family that are legally in operation (Hune, 1987). When the nuclear family is adopted as legal standard, women in extended family structures, consensual or common-law marriages may not be eligible for entry. Such a definition may also curtail the migration of dependent children of migrant heads of households who are female, as many of those originating in the Caribbean are (Garrison and Weiss, 1979; Boyd, 1987b). Although marriage with a country's citizen is often an avenue for migration, national regulations vary in their degree of stringency. Australia and Canada, for example, exempt fiancé(e)s of citizens from migration regulation, whereas the United States does not (Kritz, 1987, p. 951). Evidence that single women have more difficulty in finding legal avenues for migration and that a significant proportion of undocumented migrant women are on their own economically (Simon and DeLey, 1986; de Wenden and DeLey, 1986) should be considered in relation with the set of regulatory mechanisms that may directly or indirectly influence those outcomes.

When conditions of admission are such that women are not recognized as heads of household or are admitted subject to the sponsorship of spouses or even under a common residence permit with their spouses, one must focus not only on the implications of such conditions for the legal dependency of women but also on their indirect effects on labour market stratification and power-sharing inside the family.

Some of the issues raised by the OECD Monitoring Panel on Migrant Women (Boyd, 1988a) are of research interest in this context: (a) the extent to which existing rules for family reunification and their application are gender neutral; (b) the extent to which a migrant woman enjoys an independent status from that of her husband; (c) the consequences of linking a woman's residence permit to that of her husband in the event of marital disruption (through divorce or because of the departure or unemployment of the husband); (d) the implications of separating residence permits from work permits; and (*e*) the implications of regulations granting temporary residence permits to persons admitted because of a recent marriage to a resident.

It is important to note that women have often been admitted as temporary migrant workers in their own right. Consequently, in examining the policy context relating to those types of migrants, one needs to explore whether the legal protection accorded to them is appropriate to prevent the abuse or exploitation of migrant women. Do legally mandated contracts for temporary workers safeguard the interests and rights of female migrants? Are female migrant workers equally able as their male counterparts to sponsor the admission of close relatives? Are there any programmes in place to regulate the activity of recruitment agents and is an effort being made to derail illegal recruitment activities? In so far as the temporary migration policies of a number of countries are increasingly oriented towards admitting skilled workers, professionals or entrepreneurs, who generally receive better treatment than their unskilled counterparts, the implications of such policies for female migrants need to be considered. In Singapore, for instance, only skilled migrants are encouraged to stay for long periods (Pang and Lim, 1982).

Apart from employment-related reasons, women can be admitted under other categories of temporary migration as, for instance, students, exchange visitors, asylum-seekers or refugees. Data on the female selectivity of such temporary migration streams are needed and the constraints to which women in those migration categories are subject need to be documented. In the United States, for instance, where persons admitted temporarily can eventually adjust their status to become immigrants, it would be useful to establish whether more women than men resort to that procedure and on what grounds (Arnold, Minocha and Fawcett, 1987). One hypothesis to test is whether female temporary migrants are more likely than their male counterparts to marry citizens of the country of destination in order to stay.

In countries of origin, state policies can influence migration through prohibitive, selective, permissive, promotional and expulsive rules of exit (Weiner,

1985) that may affect male and female migrants differently. Thus, as of mid-1988, reacting to reports of exploitation and ill treatment of female migrants, Bangladesh, India, Pakistan and the Philippines had all taken measures to prevent their female citizens from departing to work abroad as domestic servants (Hugo and Singhanetra-Renard, 1989). The Government of the Philippines has gradually and selectively lifted the ban on exit to 23 countries with which it has reached bilateral agreements concerning the working conditions of Filipino domestic servants. An evaluation of the effectiveness of the measures taken by countries of origin is necessary to ascertain to what extent they have protected the interests of migrant women and whether other policies or programmes would be useful. The latter might include publicity and orientation courses to prepare migrant women for the conditions in countries of destination and a better supervision and control of the activities of recruitment agents.

The process by which the Governments of countries of origin have devised and implemented specific measures to protect migrant women deserves attention, especially to determine whether the initiative for those actions rested on the Government itself or was prompted by the actions of the migrant women themselves or by a middle class desire to protect national dignity. For instance, to what extent has Sri Lanka, a major source of female migrant workers, avoided the use of migration restrictions to prevent the exploitation of women because of the lower status of women in that country combined with the lack of influence of women's groups. The influence of social groups in receiving countries is also of interest. In Malaysia, church groups have set up a shelter and advisory centre for Filipino domestic servants and in Japan, Japanese women assist migrant women who have been exploited as "entertainers".

Social processes

A key aspect of the study of international migration is the role that women play in the social and kinship networks that sustain migration flows. The importance of social networks in linking sending and receiving countries within dynamic migration systems has been increasingly emphasized (Lim, 1987; Gurak and Caces, 1992). Social networks[3] involve not only members of a family but also persons related by other affiliation ties that involve reciprocal obligations, including kinship and friendship ties among persons sharing a common community of origin, culture or religion (Massey, 1986 and 1988). From an analytical perspective, social networks can be viewed as linking the macro-processes that set the stage for international migration and the individuals who ultimately move. Therefore, networks offer a bridge between structural approaches to the study of migration and those that emphasize the individual migrant as actor (Boyd, 1989).

To date, most research tends to assume either that the structure and functions of social networks are the same when men predominate over women in migration flows as when the reverse occurs, or that the "female" phase of migration represents the maturation of the migration network (when wives and children join husbands already established abroad). Boyd (1989) has stressed that more needs to be known about differences in how male and female migrants develop, maintain or use social networks, taking account of the social, ethnic or cultural context in which those networks function.

One needs to know whether the process of network formation differs for men and women. Given the variety of their social roles, women may have a greater number of contacts with friends and family and thus be better able to gather information and extend social networks. Women may be more likely than men to rely on informal channels which may, in turn, be more effective than the formal social groups to which men tend to belong (Smith, 1980; Foner, 1986). On the other hand, women who do not work in the formal sector or who are mostly confined to household roles may be less likely than men to have access to networks based on friendship, social or ethnic ties and may have to rely on their spouses or other kin to have such access. Constraints of that type are likely to affect their opportunities for migration (Graves, 1984). The type of migration involved may interact with gender to determine how networks are generated and used. Thus, female migrant workers or refugee women tend to have fewer kin and friendship ties than women moving in the context of family migration (Boyd, 1989). The structure and

function of social networks may be different for men and women. Migrant women may be more likely to use networks mainly to obtain information, help with housing, to meet other social needs or send remittances to the country of origin, whereas men may use them to find jobs and obtain economic assistance. Although social networks are thought to assist in the adaptation process, the exact mechanisms involved remain to be elucidated, especially where migrant women are concerned. It is also of interest to ascertain if women's roles as generators and users of social networks are the same before and after migration.

Research on social networks has relied on two basic methodologies: the ethnographic approach based on the study of individual cases within a community (Repak, 1988) and the use of surveys sometimes in conjunction with the ethnographic approach (Boyd, 1989). Surveys can gather information on the structure and function of family, kin and friendship networks, including the source of information leading to migration, the actual forms of assistance received from kin and friends, the presence of relatives or friends in the country of destination, the means of finding a job, the frequency and content of verbal or written communications with family members living elsewhere (including the country of origin), the level of remittances, the frequency of return visits, membership in voluntary associations or ethnic organizations, residence in an ethnic neighbourhood etc. (Tienda, 1980; Portes and Bach, 1985; De Jong and others, 1985/86; Massey and others, 1987).

C. WOMEN'S STATUS AS A DETERMINANT OF INTERNATIONAL MIGRATION

So far, we have discussed gender-specific concerns from a structural perspective focusing on the different processes linking countries of origin and destination in dynamic migration systems. This section focuses on the individual female migrant, viewing women not as isolated "gender entities" but rather in relation to men, both within the family and in the context of the social, political and economic conditions that shape the set of constraints and opportunities for spatial mobility across international boundaries.

37

Figure I shows that three sets of influences operate on a woman's status, on her motives or potential to migrate and on her eventual migratory experience, namely, the macro-structural context, the structure and functions of her family, and her own individual characteristics over the life cycle. This framework was originally developed to explain the linkages between macro-structural variables and the relations between women's status and migration in general (Lim, 1988a) and has been adapted here to focus on international migration in particular. Figure I shows that the forces determining a woman's status also shape the context in which her mobility takes place. The macro-structural context has four paths of direct and indirect influence—on the family, on the individual characteristics of a woman, on her roles and status, and on the decision-making processes leading to migration and carried out either at the individual or family level. Here the term "family" refers not only to the immediate domestic unit but also to the social networks in which individuals are embedded and which straddle time and space. Figure I makes a distinction between decision-making on the part of an individual woman and her involvement in a household strategy of migration in which other family members (whether male or female) take the lead in decision-making. Yet, even when a woman moves on her own (autonomous migration), the family may play an important role in decision-making and the motivation to move may be related to considerations regarding family welfare. Similarly, associational migration may involve a certain degree of choice and the active participation in the decision-making process of the woman involved.

The decision-making process at the individual level

The autonomy to decide whether to migrate or not and under what circumstances, as well as the ability to influence the migration decision of others, is itself an indicator of a woman's status. In highly traditional and patrilineal societies, one of the indicators of the subordinate position of women is that they take part only in associational migration decided by the patriarch or other male members of the family. When a woman has the autonomy to change her behaviour or when her rights and obligations within

the family or in society include a personal mobility alternative, the influence of her roles and status on the motivation to migrate can be traced. Various dimensions of the roles and status of a woman are assumed to affect her evaluation of the feasibility and attractiveness of migration as an option. It is likely that the higher her status within the family and society of origin, the lower her incentive to migrate. The greater her subordination to male authority, the stronger her motivation to migrate, although her ability to do so may be restricted.

The effects of female status can also be traced through the selectivity of the migration process. The greater selectivity evident among autonomous female migrants than among those involved in associational migration may, however, be due to the fact that economic opportunities in the country of destination attract autonomous female migrants to both the top and the bottom of the occupational scale, so that "high" status may not necessarily account for selectivity.

One important reason for the migration of women that does not apply to men is the desire to escape the constraints imposed by their subordinate position in the country of origin. As Seller points out:

"Many of these women came to the United States on their own initiative, independent of, and sometimes in opposition to, the wishes of their families. Some were motivated by the desire to send money to parents and siblings at home. For these women, immigration was an extension of the traditional female role of dutiful daughter. Others came because they preferred the freedom and independence of even poorly paid work in the United States to the dependence of unpaid work in the home of parents or a future husband. For them, immigration was a rejection, conscious or unconscious, of traditional female roles. Autobiographies also suggest that women who came to the United States on their own initiative may have been less strongly committed than other women to traditional social roles" (Seller, 1981, p. 21).

To investigate when women are motivated to migrate so as to escape forms of oppression to which they are subject by virtue of being women (Seller,

Figure I. The macro-structure, women's status and international migration

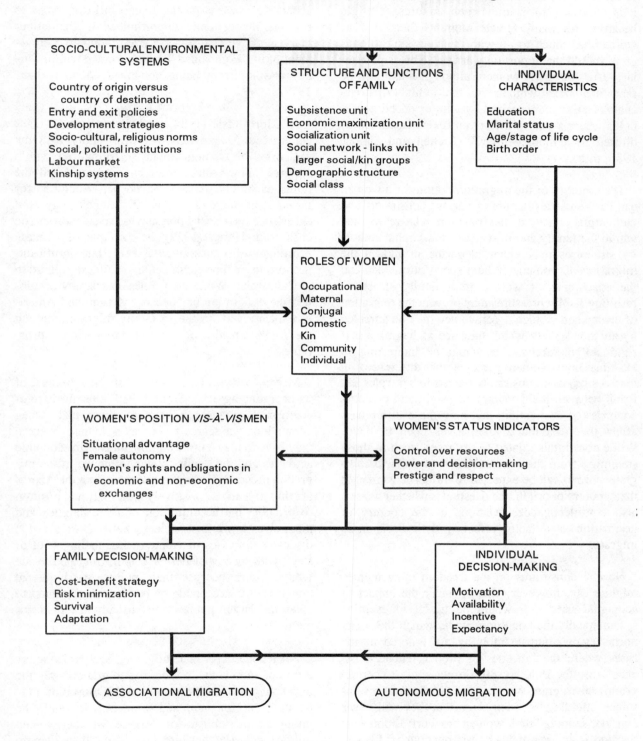

1981; Brouwer and Priester, 1983; Jackson, 1984), it is necessary to examine their cultures of origin because "for many female migrants their 'lot' as women has much to do with their decision to emigrate should the opportunity arrive. This is particularly true for single women, although it can also be seen for married women who live in highly patriarchal societies characterized by joint extended households where a young wife often finds herself subordinated to a mother-in-law" (Brettell and Simon, 1986, p. 5).

The viability of the migration option for a woman can be seen as a function of various constraints and facilitators related to her position relative to men within the family and in society. Patriarchal authority structures may either proscribe or induce the migration of women. Where social norms demand the attachment of women to a family structure, resulting family pressures may prevent the migration of unattached women. Yet women may be attracted by another society which they see as having a less rigid sex hierarchy. It would be interesting to examine how women perceive the differences in macro-structural constraints related to sex roles existing between their country of origin and potential countries of destination, and how those differences affect the behavioural alternatives open to them. While constraints related to sex roles (such as those stemming from the internalization of social or religious norms) can be expected to influence women in their country of origin, the question is whether women also consider gender relations in the country of destination as a factor affecting their decision to migrate.

Normal constraints on the freedom of women to migrate can, however, change under the impact of economic need. It would be useful to examine systematically the conditions under which the social norms against female mobility are ignored or the cases where the "niceties of proper female existence" (Smith, 1980, p. 80) do not apply to certain groups of migrant women. In Sri Lanka, for instance, middle class men claim that they will never consider sending "their women" to work as domestic servants in another man's house, but poor Sri Lankan women may not be able to afford the luxury of conforming to those social norms since, for them, becoming migrant workers may be the only option to

earn a decent wage (Brochmann, 1987). Similarly, economic necessity pushed many Turkish women to respond to economic opportunities in the labour markets of Western Europe, even though the movement of unaccompanied Turkish women within Turkey was far from being condoned (Abadan-Unat, 1977).

As Morokvasic (1984, p. 898) has noted, sociocultural constraints may not even apply to some categories of women already marginalized within society. Thus, those who have transgressed the limits of rigidly defined female behaviour by, for instance, having children out of wedlock, may even experience some social pressure to leave. Morokvasic cites from Hirata (1979) the example of Chinese prostitutes who constituted a small, but significant, proportion of nineteenth century Chinese migration to California. While the Chinese patriarchy prohibited the emigration of "decent" women and American society was hostile to family migration among the Chinese, neither prevented the migration of prostitutes.

Marginality may be a source of strength because of its liberating aspects. Smith (1980) cites the case of Azorean Portuguese women to show that, when competition for scarce resources is intense, women may have to play a more significant role in economic activities and thus gain greater influence in the migration process. Portuguese women from the Azores are thus able to use positively their marginal position to promote the acculturation of their families and themselves to the host society. Seller (1981, p. 17) discusses the cases of women who, feeling "out of step" with their societies of origin, migrated to the United States because their political activities at home were unacceptable or because they wanted to enter the larger public arena usually reserved for men.

For female as for male migrants, economic factors are commonly the reason for migration, yet the underlying economic motivations of migration may be different for men and women. It would be important to establish, for instance, whether women migrate because they are less likely than men to secure stable employment or income. When subsistence societies evolve, the economic changes that ensue may result in a greater displacement of women than of men from productive activity and such displacement may lead to out-migration. Thus, attention should be given to whether women are more seriously affected than men by agricultural mechanization or the destruction of cottage industries, and to whether women are more likely to leave areas where men control landownership and agricultural production or those where the reorganization of agriculture reduces the size of landholdings or increases the number of landless families (Boyd, 1989; Young, 1982; Sassen-Koob, 1984). It is also necessary to consider the options open to women in a system of production where they have become superfluous. Single women with few prospects of gainful employment in the area of origin may need to emigrate to find other means of support (Seller, 1981, p. 16). That is also likely to be the main option available for female heads of household struggling to bring up families on their own.

Marriage has often been cited as the main motivation for the migration of women. Thadani and Todaro (1984) and Behrman and Wolfe (1984) model the internal migration of women by emphasizing that motivational aspect.[4] After a review of the literature on female migration, Brettell and Simon (1986, p. 9) conclude that the subject of marriage as a reason for migration needs further examination. It is necessary to determine the relative importance of that motivating factor among all others and to relate it to both the various dimensions of status and the realities of international migration. In the United States, for instance, where immigrant admission is generally based on family ties, and priority is given to the admission of the spouses and children of United States citizens, family reunification and, particularly, the admission of women as wives explains the relatively high proportion of women admitted as immigrants to the United States since 1930 (Houstoun, Kramer and Barrett, 1984, p. 919). Yet, only in relatively few cases do women migrate in order to get married. Appleyard and Amera (1986) cite the case of single Greek women from villages depleted of single men for whom the prospect of finding husbands in Australia was an important motivating factor for migration. Women may also emigrate in order to avoid an unwanted marriage, to evade family pressures that push them into marriage (Connell, 1984, p. 966), to formalize a separation (Foner, 1986, p. 139) or to escape marital discord

and physical abuse from their husbands (Morokvasic, 1980). But even such motives may not be devoid of economic considerations. Thus, for Irish women migrating to the United States the desire to avoid marriage was often linked to the desire of avoiding the poverty that such marriage entailed (Seller, 1981, p. 18). The dowry system also acted as a push factor for Irish women (Schrier, 1958).

The case of "mail-order brides" deserves attention. The stereotypical image of a Filipino woman as being "a quietly spoken, docile companion who combines sexual attraction with gratitude to her 'master' for rescuing her from poverty" has increased the attraction of Filipino mail-order brides who have been sought by men in a number of countries, including Australia, Canada, Germany, Sweden and the United Kingdom (*New Straits Times*, 7 February 1988). There is a need to document the motivations and experience of mail-order brides and war brides. The latter constitute a numerically important group in countries like the United States (Tyree and Donato, 1986). It would be important to know whether women enter into such marriages because of poverty, the desire to escape the constraints to which they are subjected in their own societies, or because they expect a more egalitarian relationship with a man from a Western culture. The extent to which such expectations are fulfilled also deserves attention.

Married women may migrate on their own, move in conjunction with their husbands or stay behind in the country of origin when their husbands migrate depending, among other things, on the cultural acceptability of the separation of spouses. Prolonged separation may be more acceptable if it is forced by poverty. Thus, poor women from Indonesia, the Philippines, Sri Lanka and Thailand leave husbands and children behind to work overseas. When men migrate, the economic roles of their wives in the country of origin and the economic opportunities open for women in the country of destination are factors to consider in analysing the motivation for family reunification.

The majority of women migrate with their close family members or to join them abroad. There is little information, however, on the role that women play in making the decision to migrate. As Smith

41

(1980, pp. 79-80) points out in a study of Portuguese female migrants

"for every woman who was prompted by the male and followed willingly or regretfully, there were two who resisted and forced him to remain where he was, and there were five who had been the initiators of the idea: mothers, sisters, wives or daughters who worked at cajoling or pressuring males into taking the lead, or forced them to make the move. Women were often the pushers, the naggers, the needlers, the manipulators, the innovators, the security blankets and the teachers".

In addition to marital status, a woman's educational attainment and her stage in the life cycle are key factors to consider in relation to migration. Educated women may have a stronger incentive to move and may be more likely to qualify for legal admission.[5] Where women were previously disadvantaged, the liberalization of educational opportunities may be an important reason for migration (Zakrsewska, 1981).

Use of a life-cycle approach permits the examination of transitions in relation to migration, including changes in an individual's family configuration or the occurrence of key events such as leaving home, entering the labour force, marrying, having children or becoming widowed. Sex differentials in migration propensities should be examined in relation to events in the life cycle. Age is a particularly crucial factor. The sex selectivity of migration is often linked to age selectivity and their joint effect must be considered since they both affect and are affected by family institutions (Balán, 1983, p. 5). In so far as a woman's status changes over the life cycle, so too would her propensity to migrate. The timing of migration in relation to a woman's life cycle has major implications for the strategies a woman may adopt to deal with changes in her roles stemming from migration (Lamphere, 1986).

Depending on societal norms, changing marital status has been identified as a key motive for female migration, especially among women of working or marriageable ages. As a young bride and daughter-in-law, a woman may be in an especially weak position even though her incentive to migrate and gain independence from her husband's family in patriarchal and patrilocal societies may be strong (Ware, 1981, p. 162). As a mother of young children, a woman's ability to migrate will depend on whether she can manage multiple roles or can modify "old" ones. When society emphasizes the reproductive and domestic roles of women, female migration at certain stages of the life cycle may be curtailed. Thus, it has been argued that the underrepresentation of Mexican women in undocumented migration to the United States stems from the constraints imposed by their family responsibilities (Fernández-Kelly, 1983; Massey and others, 1987). However, women may opt for migration in order to fulfil their roles as wives and economic partners rather than as mothers. Portuguese women working in France thus left their children in Portugal, generally under the care of the maternal grandmother.

As a widow or divorcee, a woman may be marginalized in her own society or even pressured to leave. The need for support may also prompt the emigration of elderly women left alone in the country of origin. According to the OECD Monitoring Panel on Migrant Women (Boyd, 1988a and 1988c) the number of elderly migrants to Canada and the United States has been increasing and has involved a significant proportion of widowed women migrating to join their migrant sons and daughters.

Influence of the family and the decision-making process

The family context is particularly significant for the study of female migration because it is usually within the family that women's subordination to male authority plays itself out. The family assigns and defines the roles of women, which then determine their relative motivation and incentive to migrate, and the family provides the resources and information that can support or discourage migration. One can focus on the "affinity, information and facilitating" influences of the family on individual female migrants (Hugo, 1981).

The family or household can be seen as the structural or functional context within which women's status is determined, migration motivations and values are shaped, human capital is accrued, information is received and interpreted, and decisions are put into operation. Harbison (1981) argues persuasively that a more coherent treatment of the family as the immediate context of the migration decision is needed and that it is useful to consider the functions served by various aspects of the family before analysing how those functions affect the motivation to migrate. The social and demographic structure of the family is identified by Harbison as influencing the costs and benefits of migration by affecting an individual's status, well-being, rights and obligations within it.

As indicated in figure I and as set out in Harbison's model, several aspects of the functions and structure of the family can be examined as affecting women's roles and status and, indirectly, migration. Research could usefully focus on the various mechanisms through which families influence the mobility of female members. These mechanisms are related to the family as a subsistence unit: to the extent that the family assigns tasks to its members, a woman's ability to migrate would depend on whether her tasks can be fulfilled by other family members. As a subsistence unit, the family determines the access of family members to resources and it is likely that women who have limited access to resources may have stronger motivations to migrate. As an economic maximization unit, the family may encourage the migration of its female members, particularly of young women moving to get married or migrating under the auspices of an extended kin network. By encouraging migration through marriage and providing the necessary financial or social support for the process, the family increases both the chances and expectation of migration among daughters (Harbison, 1981, p. 239). Lastly, as a socialization unit, the family internalizes social norms and values that determine the roles appropriate for different family members, shape their kinship rights and obligations, and encourage the sense of affinity and dependence of women. A hypothesis that may be tested is that the stronger a woman's feelings of attachment to the family, the lower her propensity to migrate.

Perhaps the most important function of the family as a catalyst for migration is the assistance that it provides through the social networks to which it belongs, each entailing a complex set of rights and obligations. Whether women are more likely than men to make use of the assistance and services provided by networks, including transport, accommodation, information and job placement, needs to be explored. It has been argued that family structure affects the likelihood of female migration, because extended families have more members to spare and thus women belonging to them may be more likely to engage in migration and benefit from the greater integrative capacity that the extended family provides (International Center for Research on Women, 1979, p. 124). However, nuclear families, having more resources to spare, may be more likely to provide the necessary assistance for female migration.

Women in family migration strategies

The analysis of migration as a family survival strategy has gained prominence, partly because of the growing attention devoted to household processes and the household economy (Netting, Wilk and Arnould, 1984; Redclift and Mingione, 1985). This approach is advocated because households are "a primary arena for the expression of age and sex roles, kinship, socialization, and economic cooperation, where the very stuff of culture is mediated and transformed into action" (Netting, Wilk and Arnould, 1984, p. xxii). The concepts of household and family are often used almost interchangeably, though it may be useful to keep in mind their analytical distinction since a household is defined in terms of co-residence and may include non-family members sharing a common housing unit, while a family encompasses only persons related through kinship or marriage who need not reside together. In the context of migration, the family is the unit of interest, because even when its members are separated spatially their economic and social ties remain strong. Thus, the regular transmission of remittances from migrants to their families may be seen as "income pooling", a family adaptive strategy.

Migration, whether of individual family members or of the entire family, can be considered as a family strategy to achieve a better fit between resources (land or capital), consumption needs and different options to generate monetary and non-monetary income (Boyd, 1989, p. 14; Pessar, 1982, p. 348; Wood, 1982, p. 313). Such strategies include the selection of a family member for migration with the expectation that he or she will send back remittances that contribute to the family's economic portfolio; the migration of a family member with the expectation that other family members will be sent for, and the migration of complete households at one time.

These migration strategies can be viewed from two perspectives. The first is to assume that families make a cost-benefit analysis that compares the earnings expected from migration against the anticipated costs of moving. The other is that families send members abroad not only to maximize earnings but also to minimize the risks stemming from participation in the local economy (Stark and Levhari, 1982; Katz and Stark, 1986; Massey, 1988). From the second perspective, the efficacy of international migration can be gauged in terms of how it sustains the growth of social networks that progressively reduce the risks and costs of migration by providing lodging, information or assistance in job placement at the place of destination.

For those concerned with the status of women, the task is to determine the role that women play in devising or carrying out migration strategies. How often do women initiate or propose the possibility of migrating? Under what conditions are they likely to move themselves? The answer to those questions will depend on the position of women and the power structure within the family. In rural areas, single daughters may be selected for migration because they are not needed as agricultural workers or as household help and may not have any viable employment alternatives in the village. Daughters may be seen as a particularly reliable source of remittances because they are "more willing and faithful than sons in sharing their savings with the family" (Hart, 1971, p. 133). In some cases, women in the household may be the ones who secure the first labour contract to work abroad and who are therefore urged by their fathers, husbands or other relatives to migrate and to try and secure jobs for their male relatives (Abadan-Unat, 1977, p. 31).

D. Impact of international migration on women's status

Ultimately, the assessment of whether and how migration results in a redefinition of gender relations

is an empirical question to be decided on the basis of concrete situations (Tienda and Booth, 1988, p. 296). In assessing the improvement, deterioration or other changes in the status of migrant women, one needs to specify the circumstances and socio-cultural environments that mediate the influence of migration on women's status (Tienda and Booth, 1988, pp. 295-296). The circumstances under which migration occurs, including the entry status of a migrant woman, whether the woman migrates on her own or as a "dependent" family member, the reasons for the move, and the timing of migration with respect to other events, are likely to influence the outcome of migration for women and must be considered. In addition, the issue of how the juxtaposition of cultural environments brought about by migration affects the status of women needs to be explored by, among other things, determining the extent to which migrant women are exposed to new socio-cultural norms, comparing the relative position of women in the countries of origin and destination with respect to market and family relations (that is, economic and non-economic exchanges), analysing the socio-economic stratification among migrant women (which is closely associated with origin and language ability), identifying the social supports that help migrant women to cope with their changing roles in a new environment, and considering whether the situation of female migrants is determined mostly by their being foreign, by their being women or by their social class.

The importance of comparing the socio-cultural environment in countries of origin and destination cannot be over-emphasized. As Morokvasic (1988) argues, without reaching an adequate understanding of the socio-cultural background of migrant women, researchers are likely to adopt a misleading or simplistic view of migration as a linear transformation from tradition to modernity. Researchers tend to attribute to migrant women of extremely different origins one and the same simplified cultural background, that is labelled "traditional" (implying immobility and the oppression of women) and is generally contrasted with a Western model of modernity (implying emancipation or, at least, less oppression). Migrant women are placed on a continuum ranging from tradition to modernity and are assumed to be striving for modern, Western and, of course, emancipatory values (Morokvasic, 1988, p. 156). In fact, migrant women often come from cultural backgrounds that encompass many "liberating" conditions that are therefore not the result of migration.

In assessing changes in women's position brought about by international migration, it is crucial to distinguish between their status and roles at the level of ideology and those in practice (Brettell and Simon, 1986, p. 16) or, as Foner (1986, p. 141) suggests, between the objective and subjective viewpoints. To an observer, the position of migrant women may appear oppressed and dismal, but migrant women themselves may view their situation as an improvement in comparison to that before migration. It is also necessary to distinguish the different outcomes of migration and to isolate the factors responsible for each of them because migration may bring about improvements in certain aspects of the status of women but deterioration in others.

The study of changes in the status of migrant women brought about by migration should ideally be based on a comparison of female status before and after migration. However, in view of the difficulties involved in gathering the necessary information, one may gain useful insights by comparing female migrants with the generality of women in countries of origin and destination, by comparing the experience of migrant women being admitted under different conditions, by comparing women belonging to different migrant cohorts or by comparing migrant mothers with their "second generation" daughters.

Indicators of the different dimensions of women's status that should be examined include the legal and political rights of migrant women (including whether their residence and naturalization rights are dependent on the status of their male relatives or sponsors); their access to public programmes; their participation in economic activities; the relation between women's economic, domestic and reproductive roles; whether women have control over their own earnings or the earnings of other family members; women's relative authority in household decision-making, and the prevalence of female-headed households. At a more complex level, changes in gender relations in a new socio-cultural context might be examined in terms of whether there are more open family relations, greater sharing of household and child-care responsibilities between men and women,

changing attitudes towards the education of male and female children or towards the use of contraception, greater female participation in political activities, and the existence of a feminist consciousness.

In analysing the impact of migration on women's status, the importance of drawing the policy implications of the analysis must be underscored. A crucial goal should be to identify those areas of policy formulation where it is necessary to be sensitive or to provide for the special needs of migrant women in general and of special groups of migrant women in particular.

Entry status and dependency relations

The importance of understanding the intended or unintended gender biases of policies regulating the admission of migrants by the country of destination has already been pointed out. There is also a need to investigate the implications of entry status not only on the legal rights of female migrants in terms of residence, access to the labour market or to government programmes but also on gender relations within the family.

Comparing the situation of men and women who enter the country under different migration regulations allows an evaluation of how their initial entry status determines their right to set up legal residence for a certain period in the host country, their right to naturalization (in so far as women's entry status may be tied to that of men, it is important to examine whether naturalization laws are also gender biased), their right to work, their opportunities for employment, and their relative access to various types of public assistance, or to government training or integration programmes.

Such an assessment would be useful to establish both the direct and indirect implications of policy for the dependency relations within the household. Those relations stem from sex stratification and cultural conceptions of family headship that produce more men than women as principal applicants in family migration or as sponsors of family reunification. There would be a stronger case for changes of policies and regulations if it were shown that, by linking the admission, residence and other legal rights of women to the admission of male principal applicants or by assigning women to the sponsored category, the status of migrant women would be adversely affected in ways that reinforced their marginalization from society's mainstream and exacerbated their dependence on male relatives.

Potential dependence can be inferred from an examination of migration regulations or from case-studies of gender relations within the family, which often suggest that the economic, social and emotional aspects of the dependence of migrant women are mutually reinforcing (the situation in Canada is well documented by Boyd 1986, 1987a, 1987b and 1988b). In Europe, a growing body of research stresses the isolation and dependence of migrant women (Hoffman-Nowotny, 1978; Dumon, 1981; Rosen, 1981). However, a number of issues remain to be explored as, for instance, whether women admitted in the sponsored category are selectively denied access to welfare programmes or language-training courses because of the assumption that their sponsors can satisfy all their needs; the extent to which the dependent position of migrant women force them to remain in abusive situations, or the extent to which their deficient language skills condemn them to the lower rungs of the occupational scale and, consequently, to dependence, marginalization and poverty.

The implications of regulations applying to certain categories of migrant women, such as refugee women, women marrying citizens of the receiving country, women who migrate as temporary workers or on their own, still need to be understood. Women who marry citizens of the country of destination, for instance, may find it easier to secure admission, generous residence rights or access to the labour market than other female migrants. There may be differences, however, in the treatment accorded to the foreign spouses of male and female citizens that reflect a bias against women. Whether the status of women who are admitted as principal applicants for migration purposes is better than that of women whose admission is dependent on that of their male relatives is an issue to be considered. Another one is the extent to which women exercise their legal rights and entitlements. Are women who migrate in the company of their close relatives more likely than other migrant women to know and exercise those rights? Are women who migrate as contract workers equally likely as their male counterparts to know and exercise their legal rights? Are migrant women who work as domestic servants in private households less likely to exercise their rights than migrant men hired and working in turn-key projects? Differences in the rights and entitlements of male and female migrant workers need to be documented. In the United Kingdom, for instance, foreign men who hold work permits may bring in their children, but women in the same category are not permitted to do so unless they are widows or can prove that they have sole responsibility for their children's upbringing. Even immigrant women in the United Kingdom are not automatically allowed to be joined by their husbands and dependent children (Caspari and Giles, 1986, p. 156).

Labour-force status of migrant women

The patterns of labour force participation of migrant women represent an important indicator of their economic integration to the host society and of their changing roles and status. A common, though not necessarily correct, assumption is that access to employment in the host country is a major cause of women's "emancipation". While wage employment may put women (both migrant and non-migrant) in a more powerful economic position, open up more options for them and lead them to question some aspects of their status as women, more research is needed to establish whether the labour force participation of migrant women necessarily leads to an improvement in their status. Even if working for a wage frees some women from patriarchal ties by giving them control over income, their economic activity may not be free of costs, including the stress of coping with both employment outside the home and household responsibilities or the loss of prestige that may be associated with the necessity to work.

By conceiving labour markets as segmented or dual and stressing the persistence of gender hierarchies in them, researchers have emphasized the marginal situation of migrant female workers and highlighted the double-, triple- or fourfold discrimination that female migrants experience by virtue of their sex, birthplace, class and the general acceptance that their subordination is natural or inevitable. The stress has been on how the negative aspects of being a woman and a migrant condemn migrant women to the lowest rungs of the occupational scale, although it is not always clear whether being a woman or being foreign is the more important source of vulnerability[6] and although actual data show that migrant women are concentrated among both the highly skilled and unskilled occupations (Houstoun, Kramer and Barrett, 1984; Boyd, 1986).

A more accurate description would take account of the situation of women in the country of origin, of whether they had worked before migration, their age at migration, their length of stay in the host country and their marital status. Migrant women from developed countries, especially those speaking the language of the host country, are less likely to be disadvantaged in the labour market. Women who migrate at older ages are likely to be more disadvantaged than those migrating before reaching adulthood. It is also likely that, the longer the length of stay in the host country, the lower the propensity to be unemployed and the more likely that migrant women have a higher occupational status (Evans, 1984, p. 1086). Analysis of the labour force participation of migrant women should not be based on the assumption that wage employment is an indicator of modernity that did not exist either as a norm or as a behaviour prior to migration (Morokvasic, 1988, p. 156). Women who worked before migration may not experience a major change in their status but rather exchange one oppressive situation for another. However, differences in working conditions and remuneration between the country of origin and that of destination may motivate migrant women to seek changes in other aspects of their lives. It is also possible that women who enter the labour market for the first time after migration may be less prone to question occupational segregation or wage levels based on sex.

Wage comparisons are crucial because, even when a woman's occupation at the place of destination is the same as that at the place of origin, the woman herself may experience an improvement because of positive wage differentials. A positive subjective assessment may be reinforced by trips home, infor-

mation obtained through social networks and by the perception that migration is temporary (Foner, 1986, p. 145). Information on income is also necessary to establish whether migrant women tend to enter the labour force because of necessity or to improve their status (Tienda and Booth, 1988, p. 306). If household income is inadequate, migrant women may have no choice but to work (Lamphere, 1986).

The labour force participation of female migrants should be examined in relation to their domestic roles distinguishing, as Balán (1988) suggests: (a) women who do not have important domestic responsibilities and thus are potential autonomous migrants and labour force participants in the country of destination; (b) women who participate in the labour force after finding substitute houseworkers (more often than not, other women), a condition which may lead to autonomous migration and which is also typical of associational migrants working in the country of destination; (c) women who participate in the labour market provided they fulfil their domestic obligations, as is typical of associational migrants who may find employment; and (d) women involved only in household activities who make it possible for others to work.

To understand changes in women's status brought about by migration, it is necessary not only to compare their labour force participation and domestic roles before and after migration, but also to take into account the conditions of employment. For instance, migrant women may tend to work in environments conducive to social and cultural isolation, particularly if engaged in domestic service. Migrant women who have to raise children away from the support networks available to them in the country of origin may be subject to greater constraints if they decide to enter the labour market. A systematic examination of the constraints and supports shaping the labour force participation of female migrants and of their adaptation strategies would be desirable.

An evaluation of the implications of labour force participation on the status of female migrants cannot be carried out without taking into account the sociocultural context typical of the communities of origin and destination. Thus, if at the place of origin the participation of women, particularly married women, in the labour force is considered to reflect the inability of men to support their families, a working woman may be considered as having a lower social status than the one who does not need to work. When such norms persist after migration, the labour force participation of migrant women may not appear, at least subjectively, to bring about an improvement in status. For migrant women who have internalized such norms, economic activity would not be linked to any conscious desire for emancipation, self-realization or financial independence. In addition, for some migrant women cultural barriers towards employment outside the home may be practically insurmountable, as Prieto (1986) has documented for Cuban women in the United States and Andezian (1986) for Algerian women in France. Yet, when economic need is high, women may have to live with "the dishonour" of being working wives, as Lamphere (1986, p. 273) found in the case of Colombian migrants.

Awareness and sensitivity towards such socio-cultural variations are important to gauge the degree of commitment that female migrants have towards labour force participation. Those who cling to traditional norms and ideals concerning the responsibility of women towards home and family are likely to leave paid employment as soon as the family's economic situation permits. Such decision could, of course, be strongly influenced by the attitude of husbands and other male kin who may be less prepared to give up an ideology that sanctions men's roles as producers and women's as reproducers. Such ideology may, however, arise both from the persistence of traditional norms and values, and from the adoption of a new middle-class mentality after migration.

Impact of migration on family structure, women's roles and status

In studying the impact of migration on the status of women, the challenge is to take account of the circumstances of migration while elucidating changes in women's status stemming from the process of migration itself. The issue is whether changes in family and marital status combined with the new opportunities afforded by migration are the factors that alter women's position, or whether changes in the status of migrant women are precipitated by the strategies that they adopt to cope with new roles or with roles that are increasingly at odds with each other.

At the level of society, the assumption is that women's situation relative to men changes with migration because a change in social context brings about shifts in social norms, perceptions and opportunities. Yet, whether such shifts imply more or less egalitarian gender relations is only part of the question. The key to whether there is improvement or deterioration in the status of migrant women is the extent to which they are exposed to, adopt or adapt to the new social norms. The prestige or respect that the host society accords to women in general may be higher than that accorded to women in the society of origin, but if migrant women are isolated by language barriers and remain dependent and insulated within ethnic enclaves, the new social environment may have little impact on their status. Even when exposed to new social norms and behaviour, migrant women may find it too difficult to change their own behaviour and may continue to play the roles that they have always performed as, for example, doing housework with little or no help from other family members when, in the new environment, housework is usually shared among family members (Morokvasic, 1988, p. 164). Similarly, migrant women clinging to traditional family priorities and values may remain disadvantaged in the labour market of the host society when the latter has a relatively egalitarian approach, as in Australia (Evans, 1984, p. 1087).

However, the adoption of new behavioural patterns does not guarantee an improvement in all the aspects of women's status. Migrant women who join the labour force may not retain control over their earnings or improve their control over family resources. Female migrant workers may have to face a lowering of their prestige in the society of origin by the mere fact of engaging in paid employment away from home, even though they may be the main income-earners within their families (as is the case of Asian women working in Western Asia).

The crucial point to bear in mind is that changes brought about by migration should not be viewed simplistically. As Bachu (1986, p. 238) notes: "The process is not a unidirectional one of assimilation into the indigenous society, but rather one that involves constant negotiation and redefinition" of gender relations both within and outside the family. While migration may bring about changes in the allocation of productive and reproductive labour within the family, family ideology, as reflected in notions concerning authority, respect and gender roles, may remain virtually unchanged (Lamphere, 1986, p. 272).

The main task for researchers is, therefore, to identify the circumstances giving rise to conflicting roles for female migrants or affecting different dimensions of the status of migrant women in opposite directions. Such task may be accomplished by comparing how male and female migrants adapt to the host society. In doing so, it is necessary to distinguish between behavioural adjustments to the realities of everyday life in the host society and the adoption of that society's norms and values. While migrant men may find it easier to adapt behaviourally—a male migrant who can find a job and acquire a specialized job is often judged to be assimilating successfully (Smith, 1980, p. 86)—they may resist the adoption of new norms, especially those involving a loss of male authority. Migrant women, on the other hand, may face more difficulties in adjusting to a lifestyle far removed from the one that they experienced in the country of origin, but may be more willing to internalize social norms that are likely to enhance their status within the family.[7] In some contexts, migrant men may also be more likely to view migration as temporary and hence to rationalize the rejection of new norms. Thus, a thorough assessment of changes in the status of female migrants cannot be carried out without considering the responses of migrant men.

Given that the effect of migration on the status of female migrants depends on a number of contextual factors that vary from one case to another and that the various dimensions of status may be affected differently by the same intervention, attempts at generalization are ill advised. It is useful, however, to identify the relevant issues for different groups of female migrants. Relevant groups identified in terms of the position of women within the family before or during migration include: (a) single women migrating autonomously; (b) married women moving autonomously, sometimes followed by their husbands; (c) married women moving in conjunction with their families; and (d) female migrants returning to the country of origin.

(a) *Single women migrating autonomously.* Women migrating as contract workers often belong to this category. These migrants usually originate in communities where cultural values induce daughters more than sons to fulfil family obligations (Trager, 1984, p. 1274). Female migrant workers in this category generally view migration as temporary and aim at sending remittances home to support the family. Many are unskilled and may not have been in formal employment before migration. They thus exchange the sex hierarchy at home for that at the workplace, finding it natural to accept subordination in the latter. A key issue regarding these migrants is whether mobility affects different dimensions of their status in opposite directions so that, even if changes occur, their status relative to that of men in the family does not change significantly, particularly when marriage implies a definitive return to the country of origin.

(b) *Married women moving autonomously, sometimes followed by their husbands.* When migrant women who are married migrate on their own, a key issue is whether migration leads to role reversals between husbands and wives as, for example, when the husband migrates after the wife and submits to her protection and guidance (Brettell and Simon, 1986, p. 15). Migrant women in this category are likely to assume all the responsibilities of the main breadwinner within the family, at least for a period. The implications for women of assuming such a role after migration in terms of gaining independence to make decisions, controlling resources, managing child-rearing responsibilities and enhancing their economic status need to be considered.

The analysis of the family reunification process led by female migration is also important, even when it does not lead to the expected reunion of husband and wife. Foner (1986, p. 139), for instance, found that some Jamaican women in New York never sent for their husbands because they saw migration as an opportunity to formalize a separation and regain their independence. Among those migrant women who are joined by their husbands, gender relations are likely to be influenced by the length of separation of the spouses (the longer the separation, the more unwilling a woman may be to compromise her freedom and self-reliance), by whether a woman had tended to consult her husband in making major decisions when they were separated, by her willingness to reassure her husband and not challenge his authority, and by the husband's willingness to accept and adapt to changing domestic hierarchies. An increase of family instability or of the likelihood of divorce may indicate that any change in sex roles is judged to be deviant, unrealistic or a threat to male authority.

Information is also needed about the substitution of roles arising from the delegation of child-rearing activities to other women (mother, mother-in-law, sister, daughter, maid etc.) or to men (mostly the husband) in the country of origin. Migrant women who migrate accompanied by their children may also take with them other women to aid them in child-rearing.

(c) *Married women who move with their families.* Existing literature documents both gains and losses in the status of this group of female migrants. Assessments of positive changes in their status generally involve their increased participation in production and wage employment. The paliative function that the employment of migrant women has during periods of male unemployment inevitably affects sex roles and the traditional sex hierarchy within the family (International Center for Research on Women, 1979, p. 131). The status of married migrant women is judged to improve through more egalitarian and supportive husband-wife relations. Migrant women see their gain in status as related to greater independence, control over financial resources (Foner, 1986) and a greater participation in household decision-making. Another important area of change is that encompassing attitudes towards birth control and family size.

Female status tends to be adversely affected by an increase in the responsibilities assumed by women in the absence of the support traditionally provided by kinship networks.[8] An increase in the exploitation of female migrants, both within and outside the family, may arise because of the redistribution of exchanges rooted in patriarchal authority and male dominance (Tienda and Booth, 1988, p. 312). There may also be a reduction of husband-wife communication stemming, among other things, from different working shifts or from the isolation of non-working migrant women. Often, migrant women become increasingly dependent on husbands and children, have reduced authority over their children, and are more likely to experience separation or divorce because of the instability of family relations.

Even when they accept the need for their wives to adopt new roles in the host society, some migrant men may feel threatened and seek to reinforce traditional authority structures, thus producing a severe dislocation between the roles and actual status of their wives. The extent to which migrant men accept changes in domestic hierarchies will depend on the pervasiveness with which those changes are occurring in the host society and, particularly, in the migrant community to which they belong.

Changing perceptions and expectations regarding the roles of children should also be considered. Migrants are generally keen to secure academic and occupational training for both their sons and daughters because they expect their children to achieve more than they themselves did (Wilpert, 1988, p. 178). Children may enjoy relatively high status within the migrant family because they usually adjust more easily to the new environment and often have access to better schooling than their parents did (Kudat, 1974; Wilpert, 1977). By becoming more independent they may have to assume greater responsibilities at younger ages than would have been the case in the country of origin.

(d) *Returning migrants.* An investigation of whether and why migrant women are often less keen than men to return to their country of origin may provide some insight regarding the different perceptions of men and women about the changes of status that have taken place since migration and those that are expected upon return. For instance, migrant women who have experienced social and economic gains as a result of migration generally wish to remain abroad, while their husbands are strongly motivated to return home (the implicit assumption being that the family will revert to pre-migration gender asymmetries). A comparison should be made not only between male and female migrants, but also between different groups of migrant women. Are those who are less successful in adapting to the norms and attitudes of the receiving society or those who experience a change in marital status (divorce, for instance) more likely to return? How is self-selectivity related to the tendency to return? Changes in which dimension of status are more likely to influence women's motivation to return?

Research on female returnees should also compare how they cope with the discontinuities experienced upon migration and upon return. The circumstances surrounding the return are crucial. Migrant women returning voluntarily are likely to have a very different experience from that of women who are forced to return, usually by migration constraints imposed by the country of destination. Similarly, different experiences are likely to arise if return is viewed as a proof of success or of failure. A common goal of migrants is to improve their socio-economic status upon return. Consequently, female returnees may experience the adjustment problems typical of those trying to fit into a different strata of the class structure (despite being better off economically, female returnees and their families may be marginalized).

To conclude, we note that migration also affects the status of women whose close relatives migrate, although they themselves may not leave their country of origin. Women left behind may experience changes of status similar to those experienced by married women who migrate on their own and are separated from their immediate relatives. The husband's absence may allow wives to become more independent and stronger, to develop new interests and discover hidden potentials (Go, Postrado and Jimenez, 1983b, p. 231). However, the new roles assumed by married women who migrate on their own and by wives left behind may not have the same implications for their status in relation to men. A comparison of these two groups of women may reveal that, although both assume new roles and responsibilities in the absence of their husbands, the experience is more likely to be liberating for women

who migrate on their own, partly because of their contact with a new socio-cultural context and mostly because of the initiative and independence that they need to have in order to migrate at all. Women left behind, especially those relying on remittances, remain in a dependent situation facing increased responsibilities and a larger workload. Often, non-migrant male relatives are left in charge of them, an experience that can hardly be liberating. Shah and Arnold (1985, p. 45) found that women left behind by men migrating to Western Asia relied on male relatives to use banking services and make decisions about property, children's education, household purchases and financial investments. However, there is some evidence about positive changes in the status of women left behind. Egyptian women whose husbands are abroad, for instance, not only manage land and property, decide on new investments and deal with public institutions, but they also manage to reduce their housework and enjoy more free time (Saleh, 1988). Turkish women, though generally subservient to their husbands, have shown considerable determination in maintaining the gains that they made during their husband's absence (Davis and Heyl, 1986, p. 191).

NOTES

[1]Models suggesting the "double discrimination" and "threefold oppression" of female migrants have been suggested. The latter view femaleness, compounded by class (migrant worker) and nationality (foreigner) as being a particularly unfortunate situation leading to the exploitation of migrant women (Simon and Brettell, 1986). Morokvasic (1988) proposes a "fourfold" oppression model whereby migrant women are discriminated against not only because they are women, because they belong to the working class and are members of minority groups, but also because they are socialized into accepting subordination as normal.

[2]In a paper synthesizing various country reports to the OECD Monitoring Panel on Migrant Women, Boyd (1988a) noted that migrant women who work are concentrated in specific occupations, mainly in the manufacturing and service sectors, and that they are usually found in low-paid jobs with little prestige.

[3]Social networks serve several functions: they increase the flow of information about migration opportunities and the situation of migrants in the host countries and they help to reduce the costs of migration by lowering accommodation expenses and helping with job placement. As sources of information and assistance, they serve to institutionalize migration flows, thus fueling migration even after the original mobilizing forces have disappeared. The location of networks in the country of destination has important implications for the subsequent economic experiences of migrants. The effective func-

tioning of networks, however, is constrained by official policies governing the admission of migrants.

[4]Apart from focusing on internal migration, these models have been criticized for appearing "obsessed with marriage" (Ware, 1981, p. 147) and for not recognizing family strategies of migration nor the impact of different socio-cultural environments.

[5]For example, undocumented Mexican female migrants in the United States are less well educated than the documented ones (Simon and DeLey, 1986). Women account for over 40 per cent of persons admitted by Canada under student authorizations around the mid-1980s (Boyd, 1987b).

[6]Foner (1986) found evidence that the exploitation and discrimination of migrant women may derive more from the fact of their being foreign than from their being women. Thus, a number of factors divide Jamaican women from other migrant or working class women and unite them with Jamaican men in a common cause. Morokvasic (1988) also stresses that Yugoslav women in Western Europe viewed low pay and low work status as more likely to stem from their condition as foreigners than from their class affiliation or sex. Consequently, they feel solidarity with Yugoslav men.

[7]However, migrant women may be expected to be the keepers of traditional culture (Andezian, 1986), thus having to defend the traditions of their own country and maintain the cultural continuity of their family while at the same time dealing with new roles and challenges (Smith, 1980).

[8]The absence of close kin or dependable neighbours to help with child care is an important factor. Foner (1986, p. 149) found that although many young Jamaican women in New York and London complained of the added burdens of child care, they lay the blame on the absence of close kin and dependable neighbours rather than on the norms regarding sex roles, according to which women have the major child-rearing responsibilities. The women studied did not blame men for providing insufficient help.

REFERENCES

Abadan-Unat, Nermin (1977). Implications of migration on the emancipation and pseudo-emancipation of Turkish women. *International Migration Review* (Staten Island, New York), vol. 11, No. 1 (Spring).

Abella, Manolo I. (1992). Contemporary labour migration from Asia: policies and perspectives of sending countries. In *International Migration Systems*, Mary M. Kritz, Lin Lean Lim and Hania Zlotnik, eds. Oxford, United Kingdom: Clarendon Press.

Andezian, S. (1986). Women's roles in organizing symbolic life: Algerian female immigrants in France. In *International Migration: The Female Experience*, Rita James Simon and Caroline B. Brettell, eds. Totowa, New Jersey: Rowman and Allanheld.

Appleyard, Reginald, and A. Amera (1986). Postwar immigration of Greek women to Australia: a longitudinal study. In *International Migration: The Female Experience*, Rita James Simon and Caroline B. Brettell, eds. Totowa, New Jersey: Rowman and Allanheld.

Arnold, Fred, Urmil Minocha and James T. Fawcett (1987). The changing face of Asian immigration to the United States. In *Pacific Bridges: The New Immigration from Asia and the Pacific Islands*, James T. Fawcett and Benjamin V. Cariño, eds. Staten Island, New York: Center for Migration Studies.

Asia Magazine (1987). 6 September.

Bach, Robert L. (1985). International relations, economic development and migration. Paper presented at the International Migration Workshop at the Population Council, New York.

Bachu, P. K. (1986). Work, dowry and marriage among East African Sikh women in the United Kingdom. In *International Migration: The Female Experience*, Rita James Simon and Caroline B. Brettell, eds. Totowa, New Jersey: Rowman and Allanheld.

Balán, Jorge (1983). Selectivity of migration in international and internal flows. Paper presented at the UNESCO Symposium on Issues and New Trends in Migration: Population Movements Within and Across National Boundaries, Paris, October.

_____ (1988). International migration in Latin America: trends and consequences. In *International Migration Today*, vol. I, *Trends and Prospects*, Reginald T. Appleyard, ed. Paris: United Nations Education, Scientific and Cultural Organization (UNESCO).

Behrman, Jere R., and Barbara L. Wolfe (1984). Micro determinants of female migration in a developing country: labour market, demographic marriage market and economic marriage market incentives. *Research and Population Economics*, vol. 5, T. Paul Schultz and Kenneth Wolpin, eds. Greenwich, Connecticut: JAI Press.

Benería, Lourdes, and Martha Roldán (1987). *The Crossroads of Class and Gender: Industrial Homework, Subcontracting and Household Dynamics in Mexico City*. Chicago, Illinois: University of Chicago Press.

Berger, S., and M. J. Piore (1980). *Dualism and Discontinuity in Industrial Societies*. Cambridge, United Kingdom and New York: Cambridge University Press.

Boyd, Monica (1986). Immigrant women in Canada. In *International Migration: The Female Experience*, Rita James Simon and Caroline B. Brettell, eds. Totowa, New Jersey: Rowman and Allanheld.

_____ (1987a). Immigrant women in Canada: entry status and disadvantage. *International Settlement Canada (INSCAN), Research Resource Division for Refugees (RRDR)* (Ottawa), vol. 1, Nos. 2 and 3, pp. 5-10.

_____ (1987b). *Migrant Women in Canada Profiles and Policies*. Report prepared for the Research Division Immigration Canada and Status of Women Canada. (Also available as a monograph from Employment and Immigration Canada, Public Affairs Inquiries and Distribution, Fall 1988.)

_____ (1988a). Draft: synthesis report of the OECD Monitoring Panel on Migrant Women (Ottawa).

_____ (1988b). Immigrant women: language, socioeconomic inequalities and policy issues. Paper presented at the National Symposium on the Demography of Immigrant, Racial and Ethnic Groups in Winnepeg, Canada, University of Manitoba.

_____ (1988c). Immigration and income security policies in Canada: implications for elderly immigrant women. *Population Research and Policy Review* (Dordrecht, The Netherlands), vol. 8, No. 1 (January), pp. 5-24.

_____ (1989). Family and personal networks in international migration: recent developments and new agendas. *International Migration Review* (Staten Island, New York), vol. 23, No. 3 (Fall), pp. 638-670.

Brettell, Caroline B. (1985). Male migrants and unwed mothers: illegitimacy in a northwestern Portuguese town. *Anthropology* (Los Angeles, California), vol. IX, Nos 1-2, pp. 87-109.

_____ (1988). Emigration and household structure in a Portuguese parish, 1850-1920. *Journal of Family History* (Greenwich, Connecticut), vol. 13, No. 1, pp. 33-57.

_____, and Rita James Simon (1986). Immigrant women: an introduction. In *International Migration: The Female Experience,* Rita James Simon and Caroline B. Brettell, eds. Totowa, New Jersey: Rowman and Allanheld.

Brochmann, Grete (1987). *Escape Route to Dependency? Female Migration from Sri Lanka to the Middle East*. PRIO Working Paper No. 5/87. Oslo: International Peace Research Institute.

Brouwer, Lenie, and Marijke Priester (1983). Living in between: Turkish women in their homeland and in the Netherlands. In *One Way Ticket: Migration and Female Labour*, Annie Phizacklea, ed. London: Routledge and Kegan Paul.

Caldwell, John C. (1982). *Theory of Fertility Decline.* London: Academic Press.

Caspari, A., and W. Giles (1986). Immigration policy and employment of Portuguese migrant women in the UK and France: a comparative analysis. In *International Migration: The Female Experience*, Rita James Simon and Caroline B. Brettell, eds. Totowa, New Jersey: Rowman and Allanheld.

Charlton, S. E. (1984). *Women in Third World Development.* Boulder, Colorado: Westview Press.

Cleland, John, and Christopher Wilson (1987). Demand theories of the fertility transition: an iconoclastic view. *Population Studies* (London), vol. 41, No. 1 (March), pp. 5-30.

Connell, John (1984). Status or subjugation? Women, migration and development in the South Pacific. *International Migration Review* (Staten Island, New York), vol. 18, No. 4 (Winter), pp. 964-983.

Curtis, R. (1986). Household and family in theory on inequality. *American Sociological Review* (Washington, D.C.), vol. 51, No. 2.

Davis, F. J., and B. S. Heyl (1986). Turkish women and guestworker migration to West Germany. In *International Migration: The Female Experience*, Rita James Simon and Caroline B. Brettell, eds. Totowa, New Jersey: Rowman and Allanheld.

De Jong, Gordon F., and others (1985/86). Migration intentions and behaviour: decision making in a rural Philippine Province. *Population and Environment* (New York), vol. 8, Nos. 1/2.

De Wenden, Catherine Withol, and Margo C. DeLey (1986). French immigration policy reform 1981-1982 and the female migrant. In *International Migration: The Female Experience*, Rita James Simon and Caroline B. Brettell, eds. Totowa, New Jersey: Rowman and Allanheld.

Dumon, W. A. (1981). The situation of migrant women workers. *International Migration* (Geneva), vol. 19, No. 1/2, pp. 190-209.

Eisold, E. (1984). *Young Women Workers in Export Industries: the Case of the Semiconductor Industry in Southeast Asia.* World Employment Programme Research Working Paper. Geneva: International Labour Office.

Epstein, T. S. (1986). *Status of Women in Asia and the Pacific Region*, Series 2, *Socio-cultural and Attitudinal Factors Affecting the Status of Women in South Asia.* Bangkok: Economic and Social Commission for Asia and the Pacific.

Evans, M. D. R. (1984). Immigrant women in Australia: resources, family and work. *International Migration Review* (Staten Island, New York), vol. 18, No. 4 (Winter), pp. 1063-1090.

Fernández-Kelly, María Patricia (1983). Mexican border industrialization, female labor force participation and migration. In *Women, Men and the International Division of Labour*, June Nash and María Patricia Fernández-Kelly, eds. Albany, New York: State University of New York Press.

Foner, N. (1986). Sex roles and sensibilities: Jamaican women in New York and London. In *International Migration: The Female Experience*, Rita James Simon and Caroline B. Brettell, eds. Totowa, New Jersey: Rowman and Allanheld.

Froebel, F., J. Heinrichs and O. Kreye (1980). *The New International Division of Labour.* Cambridge: Cambridge University Press.

Garrison, V., and C. I. Weiss (1979). Dominican family networks and United States immigration: a case study. *International Migration Review* (Staten Island, New York), vol. 13, No. 2 (Summer).

Go, S. P., L. T. Postrado and P. R. Jimenez (1983a). Filipino overseas contract workers: their families and communities. Paper presented at the Conference on Asian Labor Migration to the Middle East, East-West Population Institute, Honolulu, September.

_____ (1983b). *The Effects of International Contract Labour*, vol. 1. Manila: De La Salle University, Integrated Research Center.

Graves, Nancy B. (1984). Adaptation of Polynesian female migrants in New Zealand. In *Women in the Cities of Asia: Migration and Urban Adaptation*, James T. Fawcett, Siew-Ean Khoo and Peter C. Smith, eds. Boulder, Colorado: Westview Press.

Granovetter, M. (1985). Economic action and social structure: the problem of embeddedness. *American Journal of Sociology* (Chicago, Illinois), vol. 91, No. 3.

Gurak, Douglas T., and Fe Caces (1992). Migration networks and the shaping of migration systems. In *International Migration Systems*, Mary M. Kritz, Lin Lean Lim and Hania Zlotnik, eds. Oxford, United Kingdom: Clarendon Press.

Hancock, Mary (1983). Transnational production and women workers. In *One Way Ticket: Migration and Female Labour*, Annie Phizacklea, ed. London: Routledge and Kegan Paul.

Harbison, Sarah F. (1981). Family structure and family strategy in migration decision making. In *Migration Decision Making: Multidisciplinary Approaches to Microlevel Studies in Developed and Developing Countries*, Gordon F. De Jong and Robert W. Gardner, eds. New York: Pergamon Press.

Hart, K. (1971). Informal income opportunities and urban employment in Ghana. *Journal of Modern African Studies* (Cambridge and New York), vol. 11.

Hirata, L. C. (1979). Free, indentured, enslaved: Chinese prostitutes in nineteenth-century America. *Signs: Journal of Women in Culture and Society* (Chicago, Illinois), vol. 5, No. 1 (Autumn).

Hoffman-Nowotny, Hans-Joachim (1978). Social and demographic aspects of the changing status of migrant women in Europe. In *Demographic Aspects of the Changing Status of Women in Europe*, M. Niphuisnel, ed. Leiden: Nijhoff.

Houstoun, Marion F., Roger G. Kramer and Joan Mackin Barrett (1984). Female predominance in immigration in the United States since 1930: a first look. *International Migration Review* (Staten Island, New York), vol. 18, No. 4 (Winter), pp. 908-963.

Hugo, Graeme J. (1981). Village-community ties, village norms and ethnic and social networks: a review of evidence from the Third World. In *Migration Decision Making: Multidisciplinary Approaches to Microlevel Studies in Developed and Developing Countries*, Gordon F. De Jong and Robert W. Gardner, eds. New York: Pergamon Press.

_____, and Anchalee Singhanetra-Renard (1989). Asian international contract labour migration: major issues and implications. Summary of the proceedings of a workshop held under IDRC auspices at Chiang Mai University, November 1987.

Hune, Shirley (1987). Drafting an International Convention on the Protection of the Rights of all Migrant Workers and their Families. *International Migration Review* (Staten Island, New York), vol. 21, No. 1 (Spring), pp. 123-127.

International Center for Research on Women (1979). *Women in Migration: A Third World Focus.* Washington, D.C.: Agency for International Development, Office of Women in Development.

Jackson, Pauline (1984). Women in 19th century Irish emigration. *International Migration Review* (Staten Island, New York), vol. 18, No. 4 (Winter), pp. 1004-1020.

Katz, E., and Oded Stark (1986). Labor migration and risk aversion in less developed countries. *Journal of Labor Economics* (Chicago, Illinois), vol. 4.

Kritz, Mary M. (1987). International migration policies: conceptual problems. *International Migration Review* (Staten Island, New York), vol. 21, No. 4 (Winter), pp. 947-966.

Kudat, A. (1974). *International Labour Migration: A Description of the West Berlin Worker Survey.* International Institute for Comparative Social Studies, Pre-print No. P/74-1a.

Lamphere, L. (1986). Working mothers and family strategies: Portuguese and Colombian women in a New England community. In *International Migration: The Female Experience*, Rita James Simon and Caroline B. Brettell, eds. Totowa, New Jersey: Rowman and Allanheld.

Laroque, P. (1987). Conference reports. The future of migration, part III, conclusions. *International Migration Review* (Staten Island, New York), vol. 21, No. 1 (Spring), pp. 145-154.

Lim, Lin Lean (1987). IUSSP Committee on International Migration, Workshop on International Migration Systems and Networks. *International Migration Review* (Staten Island, New York), vol. 21, No. 2 (Summer), pp. 416-423.

_____ (1988a). Effects of women's position on migration. In *Conference on Women's Position and Demographic Change in the Course of Development, Oslo, 15-18 June: Solicited Papers*. Liège: International Union for the Scientific Study of Population.

_____ (1988b). *Economic Dynamism and Structural Transformation in the Asian Pacific Rim Countries: Contributions of the Second Sex*. NUPRI Research Paper Series, No. 45. Tokyo: Nihon University, Population Research Institute.

_____ (1989). Processes shaping international migration flows. *International Population Conference, New Delhi, 20-27 September*, vol. 2. Liège: International Union for the Scientific Study of Population.

_____ (1992). International labour movements: a perspective on economic exchanges and flows. In *International Migration Systems*, Mary M. Kritz, Lin Lean Lim and Hania Zlotnik, eds. Oxford, United Kingdom: Clarendon Press.

Marshall, A. (1979). Immigrant workers in the Buenos Aires labor market. *International Migration Review* (Staten Island, New York), vol. 13, No. 3.

Mason, Karen Oppenheim (1984). *The Status of Women: A Review of Its Relationships to Fertility and Mortality*. New York: Rockefeller Foundation.

Massey, Douglas S. (1986). The social organization of Mexican migration to the United States. *Annals of the American Academy of Political and Social Science* (Newbury Park, California), No. 487.

_____ (1988). Economic development and international migration. *Population and Development Review* (New York), vol. 14, No. 3 (September), pp. 383-413.

_____, and others (1987). *Return to Aztlan: The Social Process of International Migration from Western Mexico*. Berkeley: University of California Press.

Morokvasic, Mirjana (1980). *Yugoslav Women in France, Germany and Sweden*. Paris: Centre national pour la recherche sociale (CNRS).

_____ (1984). Birds of passage are also women... *International Migration Review* (Staten Island, New York), vol. 18, No. 4 (Winter), pp. 886-907.

_____ (1988). Cash in hand for the first time: the case of Yugoslav immigrant women in Western Europe. In *International Migration Today*, vol. 2, *Emerging Issues*, Charles Stahl, ed. Paris: United Nations Educational Scientific and Cultural Organization (UNESCO).

Nagaraj, Shyamala, and Lin Lean Lim (1988). Investigating the relationship between status and fertility in a multi-ethnic context: some measurement issues. Paper presented at the IUSSP Conference on Women's Position and Demographic Change in the Course of Development, Oslo, 15-18 June.

Nash, June, and María Patricia Fernández-Kelly, eds. (1983). *Women, Men and the International Division of Labour*. Albany, New York: State University of New York Press.

New Straits Times (1988). 7 February.

Netting, Robert M., Richard R. Wilk and Eric J. Arnould, eds. (1984). *Households: Comparative and Historical Studies of the Domestic Group*. Berkeley and London: University of California Press.

Oppong, Christine (1980). *A Synopsis of Seven Roles and Status of Women: An Outline of a Conceptual and Methodological Approach*. World Employment Programme Research Working Paper, No. 94. Geneva: International Labour Office.

_____, and Katharine Abu (1985). *A Handbook for Data Collection and Analysis on Seven Roles and Statuses of Women*. Geneva: International Labour Office.

Organisation for Economic Co-operation and Development (1987). *Interdependence and Cooperation in Tomorrow's World*. Paris: OECD.

_____ (1988). *1987 Continuous Reporting System on Migration (SOPEMI)*. Paris: OECD.

Pang, Eng Fong, and Linda Lim (1982). Foreign labor and economic development in Singapore. *International Migration Review* (Staten Island, New York), vol. 16, No. 3 (Fall), pp. 548-576.

Pastor, R. A., ed. (1985). *Migration and Development in the Caribbean: the Unexplored Connection*. Boulder, Colorado: Westview Press.

Pessar, Patricia R. (1982). The role of households in international migration and the case of U.S.-bound migration from the Dominican Republic. *International Migration Review* (Staten Island, New York), vol. 16, No. 2 (Summer), pp. 342-364.

_____ (1984). The linkage between the household and workplace in the experience of Dominican immigrant women in the United States. *International Migration Review* (Staten Island, New York), vol. 18, No. 4 (Winter), pp. 1188-1211.

Petras, Elisabeth McLean (1981). The global labour market in the modern world economy. In *Global Trends in Migration: Theory and Research on International Population Movements*, Mary M. Kritz, Charles B. Keely and Silvano M. Tomasi, eds. Staten Island, New York: Center for Migration Studies.

Piore, M. (1983). Labour market segmentation: to what paradigm does it belong? *American Economic Review* (Nashville, Tennessee), vol. 73, No. 2.

Portes, Alejandro (1983). International labour migration and national development. In *U.S. Immigration and Refugee Policy: Global and Domestic Issues*, Mary M. Kritz, ed. Lexington, Massachusetts: Lexington Books.

_____, and Robert L. Bach (1985). *Latin Journey: Cuban and Mexican Immigrants in the United States*. Berkeley: University of California Press.

Portes, Alejandro, and Jòzsef Böröcz (1989). Contemporary immigration: theoretical perspectives on its determinants and modes of incorporation. *International Migration Review* (Staten Island, New York), vol. 23, No. 3 (Fall), pp. 457-485.

Prieto, Yolanda (1986). Cuban women and work in the United States: a New Jersey case study. In *International Migration: The Female Experience*, Rita James Simon and Caroline B. Brettell, eds. Totowa, New Jersey: Rowman and Allanheld.

Redclift, N., and E. Mingione, eds. (1985). *Beyond Employment: Household, Gender and Subsistence*. New York and Oxford, United Kingdom: Basil Blackwell.

Repak, Terry A. (1988). They come on behalf of their children: Central American families in Washington, D.C. Paper prepared for the United States Department of Labour, Bureau of International Labour Affairs and Division of Immigration Policy and Research (Institute of Liberal Arts, Emory University, Atlanta, Georgia).

Rosen, Rita (1981). On the situation of foreign women living in the Federal Republic of Germany: an outline of the problem. *International Migration* (Geneva), vol. 19, Nos. 1/2, pp. 108-113.

Roussel, L. (1975). Ivory Coast. In *Population Growth and Socioeconomic Change in West Africa*, John Caldwell, ed. New York: Columbia University Press.

Saleh, S. (1988). Egyptian women in the Gulf: response to migration. Paper presented at the International Symposium on Women in International Migration: Social, Cultural and Occupational Issues, jointly sponsored by the Sociology Institute of the Technical University, Berlin, and UNESCO, held in Berlin, Germany, 18-21 October.

Salt, John (1988). Corporations and other complex organizations that shape migration flows. Paper presented at the IUSSP Seminar on International Migration Systems, Processes and Policies, Genting Highlands, Malaysia, September 1988.

Sassen-Koob, Saskia (1983). Labour migration and the new industrial division of labour. In *Women, Men and the International Division of Labour*, June Nash and María Patricia Fernández-Kelly, eds. Albany, New York: State University of New York Press.

_____ (1984). Notes on the incorporation of third world women into wage labor through immigration and off-shore production. *International Migration Review* (Staten Island, New York), vol. 18, No. 4 (Winter), pp. 1144-1167.

Schrier, A. (1958). *Ireland and the American Emigration, 1850-1900*. Wisconsin: University of Minnesota Press.

Seller, M. S., ed. (1981). *Immigrant Women*. Philadelphia: Temple University Press.

Shah, Nasra N., and Fred Arnold (1985). The non-economic consequences of Asian labor migration to the Middle East. *International Population Conference, Florence, 5-12 June*. Liège: International Union for the Scientific Study of Population, vol. 3, pp. 43-56.

Sidhu, M.S., and Gavin W. Jones (1981). *Population Dynamics in a Plural Society: Peninsular Malaysia*. Kuala Lumpur, Malaysia: UMCB Publications.

Simon, Rita James, and Caroline B. Brettell, eds. (1986). *International Migration: The Female Experience*. Totowa, New Jersey: Rowman and Allanheld.

Simon, Rita James, and Margo C. DeLey (1986). Undocumented Mexican women: their work and personal experiences. In *International Migration: The Female Experience*, Rita James Simon and Caroline B. Brettell, eds. Totowa, New Jersey: Rowman and Allanheld.

Smith, H. L. (1986). Theory and research on the status of women and fertility: some necessary linkages. Paper presented at the Rockefeller Foundation Workshop on Women Status and Fertility, Seven Springs, New York, July.

Smith, M. E. (1980). The Portuguese female immigrant: the "marginal man". *International Migration Review* (Staten Island, New York), vol. 14, No. 1 (Spring).

Stark, Oded, and D. Levhari (1982). On migration and risk in LDCs. *Economic Development and Cultural Change* (Chicago, Illinois), vol. 31.

Tapinos, Georges (1983). European migration patterns: economic linkages and policy experiences. In *U.S. Immigration and Refugee Policy: Global and Domestic Issues*, Mary M. Kritz, ed. Lexington, Massachusetts.: Lexington Books.

Thadani, Veena N., and Michael P. Todaro (1984). Female migration: a conceptual framework. In *Women in the Cities of Asia: Migration and Urban Adaptation*, James T. Fawcett, Siew-Ean Khoo and Peter C. Smith, eds. Boulder, Colorado: Westview Press.

Tienda, Marta (1980). Familism and structural assimilation of Mexican immigrants in the United States. *International Migration Review* (Staten Island, New York), vol. 14, No. 3 (Fall).

_____, and Karen Booth (1988). Migration, gender and social change: a review and reformulation. *Conference on Women's Position and Demographic Change in the Course of Development, Oslo, 15-18 June: Solicited Papers*. Liège: International Union for the Scientific Study of Population.

Trager, Lilian (1984). Family strategies and the migration of women: migrants to Dagupan City, Philippines. *International Migration Review* (Staten Island, New York), vol. 18, No. 4 (Winter), pp. 1264-1278.

Tyree, A., and K. Donato (1986). A demographic overview of the international migration of women. In *International Migration: The Female Experience*, Rita James Simon and Caroline B. Brettell, eds. Totowa, New Jersey: Rowman and Allanheld.

United Nations (1979). *Trends and Characteristics of International Migration since 1950*. ST/ESA/SER.A/64. Sales No. E.78.XIII.5.

_____ (1988). *World Population Trends and Policies: 1987 Monitoring Report*. Sales No. E.88.XIII.3.

United Nations Industrial Development Organization (1980). *Women in the Redeployment of Manufacturing Industry to Developing Countries*. UNIDO Working Papers on Structural Change, No. 18.

Ware, Helen (1981). *Women, Demography and Development*. Canberra: Australian National University.

Weiner, Myron (1985). On international migration and international relations. *Population and Development Review* (New York), vol. 11, No. 3 (September), pp. 441-455.

Wilpert, Czarina (1977). *Children of Turkish Workers in West Berlin*. Pre-print Series. Berlin, Germany: Science Center.

_____ (1988). Migrant women and their daughters: two generations of Turkish women in the Federal Republic of Germany. In *International Migration Today*, vol. 2, *Emerging Issues*, Charles Stahl, ed. Paris: United Nations Education, Scientific and Cultural Organization (UNESCO).

Wood, Charles H. (1982). Equilibrium and historical-structural perspectives on migration. *International Migration Review* (Staten Island, New York), vol. 16, No. 2 (Summer), pp. 298-319.

Young, Kate (1982). The creation of a relative surplus population: a case study from Mexico. In *Women and Development: The Sexual Division of Labour in Rural Societies*, Lourdes Benería, ed. New York: Praeger.

Zakrzewska, M. (1981). My education and aspirations demanded more. In *Immigrant Women*, M. S. Seller, ed. Philadelphia, Pennsylvania: Temple University Press.

Zolberg, Aristide (1981). International migration in political perspective. In *Global Trends in Migration: Theory and Research on International Population Movements*, Mary M. Kritz, Charles B. Keely and Silvano M. Tomasi, eds. Staten Island, New York: Center for Migration Studies.

IV. MEASURING THE EXTENT OF FEMALE INTERNATIONAL MIGRATION

United Nations Secretariat*

The extent of female international migration, just as several other aspects of the migration of women across international borders, has been a largely neglected subject. Lack of readily available information on the participation of women in international migration is probably at the root of the conventional view that the typical migrant is a young, economically motivated male. Unfortunately, the deficiencies of migration statistics hinder attempts to challenge such a generalized misconception. Indeed, the difficulties involved in assessing recent trends in international migration are amplified when the aim is to establish such trends by sex, since a large number of countries have either no data on migration or fail to publish what data they have classified by sex.

One possible approach to assessing the extent of international migration among women is to focus on the long-term effects of the process, namely, on the stock of migrants of each sex present in different countries. At present, figures on the foreign-born population enumerated by censuses all over the world provide the most comprehensive and comparable basis for the assessment of the immediate demographic effects of migration. This paper uses that information to highlight the importance of female migration. In addition, data for specific countries will be used to explore recent trends in female migration. Lastly, the most pressing needs regarding data on international migration are discussed.

A. How many migrant women are there?

Table 1 presents the most comprehensive set of data on the number of migrants worldwide. The data were obtained from censuses that, having taken place since 1970, enumerated the foreign-born or, in some cases, the foreign population living in each country concerned. Such data were available for a total of

157 countries or areas out of the 208 constituting the world in 1989. Although, as indicated in table 1, the data for different countries usually refer to different years, their overall total is indicative of the extent of the sex imbalance in worldwide migrant stocks. Surprisingly, among the 77 million persons who at some point during 1970-1986 were enumerated outside their country of birth, 48 per cent were women. Thus, although in terms of migrant stocks worldwide migrant men did outnumber migrant women, the latter were nearly as numerous as their male counterparts. The importance of such findings cannot be overstressed.

The information in table 1 also shows that women were more numerous than men among migrants in over a quarter of the countries considered (44 countries), including the one hosting the largest number of migrants, namely, the United States of America. Data from the most recent census of that country indicate that women continue to outnumber men among the 19.8 foreign-born enumerated in 1990, constituting 51 per cent of that group (United States, 1993).

A better sense of the characteristics of the distribution of countries by the percentage of women among the foreign-born can be obtained from figure II where that percentage has been plotted against the size of the foreign-born population. The two horizontal lines depicted in the figure indicate the interquartile range of the distribution (from 44 to 51 per cent), that is, the central range within which half of the countries considered fall. Although there is no clear association between the size of the foreign-born population and the proportion of women in it, in countries with larger numbers of foreign-born, the percentage of women among them generally falls above 45 per cent. Among countries hosting more than 1 million migrants, only in the former Federal Republic of Germany, South Africa, Kuwait and Côte d'Ivoire did the percentage of female migrants fall below 44 per cent. Interestingly, all those

*Population Division of the Department for Economic and Social Information and Policy Analysis.

TABLE 1. TOTAL AND FOREIGN-BORN POPULATION, BY SEX, IN SELECTED COUNTRIES OF ENUMERATION

Country of enumeration	Year of census	Total population			Foreign-born population		
		Men	Women	Percentage of women	Men	Women	Percentage of women
Africa							
Benin[a]	1979	1 596 939	1 734 271	52.1	21 268	20 016	48.5
Botswana[a]	1981	443 104	497 923	52.9	8 788	6 831	43.7
Burkina Faso	1975	2 827 578	2 810 625	49.8	52 854	57 827	52.2
Burundi	1979	1 946 145	2 082 275	51.7	42 147	40 704	49.1
Cameroon	1976	3 491 433	3 640 400	51.0	120 442	97 627	44.8
Central African Republic	1975	861 966	919 063	51.6	21 844	22 739	51.0
Comoros	1980	167 089	168 061	50.1	6 477	7 401	53.3
Congo	1984	929 102	980 146	51.3	47 797	48 842	50.5
Côte.d'Ivoire[a]	1975	3 474 750	3 234 850	48.2	874 073	600 396	40.7
Egypt[a]	1986	24 655 297	23 549 752	48.9	63 785	44 464	41.1
Gambia	1973	250 386	243 113	49.3	33 334	21 220	38.9
Ghana[a]	1970	4 247 809	4 311 504	50.4	323 978	238 154	42.4
Guinea Bissau	1979	370 225	397 514	51.8	6 471	6 460	50.0
Kenya	1979	7 607 113	7 719 948	50.4	82 298	75 073	47.7
Liberia	1974	759 109	744 259	49.5	35 759	23 699	39.9
Libyan Arab Jamahiriya[a]	1973	1 191 853	1 057 384	47.0	133 934	62 931	32.0
Madagascar	1975	3 805 288	3 798 502	50.0	13 371	8 248	38.2
Malawi	1977	2 673 589	2 873 871	51.8	140 421	148 323	51.4
Mali	1976	3 123 733	3 271 185	51.2	73 458	72 631	49.7
Mauritania[a]	1977	658 361	680 469	50.8	16 488	11 680	41.5
Mauritius[a]	1983	498 257	502 175	50.2	2 564	2 498	49.3
Morocco[a]	1982	10 236 078	10 213 473	49.9	30 219	31 115	50.7
Mozambique[a]	1980	5 670 484	6 003 241	51.4	19 759	19 383	49.5
Reunion	1982	252 997	262 801	51.0	19 702	16 427	45.5
Rwanda[a]	1978	2 363 177	2 468 350	51.1	21 411	20 500	48.9
Swaziland	1976	231 861	262 673	53.1	12 554	13 906	52.6
Saint Helena[b]	1976	2 514	2 633	51.2	154	149	49.2
Sao Tome and Principe[a]	1980	48 031	48 580	50.3	3 518	3 102	46.9
Senegal[a]	1976	2 472 622	2 525 263	50.5	67 898	50 884	42.8
Seychelles[a]	1977	31 171	30 727	49.6	1 185	748	38.7
Sierra Leone[a]	1974	1 359 321	1 375 838	50.3	48 336	31 078	39.1
South Africa	1985	11 545 282	11 840 363	50.6	1 209 967	652 225	35.0
Sudan	1973	7 137 964	6 975 626	49.4	113 028	114 878	50.4
Togo	1970	937 481	1 013 119	51.9	69 294	74 326	51.8
Tunisia[a]	1984	3 546 040	3 429 410	49.2	18 690	19 350	50.9
United Republic of Tanzania .	1978	8 587 086	8 925 525	51.0	219 188	196 496	47.3
Zambia	1980	2 769 995	2 891 806	51.1	121 436	109 918	47.5
Zimbabwe[a]	1982	3 673 620	3 827 850	51.0	301 490	226 950	42.9
Americas							
Antigua and Barbuda	1970	30 589	34 205	52.8	3 566	3 304	48.1
Argentina	1980	13 755 983	14 191 463	50.8	954 908	957 309	50.1
Bahamas	1980	101 774	107 731	51.4	12 379	11 664	48.5
Barbados	1980	115 771	128 457	52.6	8 046	10 591	56.8
Belize	1980	71 899	70 948	49.7	6 535	5 208	44.3
Bermuda	1980	26 350	27 700	51.2	6 753	7 417	52.3
Bolivia	1976	2 276 029	2 337 457	50.7	30 866	27 166	46.8
Brazil	1980	59 146 099	59 924 766	50.3	635 627	545 558	46.2
British Virgin Islands	1980	5 617	5 368	48.9	1 987	1 884	48.7

TABLE 1 (*continued*)

Country of enumeration	Year of census	Total population			Foreign-born population		
		Men	Women	Percentage of women	Men	Women	Percentage of women
Canada	1981	11 958 360	12 125 140	50.3	1 911 130	1 956 030	50.6
Cayman Islands	1979	8 113	8 564	51.4	2 585	2 809	52.1
Chile	1982	5 553 409	5 776 327	51.0	43 072	41 273	48.9
Colombia	1973	10 124 394	10 542 526	51.0	42 950	39 898	48.2
Costa Rica	1984	1 208 216	1 208 593	50.0	45 395	43 559	49.0
Cuba	1970	4 392 970	4 176 151	48.7	91 123	37 269	29.0
Dominica	1981	36 754	37 041	50.2	893	864	49.2
Dominican Republic	1970	1 998 990	2 007 415	50.1	21 279	11 170	34.4
Ecuador	1982	4 020 383	4 030 247	50.1	38 079	37 325	49.5
El Salvador	1971	1 763 190	1 791 458	50.4	15 812	16 355	50.8
French Guiana	1982	38 448	34 564	47.3	18 200	13 594	42.8
Greenland	1976	26 856	22 774	45.9	6 228	2 645	29.8
Grenada	1981	42 943	46 145	51.8	1 228	1 181	49.0
Guadeloupe	1982	160 112	166 890	51.0	17 406	17 457	50.1
Guatemala	1981	3 015 826	3 038 401	50.2	17 634	22 583	56.2
Guyana	1980	375 841	382 778	50.5	3 552	2 850	44.5
Haiti	1982	2 449 550	2 603 639	51.5	6 978	8 075	53.6
Jamaica	1982	1 074 633	1 115 724	50.9	11 220	11 437	50.5
Martinique	1982	158 415	168 302	51.5	13 619	12 781	48.4
Mexico	1980	33 039 307	33 807 526	50.6	134 212	134 688	50.1
Montserrat	1980	5 536	5 983	51.9	722	752	51.0
Netherlands Antilles	1981	112 148	119 784	51.6	12 106	15 719	56.5
Nicaragua	1971	921 543	956 409	50.9	11 460	10 558	48.0
Panama^c	1980	883 369	854 939	49.2	25 753	21 975	46.0
Paraguay	1982	1 519 720	1 515 640	49.9	89 160	79 980	47.3
Peru	1981	8 489 867	8 515 343	50.1	34 919	32 006	47.8
Puerto Rico	1980	1 556 842	1 639 678	51.3	131 272	139 020	51.4
Saint Kitts and Nevis	1980	20 840	22 469	51.9	1 300	1 297	49.9
Saint Lucia	1980	54 509	58 900	51.9	1 733	1 782	50.7
Saint Pierre and Miquelon	1982	2 981	3 056	50.6	407	412	50.3
Saint Vincent and the							
Grenadines	1980	47 409	50 436	51.5	1 029	1 082	51.3
Trinidad and Tobago	1980	526 234	529 529	50.2	30 017	31 662	51.3
Turks and Caicos	1980	3 580	3 833	51.7	622	580	48.3
United States of America	1980	110 053 161	116 492 644	51.4	6 581 094	7 498 812	53.3
United States Virgin Islands ..	1980	46 204	50 365	52.2	22 459	25 511	53.2
Uruguay	1985	1 439 021	1 516 220	51.3	48 103	54 899	53.3
Venezuela	1981	7 258 674	7 258 061	50.0	543 938	495 168	47.7
Asia							
Bahrain^a	1981	204 793	146 005	41.6	84 869	27 509	24.5
Bangladesh	1974	37 070 694	34 406 971	48.1	407 335	351 917	46.4
Brunei Darussalam	1981	102 942	89 890	46.6	31 822	21 769	40.6
Hong Kong	1981	2 604 168	2 382 392	47.8	1 143 295	988 783	46.4
India^d	1981	354 397 884	330 786 808	48.3	4 189 298	3 749 107	47.2
Iran (Islamic Republic of)	1986	25 280 961	24 164 049	48.9	481 219	371 288	43.6
Israel^e	1983	1 662 725	1 687 272	50.4	679 673	742 463	52.2
Japan^a	1985	59 497 316	61 551 607	50.8	364 117	355 976	49.4
Jordan^a	1979	1 086 591	1 013 428	48.3	59 282	29 686	33.4

TABLE 1 (*continued*)

Country of enumeration	Year of census	Total population			Foreign-born population		
		Men	Women	Percentage of women	Men	Women	Percentage of women
Kuwait[a]	1985	965 297	732 004	43.1	626 501	389 512	38.3
Macau	1981	122 990	118 739	49.1	73 476	72 136	49.5
Malaysia	1980	6 537 109	6 533 263	50.0	357 817	315 552	46.9
Nepal	1981	7 695 336	7 327 503	48.8	71 555	162 484	69.4
Philippines	1980	24 020 641	23 929 852	49.9	26 788	15 802	37.1
Qatar[a]	1970	71 714	39 419	35.5	49 046	17 048	25.8
Republic of Korea	1980	18 139 992	18 651 007	50.7	302 008	246 834	45.0
Saudi Arabia[a]	1974	3 576 753	3 149 713	46.8	528 671	262 434	33.2
Singapore	1980	1 231 760	1 182 185	49.0	266 710	260 442	49.4
Sri Lanka	1981	7 568 092	7 280 269	49.0	28 164	19 640	41.1
Syrian Arab Republic[a]	1981	4 621 852	4 424 292	48.9	181 391	171 373	48.6
Thailand	1980	22 315 244	22 484 765	50.2	153 289	119 397	43.8
Turkey	1980	22 695 362	22 041 595	49.3	435 266	432 929	49.9
United Arab Emirates[a]	1975	386 427	171 460	30.7	281 395	74 948	21.0
Europe							
Andorra	1988	26 715	23 813	47.1	19 581	16 944	46.4
Austria[a]	1981	3 572 426	3 982 912	52.7	161 934	129 514	44.4
Belgium[a]	1981	4 810 349	5 038 298	51.2	479 352	399 225	45.4
Channel Islands	1981	62 197	67 166	51.9	24 895	27 943	52.9
Czechoslovakia[a]	1980	7 441 160	7 841 935	51.3	29 812	43 872	59.5
Denmark	1981	2 528 225	2 595 764	50.7	76 699	89 880	54.0
Faeroe Islands	1977	21 997	19 972	47.6	1 357	1 072	44.1
Finland	1985	2 377 780	2 532 884	51.6	24 032	25 708	51.7
France[f]	1982	26 530 200	27 804 800	51.2	3 136 240	2 865 120	47.7
Germany, Federal Republic of[a]	1986	29 285 400	31 855 100	52.1	2 576 700	1 936 000	42.9
Gibraltar	1981	13 824	12 647	47.8	5 327	4 506	45.8
Greece[a]	1981	4 779 571	4 960 018	50.9	92 022	88 573	49.0
Iceland	1980	115 529	113 658	49.6	2 671	3 313	55.4
Ireland	1981	1 729 354	1 714 051	49.8	115 006	117 379	50.5
Isle of Man	1981	30 901	33 778	52.2	13 945	16 335	53.9
Italy	1981	27 506 354	29 050 557	51.4	491 526	646 001	56.8
Liechtenstein[a]	1982	13 004	13 376	50.7	5 178	4 412	46.0
Luxembourg	1981	177 869	186 733	51.2	41 955	44 650	51.6
Malta[a]	1985	169 982	175 723	50.8	2 107	2 691	56.1
Monaco	1982	12 598	14 465	53.4	8 028	9 849	55.1
Netherlands[a]	1986	7 184 540	7 344 892	50.6	312 779	239 754	43.4
Norway[a]	1983	2 045 519	2 088 834	50.5	49 818	44 850	47.4
Poland	1970	15 853 618	16 788 652	51.4	961 505	1 125 610	53.9
Portugal	1981	4 737 715	5 095 299	51.8	135 508	148 520	52.3
San Marino	1976	9 654	9 495	49.6	3 801	4 372	53.5
Spain	1970	16 641 747	17 398 896	51.1	175 340	190 036	52.0
Sweden	1986	4 137 513	4 244 002	50.6	320 335	349 541	52.2
Switzerland[a]	1985	3 160 400	3 324 400	51.3	531 500	429 200	44.7
United Kingdom[g]	1981	26 053 190	27 503 721	51.4	1 680 743	1 709 182	50.4

TABLE 1 (*continued*)

Country of enumeration	Year of census	Total population			Foreign-born population		
		Men	Women	Percentage of women	Men	Women	Percentage of women
Oceania							
American Samoa	1980	16 384	15 913	49.3	6 948	6 494	48.3
Australia	1986	7 768 313	7 833 843	50.2	1 664 517	1 582 864	48.7
Christmas Island	1981	1 918	953	33.2	1 533	622	28.9
Cocos (Keeling) Islands	1981	298	257	46.3	141	97	40.8
Cook Island	1981	9 172	8 582	48.3	1 311	1 043	44.3
Fiji	1986	362 568	352 807	49.3	6 629	6 268	48.6
French Polynesia	1983	86 914	79 839	47.9	14 024	9 045	39.2
Kiribati	1978	27 726	28 487	50.7	842	684	44.8
Nauru[a]	1977	3 781	3 185	45.7	1 759	1 321	42.9
New Caledonia	1983	74 285	71 083	48.9	18 782	15 035	44.5
New Zealand	1981	1 578 927	1 596 810	50.3	236 148	228 108	49.1
Niue	1976	1 928	1 915	49.8	245	198	44.7
Norfolk Island	1981	1 067	1 108	50.9	625	674	51.9
Northern Marianas	1980	8 817	7 963	47.5	2 620	2 003	43.3
Pacific Islands[h]	1980	59 527	56 622	48.7	911	527	36.6
Papua New Guinea[a]	1980	1 575 672	1 435 055	47.7	18 595	14 075	43.1
Samoa	1981	81 027	75 322	48.2	2 429	2 097	46.3
Solomon Islands	1976	102 808	94 015	47.8	2 675	2 292	46.1
Tokelau	1976	747	828	52.6	102	72	41.4
Tonga	1976	46 036	44 049	48.9	579	502	46.4
Vanuatu	1979	59 074	52 177	46.9	2 106	1 654	44.0
Developed countries		381 885 408	401 435 885	51.2	22 236 702	22 335 842	50.1
Developing countries		839 230 864	813 281 414	49.2	18 088 238	15 047 272	45.4
TOTAL		1 221 116 272	1 214 717 299	49.9	40 324 940	37 383 114	48.1

NOTES: — Not available.
[a]Foreign population displayed instead of foreign-born.
[b]Excluding Ascension.
[c]Including Canal Zone.
[d]The total population includes an estimate for Assam, the foreign-born excludes Assam.
[e]Jewish population only.
[f]The foreign-born population includes all those born outside metropolitan France.
[g]The total population refers only to usual residents, the foreign-born includes usual residents born in the Channel Islands and the Isle of Man.
[h]Excluding the Northern Marianas.

countries have been important receivers of foreign workers.

Although figure II shows that in the majority of countries men outnumber women among the foreign-born, it also indicates that in three quarters of the countries or areas considered, women constitute at least 44 per cent of the foreign-born population. Only in six—the United Arab Emirates, Bahrain, Qatar, Christmas Island, Cuba and Greenland—were women strongly underrepresented among migrants,

constituting at most 30 per cent of the foreign or foreign-born population.

Analysis of the data by region shows that there are considerable differences in the distribution of the proportion of women among the foreign-born. In Asia and Oceania, for instance, male migrants predominate in most countries. In Africa also, 25 out of 38 countries have more men than women among the foreign-born. In the Americas, however, the situation is balanced, with half the countries having at

Figure II. Percentage of women among the foreign born, by size of foreign-born population

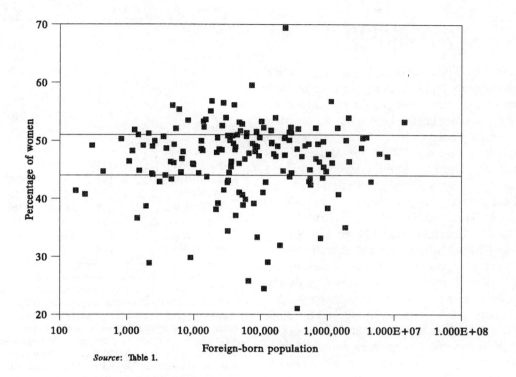

Source: Table 1.

least as many women as men among those born abroad. Only in Europe does the number of countries where female migrants outnumber their male counterparts surpass that of countries where male migrants predominate (17 against 12). These regional differences give rise to an important distinction between developed and developing countries: while in the former women tend to predominate among migrants, in the latter men do (table 1).

With respect to specific countries, it has already been pointed out that those hosting the largest number of migrants (over 1 million) tend to exhibit a fairly balanced sex distribution among the foreign-born. In fact, in 7 of the 17 countries in that group, female migrants either outnumber their male counterparts - as in the United States, Canada, Poland, Israel and Italy—or are as numerous as men, as in Argentina and the United Kingdom. In general, countries that have favoured migration for resettlement tend to have migrant populations with fairly balanced sex ratios.

As already noted, the predominance of men among migrants is often related to the promotion of migration for employment, particularly when countries have engaged in the import of unskilled labour. Such is the case of most of the oil-rich countries in Western Asia and Northern Africa or of the former labour importing countries of Western and Northern Europe. Yet, even among those countries, the presence of women among migrants is generally significant, especially as the migrant inflow matures. Thus, in most European countries at present, women constitute at least 43 per cent of the migrant population.

This brief overview of the sex composition of the stock of migrants in the world reveals not only that large numbers of women are international migrants, but also that their numbers are not so significantly different from those of men as to justify their general invisibility. Indeed, the evidence available suggests that, at the world level, women constitute nearly half of the migrant population. Consequently, even from a purely quantitative perspective, it is unconscionable to continue to ignore women as actors in the migration process.

B. Women as permanent immigrants

Although only a handful of countries in the world still admit migrants for permanent resettlement, their global importance far outweighs their limited number by virtue of counting the United States, the main migrant-receiving country in the world, among their set. Indeed, during the 1980s, the United States admitted nearly 6 million immigrants and legalized the status of another 2.6 million foreign-born persons. That country has also been unique in that, during a period of some 50 years (1930-1980), women have consistently outnumbered men among immigrants (Houstoun, Kramer and Barrett, 1984). As table 2 indicates, the proportion of women among immigrants to the United States was very high during the 1960s (over 55 per cent), but a declining trend is noticeable as of 1965. That trend reached a trough during the early 1980s when, for the first time in decades, the proportion of women among immigrants was lower than that of men (49.5 versus

TABLE 2. NUMBER OF IMMIGRANTS ADMITTED BY THE TRADITIONAL COUNTRIES OF IMMIGRATION, BY SEX AND PERCENTAGE OF WOMEN: 1960-1992

(Thousands)

Period	Both sexes	Male	Female	Percentage of women
United States				
1960-1964	1 419	635	784	55.2
1965-1969	1 795	792	1 003	55.9
1970-1974	1 923	900	1 023	53.2
1975-1979	2 413	1 136	1 276	52.9
1980-1984	2 825	835	819	49.5
1985-1989	3 028	1 511	1 518	50.1
1990-1992	2 007	903	1 104	55.0
United States legalizations				
1989-1992	2 646	1 756	889	33.6
Canada				
1960-1964	456	219	237	52.1
1965-1969	910	464	446	49.0
1970-1974	794	401	394	49.6
1975-1979	651	315	336	51.6
1980-1984	570	277	293	51.4
1985-1989	690	342	348	50.4

Table 2 *(continued)*

Period	Both sexes	Male	Female	Percentage of women
Australia				
1960-1964	558	293	265	47.5
1965-1969	781	420	361	46.2
1970-1974	612	314	298	48.6
1975-1979	345	170	175	50.7
1980-1984	468	239	230	49.0
1985-1989	616	307	310	50.2
1990-1992	305	150	156	51.0
New Zealand				
1960-1964	135	69	66	49.2
1965-1969	155	77	78	50.2
1970-1974	275	142	133	48.3
1975-1979	205	106	99	48.2
1980-1984	213	109	104	48.9
1985-1989	226	116	111	49.0
1990-1991	106	56	51	47.7

Sources: Based on Australia, Department of Immigration, *Australian Immigration: Consolidated Statistics*, Nos. 5-17, issues for 1971-1991 (Canberra); Canada, Department of Citizenship and Immigration, *Immigration Statistics*, issues for 1959-1964 (Ottawa); Canada, Manpower and Immigration, *Immigration Statistics*, issues for 1965-1976 (Ottawa); Canada, Employment and Immigration, *Immigration Statistics*, issues for 1977-1991 (Ottawa); New Zealand, Census and Statistics Department, *Population, Migration and Buildings*, issues for 1960-1970 (Wellington); New Zealand, Department of Statistics, *Population and Migration*, issues for 1971-1980 (Wellington); New Zealand, Department of Statistics, *Population and Migration Statistics*, Part B: *Migration,* issues for 1981/82, 1984/85 and 1985/86 (Wellington); New Zealand, Department of Statistics, *New Zealand Official Yearbook*, issues 1988-89 and 1992-93 (Wellington); United States of America, Department of Justice, *Annual Report of the Immigration and Naturalization Service*, issues for 1960-1977 (Washington, D.C.); United States of America, Department of Justice, *Statistical Yearbook of the Immigration and Naturalization Service,* issues for 1978-1992 (Washington, D.C.); United States of America, unpublished tabulations of the Immigration and Naturalization Service.

50.5 per cent). It must be noted, however, that for fiscal years 1980 and 1981, the distribution of immigrants by sex cannot be obtained. During the late 1980s women again became slightly more numerous than men among immigrants and their preponderance was even more marked during the early years of the 1990s. In addition, between 1989 and 1992, the United States granted immigrant status to 2.6 million persons who had been present in the country since earlier in the decade. Among the regularized population, women accounted for a relatively low proportion: 33.6 per cent.

The uniqueness of the United States experience, even with respect to that of other countries of permanent immigration, is illustrated in figure III, where the proportion of women among the annual number of immigrants is plotted for Australia, Canada, New Zealand and the United States over the period 1960-1992. Perhaps the most salient feature of that graph is that, among immigrants, the proportion of women has tended to converge towards equilibrium (50 per cent) in recent years. Indeed, whereas during most of the period 1960-1992 women tended to be underrepresented in the immigrant flows converging to Australia and New Zealand, and overrepresented in those flowing to the United States, by the late 1980s such proportions were close to 50 per cent in all three countries (table 2). Only in Canada, did the percentage of women among immigrants fluctuate almost symmetrically over a narrow band centred on 50 per cent. However, as table 2 indicates, during 1985-1989 that proportion was also close to the 50 per cent mark.

The high participation of women in migration flows converging to the traditional countries of immigration has generally been attributed to the provisions favouring family reunification that have characterized the migration policies of those countries during most of the post-war period. For instance, in analysing the sex distribution of the 1972-1979 immigrant cohort admitted by the United States,

Figure III. Percentage of women among the annual number of immigrants to the traditional countries of immigration, 1960-1992

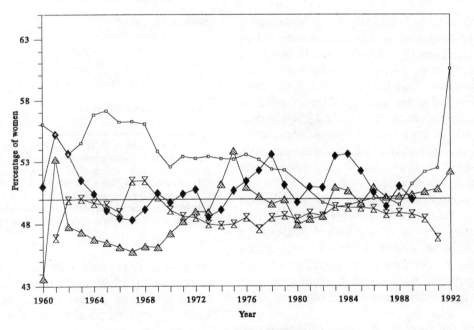

-□- United States   ◆ Canada   △ Australia   ✕ New Zealand

Sources: Based on Australia, Department of Immigration, *Australian Immigration: Consolidated Statistics*, Nos. 5-17, issues for 1971-1991 (Canberra); Canada, Department of Citizenship and Immigration, *Immigration Statistics*, issues for 1959-1964 (Ottawa); Canada, Manpower and Immigration, *Immigration Statistics*, issues for 1965-1976 (Ottawa); Canada, Employment and Immigration, *Immigration Statistics*, issues for 1977-1991 (Ottawa); New Zealand, Census and Statistics Department, *Population, Migration and Buildings*, issues for 1960-1970 (Wellington); New Zealand, Department of Statistics, *Population and Migration*, issues for 1971-1980 (Wellington); New Zealand, Department of Statistics, *Population and Migration Statistics*, Part B: *Migration,* issues for 1981/82, 1984/85 and 1985/86 (Wellington); New Zealand, Department of Statistics, *New Zealand Official Yearbook*, issues 1988-89 and 1992-93 (Wellington); United States of America, Department of Justice, *Annual Report of the Immigration and Naturalization Service*, issues for 1960-1977 (Washington, D.C.); United States of America, Department of Justice, *Statistical Yearbook of the Immigration and Naturalization Service,* issues for 1978-1992 (Washington, D.C.); United States of America, unpublished tabulations of the Immigration and Naturalization Service.

Houstoun, Kramer and Barrett (1984, p. 922) concluded that "the propensity of United States citizen and resident alien men to acquire foreign brides, reinforced by the half-century old United States policy favouring the admission of spouses" largely accounts for the predominance of women in immigrant flows. During 1972-1979, alien wives of United States citizens alone comprised 10 per cent of all immigrants. In addition, women accounted for 67 per cent of the persons admitted as parents of United States citizens (147,166 immigrants), for 61 per cent of orphans adopted by United States citizens (42,663 children) and for 49 per cent of the 154,637 alien children of United States citizens. Women also predominated among the large number of immigrants admitted under the Western Hemisphere ceiling and that of immigrants admitted as spouses or unmarried sons and daughters of permanent resident aliens (table 3).

According to table 3, the proportion of women in the different categories of immigrants admitted by the United States during 1972-1979 was always above 45 per cent, with the lowest values attained in categories having relatively little overall weight. Interestingly, even within the category of professionals or persons of exceptional ability, nearly 26,500 women were admitted as principal applicants, constituting 43 per cent of all principal applicants in the category. It must be noted, however, that when dependants are also considered, women accounted for nearly 50 per cent of all persons admitted under the professional category. Indeed, female immigrants admitted by virtue of being related to a principal applicant, a permanent resident alien or a United States citizen accounted for 60 per cent of all the admissions of female immigrants, whereas the equivalent proportion among male immigrants was 55 per cent.

By relating the number of women of various origins admitted by the United States under the different categories of immigrants to several variables indicative of possible migration determinants, Donato (1989) concluded that one of the most important determinants of the number of women immigrating as spouses or parents of United States citizens was the presence of United States military bases in the countries of origin. A high incidence of widowhood at origin was also a factor promoting migration under such

TABLE 3. IMMIGRANTS TO THE UNITED STATES, BY CLASS OF ADMISSION: 1972-1979

Class of admission	Proportion of total	Male (thousands)	Female (thousands)	Percentage female
Immediate relatives of United States citizens* ...	27.8	404	598	59.6
Western Hemisphere migrants	17.1	290	322	52.6
Siblings of adult United States citizens	14.3	269	243	47.5
Spouses and single sons and daughters of resident aliens	12.6	212	240	53.2
Refugees	11.9	214	212	49.8
Non-preference	8.0	141	147	51.0
Professionals or persons of exceptional ability	3.6	65	65	49.9
Skilled and unskilled workers in short supply .	3.1	61	51	45.6
Other	1.6	30	26	46.3
TOTAL	100.0	1 686	1 905	53.0
Of which persons admitted as relatives	58.2	933	1 157	55.3

Source: Marion F. Houstoun, Roger G. Kramer and Joan Mackin Barrett, "Female predominance of immigration to the United States since 1930: a first look", *International Migration Review* (Staten Island, New York), vol. 18, No. 4 (Winter, 1984), p. 923.

*Includes spouses, minor children, parents, married sons and daughters, and unmarried adult sons and daughters of United States citizens, as well as orphans adopted by United States citizens.

categories. In contrast, a deficit of potential grooms among young adults in the country of origin was a factor prompting women to migrate to the United States as professional or unskilled workers.

Data for Canada indicate that during 1981-1986 most of the 611,000 immigrants admitted belonged to the family class, that is, they were admitted by virtue of being close relatives of Canadian residents (table 4). The fact that women accounted for nearly 58 per cent of those immigrants is largely responsible for the overall predominance of female migrants during the period considered. Only among the category of assisted immigrants did women again

TABLE 4. IMMIGRANTS TO CANADA, BY CLASS
OF ADMISSION: 1981-1986
(*Thousands*)

Class of admission	1981-1986	Percentage female
Family	275	57.8
Independent	183	49.0
Designated	72	41.8
Assisted	56	50.5
Refugees	25	38.6
TOTAL	611	51.8

Source: Canada, Employment and Immigration, *Immigration Statistics*, various issues.

TABLE 5. IMMIGRANTS ADMITTED BY AUSTRALIA,
BY CLASS OF ADMISSION AND SEX:
FISCAL YEAR 1992/93

Class of admission	Male	Female	Percentage of women
Family class	13 165	18 937	59.0
Spouses and fiancees	5 588	10 925	66.2
Parents	1 718	2 445	58.7
Other	1 576	1 625	50.8
Concessional	4 283	3 942	47.9
Skilled workers	11 949	10 188	46.0
Employer nominees	1 027	932	47.6
Business skills	1 805	1 802	50.0
Distinguished talent	39	36	48.0
Independent	9 078	7 418	45.0
Refugees, humanitarian and special assistance	5 831	5 108	46.7
Other visaed immigrants	542	615	53.2
Special	145	159	52.3
Other	397	456	53.5
Non-visa immigrants	5 005	4 990	49.9
New Zealand citizens	4 164	4 191	50.2
Other	841	799	48.7
TOTAL	36 492	39 838	52.2

Source: Australia, Bureau of Immigration and Population Research, *Immigration Update*, June quarter 1993 (Canberra, Government Publishing Service), October, p. 11.

show a slight advantage over men. Women were strongly underrepresented among refugees (39 per cent) and among immigrants admitted as members of the designated classes[1] (42 per cent). Yet, among independent migrants, the second largest category during the period considered, women were nearly as numerous as men (49 per cent).

In Australia, Hugo's evaluation of the Points Assessment Scheme used to select immigrants (i.e., permanent settlers) showed that during 1984-1986 men outnumbered women among principal applicants in each of the following categories: (*a*) nondependent children of Australian residents; (*b*) siblings of Australian residents; (*c*) employer nominees; and (*d*) independent skilled workers or businessmen (Hugo, 1988, pp. 74-75). The distribution by sex, however, became fairly balanced when the dependants of principal applicants were considered. Women tended to be more numerous among dependants. Table 5 shows the distribution by sex of immigrants admitted by Australia during the fiscal year 1992/93 by class of admission. The data available do not distinguish between principal applicants and dependants. Nevertheless, they indicate that women tend to outnumber men among immigrants admitted in the family class, particularly among persons admitted as spouses, fiancées and parents of Australian citizens. Women are also overrepresented among the small number of immigrants receiving special or other visas. In most of the other classes of admission, men outnumber women, particularly among skilled workers and among immigrants admitted on humanitarian grounds. However, the relatively high weight of admissions under the family class (they account for 42 per cent of the total) and the high overrepresentation of women among them tilts the balance towards women in terms of overall admissions, of which women constituted 52 per cent.

Thus, available admission statistics indicate that in most cases women attain immigrant status by virtue of their family ties with other immigrants or with residents or citizens of the receiving country. The number of women acquiring immigrant status by virtue of their own personal attributes, as professionals, refugees etc., is fairly small. Yet, so are the numbers of men achieving admission under such categories and, although they outnumber women, the latter constitute sizeable proportions of the categories concerned.

Indeed, in interpreting official statistics one must bear in mind that they are coloured by the policy biases of the receiving State. When the latter accords priority to the admission of close relatives, persons wishing to migrate, whatever their sex, are likely to make that priority work for them. When a traditional view of the roles of women is an implicit premise for the application of rules and regulations controlling immigrant admission, official statistics are more likely to reflect such views than reality. The case of a married woman wishing to apply as a business immigrant comes to mind. After her application was considered, admission was granted provided her husband would appear as principal applicant and as eventual manager of the business she was planning to set up. A Rose by any other name... becomes a dependant.

C. Migrant women in the Western-bloc countries of Europe

It is estimated that by 1990, the Western-bloc countries of Europe were hosting about 16 million foreigners, most of whom had been admitted as workers or as immediate family members of those workers. Indeed, during the second half of the 1950s and the 1960s, the major Western-bloc countries in Europe had resorted to the importation of foreign workers in order to combat the labour shortages that resulted from their expanding economies and the manpower losses experienced during the Second World War. However, during the early 1970s, as economic recession loomed because of rising oil prices, most of the labour-importing countries in Europe adopted measures to stop the inflow of foreign workers and stabilize the size of the foreign populations already present in their territories. Such measures generally included both the possibility of family reunification and the promotion of the voluntary return of migrants to their home countries. As a result, the presence of women among the foreign population grew. Yet, women had not been entirely absent from the flows occurring before the stoppage of labour migration. In France, for instance, data on worker migration for the period 1967-1974 show that 23 per cent of the Portuguese workers introduced by the National Office for Immigration (ONI) were women (Tribalat, 1989, table II-3). Furthermore, the censuses con-

ducted before 1965 in France, Western Germany, Luxembourg, Sweden and Switzerland, all indicate that women accounted for considerable shares of the foreign population, ranging from a low of 31 per cent in Western Germany in 1961 to a high of nearly 49 per cent in Luxembourg in 1960 (see table 6).

TABLE 6. FOREIGN POPULATION IN SELECTED EUROPEAN COUNTRIES, BY SEX, AND PERCENTAGE OF WOMEN: VARIOUS YEARS
(Thousands)

Country	Both sexes	Male	Female	Percentage of women
Belgium[a]				
31-Dec-70	696.3	377.7	318.6	45.8
01-Mar-81	878.6	479.4	399.2	45.4
01-Mar-91	900.9	485.1	415.8	46.2
Denmark				
01-Jan-76	90.9	49.6	41.2	45.4
01-Jan-81	101.6	53.7	47.9	47.2
01-Jan-86	117.0	62.9	54.0	46.2
01-Jan-92	169.5	89.0	80.6	47.5
France[a]				
10-Mar-46	1 743.6	1 001.5	742.2	42.6
10-May-54	1 765.3	1 089.3	676.0	38.3
07-Mar-62	2 169.7	1 339.9	829.7	38.2
01-Mar-68	2 621.1	1 592.2	1 028.9	39.3
20-Feb-75	3 442.4	2 060.8	1 381.6	40.1
04-Mar-82	3 714.2	2 119.6	1 594.6	42.9
05-Mar-90	3 607.6	1 988.3	1 619.3	44.9
inland				
31-Dec-60[a]	5.2	3.4	1.8	34.7
31-Dec-70[a]	5.5	3.2	2.3	41.8
31-Dec-75[a]	12.2	7.1	5.1	41.6
31-Dec-80[a]	12.7	7.2	5.5	43.0
1984	16.8	9.4	7.3	43.7
1985	17.0	9.7	7.4	43.2
Germany (Western)				
30-Sep-73	3 966.2	2 482.4	1 483.8	37.4
30-Sep-75	4 089.6	2 439.8	1 649.8	40.3
30-Sep-80	4 453.3	2 619.2	1 834.1	41.2
31-Dec-85	4 378.9	2 504.9	1 874.1	42.8
31-Dec-87[b]	4 630.2	2 627.7	2 002.5	43.2
31-Dec-87[b]	4 240.5	2 406.5	1 834.0	43.2
31-Dec-89	4 845.9	2 666.5	2 179.4	45.0
30-Sep-90	5 241.8	2 945.9	2 295.9	43.8
Germany (Western)[a]				
06-Jun-61	686.2	472.8	213.4	31.1
27-May-70	2 438.6	1 525.3	913.3	37.5
25-May-87	4 145.6	2 297.5	1 848.1	44.6

TABLE 6 (continued)

Country	Both sexes	Male	Female	Percentage of women
Luxembourg[a]				
31-Dec-60	41.5	21.2	20.3	48.9
31-Dec-66	56.7	28.7	28.1	49.5
31-Dec-70	62.5	31.5	31.0	49.6
31-Mar-81	95.8	48.1	47.7	49.8
01-Jan-89	100.9	49.7	51.2	50.8
Netherlands				
01-Jan-76	350.5	217.6	132.9	37.9
01-Jan-80	473.4	275.8	197.6	41.7
01-Jan-85	558.7	317.6	241.1	43.2
01-Jan-90	642.0	354.0	288.0	44.9
Norway				
06-Dec-60[a]	24.8	13.3	11.6	46.5
01-Jan-75	64.9	34.2	30.7	47.3
01-Jan-81	82.6	43.3	39.2	47.5
01-Jan-86	101.5	53.4	48.1	47.4
Spain[a]				
31-Dec-70	291.0	149.4	141.6	48.7
01-Mar-81	234.0	113.1	120.9	51.7
Sweden				
01-Nov-60[a]	299.9	165.1	134.8	45.0
01-Nov-70[a]	407.8	219.4	188.4	46.2
01-Jan-76	409.9	214.0	195.9	47.8
01-Jan-80	424.1	218.7	205.4	48.4
01-Jan-85	390.6	196.7	193.9	49.6
01-Jan-90	456.0	232.6	223.5	49.0
Switzerland[a]				
01-Dec-60	584.7	330.7	254.1	43.5
01-Dec-70	1 080.1	603.0	477.1	44.2
01-Dec-80	945.0	529.9	415.1	43.9
04-Dec-90	1 246.6	725.1	521.6	41.8
Switzerland[c]				
01-Jan-71	1 001.9	538.5	463.4	46.3
01-Jan-75	1 084.3	579.3	505.1	46.6
01-Jan-80	904.3	490.9	413.5	45.7
01-Jan-85	953.4	525.4	428.0	44.9
01-Jan-90	1 066.1	595.0	471.2	44.2
01-Jan-92	1 191.0	666.8	524.2	44.0

Sources: Belgium, Institut national de statistique, *Recensement de la population du 31 décembre 1970*, vol. 4, *Population selon la nationalité* (Brussels, 1974), table II; Belgium, Institut national de statistique, *Recensement de la population et des logements au 1er mars 1981*, No.1: *Résultats généraux* (Brussels, 1982), table 00.01; Belgium, Institut national de statistique, *Recensement de la population et des logements au 1er mars 1991*, vol. 1B, *Chiffres de la population* (Brussels, 1992), table 00.01; Denmark, Danmarks Statistik, *Befolkningens bevaegelsed*, various years (Copenhagen); *Statistisk arbog 1992* (Copenhagen, 1992), table 46; France, Institut national de la statistique et des études économiques, *Recensement de la*

population de 1990: nationalités, Résultats, No. 197; *Démographie-Société*, No. 19, juin 1992 (Paris), table R8; Finland, Official Statistics of Finland, *General Census of Population 1960*, vol. VIII: *Population by birthplace and by education, displaced population, etc.* (Helsinki), table 7; Finland, Central Statistical Office, *Population and Housing Census 1980* (Helsinki, 1983), vol. XVI, *Foreign citizens*, p.43; Germany, Statistisches Bundesamt, *Volks- und Berufszählung vom 6 Juni 1961: Ausländer*, Fachserie A: *Bevölkerung und Kultur* (Wiesbaden, 1961); *Vokszählung vom 27 Mai 1970: Bevölkerung und Bevölkerungsentwicklung nach Alter und Familienstand*, Fachserie A: *Bevölkerung und Kultur* (Wiesbaden); *Statistisches Jahrbuch*, various years (Wiesbaden); Luxembourg, Service central de la statistique et des études économiques, *Statistiques historiques 1839-1989* (Luxembourg, 1990), table B.100; Netherlands, Central Bureau of Statistics, *Statistical Yearbook of the Netherlands*, various years (The Hague); Nordic Council of Ministers and Nordic Statistical Secretariat, *Yearbook of Nordic Statistics 1987*, vol. 26 (Stockholm, 1987), table 14; Norway, Statistisk Sentralbyra, *Flyttestatistikk*, various years (Oslo); Spain, Instituto Nacional de Estadística, *Anuario Estadístico de España*, various years (Madrid); Sweden, Statistiska Centralbyran, *Statistisk arsbok (Statistical Abstract of Sweden)*, various years (Stockholm); Switzerland, Office fédéral de la statistique, *Annuaire statistique de la Suisse*, various years (Basel).

NOTE: Unless otherwise indicated, the data are obtained from registers, either of the population in general or of the foreign population in particular.

[a]Data obtained from population censuses.

[b]The data shown represent the number of registered foreigners before and after the adjustment carried out on the basis of the results of the 1987 population census.

[c]Includes only resident foreigners. Seasonal workers are excluded.

Table 6 presents data indicating the evolution of the proportion of women among the foreign population present in selected European countries. Attention is focused on the foreign population because most European countries equate foreigners with migrants. However, not only is it possible for foreigners not to be migrants (in the sense that migrants must have changed their country of residence at least once in their lifetime) but, in addition, changes in the foreign population may be brought about not only because of migration but also because of naturalization and, in countries where citizenship rights are not granted automatically to children born in their territory, by natural increase as well. Note that for Western Germany and Switzerland, two sets of figures on the foreign population are presented. In Western Germany, one is obtained from the register of foreigners and the other from censuses. The register of foreigners is known to overestimate the foreign population because foreigners who leave the country with the intention of remaining abroad for lengthy periods do not necessarily report their departure to the authorities. In 1987, when a census was carried out in Western Germany, the data from the register of foreigners were adjusted to better reflect the actual number of foreigners present in the country. Both the unadjusted and the adjusted figures are presented in table 6. The proportion of women, however, was not modified to match that yielded by the census.

In the case of Switzerland, one set of estimates is obtained from census counts and the other from data derived from the register of foreigners. The difference between the two sets stems, at least in part, from the fact that the data obtained from the register of foreigners exclude foreigners admitted as seasonal workers who may stay up to nine months in Switzerland. Because of the overrepresentation of men among seasonal workers, the proportion of women tends to be higher according to the register of foreigners than according to census counts.

One of the striking features of the data presented in table 6 is that, with the exception of the foreign population in Luxembourg and that enumerated by the 1981 census of Spain, women tend to be markedly underrepresented among the foreign population present in European countries, even during recent periods. In addition, the percentage of women among the foreign population does not necessarily increase monotonically through time. In a number of countries, increases in the percentage of women among foreigners were recorded during the 1970s and most of the 1980s, but declines are noticeable for the most recent period covered. Indeed, Switzerland has recorded a declining proportion of women among foreigners since 1975. There has been, however, a narrowing of the range of variation of the proportion of women among foreigners, whose endpoints changed from 37.5 and 48.9 per cent around 1970, to 41.8 and 50.8 per cent by 1990.

Table 6 also shows that, within countries, the range of variation of the proportion of women among foreigners has been relatively narrow during the period 1970-1990. The widest ranges, spanning 7 to 7.5 percentage points, are observed in Western Germany and the Netherlands. In France as well, the proportion of women among foreigners changed by nearly six percentage points between 1968 and 1990. In all three countries, women had accounted for a

low 37 to 38 per cent of the foreign population around 1970, before labour migration was discontinued, and it rose to 44 or 45 per cent towards 1990.

For a few European countries, there is information on the number of foreign-born persons present in their territories (table 7). Since foreign-born persons are necessarily migrants, the percentage of women among the foreign born is a better indicator of

TABLE 7. FOREIGN-BORN POPULATION IN SELECTED EUROPEAN COUNTRIES, BY SEX AND PERCENTAGE OF WOMEN: VARIOUS YEARS

Country	Both sexes	Male	Female	Percentage of women
France[a]				
04-Mar-82.......	6 001.4	3 136.2	2 865.1	47.7
05-Mar-90.......	5 895.1	3 002.5	2 892.6	49.1
Finland				
01-Jan-86	49.7	24.0	25.7	51.7
Italy[a]				
24-Oct-71........	936.9	400.7	536.3	57.2
25-Oct-81........	1 137.5	491.5	646.0	56.8
Netherlands				
01-Jan-90	1 167.0	575.0	592.0	50.7
Sweden				
01-Jan-85	731.3	351.3	380.0	52.0
01-Jan-90	847.7	412.6	435.1	51.3
United Kingdom[a]				
23-Apr-61	1 657.2	851.6	805.6	48.6
25-Apr-71	3 088.1	1 567.4	1 520.7	49.2
05-Apr-81	3 515.7	1 744.0	1 771.7	50.4

Sources: France, Institut national de la statistique et des études économiques, Recensement de la population de 1990: nationalités, Résultats, No. 197, (Paris, 1991), table R8; Italy, Istituto Centrale di Statistica, 11 Censimento Generale della Popolazione, 24 ottobre 1971, vol. IX: Risultati degli spogli campionari, Tome 1 (Rome, 1977), table 1; Italy, Istituto Centrale di Statistica, 12 Censimento Generale della Popolazione, 25 ottobre 1981, vol. II: Dati sulle caratteristiche strutturali della popolazione e delle abitazioni, Tome 3 (Rome, 1985), table 8; Netherlands, Central Bureau of Statistics, Statistical Yearbook of the Netherlands (various years), The Hague; Norway, Statistisk Sentralbyra, Flyttestatistikk, various years (Oslo); Sweden, Statistiska Centralbyran, Statistisk arsbok (Statistical Abstract of Sweden), various years (Stockholm); United Kingdom, General Register Office, Census 1961: Great Britain, Summary tables (London), table 10; United Kingdom, Office of Population Censuses and Surveys, Census 1981, National Report (London), table 8.

NOTE: Unless otherwise indicated, the data are obtained from population registers.

[a]Data obtained from population censuses.

women's participation in migration. Interestingly, the proportion of women among the foreign-born is generally higher than that among the foreign population in countries having statistics on both. Furthermore, according to the data on place of birth, women appear to be almost equally likely to be overrepresented as underrepresented among the foreign-born, and in no case is their level of underrepresentation as large as that implied by the data based on citizenship. It appears, therefore, that the data on the foreign population tend to underrepresent the participation of women in migration, probably because of differential naturalization levels by sex. That is the case in Switzerland, where the proportion of women among the foreign population has been declining despite the fact that net migration gains among foreigners have been dominated by women. Thus, whereas women constituted 65.4 per cent of the net migration gain recorded during 1980-1984, the percentage of women among the foreign population declined by nearly one percentage point between 1980 and 1985 (see table 6).

In the case of Western Germany, data on migration flows by sex indicate that men have outnumbered women among both immigrants and emigrants, usually by fairly wide margins (table 8). Thus, during 1965-1969, women accounted for only 33.4 per cent of all immigrants and, although their share rose after 1974, the highest level reached was 45.8 per cent of all immigrants during 1985-1989. However, since women also tended to be underrepresented among emigrants, their share of net migration was generally higher than that of immigration, though they were always underrepresented among the net migration gains recorded before 1975 and since 1985. During 1975-1984, net migration reached particularly low levels, becoming negative among men but remaining positive among women. Consequently, during that period migration contributed exclusively to the growth of the female population. Yet, the decomposition of migration flows by citizenship shows that during 1975-1984 net migration was negative among both foreign men and foreign women, although the losses that the foreign population underwent through migration were smaller among women than among men. The case of Germany thus illustrates the complex migration dynamics that underlie the changes observed in the sex distribution of the foreign population. The flow data presented in table 8 belie the widespread view that family reunification led to higher migration levels among women. Once the stoppage of labour migration went into effect, the immigration levels of both men and women declined significantly and, although emigration declined as well, net migration became very low. Among foreign migrants, in particular, net losses were prevalent though less marked among women. Since 1985, both immigration and net migration have increased, particularly the net migration of German citizens, among whom women have generally accounted for relatively high proportions. The net migration of foreigners has also increased and, among them, the share of men is tending to rise.

Changes in the sex composition of the foreign population do not occur homogeneously across all citizenship groups. Table 9, for instance, shows the changes recorded among the different foreign groups living in Western Germany. In 1973, just before the admission of foreign workers had come to an end, the percentage of women varied between 33.6 and 36.3 per cent for the largest citizenship groups, namely, Italians, Turks and Yugoslavs. The Portuguese and Spanish also had relatively low proportions of women (35.8 and 37.1 per cent, respectively). Only among the Greek and Dutch groups did women constitute some 46 per cent of the population. Between 1973 and 1975, the proportion of women rose markedly among most citizenship groups, including the Austrians, the Italians, the Portuguese, the Spanish, the Turks and the Yugoslavs. Moderately increasing trends have generally been the rule since then. Consequently, by 1989, the proportion of women among most citizenship groups was at least 44 per cent. Only among Italians did women constitute still only 39.3 per cent of the population.

These changes in composition by sex have been accompanied by important variations in the size of each population subgroup (table 9). The number of both men and women of Greek, Portuguese or Spanish nationality declined. Among Yugoslavs, the number of women increased, while that of men decreased. Among Italians, the number of women changed little, but that of men declined significantly. The number of Dutch and Austrian nationals increased slightly for both sexes. Yet by far the most

TABLE 8. AVERAGE ANNUAL NUMBER OF MIGRANTS TO AND FROM WESTERN GERMANY, BY SEX AND CITIZENSHIP, AND PERCENTAGE OF WOMEN AMONG IMMIGRANTS, EMIGRANTS AND NET MIGRANTS

Sex and citizenship	1965-1969	1970-1974	1975-1979	1980-1984	1985-1989	1990-1991
Average annual numbers (thousands)						
All men						
Immigrants	2 351	2 760	1 481	1 452	2 204	1 624
Emigrants	1 764	1 904	1 542	1 493	1 234	717
Net migration	587	855	-61	-41	970	907
Foreign men						
Immigrants	2 179	2 598	1 254	1 227	1 538	1 056
Emigrants	1 597	1 771	1 414	1 353	1 061	595
Net migration	582	827	-160	-126	477	461
German men						
Immigrants	173	161	228	225	666	567
Emigrants	167	133	128	140	173	122
Net migration	5	28	100	85	493	446
All women						
Immigrants	1 179	1 606	1 156	1 059	1 862	1 211
Emigrants	779	930	1 063	1 003	964	476
Net migration	400	676	93	56	898	735
Foreign women						
Immigrants	999	1 444	924	832	1 230	707
Emigrants	580	785	925	852	785	368
Net migration	419	658	-1	-20	446	338
German women						
Immigrants	180	162	232	227	632	504
Emigrants	199	145	138	151	179	108
Net migration	-19	17	94	76	452	397
Percentage of women						
All persons						
Immigrants	33.4	36.8	43.8	42.2	45.8	42.7
Emigrants	30.6	32.8	40.8	40.2	43.9	39.9
Net migration	40.5	44.1	+	+	48.1	44.8
Foreign persons						
Immigrants	31.4	35.7	42.4	40.4	44.5	40.1
Emigrants	26.6	30.7	39.5	38.6	42.5	38.2
Net migration	41.9	44.3	..	..	48.3	42.3
German citizens						
Immigrants	51.1	50.1	50.5	50.3	48.7	47.1
Emigrants	54.4	52.1	52.0	51.9	50.9	47.0
Net migration	−	38.1	48.5	47.3	47.8	47.1

Source: Unpublished tabulations by the Statistisches Bundesamt, Wiesbaden, Germany.

NOTE: A plus sign (+) indicates that the number of net migrants is positive among women and negative among men; a minus sign (−) indicates that the number of net migrants is negative among women and positive among men; two dots (..) indicate that data are not available or are not separately reported. No percentage of women is calculated when net migration is negative among both men and women.

TABLE 9. FOREIGN POPULATION IN WESTERN GERMANY BY COUNTRY OF CITIZENSHIP AND SEX: VARIOUS YEARS

Country of origin and date	Foreign population (thousands)			
	Both sexes	Male	Female	Percentage of women
Austria				
30-Sep-73	1 588	961	627	39.5
30-Sep-75	1 740	1 014	726	41.7
30-Sep-80	1 726	1 003	723	41.9
31-Dec-85	1 725	976	750	43.5
31-Dec-89	1 798	1 007	792	44.0
Greece				
30-Sep-73	3 992	2 153	1 839	46.1
30-Sep-75	3 905	2 072	1 834	47.0
30-Sep-80	2 975	1 592	1 384	46.5
31-Dec-85	2 806	1 511	1 295	46.2
31-Dec-89	3 096	1 701	1 395	45.1
Italy				
30-Sep-73	6 220	4 103	2 117	34.0
30-Sep-75	6 014	3 797	2 217	36.9
30-Sep-80	6 179	3 856	2 323	37.6
31-Dec-85	5 313	3 260	2 054	38.7
31-Dec-89	5 477	3 327	2 150	39.3
Netherlands				
30-Sep-73	1 058	574	484	45.7
30-Sep-75	1 103	590	515	46.6
30-Sep-80	1 078	570	508	47.1
31-Dec-85	1 084	572	512	47.2
31-Dec-89	1 107	584	523	47.2
Portugal				
30-Sep-73	1 117	717	400	35.8
30-Sep-75	1 185	680	505	42.6
30-Sep-80	1 123	605	518	46.1
31-Dec-85	770	412	359	46.6
31-Dec-89	822	437	385	46.8
Spain				
30-Sep-73	2 861	1 800	1 061	37.1
30-Sep-75	2 474	1 466	1 009	40.8
30-Sep-80	1 800	1 039	760	42.2
31-Dec-85	1 528	869	659	43.1
31-Dec-89	1 380	767	613	44.4
Turkey				
30-Sep-73	8 936	5 936	3 000	33.6
30-Sep-75	10 771	6 700	4 071	37.8
30-Sep-80	14 624	8 762	5 863	40.1
31-Dec-85	14 019	8 085	5 935	42.3
31-Dec-89	16 215	9 043	7 172	44.2
Yugoslavia				
30-Sep-73	6 733	4 291	2 442	36.3
30-Sep-75	6 779	4 083	2 696	39.8
30-Sep-80	6 318	3 584	2 734	43.3
31-Dec-85	5 910	3 298	2 612	44.2
31-Dec-89	6 382	3 490	2 890	45.3

Source: Based on Germany, Statistisches Bundesamt, *Statistisches Jahrbuch*, issues for 1974-1991 (Wiesbaden).

important increase was observed among Turks, whose numbers doubled between 1973 and 1989. Growth was considerably higher among Turkish women than among Turkish men (139 versus 52 per cent, respectively), though by 1989 men still outnumbered women among Turkish migrants by a wide margin.

Differentials in the composition by sex of the various citizenship groups are observed in most receiving countries. In France, for instance, migrant groups of European origin display significantly higher proportions of women than those of Northern African origin (see table 10). In the United Kingdom as well, migrants of African or Asian origin tend to exhibit lower proportions of women than those originating in the Americas, Europe and Oceania (see table 11). Among persons born in Pakistan or Bangladesh who reside in the United Kingdom, the proportion of women was particularly low in 1971 (28 per cent) and, though it rose to 41 per cent by 1981, it is still far below those exhibited by other migrant groups.

This overview of migration to the Western-bloc countries of Europe indicates that the participation of women in international migration flows converging

TABLE 10. PERCENTAGE OF WOMEN IN THE FOREIGN POPULATION PRESENT IN FRANCE, BY SELECTED COUNTRY OF CITIZENSHIP

Region or country of citizenship	1975 census	1982 census	1990 census
European Community			
Italy............................	43.7	43.2	43.0
Spain	47.2	47.2	48.0
Portugal........................	46.1	47.1	46.5
Other	43.9	47.5	49.8
Northern Africa			
Algeria	32.0	38.6	41.3
Morocco	26.7	39.1	44.1
Tunisia	30.9	37.8	42.0
World total	40.1	42.9	44.9

Source: Michèle Tribalat, "Rapport français", paper presented at the meeting of the Working Group on International Migration of the European Association for Population Studies, Paris, June 1989, table I.5; France, Institut national de la statistique et des études économiques, *Recensement de la population de 1990: nationalités*, Résultats No. 197 (Paris, 1991), table 10.

TABLE 11. PERCENTAGE OF WOMEN IN THE FOREIGN-BORN
POPULATION ENUMERATED IN THE UNITED KINGDOM,
BY REGION OF BIRTH

Region of birth	1971 census	1981 census
Africa	47.3	48.3
Americas	49.5	50.7
Asia	42.4	46.4
Europe	52.0	53.0
Oceania	56.2	55.0
Pakistan and Bangladesh	28.0	41.2
World total	49.2	50.3

Source: United Kingdom, Office of Population Censuses and Surveys and Registrar General of Scotland, *Census 1981. Country of Birth. Great Britain* (Her Majesty's Stationery Office, London), table 8.

to those countries was far from negligible even before the cessation of the male dominated labour migration of the 1950s and 1960s. However, the policy changes occurring towards 1973-1974, by reducing the inflow of workers from non-member countries of the European Community, favouring family reunification, and promoting the return of significant numbers of workers, tended to produce foreign populations with more balanced distributions by sex. Such changes in sex composition occurred concomitantly with substantial inflows and outflows of migrants, in both of which women were well represented. In general, however, the foreign populations hosted by most European countries still exhibit relatively low proportions of women, especially among certain citizenship groups. It is likely that differential naturalization levels by sex and citizenship, as well as factors influencing the sex selectivity of migration at origin are responsible for the continued underrepresentation of women among the foreign population groups in Europe.

D. WOMEN AS TEMPORARY MIGRANT WORKERS IN ASIA

Probably one of the developments that has contributed the most to increase the visibility of women as international migrants is their participation in worker migration to the oil-rich countries of Western Asia. In the early 1980s, Korale (1983) reported that the

official statistics of Sri Lanka indicated that women were outnumbering men by large margins among persons leaving the country to work abroad. Soon thereafter, similar trends were noticed in various South-eastern Asian countries known to export temporary workers, though reliable statistics on the phenomenon remain scarce.

At present, it is well known that significant numbers of women originating in Indonesia, Malaysia, the Philippines, Sri Lanka or Thailand have become temporary migrant workers. According to official statistics, during 1983-1988, Indonesia deployed 205,000 female migrant workers who constituted 65.7 per cent of the total number of persons deployed to work abroad (ILO, 1989). In 1988 alone, nearly 50,000 Indonesian women had been deployed abroad, constituting 78 per cent of all workers deployed. The equivalent numbers for Thailand and Sri Lanka were 15,000 and 9,000 female migrants, respectively.

One of the major source countries of female migrant workers in South-eastern Asia is the Philippines. With relatively high levels of educational attainment and their command of English, Filipino women have long been in demand as nurses in overseas countries. In fact, the countries of destination of Filipino female migrants are no longer, even if they ever were, located exclusively in Western Asia. Reports of Filipino women working as domestic workers in countries like Hong Kong, Singapore or even Italy abound. Filipino women are also prominent among temporary workers admitted to Japan as entertainers. Data compiled by the Philippine Overseas Employment Administration indicate that worker migration from the Philippines tripled between 1980 and 1987, passing from 137,000 to some 450,000 to 500,000 workers a year. However, no distribution by sex is provided. Data for 1987 indicated that 81,000 women were deployed as domestic workers abroad, 32,000 as entertainers and 26,000 as nurses (no classification by sex was provided for the latter), yielding a total of 139,000 female workers deployed abroad (ILO, 1989). The distribution by country of destination shows that most nurses (23,000 out of a total of 26,000) were working in Western Asia. Saudi Arabia alone accounted for nearly 18,000. Among the 81,000 domestic workers reported, the vast majority (51,000) were working in Asian countries other than the oil-rich countries of Western Asia. Thus, Hong Kong hosted some 30,000 and Singapore another 17,000. Countries in Western Asia employed an additional 24,000, concentrated mainly in Saudi Arabia and the United Arab Emirates (with about 9,000 and 8,000, respectively). Only about 4,000 were reported to be working in Europe, mainly in Greece (1,600) and Italy (1,500). Among the 81,000 women deployed as domestic workers abroad, 49,000 or nearly 61 per cent were hired for the first time, the rest were being rehired by their foreign employers.

Among the 31,579 Filipino women migrating as entertainers, virtually all (31,292) went to Japan. Only 19 were reported as rehires. Japanese statistics show that the balance of entries and departures of citizens of the Philippines has been growing steadily. Thus, while in 1980 such balance amounted only to about 1,500 persons, by 1987 it had reached 18,000 (Japan, 1988). Unfortunately, the data on entries and departures to Japan are neither classified by sex, nor jointly by place of origin and purpose of stay. Hence, it is not possible to know how many Filipino women enter the country and for what purpose. There is evidence, however, that the number of Filipino women working illegally in Japan has been rising, as discussed in the following section.

Clearly, though the data available remain sketchy, they indicate that the participation of Asian women in temporary labour migration has grown to significant levels during the 1980s, although both in absolute and relative terms it still does not match the levels that female migration to the United States or Europe has attained. However, the unequivocal economic role that women play when they engage in labour migration justifies the importance attached to such movements and has already brought to the forefront issues of migrant protection and equality of treatment that are relevant for female migrants the world over.

E. WOMEN AS UNDOCUMENTED MIGRANTS

Just as undocumented migration in general, the undocumented migration of women is very difficult to quantify. Yet, in this area again, the pervasive view is that most undocumented migrants are men. Some evidence on the extent of female participation in undocumented migration can be obtained from the results of amnesties or regularization drives carried out in different countries.

Argentina has often resorted to amnesties to regularize the situation of de facto immigrants present in its territory. During the past 40 years amnesties took place in 1949, 1958, 1964-1969, 1974 and 1984 (Mármora, 1983; Balán, 1992). Data on the number of regularizations by sex are available for 1974. Among the 147,000 persons regularized that year, 47 per cent were women. The distribution by sex varied considerably by citizenship. Thus, whereas among Chileans and Uruguayans men accounted for nearly 60 per cent of those regularized, among Paraguayans women outnumbered men slightly, accounting for 52 per cent. Among Bolivians and Brazilians, the percentages of women were 44 and 47 per cent, respectively (Mármora, 1983, p. 64).

Venezuela carried out a regularization drive in 1980 during which a total of 267,000 migrants applied for legalization (Torrealba, 1982). Among them, 144,000 were men (54 per cent) and 123,000 women (46 per cent). The vast majority of those applying for regularization were Colombians (246,000) among whom women accounted also for 46 per cent. Women tended to be more numerous than men among the relatively fewer migrants coming from Ecuador and Chile, the Dominican Republic, and Northern America and the Caribbean in general (which accounted for some 12,000 migrants).

Among the 2,003 persons who had applied for amnesty by 30 June 1980 under the Regularization of Status Programme implemented by the Australian Government in 1980, 73 per cent were men (Storer, 1982). Such imbalance in the number of persons of each sex contrasts sharply with the relatively more balanced sex ratios characterizing normal immigrant inflows to Australia. However, the number of applicants is not equivalent to the number of persons who were eventually regularized, not only because of possible rejections, but also because the dependants of applicants were also entitled to legalization. Unfortunately, no data were provided on the number and sex distribution of dependants.

The proportion of women was also very low among migrants regularizing their status in France and Italy during the drives carried out in 1981-1982 and 1987-1988, respectively (OECD, 1990). During the former, 132,000 migrants were regularized, 17 per cent of whom were women. In Italy, the number of migrants regularized was 105,000, with women accounting for only 28 per cent or some 30,000 (OECD, 1990). By far the largest group of women regularized in Italy consisted of domestic workers (17,000), although relatively large groups of women were also regularized as unskilled workers, office workers and waitresses (9,000). In Spain, the regularization programme undertaken in 1991 yielded some 133,000 applications. Among the 104,000 that had been granted by 1992, one third had been lodged by women (OECD, 1992).

The United States, as a result of the provisions of the Immigration Reform and Control Act of 1986 (IRCA), has implemented a major regularization drive that has already resulted in the legalization of 2.6 million undocumented migrants. The Act established two different regularization programmes: one providing for the legalization of undocumented aliens who had resided in the United States continuously since before 1 January 1982 and another granting first temporary and then permanent residence to persons who had worked in agriculture for at least 90 days during the 12 months preceding 1 May 1986 (United States, 1991). Persons regularized under the second programme are known as special agricultural workers (SAWs). Approximately 1.7 million persons applied for regularization under each programme (OECD, 1990). Among the SAWs, men predominated, accounting for 82 per cent of all applicants. In contrast, women accounted for 43 per cent of all applicants to the general programme. During 1989-1992, 1.6 million persons were granted permanent residence rights as a result of the general programme, 44.5 per cent of whom were women. The equivalent percentage among the 1.1 million migrants regularized under the SAW programme was 18 per cent (Zlotnik, 1993).

It is believed that many of the applications presented under the SAW programme were fraudulent.

Indeed, it is estimated that in California alone, the number of SAW applicants amounted to three or four times the number of eligible farmworkers, whether legal or illegal (Woodrow and Passel, 1989, p. 24). Since the majority of farm workers are men, persons taking the risk of presenting fraudulent applications would also be likely to be men. Thus, the results of the SAW programme are not likely to be representative of the actual sex distribution of the undocumented population.

Given the terms of the general regularization drive established by IRCA, it was not expected to reduce the undocumented population to zero. Using the results of the 1988 Current Population Survey of the United States, Woodrow and Passel (1989) have estimated that approximately 1.9 million undocumented migrants present in the country in 1988 did not apply for amnesty under the general programme. Among them, women predominated, accounting for nearly 59 per cent of the remaining undocumented population. The predominance of women would be greater if some of the men assumed to remain as undocumented migrants had in fact applied for amnesty under the SAW programme.

Apprehension statistics can also provide indications of the extent of women's participation in undocumented migration, though there is no guarantee that apprehended aliens are representative of the undocumented population in a country. Japan provides an interesting case in which data on the apprehensions of illegal migrants indicate that important changes have taken place in the participation of women through time. Table 12 shows the number of migrant workers apprehended during each year of the period 1982-1990, classified by sex and selected country of citizenship. The total number of apprehensions rose markedly during the period, passing from barely 1,900 in 1982 to nearly 30,000 in 1990, and whereas until 1987 most of the apprehended migrant workers were women (76 per cent), since 1988 women have accounted for only 26 per cent of all apprehensions. In addition, whereas during 1982-1987, 82 per cent of the migrants apprehended originated in the Philippines or Thailand, by 1988-1990 those two countries accounted for only 28 per cent of all apprehended aliens. In Japan, women have generally predominated among migrant workers originating in those two countries, thus accounting for

TABLE 12. ILLEGAL MIGRANT WORKERS APPREHENDED IN JAPAN, BY SEX AND COUNTRY OF CITIZENSHIP

Year	Male	Female	Both sexes	Percentage of women
All apprehensions				
1982	184	1 705	1 889	90.3
1983	200	2 139	2 339	91.4
1984	603	4 180	4 783	87.4
1985	687	4 942	5 629	87.8
1986	2 186	5 945	8 131	73.1
1987	4 289	7 018	11 307	62.1
1988	8 929	5 385	14 314	37.6
1989	11 791	4 817	16 608	29.0
1990	24 176	5 708	29 884	19.1
1982-1987	8 149	25 929	34 078	76.1
1988-1990	44 896	15 910	60 806	26.2
1982-1990	53 045	41 839	94 884	44.1
Philippines				
1982	13	396	409	96.8
1983	29	1 012	1 041	97.2
1984	349	2 634	2 983	88.3
1985	349	3 578	3 927	91.1
1986	1 500	4 797	6 297	76.2
1987	2 253	5 774	8 027	71.9
1988	1 688	3 698	5 386	68.7
1989	1 289	2 451	3 740	65.5
1990	1 593	2 449	4 042	60.6
1982-1987	4 493	18 191	22 684	80.2
1988-1990	4 570	8 598	13 168	65.3
1982-1990	9 063	26 789	35 852	74.7
Percentage of total				
1982-1987	55.1	70.2	66.6	
1988-1990	10.2	54.0	21.7	
1982-1990	17.1	64.0	37.8	
Thailand				
1982	25	387	412	93.9
1983	39	518	557	93.0
1984	54	1 078	1 132	95.2
1985	120	953	1 073	88.8
1986	164	826	990	83.4
1987	290	777	1 067	72.8
1988	369	1 019	1 388	73.4
1989	369	775	1 144	67.7
1990	661	789	1 450	54.4
1982-1987	692	4 539	5 231	86.8
1988-1990	1 399	2 583	3 982	64.9
1982-1990	2 091	7 122	9 213	77.3
Percentage of total				
1982-1987	8.5	17.5	15.4	
1988-1990	3.1	16.2	6.5	
1982-1990	3.9	17.0	9.7	

TABLE 12 (*continued*)

Year	Male	Female	Both sexes	Percentage of women
Other countries				
1982	146	922	1 068	86.3
1983	132	609	741	82.2
1984	200	468	668	70.1
1985	218	411	629	65.3
1986	522	322	844	38.2
1987	1 746	467	2 213	21.1
1988	6 872	668	7 540	8.9
1989	10 133	1 591	11 724	13.6
1990	21 922	2 470	24 392	10.1
1982-1987	2 964	3 199	6 163	51.9
1988-1990	38 927	4 729	43 656	10.8
1982-1990	41 891	7 928	49 819	15.9
Percentage of total				
1982-1987	36.4	12.3	18.1	
1988-1990	86.7	29.7	71.8	
1982-1990	79.0	18.9	52.5	

Sources: International Labour Office, *Statistical Report, 1989* (Bangkok, 1989); Japan, Ministry of Justice, *The Immigration Newsmagazine* (Tokyo, September 1991).

75 per cent of apprehended Filipinos and for 77 per cent of apprehended Thais during 1982-1990. Most of the women apprehended worked as hostesses, though their proportion has been declining, passing from levels above 80 per cent during 1985-1988 to 56 per cent in 1990. In contrast, the proportion of apprehended migrant women who worked in industry increased from less than 1 per cent during 1985-1987 to 13 per cent in 1990. The share of those declaring that they worked as strippers or prostitutes declined from 13 per cent in 1985 to about 5 per cent in 1990, and because the number of women apprehended changed little between those two dates, that drop implied that the number of apprehended migrant women in those occupations declined by more than half, passing from about 620 in 1985 to 300 in 1990 (Japan, 1991).

The cases reviewed above corroborate that the participation of women in undocumented migration is far from negligible. In fact, in the country hosting the largest undocumented population in the world, the United States, women are likely to outnumber men among undocumented aliens once the regularization programmes established by IRCA run their course. Although in some contexts women have been strongly underrepresented among migrants applying for legalization, their low relative weight may stem from biases against women implicit in the terms under which the regularization is carried out or from administrative practices that discourage female migrants from applying for legalization. The evidence suggests that the sex selectivity of undocumented migration varies considerably according to country of origin and that undocumented female migrants, just as their male counterparts, tend to be relegated to unskilled and less than appealing occupations.

Women as refugees

In early 1993, there were nearly 19 million refugees in the world under the mandate of the United Nations High Commissioner for Refugees (UNHCR), plus an additional 2.5 million Palestinian refugees under the mandate of the United Nations Relief and Works Agency for Palestine Refugees in the Near East (UNRWA). UNHCR sources reported that women and children were thought to constitute up to 80 per cent of the refugees present in a number of countries (UNHCR, 1993). However, in many countries, the statistics on refugees are at best rough approximations and a classification by age or sex is rarely available. Consequently, the claim that women and children constitute a large proportion of the refugee population, particularly in the developing countries of Africa, Asia or Central America, is little more than a recognition of the fact that refugees are largely a representative group of the population of high-fertility countries where the proportion of children (persons under 18) and women varies typically between 74 and 78 per cent (United Nations, 1993).

Although UNHCR has been calling for improvements in the information relative to female refugees, changes have been slow in coming. Indeed, the 1991-1992 report of UNHCR on programme planning, presented to the Executive Committee of the High Commissioner's Programme, provided some breakdown of the refugee population by sex and age for just 16 countries of asylum (UNHCR, 1992). Typically, reports included only the percentage of women among "adults" and the percentage of "children". The latter were variously defined as persons

under age 15, 16, 17 or 18 (table 13). In several cases it was indicated that the percentages reported were only "estimates" and in others they referred only to a subset of the total refugee population in a country. The proportion of women and children varied from a low of 54 per cent among Vietnamese refugees in Indonesia to a high of 82 per cent among Liberians and Angolans in Côte d'Ivoire and Zaire, respectively. Among adults, refugee women outnumbered refugee men in only three of the 12 countries with data available. They were almost as numerous as refugee men in another three countries, and they were less numerous than refugee men, often by wide margins, in the remaining six. Among the six countries for which the overall proportion of refugee women was reported, the latter outnumbered refugee men in three and were outnumbered by men in another three. That is, the data available, though partial and of uncertain quality, do not corroborate the widespread belief that women constitute especially high proportions of most refugee populations in the world.

Another indication of the extent of women's participation in refugee migration is provided by statistics gathered by third countries of asylum which admit refugees for resettlement. In the United States, for instance, among the 426,000 persons admitted as refugees during 1972-1979, nearly 50 per cent were women (table 3), but among the 888,000 refugees and asylees granted lawful permanent status during 1983-1991 the percentage of women had declined to 45 per cent (United States, 1991 and 1992). In Canada, the proportion of women admitted among the 276,000 refugees and persons in the designated classes[1] during 1981-1991 amounted to 40 per cent (Canada, 1987 and 1992); and in Australia, 47 per cent of the 11,000 persons admitted as refugees or under the Special Humanitarian Programme during fiscal year 1992/93 were women (table 5). That is, women tended to constitute less than half of the refugees reaching developed countries, partly because the criteria used to select refugees for resettlement often work to the detriment of women. Conscious of such biases against female refugees, the Government of Canada instituted in February 1988 a programme to enhance the resettlement opportunities of refugee women whose lack of language or employment skills would not allow them to qualify

TABLE 13. PERCENTAGE OF WOMEN AMONG REFUGEES IN SELECTED COUNTRIES OF FIRST ASYLUM

| Country of asylum | Origin | Number of refugees | Percentage of | | | Upper age of children |
			Women	Adult women	Women and children	
Africa						
Central African Republic	Sudanese	12 000	49	47	66	18
Côte d'Ivoire	Liberian	230 000	..	59	82	18
Senegal[a]	Various	72 000	58	..	..	..
Swaziland	Mozambicans[b]	15 500	52	..	..	..
	Total	50 000	..	..	..	..
Zaire	Angola	279 000	52	41	82	18
	Total	483 000	..	..	..	..
Latin America						
Costa Rica	Various	25 000	..	39	65	..
Guatemala	Various	5 100	40	..	76	18
Mexico	Various	51 000	..	50	82	..
Asia						
Bangladesh	Assisted	265 000	..	50	75	15
India	Non-Sri Lankan	10 600	..	50	72	18
	Total	140 600	..	..	..	..
Indonesia	Vietnamese	17 000	..	..	54	..
	Cambodian	1 700	..	..	55	..
Iran, Islamic Rep. of	Afghanistan.............	3 187 000	..	33	..	..
Malaysia	Vietnamese	12 500	..	53	66	17
Nepal	Bhutan	50 000	49	48	65	16
Pakistan[a]	Afghanistan.............	2 768 000	..	53	76	..
Thailand	Indo-chinese	86 000	..	44	65	..

Source: United Nations High Commissioner for Refugees, "UNHCR activities financed by voluntary funds: report for 1991-1992 and proposed programmes and budget for 1993", Parts I-V, 1992 (A/AC.96/793).

NOTE: Two dots (..) indicate that data are not available or are not separately reported.

[a]Estimated.

[b]Assisted refugees only.

for resettlement under normal conditions (United Nations, 1991).

Women also tend to be strongly underrepresented among persons filing asylum-claims in developed countries, although data on asylum applications by sex of applicant are rarely published. Those available for France indicate that women filed 33 per cent of the asylum claims lodged during 1991-1992.

In sum, it appears that the participation of women in refugee migration varies considerably among countries of asylum. In developing countries, women seem almost as likely to be overrepresented among refugee populations as to be underrepresented, especially among adults. In developed countries, there is a strong tendency for women to be underrepresented, especially among refugees admitted for resettlement and among asylum-seekers.

F. CONCLUSION

As shown by this overview, an assessment of the extent of female participation in international migration is far from straightforward. Differences between countries in the ways of conceptualizing migration, the resulting lack of comparability in data sources, and the general paucity of data on international migration are some of the obstacles faced in carrying out that task. Clearly, however, the sparse evidence available points to a significant participation of women in all types of migration. Rough indications provided by migrant stocks suggest that women account for over 44 per cent of the migrants present in most countries. Such numerical importance should be sufficient to justify that more attention be devoted to understanding the nature and consequences of their migratory experience.

Adequate statistical information is necessary to further our understanding of female migration. Considerable improvements might be achieved by ensuring that all countries that already publish migration data on a regular basis ensure that all tabulations published incorporate the variable "sex" explicitly. No assumptions should be made regarding the likely sex composition of migrant subgroups. For instance, it would not be acceptable to use the distinction between "migrants" and "dependants" as a proxy for a distribution by sex. Similarly, it would not be appropriate to imply that persons in certain occupations, be it nurses, domestic workers etc., are exclusively women.

Mechanisms to publish and disseminate data that are already being gathered by government agencies should be developed. In doing so, one should bear in mind that non-events are often as important as events. For instance, statistics relating to the number of work permits granted to migrants may be just as important as those on the number of applications rejected. Similarly, the number of applicants for amnesty may be more indicative of the extent of undocumented migration than the number eventually legalized by a given country.

The importance of assessing the level of female participation in every type of migration flow should be stressed. Whether a country admits migrant workers, refugees or immigrants, their distribution by sex is essential to assess the likely socio-economic impact of such flows given that equality of opportunities and treatment is not yet a reality for most women around the world.

NOTE

[1]The designated classes encompass persons who are displaced, persecuted or oppressed and are in need of protection even though they do not meet the strict definition of a Convention refugee.

REFERENCES

Balán, Jorge (1992). The role of migration policies and social networks in the development of a migration system in the Southern Cone. In *International Migration Systems*, Mary M. Kritz, Lin Lean Lim and Hania Zlotnik, eds. Oxford, United Kingdom: Clarendon Press.

Canada, Employment and Immigration Canada (1987). *Immigration Statistics, 1985*. Ottawa: Ministry of Supply and Services Canada.

_____ (1992). *Immigration Statistics, 1991*. Ottawa: Ministry of Supply and Services Canada.

Donato, Katharine M. (1989). Why some countries send women and others send men: cross-national variation in the sex composition of U.S. immigrants. Paper presented at the 1989 Meeting of the American Sociological Association. Mimeographed.

Hugo, Graeme J. (1988). Outputs and effects of immigration in Australia. Report prepared for the Committee to Advise on Australia's Immigration Policy, Flinders University, Australia.

Houstoun, Marion F., Roger G. Kramer and Joan Mackin Barrett (1984). Female predominance of immigration to the United States since 1930: a first look. *International Migration Review* (Staten Island, New York), vol. 18, No. 4 (Winter), pp. 908-963.

International Labour Organization (1989). Statistical report 1989: international labour migration from Asian labour-sending countries. Bangkok: Regional Office for Asia and the Pacific.

Japan, Statistics Bureau (1988). *Statistical Yearbook, 1988*. Tokyo.

Japan, Ministry of Justice (1991). *The Immigration Newsmagazine*. Tokyo (September).

Korale, R. B. M. (1983). Migration for employment to the Middle East: its demographic and socio-economic effects on Sri Lanka. Paper presented at the Conference on Asian Labour Migration to the Middle East, Honolulu, Hawaii, 19-23 September.

Mármora, Lelio (1983). La amnistía migratoria de 1974 en Argentina. Working Paper, International Migration for Employment Programme. Geneva: International Labour Organisation.

Organisation for Economic Co-operation and Development (OECD) (1990). Analyse comparative des récentes expériences de régularisation en France, en Italie, en Espagne et aux Etats-Unis. Paper presented at the Meeting of the Working Group on Migration. Paris. MAS/WP2(90).2.

_____ (1992). *SOPEMI: Trends in International Migration*. Paris.

Storer, Desmond (1982). Out of the shadows. A review of the 1980 Regularisation of Status Programme in Australia. Working Paper, International Migration for Employment Programme. Geneva: International Labour Organisation.

Torrealba, Ricardo (1982). La migración internacional hacia Venezuela en la década de 1970: características socio-demográficas. Paper prepared for the Intergovernmental Committee on Migration, Caracas, Venezuela.

Tribalat, Michèle (1989). Rapport francais. Paper presented at the meeting of the Working Group on International Migration of the European Association for Population Studies, Paris, June.

United Nations (1991). *World Population Monitoring, 1991*. Sales No. E.92.XIII.2.

_____ (1993). *The Sex and Age Distribution of the World Populations: The 1992 Revision*. Sales No. E.93.XIII.3.

United Nations High Commissioner for Refugees (1992). UNHCR activities financed by voluntary funds: report for 1991-1992 and proposed programmes and budget for 1993, parts I-V. Geneva. A/AC.96/793.

_____ (1993). *The State of the World's Refugees: The Challenge of Protection*. New York: Penguin Books.

United States, Immigration and Naturalization Service (1991). *1990 Statistical Yearbook of the Immigration and Naturalization Service*. Washington, D. C.: Government Printing Office.

_____ (1992). *1991 Statistical Yearbook of the Immigration and Naturalization Service*. Washington, D. C.: Government Printing Office.

United States, Bureau of the Census (1993). *1990 Census of Population: the Foreign-Born Population in the United States*. Washington, D. C.: Government Printing Office.

Woodrow, Karen A., and Jeffrey S. Passel (1989). Post-IRCA undocumented migration to the United States: assessment based on the June 1988 CPS. Paper presented at the Conference on Illegal Immigration Before and After IRCA, The Urban Institute, Washington, D. C., 21 July (revised).

Zlotnik, Hania (1993). The South-to-North migration of women: dimensions and characteristics. Paper presented at the Conference on Social and Economic Aspects of International Migration held at the Academia Sinica, Taipei, Taiwan Province of China, 4-6 June.

Part Three

FEMALE MIGRANTS IN DEVELOPED COUNTRIES

V. MIGRATION REGULATIONS AND SEX SELECTIVE OUTCOMES IN DEVELOPED COUNTRIES

*Monica Boyd**

Discussions of international migration frequently distinguish between the migrant-receiving countries of Europe on the one hand and those in Northern America and Oceania on the other. The first group is taken to represent the "labour-recruitment" countries, whereas the second is considered that of the countries of "permanent settlement" or "immigration" (United Nations, 1979, 1985a, 1985b; De Wenden, 1987). This distinction serves to capture the differences between countries regarding the objectives that they have pursued through migration as well as their immigration histories. Despite those distinctions, the migrant receiving countries of Europe share with the overseas countries of immigration—Australia, Canada, New Zealand and the United States of America—the experience of having admitted, since the mid-1970s, a majority of their migrants on the basis of family reunification and of having witnessed the development and consolidation of "the women's movement" in their midst. As a result, during the 1970s and 1980s, social, economic, political and legal inequalities between men and women have been documented and discussed in all of those countries and broad concern over gender inequality has in turn led to the explicit consideration of women's issues in research on international migration. Such research has shown that considerable numbers of women migrate internationally and has documented both the role played by women in the migration process and their experiences as migrants. Much of that research has addressed two themes that are prevalent in general studies on women: the invisibility of women in social science research and the

disadvantaged economic, social and legal status of women compared to men.

Direct or overt discrimination is considered an important cause of inequality based on gender, but the experiences of women are also shaped by practices and regulations that result in covert, indirect and systemically induced discrimination. This type of discrimination occurs when there are different outcomes for men and women as a result of practices and regulations that are not sex-specific in their terms of reference, but that become so in their implementation (Abella, 1984; Boyd, 1989a).

Because immigration regulations represent a mediating mechanism between the societies of origin and destination, they are especially likely to have embedded within them practices that lead to differential outcomes for men and women. Immigration laws and regulations can be overtly discriminatory on the basis of country of origin, citizenship, sex, race, religion and other criteria, and therefore produce differential outcomes regarding entry status, social and economic entitlements, and migration-related rights for particular groups of persons meeting the stipulated criteria. However, throughout the twentieth century, many nation States have removed overtly discriminatory criteria from their immigration laws and regulations. Such removal does not mean that all immigration regulations in all countries are free from discriminatory outcomes, but it does imply that most differential outcomes are produced indirectly or covertly. That is, outcomes that differ according to sex, race or ethnicity are produced primarily through the implementation of general laws and practices which are not discriminatory in content, but that become so in combination with other rules, regulations and practices.

This paper examines the implications of migration rules and regulations for the status of migrant women. The first section emphasizes that the sex-specific

*Department of Sociology and Anthropology, Carleton University, Ottawa, Canada. The author is grateful to Professor Mark Miller, University of Delaware, for providing statistics on migrant women from selected country reports of the 1986 SOPEMI, to the Directorate for Social Affairs, Manpower and Education at OECD for providing data from the 1989 SOPEMI report prior to its publication, and to the Australian High Commission, the British High Commission, and the embassies of Austria and Sweden for providing information on the migration situation in their countries.

effects of migration regulations need to be understood alongside systems of sex stratification and within the context of country-specific ideologies regarding migration. The second section considers to what extent the sex selectivity of migration reflects direct or systematic discrimination associated with migration regulations. The third examines the link between admission regulations and sex differentials in access to economic entitlements in the country of destination. The fourth and fifth sections discuss how migration regulations, as mediated by sex stratification and country-specific practices, can produce differential outcomes for migrant men and women in terms of the right to remain in the country of destination and in their ability to facilitate the migration of others.

A. IMMIGRATION REGULATIONS, SEX STRATIFICATION AND COUNTRY DIFFERENCES IN MIGRATION OBJECTIVES

Immigration regulations need not be overtly discriminatory to produce sex-specific outcomes. Systematic discrimination can result when migration regulations reinforce gender inequality by accepting stereotypical images of men and women and traditional sex roles in the countries of origin and destination. Practices tending to designate men automatically as heads of household confirm and perpetuate a traditional sexual division of labour, both within the immigrant family and in society at large. In countries where women's roles are confined to childbearing and child-rearing and where educational and employment opportunities are limited, men rather than women may receive higher educational and occupational training and, consequently, be more likely to meet the educational and occupational requirements set by immigration regulations. Industrial economies which view traditionally female occupations, such as clerical work or domestic service, as less skilled than equivalent male occupations, such as typesetting or driving, and which base admission criteria and entry status on those views thus incorporate and reaffirm images of female labour as less valuable in their immigration standards. In countries where women are typically paid less than men, migrant women may have more difficulty than

migrant men in meeting the financial criteria necessary for continued residence in the host country or in sponsoring the migration of close relatives.

Any analysis of the overt or covert infusion of gender roles into the implementation of immigration law and regulations needs to consider the variation stemming from country differences in immigration objectives and in the resulting immigration laws and procedures. Both European countries and the overseas countries of immigration permit the entry of migrants on the basis of social, humanitarian and economic grounds. However, they differ in the historical use of those grounds, their policy objectives and their admission and residence procedures.

In the overseas countries of immigration—Australia, Canada, New Zealand and the United States—migrants may be admitted on a short-term, long-term, temporary or permanent basis, although permanent settlement is a central objective of immigration policy and it is widely assumed that all those acquiring permanent residence rights will remain in the country; so much so, that Canada and the United States lack a formal system to monitor emigration. Although economic considerations based on labour market needs have always been, to a greater or lesser extent, a basis for the admission of some immigrants, family ties with citizens or previous immigrants have generally been the basis for the admission of a high proportion of all immigrants, particularly in the United States (United Nations, 1992). Migrants admitted on a temporary basis constitute a heterogeneous group that includes students, exchange visitors, business representatives, unskilled and highly skilled workers admitted to meet specific labour needs, asylum-seekers, the fiancés or fiancées of residents etc. All these migrants are admitted on a conditional basis and are subject to restrictions regarding their participation in the labour market, their residence rights and the right to be accompanied by close family members. Although temporary migrants are supposed to leave once their residence rights expire, some categories are allowed to become immigrants. In Canada, for instance, foreign domestic workers admitted temporarily are permitted to adjust to permanent resident status and in the United States a significant proportion of the immigrants admitted each year are persons adjusting their status from some category of temporary admission.

The history of migration to the Western-bloc countries of Europe and their current administrative structure differ substantially from those of the overseas countries of immigration. Beginning in the late 1950s, a number of European countries that faced labour shortages—especially, Belgium, France, the Federal Republic of Germany, the Netherlands, Switzerland and Sweden—recruited unskilled workers, mostly from other European countries, on a temporary basis, with the expectation of having them return to their countries of origin once their contracts expired. However, return migration did not occur as readily as expected and when the labour-importing countries decided unilaterally to stop the recruitment of foreign labour around 1973 or 1974, they allowed those foreign workers wishing to stay to remain in their territories and, provided some conditions were met, to bring in their immediate relatives. The decision to permit family reunification both recognized the long-term nature of migration and ensured that the migrants remained for good (Castles, 1984; United Nations, 1979; 1985a; 1985b).

The different positions of the overseas countries of immigration and the former labour-importing countries of Europe regarding the objectives of migration are evident in regulations governing family reunification. In Australia, Canada, New Zealand and the United States, family ties are the basis for the admission not only of spouses and children, including adult children, but also of parents and siblings. In Europe, the definition of family is more restricted, usually including only spouses and dependent children under a given age. In some European countries, such as the United Kingdom of Great Britain and Northern Ireland, elderly parents over a certain age can be admitted if they meet stringent criteria (e.g., provided they are wholly dependent on their migrant sons or daughters who have adequate means to support them and provided they lack other close relatives in their own country). The requirements for family reunification differ somewhat among European countries, but they are generally more stringent than those imposed by the countries of

immigration. Those requirements generally include one or more of the following: proof of family relationship, such as legal marriage; a minimum length of residence by the head of the household in the host country; proof of sufficient resources to support the family members that are to be admitted (usually by presenting proof of having an adequate income or employment); and ability to pay for or the existence of adequate housing. Once those conditions are met, a residence permit may be granted to the spouse and children of a resident migrant (Castles, 1984; Barisik, 1987; Lithman, 1987; Mehrlander, 1987; Federal Republic of Germany, 1988; Lemoine, 1989; Pekin, 1989; United Kingdom, 1989).

European countries, in contrast with the overseas countries of immigration, generally do not grant migrants the right to permanent residence when they are first admitted into the country, although there are considerable variations between countries (Pekin, 1989). Usually, a short-term permit is issued initially although, in some countries, persons admitted as refugees are granted at the outset a right to residence for an indefinite period. The short-term residence permit can be renewed a number of times and after a specified period (usually measured in years) it can be exchanged for a permit which confers a longer term and more solid right to residence. In some countries, such as Germany, the right to permanent residence is granted only if the migrant satisfies integration criteria related to employment, language skills and other factors. Administratively, the system of granting incremental residence rights to persons that are considered "temporary migrants" distinguishes European countries from the overseas countries of immigration where immigrants are admitted as permanent residents at the outset and temporary migrants are not necessarily granted improved residence rights over time.

The separation of employment rights from residence rights also distinguishes many European countries from those of immigration. The latter group admits immigrants with a view to making them citizens and therefore tends to extend to them equal economic, social and political rights within a relatively short period (Boyd, 1988b). In particular, immigrants have the same economic rights as citizens upon admission, so that the right to seek employment is inextricably linked to the status of immigrant. In European countries, in contrast, residence rights do not necessarily encompass the right to obtain paid work (De Wenden, 1987; Pekin, 1989) and important distinctions exist between the rights of the "bridgehead" migrant and those of accompanying family members (usually admitted long after the bridgehead migrant).

Although some simplification is necessary to make broad comparisons between the migrant-receiving European countries and the overseas countries of immigration, it is important to underscore that European countries are not homogeneous in their treatment of migrants, nor do they apply the same rules to all migrants. The member States of the European Community (EC), for instance, accord special treatment to citizens of other member States[1] by assuring them the right of residence while they seek employment and hold a job in another member State (Hovy and Zlotnik, 1993). Similar rules operate within the member States of the Nordic Common Market (Denmark, Finland, Iceland, Norway and Sweden). In addition, some countries provide work permits alongside residence permits for all family members. In the United Kingdom, for instance, no employment restrictions exist for family members of permanent settlers (excluding fiancés or fiancées who are admitted conditionally). In Belgium and Sweden, non-EC and non-Nordic nationals, respectively, must obtain both a work permit and a residence permit prior to entry but in Sweden migrants entering under family reunification are permitted to seek employment right away (Lithman, 1987, p. 15). In Belgium, in contrast, persons admitted under family reunification are not automatically entitled to a work permit, and the type of permit issued to married women is determined by the work permit held by their husbands (De Wenden, 1987; Pekin, 1989). In Germany, spouses of foreign workers must wait four years (three if they are Turkish) after admission to apply for an initial work permit.

The treatment of the offspring of migrants in general and of the dependants of those migrants moving under regimes assuring the free movement of workers, as in the European Community or the Nordic Common Market, are two additional factors to consider when discussing European migration regulations and practices. In the European Community, regulation 1612/68 of 1968 establishes that when a national of a member State pursues an economic activity as an employed or self-employed person in the territory of another member State, his spouse and those of his children under the age of 21 years or dependent on him have the right to take up any activity as employed persons throughout the territory of the host member State, even if they are not nationals of any member State (Hovy and Zlotnik, 1993). With respect to migrants who are not citizens of member States, some European countries grant to their dependent migrant children of both sexes residence rights under the permit of a parent (usually the father). The offspring of migrants may apply for residence permits in their own right by a specified age and the granting of work permits is not automatic.

B. SEX SELECTIVITY OF ENTRY REGULATIONS

The preceding discussion raises three questions. First, do migration regulations include sex as an explicit criterion for admission, thereby giving rise to sex-specific outcomes? Second, do sex-specific outcomes operate to the disadvantage of migrant women? And, third, to what extent are the answers to the preceding questions different for the overseas countries of immigration from those for European countries? This section discusses those questions with respect to entry status.

The first question can be answered in the affirmative only if regulations include sex-specific words, such as, husband or wife instead of spouse, daughter or son instead of offspring, or male or female instead of migrant.[2] Three sources were scrutinized for the appearance of sex-specific terminology: (a) entry legislation for Canada, the United Kingdom and the United States; (b) overviews of migration regulations for Austria, the Federal Republic of Germany (Federal Republic of Germany, 1988), and Sweden (Lithman, 1987); and (c) a summary article by Pekin (1989) on regulations governing family migration in Austria, Belgium, France, the Federal Republic of Germany, Luxembourg, the Netherlands, Norway, Sweden and the United Kingdom.

Generally, migration regulations governing entry are not overtly sex-specific although two types of exceptions exist. First, legislation governing the entry of "au pair" workers tends to specify "au pair girls", thus clearly targeting women. Second, legislation on family reunification for the United Kingdom and a description of family reunification regulations for Belgium (Pekin, 1989) employ, in selected instances, terminology that appears to distinguish between men and women. In the United Kingdom, for instance, section 3 of the 1989 Statement of Changes in the Immigration Rules stipulates that nothing in the rules shall be construed as allowing a woman to be granted entry clearance, leave to enter, or variation of leave as the wife of a man when the marriage is polygamous, but no stipulations exist regarding the admission of a man whose marriage is polygamous. Similarly, leave to enter may be granted to wives and children under 18 of male students who are admitted for temporary purposes (United Kingdom, 1989, section 31), but no section refers to the possible entry of the husband and children of a female student. The 1989 Immigration Rules, however, no longer incorporate other cases of overt discrimination based on sex that were present in the 1984 legislation (WING, 1985). In particular, the 1989 Rules grant both men and women equal status in sponsoring spouses if the migrants themselves have been granted unlimited leave to stay in the United Kingdom or if they have leave to enter under a work permit.[3]

Those examples notwithstanding, sex-specificity in migration regulations is the exception rather than the rule. However, the absence of sex-specific directives does not mean that immigration regulations are gender-neutral or that they produce gender-neutral outcomes. For instance, the sex composition of migration inflows to the overseas countries of immigration, among which sex is not a criterion for admission, suggests that indirect and systemic factors are at work even though, at first glance, the sex composition of migration flows buttresses the impression of gender neutrality in the admission process. Contrary to the stereotypical view of migration as male dominated, as table 14 shows, women have tended to outnumber men among immigrants admitted by the overseas countries of immigration and, particularly, by the United States before 1981

(Houstoun, Kramer and Barrett, 1984; Tyree and Donato, 1986). The importance of family reunification as the basis for immigrant admission has generally been held responsible for such pattern.

Women are less likely than men to enter on the basis of labour-market criteria. In Europe, labour migration during the 1960s and early 1970s was clearly dominated by men, although migrant female workers constituted sizeable proportions of those originating in countries such as Portugal (Caspari and Giles, 1986), Turkey (Davis and Heyl, 1986), and Yugoslavia (OECD, 1987). Table 15 shows that during the 1980s the proportion of women among migrants admitted as workers rose somewhat in France and that the proportion of women among migrants receiving initial work permits in Austria was substantial, generally surpassing 40 per cent. However, the data for Austria and the Federal Republic of Germany do not reflect the admission of migrant women as workers but rather the entry into the labour force of migrant women admitted mostly on the basis of family reunification.

Tables 16 and 17 show the percentage of women among immigrants admitted by Canada and the United States, classified by admission category. In Canada, somewhat fewer women than men were admitted in the business or "other" categories which represent the labour component of Canada's immigration intake. Consideration of family status reveals that women who enter in the business and "other" categories are seldom admitted as principal applicants but instead enter as the spouses or dependants of principal applicants. The same is true for women admitted under the third and sixth preference categories of admission to the United States which constitute the labour component of immigration to that country (table 17).

If women are less likely than men to enter both European countries and the overseas countries of immigration on the basis of labour-market criteria, on what grounds do they enter? As already suggested, the majority of migrant women are admitted on the basis of their familial ties to another person, usually male. Women who migrate under the auspices of family reunification in Europe may be termed "dependent" migrants because their admittance is

TABLE 14. PERCENTAGE OF WOMEN AMONG THE MIGRANTS ADMITTED
BY SELECTED COUNTRIES: 1973-1988

Year	Immigrants aged 15 or over				Migrants of all ages			
	Australia	Canada	United States	United Kingdom	Belgium	Germany, (Western)	Nether-lands	Sweden
1973	49.6	48.5	54.6	46.6	..	..	..	50.9
1974	49.7	49.4	54.5	43.1	..	..	..	63.1
1975	57.5	51.4	54.4	49.1	..	..	..	48.7
1976	54.5	52.4	54.8	46.9	..	..	..	46.8
1977	51.3	53.3	..	46.2	..	..	..	48.2
1978	51.2	54.8	53.4	46.9	..	..	..	49.2
1979	51.7	51.9	53.1	47.6	..	..	..	49.2
1980	49.2	50.4	..	47.4	..	..	..	49.3
1981	48.1	51.7	..	46.0	..	..	49.4	50.5
1982	49.0	51.6	50.2	51.5	..	43.7	51.1	50.7
1983	50.2	54.3	49.5	48.4	..	43.9	51.6	50.2
1984	52.4	54.6	49.5	50.0	..	44.4	50.0	47.6
1985	..	53.1	49.9	59.6	46.4	42.9	46.4	..
1986	..	51.0	50.2	51.9	46.3	43.2	47.0	47.3
1987	..	..	50.3	50.8	47.6	45.8	..	48.3
1988	..	..	49.6	..	47.6	45.5	..	..

Sources: Australia, *Yearbook of Australia, 1980* (Canberra), p. 120; Australia, *Yearbook of Australia, 1986* (Canberra), p. 118; Monica Boyd, "Migrant women in Canada: profiles and policies, 1987", Immigration Research Working Paper No. 2 (Ottawa, Employment and Immigration, 1989), table 6; United States, Immigration and Naturalization Service, *1976 Annual Report* (Washington, D. C., Government Printing Office), table 10; United States, *Statistical Yearbook of the Immigration and Naturalization Service, 1988* (Washington, D. C., Government Printing Office), table 11; United Kingdom, Office of Population Census and Surveys, *International Migration* (London, Her Majesty's Stationery Office), Series MN, No. 3 (1976), table 2.9; Series MN, No. 13 (1986), table 2.7; and Series MN, No. 14 (1987), table 2.8; Organisation for Economic Co-operation and Development, *SOPEMI 1989* (Paris, 1990), tables B2.1 and B2.2; and Sweden, *Yearbook of Nordic Statistics* (Stockholm, various years).

NOTE: The data for Australia, Canada and the United States refer only to immigrants. The data for the United Kingdom refer to persons intending to stay in the country for a year or more. The data for the Netherlands exclude migrants from other European Community countries and those for Sweden exclude migrants from the Nordic countries. Two dots (..) indicate that data are not available or are not separately reported.

conditional on the presence (and the residence permit) of another person in the receiving country. In the countries of immigration, family reunification is also the main avenue for female migration and women are frequently admitted in categories that indicate either their marital relationship or their adjunct status to a man, whether migrant himself or not.

In Canada, over 60 per cent of female migrants aged 15 or over were admitted on the basis of family ties during 1981-1986 (the family and assisted relatives classes in table 16). Women constituted 59 and 51 per cent, respectively, of the persons admitted in those admission classes. They also tended to outnumber men in the class of retired persons. How-

ever, only in the family class did women outnumber men as principal applicants, largely because wives who migrate to rejoin their husbands are administratively processed as principal applicants. Their admission, however, is conditional on the existence of sponsors, who are close relatives that agree to assume the financial and social responsibility for the care of the applicant. Note that in all admission categories, the "spouses" of the principal applicant were overwhelmingly women (table 16).

Similar patterns characterize immigration to the United States. In the categories subject to numerical limitation, women outnumbered men as spouses of aliens already residing in the United States.[4] As

TABLE 15. NUMBER OF NEW FOREIGN WORKERS ANNUALLY ENTERING THE LABOUR FORCE OF SELECTED EUROPEAN COUNTRIES AND PERCENTAGE OF WOMEN AMONG THEM: 1976-1987

| | France | | Germany | | Austria | | | |
| | | | | | Initial permits | | Extension of permits | |
Year	Number	Percentage	Number	Percentage	Number	Percentage	Number	Percentage
1976	26 949	26.5	..	..	..	..	..	..
1977	22 756	28.0	..	..	..	..	..	..
1978	18 356	28.3	..	..	..	..	..	..
1979	17 395	29.9	..	..	..	..	..	..
1980	17 370	27.7	..	..	95 425	38.7	117 367	40.7
1981	33 433	20.4	..	..	81 934	39.2	111 162	41.6
1982	96 962	18.1	..	..	57 234	39.2	91 802	41.3
1983	18 483	26.5	24 373	22.4	52 674	38.0	74 173	45.4
1984	11 804	32.6	27 511	20.0	55 239	38.0	72 182	43.9
1985	10 959	32.7	33 400	24.5	60 247	37.5	67 485	44.1
1986	11 238	32.5	37 224	24.1	50 818[a]	38.8	79 066[a]	40.4
1987	12 231	34.2	12 721[b]	21.3	46 812	40.6	86 661	38.7

Sources: France, Ministère de l'économie, des finances et du budget, *Annuaire statistique de la France, 1988* (Paris), p. 82, table B.03-04; Gudrun Biffl, "Report on labour migration" (Vienna, 1988), unpublished, tables 2 and 3; Heinrich Meyer, "SOPEMI country report for the FRG" (Paris, Organisation for Economic Co-operation and Development, 1987), table 2.

Note: Two dots (..) indicate that data are not available or are not separately reported.

[a]Administrative practice was not strictly comparable with that of previous years.

[b]Refers to the period 1 January to 31 May.

TABLE 16. SELECTED CHARACTERISTICS OF IMMIGRANTS AGED 15 OR OVER ADMITTED BY CANADA, BY CLASS OF ADMISSION AND FAMILY STATUS: 1981-1986

| | Total | Family class | Refugees and designated classes | Assisted relatives | Independent classes | | |
					Retired	Business	Other
Number of immigrants							
Female	259 563	140 970	27 904	21 202	6 638	12 582	50 267
Male	234 365	98 758	43 883	20 358	5 510	14 351	51 505
Percentage distribution by class of admission							
Female	100.0	54.3	10.8	8.2	2.6	4.8	19.4
Male	100.0	42.1	18.7	8.7	2.4	6.1	22.0
Proportion of women	52.6	59.0	38.9	51.0	54.6	46.7	49.4
Proportion of women by family status							
Principal applicant	42.6	55.2	20.4	38.3	37.2	11.3	34.2
Spouse	94.6	96.1	97.0	89.0	93.5	93.9	93.9
Dependant	47.0	47.2	44.6	47.9	47.3	46.0	48.4

Source: Special tabulations provided by Employment and Immigration Canada, Policy Analysis Directorate, Immigration Branch.

shown in table 17, in 1986, 59 per cent of the principal applicants entering the United States as spouses of aliens under the second preference were women. The data also show that fewer women than men entered as principal applicants in the worker categories (third and sixth preferences). However, women outnumbered men among the spouses of immigrants admitted on the basis of labour-market needs.

Patterns of sex-selectivity by family status are also evident in the admission of refugees. Immigration

TABLE 17. PERCENTAGE OF WOMEN AMONG IMMIGRANTS ADMITTED BY THE UNITED STATES, BY CLASS OF ADMISSION AND RELATIONSHIP TO PRINCIPAL APPLICANT: FISCAL YEAR 1986

	Total	Principal applicant	Spouse	Children
Total subject to numerical limitation	49.8	..	..	..
First preference Unmarried sons and daughters of U.S. citizens	47.6	47.1	..	49.8
Second preference ...	50.7	..	..	48.9
Spouses of aliens	..	58.9	..	..
Unmarried children of aliens	..	45.7	..	..
Third preference Professional or highly skilled	45.7	19.9	85.9	47.5
Fourth preference Married sons and daughters of U.S. citizens	49.1	52.2	47.3	48.2
Fifth preference Siblings of U.S. citizens	50.3	48.5	54.9	48.4
Sixth preference Needed unskilled workers	51.9	45.5	69.9	48.3

Source: Special tabulations provided by the United States Immigration and Naturalization Service, Statistics Branch.
NOTE: Two dots (..) indicate that data are not available or are not separately reported.

regulations regarding the granting of refugee status do not specify sex as a criterion, although Gottstein (1988) suggests that certain biases may exist. However, the selection practices used to identify refugees for resettlement tend to designate men as principal applicants. Thus, in both Canada and the United States, men outnumber women, sometimes by wide margins, as refugees admitted in the role of principal applicants, whereas women outnumber men in the category of spouses of principal applicants (tables 16 and 18).

The sex selectivity of migration cannot be readily explained by explicit sex-specific migration regulations, for such directives generally do not exist. Instead, indirect factors, notably sex stereotypes and sex stratification, are at work. In receiving countries, occupational segregation by sex implies that the admission of migrants as workers is sex-specific, although that fact is not stated. Thus, migrants admitted as seasonal agricultural workers are usually men, whereas domestic workers are generally women. In sending countries, sex stratification in education and in the labour force may enhance the ability of men and not that of women to meet admission criteria based on economic considerations. In both societies, practices that automatically assign the role of head of household to men increase the probability that women are administratively designated as

TABLE 18. PERCENTAGE OF WOMEN AMONG IMMIGRANTS ADMITTED BY THE UNITED STATES UNDER SELECTED REFUGEE AND ASYLEE ADJUSTMENT LEGISLATION: FISCAL YEAR 1986

	Total	Refugee or asylee	Spouse	Children
Total....................	43.9	..	..	..
Cuban refugees Act of 11/2/66.....	43.8	43.4	..	..
Refugees Act of 3/17/80.....	44.1	32.9	96.6	47.1
Asylees Act of 3/17/80.....	41.7	30.6	92.2	47.1

Source: Special tabulations provided by the United States Immigration and Naturalization Service, Statistics Branch.
NOTE: The total includes data for persons admitted under the Indochinese Refugee Act of 10/28/77 and the Refugee Parolees Act of 10/5/78. Two dots (..) indicate that data are not available or are not separately reported.

spouses, both by visa officers and by the immigrant family itself (Boyd, 1989c).

Sex stereotypes and sex stratification not only explain why more men than women are admitted on labour-market grounds and more women than men enter as dependent family members, they also influence the type of work for which migrant female labour is recruited. When women enter on the basis of labour-market skills, many are in service occupations.[5] In the United States, among female immigrants admitted as principal applicants in the third and sixth preference categories during 1985-1987, nearly half (45.7 per cent) were in service occupations compared to only 11 per cent of the male principal applicants in those categories (United States Department of Labor, 1989, table 2.3, p. 27). In Canada, between 1981 and 1986, 26.9 and 22.2 per cent of the female immigrants admitted in the independent class held previous or arranged employment in service and clerical occupations, respectively, compared to 6.8 and 3.4 per cent of their male counterparts. Furthermore, in countries that recruit migrant workers on a temporary basis, women are admitted largely as domestic workers, which include those specializing in child care. Case-studies indicate that in the United Kingdom and the United States, Jamaican and Portuguese women are often recruited as domestic workers (Caspari and Giles, 1986; Foner, 1986). "Au pair" arrangements which recruit young women are common in many countries. Regrettably, the lack of sex-specific data prevents an analysis of the extent to which migrant women are admitted to work in occupations that are extensions of the traditional female roles of care-giving and cleaning (United States Department of Labor, 1989, pp. 42-43). However, Canadian data are indicative of the admission of female temporary workers employed in low-skilled, sex-typed occupations. Between 1979 and 1986, women constituted over half of all validated employment authorizations in domestic occupations. In contrast, about one fifth of the male workers admitted temporarily by Canada were issued authorizations for farm work, over one third were engaged in managerial, science and engineering jobs, and another third worked in medical and health-care occupations (Boyd and Taylor, 1986).

C. ADMISSION REGULATIONS AND ACCESS TO ENTITLEMENTS IN THE RECEIVING COUNTRY

Entry and employment entitlements

Entry status and migration regulations generally influence the experiences of migrants after they establish residence in a country. A comparison of selected European countries with the overseas countries of immigration indicates that such impacts are more likely to handicap female migrants than their male counterparts, not because of overt discrimination but because entry status and related entitlements differ by gender. The comparison also indicates differences between the countries of immigration and European countries in the nature and degree of those handicaps. Generally, in countries where it takes a long time for migrants to acquire social, economic and political rights equal to those of citizens, migration regulations have more severe negative effects on migrant women than in countries where the acquisition of those rights is more rapid. Although some European countries, such as Sweden, tend to grant full rights to migrants fairly quickly, most belong to the first category described above.

The separation of residence and employment permits that distinguishes most migrant-receiving European countries from the countries of immigration provides an example of how migration regulations can affect the position of migrant women in receiving societies. In the countries of immigration, the fusion of entry and employment rights means that persons who enter illegally, if employed, also work illegally. In European countries, in contrast, migrants may have a legal right to residence but no right to be employed and may therefore be in an illegal situation in terms of employment but not in terms of residence. In a number of European countries, service work is often performed by legally resident migrant women who work illegally. That is the case of a number of Portuguese women in France and of Turkish women in the Federal Republic of Germany (Caspari and Giles, 1986; De Wenden and DeLey, 1986; Goodman, 1987). The separation of residence and work permits leads migrant women admitted as dependants to engage in illegal employment and ensures that a cheap labour force is available for certain sectors of the economy, particularly domestic service and manufacturing (De Wenden and DeLey, 1986; Goodman, 1987).

Separating residence permits from employment permits has at least two consequences for migrant women.[6] First, in those European countries where the spouses and children of migrants are allowed to enter the labour force only after a number of years have elapsed since their arrival (Pekin, 1989), the newly arrived have no choice but to be economically dependent on other family members. Second, those migrants who decide to engage in clandestine employment become dependent on their employers and are more vulnerable to exploitation. That dependency can influence their eventual application for a work permit and perpetuate the low wages and poor work conditions that they are forced to accept. Goodman (1987, p. 246) describes clandestine workers in the former Federal Republic of Germany as caught in a "work permit round robin". Under German regulations, employers have to petition the Ministry of Labour for the required work permit. The employer has therefore the means to control the worker, since clandestine workers wishing to obtain a work permit are not likely to resist unfair labour practices.

European countries vary in the mandatory period that must elapse between the issuance of a residence permit and that of a work permit, and even when the conditions in terms of length of stay are met, the issuance of a work permit is not automatic, depending on the type of residence permit of the migrant concerned and his or her employment situation. In the Federal Republic of Germany, for instance, work permits for first employment and for the resumption of employment are granted only if no German citizen or a foreigner who is a national of a member State of the European Community is available to fill a given vacancy (Federal Republic of Germany, 1988, p. 23). The effects of such regulations are difficult to ascertain. On the one hand, only 6.3 per cent of all foreign workers had that type of work permit in 1986 but few applications for an initial work permit were turned down (less than 5 per cent in 1986). On the other hand, the regulation stipulates that access to employment, even after years of residence, is a privilege, not a right. Such messages may reinforce the tendency to seek clandestine employment among migrant women and contribute to reducing the number of applications for work permits.

Economic and income security

In addition to influencing residence and employment rights, entry status can be part of the eligibility criteria for social welfare programmes. In the United States, for instance, the income and assets of sponsors are considered in determining the eligibility of immigrants who have been in the country for less than three years to obtain assistance through the following programmes: food stamps; aid to families with dependent children; and the supplemental security income for the aged, disabled and the blind. Consequently, sponsored immigrants are unlikely to be eligible for assistance from such programmes (Kramer, 1987, p. 54). In Canada, sponsors are viewed by the federal and provincial governments as making a commitment that the designated immigrants will not require any public assistance during a specified period, ranging from 5 years in the case of immigrants admitted under the assisted relatives category up to 10 years in the case of immigrants admitted under the family class. Such immigrants can be denied, on that basis, access to welfare assistance programmes ranging from income assistance to public housing (Boyd, 1989b). Although practices vary within municipalities and provinces, agencies in charge of implementing the various programmes may not extend aid until evidence is provided that the sponsorship relation has broken down.

Once again, consideration of the sponsor's role in establishing the eligibility criteria for social welfare and income assistance programmes does not explicitly use the sex of the applicant as a criterion. However, since the majority of migrants in the sponsored categories are women, they are more likely to be negatively affected by such regulations. Migrant women who experience marital breakdown are the most vulnerable, particularly because they are less likely to be employed and, if employed, they are likely to earn less than their husbands. Furthermore, they are also more likely to be living with dependent children.

For migrant women in Europe, marital breakdown may also prevent them from receiving needed assistance (OECD, 1985 and 1989). Married migrant women whose marriage breaks up may not be immediately eligible for social welfare assistance, and the practice of giving child allowances to the head of household irrespective of who actually takes care of the children can create difficulties. However, more information is needed to understand how migration procedures linking the residence statuses of wives and husbands are the source of problems in such circumstances.

D. THE RIGHT TO REMAIN: ADMISSION, DEPORTATION AND DEPARTURE

Immigration regulations embody more than rules and criteria for admission, they also govern departures and deportations. Entry status and the right to remain are often linked. Given that women tend to be admitted in certain categories more than in others, one can ask if rules governing exits have a greater impact on women than on men. The answer is in the affirmative, less because sex is an explicit criterion for deportation and enforced departure than because there is an association between entry status and the right to remain in the receiving country. Rules governing entry affect exits in at least three ways: (*a*) by specifying that welfare assistance cannot be sought; (*b*) by linking the entry status and the right to remain of dependent migrants with those of the principal applicant or sponsoring migrant; and (*c*) by stipulating conditions on the admission and stay of migrants. In the overseas countries of immigration, regulations on entry rarely fall in the first two categories.

Limitations on welfare assistance

As already discussed above, migrant women are more likely than migrant men to need welfare assistance. In Canada, making use of welfare programmes is not a condition for deporting permanent residents. In the United States, becoming a public charge can be grounds for deportation and for being refused re-admission but, in practice, those grounds are almost never invoked. The situation in European countries varies and deserves greater study. Migrants in

Sweden are allowed access to social programmes without negative consequences on their residence rights, but in other countries it can be a criterion for withdrawing residence privileges. In the United Kingdom, for instance, "in considering whether to require a wife and children to leave with the head of family, the Secretary of State will take into account all relevant factors including ... the ability of the wife to maintain herself and children or to be maintained by relatives or friends without charge to public funds, not merely for a short period but for the foreseeable future" (United Kingdom, 1989, p. 30). In the Federal Republic of Germany, "[a]s a matter of principle aliens can be expelled if they cannot or do not cover the subsistence costs for themselves and their dependants without receiving social assistance. If social assistance is needed only for a transitory period the alien shall not be expelled as a rule..." (Federal Republic of Germany, 1988, p. 21).

Because of the European Convention on Social and Medical Assistance, nationals of contracting States can be expelled on the grounds of need for assistance only if certain conditions are met, such as less than five uninterrupted years in the Federal Republic of Germany if they entered when they were under 55 years of age. However, in the case of Germany, such rules hold only if the alien has a valid residence permit. After the permit expires, the authorities need not grant an extension if the alien is dependent on public assistance (Federal Republic of Germany, 1988, p. 21). Thus, in some European countries, migrants who hold renewable resident permits will not be immediately expelled if they seek social assistance, but they will not necessarily have their residence permits renewed once they expire and will therefore be liable for deportation.

Limitations on the right of residence

Women may also be compelled to leave or be deported if their right to remain is tied to that of a principal applicant or resident migrant. However, in the overseas countries of immigration, women who secure permanent residence rights on the basis of their relationship to other migrants are treated as if they had secured those rights on their own. Thus, in Canada, deportation or departure notices do not apply to dependants who are either Canadian citizens or permanent residents aged 18 or over. In contrast, women admitted to Canada on a temporary basis may be subject to deportation if the person on whom they are dependent for support is deported or compelled to leave. Women admitted as fiancées or those attached to persons whose application for residence is under review (such as refugee claimants) often find themselves in such situations.

In the United Kingdom, authorities can issue a deportation order for the wife and children under 18 of a person that is being deported. However, mitigating circumstances are taken into account. Thus, a deportation order for dependants cannot be issued if more than eight weeks have elapsed since the enforced departure of the person concerned. Furthermore, the Secretary of State may take into account factors such as the ability of dependants to support themselves, their length of residence in the United Kingdom, the ties that the wife or children have to the United Kingdom, or any compassionate or other special circumstances, in determining whether deportation orders are to be issued for dependants. If the wife qualifies for settlement in her own right, usually after four years in approved employment, or if she is living apart from her husband, she will not be included in a deportation order directed at the husband.

As already noted, several European countries follow the practice of issuing residence permits that consolidate over time the right to residence. While the sex of the applicant is usually not an explicit criterion for obtaining a residence permit of longer validity, migrant women may be handicapped in meeting the conditions necessary to obtain enhanced permits. In the Federal Republic of Germany, for instance, an unlimited right to residence can be granted to migrants who have been living in the country for eight years and who can prove that they are sufficiently integrated into its economic and social life. Integration implies meeting the following conditions: having a secure means of subsistence that excludes unemployment benefits or benefits under the Federal Act on Social Assistance, having sufficient knowledge of the German language, having adequate housing, holding a special work permit, proving that one's children attend school and observing the legal order. Obtaining a sufficient level of

language proficiency may be more problematic for migrant women than for migrant men, especially if the former remain at home or if they hold jobs that do not require a good knowledge of the host country's language. In addition, unless the applicant is married to a German citizen or is entitled to asylum, receipt of a special work permit requires the continuous exercise of a legitimate salary-earning activity during five of the eight years of stipulated residence (special provisions for Turkish citizens reduce the required time from five to four years). However, spouses of foreign workers must wait for four years (three if they are Turkish) after admission before they can apply for an initial work permit. Consequently, women who are admitted as spouses must wait a long time to qualify for a more secure resident status and may be prevented from obtaining it altogether by this complex web of requirements regarding residence and work permits.

Conditional admission related to marriage

Because entry status and residence rights are related, the foreign women admitted for family reunification in European countries can be considered to be admitted conditionally. Such conditionality is stronger in the case of migrants who enter on the basis of intended or newly formed family ties. In fact, all receiving countries in the developed world are concerned about the use of marriage for the sole purpose of gaining admission. This concern underlies the conditional admission of fiancés or fiancées and newly married spouses. Thus, the United States admits fiancés or fiancées of foreign citizens in the non-immigrant class and a marriage must occur within 90 days of entry if the fiancé or fiancée is not to be deported. In Canada, admission of fiancés or fiancées is conditional on marriage occurring within six months of entry. Similarly, in the United Kingdom, fiancés and fiancées arriving with entry clearances for the purpose of marriage are normally admitted for six months. If the marriage does not take place, an extension of stay subject to a prohibition on employment is to be granted only if good cause is shown for the delay and there is satisfactory evidence that the marriage will take place. In the Federal Republic of Germany concern also exists about the extent to which marriage is used as a means of fueling migration. In December 1981, the Federal Government recommended that spouses of second-generation migrants be excluded from provisions for family reunification if the foreigner concerned has not been resident in the country for at least eight years, has not yet attained age 18 or if the marriage has not existed for at least one year. Not all Länder adopted those guidelines, but discussion continues over restricting the admission of the spouses of second and subsequent generations of migrants (Federal Republic of Germany, 1988, pp. 34-35).

Receiving countries also monitor newly formed marriages and make conditional the residence of the migrant spouse on the continuation of the marriage. In the United Kingdom and the United States, an application for longer term residence can be filed once marriage occurs. In the United Kingdom, the applicant is allowed to remain for one year provided the authorities are satisfied that a number of conditions are met, including that the primary purpose of the marriage is not to obtain entry to the United Kingdom (United Kingdom, 1989, paragraph 131). After a year, if the Secretary of State is satisfied that the marriage has not terminated and that each of the parties has the intention of living permanently with each other, the time limit on the stay of the migrant spouse is removed.

Similar procedures are followed for the admission of persons wishing to join their spouses. In the United States, conditional admittance for a two-year period is granted after marriage. A petition to terminate conditional admittance must be filed 90 days prior to the second anniversary of the alien's admission. As in the United Kingdom, a number of conditions must be met if the foreign spouse is to be granted permanent residence (United States Immigration and Nationality Act, Section 216, Publication 99-639, November 10, 1986). Sweden also provides conditional admittance for a period of up to two years to spouses who are newly married to citizens or foreigners holding a permanent residence permit. During that time, temporary residence permits of six months are issued to the foreign spouse, a practice designed to deter the use of bogus marriages or relationships as a means of immigrating to Sweden (Lithman, 1987, pp. 15-16).

Laws and regulations governing migration for the purposes of marriage appear gender neutral. Neither men nor women are explicitly identified as targets of conditional entry. However, migration for marriage may nevertheless be selective in terms of sex. If sex selectivity exists, gender neutrality in the formulation of migration regulations will not prevent a gender-specific outcome. Thus, unpublished tabulations produced by the Statistics Branch of the United States Immigration and Naturalization Service reveal that women constituted nearly three fourths of the 1987 adjustments to immigrant status by persons admitted as fiancés or fiancées of United States citizens. In Sweden, about two thirds of migrants admitted for family reunion are on the basis of marriage or common-law relationships that have lasted a short time (Lithman, 1987, p. 16). These statistics suggest that women, more than men, are likely to be admitted conditionally for marriage-related reasons. One possible consequence is that those women may be reluctant to leave situations of domestic violence during the period of conditional residence (Lithman, 1987; Boyd, 1989b).

E. CAPACITY TO FACILITATE THE MIGRATION OF OTHERS

Migration regulations usually establish procedures under which citizens or resident migrants can facilitate the admission of close relatives. There is little evidence on whether women have equal chances as men to foster such migration, but it appears that women are less likely to sponsor additional migration, not because they are prevented from doing so explicitly by migration regulations but rather because gender roles and stratification make women less likely to meet the criteria necessary to facilitate the migration of others.

In the overseas countries of immigration, immigrants must petition the authorities to bring in relatives. The exact procedure varies by country but, in general, the sponsor must indicate a willingness to assume financial responsibility for the designated person or persons. Approval of the application is based in part on an assessment of the sponsor's ability to support the persons in question. In Canada and the United States, household income is used as an indicator of such ability. If it is too low according to a specified set of criteria, such as low-income cut-offs or poverty lines, the applicant is not judged as qualified to fulfil the legal agreement to support the would-be migrant relatives and the application is denied. Because women's incomes are generally substantially lower than those of men, they are considerably less likely than men to be successful in sponsoring the migration of relatives, especially if the women concerned are heads of household or single.

In the main receiving countries of Europe, regulations governing family reunification are gender neutral in their wording, though exceptions exist (see, for instance, the cases of Belgium and Luxembourg as reported by Pekin, 1989). However, those regulations generally stipulate more stringent criteria than those set by the countries of immigration. Thus, in order to facilitate the migration of spouses, migrant women must have been employed for a certain period, earn sufficient income and have access to suitable housing. Since standards of adequate income, length of employment or housing are based, often without acknowledgement, on the experiences of male wage-earners, migrant women usually have difficulty meeting them.

F. CONCLUSION

Several conclusions derive from the preceding analysis of migration regulations and their impacts. Empirically, in both the overseas countries of immigration and in the former labour-importing countries of Europe, the migration of women during the 1970s and 1980s occurred largely under family reunification. Men predominated in the earlier flows of workers to Europe and they generally outnumber women as principal applicants in the labour-related categories of immigrants admitted by the countries of immigration. Migrant women are admitted largely on the basis of their familial ties to citizens or to other migrants and, consequently, their dependent status with respect to others is perpetuated.

Although migration regulations governing entry do not generally make an explicit differentiation between male and female migrants, their sex-selective outcomes stem from traditional sex roles and stereotypical images regarding the place of women in society. Thus, women admitted as workers are generally concentrated in the traditional "female" occupations, such as domestic service or nursing.

In a number of European countries, migrant women admitted on the basis of family ties become legally dependent on the migration and residence status of others. The complexity of regulations governing the acquisition of residence and employment rights, which are mostly based on a male-oriented migration experience, means that migrant women are less likely than migrant men to obtain those rights on their own. Migrant women, therefore, often lack rights to entitlements, their ability to enter the workplace legally is considerably more restricted than that of migrant men and, if they lose the support of their husbands or parents and are forced to seek welfare benefits, they may be deported. Furthermore, if their husbands or parents are deported, they may be summarily subject to the same expulsion orders.

These findings underscore the differences in the migration experiences of men and women, and the handicaps faced by migrant women. Both themes dovetail with a literature that studies the process of adaptation of migrant groups while recognizing that social stratification along sex, racial and ethnic dimensions can influence such process. Well into the 1970s, the literature on assimilation often drew upon a nineteenth century liberal paradigm of equality in which individual achievements were stressed and the crucial question was whether some individuals, by virtue of ascriptive criteria (birthplace, sex etc.), were unfairly handicapped.

The findings of this paper are also understandable within two more recent bodies of literature on the welfare State and on feminist analyses of the oppression of women. Recent writing on the welfare State emphasizes that State policies determine the nature of the stratification system by structuring the distribution of resources which range from income transfers and social security to the organization and management of the economy (Esping-Anderson, 1990, pp. 1-3). The welfare State does not necessarily create a more egalitarian society through its social policies, but rather such policies can maintain existing cleavages or even create new ones (Esping-Anderson, 1990, p. 23). As State policies, migration policies often define the entitlements of newcomers to a nation State, thus creating or maintaining inequalities based on nativity. For example, in Europe, the practice of separating work and residence permits and of allowing the consolidation of residence rights over time derives from an earlier era in which Governments did not view migrants as full participants and members of their societies. Such practices contrast with those of the countries of immigration which tend to extend economic, social and political rights to immigrants either upon entry or within a short period after admission.

As this paper has shown, the position of migrants within host countries varies by sex. Where migrants admitted as dependants have different residence and employment rights than migrants admitted on their own right, the status of female migrants is likely to be negatively affected. Such sex-specificity is not surprising in light of recent analyses relative to the welfare State. State policies are increasingly seen as perpetuating the dependency of women on men, largely through welfare programmes which determine eligibility to benefits on the basis of family structure and which assume that women and children are dependent on male wages (Barrett, 1980; Quadagno, 1990). From this perspective, migration policies are part of the large domain of State policies that assume and sustain female dependency. In fact, the admission of women on the basis of family ties and their vulnerability to deportation for no fault of their own are consistent with the argument that State actions emphasize female familial roles and devalue the economic contributions of women. As with other social policies, the ones relative to migration need not be overtly sex-specific since outcomes that vary by sex can be generated by sex-specific ideologies and entrenched systems of sex stratification (McKinnon, 1989, chapter 8).

NOTES

[1]As the membership of the European Community has expanded, lengthy transition periods between accession to the Community and the entry into force of freedom of movement provisions have been established for new member countries. Thus, Greek nationals acquired the right of free movement of workers only on 1 January 1988 and Portuguese and Spanish nationals acquired such right only as of 1 January 1992, except with respect to Luxembourg where the time limit extends to 1 January 1996 (see Hovy and Zlotnik, 1993).

[2]Immigration rules or regulations may also use the pronoun "he" to refer to a migrant (see, for example, United Kingdom, 1989). However, sex-specific reference cannot necessarily be assumed in that case because "he" is generally used as a generic pronoun.

[3]The 1989 Immigration Rules, however, have done nothing to remove the burden of proof regarding marriage that the migrants themselves must assume (WING, 1985).

[4]In the United States, spouses of United States citizens are permitted to immigrate without regard to numerical limitations. According to unpublished 1986 immigration data, men slightly outnumbered women as spouses of citizens (69,286 men versus 68,311 women).

[5]Women who are admitted as family migrants also enter the labour force. Many are found in service occupations and manufacturing (De Wenden and DeLey, 1986; Boyd, 1989a).

[6]Depending on the country, another consequence is the drop in the labour force participation rates. For example, in the former Federal Republic of Germany, the labour force participation of foreign women dropped between 14 and 20 per cent from 1968 to 1980 as a result of the entry of foreign women who were not in the labour force (Mehrlander, 1987, p. 89). However, in France, the labour force participation of women seems to have increased slightly between 1968 and 1975. The number of foreign women in the labour force increased by 32 per cent, compared to an increase of 29 per cent for the foreign female population as a whole (De Wenden and DeLey, 1986, p. 200).

REFERENCES

Abella, R. S. (1984). *Equality in Employment: A Royal Commission Report*. Ottawa, Canada: Ministry of Supply and Services Canada. Catalogue No. MP43-157/1-1984E.

Barisik, A. (1987). Turkish Government policy in relation to women from ethnic minority groups. Paris: Organisation for Economic Co-operation and Development, Directorate for Social Affairs, Manpower and Education, Monitoring Panel on Migrant Women. SME/MP/W/87.5.

Barrett, M. (1980). *Women's Oppression Today*. Thetford, Norfolk (England): Thetford Press.

Biffl, Gudrun (1988). Report on labour migration. Vienna. Unpublished report.

Boyd, Monica (1988a). Immigration, income security programs and social policy issues. In *Policy Forum on the Role of Immigration in Canada's Future*, Charles M. Beach and Alan A. Green, eds. Policy Forum Series, No. 15. Kingston, Ontario: Queens University, John Deutsch Institute for the Study of Economic Policy.

_____ (1988b). Immigration and income security policies in Canada: implications for elderly immigrant women. *Population Research and Policy Review* (Dordrecht, Netherlands), vol. 8, No. 1 (January), pp. 5-24.

_____ (1989a). Family and personal networks in international migration: recent developments and new agendas. *International Migration Review* (Staten Island, New York), vol 23, No. 3 (Fall), pp. 638-670.

_____ (1989b). Migrant women in Canada: profiles and policies, 1987. Immigration Research Working Paper, No. 2. Ottawa, Canada: Employment and Immigration Canada.

_____ (1989c). *Synthesis Report of the OECD Monitoring Panel on Migrant Women*. SME/MP/MIG.W/2769. Paris: Organisation for Economic Co-operation and Development.

_____, and Charles Taylor (1986). The feminization of temporary workers: the Canadian case. *International Migration* (Geneva), vol. 24, No. 4 (December), pp. 717-734.

Caspari, A., and W. Giles (1986). Immigration policy and the employment of Portuguese migrant women in the United Kingdom and France: a comparative analysis. In *International Migration: The Female Experience*, Rita James Simon and Caroline B. Brettell, eds. Totowa, New Jersey: Rowman and Allanheld.

Castles, Stephen (1984). *Here for Good*. London: Pluto Press.

Davis, F. J., and B. S. Heyl (1986). Turkish women and guestworker migration to West Germany. In *International Migration: The Female Experience*, Rita James Simon and Caroline B. Brettell, eds. Totowa, New Jersey: Rowman and Allanheld.

De Wenden, Catherine Withol (1987). National policies and practices of entry control in OECD Member Countries. In *Continuous Reporting System on Migration: SOPEMI 1986*. Paris: Organisation for Economic Co-operation and Development.

_____, and Margo C. DeLey (1986). French immigration policy reform 1981-1982 and the female migrant. In *International Migration: The Female Experience*, Rita James Simon and Caroline B. Brettell, eds. Totowa, New Jersey: Rowman and Allanheld.

Esping-Andersen, G. (1990). *The Three Worlds of Welfare Capitalism*. Cambridge: Polity Press.

Foner, N. (1986). Sex roles and sensibilities: Jamaican women in New York and London. In *International Migration: The Female Experience*, Rita James Simon and Caroline B. Brettell, eds. Totowa, New Jersey: Rowman and Allanheld.

Germany, Federal Republic of, Federal Ministry of the Interior (1988). *Survey of the Policy and Law regarding Aliens in the Federal Republic of Germany*. VII 1-937 020/15. Bonn.

Goodman, C. (1987). Immigration and class mobility: the case of family reunification wives in West Germany. *Women's Studies* (New York), vol. 13, pp. 235-248.

Gottstein, M. (1988). Women, rights and asylum in the Federal Republic of Germany. *Refugees* (Geneva), No. 56 (September), p. 27.

Houstoun, Marion F., Roger G. Kramer and Joan Mackin Barrett (1984). Female predominance of immigration to the United States since 1930: a first look. *International Migration Review* (Staten Island, New York), vol. 18, No. 4 (Winter), pp. 908-963.

Hovy, Bela, and Hania Zlotnik. Europe without internal frontiers and international migration. *Population Bulletin of the United Nations*, No. 36. New York, pp. 19-42.

Kramer, Roger G. (1987). United States government policy in relation to women from ethnic minority groups. Paris: Organisation for Economic Co-operation and Development, Directorate for Social Affairs, Manpower and Education, Monitoring Panel on Migrant Women. SME/MP/W/87.6.

Lemoine, M. (1989). Effects of migration on family structure in the receiving country. *International Migration* (Geneva), vol. 27, No. 2 (June), pp. 271-279.

Lithman, E. Lundberg (1987). Swedish government policy in relation to women from ethnic minority groups. Paris: Organisation for Economic Co-operation and Development, Directorate for Social Affairs, Manpower and Education, Monitoring Panel on Migrant Women. SME/MP/W/87.8.

Mackinnon, C. (1989). *Toward a Feminist Theory of the State*. Cambridge, Massachusetts: Harvard University Press.

Mehrlander, Ursula (1987). Sociological aspects of migration policy: the case of the Federal Republic of Germany. *International Migration* (Geneva), vol. 25, No. 1 (March), pp. 87-96.

Meyer, Heinrich (1987). SOPEMI country report on the FRG. Organisation for Economic Co-operation and Development. Paris. Unpublished report.

Organisation for Economic Co-operation and Development (1985). *The Integration of Women into the Economy*. Paris.

_____ (1987). Yugoslavian government policy in relation to women from ethnic minority groups. Directorate for Social Affairs, Manpower and Education, Monitoring Panel on Migrant Women. SME/MP/W/87.4. Paris.

_____ (1989). *Synthesis Report of the OECD Monitoring Panel on Migrant Women*. SME/MP/MIG.W/2769. Paris.

Pekin, H. (1989). Effects of migration on family structure. *International Migration* (Geneva), vol. 27, No. 2 (June), pp. 281-293.

Quadagno, J. (1990). Race, class and gender in the U.S. welfare state: Nixon's failed family assistance plan. *American Sociological Review* (Washington, D.C.), vol. 55 (February), pp. 11-28.

Tyree, Andrea, and Katharine Donato (1986). A demographic overview of the international migration of women. In *International Migration: The Female Experience*, Rita James Simon and Caroline B. Brettell, eds. Totowa, New Jersey: Rowman and Allanheld.

United Kingdom (1989). *Statement of Changes in Immigration Rules* (laid before Parliament on 14 June 1989). London: Her Majesty's Stationery Office.

United Nations (1979). *Trends and Characteristics of International Migration since 1950*. Sales No. E.78.XIII.5.

_____ (1985a). *World Population Trends, Population and Development Interrelations and Population Policies*, vol. I, *Population Trends*. Population Studies, No. 93. Sales No. E.84.XIII.10.

_____ (1985b). *World Population Trends, Population and Development Interrelations and Population Policies*, vol. II, *Population and Development Interrelations and Population Policies*. Population Studies, No. 93. Sales No. E.85.XIII.2.

_____ (1992). *World Population Monitoring, 1991*. Population Studies, No. 126. Sales No. E.92.XIII.2.

United States Department of Labor, Bureau of International Labor Affairs (1989). *The Effects of Immigration on the U.S. Economy and Labor Market*. Immigration Policy and Research Report 1. Washington, D. C.: Government Printing Office.

Women, Immigration and Nationality Group (WING) (1984). *Worlds Apart: Women under Immigration and Nationality Law*. London: Pluto Press.

VI. FEMALE MIGRATION AND THE STATUS OF FOREIGN WOMEN IN FRANCE

*Georges Photios Tapinos**

This paper describes and analyses the changes that have taken place in the status of foreign women in France and the nature of the discrimination to which they may be subject. To avoid confusion in an area where concepts are often vague, one must first make clear what and who are the subjects of study. The first part of the paper delimits therefore the universe of interest. The changing characteristics of female migration are discussed next. Being initially induced by the entry of male workers to France, female migration, as a result of the dynamics of the migration process and changes in the status of women, later became an essential element of migration to France and of the foreign presence in it. The analysis of this evolution illustrates the differential impact—on men and women—of migration policies, which are discussed briefly. The analysis of the evidence regarding changes in the status of women both with regard to economic activity and to demographic processes is undertaken last.

Studying the status of women in relation to fertility and mortality, Mason points out that it is only recently that women have ceased to be considered as a special subject, rather than as a central one to mainstream theories of reproductive change (Mason, 1984). This advancement of the subject has been accompanied by a reflection on the meaning and scope of the concept of status itself and its elements of definition: prestige, power, control over resources, freedom from the control of others. Other authors have preferred to identify female roles and have sought to describe the exercise of those roles and their transformations in different societies. Along these lines, Oppong (1985) distinguishes seven roles of women: producers, wives, mothers, housewives, kin, community members and individuals.

*Institute national d'études démographiques (INED), Paris, France. The author would like to thank Isabelle Palluel-Lafleur and Sophie Pennec for their assistance and Michèle Tribalat for the remarks that she kindly made on the first version of this paper.

These classifications may have been used by researchers but they have hardly affected the decision-making process. In France, public authorities have paid no specific attention to either migrant or foreign women. Although a report dating from 1975, when social action on behalf of migrants was being relaunched, put forward some proposals regarding migrant women (Secrétariat d'état auprès du Ministère du travail, 1975), no mention was made of foreign or migrant women in the "hundred measures for women" proposed in 1976 by the *Secrétariat d'état à la condition feminine* (1976) in light of a study that sought to establish a clear picture of the objective situation of French women. The report of the Minister for the Rights of Women, entitled *Les femmes en France dans une société d'inégalités* (Women in France in a society of inequalities) sought to identify forms of discrimination rather than to put forward proposals for action (Ministre des droits de la femme, 1982).

A. WHAT CONSTITUTES DISCRIMINATION? A REVIEW OF METHODOLOGICAL ISSUES

The obstacles facing migrant women in host countries are extremely hard to grasp and measure. Problems arise both at the conceptual and at the statistical level. At the conceptual level one must make clear who is the object of discourse. Is one considering migrants or foreigners? In the case of France, if migrant women are defined as women who were born outside the country, they may be foreigners or they may be French, having, for instance, acquired French nationality by marriage or naturalization. Foreign women, whether born in or out of France, are distinguished by their citizenship, although this criterion is not devoid of ambiguity, especially in cases of double nationality or when the distinction is based solely on the declaration made by a respondent (as in censuses). Although the set of migrant women is not disjoint from that of foreign women, the distinction between the two is nevertheless essential, since it reflects the nature of the obstacles or the discriminatory practices that need to be studied. Thus, migrant women who have become French citizens escape from any legal discrimination linked to citizenship, although they may still face other forms of discrimination.

What is the significance of the differences observed? Among the discriminatory measures based on law and the obstacles facing both foreign and migrant women by virtue of their foreign origin or of their being women, there is a continuum of situations, some reflecting effective discrimination, others reflecting the particular impact on women of provisions that are general in nature. One may ask if one must consider as discriminatory restrictions on the immigration of female workers that may have resulted from the structure of labour demand in the industrial sector during the years of economic growth or restrictions on the range of employment opportunities open to foreign women stemming from their being banned from occupying tertiary jobs in the public sector.

Indeed, one may reach different conclusions regarding the extent to which foreign women are subject to discrimination depending on whether one addresses the issue from the point of view of, say, social workers, who are familiar with the actual experiences of migrants and are ready to mention countless limitations of the rules of law, or from a more theoretical perspective, through, for instance, a meticulous examination of existing legal provisions. The latter will almost surely show that openly discriminatory rules are practically non-existent. Such divergent conclusions not only reflect the limitations of the different perspectives used, they also underscore the significance of the particularities that one is trying to seize. In this paper the legal provisions that limit the rights of foreigners in relation to those enjoyed by citizens are considered only tangentially. Instead, attention is centred on those that lead to a differential treatment of foreign women in relation to either all foreigners or French women in general.

Even in the absence of statutory discrimination, the legal position of foreign women may be compromised as a result of the impossibility of reconciling different interpretations of equality of rights and individual autonomy, or rigid socio-juridical systems lacking common principles, or the divergent legal practices of judicial authorities in the countries of origin and the host country. The access to French nationality by marriage, polygamy and the exercise of parental authority in cases of separation of spouses illustrate those three dimensions of discrimination.

The evolution of legislation relating to the acquisition of French nationality by marriage underscores the conflict between the general principles of law and the affirmation of the equality of treatment of spouses. The Civil Code of 1804 provided that a woman should acquire the same nationality as her husband: thus, a foreign woman who married a Frenchman became French, but a French woman who married a foreigner lost her French citizenship. The 1927 reform gave priority to personal status: a French woman who married a foreigner kept her French citizenship, but a foreign woman who married a Frenchman remained foreign. The situation changed again in 1945 when new regulations established that a foreign woman who married a Frenchman became automatically a French citizen and a French woman who married a foreigner remained French, though she could renounce her French citizenship in order to acquire that of her husband. The 1973 reform, which established the conditions in force today, reflected a new conception of conjugal relations. Since then, a foreign woman who marries a Frenchman no longer becomes French automatically but she may acquire French citizenship by declaration (a fairly simple administrative procedure). The rule applies equally to a foreign man marrying a French woman. The Law of 1973 also eliminates all "asymmetrical" rules concerning the transmission of citizenship by either a father or a mother (Belorgey, 1987).

The legal texts that provide the basis for the rights and duties of spouses are of general application. With the exception of polygamy, they include no special disposition for foreign couples. Since French law prohibits polygamous unions, problems arise only with regard to aliens residing in France whose polygamous unions were contracted abroad. However, existing law recognizes that the wives of polygamous husbands have the right to join them in

France. In addition, persons in polygamous unions are entitled to receive child allowances under the same conditions as persons in monogamous unions. Yet, since persons applying for family reunification need to meet certain conditions regarding financial resources and adequate housing, those in polygamous unions may find it more difficult to qualify. Moreover, only one spouse is entitled to the social security benefits accrued by a working husband, including any pension benefits. Thus, if the husband dies, only one wife has the right to a pension. Since these regulations conform to the general principles governing marriage in France, they cannot be construed as discriminatory, although the legislator, taking into account changing customs, has been led to grant social security benefits both to the concubine and the spouse of the same partner and, in cases of divorce and remarriage, to divide pension benefits between successive wives in function of the respective durations of their unions.

The question of polygamy is not relevant from a statistical perspective. Most migrants in France come from countries where polygamy is rare (Algeria) or even prohibited (Portugal, Spain, Tunisia etc.). Yet the issue illustrates possible quandaries in assessing the detrimental effects of legal provisions on the status of women or on their autonomy. Thus, whereas the French legislator who undermines the legal position of women in polygamous unions must consider how common a social practice must be to merit incorporation into the dominant legal system, those who consider such restrictions discriminatory need to establish first whether the infringement of the rights of polygamous women is more discriminatory than polygamy itself.

With regard to the exercise of parental authority in the case of separation or divorce, the return of one spouse to the country of origin creates difficult and traumatic situations regarding the custody of children and visiting rights, particularly when judgements rendered by different national jurisdictions are inconsistent and parents have different citizenships. The problem has been especially acute in the case of Franco-Algerian marriages. After a protracted negotiation, an agreement between Algeria and France signed in July 1978 established a certain balance in favour of mothers. The agreement is yet another of a series of international, multilateral (c.f. the European Convention of Luxembourg of 20 May 1980 and The Hague Convention of 1980) and bilateral (between France and Morocco, Turkey, Egypt and Portugal) instruments whose impact has been fairly weak and that are relevant for a relatively small number of cases.

B. PROBLEMS OF MEASURABILITY

The identification of discriminatory aspects of the law must be buttressed with evidence indicating that the number of women affected is significant. Although the overall prevalence of certain situations may not reflect their intrinsic gravity, when only small numbers are involved it is hard to make a case for the need to prevent them altogether. Thus, although separation or divorce may have dramatic consequences for foreign women admitted only by virtue of being married to a migrant, the number of such cases is relatively small. In contrast, less serious discriminatory practices may be pervasive. That was the case before 1980 when French authorities refused to give priority cards to foreign women who were pregnant or had small children.

When discrimination, rather than stemming from regulations that explicitly deprive certain categories of persons from certain rights or privileges, arises instead from administrative practice or the interplay of market forces, adequate statistical evidence is hard to find. Generally, the statistics flowing from administrative practice refer to the cases approved or processed successfully and no information is available about those rejected. Thus, little is known about rejected applications for family reunification, for access to the labour market for family members or for the acquisition of French nationality by marriage or naturalization. When such statistics exist, they are rarely classified by sex and there is usually no information on the population subject to risk. The same observation can be made with regard to market-based discrimination. At equilibrium, even a market that works perfectly in terms of the flow of information and access to opportunities, still shows a gap between the curves of supply and demand.

Given the lack of longitudinal data that would allow the measurement of changes in the status of women linked to migration, recourse to the hypothetical cohort—the last resort of the demographer—is meaningless. Given the selectivity of migration, a comparison of the characteristics of migrant women with aggregate indicators referring to countries or areas of origin is not justified and may lead to erroneous conclusions regarding changes in the status of women.

A further limitation arises from the level of aggregation used. Research on migration has established that national origin is, statistically, the most discriminating variable. In the case of France, a systematic analysis by nationality has not been possible either because the disaggregated data are lacking or because they have not been classified with the necessary degree of detail. When the different foreign or migrant populations have characteristics of variable intensity but of the same nature, the bias involved in considering them as a whole is not too serious. However, that is not always the case. Thus, as figure IV shows, the marital status by age of women with foreign mothers appears to be the same as that of women whose mothers are French. Yet, the overall profile of women with foreign mothers is the result of diverging patterns by nationality, especially among daughters of Algerian and Portuguese women.

In these circumstances, the attempt to compare the status of foreign women in several host countries is almost heroic, not only because of the diversity of institutional rules, administrative practices and market mechanisms operating in those countries or because of the pace and intensity of the changes taking place in countries groping to redefine their migration policies, but mainly because the regulations and practices of interest make sense only within each national system.

Figure IV. Proportions of single women among the daughters of women interviewed in 1982, by year of birth of daughter and mother's citizenship

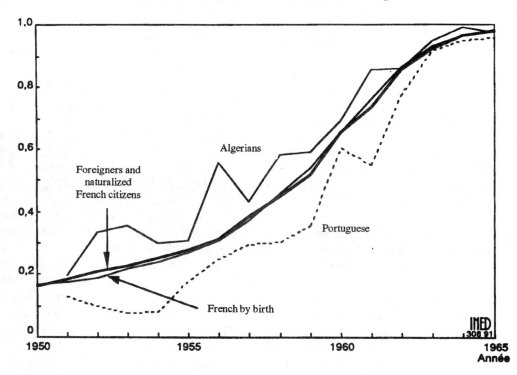

Source: Michèle Tribalat, ed., *Cent ans d'immigration, étrangers d'hier, français d'aujourd'hui*, Institut national d'études démographiques, Travaux et documents, cahier No. 131 (Paris, 1991), p. 152.

C. TRENDS AND CHARACTERISTICS OF FEMALE MIGRATION TO FRANCE

The presence of foreign workers and their families in the countries of Western Europe stems from the strong economic growth that they experienced during the 1950s and 1960s. Although the socio-economic conditions in the countries of origin had some influence, migration flows were mostly determined by the demand for unskilled labour in the industrial sector of the receiving countries. Consequently, migration consisted at first mostly of male workers. Female migration stemmed mainly from the inflow of spouses and children of male workers, although some female worker migration was also registered (United Nations Secretariat, chapter IV). The segregation by sex was such that the National Office for Immigration (Office nationale d'immigration) did not consider it necessary to record the sex of spouses entering for the purpose of family reunification. That practice reflected the narrow conceptualization of the migration process that prevailed during the 1950s and 1960s. During the 1960s, the trend towards an increase in the number of women among workers and the rise in family migration (see table 19) resulted in a growing feminization of admissions and of the foreign population in general (see table 20). By the late 1970s, when nearly 3 out of every 10 workers admitted were women, the practice of assuming that all spouses were female was clearly unwarranted.

After the Second World War, French migration policy was motivated both by the desire to promote

TABLE 19. FEMALE COMPONENT IN ADMISSIONS OF WORKERS AND
FAMILY MEMBERS TO FRANCE: 1967-1988[a]

	Workers admitted		Migrants admitted under family reunion			
Year	Total (base year 1967)[b]	Percentage of women	Total (base year 1967)[b]	Percentage of spouses	Percentage of children	Percentage female among children
1967	100	16.7	100	38.0	56.4	49.4
1968	86	18.1	102	39.4	55.1	49.3
1969	63	14.2	105	39.7	56.3	49.2
1970	162	17.8	149	39.0	56.9	48.7
1971	126	21.1	150	40.8	55.0	48.8
1972	91	20.8	138	41.2	53.9	48.9
1973	122	15.4	133	41.4	53.5	48.6
1974	60	18.3	125	41.3	54.3	48.4
1975	24	29.2	95	44.1	52.3	47.9
1976	25	26.5	105	43.7	53.4	48.1
1977[c]	21	28.0	96	45.6	51.6	47.9
1978	17	28.3	74	46.7	51.1	47.9
1979	16	29.9	72	44.6	52.7	47.8
1980	16	27.7	77	42.3	55.3	47.2
1981	31	20.4	76	41.9	55.6	47.0
1982	90	18.1	87	41.7	55.1	47.6
1983	17	26.5	84	44.7	52.5	47.4
1984	11	32.6	73	48.8	48.8	48.1
1985	9	33.2	60	52.3	45.7	47.5
1986	9	33.8	50	52.1	46.7	46.4
1987	10	35.0	49	49.3	49.5	46.5
1988	12	33.8	54	47.2	51.5	45.3

Source: Office des migrations internationales (OMI), *OMISTATS*, various years.
[a]Statistics on admissions by sex are available only from 1967 onwards.
[b]For the base year 1967, the total number of long-term workers was 107,833 and that of family members was 54,479.
[c]Between 1977 and 1982, provisional work permits are included.

TABLE 20. WOMEN AS A PERCENTAGE OF THE FOREIGN POPU-
LATION ENUMERATED IN FRANCE, BY COUNTRY OF CITIZENSHIP

Country of citizenship	Census year				
	1954	1962	1968	1975	1982
Total foreign	38.3	38.2	39.2	40.1	43.0
Africa					
Algeria	6.4	16.5	26.7	32.0	38.6
Morocco	9.3	16.2	21.8	26.7	39.1
Tunisia	24.6	31.5	33.3	31.0	37.8
Asia					
Turkey	53.3	..	38.7	25.7	42.3
Europe					
Italy	42.6	42.7	44.0	43.7	43.3
Portugal	27.0	30.1	35.4	46.2	47.1
Spain	42.0	44.1	46.8	47.3	47.2
Yugoslavia	39.7	36.7	37.1	42.1	46.0

Sources: France, Institut national de la statistique et des études
économiques, *Recensement général de la population 1954*, volume:
France entière, population, ménages, logement, table N; *Recensement
général de la population, 1962*, volume: *Structure de la population*,
table 7; *Recensement général de la population, 1968*, volume: *Structure de la population totale*, table 13; *Recensement général de la
population, 1982*, volume: *Etrangers*, tables 3 and R8.

demographic recovery and by the imperative need to
pursue economic reconstruction. Consequently, the
right to family reunification was recognized and
encouraged. Regulations provided not only for the
possibility of family members joining migrant workers but also for their accompanying the worker upon
first entry. However, the conditions that migrants
had to meet to qualify for family reunification, especially in regard to housing, were not applied with
equal severity to all nationalities, a practice that may
explain, at least in part, that the pace of family
reunification and the consequent feminization of the
population differ substantially from one nationality
group to another. Yet, at the time of the cessation of
labour migration, family reunification was more advanced in France than in other European countries
that had also resorted to foreign labour. The attempts made to restrict family reunification after
1974 took a long time to get a hold and constituted a
clear case of discrimination against female migration.

At present, family reunification is possible for any
foreigner living in France and holding a yearly
residence permit. Unlike the American system of
preferences, family reunification is strictly limited to
the spouse and children under 18, with a few exceptions made for collaterals and ascendants. A foreigner applying for family reunification must have a
stable and adequate income and a dwelling fulfilling
certain conditions regarding size and amenities. Family members to be admitted are subject to a medical
examination. The acceptance of the application for
family reunification depends on an administrative
decision by the prefect of the *département* in which
the migrant lives. Family members are granted
residence permits of the same kind as the migrant
already present in France.

Family reunification and its meaning have changed
in the course of time. Originally, family reunification
was spoused because of a dual concern: the
affirmation of an expatriate worker's right to be
joined by close family members and the desire to
promote the long-term settlement of migrants and
their integration into French society. However, the
liberal way in which family reunification was implemented with respect to migrant workers led to the
entry of spouses, many of whom joined the labour
force. This inflow of economically active persons,
most of whom are women, under the cover of family
reunification has compromised migration policy and
may be detrimental to the status of migrants.

Indeed, in recent years it can be said that family
reunification has become a vehicle for the admission
of foreign labour through the inflow of children of
migrants who then marry persons from the home
country and are joined by the latter. This practice
departs considerably from the initial justification of
family reunification which sought to avoid the breakup
of existing families. Nowadays, family reunification
depends less on the initial flows of workers than on
the matrimonial preferences of foreigners already
present in France.

Among the work permits ("admissions au travail")
granted during the late 1970s to aliens intending to
work and who were either admitted under family
reunification or were born in France but had kept
their foreign status, more than half went to women
(their share ranged from 55 per cent in 1976 and
1977 to 52 per cent in 1980). However, since

regulations concerning the "opposability of employment" and the practice of local authorities varied considerably from one nationality to another, from region to region and from sector to sector, no general conclusion can be drawn from such data. The situation changed as of August 1981, when it was established that women who entered France legally for the purpose of family reunification could not be barred from employment.

D. FOREIGN WOMEN AND THE LABOUR MARKET

Since the presence of foreign women in France is so highly determined by family reunification, their economic activity becomes crucial in assessing changes in their status. Both among the foreign population and the French, the trend in economic activity is similar: women are working more, men are working less, although the feminization of the active population is less marked among foreigners (from 1962 to 1982 the percentage of women among the foreign active population rose from 16 to 24 per cent) than among the French (the equivalent change was from 35 to 41 per cent among the French active population, as shown in table 21). Owing to the decline in male activity and the slow increase in female activity among the foreign population, in 1982, for the first time since the Second World War, the activity rate among the foreign population (both sexes combined) was lower than that among French nationals (table 21).

The activity rates of foreign women by nationality reveal the existence of wide differences (table 22). However, the interpretation of levels and trends on the basis of cross-sectional data is hazardous because, aside from the problem of distinguishing between behavioural and cohort effects, one would need to control for the duration of stay in France and the stage in the migration cycle in which the women find themselves. Nevertheless, the data reveal a clear difference between foreign women of European origin (Italians, Portuguese, Spanish and Yugoslavs) and women from Northern Africa and Turkey. The former display substantially higher activity rates, closer to those recorded among French women. Such high rates reflect, in part, the effects of migration dynamics and the completion of family reunification, confirming that duration of stay has a decisive influence on the status of migrant women. Yet one must also make allowance for the special traits associated with national behaviour. Yugoslav female migrants, for instance, whether in France or in the former Federal Republic of Germany, have always displayed relatively high activity rates, higher even than those of French women. Such outcome reflects both the influence of the country of origin (the activity rates of women in the former Yugoslavia were higher than those recorded in many Western European countries) and the selectivity of migration (economically active women are more likely to migrate). Since the statistical evidence available provides no indication about whether the activity rates of Yugoslav women in France are higher than would be expected given the factors outlined above, the high values recorded cannot be automatically interpreted as indicating a change of status due to migration.

Lacking longitudinal data, the analysis of activity rates by age can only allow the exploration of changes in labour force participation if one assumes stability of behaviour from one generation to the next (table 22). Unlike the patterns observed at present among French women, the bimodal curve characterizing the economic activity rates of foreign women by age is similar to what used to be considered the typically "feminine" pattern of activity characterized by low rates among young married women who discontinue economic activity when their children are young (figure V). The difference in patterns of economic activity by age underscores generational effects. Northern African women have lower activity rates at all ages, but differences are less marked at younger ages, suggesting that younger generations of Northern African women are tending to behave more and more like French women and other foreigners.

The distributions of economically active foreign women by sector of activity (table 23) and by socio-professional category (table 24) suggest that foreign women face serious constraints in choosing an economic activity: they remain markedly concentrated in the tertiary sector (working mostly by providing

105

TABLE 21. TOTAL AND ACTIVE POPULATION, BY NATIONALITY: CENSUSES OF FRANCE, 1954-1982

	1954[a]	1962[a]	1968	1975[b]	1982[b]
Base year 1954					
Total population	100	108.6	116.1	122.9	126.9
Foreign population					
Male	100	123.0	146.0	190.0	193.2
Female	100	122.7	152.2	204.4	233.1
Active population					
Male	100	102.2	107.8	110.8	113.2
Female	100	102.0	109.0	124.4	146.7
Active foreign population					
Male	100	116.2	132.8	161.2	148.8
Female	100	109.2	137.7	196.7	243.4
Percentage					
Foreigners in total population	4.1	4.7	5.3	6.5	6.8
Women in foreign population.................	38.3	38.2	39.2	40.1	42.8
Active persons in total population					
Male	60.0	55.8	54.8	53.0	52.6
Female	29.3	27.9	28.0	30.3	34.6
Both sexes	44.1	41.4	41.1	41.4	43.3
Active persons in foreign population					
Male	73.2	69.2	66.5	62.4	56.4
Female	22.4	20.0	20.3	21.6	23.4
Both sexes	53.8	50.4	48.4	46.0	42.3
Foreigners in active population					
Male	6.5	7.4	8.0	9.4	8.5
Female	2.3	2.5	2.9	3.7	3.9
Both sexes	5.0	5.7	6.2	7.3	6.6
Women in active population	34.7	34.6	34.9	37.3	40.7
Foreign women in foreign active population......................................	16.0	15.2	16.5	18.8	23.7

Source: Institut national de la statistique et des études économiques, *Recensement général de la population 1982*, volume: *Etrangers* (Paris), table R8.

[a]Algerians, although legally French nationals, are classified as foreign. In 1954, however, nationals of the French Union were classified as French.

[b]In 1975 and 1982, persons aged 15-16 were subject to compulsory schooling and were not considered in determining the active population, a practice not followed in previous censuses.

services to private persons) and in manual jobs. Such distribution reflects the negative effects of excluding foreign women from the public sector.

Must one conclude from the evidence available that there is a segmented labour market with only one section open to foreign women and operating under its own logic? To answer this question, let us consider the different facets of employment equilibrium in terms of differential unemployment, relative wages and legality (legal, clandestine or informal employment).

TABLE 22. ACTIVITY RATES AMONG WOMEN, BY COUNTRY OF CITIZENSHIP: CENSUSES OF FRANCE, 1975 AND 1982

Country of citizenship	1975[a]	1982[a]	1982 Census				
			15-24	25-34	35-54	55+	Total[b]
France	50.0	55.0	39.5	66.0	57.8	14.4	41.3
Total foreign	37.1	38.3	33.2	41.5	40.8	12.2	33.3
Africa							
Algeria	16.2	23.6	30.6	25.7	14.8	9.0	23.1
Morocco	24.9	20.4	20.4	18.7	22.4	18.4	20.1
Tunisia	24.6	20.9	20.4	20.2	22.5	8.7	20.0
Asia							
Turkey	19.4	14.7	21.9	11.3	12.2	7.3	14.2
Europe							
Italy	33.8	36.3	35.7	52.2	36.1	9.2	24.7
Portugal	48.6	55.8	48.5	62.7	57.0	29.7	36.3
Spain	39.7	44.6	37.6	55.4	46.0	15.0	33.9
Yugoslavia	59.1	57.5[b]	32.8	64.5	71.6	21.6	57.5

Source: Institut national de la statistique et des études économiques, Recensement général de la population, 1982, volume: Etrangers (Paris), tables 3 and 8.

[a]Activity rates calculated as the percentage of active persons among the population aged 15-64.

[b]Activity rates calculated as the percentage of active persons among the population aged 15 or over.

TABLE 23. FOREIGN FEMALE POPULATION, BY SECTOR OF ECONOMIC ACTIVITY AND COUNTRY OF CITIZENSHIP: 1982

(Percentage)

Sector of economic activity	Africa			Asia	Europe			Total
	Algeria	Morocco	Tunisia	Turkey[a]	Italy	Portugal	Spain	
Industrial production								
Intermediate goods	4.6	5.8	4.0	9.9	6.4	6.4	3.4	5.1
Capital goods	5.4	4.6	6.0	7.2	7.2	6.5	4.7	6.0
Consumer goods	11.4	9.7	12.0	40.5	16.1	13.3	9.4	13.3
Textile and clothing industry	7.9	6.1	8.4	31.5	11.3	8.2	5.3	8.5
Commerce[b]	14.6	10.7	11.6	6.3	14.4	9.6	12.1	11.2
Commercial services	36.8	33.2	39.4	11.7	25.9	29.9	28.1	30.5
Hotels, cafés, restaurants	9.5	9.0	10.8	1.8	5.6	5.3	5.0	6.5
Commercial services to enterprises	5.9	6.6	15.7	5.4	7.8	9.5	11.9	9.3
Commercial services to individuals	20.2	17.5	12.4	3.6	11.6	14.6	10.8	14.1
Non-commercial services	17.5	23.1	17.3	8.1	18.1	23.8	31.6	23.5

Source: Institut national de la statistique et des études économiques, Recensement général de la population, 1982, volume: Etrangers (Paris), table 9.

NOTE: The entries do not add up to 100 because only the main categories are shown.

[a]Agricultural activities (farming, forestry, fishing) and agricultural and food industries account for 12.6 per cent of the economically active female Turkish population.

[b]Mainly food and non-food retail activity.

107

Figure V. Economic activity rates among women in France, by age group and citizenship: 1975 and 1982

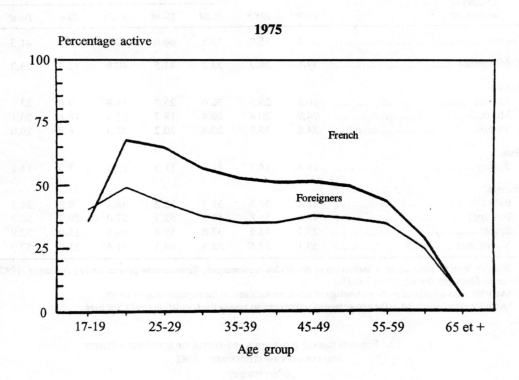

1975

Percentage active

French

Foreigners

Age group

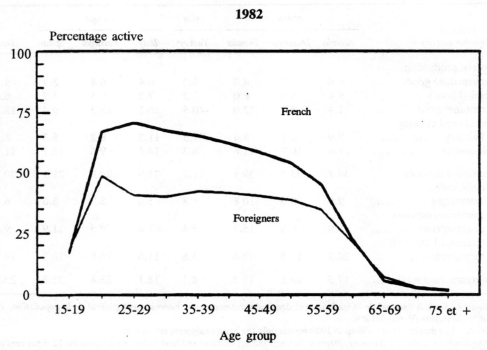

1982

Percentage active

French

Foreigners

Age group

108

TABLE 24. ACTIVE POPULATION, BY SEX, NATIONALITY AND
SOCIO-PROFESSIONAL CATEGORY: 1982

(*Percentage*)

Socio-professional category	Foreign men	Foreign women	French women
Artisans, tradespeople, heads of enterprise	4.7	1.9	6.6
Highly-skilled professionals	3.6	2.1	5.0
Intermediate professions ...	5.2	5.2	17.2
Teaching, health and public service	0.9	3.0	11.9
Employees	9.0	43.2	47.3
Public service	1.2	5.0	14.0
Administrative (enterprises)	4.8	11.2	20.1
Commercial	0.9	4.4	6.2
Direct services to individuals	2.2	22.5	7.1
Workers	75.5	39.6	15.8
Skilled	31.4	5.9	3.6
Unskilled	40.0	32.0	11.7
Unemployed who have never worked	1.3	7.4	2.1

Source: Institut national de la statistique et des études économiques,
Recensement général de la population, 1982, volume: *Etrangers*
(Paris), table 8.

The data on unemployment presented in table 25
indicate that women are more likely than men to be
unemployed and so are foreigners with respect to
French nationals. According to the 1982 census, the
unemployment rate among foreign women (over
20 per cent) was nearly twice that recorded among
foreign men (12 per cent) or that prevalent among all
women (12 per cent). In interpreting the unemployment rate among foreign women one must bear in
mind that we are not considering here all migrant
women, that foreign women in general show relatively low activity rates and that they often work in
the informal sector where their activity goes
unrecorded. The high unemployment rates prevalent among foreign women may stem from their own
handicaps (age, language abilities or low skill levels)
but, in addition, they reflect the difficulties that
foreign women face in "entering" the labour market.
Indeed, among foreign women originating in countries outside the European Community and registering as unemployed (job applications at the end of the

month as of 31 December 1985), 30 per cent reported to be registering for the first time. The
equivalent proportion among unemployed foreign
men from non-EC member States was 11 per cent
and it was 17 per cent among unemployed French
women (see table 26). Consequently, one is tempted
to interpret the lower activity rates prevalent among
foreign women of all ages not merely as a result of
less willingness to become economically active but
mainly as a reflection of the obstacles that foreign
women face in entering the labour market.

With regard to unemployment rates, the differences by nationality remain marked and confirm, in
particular, the greater vulnerability of Northern African and Turkish women. In the age group 15-24,
their unemployment rates exceed 50 per cent. Among
Algerian women, unemployment rates reach 61.2 per
cent (see table 25). Once more, nationality is a
strongly discriminating factor among foreign women.

Statistics on "annual income statements" show, for
wage-earners (excluding agricultural workers, domestic workers and most civil servants), total remuneration by sex, economic sector, socio-professional
activity and nationality (French versus foreign).[1]
Average wages in all sectors order themselves in the
following way: French men have the highest, followed by foreign men, French women and foreign
women (INSEE, 1985). Unfortunately, the statistics
available provide little insight into the causes of the
differences observed. Thus, one cannot assess the
influence of seniority (which is usually lower among
women), level of education, location and size of
enterprise, and discriminatory practices linked to
foreign or female status.

When one considers average wages for workers in
different occupations, although the ordering remains
the same (French men, foreign men, French women
and foreign women), the largest gap in mean wages
sometimes is found between men and women (as in
the case of unskilled workers in the industrial sector)
and sometimes between French men and all other
categories (as in the case of persons providing direct
services to private individuals).[2]

These statistics neither confirm nor invalidate the
hypothesis that there is a labour market specific to

TABLE 25. UNEMPLOYMENT RATES AMONG THE ECONOMICALLY ACTIVE POPULATION,
BY SEX, COUNTRY OF CITIZENSHIP AND AGE: 1982

Country of citizenship	Total population			Female population			
	Male	Female	Both sexes	15-24	25-34	35-54	55+
Total active population	6.7	11.7	8.8	27.7	10.4	6.2	7.6
Foreign active population	12.1	20.2	14.0	37.7	19.5	11.5	11.2
Africa							
Algeria	18.3	45.1	21.9	61.2	36.5	26.1	13.8
Morocco	12.3	36.3	15.0	55.3	32.9	18.3	15.1
Tunisia	15.5	35.3	17.6	52.1	32.5	23.8	22.7
Asia							
Turkey	11.2	38.2	13.8	55.9	27.7	23.2	23.1
Europe							
Italy	7.4	17.0	9.5	34.9	16.5	12.6	10.9
Portugal	6.3	10.3	7.7	20.7	8.3	6.2	8.3
Spain	8.6	12.7	9.9	32.7	12.0	6.9	8.5
Yugoslavia	10.0	12.3	10.8	26.0	12.0	10.6	11.3

Source: Institut national de la statistique et des études économiques, *Recensement général de la population, 1982*, volume: *Population active* (Paris), tables 7 and 8.

NOTE: The unemployment rate is the percentage of the active population that is unemployed.

TABLE 26. FOREIGN POPULATION REGISTERED AS UNEMPLOYED, BY SEX,
NATIONALITY AND MOTIVE FOR REGISTRATION: 1985
(Percentage)

Motive for registration	Citizens of non-EC countries			French		
	Male	Female	Both sexes	Male	Female	Both sexes
Economic dismissals	26.6	15.4	23.5	23.0	17.6	20.3
Other dismissals	12.9	9.5	12.0	11.9	8.3	10.0
Resignation	2.9	5.1	3.6	5.0	8.5	6.7
End of contract	27.7	22.5	26.2	33.5	33.8	33.7
End of interim period	6.8	2.0	5.4	4.9	2.3	3.7
First entry	10.7	30.4	16.2	10.5	17.0	13.8
Renewal of activity	8.2	10.2	8.7	7.9	8.8	8.3
Other cases	4.2	4.9	4.4	3.3	3.7	3.5
Total registered (thousands)	196	76	272	1 056	1 089	2 145

Source: Ministry of Labour, Agence nationale pour l'emploi, special tabulations.

foreign women. In fact, the mean wage of French nationals is higher in enterprises having foreign employees. This outcome can be interpreted either as showing the complementarity of the foreign and national labour force or as an indication of discriminatory practices with regard to foreigners and, especially, to women.

Fragmentary evidence corroborates the significant participation of foreign women in clandestine and informal employment. Thus, women constituted some 20 per cent of the workers regularized during the 1981-1982 regularization drive. There were, however, considerable differences between the various nationality groups: among Turks, only 3.4 per cent of the regularized workers were women, whereas that proportion amounted to 43.5 per cent among Yugoslavs (Marié, 1983; Moulier-Boutang, Garson and Silberman, 1986). Single, widowed and divorced persons accounted for over 75 per cent of the regularized female population as compared to 60 per cent among men. Indeed, among currently married women who applied for regularization, the very small proportion who had a spouse in France—16.2 per cent—indicates the existence of a marginalized and vulnerable segment of the female foreign population in France. One must, however, be prudent in the interpretation of these data since married women are more likely to regularize their status through family reunification and would consequently not have applied for regularization under the 1981-1982 drive.

Women of Northern African origin show a marked tendency to engage in informal employment, a fact that explains, to some extent, their low participation rates. However, in contrast to clandestine employment, participation in the informal sector may be considered the result of deliberate choice. Northern African women may prefer informal jobs where they can obtain cash earnings outside their husband's control (Boulahbel-Villac, 1989). Consequently, their low participation rates may stem from supply constraints rather than from the difficulties that they face in obtaining formal employment or from the discrimination of employers. In order to reconcile such an interpretation with the high unemployment rates recorded among Northern African women, one can hypothesize the existence of different behaviours according to age group: younger women would be more likely to join the formal sector and would therefore be more vulnerable to overt unemployment, while older women would tend to work in the informal sector and would be less likely to appear in the unemployment rolls. Unfortunately, the data on unemployment claims do not allow the examination of this issue since they are not classified by age.

E. THE MIGRATION PROCESS AND THE STATUS OF MIGRANT WOMEN

As migration flows evolved and the distribution of the foreign population by sex became more balanced, the status of foreign women underwent certain changes. Not only were migrant women faced with significantly different lifestyles and socio-cultural models but, in addition, they were not immune from the changes brought about by the more comprehensive movement advocating women's rights in Europe. In this section, the effects that such experiences have had on the nuptiality patterns of foreign women, their control of fertility and naturalization trends are explored.

Age at marriage or at cohabitation

In the absence of longitudinal data, the 1982 family survey (Tribalat and others, 1991) has been used to compare the experience of different birth cohorts so as to grasp the behavioural changes that have taken place. The comparison of nuptiality patterns by nationality reveals striking differences. Among Algerian women, 70 per cent of mothers whose daughters were born in 1961 were married before they were 20, as against only 15 per cent of their daughters at the time of the survey. The equivalent proportions among French women were 40 per cent for the mothers and 25 per cent for the daughters. Although the trend among Algerian women and their children can be associated with the rising age at marriage observed in Algeria itself during the same period, it is also a reflection of changes in the status of women resulting from migration. Indeed, according to the 1981 Algerian census the proportion of single women aged 20-24 was only 53 per cent compared to 73 per cent among second-generation migrants of Algerian descent in France belonging to the same age group (Tribalat and others, 1991).

Data on the situation of young adults who still live in their parents household and on those who have already left home (table 27) indicate that women leave home earlier than men, a phenomenon that is more accentuated among foreign women. In addi-

TABLE 27. YOUNG ADULTS, BY PLACE OF RESIDENCE (PARENTS' HOUSEHOLD
OR ELSEWHERE) AND WORKING STATUS: 1982

(*Percentage*)

Nationality of mother and sex	Young adults who left home at 18 (19 for men) by age group of mother		Situation of young adults (aged 18) present in the household in 1981			
	50-54	55-59	In school	Employed	Un-employed	Others
French						
Male	8	7	41	25	13	21
Female	12	13	57	19	17	7
Portuguese						
Male	10	7	14	61	12	13
Female	30	23	24	36	18	22
Algerian						
Male	7	5	32	11	37	20
Female	26	17	51	10	29	10

Source: Derived from the "Enquête famille 1982" (Tribalat, 1991).

tion, the situation of young women still living at home varies considerably from one nationality group to another. Women of Algerian descent tend to stay longer in school and are more likely to be unemployed when they seek to enter the labour market. The two phenomena are interrelated, since Algerian women face special difficulties securing employment for the first time both because of biases in the labour market and constraints stemming from their family environment. Consequently, they stay in school longer. In contrast, women of Portuguese descent leave school earlier and find jobs more easily. It is noteworthy that, in general, young women have higher educational attainment than their male counterparts.

Although the foregoing evidence indicates that there have indeed been some changes in the status of women, they cannot be ascribed exclusively to migration. Indeed, migration is probably less of a causal factor than a means to an end. The mere act of engaging in migration is a manifestation of change and of the willingness to adapt. In addition, when the migration process has involved, as in the case of France, the initial migration of men followed by their wives and children, male emigration itself has had some impact on the status of women left behind. Consequently, changes in the attitude and behaviour

of the second generation are just the crystallization of a long-term process in which migration plays a crucial role but is probably not the main determinant of change.

Control of fertility

Regulations regarding access to contraceptive methods and counselling call for no special comments. Abortion has been legal in France since 1975, provided it is performed before the tenth week of gestation by a doctor in an approved medical establishment. Technically, the law of 17 January 1975 relative to the voluntary interruption of pregnancy put in abeyance during five years the application of the dispositions contained in the Penal Code on the matter of abortion, and the law of 31 December 1979 established the permanence of those dispositions. Since at the time abortion was made legal in France, French legislation was more liberal than that of neighbouring countries, it was feared that foreign women residing abroad might flock to France to interrupt their pregnancies. The law therefore stipulated that a woman had to reside in France for a period of at least three months before resorting to an abortion. However, the law also established that an abortion could be performed at any time for therapeutic reasons, apparently without any conditions on length of residence.

In addition to the legal aspects of abortion, its significance for foreign women must be assessed. Indeed, the age-specific abortion rates among foreign women (all nationalities combined) tend to be higher than among French women, especially among women aged 20 or over (table 28). Tribalat and Muñoz-Perez (1989) consider that such differences are indicative of the fact that foreign women are more likely than French women to use abortion to control family size within marriage. There have been important changes in the recourse to abortion by foreign women over time. As table 29 shows, in 1976 the number of abortions per birth was lower among foreign women than among French women, but by 1985 both groups of women registered similar levels. The growth of the number of abortions among foreign women also suggests that abortion is being used as a key method of birth control within marriage. Women of European origin, particularly Italian and Spanish women, are the most likely to resort to abortion (table 29).

Naturalization

French legislation distinguishes between the attribution of French nationality at birth and the acquisition of French nationality, be it by declaration (through marriage) or by decree (naturalization). Current law on the attribution or acquisition of French nationality contains no provisions that differentiate between the sexes. If a foreign man or woman marries a French national, he or she can acquire French citizenship by declaration after six months of marriage. The only condition is that the spouses live together during that period. By imposing this condition, the legislator has tried to avoid the use of "marriages on paper" as a means of acquiring French citizenship. The concern of authorities and public opinion in this regard has been echoed by the Commission on Nationality which proposed to increase from six months to a year the required length of life in common. Whereas naturalization is granted at the discretion of the Administration, access to French citizenship through marriage cannot be refused except for indignity or lack of assimilation (Law of 7 May 1984).

TABLE 28. ABORTION RATES PER 1,000 WOMEN, AMONG FRENCH AND FOREIGN WOMEN IN EACH AGE GROUP: 1982

Age group	French women	Foreign women
15-19	10.5	9.4
20-24	20.5	36.6
25-29	19.5	34.9
30-34	16.9	26.1
35-39	12.5	18.6
40-45	5.8	9.0
45-49	0.8	1.6

Source: Michèle Tribalat and Francisco Muñoz-Pérez, "Rapport français", paper prepared for the Meeting of the Working Group on Immigrant Populations of the European Association for Population Studies held in Paris, 14-15 June 1989, table 24.

TABLE 29. ABORTIONS PER BIRTH, BY COUNTRY OF MOTHER'S CITIZENSHIP

	1976	1982	1983	1984	1985
France	0.187	0.229	0.244	0.236	0.222
Total foreign	0.142	0.209	0.222	0.225	0.228
Africa					
Algeria	0.069	0.141	0.150	0.160	0.169
Morocco	0.054	0.087	0.108	0.114	0.120
Tunisia	0.086	0.130	0.137	0.141	0.137
Europe					
Italy	0.228	0.308	0.376	0.331	0.319
Portugal	0.164	0.271	0.304	0.292	0.286
Spain	0.218	0.377	0.374	0.368	0.333
Others	0.231	0.321	0.320	0.321	0.322

Source: Michèle Tribalat and Francisco Muñoz-Pérez, "Rapport français", paper prepared for the Meeting of the Working Group on Immigrant Populations of the European Association for Population Studies held in Paris, 14-15 June 1989, table 26.

Statistics on mixed marriages, defined as those in which one spouse is foreign and the other French, show a predominance—constant over time—of marriages between French women and foreign men, which account for some 60 per cent of all mixed marriages. Although there is an increasing trend in the incidence of mixed marriages, it cannot be interpreted as indicating the increasing integration of foreigners (Muñoz-Pérez and Tribalat, 1984). Indeed, since according to French nationality law, children born in France of Algerian parents born in Algeria before 1964 are French at birth and children born in France of foreign parents automatically become French when they reach age 18, growing numbers of mixed marriages can be expected as these "new French citizens" contract marriages with persons of foreign origin.

With regard to naturalization proper, the law again is neutral in the treatment of men and women, although the administration has the discretionary power to accept or reject an application. Hence, in practice women and men may be treated differently, especially since the administration is free to set quantitative goals or criteria for acceptance of applications which are not made explicit.[3]

Census data on persons who have been naturalized are not the best basis for assessing the even-handedness of administrative practice with respect to sex. In 1982, if one compares the sex distribution of persons acquiring French citizenship with that of foreigners, an overrepresentation of women is evident. The difference is partly imputable to the age structure of naturalized persons. The differences by sex, however, are smaller than those by nationality. In recent years, although the number of naturalizations has been the same for women and men, unfavourable decisions have been higher for men. Yet the period of observation is too short for the comparison to be meaningful and there are no statistics on the number of applications by sex that would permit an assessment of the possible biases of positive or negative decisions by sex. In addition, the variable duration of the administrative procedure involved does not warrant the practice of relating naturalizations granted to the number of applications made during any given year. Lack of information classified by sex is also a problem. For example, for the 8.6 per cent unfavourable decisions taken in 1985 a breakdown by sex is not available.

F. Women's role in the integration process

Changes in the status of migrant women and their consequences are part of the critical process of integration to the host society. However, the issue of whether and how the presence of female migrants contributes to integration is still controversial. Thus, although the increasing presence of foreign women in France has promoted the re-establishment of a

normal family life among migrants who had previously been characterized by high proportions of men living in collective dwellings largely isolated from the host society, the reunification of families has often implied a return to traditional sex roles and the reassertion of the power of the male head of household. That has been particularly true about families of Northern African origin, who were reunited at a later stage than those of migrants from Southern Europe. It has been suggested that the consolidation of the family unit among Northern African migrants has contributed to strengthening the influence of Islam during the 1980s (Kepel, 1992). The ambivalent feelings of the general public regarding migration and the ideological slant of analyses of the phenomenon colour this controversy. During the 1960s and 1970s it was thought that the very structure of the Northern African migrant population prevented its successful integration to French society, since single males living in collective dwellings had little enticement or opportunity to interact with the rest of society. Today, when the Northern African population present in France has moved closer to a normal demographic and social profile, those very characteristics are claimed to be detrimental to its successful integration. Clearly, these contradictory perspectives fail to take serious account of the changes that have taken place and continue to take place in the migrant community.

Another area where the presence of migrant women has had a decisive impact is on the attitudes of migrants towards return migration. France has adopted a series of measures to promote the return of migrants, including the granting of financial assistance. During 1984-1987, the proportion of economically active foreign women who received assistance for their return amounted to only 6 per cent, a level far below that of the total economically active female population among foreigners. Although the tendency to return is stronger among married men than among those who are single, the presence in France of their wives and children reduces the likelihood of return. Thus, the wives of Moroccan workers who were offered financial aid to return home did everything possible to ensure that their families stayed in France. Among the single foreign population and particularly among single persons from Northern Africa, the propensity to return is probably weaker among young women, mainly because they fear losing the opportunities and freedom of action that they have become accustomed to (Boulahbel-Villac, 1989).

As the migration process unfolds, female migration sheds its induced or subordinate nature to become a critical element in the dynamics of integration. The statistics available have allowed us to suggest a number of hypotheses concerning the impact that public policies have had on foreign women. In addition, changes in the behaviour of migrant women have been explored with respect to both market and non-market activities. Unfortunately, the data available are insufficient to establish clearly the causes of the changes observed and, consequently, are still a poor basis for the formulation of adequate interventions.

NOTES

[1]According to the General Code on Taxes, every person, whether physical or moral, domiciled or established in France who pays wages or salaries must present an "Annual declaration on social data". Such information is available for about 70 per cent of salaried jobs and for three quarters of full-time jobs.

[2]Mean yearly salary based on annual declarations (in French Francs):

	Unskilled workers in industry	Persons providing services for individuals
French men	68 550	77 170
Foreign men	64 835	62 265
French women	54 233	56 441
Foreign women	50 630	52 555

Source: Institut national de la statistique et des études économiques, *Déclarations annuelles de salaires 1985*.

[3]Some dispositions favouring the naturalization of certain categories of aliens were made explicit, as in the case of persons participating voluntarily in the French Army in 1939, foreigners under the flag in 1946 or certain categories of workers—miners, in particular, in 1947 (Lebon, 1980).

REFERENCES

Belorgey, J. M. (1987). Le droit de la nationalité: évolution historique et enjeux. In *Questions de nationalité. Histoire et enjeux d'un code*, S. Laacher, ed. Paris: L'Harmattan.

Boulahbel-Villac, Yeza (1989). *Stratégies professionnelles et familiales des femmes algériennes*. Rapport final sous la direction scientifique de D. Schnapper, Ecole des hautes études en sciences sociales. Paris: Convention caisse nationale des allocations familiales.

France (1985). *Déclarations annuelles de salaires 1985*. Paris: Institut national de la statistique et des études économiques (INSEE).

France, Ministère des droits de la femme (1982). *Les femmes en France dans une société d'inégalités. Rapport au Ministre*. Paris: La documentation française.

France, Secrétariat d'état à la condition feminine (1976). *Cent mesures pour les femmes*. Rapport présenté par F. Giroud. Paris: La documentation française.

France, Secrétariat d'état auprès du Ministère du travail (1975). Les femmes immigrées. Rapport présenté à M. P. Dijoud par la Commission présidée par Mme G. Tillion. Paris: Secrétariat d'état auprès du Ministère du travail—Travailleurs immigrés.

Kepel, Gilles (1992). Les populations d'origine musulmane en France: insertions ou intégration. In *La France dans deux générations*, Georges P. Tapinos, ed. Paris: Fayard.

Lebon, André (1980). *Démographie, immigration, naturalisation*. Report presented to Mr. Mattéoli, Ministre du travail et de la participation. Paris: Haut comité de la population.

Marié, C. M. (1983). L'immigration clandestine et le travail clandestin des étrangers en France à travers la régularisation des "sans-papiers" de 1981-82. Paris: Ministère des affaires sociales et de la solidarité nationale.

Mason, Karen Oppenheim (1984). *The Status of Women. A Review of its Relationship to Fertility and Mortality*. New York: The Rockefeller Foundation.

Moulier-Boutang, Yann, Jean-Pierre Garson and Roxane Silberman (1986). *Economie politique des migrations clandestines de main-d'oeuvre: comparaisons internationales et exemple français*. Paris: Publisud.

Muñoz-Pérez, Francisco, and Michèle Tribalat (1984). Mariages d'étrangers et mariages mixtes en France: évolution depuis la première guerre. *Population* (Paris), vol. 3, pp. 427-461.

Oppong, Christine, and Katharine Abu (1985). *A Handbook for Data Collection and Analysis on Seven Roles and Statuses of Women*. Geneva: International Labour Office.

Tribalat, Michèle, and Francisco Muñoz-Pérez (1989). Rapport français", paper prepared for the Meeting of the Working Group on Immigrant Populations of the European Association for Population Studies held in Paris, 14-15 June.

_____, and others (1991). *Cent ans d'immigration, étrangers d'hier, français d'aujourd'hui*. Travaux et documents. Cahier No. 131. Paris: Institut national d'études démographiques.

United Nations Secretariat (1995). Measuring the extent of female international migration. Chapter IV in the present volume.

VII. THE INTEGRATION OF ALGERIAN WOMEN IN FRANCE: A COMPROMISE BETWEEN TRADITION AND MODERNITY

Yeza Boulahbel-Villac*

The integration of Algerian women into the socio-economic and cultural life of France takes a paradoxical form. Unlike that of men, for whom employment is the primary route to integration, and a narrow one at that, the integration of women takes place mostly in the domestic sphere and remains within the traditional context. In order to illustrate the unique path towards integration followed by Algerian women in France, this paper focuses on three aspects of their integration strategies. The first concerns the relation of Algerian migrant women to work and the economic sphere in general. Their low labour force participation rates fail to reflect their considerable involvement in informal economic activities, adapted from traditional practices that provide women with some degree of financial independence. The second concerns family and marriage, areas in which the traditional sex roles appear to prevail. However, demographic indicators reveal a gradual convergence towards the parameters characterizing the native population. The third concerns the extent to which Algerian women make use of the welfare system, whose assistance, reinterpreted by Algerian women in the light of tradition, is used as a means of contact with the host society that results in a gradual integration into it. Thus, far from being confined to the domestic sphere, to cultural isolation and tradition, Algerian female migrants in France create their own opportunities. Their dynamism is not only likely to foster their own integration but also that of the second generation. Algerian women may thus spearhead the integration of the whole Algerian population in France.

A. ALGERIAN MIGRATION TO FRANCE

Algerian migration to France has a long history. Algerian men were recruited as soldiers and workers during the First World War. Later in the century,

Algerian men were prompted to move to France because of the economic changes that Algeria was undergoing. Their migration was part of the process that Sayad (1977) has called the "separation from the land" and that comprises three major phases. During the first phase, migrants left their homes and families in rural areas only for limited periods and remained attached to the peasant society. During the second phase, individualism grew and emigration provided an opportunity for breaking the migrant's ties with the rural community of origin, especially by escaping from its control. In the third phase, the process of separation from the land was completed and migrants emerged as a group capable of developing independently from both Algerian and French society. During the last phase, emigration from Algeria involved large numbers of people from all regions of the country, both rural and urban areas, including both families and men migrating on their own. It was precisely at that stage that women began migrating in large numbers and their migration may be considered to characterize the most mature phase of Algerian emigration to France.

Although the migration of Algerian women occurs mostly as part of family migration, migrant women should not be considered merely as dependants of their husbands and dominated by them. The difference in the timing of the migration of men and women reflects their different migration strategies. Whereas men moved largely because of economic motives, women, being traditionally excluded from the economic sphere, had to devise a different strategy to migrate. Their preferred path to emigration has been through marriage. Thus, Algerian women wishing to emigrate marry Algerian men already living abroad. A few make a more significant break with tradition and marry Frenchmen, and yet another group seeks further education abroad.

For many Algerian women, the decision to emigrate reflects a conscious choice of society, a desire

*Université Tolliac, Paris.

to have greater freedom, to live in an urban environment, to have access to more consumer goods etc. According to interviews carried out among Algerian migrants, most female migrants have no plans to return to their country of origin. The view of one of them is typical: "My country is where my children and family are". In contrast, migrant men tend to maintain alive the expectation of return. Embedded in this notion is the idea of being part of the community of origin, being attached to the land and to one's roots. Women have, in contrast, a more individualistic sense of themselves and their families, and their plans and expectations give greater weight to the future.

B. THE ALGERIAN COMMUNITY IN FRANCE:
ITS DIMENSIONS AND CHARACTERISTICS

In 1982, Algerians constituted the largest migrant community in France, accounting for 21.7 per cent of the foreign population present in the country and for 1.5 per cent of the total population. Women constituted only 38.6 per cent of the 805,000 persons declaring themselves as having Algerian citizenship in the 1982 census. However, because Algeria was part of France until it gained independence in 1962, many persons declaring themselves as Algerian in the census had, in fact, the right to French citizenship by virtue of having been born in French territory, that is, in Algeria before independence. Consequently, the 1982 census data on Algerian citizens are better indicators of the population of Algerian origin than normal data on citizenship would be. Nevertheless, most of the data discussed below, based on information on citizenship at the time of birth as declared by persons enumerated by the census, are a better indicator of ethnic or cultural origin than citizenship at the time of the census. That is, in most of what follows, "Algerians" include both persons who declared to have kept their Algerian citizenship since birth and former Algerian citizens.

As expected, the proportion of women among the Algerian population in France has been increasing. Thus, whereas in 1975, women accounted for 32 per cent of the 711,000 Algerian citizens enumerated by the census, by 1982 the equivalent proportion had

risen to 38.6 per cent and in 1990 it had reached 41.3 per cent (France, n.d. and 1992). The proportions of women among both those declaring their current citizenship as Algerian and those whose previous citizenship was Algerian was slightly higher, amounting to 38.9 per cent in 1982 and to 42.2 in 1990.

According to the 1982 census, there were considerable differences between the male and female populations of Algerian origin. As table 30 indicates, Algerian men aged 25-54 were considerably less likely than Algerian women to be living as one of a couple. Thus, whereas 46.5 per cent of Algerian men lived with their spouse, 83.2 per cent of Algerian women did so. Relatively high proportions of Algerian men lived outside ordinary households, mostly in collective dwellings or dormitories (21.4 per cent), in shared accommodations (16.2 per cent) or alone (15.1 per cent). In contrast, barely 9.6 per cent of all Algerian women had those living arrangements. However, Algerian women were nine times more likely than Algerian men to be living in single-parent families (7.2 versus 0.8 per cent).

There were also important differences between the sexes in the types of couples they belonged to. While 87.7 per cent of Algerian women living in conjugal unions had as partners Algerian men, only 68.5 per cent of their male counterparts had Algerian women as partners. That is, Algerian men were considerably more likely than Algerian women to enter into mixed marriages, an outcome that reflects the different impact that norms against mixed marriages have on men and women.

Information on living arrangements by age shows that older Algerian men were less likely to live as part of a couple and more likely to live either in collective dwellings or alone (see table 31). Algerian men aged 25-34, as well as their female counterparts, were more likely to live in shared accommodations, and Algerian women in that age group were also the least likely to live as part of a couple. Furthermore, both men and women aged 25-34 were the most likely to live with partners who were not Algerian. Those differences by age may be indicative of the better relative adaptation of younger migrants to the host society.

	Algerian population		Percentage distribution				
	All ages	25-54	All ages	25-54	25-34	35-44	45-54
A. Men							
Children living with parents	189 740	-	35.8	-	-	-	-
Living as a couple	157 380	126 814	29.7	46.5	49.4	46.8	44.5
Both partners Algerian	107 840	87 815	20.3	32.2	27.6	34.2	32.5
French-Algerian couple	46 100	35 999	8.7	13.2	20.5	11.4	10.9
Other living arrangements	183 460	145 904	34.6	53.5	50.6	53.3	55.4
Single-parent family	2 860	2 182	0.5	0.8	0.4	0.7	1.1
Living alone	53 740	41 180	10.1	15.1	13.1	14.8	16.9
Sharing accommodation	54 540	44 180	10.3	16.2	22.4	14.7	14.1
Collective dwelling	72 320	58 362	13.6	21.4	14.7	23.1	23.3
TOTAL	530 580	272 718	100.0	100.0	100.0	100.0	100.0
B. Women							
Children living with parents	175 480	-	52.0	-	-	-	-
Living as a couple	122 960	103 951	36.4	83.2	80.3	88.1	82.8
Both partners Algerian	107 840	93 706	31.9	75.0	70.7	81.6	75.3
French-Algerian couple	12 120	7 871	3.6	6.3	7.4	4.8	5.9
Other living arrangements	39 240	20 990	11.6	16.8	19.6	12.0	17.3
Single-parent family	11 100	8 996	3.3	7.2	4.7	8.1	12.1
Living alone	6 860	3 124	2.0	2.5	3.2	1.7	2.2
Sharing accommodation	16 660	7 871	4.9	6.3	10.6	1.6	2.4
Collective dwelling	4 620	1 000	1.4	0.8	1.1	0.6	0.6
TOTAL	337 680	124 942	100.0	100.0	100.0	100.0	100.0

Source: France, Population census, 1982, unpublished tabulations.

Because the living conditions of a migrant condition his or her experience in the host society, it is important to control for them to the extent possible. In what follows, attention is focused on the most sizeable groups of migrants according to living conditions. Among Algerian women, a distinction is made between those living as part of a couple with an Algerian partner, those with a French partner, those living in single-parent households, and those living alone. Those four groups of women account for 91 per cent of Algerian women aged 25-54. Among Algerian men, a distinction is made between those living with an Algerian spouse, those living with a French spouse, those living alone, those sharing accommodation with other persons, and those living in collective dwellings or dormitories. Those five groups of migrant men account for 98 per cent of all Algerian men aged 25-54 (see table 30).

Educational level and age are the first two variables which must be taken into account to understand women's various family and occupational situations. Among both natives and migrants, education, by promoting modern values and reducing the influence of traditional norms and practices, has been a means of acculturation, particularly among women. Thus, it can be argued that the most influential process leading to a break or compromise with tradition and

118

TABLE 31. POPULATION OF ALGERIAN ORIGIN IN FRANCE, BY SEX,
TYPE OF LIVING ARRANGEMENT AND AGE GROUP: 1982

(Percentage)

			Age			
	Under 25	25-34	35-44	45-54	55 and older	Total
A. Men						
Total male population	21	21	16	15	27	100
Population of Algerian origin	18	15	30	24	13	100
Both partners Algerian	1	15	39	28	17	100
French-Algerian couple	4	26	30	22	18	100
Living alone	3	14	33	30	20	100
Sharing accommodation	9	24	33	24	10	100
Collective dwelling	8	12	39	30	11	100
B. Women						
Total female population	19	19	14	14	34	100
Population of Algerian origin	32	29	18	12	9	100
Both partners Algerian	7	40	29	18	6	100
French-Algerian couple	19	38	15	12	16	100
Single-parent family	6	26	28	28	12	100
Living alone	13	29	9	8	41	100

Source: France, Population census, 1982, unpublished tabulations.
NOTE: Coverage: persons aged 15 or older.

its concept of the family is not international migration *per se* but rather the shift from a traditional educational system to a modern one.

In terms of both age and education, two subgroups of women can be distinguished among those of Algerian origin. The first and most numerous is constituted by women who live in conjugal union with Algerian men, who tend to be concentrated in age groups 25-34 and 35-44, and whose educational attainment is very low (90 per cent did not complete primary school). The second comprises a group of younger and better educated Algerian women who tend either to live alone or be married to Frenchmen (see tables 31 and 32).

Algerian women living in single-parent households tend to be older than those in unions (40 per cent are aged 45 or over, compared to 24 per cent of those married to Algerian men) and also have very low levels of educational attainment (83 per cent did not complete primary school). Many of them are

likely to be widows whose origin and type of migration was similar to those of Algerian women still married to Algerian men.

Algerian women living alone, though few in number, constitute a more diversified group, with over 40 per cent aged 55 or over, and 62 per cent having minimal levels of educational attainment. Since older Algerian women are more likely to be those having little education, they represent a group similar to those living in single-parent households, that is, women who migrated to join their husbands but who have become widowed since then and whose children have left home. In contrast, younger Algerian women living alone tend to have higher levels of educational attainment, comparable to those of French-born women of similar age (see table 33).

Algerian women married to French men also seem to encompass two distinct subgroups: younger women with relatively high levels of educational attainment; and older women with little education. Over half of

119

TABLE 32. POPULATION OF ALGERIAN ORIGIN IN FRANCE, BY HIGHEST EDUCATIONAL CERTIFICATE OBTAINED, TYPE OF LIVING ARRANGEMENT AND SEX: 1982

(Percentage)

| | | Highest educational certificate obtained | | | | | |
	None	Primary-school certificate	Junior high-school diploma	Technical proficiency certificate	High-school diploma	Higher degree	Total
A. Men							
Total male population	39	18	7	18	10	8	100
Population of Algerian origin	84	4	2	7	2	1	100
Both partners Algerian	88	4	1	5	1	1	100
French-Algerian couple	66	8	3	14	4	5	100
Living alone	89	3	1	3	2	2	100
Sharing accommodation............	87	3	1	6	1	2	100
Collective dwelling	94	2	0	2	1	1	100
B. Women							
Total female population	41	22	10	11	9	7	100
Population of Algerian origin	79	6	4	7	3	1	100
Both partners Algerian	90	4	1	3	1	1	100
French-Algerian couple	51	14	7	12	7	9	100
Single-parent family	83	6	2	6	2	1	100
Living alone	62	9	4	12	7	6	100

Source: France, Population census, 1982, unpublished tabulations.

NOTE: Coverage: persons aged 15 or older.

all Algerian women in mixed marriages had not completed primary school. They are likely to be part of the first wave of Algerian women migrating to France, namely, those married to French men who had worked in Algeria before independence.

The differences between the distributions by age and educational attainment among Algerian men having different living arrangements are less striking than among Algerian women. Algerian men living in conjugal union with Algerian women tend to be older than men sharing accommodation, or than those married to French women. Algerian men living alone tend to be older than those living in a union. Educational attainment is very low among most groups of Algerian men. The group with the most favourable distribution by educational attainment was that of Algerian men married to French women, only a third of whom had completed primary school or a higher degree. Indeed, Algerian women married to French men display a slightly more favourable distribution by educational attainment than their male counterparts.

C. EMPLOYMENT AS AN INDICATOR OF ADAPTATION

Given the traditionally low labour force participation rates characterizing Algerian women, it is important to consider factors that may increase them. Education plays a major role in fostering a break with tradition, especially by imparting values that are no longer based on female seclusion, but that stress instead success in male-dominated areas through the acquisition of skills and the freedom of choice. To assess the impact of education one may focus on the experience of different generations, represented by persons in different age groups. Thus, younger women, who are more likely to be better educated, are also the most likely to be employed in the formal sector of the economy. As table 34 indicates, such a difference is evident within the group encompassing

TABLE 33. POPULATION OF ALGERIAN ORIGIN IN FRANCE BY HIGHEST EDUCATIONAL CERTIFICATE
OBTAINED, TYPE OF LIVING ARRANGEMENT, AGE GROUP AND SEX: 1982
(*Percentage*)

Age and educational certificate obtained	Algerian origin						French living as couples
	Both partners Algerian	French-Algerian couple	Living alone	Sharing accommodation	Collective dwelling	Single-parent family	
A. Men							
15-29							
Primary school certificate, at most	61	43	51	61	75	..	34
Junior high-school diploma	3	7	3	5	3	..	8
Technical proficiency certificate	26	32	18	23	8	..	36
High-school diploma or higher	10	18	28	11	14	..	22
30-44							
Primary school certificate, at most	90	71	92	95	98	..	41
Junior high-school diploma	1	3	0	1	0	..	5
Technical proficiency certificate	7	17	3	2	1	..	28
High-school diploma or higher	2	9	5	2	1	..	26
45-59							
Primary school certificate, at most	98	90	97	99	99	..	65
Junior high-school diploma	0	2	0	0	0	..	4
Technical proficiency certificate	1	5	1	0	1	..	15
High-school diploma or higher	1	3	2	1	0	..	16
B. Women							
15-29							
Primary school certificate, at most	84	54	41	..	..	74	41
Junior high-school diploma	3	10	7	..	..	3	11
Technical proficiency certificate	8	20	24	..	..	16	23
High-school diploma or higher	5	16	28	..	..	7	25
30-44							
Primary school certificate, at most	96	61	65	..	..	88	52
Junior high-school diploma	1	6	2	..	..	3	8
Technical proficiency certificate	2	10	17	..	..	4	18
High-school diploma or higher	1	23	16	..	..	5	22
45-59							
Primary school certificate, at most	99	83	96	..	..	98	75
Junior high-school diploma	0	4	4	..	..	1	7
Technical proficiency certificate	0	6	0	..	..	1	8
High-school diploma or higher	1	7	0	..	..	0	10

Source: France, Population census, 1982, unpublished tabulations.
NOTE: Coverage: persons aged 15 or older.

the highest proportion of Algerian women, namely, those living in conjugal union with Algerian men.

Education is not the only factor leading to higher labour force participation rates. Economic necessity may also lead women to break with tradition. Thus, Algerian women living in single-parent households and those living alone have higher labour force participation rates than Algerian women living with Algerian men. Indeed, the labour force participation rates of Algerian women living alone are even higher than those of French women living with a spouse.

TABLE 34. LABOUR FORCE PARTICIPATION RATES FOR FRENCH POPULATION AND ALGERIANS IN FRANCE,
BY AGE GROUP, SEX AND TYPE OF LIVING ARRANGEMENT: 1982

(Percentage)

	Age				
	Under 25	*25-34*	*35-44*	*45-54*	*55-64*
A. Men					
Total male population in France	45	95	97	93	60
French men living with a spouse	94	98	98	95	61
Population of Algerian origin	40	87	93	90	67
Both partners Algerian	90	96	96	92	61
French-Algerian couple	92	94	96	90	56
Living alone	68	85	93	91	70
Sharing accommodation....................................	55	89	92	93	70
Collective dwelling	18	64	86	84	71
B. Women					
Total female population in France	42	69	64	56	35
French women living with a spouse	69	65	60	52	31
Population of Algerian origin	30	25	15	13	15
Both partners Algerian	27	13	9	8	10
French-Algerian couple	60	53	52	34	16
Single-parent family	49	72	55	37	18
Living alone	77	83	94	82	39

Source: France, Population census, 1982, unpublished tabulations.
NOTE: Coverage: persons aged 15 or older.

Although for some of the Algerian women living on their own or in single-parent households, holding a job may be a choice reflecting a conscious break with tradition, for many choice is not an issue. Lack of male support forces them to earn their living, often by taking low-status and low-paid jobs.

The case of women married to French men illustrates yet another mechanism leading to economic participation. Their labour force participation rates, though not as high as those of women living alone, are nevertheless considerably higher than those of Algerian women living with Algerian men. In the case of Algerian women in mixed marriages, necessity is likely to play a smaller role in prompting them to work. Rather, their labour force participation may be seen as a clearer break with tradition, stemming from a conscious decision to depart from the norms and values of the society of origin. Of course, marriage to a non-Algerian man already indicates a similar departure, but their tendency to conform to

the patterns of labour force participation observed among married French women corroborates their break with tradition.

In contrast with Algerian women, Algerian men not living with a spouse tend to have lower labour force participation rates than men living in conjugal union. Particularly low labour force participation rates characterize men living in collective dwellings, yet their economic activity tends to be considerably higher than that recorded among most groups of Algerian women. The high labour force participation rates characterizing Algerian men aged 25-55 corroborate that prevailing norms and values allow men few choices: in both the society of origin and that of destination, men are expected to assume an economic role, being the main breadwinners in a household.

The distribution by occupation indicates that Algerian women who are gainfully employed tend to be

122

concentrated in white or blue-collar occupations (see table 35). The proportion working as white-collar workers is specially high among Algerian women living alone (28 per cent), among those whose spouses are French (25 per cent) and among those living in single-parent households (24 per cent). There is a relatively high proportion of retired workers among Algerian women living alone (21 per cent) and also of those in blue-collar occupations (18 per cent). Blue-collar workers also account for a substantial proportion of the gainfully employed women living in single-parent households. In general, low proportions of Algerian women work as managers, supervisors or in intermediate professions. Women living alone or those living with French men are the most likely to belong to those occupational groups. These differentials serve to confirm the inferences made on the basis of labour force participation rates: Algerian women who can choose the economic activity they engage in (i.e., women married to French men or younger women living alone) are more likely to obtain better jobs than women who are forced to become economically active because of necessity (i.e., women in single-parent households or older women living alone).

It is worth noting that Algerian men tend to be concentrated in blue-collar occupations to a greater extent that Algerian female workers and that, just as Algerian women, Algerian men married to French women or those living alone are somewhat more likely to have better occupations.

TABLE 35. POPULATION OF ALGERIAN ORIGIN IN FRANCE, BY SEX, OCCUPATION AND TYPE OF LIVING ARRANGEMENT AND TOTAL POPULATION IN FRANCE BY SEX AND OCCUPATION: 1982

(Percentage)

Occupational category	Algerian origin							Total population
	Total	Both partners Algerian	French-Algerian couple	Living alone	Sharing accommodation	Collective dwelling	Single-parent family	
A. Men								
Farm workers	0	0	0	0	0	0	..	5
Artisans, tradesmen	3	4	8	4	3	0	..	6
Managers and supervisors	1	0	3	1	0	0	..	7
Intermediate professions	2	2	7	2	1	0	..	11
White-collar workers	8	7	9	13	10	7	..	8
Blue-collar workers	61	73	56	63	71	68	..	30
Retired	5	8	11	6	3	2	..	17
Not gainfully employed	20	6	6	11	12	23	..	16
TOTAL	100	100	100	100	100	100	..	100
B. Women								
Farm workers	0	0	0	0	..	..	0	3
Artisans, trades people	1	1	1	1	..	..	2	3
Managers and supervisors	0	0	2	1	..	..	0	2
Intermediate professions	1	1	5	6	..	..	3	7
White-collar workers	11	5	25	28	..	..	24	20
Blue-collar workers	7	4	9	18	..	..	17	7
Retired	2	0	5	21	..	..	0	17
Not gainfully employed	78	89	53	25	..	..	54	41
TOTAL	100	100	100	100	..	..	100	100

Source: France, Population census, 1982, unpublished tabulations.

NOTE: Coverage: persons aged 15 or older.

D. Detailed information on the migration experience of Algerian women: in-depth interviews

To obtain a better grasp of the experience of Algerian migrants in France, in-depth interviews were conducted with Algerian families, both in their home country and in France. Most of the interviews were carried out in three communes of the Parisian suburbs:

(a) Trappes, a neighbourhood with a large concentration of foreigners, including Algerians, Moroccans and persons from French-speaking countries of sub-Saharan Africa. 21 families were interviewed. Persons of French origin living in the low-cost housing of the area are generally very poor. Living in Trappes is not a matter of choice, as families in the neighbourhood usually cannot afford housing elsewhere;

(b) Chanteloup-les-Vignes, a nearby community located in a considerably smaller commune than the new town of Trappes. Many Algerians work in nearby car factories. As in the case of Trappes, Algerians living in Chanteloup-les-Vignes do so because they cannot afford better housing;

(c) Bagneux, a Parisian suburb closer to the city whose social composition is more varied, with foreigners accounting for a large proportion of the population in some neighbourhoods where they nevertheless live side-by-side with French people, such as civil servants, with good jobs.

Some interviews were also conducted among "French-Muslim" families living in Corsica, south of Bastia, on the east coast of the island. Scattered communities of *harkis* settled there at the end of the Algerian war and those remaining are still employed by the Forestry Department, although they lack civil-service status. Some live in housing estates on the outskirts of medium-sized communes. Lastly, to be able to compare the situation of Algerian migrants in France with non-migrants in the country of origin, interviews of Algerian families living in a small town in eastern Algeria were also carried out. Those families were assumed to represent the traditional behaviour typical of the communities of origin of Algerian migrants in France.

Some 50 interviews were conducted in total, not only with Algerian families, but also with social workers or important informants in the different localities considered. Clearly, the persons interviewed were not a representative sample either of the Algerian population in France or of that in Algeria. Nevertheless, the approach used ensured that qualitative information regarding the migration experience of women would be more likely to emerge.

E. Methodology: seeing and listening

Admission into the families interviewed was generally not immediate. Usually, an acquaintance was developed and a relatively long stage of interaction preceded the formal interview so as to elicit the necessary trust on the part of the respondent, thus making it possible to obtain information on experiences and assessments not ordinarily revealed to an outside observer. In most cases, the persons approached remained diffident for several days before agreeing to a formal interview, but during those waiting periods the researcher had the opportunity to establish a better rapport with interviewees and prompt their cooperation. Being invited and received several times in the interviewee's home was necessary before an appointment for an interview could be made.

The visits made to the interviewee's home were especially useful for observation purposes. Daily behaviour, attitude towards food, table manners, languages spoken, and actual solidarity within the family group are better observed than expressed. Such observations were made systematically on the basis of lists of behaviours or attitudes that are not verbalized. Particular attention was paid to the interviewee's attitude towards money, French culture in a broad sense and France itself. Details regarding daily activities, behaviours absorbed subconsciously, table manners, the upbringing of children etc. were noted. Such observations were made not only at the homes of interviewees but also at common meeting-places, such as the Friday market.

The interviews themselves were carried out in Arabic, with French words or phrases used where necessary. Use of the interviewee's native language made it easier to deal with matters that are usually not expressed or made explicit because of their sensitive nature. Furthermore, the use of Arabic was mandatory when interviewees had a poor command of French and it contributed to enhancing the rapport between the researcher and those interviewed who tended to associate the use of French with official business. Generally, husband and wife were interviewed together. A full interview lasted more than two hours and, in some cases, it was followed by an additional session with the wife alone, especially when she showed signs of being embarrassed to say certain things in front of her husband. Interviews usually took place in the homes of those interviewed and could thus be recorded.

F. INFORMAL ACTIVITY AS A MEANS OF ACHIEVING INDEPENDENCE

As noted above, Algerian women in France are characterized by very low rates of labour force participation. In 1982, only 22 per cent of the Algerian women aged 15 or over were economically active. The labour force participation rate of French women was twice as high. Thus, Algerian women seem to abide by traditional norms that discourage their participation in gainful employment outside the home. If, as the feminists claim, without financial independence there is no salvation, Algerian women in France have a long way to go to be "saved". However, official data on labour force participation are often deficient, since they tend to reflect only employment in the formal sector of the economy. Women the world over and, particularly, Algerian women in France have developed a series of informal economic activities that provide them some means of economic independence. It is, however, difficult to obtain adequate indicators of the extent of women's participation in the informal sector. In France, estimates of the number of women who are not wage-earners but who are nevertheless economically active fluctuate widely (Huet, 1981).

Information regarding the labour force participation of women in Algeria is not much better. According to Algerian sources (Hakiki-Talahite, 1986), the female economically active population is concentrated mostly in urban areas (86 per cent), where the modern sector of the economy tends to be located. Indeed, the labour force participation rate of Alge-rian women living in France is seven times higher than that of women in Algeria (3 per cent). In Algeria, women working for wages are still the exception. That does not mean, however, that women are cut off from economic activity. In traditional Algerian society women have created, within certain limits established by pre-existing economic practice, an informal sector in which their earnings permit the accumulation of some personal property (jewellery, clothing etc.). Thus, women become economic actors not through work outside the home but rather within the shadow of tradition.

Women's work, however, does not have the same function as that of men, whose purpose is to ensure the survival of the family. For women, work is a means of saving. Traditionally, any remuneration that women obtain through work is for their personal use. In Algerian society it is a disgrace for a husband or father to depend upon the earnings of women. A man who can provide enough for his clan or family to live on must, as a sign of wealth, flaunt the fact that neither his wife nor his daughters have the need to work.

In such a society, female work is mostly linked to the world of women. Women engage in home production, buying and selling among themselves. The income they raise through such activities is rarely devoted to covering household expenses. Only when women lack the support of men do they work to feed or clothe the family.

This type of female economic activity is rarely reflected in official statistics, because it is generally not reported. Consequently, the work of women lingers in the collective subconscious and is not considered economic in character. The money they earn is not reckoned as part of household income but is instead left for their personal use. They thus acquire a certain measure of independence that is consistent with tradition.

G. IN THE IMMIGRANT COMMUNITY, TRADE HAS REPLACED HANDICRAFTS

To what extent have traditional attitudes towards women's economic activity managed to survive among Algerian migrants in France? There are a number of indications that there is a continuity of practice regarding the participation of Algerian migrant women in informal activities. For instance, Algerian women engage in small-scale commerce between Algeria and France, taking to Algeria for sale a wide range of products that are symbols of the French style of life (e.g., perfumes, cosmetics, fabrics, clothing, small appliances and even automotive parts). Inter-community trade also flourishes. Thus, Moroccan women sell traditional products (gold jewellery in particular) to Algerian women in France, who some-times take them back to Algeria. Many Algerian female migrants have thus become businesswomen on their own right, fostering a type of trade that caters to the demand for consumer goods among Algerian women back home.

The interviews carried out in the Parisian suburbs confirm and clarify the nature of the informal activi-ties of migrant women. Algerian women who decide to abide by tradition and remain outside the formal economic sphere nevertheless engage in such activi-ties and therefore, in a way, defy tradition. Their participation in the informal sector constitutes a sort of compromise that allows them to strike a balance between the norms of the two societies to which they belong. While avoiding conflict and discord, they establish a bridge between the two on the basis of a reinterpretation of traditional values within permis-sible limits. Trade among women revives the tradi-tional role of women as links between closed interi-ors (harems), the sanctuary, the home. Though women engaging in those activities were usually older, widowed or sterile, they are now young, ready to travel and make decisions, though normally within the confines of tradition.

Reliable information on such types of informal activity is difficult to obtain, mostly because even the women themselves tend to dismiss them as insignifi-cant. According to traditional norms, women do not work, they "manage", do "odd jobs", "get by". Even the terms used suggest the lack of importance attached to their activities. Furthermore, the infor-mal work of women must be distinguished from the moonlighting or odd jobs carried out by men. Since most Algerian men in France are wage-earners, their informal economic activities do not have the same meaning as those of women. They usually engage in

such activities to improve household income or meet exceptional household expenses.

During the interviews carried out, the informal work performed by men was practically never re-ported, mostly because it was considered insignifi-cant, not being the main source of male income. Yet, many Algerian men who were unemployed at the time of interview "did odd jobs" as a way of reducing the anxiety associated with unemployment. For men, being a wage-earner ensures their dignity and legitimizes their status. Often, securing a job in the formal sector was the reason for their migration. Even being unemployed confers them a sort of sta-tus, derived from the fact that they were previously employed (Schnapper, 1989).

In Algeria, the interviews carried out revealed that a number of women had given up paid employment to work at home, sewing, knitting or serving as intermediaries between Algerian women in France and those in Algeria. Interestingly, the money those women earned through their informal activities, which had traditionally been hoarded as a protection against bad times, was being invested. Thus, women were cashing in their savings to set up businesses in conjunction with their husbands. Such transition to investment, even if still guided by the husband, indicates that economic calculation is not absent from the strategies of "traditional" women.

Algerian women in France are also starting to invest, but in a different way. For them, the priority is to improve their housing. Although Algerian households had until recently failed to follow the trend of French households in acquiring real estate, they are increasingly joining that trend, often thanks to the money saved by women.

H. THE FAMILY: BETWEEN TRADITION AND MODERNITY

Changes within the family of migrants provide yet another example of the paradoxical form of integra-tion that Algerian women in France are experienc-ing. In Western societies, the family has undergone changes as a result of the emergence of the wage-earning class. There has thus been a transition from a normative family, operating as an institutional group, to a contractual family, based on the union of two free and equal individuals. Immigrant Algerian families, however, show a different kind of evolution.

In contemporary French society, the basis of the family is the couple, constituted by the union of two independent individuals who enter freely into a partnership. That partnership, however, is subject to change and may be broken, as the rising divorce rate makes plain. Moreover, unions need not be based on the traditional marriage contract. The expansion of the wage-earning class has promoted the individualization of commitments: one signs a contract with one's employer just as one makes one with one's spouse or partner. Consensual unions have therefore become a common option for members of the working class.

In contrast, the traditional marriage represents a collective contract. Marriages based on love are, after all, only a recent development that has varied according to a person's social milieu. Marriages of convenience or arranged marriages were still frequent in French society in the 1960s. They represented in most cases the alliance of two families, two sets of interests, two collective plans of which those contracting marriage were the symbol. From that perspective, the family is an institution which must be preserved and whose survival depends on collective interests far broader than those of the individual.

Most Algerian families, whether constituted of migrants or not, still abide by the rules governing the family as an institutional group. They thus adhere to a tradition in which there is a marked spatial division between the sexes. Men, being in charge of supporting the family, interact with the outside world, while women, charged with household duties and the care of the children, remain within the home. Marriage is still primarily a system of family alliances. Even when they have settled in another country, Algerian men return home to marry women selected by their families.

There are, however, some changes taking place among Algerian families in France. Yet, they occur largely within the confines of tradition. With the increasing educational attainment of Algerian women in France, particularly those belonging to the second generation, the traditional arranged marriage is shifting towards a kind that is halfway between tradition and modernity. Thus, love and the individual's role in choosing a spouse are increasingly playing a role. However, marriages based on mutual affection have not yet become the prevailing type. Often, the only concession made by the family is to give the woman the option of accepting or refusing an arranged match. In Algeria, marriage by mutual agreement of the individuals involved is generally confined to cities. In villages or small towns, the weight of tradition and social pressure is still too great to allow that form of marriage to become frequent.

Arranged marriages where the woman is given the possibility of rejecting the selected husband are the most common among Algerian migrants in France, mainly because most migrants originate in rural areas or small towns. During our interviews, few men or women admitted that their marriage had been arranged, that is, that it had been contracted without their consent. In many cases, however, marriages could not be said to be based on love, since husbands were generally older, less educated and of rural origin, while wives were younger, better educated and belonged to the lower rungs of the wage-earning class. According to the logic of social mobility through marriage, such women should have married men with a slightly higher social standing, preferably city dwellers. That women marry migrant men even when their socio-economic profiles in other respects fail to meet the expected standards says much about marriage as a migration strategy.

Algerians have ambivalent feelings about migrants. On the one hand, migrants are persons who deserted the home country and who have adopted foreign mores. On the other, they are persons who have access to foreign currency, French products, and a better standard of living abroad. From the family perspective, an alliance with a migrant is a type of investment. Through the migrant, a family can obtain access to French goods and foreign currency, as well as a link with France, at least in terms of having free lodging during visits abroad. By marrying a migrant, a woman can improve her position. Marriage thus becomes a strategy for geographical as well as social mobility for the woman concerned, a strategy that also involves a choice of society and a new way of life. In addition, for the male migrant it is advantageous to marry a younger woman with some education who is more likely to adapt to living conditions in the country of destination.

Marriage becomes therefore an economic alliance between the family of the bride and the groom. In Algeria, where village endogamy is still prevalent, such types of alliances promote exogamy. Marriages between members of different clans or tribes, whose alliances have political implications, are replaced by marriages contracted on the basis of economic considerations.

I. Marriage among the second generation

The marriage practices of the second generation, that is, of the children of Algerian migrants, are evolving rapidly (Desplanques, 1985). Young North African women, particularly those of Algerian origin, are tending to conform to the marriage patterns of young French women. Perhaps the most striking change relates to the average age at first marriage. According to retrospective information obtained from the Family Survey conducted in France in 1982, the average age at first marriage of women marrying during 1960-1964 was 19.1 years for Algerian women and 22.4 years for French women. Among Algerian women marrying for the first time during 1975-1979, the average age had increased to 22.6 years, whereas that among French women had decreased somewhat to 22.1 years. Delays in the timing of first marriage, however, do not in themselves prove that there is an assimilation of the practices of the host society. It might be, for instance, that marriage was being delayed because Algerian women in France could not find suitable partners within the Algerian community.

That the process of adaptation is indeed taking place is further validated by changes in fertility. Regardless of the indicator used, the fertility of Algerian women is higher than that among French women. However, there are incontrovertible signs of convergence towards the French norm. Thus, the total fertility of Algerian women living in France

dropped from 8.54 children per woman in 1962 to 4.35 in 1980 (Desplanques, 1985).

Another indication of the adoption of the host society's norms and values is the increasing number of consensual unions with at least one partner of Algerian origin. Consensual unions were practically non-existent among migrants of the first generation (Audirac, 1986). Yet, Algerian women are still considerably less likely to live in consensual unions than their male counterparts. Young Algerian men are freer than their sisters to adopt the mores of the host society, particularly when there is still a deficit of women in the Algerian community in France.

J. Use of social services

For Algerian women, recourse to social workers and to various forms of social assistance is not only a source of direct benefits but also a means of defining their identity by establishing a rapport with members of the host society. Algerian women want to get to know French women in order to be like them. The cultural isolation in which migrant women live needs to be understood. For their husbands and children, migration has generally been accompanied by activities that can promote their adaptation to the host society, such as working or attending school. Women migrating as adults do not have the same opportunities. Their living conditions, their working-class milieu and large families leave them little time to socialize. Their direct contacts with the host society are restricted and their relative isolation is exacerbated when they live in neighbourhoods heavily populated by foreigners, where even the shopkeepers are migrants. Their exposure to French people and society is often reduced to watching television or interacting with social or health workers.

In this context, the relationship of Algerian families with social workers is not neutral and must be seen as part of an integration strategy, especially in the case of women. In a difficult social environment, social workers are the only French people who are approachable and with whom one can interact. The French population living in neighbourhoods where foreigners tend to be concentrated often have a style of life that migrants reject. As in many other countries, poverty goes hand in hand with a higher prevalence of drug or alcohol abuse, a higher number of school dropouts, teenage pregnancies, single mothers, broken homes and consensual unions, all of which are taken as proof of slackening family values by the migrant.

Given their limited opportunities, migrant women devise their integration strategies according to the means at their disposal. Their contacts with social workers should therefore be interpreted within such a context. Migrant women obtain from social workers information that enables them to react better to their new environment; they find out about their rights and those of their family in regard to social security, unemployment benefits, family allowances and loans. Because of their active participation in initiating such contacts, women gain confidence and see their authority within the family enhanced. Since women are traditionally the ones fostering the cohesion of the family, their contacts with social workers reinforce such a role.

Because of the strong family values characterizing the Algerian community, social services have a different impact among them than among the French population. French people seeking public assistance are usually forced to do so because poverty has condemned them to the fringes of society. North African migrants, in general, seek assistance to improve their status and that of their family. The cohesion of the migrant community protects it from being pushed to the fringes of society and enables it to make good use of the support which it can receive from public assistance.

It is important to understand how Algerian migrants link public assistance with traditional practices in order to assess the special relationship that they establish with welfare agencies. Two types of public assistance must be distinguished. The first includes transfer payments, such as family or housing allowances, that are established by law and form an integral part of the labour code (Schnapper, 1989). Because only persons having a regular job and a work permit are eligible for them, such transfer payments are linked, in the perception of migrants, to labour force participation and the earning of wages. All other types of assistance are associated

by the migrant with a kind of solidarity that is akin to that existing traditionally within the family or the village. Such reinterpretation stresses the positive aspects of public assistance and contributes to strengthening the relationship between migrant women and social workers.

However, such a relationship is based on a certain ambiguity, since modern social work is based on the individualism characterizing Western society whereas, according to the migrant, it is a new version of the traditional solidarity characterizing the extended family. There results a dialogue at cross purposes, where social workers speak of values and norms characterizing the host society (e.g., the protection of children, the role of hygiene and education, women's liberation), and migrants cling to their traditional norms. Yet, as key players in ensuring the cohesion of the Muslim family, migrant women learn to negotiate their way in the host society and manage to use public services to the advantage of their families.

K. Conclusion

The Algerian population in France is often discussed in relation to a host of problems: problems of adaptation or return; unemployment; poverty; and even delinquency. However, our research shows that Algerians in France are not passive actors, nor are they more vulnerable than the rest of the population. Indeed, despite their limited economic means, Algerian migrants are pursuing their own integration strategies to fit better in the mosaic that constitutes the host society. Migrant women, in particular, are taking action to become better adapted to their new environment. While deriving support from traditional norms and values, they are not averse to transforming them in ways that facilitate their integration and that of their families. In a sense, migrant women are more oriented towards the host society than migrant men, since the former migrated with the intention of accumulating some capital and returning to the home country. Migrant women, in contrast, move to France with the intention of staying and making a new home for their families. They have, therefore, a greater stake in the integration process.

Yet, Algerian women have the double burden of becoming part of the new society without abandoning the norms and values of the society of origin. They therefore have to opt for a series of compromises between the traditional and the modern way of life. With respect to employment, for instance, Algerian women, both in Algeria and France, have low labour force participation rates. Yet, their low participation in the formal sector of the economy does not preclude the pursuit of a number of informal economic activities that are a source of personal income. Traditionally, by engaging in petty trade or in the production of handicrafts, women have an independent source of income that they jealously guard. As migrants, they have expanded somewhat their range of activities and there are indications that some women are gaining authority within the household because of their earning capacity.

A sort of compromise is also being forged regarding family building processes. Despite the dictates of tradition, Algerian women are exercising greater freedom in choosing marriage partners and the second generation is adopting marriage patterns similar to those of the French population. Fertility levels, though still high among Algerians, also show signs of convergence to the French norm.

The desire to conform and yet to maintain the culture of the society of origin has thus led to a paradoxical form of integration where tradition is reinterpreted and viable compromises are reached. Such strategies are not yet properly understood by the host society which, making use of its own moral and social standards, often stigmatizes Muslim migrants. They are thus often treated as underprivileged groups in need of special public assistance. However, even that assistance is used by Algerian women as a means of contact with the host society that can enhance integration.

REFERENCES

Audirac, P. A. (1986). La cohabitation: un million de couples non mariés. *Economie et statistique* (Paris), No. 185 (February).

Desplanques, G. (1985). Nuptialité et fécondité des étrangères. *Economie et statistique* (Paris), No. 179 (July-August).

France (n.d.). *Recensement général de la population de 1982. Les étrangers. Sondage au 1/20—France métropolitaine.* Paris: Institut national de la statistique et des études économiques (INSEE).

_____ (1992). *Recensement de la population de 1990. Nationalités. Résultats du sondage au vingtième.* Paris: Institut national de la statistique et des études économiques (INSEE).

Hakiki-Talahite, F. (1986). Le salariat féminin en Algérie: données et pratiques. University of Oran. Mimeographed.

Huet, M. (1981). Les catégories statistiques utilisées pour classer les épouses et enfants d'agriculteurs; des principes à l'usage effectif. *Archives et documents* (Paris), No. 38 (December).

Sayad, A. (1977). Les trois âges de l'émigration Algérienne. *Actes de la recherche en sciences sociales* (Paris), No. 15 (June).

Schnapper, D. (1989). Rapport à l'emploi, à la protection sociale et statuts sociaux. *Revue française de sociologie* (Paris), vol. 40, No. 1 (January-March).

VIII. COMPARING THE POSITION OF MOROCCAN AND TURKISH WOMEN IN THE NETHERLANDS AND IN THE COUNTRIES OF ORIGIN

Jeannette J. Schoorl*

Migration from Morocco and Turkey to the Netherlands started in the early 1960s. Even though the Dutch labour force was then increasing rapidly, labour shortages were becoming more pronounced. Therefore, industrial employers began recruiting workers in a number of Mediterranean countries. By the beginning of 1967 there were 74,000 persons from the so-called recruitment countries[1] in the Netherlands, 39 per cent of whom were from Morocco or Turkey. Very few of those migrant workers were women: in 1967 there were only about 400 Turkish and 40 Moroccan women in the Netherlands (3.3 and 0.3 per cent, respectively, of all Turks and Moroccans in the country). Labour recruitment came to a virtual standstill after the 1973 oil crisis. Nevertheless, migrant inflows from Morocco and Turkey, though fluctuating, showed a generally increasing trend during the 1970s, mainly because of family reunification.[2] More recently, family reunification and the granting of asylum have become practically the only grounds for the admission of long-term migrants into the Netherlands (see figures VI and VII). As a result, the number of women and children in the migrant population has increased rapidly. In 1980, for instance, among the 120,000 Turks and 72,000 Moroccans living in the Netherlands, 43 and 35 per cent, respectively, were women.

During the first half of the 1980s there was a considerable drop in the migrant inflows to the Netherlands, followed by a rise that is no longer being fueled by the family reunification of the original group of migrant workers, whose immediate relatives have mostly joined them already, but rather by the admission of the spouses of the grown-up children of the original migrants.

The process of family reunification has been particularly important for the Moroccan and Turkish communities in the Netherlands. Migrant groups from other Mediterranean countries have been more likely to opt for return migration rather than for family reunification. Furthermore, because the fertility of Moroccans and Turks is comparatively high and naturalization rates have been low, the population of Moroccan or Turkish citizenship has become one of the largest foreign groups in the Netherlands. Indeed, the population subgroups of Moroccan and Turkish origin[3] are among the four most numerous in the country, together with the Surinamese and those originating in Indonesia or the Dutch East Indies.[4] By early 1989, there were 177,000 Turkish citizens and 139,000 Moroccans in the Netherlands, accounting together for about 2 per cent of the total population of the country. The number of women and girls stood at 80,000 among Turks and 61,000 among Moroccans, with the proportion aged 15 or over amounting to 65 per cent in the female Turkish population and to 54 per cent in the Moroccan. Furthermore, about 27 per cent of the population of Moroccan or Turkish origin has been born in the Netherlands, thus giving rise to a sizeable second generation[5] which already encompasses most children of Moroccans and Turks: about 90 per cent of those under age 4, 76 and 88 per cent, respectively, of the Moroccan and Turkish children in age group 4-7, and 48 and 73 per cent, respectively, of those in age group 8-11 (Voets, 1989).

About 43 per cent of Moroccans and Turks live in the four large cities in the western part of the country—Amsterdam, the Hague, Rotterdam and Utrecht— where they constitute 6.5 per cent of the local population. Moroccans and Turks tend to be concentrated in nineteenth century neighbourhoods which surround the centres of those cities, and in other neighbourhoods having cheap housing.

*Netherlands Interdisciplinary Demographic Institute (NIDI), The Hague, Netherlands.

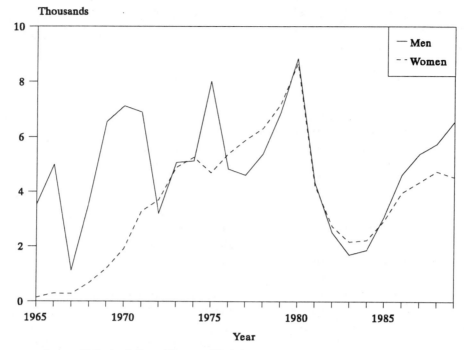

Figure VI. Immigration of Turks to the Netherlands, by sex, 1965-1989

Source: Netherlands Central Bureau of Statistics.

NOTE: The peak among men observed in 1975 is due to the regularization of undocumented migrants, most of whom had arrived in the Netherlands before 1975.

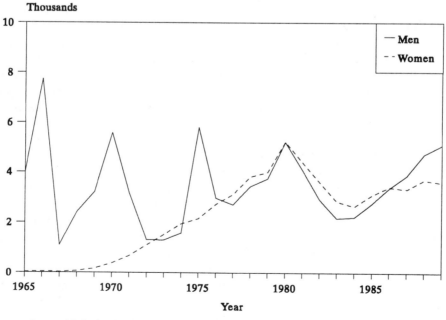

Figure VII. Immigration of Moroccans to the Netherlands, by sex, 1965-1989

Source: Netherlands Central Bureau of Statistics.

NOTE: The peak among men observed in 1975 is due to the regularization of undocumented migrants, most of whom had arrived in the Netherlands before 1975.

This paper compares the position of Moroccan and Turkish women in the Netherlands with that of women in the countries of origin and that of other women (mostly Dutch women) in the host country. There are several interrelated aspects to the notion of "position": one's position in a social class or stratum; one's position as a foreigner (ethno-cultural aspect); and one's social position or role as a woman or man. Furthermore, positions may be acquired or allocated. Allocation and acquisition of position can manifest themselves at several levels: the institutional; the organizational; the familial; and the individual (Penninx, 1988; Lim, chapter III in this volume).

Personal characteristics, choices and efforts are important in the process of acquiring a position, including one's educational attainment, professional qualifications, family situation, language proficiency, the timing of migration in the life cycle etc. Consideration of the allocation of position generally involves an approach of the issue at the macrolevel, considering factors such as regulations determining admission and residence status, economic conditions in the host country, access to public facilities and programmes, access to education and jobs etc. This paper focuses on the interrelations between, on the one hand, education, labour force participation and fertility behaviour and attitudes, and on the other, the status of migrant women and the role of migration.

A. DATA USED

Few data sources permit the study of the status of migrant women in the Netherlands and there is even less information regarding changes in their status. The two main types of data sources on international migration and migrants in the Netherlands are: (*a*) the population registration system and other registration systems, such as those on unemployment and school enrolment; and (*b*) surveys. Censuses have less importance because no census has been carried out in the country since 1971.

The population registration system yields flow and stock statistics by citizenship and a number of demo-

graphic and geographic characteristics of migrants. The data are processed and published by the Netherlands Central Bureau of Statistics (NCBS).[6] Several other registration systems also yield data classified by citizenship (Schoorl, 1982; Roelandt and Veenman, 1986 and 1987). Since 1986 these data have become more widely available through the annual publications of the programme on "Reporting system accessibility and proportionality" (Ankersmit, Roelandt and Veenman, 1987). Topics covered include population, education, labour force participation, housing and health.

Despite their richness, the data yielded by registration systems generally do not provide sufficient information on socio-economic characteristics, opinions or attitudes. National surveys fill some of the existing gaps. The main ones are the National Labour Force Survey, which was carried out every two years until 1985 and since then is carried out on a continuous basis; the National Housing Survey, taking place every four years; and the National Fertility Survey, undertaken every three years. In addition, special surveys targeting only minority groups have been carried out: a survey on conditions of life (1984-1985); a fertility survey among Moroccan and Turkish migrant women (1984); and a survey on social position and use of public facilities (1988). In addition, a number of small-scale in-depth studies that provide valuable information on the position of women have been undertaken, although they are not representative of the migrant population (van den Berg-Eldering, 1981; Priester and Brouwer, 1982; Brassé, and others, 1983; Gemeente Utrecht, 1984; van der Most van Spijk, 1985; Sieval, 1985; Bouw and Nelissen, 1986; Rivanoglu-Bilgin, Brouwer and Priester, 1986; de Vries, 1987).

Many of the large-scale surveys mentioned above cover the general population and fail to include sufficiently detailed questions on migration. Since they are carried out only in Dutch, they usually record high non-response rates among migrants, thus compromising the reliability of their results regarding the migrant community. Furthermore, most of those surveys are of the single-round type and, consequently, are not ideally suited to measure change. Lastly, they usually obtain information from male respondents (heads of household) who are unlikely to reflect adequately the experience or the concerns of women.

Better information specific to the experience of migrant women was obtained by the 1984 Immigrant Fertility Survey (IFS) carried out by the Netherlands Interdisciplinary Demographic Institute (NIDI) on the fertility of Moroccan and Turkish migrant women in the Netherlands. Data from that survey will be the major source of information used in this paper, supplemented with published data from the large-scale surveys and registration systems and with qualitative information from micro-studies referring to migrant women and their families. Data on the experience of women remaining in Morocco and Turkey were obtained from the World Fertility Survey (WFS) and Demographic and Health Surveys (DHS) carried out in Morocco and Turkey during the 1970s and 1980s.

The NIDI Immigrant Fertility Survey was carried out in a manner comparable to that of the surveys undertaken in Morocco and Turkey as part of the World Fertility Survey programme. In the NIDI survey, 177 Moroccan and 225 Turkish ever-married women aged 15 to 49 were interviewed, representing 0.8 and 1.1 per cent of the respective populations present in the Netherlands.[7] A representative sample was drawn from the population registers of eight municipalities. Interviews were conducted by bilingual or trilingual female interviewers in Turkish, Moroccan Arabic, Berber or Dutch, using structured questionnaires (Schoorl, 1985 and 1987a). Since most of the interviewers were themselves of Moroccan or Turkish origin, their rapport with those interviewed was generally good.

B. Legal regulations

The migration and minorities policy of the Netherlands is based on two main stances: (a) restriction of immigration; and (b) improvement of the legal position of foreigners who have been granted the permission to reside permanently in the Netherlands. Therefore, except for residence permits issued in accordance with international commitments (e.g., those granted to citizens of member States of the European Community or to refugees), residence permits are only issued if the presence of a migrant is essential to Dutch society or for humanitarian reasons, including family reunification.

At present, foreigners wishing to live in the Netherlands are usually granted a temporary residence permit provided that their purpose of stay is sanctioned. A temporary permit is generally valid for one year and may be renewed annually. However, it may be withdrawn or may not be renewed if the migrant lacks funds to stay in the Netherlands, has violated the Law on Foreign Employees or has seriously infringed public order or national security. Other grounds for termination of a temporary residence permit are stipulated in each individual permit. If the purpose of stay changes at any time during the migrant's stay, a change of permit can be requested.

A permanent residence permit is issued to a foreigner who is at least 18 years old and has resided in the Netherlands for at least five years under a temporary permit. A permanent residence permit can be refused only if there is no reasonable guarantee that the foreigner will have sufficient income, or if he or she has seriously infringed the public order or national security. A permanent permit can only be withdrawn if fraud has been committed to obtain it, if the migrant has committed a serious crime or if he is a threat to national security.

Generally, foreigners still need to obtain a work permit even if they hold a temporary residence permit issued for the purpose of work.[8] After three years of employment, a work permit is no longer needed in most cases. Foreigners with a permanent residence permit, their spouses and children under 18 are exempt from the work permit requirement (Handboek Minderheden, 1984).

The temporary residence permit issued for the purpose of family reunification to the foreign immediate relatives of Dutch citizens or of foreigners holding permanent residence permits is changed into a "dependent permanent residence permit" after one year, so that the condition of living with the Dutch citizen or with the holder of the original permanent residence permit remains. Children lose that permit automatically upon reaching age 18, but may then apply for another type of permit: either a permanent residence permit of their own if they have resided in the Netherlands for at least five years, or a normal temporary residence permit. In the latter case, the requirement of employment is waived for persons aged 15-18 who were born in the Netherlands and for those aged 15 or over who have been admitted for family reunification purposes at least a year before application (Handboek Minderheden, 1984). Due to the high unemployment rate among young people, the legal position of young migrants who arrived in their teens is weak (Brassé and others, 1983). Generally, women are more likely than men to be holding permanent residence permits for dependants. However, that situation is changing as the children of migrants seek spouses abroad and are joined by them in the Netherlands. Consequently, a higher proportion of the permanent residence permits for dependants issued annually is going to young men.

Most Moroccan and Turkish women have been admitted under residence permits for dependants, issued conditionally on their reunification with their husbands already living in the Netherlands. The duration of marriage is immaterial for the granting of such permits and, indeed, marriage need not have been contracted because proof of cohabitation is sufficient. In the case of polygamous marriages, only one wife can be admitted legally in the Netherlands. The regulations governing the family reunification of holders of permanent residence permits are less stringent than those relative to the family reunification of persons admitted under temporary permits, whose income must meet certain standards if immediate relatives are to gain admission. For holders of permanent residence permits, involuntary unemployment is not a ground for refusing the admission of immediate family members and there are no requirements regarding duration of marriage for the admission of spouses. However, a person admitted on a family reunification permit can obtain a permit on his or her own right only by becoming employed.

In the event of divorce, a person on a dependant residence permit risks deportation unless he or she has been married for at least three years of which one year should have been spent in the Netherlands. If the divorce takes place after those conditions have been fulfilled, the person concerned receives a temporary residence permit which may be renewed annually for five years, on the condition that he or she has a job and is likely to have a job in the coming year. Only women or men who have to take care of young children are temporarily exempt from the requirement of having paid employment. Instead, they are eligible for welfare benefits on the same basis as other single unemployed parents. Conversion to a permanent residence can take place after five years as in the case of any other holder of a temporary residence permit (Handboek Minderheden, 1984).

Although there are no restrictions on the employment of holders of family reunification or dependant permanent residence permits, because women are generally admitted in a "dependant" category their status with respect to men is hardly enhanced by their legal position. In fact, migrant women are especially dependent on their husbands shortly after migration, when they have to adapt to a new situation, sometimes after lengthy separations. If conflict between the spouses arises, women are particularly vulnerable since divorce can curtail their right to remain in the Netherlands. Furthermore, migrants with low incomes, especially the young, may find it difficult to qualify for family reunification.

C. Migration

Because the migration of women from Morocco and Turkey to the Netherlands is a relatively recent phenomenon, most of the Moroccan and Turkish women in the country grew up in the countries of origin (table 36). Thus, 42 per cent of the Moroccan migrant women interviewed by the 1984 IFS originated in the eastern part of Morocco, especially at Nador, a poor rural area characterized by heavy out-migration. Altogether, 83 per cent of the Moroccan female migrants originated in northern or northeastern Morocco, though only 43 per cent of the population of Morocco lives there. In the case of Turkish women, migration was less selective by region, though some concentration can nevertheless be observed. Central Anatolia, a vast, predomi-

TABLE 36. MAIN REGION OF RESIDENCE UNTIL AGE 14 OF
MOROCCAN AND TURKISH WOMEN IN THE NETHERLANDS
AND IN THE COUNTRIES OF ORIGIN
(*Percentage*)

Region	Migrants in the Netherlands	Women in the country of origin
Moroccan women		
East	42	7
Centre-North	23	14
Northwest	18	23
Centre	6	5
Centre-South	4	25
Tensift	2	14
South	2	12
Abroad	3	-
TOTAL	100	100
Number interviewed	(177)	(4 105)
Turkish women		
Centre	58	28
North	12	12
West	11	29
East	11	20
South	9	12
Abroad	1	-
TOTAL	100	100
Number interviewed	(225)	(4 431)

Sources: 1984, Immigrant Fertility Survey (IFS); 1979-1980
Moroccan Fertility Survey (MFS); 1978 Turkish Fertility Survey
(TFS).

nantly rural area, in which the country's capital is located, was the region of origin of 58 per cent of the Turkish female migrants interviewed, although only 28 per cent of the Turkish population lives in that region. With the exception of northern Turkey, migrants from all other areas are underrepresented.

As expected, the women interviewed by the 1984 IFS have relative short durations of residence in the Netherlands, averaging seven to eight years. Most had migrated as young adults to join their husbands, though one in 10 Moroccan women and one in five Turkish women arrived in the Netherlands as children (before age 15). Overall, the average age at migration was low: 23 years for Turkish women and 27 for Moroccan women. The duration of residence of Turkish husbands was on average three years longer than that of their wives, but between Moroc-

can wives and husbands the difference was almost eight years. Clearly, family reunification has often been preceded by long periods of separation: 10 years or longer were no exception, especially among Moroccan couples. However, as the first wave of family reunification has run its course, marriage migration has increasingly taken the place of the reunification of couples married long before migration and the periods of separation have tended to decrease.

Several researchers have pointed out that the separation of families has led to a change in women's roles. When the women left behind lived in urban areas, they were more likely to live separately from relatives and in-laws and, consequently, to gain decision-making power regarding financial and other matters after their husband's migration. However, for women who stayed behind in the company of relatives to whom their husband had delegated his decision-making power, the potential for a change in the roles of women was considerably more limited (Kudat, 1975; Abadan-Unat, 1977; van den Berg-Eldering, 1981; Gemeente Utrecht, 1984).

Having a husband in the Netherlands or getting married to a man already living there was the basic reason for the migration of most of the women interviewed. When asked about their attitude towards migration, 90 per cent of the women interviewed by the 1984 IFS replied that, at the time of migration, they had wanted to move to the Netherlands. Such positive answers may be the result of rationalization after the fact and of women's reluctance to admit negative feelings. Furthermore, women who were opposed to migration may not have migrated at all or may have returned to the country of origin. The replies of the women interviewed tended to be straightforward and practical, reflecting the ambivalence or doubts that some of them felt at the time of migration. As factors prompting their migration in the country of origin they mentioned being tired of living alone, their hard life at home, problems with their in-laws, and having few or no relatives left in the country of origin. As attractive factors in the country of destination they mentioned their expectations regarding employment opportunities, a better life and future for the family and for the children, better educational facilities, medical services etc.   One fifth of the women interviewed mentioned considerations about their children as reasons to migrate, including the difficulty of raising them in the absence of their father and the existence of better educational opportunities in the Netherlands. Lastly, 8 per cent of the women said that they were curious about life in Europe, and 5 per cent of Moroccan women and 8 per cent of Turkish women declared that they had not wanted to migrate because they liked life in the country of origin better, they had wanted to stay near their relatives, or they were afraid to live in a foreign country.

These results are confirmed by a study of 105 Moroccan and Turkish women in the city of Utrecht (Gemeente Utrecht, 1984), and by an earlier study by van den Berg-Eldering (1981) among 45 Moroccan families interviewed in the Netherlands during the mid-1970s. Van den Berg-Eldering found that the more important the position of a woman within the household, the greater her decision-making power regarding migration. Indeed, some women forced their husbands to choose between returning to Morocco or arranging for family reunification. Marriages contracted with Moroccan men that already worked in the Netherlands often ended in divorce if the wives did not join their husbands abroad. In some cases, the bride's migration to the Netherlands was one of the conditions for the marriage to take place, but the women involved often did not have a say in that decision (van den Berg-Eldering, 1981, pp. 60-61).

Once family reunification takes place, a woman is likely to lose whatever independence she might have acquired while her husband was working abroad since the husband will, in all likelihood, reclaim his pre-migration roles and position. In addition, migrant women depend on their husbands while they become adapted to their new environment, especially since they rarely speak Dutch. Consequently, migration may, at least initially, affect negatively their position within the family (Gemeente Utrecht, 1984).

At any particular point in time the total population of migrant women residing in a country is composed of a rather heterogeneous group in terms of migration history. Table 37 displays the distribution of the

TABLE 37. MOROCCAN AND TURKISH MIGRANT WOMEN IN THE NETHERLANDS, AGED 15-49 AND STILL IN THEIR FIRST MARRIAGE, BY TIMING OF FAMILY REUNIFICATION: 1984
(*Percentage*)

Type	Turkish women	Moroccan women
Marriage precedes husband's migration and the wife's migration occurs over six months after marriage	47.0	43.7
Husband's migration precedes marriage and marriage precedes woman's migration by over six months	10.1	30.5
Marriage and woman's migration occur within six months of each other	24.0	18.0
Woman's migration precedes marriage by more than six months	18.9	7.8
TOTAL	100.0	100.0
Number of women.........................	(217)	(167)

Source: 1984 Immigrant Fertility Survey (IFS).

women interviewed by the 1984 IFS according to type of family reunification. The largest group (44 per cent of the Moroccan women and 47 per cent of the Turkish women) consists of the wives of the original group of migrant workers, that is, women who were married in their country of origin, were separated from their husbands for more than six months after the latter migrated to the Netherlands, and then joined them abroad. Prior to their migration these Moroccan and Turkish women had, on average, 5.3 and 3.2 children, respectively.

Moroccan men were more likely than Turkish men to be single at the time of migration, then marry a woman from the home country and apply still later for family reunification in the Netherlands, with the interval between marriage and the migration of the wife exceeding six months. Among the women interviewed, almost one third of those from Morocco belonged to that category, against just 10 per cent of the Turkish women.

Women migrating as children (before age 15) or within six months of their marriage constituted 43 per cent of the Turkish women interviewed and 26 per cent of the Moroccan women. Many of them were the daughters or daughters-in-law of the original migrant workers. Their lower percentage among

Moroccan women may be attributed to the tendency of Moroccan newly-wed women to remain in the home country for relatively lengthy periods. Furthermore, the Moroccan migration process to the Netherlands is somewhat more recent than that of the Turkish population.

Though the data available do not allow more precise characterizations of the different groups of female migrants, those identified above are adequate proxies for the different waves or generations of migrants. Therefore, the groups identified differ not only in their marriage and migration histories but also in a number of other demographic and socio-cultural characteristics (table 38). As expected, women who migrated as children or shortly after

TABLE 38. SELECTED CHARACTERISTICS OF MOROCCAN AND TURKISH MIGRANT WOMEN IN THE NETHERLANDS, AGED 15-49 AND STILL IN THEIR FIRST MARRIAGE, BY TYPE OF MIGRATION: 1984

	Turkish women		Moroccan women	
	Marriage precedes migration by over six months	Other	Marriage precedes migration by over six months	Other
Mean age (years)	36	24	37	25
Mean duration of marriage (years)	18	6	19	6
Mean age at immigration (years)	28	16	30	18
Mean duration of residence (years) ...	8	8	7	7
Of urban origin[a] (percentage)	37	67	56	84
Owning home in country of origin (percentage)	82	47	63	33
Completed at least primary education (percentage)	29	84	16	58
Speaking Dutch (percentage)	12	54	19	65
Currently employed (percentage)	20	37	5	15
Number of women	(124)	(93)	(124)	(43)

Source: 1984 Immigrant Fertility Survey (IFS).
NOTE: The first type of migration considered corresponds to the sum of the first two types identified in table 37, the second type (category denominated "other") corresponds to the sum of the last two types listed in table 37.
[a]Type of place where woman lived during most of her life before reaching age 14.

marriage are, on average, younger, better educated, more likely to originate in an urban area and have a better command of the Dutch language than women who migrated at least six months after marriage. In addition, the ties of the first group of women with the country of origin are probably weaker. Since many women in that group married only after they migrated, they are less likely to have owned a house in Morocco or Turkey and, because their financial position in the Netherlands is weak (they are young and have relatively low incomes), they are unlikely to acquire real state in that country over the short run.

D. EDUCATION

Among the Moroccan and Turkish women interviewed, 60 and 29 per cent, respectively, have never learned to read and write. Illiteracy is highly correlated with age (table 39) and is more widespread among the general female population of Morocco and Turkey than among migrant women from those countries in the Netherlands. Indeed, the younger the women, the larger the literacy gap between migrants and the general female population of the countries of origin. Clearly, young migrant women in the Netherlands have had educational opportunities that are not available in their home countries. About 20 per cent of the Moroccan and Turkish migrant women aged 15-29 have completed secondary school or earned a higher degree, a figure that compares positively with the 5 and 10 per cent, respectively, of women aged 15-29 in Morocco and Turkey who have achieved a similar level of educational attainment. Yet, overall, the proportion of migrant women who have attended school in the Netherlands is small (10 per cent of both Moroccan and Turkish female migrants). Among Turkish migrants, another 60 per cent attended school only in Turkey and 30 per cent never attended school. In the case of Moroccan women, 60 per cent never attended school and 30 per cent only attended school in Morocco (table 40).

A high proportion of Moroccan and Turkish women have a poor command of Dutch: 30 per cent declared that they spoke no Dutch at all and 40 per cent said they spoke only a "little". About 30 per cent

TABLE 39. EDUCATIONAL ATTAINMENT OF MOROCCAN AND TURKISH EVER-MARRIED WOMEN IN THE NETHERLANDS AND IN THE COUNTRIES OF ORIGIN, BY AGE GROUP
(*Percentage*)

| | Turkish women | | | Moroccan women | |
| | Netherlands 1984 | Turkey | | Netherlands 1984 | Morocco 1979-1980 |
		1978	1983		
15-29					
Illiterate	9	38	30	40	85
Incomplete primary	9	11	8	16	1
Completed primary	61	42	51	21	10
Secondary or higher	20	10	11	23	5
30-39					
Illiterate	38	54	46	52	89
Incomplete primary	27	14	13	11	0
Completed primary	25	24	32	17	7
Secondary or higher	10	8	9	20	4
40-49					
Illiterate	63	65	56	96	98
Incomplete primary	30	14	13	4	1
Completed primary	7	17	25	0	1
Secondary or higher	0	5	5	0	0
All ages (15-49)					
Illiterate	29	49	41	60	89
Incomplete primary	19	12	11	11	1
Completed primary	39	30	39	14	7
Secondary or higher	13	8	9	15	3

Sources: 1984 Immigrant Fertility Survey (IFS); 1979-1980 Moroccan Fertility Survey (MFS); 1978 Turkish Fertility Survey (TFS); Hacettepe University, 1987.

NOTE: In the case of women in Morocco, the data seem to refer to the highest type of schooling attended, rather than to that completed. In particular, those reported here as having incomplete primary education are women who can read and write but who did not attend school, and those reported as having completed primary education are women who attended primary school.

had tried or were trying to improve their command of Dutch by taking language courses. Without adequate language skills, migrant women have few opportunities for continuing their education. That is more likely to be the case for women who migrated to join their husbands than for those who migrated as children.

However, even Moroccan and Turkish women who arrived in the Netherlands as children may not have equal educational opportunities as their male counterparts. Van Praag and Muus (1987) found that the school enrolment of Dutch, Moroccan and Turkish boys and of Dutch girls in age groups 12-14

and 15-17 was similar, but that the enrolment of Moroccan and especially Turkish girls aged 12-14 was 2-8 percentage points lower than the school enrolment of other groups; and of those aged 15-17, enrolment was 8-15 points lower. Other studies have also documented the relatively low levels of school enrolment among Moroccan and Turkish girls, especially those who were older when they arrived in the Netherlands. Causes cited for staying away from school include that girls have to help in the home because of their mothers' illness; that girls do not feel at ease in school; or that the father opposes the daughter's school attendance (De Vries, 1987; Penninx, 1988). Furthermore, Moroccan and Turk-

TABLE 40. MOROCCAN AND TURKISH WOMEN IN THE
NETHERLANDS, BY COUNTRY IN WHICH THEY ATTENDED SCHOOL
(Percentage)

Country	Turkish women	Moroccan women
Never attended school	32	61
Morocco/Turkey only	56	29
Morocco/Turkey and the Netherlands[a]	11	7
Netherlands only	0	3
TOTAL	100	100
Number of women.......................	(225)	(177)

Source: 1984 Immigrant Fertility Survey (IFS).

[a]Including a few women (1 per cent per nationality) who went to school in other Western European countries than the Netherlands.

ish children do not pursue their education to the same advanced levels that Dutch children attain. A study among students registered in kindergarten, primary and secondary schools in Amsterdam in 1982 indicates that, to a large degree, the outcome is a function of migration at higher childhood ages and therefore is associated with a late start in the Dutch educational system (Hoolt, 1987a and 1987b, also reported in Penninx, 1988, pp. 115-116). However, Moroccan and Turkish students born in the Netherlands are still a small and atypical group, dominated by children of mixed marriages, and those who arrived as pre-schoolers seem more likely to reach only lower rather than higher secondary education in comparison to Dutch students (Hoolt, 1987a). A recent study among Moroccan and Turkish students aged 12-18 confirms Hoolt's main findings: migration at older childhood ages and low socio-economic status have a negative effect on school careers, but those factors do not completely explain differences in educational attainment between different groups of students (Roelandt and Veenman, 1990).

E. LABOUR FORCE PARTICIPATION

Among married female migrants, Turkish women are more likely to work for wages than Moroccan women, and the difference is most striking among women under age 25 (table 41). Overall, 27 per cent of Turkish married women and only 8 per cent of Moroccan married women have a job according to the 1984 IFS. Furthermore, whereas working Turk-

ish women have varied backgrounds, those from Morocco are highly selected, originating mostly in the urban areas of the home country (Bouw and Nelissen, 1986). The percentage of married women having a job is highest among those in age group 25-39: 32 per cent among Turkish women and 13 per cent among Moroccans. Among women under 40, the proportion having a job varies little between Turkish migrants, Dutch women and women in Turkey. In contrast, very few Moroccan female migrants aged 15-29 and 40-49 work, even in comparison with women in Morocco.

Within the age range 15-49, married migrant women in their forties are the least likely to have a job. The proportion holding a job is lower than that of Dutch women aged 40-49 or of women in that age group living in the countries of origin (table 42). The nature of the jobs open to unskilled migrant women doubtless contributes to that outcome. Women in Morocco and Turkey are more likely to be engaged in unpaid family work or in doing piece-work at home (Bouw and Nelissen, 1986). In the Netherlands, in contrast, they must compete for low-paid jobs outside the home. Given the shortage of jobs, employers are more likely to hire younger women and, consequently, older women experience greater unemployment and often drop out from the labour force altogether. Unemployment levels may be inferred from a comparison of tables 41 and 42, which show, respectively, the proportion of women actually employed and that of women who either have a job or are looking for one (the labour force participation rates). The proportion of women aged 40-49 in the labour force is twice as high as those holding a job, meaning that half are looking for work. Among younger migrant women (under 25), the proportion looking for work amounts to 7 per cent among Turks and 10 per cent among Moroccans. The desire to have a job is strongest among women who have previous work experience: one in three is looking for a job. Very high unemployment rates among migrant women were also recorded by the 1985 National Labour Force Survey, which showed that, whereas 16 per cent of all women in the labour force were unemployed, the proportion unemployed reached 66 and 49 per cent, respectively, among Moroccan and Turkish migrant women.[9] The equivalent figures for men were 11 per cent for the

TABLE 41. Employed[a] Moroccan and Turkish women in the Netherlands and in the countries of origin, by age group
(Percentage)

Age	Turkish women		Moroccan women	
	Netherlands	Turkey	Netherlands	Morocco
15-24	29	35	3	13
25-39	32	39	13	18
40-49	13	42	2	18
15-49	27	39	8	17

Sources: 1984 Immigrant Fertility Survey (IFS); 1978 Turkish Fertility Survey (TFS); 1979-1980 Moroccan Fertility Survey (MFS).
[a]Irrespective of the number of hours per week.

TABLE 42. Moroccan, Turkish and Dutch women in the Netherlands who are working or looking for work[a], by age group
(Percentage)

Age	Turkish women	Moroccan women	Dutch women
15-24	36	13	52
25-39	41	13	43
40-49	26	4	36
15-49	36	10	44

Sources: 1984 Immigrant Fertility Survey (IFS); 1981 Netherlands Labour Force Survey.
[a]Women working for pay at least 20 hours per week or looking for paid work. Dutch women irrespective of marital status; among migrant women only the ever-married are considered.

total male population, 42 per cent for Moroccans and 34 per cent for Turks (Ankersmit, Roelandt and Veenman, 1988, p. 53).

In the Netherlands, migrants work predominantly as unskilled or semi-skilled workers in the industrial or service sectors where most of the reductions in employment have occurred. However, such reductions cannot explain the difference between the unemployment rates of native and foreign workers. Unequal access to the labour market due to conscious or unconscious discrimination undoubtedly also plays a part (Penninx, 1988).

About one third of married female migrants from Turkey did not have a job at the time of interview but had had one before (table 43). Differences in work

experience, measured in terms of having had a job, between the various age groups may result from a generation effect, in the sense that working outside the home has become more acceptable than it used to be; a reporting effect, in the sense that women may not consider work carried out at home in the country of origin as "a job" and may not report it; and a selection effect, in the sense that women marrying young are, at least temporarily, opting for marriage and child-bearing rather than for paid work.

In addition to the general economic situation and the potential existence of discrimination on the part of employers, personal characteristics are also important determinants of a woman's decision to work and of her chances of being employed. Multivariate analysis has been used to determine the relative importance of such factors in determining women's employment status, that is, whether a woman was working or not at the time of interview[10] (Schoorl, 1987b). Turkish women who migrated at a young age, have lived for a relatively long time in the Netherlands, have few children living at home, and have a good command of Dutch are most likely to work. After other factors are controlled for, the influence of education diminishes considerably.

As in the case of Dutch women with comparable educational attainment levels, the need for income is the most important reason compelling migrant women to work (Bouw and Nelissen, 1986). The income earned by migrant women contributes to support the family and about half the migrant women who work send part of their income to relatives in the home country. Migrant women, just as Dutch women, are also prompted to work outside the home so as to get to know other people, avoid the social isolation of remaining at home, or gain independence and control over their own lives. Although Turkish migrant women do not mention contact with other people as a reason to work, they actually have more contacts with colleagues than Moroccan women (Bouw and Nelissen, 1986). The majority of the working Moroccan and Turkish female migrants (60 per cent) and 40 per cent of a group of comparable Dutch women do not receive any help with household chores from their husbands. Husbands also provide little assistance with child care: among Dutch and Moroccan working women, the husband helps in

TABLE 43. PAST AND CURRENT LABOUR FORCE PARTICIPATION OF MOROCCAN AND TURKISH WOMEN
IN THE NETHERLANDS, BY AGE GROUP
(Percentage)

Age	Turkish women				Moroccan women			
	Currently employed	Previously employed	Total ever employed	Number of women	Currently employed	Previously employed	Total ever employed	Number of women
15-24	29	25	54	(69)	3	29	32	(31)
25-39	32	33	65	(110)	13	13	26	(94)
40-49	13	44	57	(46)	2	4	6	(52)
15-49	27	32	59	(225)	8	13	21	(177)

Source: 1984 Immigrant Fertility Survey (IFS).
NOTE: All women, including those who never worked, make 100 per cent.

about half the cases, otherwise daughters, mothers or other women assist. Moroccan women sometimes use the very limited day-care facilities available in the Netherlands. In Turkish families, female relatives usually help with child care, although some husbands also assist (IFS, 1984; Rivanoglu-Bilgin, Brouwer and Priester, 1986). According to Bouw and Nelissen (1986), one third of Turkish women sent their children to Turkey, where grandmothers took care of them. Turkish women whose husbands help with child care are likely to be those who managed their households on their own while they were separated from their husbands, or young educated women belonging to couples that consider it normal for husband and wife to share household tasks. The existence of these couples does not necessarily indicate that Turkish migrants are adapting to Dutch norms since, as Rivanoglu-Bilgin, Brouwer and Priester (1986) point out, similar changes in gender roles are taking place in Turkey.

Given that most women who work do so full time (IFS, 1984; Bouw and Nelissen, 1986) and that they tend to carry the full burden of household and child-care tasks, it is no surprise that many complain of tiredness and bad health. Some even stop working after a number of years (Rivanoglu-Bilgin, Brouwer and Priester, 1986). In those cases, the incursions of men and women into each other's domains are only temporary, to provide needed help, and do not represent lasting changes in gender roles within the family (Bouw and Nelissen, 1986).

The occupational distribution of Moroccan and Turkish female migrants is presented in table 44. Differences in the age groups used reduce the comparability of the figures across sources. Moreover, the data span a period of seven years and the samples used, especially where Moroccan women are concerned, are very small. Therefore, the data in table 44 should only be taken as indicative. Nevertheless, those data in conjunction with several studies concerning the position of migrant women[11] indicate that they work mainly in the service sector as cleaners or in laundries, in the food and textile industries, or in sweat-shops doing piece-work for the clothing industry. Overall, 90 to 95 per cent of migrant women work in occupations of the service or the manufacturing sector, as compared to only 28 per cent of all working women aged 15-44 in the Netherlands. However, Ankersmit, Roelandt and Veenman (1989) report lower proportions of migrant women engaged in those occupations and higher proportions in the scientific or professional, commercial and administrative occupational groups.[12]

In the Netherlands, as in virtually every country, a strong distinction exists between men's and women's jobs. In addition, migrant women tend to concentrate in jobs or occupations that few Dutch women occupy. Even when Dutch and migrant women work in similar occupations (as cleaners, for instance), the terms of work are not always equal. Generally, Dutch women secure higher paid jobs with better benefits than migrant women, and the jobs of Moroccan female migrants also tend to be better than those occupied by Turkish migrant women (Bouw and Nelissen, 1986). Some low-paying and generally unattractive jobs and occupations seem to be reserved for migrant women.

Only a minority of migrant women have higher education and work in scientific or professional occupations, including as civil servants or social workers. So far, the only indication of upward social mobility or at least of diversification in the occupational structure is that younger migrant women who are employed are more likely to work in administrative jobs than older women (Schoorl, 1987b; Ankersmit, Roelandt and Veenman, 1989). The data in table 44 further suggest that there may be an increase in the percentage of migrant women working in administrative, commercial and scientific or professional occupations. However, several studies point out that migrant women with an urban background experience a loss of status relative to their position before migration, partly because they are compelled to work outside the home in order to maintain the same standard of living that they had enjoyed prior to migration. Although the position of migrant women in the Dutch labour market is indeed weak, most of them have experienced improvements in their material position after migration (Bouw and Nelissen, 1986).

F. FERTILITY

The timing of migration during a woman's life may influence many aspects of her life, including her educational opportunities, labour force participation and fertility behaviour. Thus, women who have spent most of their marital and reproductive life in their country of origin are less likely to have experienced changes in their fertility behaviour and attitudes than women who migrated at the beginning of their marriage. Women who migrated as children are even more likely to adapt to the norms and behaviour of the host society.

TABLE 44. EMPLOYED MOROCCAN, TURKISH AND DUTCH WOMEN IN THE NETHERLANDS, BY OCCUPATION: SELECTED YEARS[a]

(Percentage)

| Occupation | Turkish | | | Moroccan | | | Dutch |
	1981[b]	1984[c]	1988[d]	1981[b]	1984[c]	1988[d]	1988[e]
Scientific/professional	—	1	6	—	—	23	27
Management	—	—	1	—	—	—	1
Administrative	2	1	4	8	3	3	29
Commercial	—	—	5	3	3	13	13
Services	37	44	38	55	60	13	22
Agricultural	8	3	10	—	—	—	2
Industrial	53	51	37	35	34	49	6
TOTAL	100	100	100	100	100	100	100
Number of women	(92)	(134)	(136)	(40)	(37)	(31)	..

Sources: P. Brassé, and others, "Jonge Turken en Marokkanen op de Nederlandse arbeidsmarkt" (Amsterdam, Universiteit van Amsterdam, Instituut voor Sociale Geografie, 1983); T. Ankersmit, T. Roelandt and J. Veenman, "Minderheden in Nederland", *Statistisch Vademecum 1989* (The Hague, Central Bureau of Statistics, 1989); and Centraal Bureau voor de Statistiek, "Enquête Beroepsbevolking 1988", ('s Gravenhage, 1989).

NOTE: Em dash (—) indicates that the amount is nil or negligible; two dots (..) indicate that data are not available or are not separately reported.

[a]1981 and 1984: Women who are currently working or have previously worked for pay; 1988: Women who are currently working for pay.

[b]1981: Women aged 16-24 years.

[c]1984: Ever-married women aged 15-49 years.

[d]1988: Moroccan and Turkish women aged 16-44 years, but labour force participation among the Moroccan women in the sample was heavily concentrated in age group 16-29.

[e]1988: All women in the Netherlands aged 15-44 years.

143

The total fertility of Moroccan and Turkish migrant women has declined continuously since 1976, passing from 8.1 children per woman to 5.2 in 1988 among Moroccan women and from 5.1 to 3.2 children per woman among their Turkish counterparts. Fertility has declined in Morocco and Turkey as well. In Morocco, total fertility dropped from an estimated average of 5.9 children per woman in 1979 according to the Moroccan Fertility Survey carried out in 1979-1980 to 4.8 children per woman in 1987 according to the 1987 Enquête nationale sur la planification familial et la santé de la population (part of the DHS programme). In Turkey, total fertility has decreased from 4.6 children per woman in 1974-1979 to 4.1 in 1983 (Hacettepe University, 1987) and to an estimated 3.8 in 1988 (Hacettepe University, 1989). Compared to the Dutch fertility level of about 1.6 children per woman, those of Moroccan and Turkish women, both as migrants and in their home countries, are high. Although the interpretation of these total fertility levels is fraught with difficulties (see, for instance, the discussion in Schoorl, 1989), it is clear that fertility behaviour is changing among Moroccan and Turkish women, irrespective of whether they are migrants or have remained in the countries of origin.

The downward trend in fertility is confirmed by retrospective survey data on the number of children ever born to successive cohorts of Moroccan and Turkish women interviewed in the Netherlands (table 45). For instance, Moroccan migrant women born in 1935-1939, 1940-1944 and 1945-1949 had given birth, on average, to 6.4, 5.9 and 4.1 children, respectively, by the time they were 35-39 years old. The same cohorts of Turkish migrant women reported, on average, to have had 4.5, 4 and 3.5 children, respectively, by the time they reached ages 35-39.

A comparison of the fertility of migrant women with that of women in the countries of origin shows that, in general, the fertility of migrant women has been lower than that of women remaining in Morocco or Turkey (table 46). For instance, in 1984, 35-39 year-old Moroccan migrant women in the Netherlands had given birth, on average, to 4.2 children, while in Morocco, women aged 35-39 in 1979-1980 had had, on average, 6.1 children and those aged 35-39 in 1987 had had 5.5 children on average. Comparable estimates for Turkish women are 3.9 children per woman among migrants aged 35-39 in the Netherlands in 1984, compared to 5.5 and 4.9 chil-

TABLE 45. CHILDREN EVER BORN TO MOROCCAN AND TURKISH WOMEN IN THE NETHERLANDS, BY BIRTH COHORT AND AGE GROUP OF MOTHER

(*Mean number*)

Age group	Birth cohort						
	1935-1939	*1940-1944*	*1945-1949*	*1950-1954*	*1955-1959*	*1960-1964*	*1965-1969*
Moroccan women							
15-19	0.9	0.2	0.4	0.3	0.3	0.2	(0.4)
20-24	1.1	1.9	1.0	1.4	1.2	1.6	
25-29	3.2	3.9	2.5	2.9	2.6		
30-34	5.2	5.2	3.4	3.9			
35-39	6.4	5.9	4.1				
40-44	6.8	6.3					
45-49	7.4						
Turkish women							
15-19	0.2	0.4	0.3	0.2	0.3	0.3	(1.0)
20-24	1.0	1.4	1.2	1.4	1.3	1.7	
25-29	2.6	2.5	2.2	2.5	2.4		
30-34	3.6	3.6	3.0	3.3			
35-39	4.5	4.0	3.5				
40-44	4.9	4.4					
45-49	5.1						

Source: 1984 Immigrant Fertility Survey, 1984.

NOTE: Numbers in parentheses ( ) indicate that observations are fewer than 10.

TABLE 46. CHILDREN EVER BORN PER EVER-MARRIED WOMAN, BY CITIZENSHIP,
COUNTRY OF RESIDENCE AND AGE GROUP
(Mean number)

| Age group | Turkish women | | | Moroccan women | | | Netherlands |
| | Netherlands 1984 | Turkey | | Netherlands 1984 | Morocco | | Dutch women |
		1978	1983		1979-1980	1987	
15-19	(0.8)	0.7	0.7	(0.4)	0.8	0.5	0.2
20-24	1.7	1.8	1.7	1.6	1.9	1.5	0.5
25-29	2.4	3.0	2.9	2.6	3.3	2.8	1.1
30-34	3.4	4.3	4.1	3.9	4.9	4.2	1.8
35-39	3.9	5.5	4.9	4.2	6.1	5.5	2.0
40-44	4.6	6.0	5.4	6.7	7.1	6.8	..
45-49	6.0	6.3	5.7	7.4	7.1	7.4	..
TOTAL	3.1	3.9	3.7	4.1	4.6	4.3	..
Standardized[a]	3.3	4.0	3.7	3.8	4.5	4.1	..
Number of women	(225)	(4 431)	(5 398)	(177)	(4 105)	(5 982)	..

Sources: 1984 Immigrant Fertility Survey (IFS); 1978 Turkish Fertility Survey (TFS); 1979-1980 Moroccan Fertility Survey (MFS); Hacettepe University, 1987; Enquête nationale, 1989.

NOTE: Numbers in parentheses ( ) indicate that there were fewer than 10 observations; two dots (..) indicate that data are not available or are not separately reported.

[a]The standard used is the population of Moroccan and Turkish women in the Netherlands.

dren per woman among those aged 35-39 in 1978 and 1983, respectively, living in Turkey. Dutch women in that age group had, on average, only two children.

There is, however, little difference in the average number of children ever born declared by older migrant women and those living in the countries of origin (women aged 40-44 and 45-49). The small differences detected may be the result of the relatively late timing of migration in the lives of Moroccan and Turkish women aged 40 or over in 1984. Most of those women had most or all of their children in the country of origin, before migration. Indeed, 60 per cent of the migrant women aged 45-49 at the time of interview had arrived in the Netherlands after age 40, and among the remaining 40 per cent, most were aged 35-39 at the time of migration.

Interestingly, the average number of children desired[13] is lower among Moroccan and Turkish women in the Netherlands than among those in the countries of origin (table 47). The differences are more pronounced among Moroccan women and are more concentrated in the younger age groups than they are in the case of the two groups of Turkish women

being compared. Relative to the average number of children wanted by Dutch women, the numbers desired by Moroccan and Turkish women in the Netherlands are still fairly high, amounting to 4.7 children, on average, among Moroccan women and 3.4 children among their Turkish counterparts. However, younger migrant women in the Netherlands, whether Moroccan or Turkish, wish to have only three children, on average. Note that, because of the way in which the number of children wanted was estimated, that measure increases with age.

The generally lower actual and desired fertility of migrant women in the Netherlands may result not only from the adaptative behaviour of migrants but also from the selectivity of migration and from the disruptive effects of migration on fertility and nuptiality (Michel, 1974; Friedlander, 1978; Kane, 1984 and 1986; Goldstein and Goldstein, 1985; Ford, 1985; Hervitz, 1985; Carlson, 1985a, 1986; Santow, 1986 commenting on Carlson, 1985b; Nauck, 1987; Schoorl, 1990). However, the 1984 IFS indicates that the Moroccan women who migrated to the Netherlands were not selected in terms of fertility behaviour, that is, women who were already married before their husband migrated had, in general, as

145

TABLE 47. CHILDREN DESIRED PER WOMAN,[a] BY CITIZENSHIP,
COUNTRY OF RESIDENCE AND AGE GROUP
(Mean number)

| Age group | Turkish women | | Moroccan women | |
	Netherlands 1984	Turkey 1978	Netherlands 1984	Morocco 1979-1980
15-19	(2.9)	2.5	(2.5)	4.0
20-24	2.6	2.8	3.1	4.2
25-29	3.2	3.2	3.3	4.3
30-34	3.3	3.8	4.2	5.3
35-39	3.9	4.5	4.4	5.9
40-44	4.3	4.5	6.1	6.1
45-49	4.7	4.7	7.0	6.0
TOTAL	3.4	3.7	4.7	5.1
Standardized[b] ..	3.5	3.8	4.4	5.2
Number of women	(199)	(3 979)	(136)	(3 099)

Sources: 1984 Immigrant Fertility Survey (IFS); 1978 Turkish Fertility Survey (TFS); 1979-1980 Moroccan Fertility Survey (MFS).

NOTE: Numbers in parentheses ( ) indicate that observations are fewer than 10.

[a]The number of children desired was defined as the number of children surviving plus the number of additional children wanted by currently married women who supplied a numerical answer. Women who were not fecund (i.e., women who reported that they had been sterilized or were otherwise unable to have more children) were assumed not to want any more children.

[b]Standard is the combined population of Turkish and Moroccan women in the Netherlands.

many children prior to the husband's migration as women who were to stay in Morocco, once factors such as duration of marriage, regional origin and education were controlled for. Yet, when the husband migrated, the process of family formation was disrupted, causing the fertility of Moroccan and Turkish women just prior to their own migration to be significantly lower than that of women in the countries of origin who did not migrate.

Ideally, the study of the adaptation process should be based on longitudinal data. However, since those data are normally lacking, retrospective information[14] and data on duration of residence obtained from single-round surveys can be used to assess adaptation, assuming that a longer duration of residence provides greater opportunities for improving contacts with the host society. Such contacts may

take a variety of forms, including enrolling in further education or language courses, obtaining a job or making efforts to interact with the local population etc. Furthermore, the opportunities open or accessible to migrant women in the country of destination may, by themselves, influence fertility behaviour. For instance, if migrant women are more likely to work outside the home than in their country of origin or if child-care facilities are more easily accessible than in the home country, the opportunity costs of child-bearing will be assessed differently than prior to migration and are likely to lead to attitudinal changes. In addition, irrespective of migration, higher educational attainment among women and women's participation in the labour force usually lead to lower fertility (Singh and Casterline, 1985; Freedman, 1987). It is also likely that factors related to the country of origin, such as a migrant woman's socio-cultural background or the strength of her contacts with the country of origin after migration, may influence her fertility behaviour and attitudes, although such contacts will likely grow weaker as time since migration elapses.

In the case of Moroccan and Turkish female migrants in the Netherlands, factors related to the country of destination explain most of the differences in fertility levels and desires among migrants (Schoorl, 1989 and 1990). Labour force participation and education obtained in the Netherlands were major explanatory factors. Education obtained in the country of origin was also a significant factor explaining fertility differentials, but it applied mostly to older women. Other variables related to the country of origin were not statistically significant once other factors were controlled for, with the exception of type of background (urban or rural) in the case of the desired fertility of Turkish women. Variables related to the migration process, such as type of family reunification and duration of residence, lost most of their significance once other factors were controlled for. The role of duration of residence is ambiguous in any case: in the short run, the disruption of family formation due to migration may play a role. Among women who have lived in the Netherlands for a relatively long time, fertility seems to be somewhat lower, but the relationship is weak. It should be kept in mind, however, that, on average, Moroccan and Turkish migrant women have lived in the Netherlands for a period of only seven to eight years.

The fact that adaptative processes are at work is corroborated by the importance of education and labour force participation in the Netherlands as explanatory variables for differential fertility behaviour. In addition, overall fertility levels are probably influenced by a change in the composition of the migrant population. The group of migrant wives of men belonging to the first wave of migrant workers is declining relative to the group of migrant daughters and daughters-in-law, who not only come from generations that are themselves undergoing a process of change in the countries of origin (Allman, 1978; Abadan-Unat, 1981; Erder, 1985; Mernissi, 1985; United Nations, 1985), but who also migrate at younger ages and are therefore more likely to get at least part of their education in the Netherlands, are more likely to speak Dutch and, consequently, are more likely to become integrated to Dutch society.

G. Contraceptive use

The changes in fertility behaviour documented above are made possible by changes in contraceptive use. Thus, in every age group, the percentage of women using contraceptives is considerably higher among Moroccan and Turkish women in the Netherlands than among those living in Morocco or Turkey (table 48). In 1978, less than half the 30-34 year old women in Turkey and only one fourth of those in Morocco in 1979-1980 used contraception, whereas in 1984, 80 per cent of the 30-34 year-old migrant women from those countries living in the Netherlands were contraceptive users. More recent data from surveys in Morocco and Turkey indicate that contraceptive use has been increasing, nearly doubling in Morocco between 1979-1980 and 1987. Nevertheless, a considerable difference in contraceptive use remains between women in the countries of origin and female migrants in the Netherlands (Hacettepe University, 1987; Morocco, 1987).

Levels of contraceptive use among Moroccan and Turkish migrant women in the Netherlands are almost as high as those of Dutch women. The main exception is constituted by 15-24 year-old Moroccan women whose level of contraceptive use is relatively low because many of them are pregnant or want to become pregnant. The difference in levels of contraceptive use between Moroccan and Turkish migrant women and those in the countries of origin seems to be influenced primarily by differences in the availability and accessibility of contraceptive supplies and only secondarily by differences in the demand for contraception.

In the Netherlands the pill and, among women aged 30 or over, sterilization are the most popular contraceptive methods (table 49). These contraceptive attitudes of the whole population are likely to influence the choices and options open to migrant women. Thus, the pill and Depoprovera are not only the methods most often used by Dutch women but also by Moroccan and Turkish women. Dutch women aged 30 or over are more likely to opt for sterilization than migrant women. Even so, sterilization is the method of choice of a higher proportion of older migrant women in the Netherlands than of their counterparts in Morocco and Turkey: among women aged 35-44 in Morocco and Turkey, only 3 and 5 per cent, respectively, have been sterilized whereas among Moroccan and Turkish women in the Netherlands the equivalent proportions are 28 and 21 per cent, respectively. The comparable figure for Dutch women is 43 per cent.

In Turkey, young women tend to use the pill or the intra-uterine device (IUD), older women opt for sterilization. In 1978, 75 per cent of contraceptive users in Turkey resorted to methods other than the pill, IUD or sterilization. The most widely used method was withdrawal (Bulut, Cilingiroglu and Bertan, 1986). Data for 1983 indicate both an increase in the percentage of contraceptive users and an increase in the proportion using the pill or IUD. Nevertheless, still about half the women who reported using a contraceptive relied on withdrawal (Hacettepe University, 1987).

Regarding the type of contraceptive used, there are only small differences between women in Morocco and Moroccan women in the Netherlands. The pill is the method most commonly used, followed far behind by the IUD, sterilization and, other methods such as withdrawal and periodic abstinence which

TABLE 48. MARRIED WOMEN CURRENTLY USING CONTRACEPTION, BY CITIZENSHIP, COUNTRY OF RESIDENCE AND AGE GROUP
(*Percentage*)

| Age group | Turkish women | | Moroccan women | | | Female population |
| | Netherlands | Turkey | Netherlands | Morocco | | Netherlands |
				1979-1980	1987	
15-19	80	15	40	9	17	81
20-24	75	32	52	15	26	78
25-29	81	41	70	19	36	76
30-34	81	51	85	23	43	77
35-39	78	45	73	20	43	76
40-44	60	37	68	20	42	65
45-49	45	20	45	10	30	57

Sources: 1984 Immigrant Fertility Survey (IFS); 1978 Turkish Fertility Survey (TFS); 1979-1980 Moroccan Fertility Survey (MFS); Dutch Fertility Survey, 1982 (DFS); and the study "Sex in the Netherlands 1981".

TABLE 49. MARRIED WOMEN AGED 15-44 CURRENTLY USING CONTRACEPTION, BY CITIZENSHIP, COUNTRY OF RESIDENCE AND TYPE OF CONTRACEPTIVE METHOD USED

Citizenship and country of residence	Pill[a]	IUD	Sterilization	Other	Total	Percentage of users[b]
Turkish women						
Netherlands	61	16	11	11	100	75
Turkey	18	8	2	73	100	40
Moroccan women						
Netherlands	85	5	8	2	100	70
Morocco	72	8	3	17	100	20
Netherlands[c]	39	11	29	21	100	78

Sources: 1984 Immigrant Fertility Survey (IFS); 1978 Turkish Fertility Survey (TFS); 1979-1980 Moroccan Fertility Survey (MFS); Dutch Fertility Survey, 1982 (DFS); and the study "Sex in the Netherlands 1981".
[a]Including injections.
[b]Percentage of all married women aged 15-44 using contraception at the time of the survey.
[c]Estimate based on the Dutch Fertility Survey, 1982 (DFS) and the study "Sex in the Netherlands 1981".

are more commonly used in Morocco than in the Netherlands (see table 49 and Morocco, 1987).

Although abortion generally tends to be under-reported, 14 per cent of the Turkish women interviewed by IFS, and more than one in four of those aged 40-49, reported that they had had at least one induced abortion. High abortion rates are reported in Turkey as well (Hacettepe University, 1987). An in-depth study of 38 Turkish migrant women who applied for abortion revealed that many were ambivalent about the use of contraception and that being proved fecund was one of the factors prompting them to prefer abortion (Sieval, 1985).

As expected, the duration of marriage, the number of children a woman has had, and the desire to postpone the next pregnancy are the most important factors influencing contraceptive use among migrant women. In addition, women from a rural background are less likely to use contraception than women from an urban background. Factors related to migration as, for instance, duration of residence in the Netherlands and age at migration, did not affect significantly the likelihood of using contraception, except in the case of women who were already in their forties when they migrated: they were unlikely to start using contraception after migration. Migrant women with Dutch friends and acquaintances are more likely to use contraception than women who have no contact with Dutch women (Schoorl, 1987a).

In conclusion, migrant women appear to have already been motivated to use contraception prior to migration; however, lack of access to contraceptive supplies prevented their widespread use. Migration, by improving women's access to contraceptive supplies, contributed to increasing their use among migrants. As to the choice of method, migrant women generally followed the patterns set by Dutch women.

The fact that so many migrant women use contraception does not preclude them from having doubts about the methods they use or from being dissatisfied with them. Women in general report problems in using the pill correctly and have complaints about the pill's side effects, including irregular periods, a general feeling of illness, nausea, headaches, weight gain etc. Among Moroccan and Turkish women, such problems are likely to lead to a discontinuation of pill use or to the use of an alternative method (1984 IFS; Sieval, 1985; Rivanoglu-Bilgin, Brouwer and Priester, 1986; Morocco, 1987).

H. Conclusion

This analysis of some of the indirect indicators of the status of Moroccan and Turkish migrant women in the Netherlands provides valuable insights regarding the changes that women have experienced because of migration. However, it is difficult to determine the causes of changes in the status of migrant women because such changes may have been initiated in the society of origin prior to migration, they may have been triggered mostly by the migration process or they may result from changing behaviour as a response to new opportunities or from changes in attitude stemming from the adaptation process. As this paper shows, the data available do not permit a thorough assessment of the different components of change.

Moroccan and Turkish women in the Netherlands constitute at the same time a selected group, in the sense that they are not representative of the total female population of their countries of origin, and a heterogeneous group. They are, for instance, se-

lected in terms of place of origin, and a high proportion has rural backgrounds. They are heterogeneous in that several distinct groups coexist, in particular, women who migrated relatively late in their lives after lengthy separations from their husbands; women who migrated soon after they married; and women who migrated as children. The timing of migration in a woman's life is likely to be crucial in determining her position within the family and in society. Women whose husbands migrated after they had started a family were more likely to reach a certain independence during the years of separation. However, they also had to assume the responsibility of raising the children largely on their own. If they lived with their in-laws or other close relatives while the husband was abroad, their roles are less likely to have changed. Hopes for a better life and future, but also conflict with relatives or concern about the behaviour of children in the absence of the father were some of the main factors leading to the migration of the whole family. Not much is known about the role women played in making the decision to migrate, but communication between husbands and wives regarding migration seems to be the rule rather than the exception. Yet, many women may have felt that the final choice was not up to them. In general and other things being equal, young women without children tend to have less say in the matter than older women with children.

After migration, women run the risk of becoming highly dependent on their husbands and children, at least initially, given their lack of familiarity with the host society and their deficient command of the local language. Moreover, their dependent legal status increases their dependence on their husbands. Learning the receiving country's language or finding a job are ways of gaining some measure of independence.

On average, Moroccan and Turkish migrant women have higher levels of educational attainment than women in Morocco or Turkey, mostly because those who migrated as children have had better educational opportunities in the Netherlands. However, the educational attainment of Moroccan and Turkish women in the Netherlands is considerably lower than that of Dutch women. That outcome is related to the timing of migration: children born in the Netherlands to migrant parents are performing considerably better in school than children who arrived in the Netherlands at age 6 or later and who not only had to learn a new language but often had to adapt to a new educational system. Currently, second generation Moroccans and Turks in the Netherlands reach considerably lower levels of educational attainment than their Dutch counterparts, and among Moroccan and Turkish girls relatively low school enrolment rates prevail.

Since educational attainment largely determines the type of job and the income level one can secure, migrants who, for the most part, have received their education abroad, tend to be relegated to relatively undesirable and low-paid jobs. Female migrants are in a particularly weak position regarding their possible insertion into the Dutch labour market. Given the worsening economic situation and the increasing use of automation, jobs for unskilled workers are declining. When unemployment is high, the migrant's poor language proficiency, the need to secure work permits for family migrants, as well as a conscious or unconscious tendency among employers to discriminate, all militate against the employment of Moroccan or Turkish migrant women. To the extent that migrant women have been able to penetrate the partially sex-segregated Dutch labour market, they have been relegated not just to women's jobs but to migrant women's jobs, that is, jobs that have low wages and status.

Though most Moroccan and Turkish migrant women have improved their material position after migration to the Netherlands, the status of some women with urban backgrounds may have declined. These are women whose position in Morocco or Turkey, as wives of migrants, was relatively good but who find themselves after migration in the lower socio-economic groups, being faced with the need to work in order to meet the family's needs and to try to reach the standard of living that they had before migration.

Employed migrant women tend to work full time and bear, at the same time, full responsibility for managing the household and caring for the children. While in many families the husband helps with both household chores and child care, especially among the small and selected group of Moroccan working

women, women still undertake most domestic and child-rearing tasks. Furthermore, it is not clear to what extent the changes in gender-roles taking place among migrant couples are influenced by Dutch norms and values, or by the occurrence of similar changes in Morocco and Turkey.

Moroccan and Turkish women in the Netherlands have, on average, lower fertility and want fewer children than women in Morocco or Turkey, where fertility is also declining. This outcome seems to stem primarily from the better availability of and access to contraceptive supplies in the Netherlands as compared to Morocco and Turkey. Furthermore, increased education and labour force participation after migration are playing a role in the overall decrease of family size and the average number of children wanted. Although the relation between fertility levels and duration of residence is weak, it may be premature to draw conclusions about "assimilation": part of the changes observed have probably been initiated before migration, in the changing societies of origin, and the average duration of residence of Moroccan and Turkish women in the Netherlands is still relatively short, with most female migrants arriving in the country after they had had several children. Indeed, the orientation of the majority of those women is towards their own ethnic group, in which they have most of their contacts. In contrast, their daughters or daughters-in-law form a more diverse group in terms of migration history, education, language proficiency or legal position. Consequently it is still hazardous to make generalizations about the prospective socio-economic position or the changing status of Moroccan and Turkish migrant women in the Netherlands.

NOTES

[1]Greece, Italy, Morocco, Portugal, Spain, Tunisia, Turkey and Yugoslavia.

[2]Basically, family reunification is allowed in the case of spouses (irrespective of the duration of marriage), cohabiting couples and dependent children under 18 years of age who are still single (until 1 January 1991 the upper age limit was 21 years of age). Other requirements have gradually been relaxed, but a number of conditions remain, the most important being that "suitable" housing be available and that the principal migrant earn "sufficient" income to support those joining him or her.

[3]Defined as persons with Turkish or Moroccan citizenship plus persons born in Turkey or Morocco who have acquired Dutch

citizenship and those born in the Netherlands with at least one parent born in Turkey or Morocco.

⁴The number of Surinamese in the Netherlands—defined as persons who have Surinamese nationality (a small minority), who were born in Suriname and at least one of whose parents was born in Suriname—is estimated at 230,000-246,000 (Voets, 1990). The population of Moroccan or Turkish origin, if defined according to the same criteria, would number 147,000 and 186,000, respectively (Voets, 1989). Little is known about the demographic dynamics of an earlier group of migrants from Indonesia or the Dutch East Indies (some of whom were repatriating Dutchmen), who entered the Netherlands between 1945 and 1968. By the end of the 1960s this population subgroup was estimated at 250,000 persons excluding children born in the Netherlands (Surie, 1973). Ellemers and Vaillant (1985) estimate that the second and third generations include another 200,000 to 300,000 persons.

⁵"Second generation" is defined here to include all persons born in the Netherlands with at least one parent born abroad.

⁶A detailed description of the population registration system and the demographic statistics derived from it can be found in van den Brekel (1977), Storm and Verhoef (1987) and, with regard to foreign nationals and ethnic minority groups, in Schoorl (1982).

⁷The survey was carried out at the Netherlands Interuniversity Demographic Institute (NIDI) and was financed by the Netherlands Organization for the Advancement of Pure Research, The Interdepartmental Committee for Minorities Policy, and the National Programme for Demographic Research.

⁸Citizens of European Community countries, as well as foreigners with permanent residence permits, refugees, the spouses and minor children of permanent residents and refugees, and a number of other categories of foreigners are exempted from securing work permits. The Law on Foreign Employees establishes the requirements to obtain a work permit.

⁹The total participation rate, that is, the percentage of working and unemployed women aged 15-64 years among the total female population aged 15-64, was 39 per cent among Turkish women in the Netherlands and 17 per cent among Moroccan women (Ankersmit and others, 1988, p. 52).

¹⁰Nested logistic regression was used to test the strength of the relations between the independent and the various dependent variables considered. The dependent variables used included: citizenship, age, duration of residence, educational attainment, country where the person studied, municipality of residence, place of origin (village, town or city), number of children living at home, desire for more children, language proficiency, degree of contact with Dutch women, attitude towards the labour force participation of a daughter, husband's education, husband's employment situation.

¹¹See, for example, Brassé and others, 1983; Gemeente Utrecht, 1984; Bouw and Nelissen, 1986; Rivanoglu-Bilgin and others, 1986; Schoorl, 1987b.

¹²It is not clear if the lower figures cited by Ankersmit and others (1989, p. 65) are a function of time (late 1980s versus early to mid-1980s) or a function of sample size and structure. The high percentage of Moroccan women (mainly those aged 16-29) engaged in scientific or professional occupations seems particularly noteworthy.

¹³The measure of children wanted used here is based on a combination of past behaviour (the number of children a woman has already had) and desires for additional children. Women who are not fecund (i.e., women who have been sterilized or are otherwise unable to have any more children) have been assumed not to want any more children, while women who are not currently married have been excluded from the calculation of children wanted.

¹⁴Problems in using retrospective data stem from the fact that their quality can be impaired by memory lapses, errors in reporting the timing of events, adjustment of a person's evaluation of past attitudes or opinions depending upon consequent events.

REFERENCES

Abadan-Unat, Nermin (1977). Implications of migration on emancipation and pseudo-emancipation of Turkish women. *International Migration Review* (Staten Island, New York), vol. 11, No. 1 (Spring), pp. 31-57.

_____ (1981). *Women in Turkish Society*. Leyden, Netherlands: E. J. Brill.

Allman, J., ed. (1978). *Women's Status and Fertility in the Muslim World*. New York: Praeger Publishers.

Ankersmit, T., T. Roelandt and J. Veenman (1987). Minderheden in Nederland. *Statistisch Vademecum 1987*. 's Gravenhage: Staatsuitgeverij. The Hague: Central Bureau of Statistics.

_____ (1988). Minderheden in Nederland. *Statistisch Vademecum 1988*. 's Gravenhage: Staatsuitgeverij. The Hague: Central Bureau of Statistics.

_____ (1989). Minderheden in Nederland. *Statistisch Vademecum 1989*. 's Gravenhage: Staatsuitgeverij. The Hague: Central Bureau of Statistics.

Bouw, C., and C. Nelissen (1986). *Werken en zorgen. Een vergelijkend onderzoek naar de arbeidservaringen van Turkse, Marokkaanse en Nederlandse vrouwen*. 's Gravenhage: Ministerie van Sociale Zaken en Werkgelegenheid.

Brassé, P., and others (1983). *Jonge Turken en Marokkanen op de Nederlandse arbeidsmarkt*. Amsterdam: University of Amsterdam, Institute for Social Geography.

Bulut, A., N. Çilingiroglu and M. Bertan (1986). Is withdrawal a handicap for fertility regulation? *Nüfusbilim Dergisi* (Ankara, Turkey), vol. 8, pp. 45-55.

Carlson, E. (1985a). Marriage, childbearing and migration to Australia. Paper prepared for the International Union for the Scientific Study of Population (IUSSP) General Conference, Florence, June 1985.

_____ (1985b). The impact of international migration upon the timing of marriage and childbearing. *Demography* (Washington, D.C.), vol. 22, No. 1, pp. 61-72.

_____ (1986). Using the Melbourne Family Survey in migration research: reply to Santow. *Demography* (Washington, D.C.), vol. 23, No. 3, pp. 469-471.

Central Bureau of Statistics (1984). *Onderzoek Gezinsvorming 1982*. 's Gravenhage: Staatsuitgeverij.

_____ (1989). *Enquête Beroepsbevolking 1988*. 's Gravenhage.

de Vries, M. (1987). *Ogen in je rug. Turkse meisjes en jonge vrouwen in Nederland*. Alphen aan de Rijn: Samsom.

Ellemers, J. E., and R. E. F. Vaillant (1985). *Indische Nederlanders en gerepatrieerden*. Muiderberg: Coutinho.

Erder, T., ed. (1985). *Family in Turkish society*. Ankara: Turkish Social Science Association.

Ford, K. (1985). The fertility of immigrants to the United States: evidence for the disruption model. Paper prepared for the International Union for the Scientific Study of Population (IUSSP) General Conference, Florence, June 1985.

Freedman, R. (1987). Fertility determinants. In *The World Fertility Survey. An Assessment*, J. Cleland and C. Scott, eds. New York: Oxford University Press.

Friedlander, D., and C. Goldscheider (1978). Immigration, social change and cohort fertility in Israel. *Population Studies* (London), vol. 32, No. 2, pp. 299-317.

Gemeente Utrecht (1984). *Turkse en Marokkaanse vrouwen in Utrecht: Een verkennend onderzoek naar hun positie en ervaringen.* Utrecht: afdeling onderzoek, ROVU.

Goldstein, S., and A. Goldstein (1985). Migration/fertility inter-relations: methodological concerns and findings from Thailand and Malaysia. Paper prepared for the International Union for the Scientific Study of Population (IUSSP) General Conference, Florence, June 1985.

Hacettepe University, Institute of Population Studies (n.d.). *Turkish Fertility Survey 1978, First Report.* Ankara.

_____ (1987). *1983 Turkish Population and Health Survey.* Ankara.

_____ (1989). *1988 Turkish Population and Health Survey.* Ankara.

Handboek Minderheden (1984). Alphen aan den Rijn: Samsom.

Hervitz, H. M. (1985). Selectivity, adaptation, or disruption? A comparison of alternative hypotheses on the effects of migration on fertility: the case of Brazil. *International Migration Review* (Staten Island, New York), vol. 19, No. 2 (Summer), pp. 293-317.

Hoolt, J. (1987a). *Het onderwijsniveau van migrantenkinderen. Deel A: Samenvatting van de onderzoeksresultaten en beleidsconsequenties.* Gemeente Amsterdam: Afdeling Bestuursinformatie, Afdeling Onderzoek en Statistiek, 1987.

_____ (1987b). *Het onderwijsniveau van migrantenkinderen. Deel B: Resultaten van het onderzoek naar de onderwijspositie van etnische groepen in het Amsterdams onderwijs.* Gemeente Amsterdam: Afdeling Bestuursinformatie, Afdeling Onderzoek en Statistiek, 1987.

Kane, T. T. (1984). The fertility of guestworker populations in the Federal Republic of Germany. Unpublished doctoral dissertation. Princeton, New Jersey: Princeton University, Ph.D.

_____ (1986). The fertility and assimilation of guestworker populations in the Federal Republic of Germany: 1961-1981. *Zeitschrift für Bevölkerungswissenschaft* (Boppard am Rhein, Germany), vol. 12, No. 1, pp. 99-131.

Kudat, A. (1975). *Stability and Change in the Turkish Family at Home and Abroad: Comparative Perspectives.* Berlin: International Institute for Comparative Social Research.

Lim, Lin Lean (1995). The status of women and international migration. Chapter III in the present volume.

Mernissi, F. (1985). *Vrouwen in Marokko aan het woord.* Weesp: Het Wereldvenster.

Michel, A. (1974). *The Modernization of North African Families in the Paris Area.* 's Gravenhage: Mouton.

Morocco, Ministry of Public Health (1984). Enquête nationale sur la fécondité et la planification familiale au Maroc. Rapport national 1979-80. Rabat.

_____, Service des études et de l'information sanitaire and Demographic and Health Surveys, Westinghouse (1987). Enquête nationale sur la population et la santé (ENPS-I). Rabat, and Columbia, Maryland: 1989.

Nauck, B. (1987). Individuelle und kontextuelle faktoren der kinderzahl in Türkischen migrantenfamilien. *Zeitschrift für Bevölkerungswissenschaft* (Boppard am Rhein, Germany), vol. 13, No. 3, pp. 319-344.

Ouakrim, M., and M. Ayad (1985). *Planification Familiale, Fécondité et Santé Familiale au Maroc 1983-84.* Rapport de l'Enquête nationale de prévalence contraceptive. Rabat and Columbia, Maryland: Ministry of Public Health/Westinghouse Public Applied Systems.

Pennix, R. (1988). *Minderheidsvorming en emancipatie: Balans van kennisverwerving ten aanzien van immigranten en woonwagenbewoners.* Alphen aan den Rijn: Samsom.

Priester, M., and L. Brouwer (1982). *Vrouwen tussen heden en weleer. Turkse vrouwen in Nederland en Turkije.* Amsterdam: University of Amsterdam, Anthropology-Sociology Centre.

Rivanoglu-Bilgin, S., L. Brouwer and M. Priester (1986). *Verschillend als de vingers van een hand. Een onderzoek naar het integratieproces van Turkse gezinnen in Nederland.* Leyden: State University.

Roelandt, T., and J. Veenman (1986). *Minderheden in Nederland. Achtergrondstudie 1986 bij het rapportagesysteem Toegankelijkheid en Evenredigheid.* Rotterdam: ISEO.

_____ (1987). *Minderheden in Nederland. Achtergrondstudie 1987 bij het rapportagesysteem Toegankelijkheid en Evenredigheid.* Rotterdam: ISEO.

_____ (1990). *Allochtonen van school naar werk.* 's Gravenhage: SDU.

Santow, G. (1986). A comment on Elwood Carlson's "The impact of international migration upon the timing of marriage and childbearing". *Demography* (Washington, D.C.), vol. 23, No. 3, pp. 467-468.

Schoorl, Jeannette J. (1982). *Allochtone deelpopulaties in Nederland. Een inventariserende studie van bronnen van statistische gegevens en demografisch onderzoek.* Voorburg: NPDO.

_____ (1985). Geboorteregeling van Turkse en Marokkaanse vrouwen benadert Nederlands niveau. *Demos* (The Hague), vol. 1, No. 6, pp. 41-43.

_____ (1987a). Contraceptive use among Turkish and Moroccan immigrants in the Netherlands. Paper prepared for the European Population Conference, Jyväskylä, 1987.

_____ (1987b). Turkse en Marokkaanse vrouwen op de Nederlandse arbeidsmarkt. *Demos* (The Hague), vol. 3, No. 8, pp. 62-64.

_____ (1989). Kindertal en geboorteregeling bij Turkse en Marokkaanse vrouwen in Nederland: "assimilatie"? *Migrantenstudies*, vol. 5, No. 3, pp. 55-69.

_____ (1990). Fertility adaptation of Turkish and Moroccan women in the Netherlands. *International Migration* (Geneva), vol. 28, No. 4 (December), pp. 477-496.

Sieval, Z. (1985). *Anticonceptie: bevrijding of bedreiging?* 's Gravenhage: Stimezo.

Singh, S., and J. Casterline (1985). The socio-economic determinants of fertility. In *Reproductive Change in Developing Countries*, J. Cleland and J. Hobcraft, eds. Oxford: Oxford University Press.

Storm, H., and R. Verhoef (1987). Bevolkingsstatistieken in Nederland. Maandstatistiek van de Bevolking (Central Bureau of Statistics), vol. 35, No. 5, pp. 24-34.

Surie, H. G. (1973). De gerepatrieerden. In *Allochtonen in Nederland*, H. Verwey-Jonker, ed. 's Gravenhage: Staatsuitgeverij.

United Nations (1985). Socio-economic development and fertility decline in Turkey. Background paper prepared for the Project on Socio-economic Development and Fertility Decline. New York.

van den Berg-Eldering, L. (1981). *Marokkaanse gezinnen in Nederland.* Alphen aan den Rijn: Samsom.

van den Brekel, J. C. (1977). *The use of the Netherlands system of continuous population accounting for the population statistics.* Voorburg: Netherlands Central Bureau of Statistics.

van der Most van Spijk, M. (1985). *Gezondheidszorg voor Turkse en Marokkaanse Kinderen in Amsterdam.* Amsterdam: Gemeentelijke Geneeskundige en Gezondheidsdienst.

van Praag, C. S., and P. J. Muus (1987). Achterstand maar geen stagnatie. Etnische groepen in het onderwijs. *Migrantenstudies*, vol. 3, No. 2, pp. 14-27.

Voets, S. Y. (1989). *Allochtonen in Nederland. Demografische ontwikkeling en samenstelling naar nationaliteit, geboorteland en geboorteland van de ouders.* The Hague: Netherlands Interdisciplinary Demographic Institute.

IX. THE EXPERIENCE OF FILIPINO FEMALE MIGRANTS IN ITALY

Odo Barsotti* and Laura Lecchini**

Italy, a country that until the mid-1970s had been a source of numerous emigrants, began attracting migrants when the traditional labour-importing countries of Europe put a stop to the recruitment of foreign labour. During the 1980s, in particular, Italy became the destination of significant numbers of migrants from developing countries. However, because the country lacked policies geared towards the admission of foreign workers, migration occurred largely at the margin of the law. Consequently, towards the late 1980s Italy found itself hosting a significant number of undocumented migrants. To cope with such developments and introduce adequate migration controls, laws regulating the migration of citizens of countries that did not belong to the European Community were adopted in 1986 and 1990. Both laws established, among other things, regularization drives for undocumented migrants already present in Italy. Consequently, 105,000 and 216,000 foreigners regularized their status in 1986 and 1990, respectively. Including those persons, official statistics indicated that towards the end of 1990, 635,000 citizens of non-member countries of the EC were legal residents of Italy (OECD, 1991). Among them, 23 per cent originated in Northern Africa, 12 per cent in sub-Saharan Africa and 18 per cent in Asia. Moroccans (78,000), Tunisians (41,000), Filipinos (34,000) and Senegalese (25,000) constituted the largest citizenship groups originating in developing countries.

This paper focuses on the migration experience of Filipinos in Italy, a high proportion of whom are women. The analysis presented is based on a survey carried out during late 1986 and 1987 among migrants living in Tuscany, particularly in the metropolitan area of Florence and along the coast. The survey covered six of the most numerous groups of migrants from developing countries in that region, namely, citizens from Cape Verde, the Islamic Republic of Iran, Morocco, the Philippines, Senegal and Tunisia. There are considerable differences between the different citizenship groups. In particular, whereas nearly all Senegalese migrants are men, women account for the majority of Filipino migrants. Given that, despite the differences in their distribution by sex, those two migrant groups report economic reasons as the main ones prompting their migration, their experiences regarding the outcome of migration are contrasted below.

A. DATA USED

Because of the recency of the migration flows being studied and of the irregular legal status of most of the migrants concerned, it was not possible to obtain an adequate sampling frame on which to base the selection of a representative sample of migrants. Instead, one had to resort to indirect and partial information on the groups of migrants present in Tuscany and their likely location. During a first stage, the data from the 1981 census and those derived from the number of residence permits granted in 1984 were used to identify the main groups of migrants from developing countries living in Tuscany. However, it was soon recognized that those data failed to be representative of the true situation because of the undocumented nature of the migration involved. Consequently, an effort was made to gather information on the likely geographical and occupational distribution of migrants from representatives of political, trade union and religious organizations, from the migrants themselves, and from other informants. Official data were useful in establishing the likely demographic and occupational characteristics of the main migrant groups. Based on

*Dipartimento di Scienze Sociale, Università degli Studi di Pisa, Pisa, Italy.

**Dipartimento di Statistica e Matematica Applicata all'Economia, Università degli Studi di Pisa, Pisa, Italy.

Although both authors share responsibility for this paper, Odo Barsotti was responsible for sections A, B, C and D, while Laura Lecchini was in charge of sections E, F, G and H.

both official statistics and reports by knowledgeable informants, a rough demographic profile of the different migrant groups was derived and it was used to select purposely the individual migrants to be interviewed. Thus, the final group of migrants interviewed had distributions by age, sex and marital status similar to those derived in advance. About 70 interviews were completed in each, the Filipino and the Senegalese migrant communities. Although there was no statistical basis to establish an adequate sample size, the number of interviews was not increased because there was considerable homogeneity in the responses obtained to most of the questions posed.

The actual fieldwork to identify the migrants that would be interviewed varied considerably from one migrant group to another, depending on the types of occupations that their members engaged in. Iranians, for instance, were known to work as petty traders in specific sites, as rug dealers and in the restaurant business. By covering systematically the locations in which such activities took place, a sample of individuals could be selected for interview. Senegalese were similarly concentrated in petty trade and in agriculture, activities taking place in specific locations. Filipinos, in contrast, were engaged mostly in domestic service within private households and were, therefore, more difficult to locate. In their case, snow-ball sampling techniques were used to identify the individuals to be interviewed (Barsotti, 1988).

The questionnaire used gathered general socio-demographic information on the migrant as of the time of interview, including sex; date and place of birth; citizenship; marital status; educational attainment; language ability, particularly regarding Italian; use of the mass media; place of residence of immediate relatives; and number and demographic characteristics of relatives living with the migrant. It further recorded detailed information about the current labour force participation of the migrant, the type of occupation, sector of economic activity etc.; about any economic activity that the migrant was engaged in just before migration, and about the migrant's first employment experience in Italy. Questions were also asked about the migrant's motives in leaving the country of origin and choosing Italy as a

country of destination, and about intermediaries that might have helped the migrant to reach Italy and find a job there. Several questions were geared to assess the migrant's satisfaction with his or her current job and housing facilities, and the migrant's level of interaction with the host society, including the use of social and health services. Lastly, migrants were asked about their intentions regarding settlement in Italy, family reunification or their eventual return to their countries of origin.

In order to elicit truthful responses from the migrants interviewed and to facilitate communication with those whose command of Italian was poor, interviews were carried out by well-trained interviewers who already had experience working with migrant communities. The research team included a Filipino and a Senegalese who carried out interviews in the language of the migrants concerned. Their participation in the fieldwork contributed to allaying the fears and reducing the diffidence of the persons interviewed.

B. Characteristics of Filipino migrants

Among the 70 Filipino migrants interviewed, 67 per cent were women. Although the distribution by marital status of male and female Filipino migrants aged 14 or over was similar, with the majority being single (57 per cent of men and 55 per cent of women) and nearly 4 out of every 10 being married, the Filipino migrant women interviewed were considerably older than their male counterparts. Thus, 55 per cent of Filipino women were aged 30 or over compared to 35 per cent of Filipino men. Filipino women also displayed considerably higher levels of educational attainment than Filipino men. In particular, 78 per cent of Filipino women had completed at least 13 years of schooling while the equivalent proportion among Filipino men amounted to just 48 per cent. In addition, whereas 13 per cent of the women reported having completed at least 16 years of schooling, no men had reached similar educational levels. However, despite their high level of schooling, Filipino women had generally found employment only as domestic workers. Male Filipino migrants had not done much better. Indeed, both male and female Filipinos were highly concentrated

154

in the personal services group of occupations (see table 50). Yet, male migrants were considerably less likely than female migrants to be holding jobs at all: 26 per cent of male Filipinos were unemployed and looking for work at the time of interview while no Filipino women were in that category.

Prior to migration, both Filipino men and women displayed lower rates of labour force participation than at the time of interview, but whereas men were

TABLE 50. CHARACTERISTICS OF FILIPINO MIGRANTS INTERVIEWED IN THE REGION OF TUSCANY, ITALY

| | | | Percentage | |
	Male	Female	Male	Female
Number of interviewees ..	23	47	33	67
Marital status				
Single	13	26	57	55
Married	9	19	39	40
Divorced	1	1	4	2
Widowed	0	1	0	2
Age group				
14-19	2	1	9	2
20-24	5	8	22	17
25-29	8	12	35	26
30-34	3	8	13	17
35-39	3	8	13	17
40-49	2	8	9	17
50-59	0	2	0	4
Years of schooling				
Less than 4	0	0	0	0
4-8	5	3	22	6
9-12	7	11	30	23
13-15	11	27	48	57
16 or over	0	6	0	13
Employment status				
Employed	17	46	74	98
Looking for work	6	0	26	0
Other	0	1	0	2
Occupation				
Domestic worker	15	46	88	100
Commerce	1	0	6	0
Food-processing	1	0	6	0
Employment status before migration				
Employed	14	31	61	66
Looking for job	5	5	22	11
Student	4	4	17	9
Home	0	7	0	15

TABLE 50 (continued)

| | | | Percentage | |
	Male	Female	Male	Female
Reason for migration				
Economic	16	40	70	85
Political	1	0	4	0
Family	4	3	17	6
Other	2	4	9	9
Year of arrival in Italy				
1972-1976	0	3	0	6
1977-1981	5	18	22	38
1982-1985	17	24	74	51
1986	1	2	4	4
Number of years in Italy				
Less than 1	1	2	4	4
1	9	6	39	13
2-3	6	12	26	26
4-6	6	20	26	43
7-10	1	6	4	13
More than 11	0	1	0	2
Continuity of presence in Italy				
Continuously	21	37	91	79
Short return to origin ..	1	9	4	19
Long return to origin ..	1	1	4	2
Type of dwelling				
Independent	1	3	4	6
With family or friends .	4	4	17	9
Rooming house	1	0	4	0
Shared room	1	0	4	0
In employer's home	15	38	65	81
Other	1	2	4	4
Intentions to stay in Italy				
4-6 months	1	0	4	0
7-12 months	1	0	4	0
2-3 years	4	4	17	9
More than 4 years	4	7	17	15
Indefinite	8	26	35	55
Permanent	0	3	0	6
Not known	5	7	22	15

more likely to be unemployed and looking for work, women tended to be engaged instead in household activities. However, whatever their employment experience in the country of origin, most migrants reported economic reasons as the main motive for their migration. Interestingly, female Filipino migrants were more likely to cite economic reasons than Filipino men and the latter were more likely to cite family reasons than Filipino women. Generally, differentials regarding the reasons for migration cited by men and women run in the opposite direction.

There are other indications that female Filipino migrants represent a rather special group. Data on the year of arrival in Italy or on the length of stay in the country indicate that Filipino women had a head start as migrants: they are the ones who started the migration chain. Thus, whereas none of the men interviewed had arrived in Italy before 1977, 6 per cent of the women declared that their arrival date fell within the period 1972-1976. In terms of length of stay, 30 per cent of male Filipino migrants had lived in Italy for at least four years, compared with 58 per cent of Filipino women. Probably because of their shorter average length of stay, Filipino men were more likely to have stayed continuously in Italy since their arrival (91 per cent had done so) than Filipino women (79 per cent had not left Italy since arrival).

C. FILIPINO AND SENEGALESE MIGRATION COMPARED

If, as documented above, there are significant differences between male and female Filipino migrants who, despite having a common socio-cultural background, seem to be responding differently to the opportunities that they perceive to exist abroad, there are even more marked differences between female Filipino migrants and male Senegalese in Italy. A comparison between the two groups is enlightening because it suggests that the socio-cultural characteristics of the societies of origin condition differentially the ability of men and women to respond to employment opportunities abroad.

In terms of demographic characteristics, Filipino migrant women resemble Senegalese migrant men in that both groups have a high proportion of single persons, though Filipino women are considerably older than Senegalese men (38 per cent of Filipino women were aged 35 or over at the time of interview compared with only 6 per cent of Senegalese men). Furthermore, as already noted, Filipino women have high levels of educational attainment that are simply not matched by those of Senegalese men. Among the latter, 4 per cent were illiterate, 50 per cent had at most attended Koranic school and not a single one had more than 16 years of schooling (see table 51).

TABLE 51. CHARACTERISTICS OF FILIPINO MIGRANT WOMEN AND SENEGALESE MIGRANT MEN COMPARED

(*Percentage*)

Age	Filipino women	Senegalese men
Age group		
18-19	2	2
20-24	17	23
25-29	26	40
30-34	17	28
35 or over	38	6
Marital status		
Unmarried	55	64
Married	43	36
With children	30	32
Without children	13	4
Widowed or divorced	2	0
Educational attainment		
Illiterate	0	4
Koran school	0	49
Years of study		
4-8	6	30
9-12	23	4
13-15	57	13
16 or over	13	0
Economic activity and occupation		
Occupied	71	79
Clerical worker	50	4
Blue collar worker	9	16
Self-employed	12	9
Petty trader	0	17
Agricultural worker	0	34
Looking for work	6	21
No fixed occupation	23	0
Place of previous residence		
Rural area	2	45
Small town	81	38
Big city	17	17

Before migration, 79 per cent of the Senegalese migrants had held a job, most of them in agriculture (34 per cent), as petty traders (17 per cent) or as unskilled workers (16 per cent). In contrast, half of the Filipino women interviewed had been employed as clerical workers. Furthermore, whereas most Filipino women had lived in an urban environment before migration (81 per cent came from small towns and 17 from large urban areas), the proportion of Senegalese men with an urban background was lower (38 per cent had lived in small towns and 17 per cent in large urban centres). Consequently, when Filipino women reached Italy, they were already accustomed to the type of life characteristic of urban environments, with high educational levels and familiarity with a Western mode of life. Senegalese men, on the other hand, are not only less likely to have urban backgrounds, but also have been less exposed to Western cultural values, mainly because of their low educational attainment and the religious nature of the education that most have received.

These profiles suggest that Senegalese men are more likely to experience greater difficulties in adapting to Italian society than Filipino women and that the latter are likely to benefit the most from migration. However, as the discussion below shows, the opportunities open for developing-country migrants in the host society do not allow the full realization of their potential for advancement, particularly in the case of Filipino women.

D. Migrants and the labour market

Most migrants from developing countries in Italy find jobs in the least qualified occupations of the service sector or in seasonal agricultural work, fishing, construction and some branches of industry. Often, they work in the informal sector or in that part of the labour market known as the "hidden economy", which operates at the margin of State and trade union regulations (Pugliese, 1983). The marginal and precarious position of recent developing country migrants in developed countries is associated with their growing numbers and their irregular status (Calvanese and Pugliese, 1989). During the 1980s, there was hardly any expansion of labour demand in European countries but, increasingly, unappealing jobs that were rejected by native workers have been filled by migrants. Migrants are thus found working in low-paid jobs, lacking long-term security and the possibility of advancement (Mingione, 1985; Pugliese, 1985).

In this context, migrant women are usually highly segregated in terms of employment. Most find work in domestic service, often living with the family that employs them. In Tuscany, 85 per cent of the female migrants from developing countries regularizing their status in 1987 were employed as domestic workers

TABLE 52. DOMESTIC WORKERS AMONG MIGRANTS FROM DEVELOPING COUNTRIES WORKING IN TUSCANY AND REGULARIZED ACCORDING TO LAW NO. 943/87

(*Percentage*)

Area of origin	Domestic workers	Others
Asia	90	10
Sub-Saharan Africa	92	8
Northern Africa	53	47
Latin America	74	26
Total	85	15

Source: Provincial Offices for Labour and Full Employment, Tuscany, unpublished tabulations.

(see table 52). Clearly, well-educated women, such as most of those originating in the Philippines, are overqualified for domestic service. However, they are at a disadvantage in competing for other types of jobs, particularly since they often lack a good command of Italian. Furthermore, Italian women themselves have been joining the labour force in growing numbers and, consequently, competition for the better paid jobs that are normally performed by women has been increasing.

Migrant women thus satisfy a labour demand that does not originate in the productive sector of the economy but answers rather to the needs of middle-class families and serves mostly to redistribute income. Indeed, the growing demand for domestic workers may be at the root of growing female migration to Italy, given that Italian women are no longer willing to perform such work, especially because of the relatively low salaries paid, the low status of domestic workers and the long hours of work involved. Only migrant women are still willing to live in the employer's home and be ready to serve at almost any time.

In the case of Filipino female migrants, becoming domestic workers in Italy certainly represents a loss of status in terms of occupation. Given the nature of domestic work, for most of them migration has meant deskilling rather than acquiring new skills. Furthermore, because there are few prospects for occupational mobility in Italy, the change experienced is not likely to be transitory. Yet, Filipino women accept such a situation and even find satisfaction in their work. Thus, 60 per cent of those interviewed declared themselves satisfied, and among the rest only half declared that they were not satisfied because their professional qualifications were neither used nor recognized. The reason for such apparently contradictory answers lies in that Filipino women earn considerably more as domestic workers in Italy than they would in better occupations in the Philippines. Thus, 68 per cent of those interviewed reported that they became domestic workers because there were no other employment opportunities open to them in Italy and that their salaries in domestic service were better than those earned in the Philippines.

An indication that there is a high demand for Filipino domestic workers is that, among the migrants interviewed, 40 per cent had signed a contract before emigrating and a further 44 per cent found a position soon after they reached Italy. Prospective migrants in the Philippines are attracted by the possibility of securing contracts before migration and of being assured relatively high salaries by Filipino standards. In addition, the fact that most domestic workers are offered accommodation in the employer's home is a further incentive for the migrant, who is generally intent on maximizing savings. Among the Filipino migrants interviewed, 81 per cent lived at their work site and 75 per cent of them reported that they were satisfied with their living conditions. Furthermore, almost 80 per cent expressed satisfaction with their level of earnings and 85 per cent reported that they sent money regularly to their families in the Philippines. Thus, from the migrant's perspective, the outcome of migration has many positive aspects. Consequently, women are willing to sacrifice their skills and career prospects, not to mention a normal family life, in order to ensure the financial means needed to support the family remaining in the home country.

Although male migrants from developing countries are also subject to marginalization within the labour market, especially if they lack education and skills, the employment opportunities open to them are more varied. Thus, members of some citizenship groups have managed to carve certain labour-market niches for themselves and have achieved considerable occupational mobility. That is the case of Iranian men, whose relatively high levels of edu-

cational attainment have certainly contributed to a positive labour market experience (Barsotti, 1988). Even among the Senegalese, whose low levels of educational attainment and lack of skills are likely to relegate them to low-status jobs, there is some evidence of a measure of occupational mobility as their length of stay in Italy increases. Thus, among the Senegalese male migrants interviewed, a quarter had given up petty trade, the economic activity that they performed when they first arrived in Italy, and were holding jobs as unskilled workers in industry or small-scale production.

Considering the restricted employment opportunities open to Senegalese men in their home country and their relative lack of work experience in the modern manufacturing sector, their work in Italy is likely to represent for them both an improvement in status and a useful training experience. However, this does not mean that their economic situation is other than precarious. Indeed, although Senegalese men tend to have earnings similar to those of Filipino women, they are likely to save less partly because they do not receive free lodging. As a result, Senegalese men are less likely to send regular remittances to the family left behind (80 per cent of those interviewed declared that they had never sent remittances or that they had sent them only sporadically).

Since providing financial help to the family of origin is one of the main objectives of migrants from developing countries (80 per cent of Filipino women and over 70 per cent of Senegalese men indicated that sending money to the family left behind was one of their reasons for migration), it is not surprising that over 75 per cent of Senegalese men declared that they were completely dissatisfied with their current earnings. In contrast, only 20 per cent of Filipino women expressed the same opinion.

E. MIGRATION AND THE ROLE OF THE FAMILY

It has been suggested that the immediate family of migrants plays a significant role in determining who migrates and when, since the family has a stake in ensuring its survival by diversifying its sources of income. Although the survey did not inquire about the influence that close family members played in reaching the decision to migrate, it included several questions about the family of origin that provide some information about the likely role of the family in the migration process. As already noted, single persons predominate among the Filipino migrant population. Migrant women, in particular, tend to be single at the time of migration (among those interviewed, over two thirds were single when they left the Philippines). In general, Filipino female migrants belong to large families, averaging 5.6 children, among whom, on average, two are abroad.

Because of the marked sex imbalance characterizing the Filipino population in Italy, Filipino women are unlikely to find husbands among their co-citizens, especially since the nature of their work leaves them relatively little time to socialize. Consequently, only 18 per cent of the Filipino women who were single when they arrived in Italy have married since. That proportion is especially low if one considers that the average age of Filipino migrants upon arrival was 24 years and their average length of stay in the country is close to five years. That is, a considerable proportion of Filipino migrant women find themselves in the ages where marriage is common. It thus appears that, by migrating to Italy, Filipino women are likely to remain single or, at the very least, are constrained to postpone marriage for a long time, especially considering that most of the migrants interviewed expressed the intention of staying in Italy for at least four more years (76 per cent did so).

Among the Filipino women who were married when they left the Philippines (32 per cent of those interviewed), the majority (87 per cent) left husband and children behind. For them, therefore, migration has meant a long-term separation from their family of procreation. Even after an average of almost six years in Italy, over 60 per cent of those migrants still have their husband and children (on average four per woman) in the Philippines. Indeed, those who have managed to initiate the process of family reunification, have been joined mostly by the husband (23 per cent) rather than by the children (15 per cent), but in no case by both. The lower likelihood that a woman may choose to be rejoined by her children than by her husband is attributable to the type of work women perform, which is not compatible with the upbringing of young children. Indeed, among the Filipino women who got married in Italy, only one third have had children and several of them (30 per cent of the cases) have sent the children back to the Philippines to be cared for by the family of origin.

Usually, the family of origin plays a role in selecting who will migrate. Younger members are normally selected for emigration and, if they are married, the family of origin undertakes the responsibility of caring for the children and husband left behind. The family not only liberates its labour force to engage in migration, it also plays a role in selecting the country of destination and in placing the migrant abroad. Thus, family ties are crucial in eliciting help from relatives already established abroad. Most Filipino woman arriving in Italy can rely on a network of friends and relatives to help them adapt to the new society and find a job. Such networks help migrants feel less separated from their families of origin and are also a means of social control. The extent of existing networks can be gauged by noting that nearly 60 per cent of Filipino women share accommodations with relatives (uncles, aunts, cousins etc.) during their time away from work and spend much of their free time with them.

The prospects for family reunification vary according to the family and legal status of Filipino migrant women. The majority of married women (two thirds) wish to be joined in Italy by their husband and children. The rest wish to return to the Philippines. The latter include women who have disagreements with their husbands that induced them to leave their country or whose children are grownups with families of their own.

Single women also wish to be reunited with their families (38 per cent declared that they did). Most of them see the possibility of family reunification as providing an opportunity for their siblings to share their positive migration experience. Interestingly, Filipino women who married after migration expressed no wish to be joined by family members left behind.

In contrast with Filipino women, married Senegalese men have generally not been joined as yet in Italy by their wives or children. Neither is there much evidence suggesting that single Senegalese men have been joined by their siblings. However, within occupations, there is a strong solidarity among Senegalese nationals working in Italy. They often live together in groups constituted by persons originating from the same village in the country of origin. Thus, 90 per cent of the Senegalese migrants interviewed reported that they lived together with co-nationals and shared living expenses with them. Once more, in contrast with Filipino women, Senegalese migrant men have the intention of returning to Senegal within the short term. Consequently, family reunification is not part of their immediate plans.

F. NATURE AND ROLE OF INTERMEDIARIES

Given that the migration of Filipino women to Italy is driven by the demand for their services, it encourages the intervention of intermediaries during the various stages of the migration process. Officially, an Italian wishing to hire a domestic worker abroad should present an application to the Consulate or Embassy of the country concerned. As is well known, private recruitment agencies are common in the Philippines and relatives already working abroad often help in the recruitment process.

According to the reports of the women interviewed, both private agencies and relatives or friends already present in Italy played a key role in furnishing information about living conditions and employment opportunities in Italy. Relatives also provided financial assistance to help defray the costs of migration. Thus, 23 per cent of the Filipino women interviewed declared that they had received help from relatives and friends to travel to Italy and secure a job there, 58 per cent had had recourse to private agencies, 11 per cent had depended on their prospective employers, and only 9 per cent had migrated entirely on their own (see table 53). In addition, 55 per cent of the migrant women interviewed reported that, in making the decision to migrate, they had relied on information, as well as on assistance to defray the costs of migration, received from relatives already abroad. Relatives abroad were often instrumental in securing a first job for the migrant. Thus, 41 per cent of the Filipino

women interviewed reported that relatives had arranged their first job (table 54).

In contrast to the migration of Filipino women, that of Senegalese men is supply driven. The demand for their services in Italy does not appear to be the factor determining their migration. Rather, the socio-economic conditions in Senegal trigger their emigration. Under those conditions, recruitment agencies have no role to play and, consequently, 83 per cent of the Senegalese men interviewed reported that they had arranged their migration to Italy on their own (table 53). Furthermore, given that Senegalese migrants still lack an extensive network of relatives in Italy that could provide assistance during the migration process, only 17 per cent had relied on relatives and friends to assist in making migration possible and most of them (89 per cent) had relied on friends and co-citizens to secure a job once in Italy. Although the assistance obtained from relatives and friends usually involved only the provision of general information, it was decisive in prompting Senegalese men to select Italy as their country of destination. Once in Italy, Senegalese men could

TABLE 53. INTERMEDIARIES AIDING IN THE MIGRATION PROCESS AS REPORTED BY MIGRANTS
(*Percentage*)

Intermediary	Filipino women	Senegalese men
Family members	19	15
Friends	4	2
Private agencies	58	0
Employers	11	0
None	9	83

TABLE 54. INTERMEDIARIES USED TO SECURE A FIRST JOB IN ITALY AS REPORTED BY MIGRANTS
(*Percentage*)

Intermediary	Filipino women	Senegalese men
International agency	7	0
Private agency	27	0
Family members	41	2
Friends or co-nationals	19	89
Others	7	9

count on the solidarity of their co-nationals and, especially, on that of their co-villagers to get settled.

G. Migration projects and the impact of migration on the host society

Although both Filipino women and Senegalese men move to Italy with the purpose of increasing their earning capacity, the two groups have nevertheless different migration plans and expectations. Thus, while Senegalese migrants aim at accumulating capital to set up some commercial activity in the home country, pay for a dowry, or buy land or a home, Filipino women aim instead at remaining in the host country.

Given their project of return, Senegalese men are intent not only on accumulating savings but also on gaining skills. Thus, two thirds of the Senegalese migrants interviewed said that they were willing to attend courses, especially those providing technical skills that were in demand in Senegal (e.g., to become mechanics, electricians, plumbers etc.). Most Senegalese migrants reported that their intention was to stay in Italy only a short time and that they did not want to be joined by their immediate relatives.

In contrast, Filipino women are interested in adapting fully to the Western style of life, a style that is already making inroads in their home country but whose expression is limited by the low levels of living of the majority of the Filipino population. Women with high levels of educational attainment are particularly conscious of the limitations imposed by their society of origin and see migration as a way of reaching their goals. Even when they can only secure low-status jobs in Italy, Filipino women have, in general, no intention of trying to improve their prospects by acquiring better qualifications. Thus 64 per cent of those interviewed declared that they did not want to attend any course to improve their credentials. Given that Filipino women devote most of their salary to sending remittances to their families back home and that such remittances are mostly used to meet daily survival needs, women and their families have little possibility of capital accumulation. Hence, the prospects facing migrants if they were to return to their home country are less than appealing.

From the perspective of Italian society, the migration of Filipino women poses few problems because they do not compete for jobs with the native population and satisfy a labour demand that would otherwise go unmet. Furthermore, because most Filipino women live in the home of their employers, they do not compete for housing with the native population and their need for social services is minimal given that they are still young and have few dependants living with them in Italy. Their social isolation may also be considered positive, since it leads to minimal friction with the host society. However, it also prevents Filipino women from becoming truly integrated into their new environment. One may even argue that Italian society feels that Filipino women pose no threat precisely because they are women and, therefore, obedient and malleable. In contrast, Senegalese men, though less in number, are seen as competing for scarce jobs with lower class Italians and as a threat to the cultural identity of Italian society.

In terms of policy, this assessment suggests that the repatriation intentions of Senegalese migrants should be reinforced by helping them acquire the skills that they seek and promoting their return to Senegal as part of international cooperation. In the case of Filipino women, measures to favour family reunification would allow them to normalize their family life in Italy and contribute to foster their adaptation to the host society. Although family reunification would also increase the demand of the Filipino community for housing and social services, it would be the first step towards a diversification of the activities that migrant women could perform in Italy and would, in the long run, reduce their concentration in a single occupation. Yet, as the visibility of Filipino women in society increases, frictions with the host society are likely to rise. The extent to which such frictions are forestalled will be a measure of the effectiveness of migration and social policies.

H. Migration and the status of migrant women

Ideally, to assess the impact of migration on the status of migrant women, it would be necessary to compare such status before and after migration. However, since migrants are generally interviewed only after migration has occurred, the only possibility of assessing their previous status is through retrospective information that is likely to be coloured by the migration experience itself. Given that the survey did not ask sufficiently detailed questions on the status of female migrants before migration, we decided to rely on information provided by leaders of the Filipino community in Italy, Filipino women involved in the trade union movement or in political activities in Italy, and representatives of private and religious organizations working with migrants from developing countries in Italy.

Focusing first on Filipino migrant women who were married at the time of migration and who therefore left their husbands and children behind, an interesting question to address is whether and to what extent migration has resulted in their gaining decision-making power within the family or in a more egalitarian relationship between husband and wife. Although by migrating and working abroad, married women have become the main source of income for their families, it does not seem that they have gained much in terms of decision-making power or influence within the family. The long-term separation of the family that migration entails seems to be partly responsible for that outcome, especially because, while they are abroad, women relinquish their roles as wives and mothers, and have difficulty asserting their views or opinions about family matters. The separation of the family reduces the interaction of its members and leaves few opportunities for roles to evolve as a result of changed circumstances. Given their social isolation in the host society, Filipino women, especially if married, tend to uphold their family's values and, considering their migration as essential for their family's well-being, see themselves mostly as instruments of the family rather than as independent actors. Thus, their separation from their immediate family, rather than weakening family ties, strengthens them. The success of the Filipino female migrant is equated with the success of her family. Yet, acceptance of traditional roles seems to be at the basis of such family cohesiveness and, when family reunification takes place, the husband has no problem in reasserting his role as head of the family and main, if not sole, decision maker.

Although it would seem more likely that single Filipino women would adopt the norms and values of the host society, particularly given their intention to stay in Italy over the long run, their desire to conform with the host society conflicts with the norms of the Filipino community from which they derive all kinds of support. Consequently, few have as yet embarked on the road to emancipation. Furthermore, Filipino migrant women in general have few opportunities to change their frame of reference given their limited exposure to the social and behavioural norms of the host society. Undoubtedly, their low-status jobs reduce their ability to respond to the opportunities for emancipation that the new socio-cultural surroundings offer them. A poor command of Italian also contributes to their isolation. Indeed, about 75 per cent of the Filipino women interviewed said that their command of Italian was not adequate. However, only 20 per cent were prepared to attend courses to improve their language abilities.

There are other indications of the relative social isolation of Filipino women working in Italy. Most of the women interviewed had no Italian friends or acquaintances aside from their employers. Only one quarter of the women interviewed met during their free time with Italians or with non-Filipino migrants. The rest socialized only with fellow Filipinos. Such segregation results in the maintenance of the norms and values of the society of origin, including those determining the status of women. Consequently, Filipino women are still far from emulating the ways of their Italian counterparts. As one migrant suggested, Filipino women find themselves squeezed between two walls: one that they do not as yet manage to climb, representing emancipation and integration into the host society, and another which they have already managed to transcend, representing tradition. Although the latter still exerts a powerful shadow, it is unlikely that over the long run Filipino migrant women will remain within its bounds.

Barsotti, Odo (1988). L'indagine sul campo: modalità di approccio e metodologia di campionamento. In *La Presenza Straniera in Italia: Il Caso della Toscana*, Odo Barsotti, ed. Milan, Italy: Franco Angeli.

Calvanese, F., and E. Pugliese (1989). Emigrazione e immigrazione in Italia: tendenze recenti. Paper presented at the International Meeting on Emigrazione e Politica Migratoria negli Anni Ottanta held in Salerno-Fisciano, Italy.

Mingione, E. (1985). Marginale e povero: il nuovo immigrato in Italia. *Politica e Economia* (Rome), No. 6.

Organisation for Economic Co-operation and Development (OECD) (1991). Continuous Reporting System on Migration (SOPEMI), 1990. Paris.

Pugliese, E. (1983). Continuità e innovazioni nell'emigrazione italiana. *Inchiesta* (Rome), vol. 13, No. 62.

_____ (1985). Quale lavoro per gli stranieri in Italia? *Politica e Economia* (Rome), No. 9.

X. ANALYSIS OF CHANGES IN THE STATUS OF FEMALE RETURNEES IN GREECE

*Ira Emke-Poulopoulos**

Since 1974, when the main receiving countries in Europe decided unilaterally to stop the inflow of migrant workers, the nature of migration flows in Europe changed considerably as sizeable numbers of migrant workers and their dependants decided to return to the countries of origin. Greece, which had been an important source of migrant workers, experienced the return of some 325,000 Greek men and 302,000 Greek women during 1971-1985 (Petropoulos and others, 1990). In addition, the country started attracting foreign immigrants, some of whom were admitted because of their ties to Greece (they originated mostly in the former Eastern-bloc countries). Although Greece lacks immigration statistics allowing the estimation of migration inflows, there are indications that the number of immigrants has been growing and, since 1985, the number of residence permits granted to women has outnumbered those granted to men. In 1988, for instance, 31,277 residence permits were granted to foreign women against 30,284 granted to foreign men (as reported by the Directorate for National Security, Ministry of Social Order).

The literature on return migration does not generally focus on female returnees or on how the reasons for returning vary by sex (Kubat, 1984; ICM, 1986; Pessar, 1984; Pereira-Perista, 1988). Most studies relative to returning Greek migrants focus exclusively on men (Unger, 1981 and 1984; Fakiolas, 1984), although there is some information about the economic and social roles of female migrants in the countries of destination and on the reintegration problems that they face when returning to Greece (Emke-Poulopoulos, 1986 and 1988).

In analysing the effects of return migration, several groups of returnees can be distinguished. For instance, a distinction can be made in terms of the

country of previous residence since the experience of Greek citizens returning from the former Federal Republic of Germany is likely to differ significantly from the experience of those returning from the overseas countries of immigration (Australia, Canada or the United States of America) or from the experience of second and third generation Greeks returning from Eastern Europe. The latter constitute a very special group, being the descendants of former Greek citizens who fled the country at the time of the 1947-1949 civil war and who had been living in Eastern European countries and the former USSR since then. Until 1974, those Greek refugees were not allowed to return to Greece, but as of that year restrictions on their return were lifted and both the original refugees and their descendants have been returning to Greece where they are generally granted Greek citizenship. There have also been provisions allowing the return of Pontian Greeks, people of Greek ancestry from Pontus, Asia Minor. Pontian Greeks arrived in Russia as early as 1416, but most moved there during 1916-1923 after the Turks killed a large number of Pontian people. Pontian Greeks have their own religion and language. By the early 1990s, an estimated 45,000 Pontian Greeks lived in Greece (Petrinioti, 1993).

A. THE EXTENT OF RETURN MIGRATION TO GREECE

One of the most deficient areas with regard to statistics on international migration is that related to the measurement of return flows. In most countries, statistics on returning migrants do not even exist. In Greece, data on return migration were compiled during 1968-1977 by asking all citizens upon arrival whether they had been emigrants and whether they were returning. However, as a result of changes in the arrival and departure cards ordered by a Ministerial decision, data on the emigration and return migration of Greek citizens ceased to be collected as of October 1977 (National Statistical Service of

---

*Institute for the Study of Greek Economy (IMEO), Athens, Greece.

Greece, 1987, p. 51). Even when data were collected, their coverage was deficient. Thus, Greeks returning from socialist countries were usually not included in the statistics on return migration (Fakiolas, 1984, p. 37). Furthermore, there is little statistical information on the Greeks who returned from Egypt and Turkey before 1968.

Table 55 shows the evolution of Greek return migration during 1968-1977. The proportion of women among returning Greek emigrants has been somewhat low, oscillating around 46 per cent. A particularly low proportion of female returnees was recorded in 1974 (44.4 per cent), although two years later it registered a high of 48 per cent. The number of returning migrants increased markedly in 1975-1976. Unfortunately, there are no data for more recent periods. Given the important return flows experienced by Greece since the mid-1970s, a microcensus of migrants who returned during 1971-1985 was conducted in 1985-1986. The microcensus found 627,625 returnees in Greece, among whom women accounted for 48.2 per cent. In comparison, the proportion of women among the rest of the population (non-returnees) was 51 per cent (table 56). Member States of the European Community had been the major source of Greek returnees (55 per cent originated there). The former Federal Republic of Germany, in particular, was reported as the previous country of residence of 43 per cent of the returnees enumerated in Greece. There had been a

relatively high proportion of returnees from overseas countries (23 per cent). There had also been sizeable numbers of returnees from Middle Eastern countries, including Cyprus and Turkey, and Eastern-bloc countries (7.4 and 5.6 per cent respectively). Although women were underrepresented among the returnees of all major regions of previous residence, they rarely accounted for proportions below 47 per cent. Women constituted a slightly smaller proportion of the returnees whose previous residence was a member State of the European Community than of those returning from the overseas countries of immigration. Among the source countries accounting for more than 10,000 returnees, women outnumbered men only among the returnees from Australia, Cyprus and Turkey (table 56).

Returnees as a whole accounted for 6.8 per cent of the total Greek population enumerated by the microcensus. Yet, because of the differential distribution by sex of the returnee population, returnees accounted for a slightly higher proportion of the male population (6.8 per cent) than of the female population (6.1 per cent). In addition, there were important differences in the distribution by sex of the returnee population in different age groups and that of the rest of the population (table 57). Thus, women tended to be overrepresented among returnees aged 20-39 and underrepresented, often by very considerable margins, over age 40. At younger ages (under 20), the proportions of women were generally similar among both returnees and the rest of the population.

TABLE 55. MIGRANTS RETURNING TO GREECE,
BY SEX: 1968-1977

Year	Both sexes	Male	Female	Percentage female
1968	18 882	10 165	8 717	46.2
1969	18 132	9 489	8 643	47.7
1970	22 665	12 284	10 381	45.8
1971	24 709	13 531	11 178	45.2
1972	27 522	15 088	12 434	45.2
1973	22 285	12 210	10 075	45.2
1974	24 476	13 597	10 879	44.4
1975	34 214	18 421	15 793	46.2
1976	32 067	16 676	15 391	48.0
1977[a]	12 572	6 609	5 963	47.4

Source: National Statistical Service of Greece, Concise Statistical Yearbook 1987, p. 50.
[a]Refers to the period January-September 1977.

B. CIRCUMSTANCES SURROUNDING THE RETURN
MIGRATION OF GREEK CITIZENS AND ITS CAUSES

The return of Greek citizens from the former labour-importing countries of Europe was part of more general return flows triggered by a number of developments, including the cessation of labour recruitment in the main receiving countries, the effects of the rising price of oil that caused the crisis of 1973, the resulting economic slowdown, and the widespread and persistent unemployment experienced by receiving countries (Council of Europe, 1982; Chepulis, 1984; Kubat, 1984; ICM, 1986; Ohndorf, 1986). Recession in the receiving countries caused

TABLE 56. RETURNEES ENUMERATED IN GREECE, BY COUNTRY OF PREVIOUS RESIDENCE AND SEX: 1985-1986

Country of previous residence	Male	Female	Both sexes	Percentage by origin	Percentage of women
Overseas countries	72 834	71 672	144 506	23.0	49.6
United States	32 813	31 475	64 288	10.2	49.0
Australia	20 772	21 288	42 060	6.7	50.6
Canada	16 337	15 796	32 133	5.1	49.2
European Community	180 152	163 027	343 179	54.7	47.5
Germany, former Fed. Rep. of	139 335	131 248	270 583	43.1	48.5
Italy	14 769	8 867	23 636	3.8	37.5
Belgium	4 721	4 492	9 213	1.5	48.8
Other Western-bloc countries	9 571	9 201	18 772	3.0	49.0
Sweden	4 968	4 882	9 850	1.6	49.6
Eastern-bloc countries	17 846	17 478	35 324	5.6	49.5
USSR (former)	7 020	6 552	13 572	2.2	48.3
Romania	3 637	3 287	6 924	1.1	47.5
Bulgaria	1 713	1 862	3 575	0.6	52.1
Yugoslavia	643	654	1 297	0.2	50.4
Northern Africa	5 071	3 935	9 006	1.4	43.7
Egypt	2 179	2 031	4 210	0.7	48.2
Sub-Saharan Africa	9 229	9 228	18 457	2.9	50.0
South Africa	4 759	4 479	9 238	1.5	48.5
Ethiopia	679	879	1 558	0.2	56.4
Middle Eastern countries	23 742	22 679	46 421	7.4	48.9
Cyprus	8 766	9 917	18 683	3.0	53.1
Turkey	7 186	8 712	15 898	2.5	54.8
Saudi Arabia	4 924	2 143	7 067	1.1	30.3
Rest of Asia	419	866	1 285	0.2	67.4
Other countries and not stated	6 430	4 245	10 675	1.7	39.8
Total returnees	325 294	302 331	627 625	100.0	48.2
Non-returnees	4 468 173	4 655 955	9 124 128	-	51.0
Total population	4 793 467	4 958 286	9 751 753	-	50.8
Returnees as percentage of the total population	6.8	6.1	6.4	-	-

Source: N. Petropoulos, and others, Greek Return Migration 1971-1986: Results from the 1985-86 Microcensus of the National Statistical Service of Greece (Athens, Council of Europe Research Project on Migration and Return Migration, Ministry of National Economy, General Secretariat for Greeks Abroad and National Center for Social Research, 1990).

Note: Hyphen (-) indicates that the item is not applicable.

factory shutdowns and rising unemployment that affected the immigrant population more severely than the national population and led to more restrictive immigration policies. The former Federal Republic of Germany, in particular, adopted a series of measures promoting return migration. Furthermore, the economic situation in Greece improved, particularly during the 1980s, so that migrants found it in

their interest to return (Emke-Poulopoulos, 1986, pp. 190-235; Collaros, Moussourou and Papantoniou, 1978, p. 68).

In a survey of 255 men and 245 women returning to Macedonia, Greece, from the former Federal Republic of Germany and carried out in 1975-1976, migrants were asked about the reasons that prompted

TABLE 57. POPULATION OF GREECE, BY RETURNEE OR NON-
RETURNEE STATUS AND PERCENTAGE OF WOMEN:
1985-1986 MICROCENSUS

	Returnees		Rest of the population	
Age group	Number	Percentage of women	Number	Percentage of women
0-4	4 946	50.1	503 579	48.3
5-9	22 411	47.0	706 168	47.6
10-14	53 624	48.4	689 364	48.7
15-19	58 733	46.5	703 687	49.2
20-29	91 270	54.4	1 260 673	50.9
30-39	130 695	53.4	1 174 831	50.4
40-49	135 976	45.2	1 076 446	51.8
50-59	81 584	39.0	1 217 648	51.5
60-69	31 175	46.2	876 117	53.3
70+	17 011	51.9	915 618	55.7
Total	627 625	48.2	9 124 128	51.0

Source: N. Petropoulos, and others, *Greek Return Migration 1971-1986: Results from the 1985-86 Microcensus of the National Statistical Service of Greece* (Athens, Council of Europe Research Project on Migration and Return Migration, Ministry of National Economy, General Secretariat for Greeks Abroad and National Center for Social Research, 1990).

them to return to Greece (Collaros, Moussourou and Papantoniou, 1978, pp. 63-68). The question used was open-ended. Women and men were interviewed separately from one another. The percentage of respondents citing specific reasons is shown in table 58. Reasons related to the family or to children's well-being were those most often cited by both returning men (58 per cent) and returning women (60 per cent). Relatively low proportions of returning migrants mentioned economic reasons as those prompting return (loss of a job or achievement of goals). Interestingly, only 4 per cent of both male and female respondents cited the loss of a job as the reason for returning. A somewhat higher proportion of men than of women reported that they had returned because they had achieved their goals (9 per cent versus 6 per cent), and men were also more likely to cite health problems as a reason for returning (10 per cent versus 7 per cent). Researchers argued that the reasons given by men for returning were more "rational" than those of women, since women were more likely to report that they returned because they "missed Greece" or "were tired", or

because they "missed the children", than men (30 per cent versus 21 per cent, respectively). According to Collaros, Moussourou and Papantoniou (1978, p. 65), the ratio of rational to emotional reasons cited by men was 10 to 9, while the ratio of those cited by women was 10 to 18.

One may question why women are considered less than rational when their decisions are aimed at achieving the well-being of their children. Several studies have documented that women decide to return because of concern about the future of their children or in order to be reunited with them after lengthy periods of separation (Panayotakopoulou, 1981; Council of Europe, 1982). In many cases return is timed so that children can begin their schooling or continue their high school studies in the home country. Health problems are also a cause for the return of migrants. German doctors have been known to recommend that sick foreigners return to their home country. Women are also concerned about the economic future of their family and realize that the savings made abroad can be better used in the country of origin (Panayotakopoulou, 1981; Council of Europe, 1982; Emke-Poulopoulos, 1986).

TABLE 58. RESPONDENTS BY SEX AND REASON FOR
RETURNING TO GREECE

Reason for returning	Men	Women	Total
Family-related reasons	58	60	60
Children's studies	22	13	18
Missed the children............	10	16	13
Children growing older	2	3	3
Problems with children	5	4	5
Reasons related to children ..	5	5	5
Family reasons	13	16	14
Followed the family	1	3	2
Tired, missed Greece	11	14	12
Health problems	10	7	8
Achieved goals	9	6	7
Lost job	4	4	4
Military service	2	0	1
Other reasons	5	8	6
No answer	3	3	3

Source: T. Collaros, L. Moussourou and A. Papantoniou, *The Return Home* (Athens, Greece, Re-integration Center for Migrant Workers, 1978), p. 64.

Several studies have indicated that migrants, especially female migrants, wish to return to the home country, but that economic realities do not always favour such a decision (Chepulis, 1984; Münscher, 1984; Der Bundesminister für Arbeit und Sozialordnung, 1985; Ohndorf, 1986). Thus, a study of Turkish women in Germany notes that repatriation is the dream of every migrant, but that both objective and subjective considerations prevent it from happening (Wilpert, 1984). Social workers dealing with Greek migrant women in Germany report that their experience regarding the desire to return is similar to that of Turkish women.

The situation of women within the family determines both their propensity to return and the effects that return migration will have on them. Just as with migration in general, a distinction may be made between autonomous return migration, when the woman herself makes the decision to return, and dependent return migration, when the decision for the woman's return is made by other family members. Single, divorced or separated women are more likely to decide on their own to return, though their decision may be influenced by considerations regarding their children, if they have any. When women live in unions, the question arises of whether the decision to return is made mainly by the partner, by the woman herself or by both jointly. Pessar (1984), studying Dominican immigrants in the United States, found that women who had experienced social and economic gains as a result of migration generally wished to remain abroad, although their husbands were strongly motivated to return to the country of origin. Different views have been expressed regarding Greek returnees. Social workers have argued that among those returning from the former Federal Republic of Germany, it is the women who do not feel integrated into the host society and wish to return. In contrast, Defingou (1988) has argued that men are more often inclined to return than woman. According to the experience of the Reintegration Center for Migrant Workers, return often results from a decision taken jointly by both spouses (RCMW, 1985). However, if upon return children fail to reintegrate, it is the women who feel more guilty about the decision taken.

The timing of the return of different family members may also vary. In a number of cases, it is the woman, sometimes accompanied by the children, who returns first in order to make arrangements for the reinstallation of the family and the children's schooling, while the husband stays in the country of immigration to continue accumulating income, qualify for a pension, or take care of personal or family affairs (Moussourou, 1984).

The Council of Europe (1982, pp. 10-11) suggests that female migrants may be reluctant to return because their status in Greece may not be totally satisfactory. Female returnees are likely to confront a number of problems. For instance, those returning from countries that are not member States of the European Community and those who returned from member States before 1981 have no social security coverage upon repatriation, so that they have no right to pensions or free health care services. Female returnees find it especially difficult to find employment in Greece, particularly if they have been outside the country for a time and they wish to secure jobs similar to the ones they had while abroad. Wages and workers' benefits in Greece are low compared with those obtained abroad and Greek society may have more restrictive norms regarding the type of employment that women may engage in. Lastly, because women have less business experience than men, they have fewer opportunities to become entrepreneurs upon return or, if they do, they are more likely to be unsuccessful in their entrepreneurial ventures.

C. Social and family status of female returnees

Changes in the social position of women resulting from return migration are mediated by their family and marital status, their socio-economic position, their length of stay abroad, their experience while abroad, and by whether they resettle in rural or urban areas. During the migration process, the Greek working-class family has had to cope with a number of problems that affect the likelihood of return, including the separation of close family members, the varying degree of adaptation of different family members, poor housing conditions in the host country, relative isolation from the host society, and long working hours that conflict with a normal family life. Migrants who have been abroad for a number of years may not have a realistic view of the current situation in Greece. In addition, their exposure to different norms and values while abroad and changes in their lifestyles may make reintegration difficult. Female returnees are more likely to experience the conflicts inherent in readapting to the society of origin.

It has been suggested that female returnees find reintegration easier if they settle in small communities, where they find themselves among relatives, friends and acquaintances. In such a setting, they are more likely to get recognition for their achievements (Panayotakopoulou, 1981). However, in Greek villages and in the less prestigious neighbourhoods of Athens where community spirit prevails, returnees are often regarded as outsiders and are accepted only in so far as they conform to local standards (RCMW, 1985). In some cases, neighbours and relatives are critical of the attitudes and activities of female returnees who have gotten used to different lifestyles and a greater degree of freedom (ICM, 1981, p. 26). Female returnees are not always ready to make concessions in their home country. Thus, mutual exclusion and a lack of willingness to communicate often arise. The few migrants who return after becoming wealthy abroad represent an exception in that, although they might not adopt the ways of the society of origin, their prestige inspires respect among their compatriots and leaves them free to behave differently.

Women who return to the agricultural and semi-agricultural areas from which they originated face fewer difficulties in readaptation (Panayotakopoulou, 1981, p. 221). If extended families or close family networks are common, children can be left behind with close relatives (grandparents, uncles or aunts) and their reunion with the parents upon the return of the latter may entail less problems regarding mutual expectations and behaviour.

Migrants of rural origins who return to urban areas face problems akin to those of first-time migrants, especially if they have to resettle without the help of friends or relatives (ICM, 1981, p. 27). In those circumstances, returning migrants, and especially women, may face social isolation and may find it difficult to develop social networks, particularly if they do not work outside the home and have little leisure time because of their domestic duties (RCMW, 1985).

D. Changes in women's position within the family

While abroad, Greek women who work outside the home are usually responsible for most domestic duties as well, including cooking, cleaning and doing the washing. Husbands and children help them mostly with activities outside the home, such as shopping. Older children may also help by looking after younger children. A study comparing Greek families in Greece and in Canada found that the traditional sex roles within the family had undergone a considerable transformation among Greeks abroad. The authority of fathers had been reduced and the role of mothers in the decision-making process had become more egalitarian and independent. Although similar changes were detectable in families remaining in Greece, they were occurring more slowly.

There are few studies exploring how return migration affects the relationship between husbands and wives or between parents and children. Several authors have found that migration is associated with more egalitarian relationships within the family (Abadan-Unat, 1977; Mantzouranis, 1977). The survey of Greek returnees from the former Federal Republic of Germany carried out in 1975-1976 showed that the proportion of respondents who believed that men should help with domestic chores and in taking care of children was 64 per cent among men and 70 per cent among women (Collaros, Moussourou and Papantoniou, 1978).

The decline of dowry practices documented in a study on Greek Cypriot women living in England (Anthias, 1983, p. 91) was also found among the returnees interviewed in 1975-1976 (Collaros, Moussourou and Papantoniou, 1978, pp. 220-224), and it was found that the attitude of returnees towards the dowry system depended on their length of stay in the former Federal Republic of Germany. The longer the stay, the stronger the view that the dowry ought to be abolished.

Despite some progressive attitudes, women's subordination to male authority remains high when migrants return to rural areas where the relations between men and women have changed little. In urban areas the effects of return migration on gender relations depend not only on the employment opportunities open for women but also upon the age and educational attainment of female returnees and the socio-economic position of the couple. More research is needed to ascertain whether the division of labour within the family that generally prevails in Greece is acceptable to returning female migrants and on the extent to which their experience while abroad produces lasting changes in their roles and status within the family.

The incidence of divorce is also associated with return migration. Migrants who have been abroad for a long time and who return from countries where the dissolution of marriage is socially acceptable may be more likely to view divorce as an option when marital relations are poor. In some cases, divorce may trigger return migration, since migrant women who divorce their husbands while abroad may not have the right to stay in the countries of immigration if they were admitted there as dependants. In the case of mixed marriages, Greek women returning after the dissolution of marriage may find it difficult to secure adequate child support. In other cases, divorce may be postponed until the return of the whole family so that the woman can secure the support of relatives. However, the society of origin may not condone divorce and may lay the blame for the dissolution of marriage on the migrant woman or on migration itself.

E. RETURNING FEMALE MIGRANTS AND THEIR CHILDREN

In general, the money earned by migrants abroad contributes to the improvement of the standard of living of their children, whether the latter accompany their parents abroad or remain behind in the country of origin. Migration also has a generally positive effect on the education of the children of migrants (Emke-Poulopoulos, 1986, pp. 399-425). Yet, the social cost of migration for the children of migrants may be high. Children who migrate with their parents or are born while their parents are abroad usually are socialized in a different environment and have to undergo a process of adaptation when they return to Greece. One of the major hurdles for returning children is to become integrated into the Greek educational system, since they often face both language and adaptation barriers. Mothers are more likely to be aware of the problems being faced by their children and may feel that the decision to return was ill-advised.

A survey about the maternal attitudes of Greek migrant women showed that recently returned women differed from other migrant and non-migrant women in their attitudes on child-rearing practices (Dikaiou, Sakka and Haritos-Fatouros, 1987, pp. 77-78). They were more restrictive, over-protective and controlling with their children. In particular, female returnees appeared to be more overprotective towards boys than towards girls. Researchers offered three explanations for those attitudes: (a) both mothers and children face anxiety-provoking situations in their effort to redefine family roles and readjust to the society of the country of origin; (b) those attitudes may be related to the conditions under which migrant women lived while abroad; (c) their returnee status is responsible for the type of discipline they use towards their children. The financial situation of returnees did not seem to influence maternal attitudes towards children.

A survey of the interactions of migrant children with non-migrant children in both the host country and in the country of origin upon return showed that there is a general feeling of insecurity about identity and sense of belonging among migrant Greek children (Dikaiou, 1989). Concerning the children's sociability with adults, the survey showed that, among children who remained in Greece and lived in an extended-family environment, girls tended to make contacts easily with adults outside the family. The opposite was true of girls living abroad, where the social environment was probably perceived as unsafe. While abroad, boys were more sociable with adults than girls (Dikaiou, 1989, p. 60).

The expectations that female returnees have about the future of their children is affected by their migration experience. Thus, interviews with four returning female migrants indicated that they gave highest priority to their children (both sons and daughters) `finding a good job. They also hoped that daughters and sons would find good spouses and have children. These results are similar to those obtained from surveys carried out in other countries (Ley, 1981), but the sample is too small to draw any firm conclusions.

F. LABOUR FORCE PARTICIPATION AND RETURN MIGRATION

One important aspect of the status of women and the changes it undergoes because of migration and return is their participation in the labour force. The majority of Greek women who were working before emigration in the primary sector of the economy, usually as unpaid family members, joined the secondary and tertiary sectors of the economy as salaried workers while abroad (Emke-Poulopoulos, 1988). Their experience in selected host countries is important as a basis for comparison with the situation of female returnees.

In 1980, 67 per cent of Greek women in the former Federal Republic of Germany were working, but by 1985 that figure had declined to 55 per cent (Bundesminister für Arbeit und Sozialordnung, 1985, p. 217). Both figures, however, probably underestimate the level of labour force participation, since women working illegally are unlikely to be counted. Generally, Greek workers of both sexes occupied jobs shunned by German workers, which generally offered low pay and involved poor working conditions. Particularly after 1981, some Greek migrants started small businesses which required the active participation of both spouses (Emke-Poulopoulos, 1988). As table 59 indicates, between 1980 and 1985 there was a significant change in the distribution of Greek migrants employed in the former Federal Republic of Germany by the type of work performed. Among both men and women, the proportion of unskilled workers rose as did that of white-collar workers. There was, however, a sharp drop in the proportion of both men and women performing skilled work and women also experienced a drop in the proportion performing semi-skilled work. That is, between 1980 and 1985, Greek men and particularly Greek women in the

TABLE 59. GREEK MIGRANTS IN THE FORMER FEDERAL REPUBLIC OF GERMANY, BY SKILL CATEGORY: 1980 AND 1985

(Percentage)

Skill category	Men		Women	
	1980	1985	1980	1985
White-collar	5.7	8.5	9.6	14.1
Skilled	31.3	19.7	26.2	11.0
Semi-skilled	43.2	45.8	40.4	33.6
Unskilled	13.2	20.4	15.4	35.2
Apprentices	1.8	3.5	4.5	0.8
Others	4.8	2.1	3.8	5.5

Source: Bundesminister für Arbeit und Sozialordnung (1985). *Situation der ausländischen Arbeitnehmer und ihrer Familien: Angehörigen in der Bundesrepublik Deutschland; Repräsentativuntersuchung '85* (Bonn, Friedrich Ebert Stiftung, 1985), p. 85.

former Federal Republic became increasingly concentrated in unskilled jobs.

In Australia, women born in Greece have tended to hold jobs of lower status than those performed by native-born Australian women. Among the latter, 53 per cent were in the labour force, compared to 58 per cent of women born in Greece (Evans, 1984, pp. 1077-1079). In Australia, migrant women who speak little English usually find employment within their ethnic community or within ethnically based work-groups in large firms or factories. In the early 1980s, native-born Australian women and women born in Greece were equally likely to be unemployed (2 per cent, respectively). The lower educational attainment of Greek women and their length of residence in Australia were found to be crucial determinants of their lower status occupations. Australian-born women had, on average, 10.3 years of completed education, compared to 7.8 among immigrant women born in Greece (Evans, 1984, table 2). About 13 per cent of immigrant women from the Mediterranean region and 14 per cent of Australian-born women owned a business and worked either as self-employed workers or as entrepreneurs with paid employees.

In Canada and the United States, Greek immigrant women have not been the subject of much research, despite the size of the population of Greek origin in both countries. It is known, however, that immigrant women in those countries tend to cluster in low-status and typically low-wage occupations (Houstoun, Kramer and Barrett, 1984, pp. 942-963; Skodra, 1987).

According to the 1985-1986 microcensus of Greece, the proportion of economically active women was higher among female returnees than among the rest of the female population in Greece: 37.2 versus 29.7 per cent (table 60). A similar differential was found between male returnees and the rest of the male population. Therefore, although women in general tended to be about half as likely to be in the labour force than men, returnees of both sexes were more likely to be in the labour force. The relative concentration of returnees in the main working ages may be partly responsible for this outcome. Thus, returnees accounted for 9.2 per cent of the population aged 20-49, whereas they constituted only 6.1 per cent of the total population. These data are consistent with the findings of the 1976-1977 survey of returnees from Germany according to which 18 per cent of the women interviewed wanted to remain out of the labour force, 50 per cent wanted to work and

32 per cent did not answer (Collaros, Moussourou and Papantoniou, 1978, p. 143). That is, female returnees appear to value economic activity and the opportunities it brings, so that a high proportion of them wish to remain economically active. That a lower proportion than those who want to work actually remain in the labour force is probably the result of difficulties in finding acceptable jobs. Thus, as table 60 shows, female returnees are more likely to be unemployed than other women (13.9 per cent versus 10.9 per cent). However, female returnees appear to be just as successful as other women in securing salaried employment or in becoming employers, and they are somewhat less likely to be unpaid family workers. It appears therefore that female returnees in Greece have been fairly successful in penetrating the local labour market.

Another indication of the relative success of female returnees in the labour market is the distribution of those who are employed according to type of occupation. As table 61 shows, the proportion of female returnees working in professional and technical occupations is considerably higher than that among

TABLE 60. RETURNEES AND REST OF THE POPULATION IN GREECE,
BY ECONOMIC ACTIVITY AND SEX: 1985-1986

	Men		Women	
	Number	Percentage	Number	Percentage
Returnees				
Not economically active	64 279	23.9	161 650	62.8
Economically active	204 410	76.0	95 793	37.2
Of which:				
Employers	83 340	40.8	15 972	16.7
Salaried workers	100 155	49.0	45 097	47.1
Unpaid family workers	3 089	1.5	21 445	22.4
Unemployed	17 826	8.7	13 279	13.9
Rest of the population				
Not economically active	1 072 871	32.3	2 581 784	70.2
Economically active	2 248 637	67.8	1 096 162	29.7
Of which:				
Employers	928 415	41.3	180 202	16.4
Salaried workers	1 129 938	50.2	519 717	47.4
Unpaid family workers	71 963	3.2	284 980	26.0
Unemployed	118 321	5.3	111 263	10.2

Source: N. Petropoulos, and others, *Greek Return Migration 1971-1986: Results from the 1985-86 Microcensus of the National Statistical Service of Greece* (Athens, Council of Europe Research Project on Migration and Return Migration, Ministry of National Economy, General Secretariat for Greeks Abroad and National Center for Social Research, 1990).

all other women: 23.2 per cent compared to 15.5 per cent. Female returnees are also more likely to work in service occupations or in manufacturing than other women. The relative importance of female returnees as workers can be gauged by considering their proportions within each occupational group (see table 61). Whereas female returnees account for 7.7 per cent of all employed women, they constitute 11.1 per cent of all female professional and technical workers, 10.5 per cent of all female service workers and 9.6 per cent of all women in manufacturing. These data indicate that the contribution of female returnees to the Greek labour market is significant, especially in regard to the availability of skilled workers.

G. Income, savings and investment

The extent to which Greek migrants manage to accumulate savings before their return depends on the income they have while abroad. Although in some contexts the wages of migrant workers are lower on average than those of nationals, the income of the migrant family may be relatively high if both spouses work or if those family members in the labour force work overtime (sometimes holding two jobs). Through such strategies, some Greek families in Germany managed to have a family income higher than that of the average German family in the lower economic brackets (Emke-Poulopoulos, 1988). According to German statistical sources, in 1985 the average wage of a Greek woman was 1,564 deutschmarks (DM), lower than the average wage of a Greek man, which stood at DM2000 (Bundesminister für Arbeit und Sozialordnung, 1985, p. 157). Furthermore, the average hourly salary for Greek men (DM16.02) was higher than that for Greek women (DM14.21) (Bundesminister für Arbeit und Sozialordnung, 1985, p. 149). Greek women also had lower average salaries than German women. However, Greek women who worked overtime or had two jobs—usually as cleaners—could earn a

TABLE 61. EMPLOYED RETURNEES AND REST OF THE POPULATION ENUMERATED IN GREECE, BY TYPE OF ACTIVITY AND SEX: 1985-1986

Type of worker	Male		Female	
	Number	Percentage	Number	Percentage
Returnees				
Total employed	186 584	100.0	82 514	100.0
Professional and technical	37 261	20.0	19 125	23.2
Service	16 397	8.8	11 372	13.8
Clerical and related	10 177	5.5	8 811	10.7
Agricultural	32 735	17.5	17 921	21.7
Craftsmen and labourers	64 680	34.7	15 424	18.7
Rest of the population				
Total employed	2 130 316	100.0	984 899	100.0
Professional and technical	241 842	11.4	152 772	15.5
Service	162 181	7.6	97 200	9.9
Clerical and related	168 879	7.9	156 026	15.8
Agricultural	451 131	21.2	310 800	31.6
Craftsmen and labourers	795 870	37.4	145 590	14.8
Returnees as percentage of				
Total employed	8.1	-	7.7	-
Professional and technical	13.4	-	11.1	-
Service	9.2	-	10.5	-
Clerical and related	5.7	-	5.3	-
Agricultural	6.8	-	5.5	-
Craftsmen and labourers	7.5	-	9.6	-

Source: N. Petropoulos, and others, *Greek Return Migration 1971-1986: Results from the 1985-86 Microcensus of the National Statistical Service of Greece* (Athens, Council of Europe Research Project on Migration and Return Migration, Ministry of National Economy, General Secretariat for Greeks Abroad and National Center for Social Research, 1990).

Note: Hyphen (-) indicates that the item is not applicable.

higher income than the average for German women (Rosen, 1981, p. 111).

Despite the difficulties they faced, Greek migrants managed to amass some savings while abroad. According to German sources, in 1980 the proportion of Greek women having some savings stood at 68.2 per cent (Bundesminister für Arbeit und Sozialordnung, 1985). Although that figure declined to 50.8 per cent by 1985, it nevertheless represented a relatively high level of savings. The propensity to save was somewhat lower among Greek men, 62.3 per cent of whom reported to have some savings in 1980 and only 45.4 per cent of whom did so in 1985. On the whole, men tended to save higher amounts than women. Thus, 46.9 per cent of men and 44.2 per cent of women had monthly savings ranging from DM300 to 600, and 11 per cent of men but only 3 per cent of women saved more than DM1,200 per month (Bundesminister für Arbeit and Sozialordnung, 1985, p. 184).

Although not all returning migrants managed to accumulate savings while abroad, those who did generally put the money to use when they returned to Greece. In general, the most common uses of savings were to purchase a dwelling or some other form of real estate, to establish a business, to buy farming equipment or household goods, to pay for children's education, and to supplement current income or provide support for those unemployed (Emke-Poulopoulos, 1986, pp. 368-373; Reyneri and Mughini, 1984, pp. 31-36). According to the 1976-1977 survey of Greek returnees in Macedonia, buying a dwelling was the most common investment that migrants made upon their return, particularly if they were women not in the labour force or were unemployed (Collaros, Moussourou and Papantoniou, 1978, pp. 119-222). Returnees working in industry at the time of interview generally reported that they had no savings. According to the plans that returnees reported regarding the future use of any savings they still had, farmers and some women living in villages intended to buy farming equipment. About 10 per cent of respondents already had their own businesses and another 8 per cent planned to start one. Relatively few planned to invest in their children's education, half of them women.

As Morocvasic (1984) has suggested, women who earn a salary or have some independent source of income are more likely to have decision-making power regarding the distribution of family resources. However, although the data on the labour force participation of returnee women do not allow a firm conclusion to be reached, it appears that the labour force participation of migrant women and, consequently, their capacity to generate income, declines considerably upon their return to Greece. Although the statistics available probably do not reflect well the participation of women in the labour force, especially if they work in the informal sector, there is reason to believe that their income in Greece is generally low. It is estimated that in September 1990 the average wage of women working in the informal sector was about DM600 a month.[1] Women who work in the formal sector or are self-employed earn, on average, a lower income than men.

Unfortunately there is no direct evidence on the extent to which married female returnees have decision-making power within the family with regard to the use of income or savings, and on how that power changed through the migration process. However, social workers report that if a house is purchased with the savings of both spouses, ownership is shared. That is generally not the case when a business is set up, since in the majority of cases the business belongs legally to the husband. However, cases of joint ownership are not rare and in some cases the business belongs only to the wife, often because of tax advantages.

Decisions regarding business ownership are not the only ones that may result in detrimental effects on the position of women. A survey of 800 women in rural areas indicated that the mechanization of agriculture tends to broaden the employment opportunities for men rather than women because men are more likely to learn how to use the new machinery (Papandreou and Gourdomihali, 1987). In fact, mechanization may limit women's participation in agricultural work if social norms prevent them from being trained in the use of machinery. In such a context, the use of returnees' savings to purchase new machinery may lead to an erosion of women's position within the farm.

H. EDUCATIONAL ATTAINMENT OF FEMALE RETURNEES

Educational attainment is probably the main factor determining the occupation of migrant women while abroad. Migrants with low educational attainment are generally concentrated in low-paying jobs in the service sector or in manufacturing. For many migrants, inadequate language skills and basic training are the main obstacle preventing them from securing better paid jobs (Palmgren, 1981, p. 166). Although migrants tend, on average, to have a higher educational attainment than the average person in the country of origin, they also tend to be below the average of the country of destination (Emke-Poulopoulos, 1986, pp. 106-110). It is worth asking whether migrants improve their educational attainment while abroad. Among Greek migrant workers of both sexes in the former Federal Republic of Germany, the desire to earn as much as possible in the shortest time and the tendency to work overtime leaves little time for educational activities, especially for women who generally have to combine employment outside the home with domestic responsibilities. Although vocational training was available in the Federal Republic of Germany for migrants of both sexes, few women enrolled in it. It has been argued that migrants who were intending to return to Greece could derive few benefits from the vocational training offered since the possibility of applying in Greece the skills that migrants acquired in Germany was limited (Pekin, 1986, p. 167).

In Canada, free English courses are offered to immigrants. However, few immigrant women attend those courses, partly because the schedules and location of the courses often conflict with women's domestic or employment responsibilities. Furthermore, the manpower criteria used to screen potential students and the priority accorded by Canadian authorities to teach English to the main breadwinner of the family also contribute to reducing the accessibility of those courses to married women.

With respect to second-generation migrants, young foreigners in the former Federal Republic of Germany have generally been at a disadvantage in relation to their German peers as they move from school to vocational training and then to a working life (Beer and Granato, 1988). Young foreign women face even greater disadvantages because of their sex, their foreign status and their working-class background. Yet, in recent years, far more foreign women than foreign men have completed their schooling in the former Federal Republic of Germany and women have generally met higher standards of achievement. Although an increasing number of foreign women want vocational training, training places are limited. Second-generation migrants returning to Greece confront problems in getting readapted to Greece's school system and some drop out (Emke-Poulopoulos, 1986, pp. 412-421). Yet there is evidence that, on average, female returnees have a higher level of educational attainment that the rest of the women in Greece. Thus, according to the 1985-1986 microcensus, female returnees are overrepresented in the higher educational category (10.3 per cent) in comparison with the rest of the female population (4.6 per cent). In addition, the proportion of female returnees who did not complete elementary education is about half of that registered among the rest of the female population (11.6 per cent versus 22.7 per cent) and, although the percentage of female returnees with only a completed elementary education is slightly higher than that among other women, in all other categories with higher educational attainment the proportion of female returnees surpasses that registered among other women (table 62). The differences in educational attainment are particularly marked in age groups 25-29 and 30-44, where female returnees display higher levels of educational attainment than other women. Although differences between the educational attainment of male returnees and that of the rest of the male population are considerably more marked, they are in the same direction. That is, returning migrants of both sexes are positively selected in terms of educational attainment. This result may be associated with the fact that both men and women often migrate to study abroad. Thus, a survey of Greek scientists returning to Greece during 1960-1971 indicated that the proportion of women among them was 9.5 per cent (Amera, 1980). During 1971-1986 the number of migrant women returning to Greece after obtaining a higher degree abroad increased substantially, but men still outnumbered them.

TABLE 62. RETURNEES AND REST OF POPULATION ENUMERATED IN GREECE, BY EDUCATIONAL ATTAINMENT AND SEX: 1985-1986

Type of worker	Male		Female	
	Number	Percentage	Number	Percentage
Returnees	277 580	99.9	257 950	100.0
Higher education	51 190	18.4	26 560	10.3
Intermediate	8 430	3.0	6 740	2.6
High school (6 years)	49 320	17.8	55 730	21.6
High school (3 years)	35 500	12.8	30 120	11.7
Elementary	111 410	40.1	108 950	42.2
Incomplete elementary	21 730	7.8	29 850	11.6
Rest of the population	3 418 640	100.0	3 679 460	100.0
Higher education	282 980	8.3	168 340	4.6
Intermediate	93 120	2.7	59 910	1.6
High school (6 years)	707 430	20.7	764 450	20.8
High school (3 years)	455 810	13.3	344 720	9.4
Elementary	1 458 360	42.7	1 506 310	40.9
Incomplete elementary	420 940	12.3	835 730	22.7

Source: N. Petropoulos, and others, *Greek Return Migration 1971-1986: Results from the 1985-86 Microcensus of the National Statistical Service of Greece* (Athens, Council of Europe Research Project on Migration and Return Migration, Ministry of National Economy, General Secretariat for Greeks Abroad and National Center for Social Research, 1990).

Lastly, it is worth noting that Greek refugees returning from the former USSR and other Eastern-bloc countries have, in general, relatively high levels of educational attainment. However, several studies have found that returning Greek refugees tend to be underemployed, working in occupations that do not make proper use of their qualifications. Although no information is available specifically on the women among this group of returning migrants, it is likely that they too have experienced a deterioration of occupational status (Mestheneos, 1988; Emke-Poulopoulos, 1990; Kassimati and others, 1992).

I. CONCLUSION

This brief overview of the experience of Greek female migrants who have returned to Greece indicates that there is much in that experience that is positive. Greek return migration is generally a family strategy, so that the goal of both migrant men and women is to maximize family rather than individual welfare. The length of stay abroad influences the way returnees confront their readaptation to Greek society. The longer the time abroad, the more likely that members of the Greek family have adopted norms and values that differ from those of the society of origin. However, migrants who have spent more time abroad are also more likely to have accumulated sufficient savings to make readaptation easier.

While abroad, the economic activity rates of Greek women tend to be high, even if they often work in low-paid occupations with little prestige. Upon their return to Greece, female returnees exhibit lower activity rates than do Greek women abroad, but returning female migrants are more likely to be in the labour force than the rest of the female population in Greece. In terms of both type of occupation and educational attainment, female returnees show more favourable distributions than those of other women in Greece. Thus, although return is not an easy process, involving always some degree of readaptation to the host society, female returnees do not appear, on average, to be worse off than the rest of the female population. That is not to negate the fact that particular groups of returnees require special assistance. Female children and young women who have spent most of their formative years abroad may need special training courses to become reintegrated into the educational system of Greece, as do their male counterparts. Divorced or separated female returnees may also require special assistance to secure child-support payments or obtain jobs that allow them to support their children. It is also important to ensure that women who acquire higher education or special training while abroad have the opportunity of using it in Greece. On the whole, female returnees represent an important component of the Greek population whose energy and resources ought to be channelled into productive activities. Facilitating their engagement in such activities should be a priority.

NOTE

[1] Exchange rates for September 1990 have been used.

REFERENCES

Abadan-Unat, Nermin (1977). Implications of migration on the emancipation and pseudo-emancipation of Turkish women. *International Migration Review* (Staten Island, New York), vol. 11, No. 1 (Spring), pp. 31-57.

Anthias, F. (1983). Sexual divisions and ethnic adaptations: the case of Greek Cypriot women. In *One Way Ticket: Migration and Female Labour*, Annie Phizacklea, ed. London: Routledge and Kegan Paul.

Amera, A. (1980). Socio-economic characteristics and motives for Greek scientists returning during the period 1960-1971 (in Greek). *The Greek Review of Social Sciences* (Athens), Nos. 39-40, pp. 221-232.

Beer, Dagmar, and M. Granato (1988). The vocational training of young female foreigners in the Federal Republic of Germany. Paper presented at the International Symposium on Women in International Migration: Social, Cultural and Occupational Issues, jointly sponsored by the Sociology Institute of the Technical University, Berlin, and UNESCO, held in Berlin, Germany, 18-21 October.

Bundesminister für Arbeit und Sozialordnung (1985). *Situation der ausländischen Arbeitnehmer und ihrer Familien: Angehörigen in der Bundesrepublik Deutschland. Repräsentativuntersuchung 1985.* Bonn, Germany: Forschungsinstitut des Friedrich Ebert Stiftung.

Chepulis, Rita L. (1984). Return migration: a theoretical framework. In *The Politics of Return: International Return Migration in Europe*, Daniel Kubat, ed. Staten Island, New York: Center for Migration Studies.

Collaros, T., L. Moussourou and A. Papantoniou (1978). *The Return Home.* Athens: Re-Integration Center for Migrant Workers.

Council of Europe (1982). *Report on Migrant Women.* Strasbourg: Parliamentary Assembly.

Defingou, M. (1988). Paper presented at the Educational Programs for Greek Migrant Women, Petra-Lesvos-Greece, General Secretariat for Greeks Abroad (in Greek).

Dikaiou, M. (1989). Peer interaction in migrant children: observational data and parents' evaluations. *International Migration* (Geneva), vol. 27, No. 1 (March), pp. 49-67.

_____, D. Sakka and M. Haritos-Fatouros (1987). Maternal attitudes of Greek migrant women. *International Migration* (Geneva), vol. 25, No. 1 (March), pp. 73-86.

Emke-Poulopoulos, Ira (1986). *Problems of Emigration and Return Migration. The Case of Greece.* Athens: IMEO-EDHM.

_____ (1988). The occupational integration of women migrants returning to Greece from the Federal Republic of Germany. Paper presented at the International Symposium on Women in International Migration: Social, Cultural and Occupational Issues, jointly sponsored by the Sociology Institute of the Technical University, Berlin, and UNESCO, held in Berlin, Germany, 18-21 October.

_____, (1990). Immigrants and refugees in Greece 1970-1990. *Eklogi* (Nicosia), June-September, pp. 1-112.

Evans, M. D. R. (1984). Immigrant women in Australia: resources, family and work. *International Migration Review* (Staten Island, New York), vol. 18, No. 4 (Winter), pp. 1063-1090.

Fakiolas, Ross (1984). Return migration to Greece and its structural and socio-political effects. In *The Politics of Return: International Return Migration in Europe*, Daniel Kubat, ed. Staten Island, New York: Center for Migration Studies.

Houstoun, Marion F., Roger G. Kramer and Joan Mackin Barrett (1984). Female predominance of immigration to the United States since 1930: a first look. *International Migration Review* (Staten Island, New York), vol. 18, No. 4 (Winter), pp. 908-963.

Intergovernmental Committee for Migration (1981). Situation and role of migrant women: specific adaptation and integration problems. *International Migration* (Geneva), vol. 19, No. 1/2 (Special issue).

_____ (1986). Seventh Seminar on Adaptation and Integration of Migrants, Geneva, 9-13 December 1985. *International Migration* (Geneva), vol. 24, No. 1 (March).

Kassimati, K., and others (1992). *Pontian Immigrants from the Former USSR: Their Social and Economic Integration.* Athens: General Secretariat of Greeks Abroad and Panteion University. (In Greek).

Kubat, Daniel (1984). Introduction. In *The Politics of Return: International Return Migration in Europe*, Daniel Kubat, ed. Staten Island, New York: Center for Migration Studies.

Ley, Katharina (1981). Migrant women: is migration a blessing or a handicap? Situation of migrant women in Switzerland. *International Migration* (Geneva), vol. 19, No. 1/2, pp. 83-93.

Mantzouranis, J. (1977). They Call Us "Gastarbeiter". Athens: Themelio. (In Greek).

Mestheneos, Liz (1988). The education, employment and living conditions of refugees in Greece and possibilities for self employment. Geneva: Office of the United Nations High Commissioner for Refugees (UNHCR). Mimeographed.

Morocvasic, Mirjana (1984). Birds of passage are also women.... *International Migration Review* (Staten Island, New York), vol. 18, No. 4 (Winter), pp. 886-907.

Moussourou, L. (1984). Emigration, return migration and family: research programme. Athens, Greece: National Centre for Social Research. Mimeographed.

Münscher, Alice (1984). The workday routines of Turkish women in the Federal Republic of Germany: results of a pilot study. *International Migration Review* (Staten Island, New York), vol. 18, No. 4 (Winter), pp. 1230-1246.

National Statistical Service of Greece (1987). *Statistical Yearbook of Greece, 1986.* Athens.

Ohndorf, Wolfgang (1986). The various forms, reasons and motivations for return migration of persons who voluntarily decide to return to their countries of origin. *International Migration* (Geneva), vol. 24, No. 1 (March), pp. 213-217.

Palmgren, Irene (1981). Situation of immigrant women in Sweden. *International Migration* (Geneva), vol. 19, No. 1/2, pp. 153-189.

Panayotakopoulou, E. (1981). Specific problems of migrant women returning to the country of origin, particularly as regards employment and social services. *International Migration* (Geneva), vol. 19, No. 1/2, pp. 219-224.

Papandreou, S., and A. Gourdomihali (1987). The Greek farmer women today, Mediterranean women. *KEGME Review* (Athens), vol. 1, Nos. 3/4.

Pekin, Hüseyin (1986). Measures to facilitate the reintegration of returning migrants into their countries of origin. *International Migration* (Geneva), vol. 24, No. 1 (March), pp. 163-178.

Pereira-Perista, Heloisa Maria (1988). Work and the occupational situation of Portuguese women returnees. Paper presented at the International Symposium on Women in International Migration: Social, Cultural and Occupational Issues, jointly sponsored by the Sociology Institute of the Technical University, Berlin, and UNESCO, held in Berlin, Germany, 18-21 October.

Pessar, Patricia R. (1984). The linkage between the household and workplace in the experience of Dominican immigrant women in the United States. *International Migration Review* (Staten Island, New York), vol. 18, No. 4 (Winter), pp. 1188-1211.

Petrinioti, X. (1993). *Immigration to Greece. A First Registration.* Athens: Odysseas.

Petropoulos N., and others (1990). *Greek Return Migration 1971-1986. Results from the 1985-1986 Microcensus of the National Statistical Service of Greece.* Council of Europe Research Project on Migration and Return Migration. Athens: Ministry of National Economy, General Secretariat for Greeks Abroad and National Center for Social Research. (In Greek).

Reintegration Center for Migrant Workers (1985). Return migration and the problem of women. Athens. Mimeographed.

Reyneri, Emilio, and Clara Mughini (1984). Return migration and sending areas: from the myth of development to the reality of stagnation. In *The Politics of Return: International Return Migration in Europe*, Daniel Kubat, ed. Staten Island, New York: Center for Migration Studies.

Rosen, Rita (1981). On the situation of foreign women living in the Federal Republic of Germany: an outline of the problem. *International Migration* (Geneva), vol. 19, No. 1/2, pp. 108-113.

Skodra, E. (1987). *Patriarchal Family Relations: The Threat of Change for First Generation Immigrant Women.* Toronto, Canada: Queen St. Mental Health Center.

Unger, Klaus (1981). Greek emigration to and return from West Germany. *Ekistics* (Athens), vol. 48, No. 290, pp. 369-374.

_____ (1984). Occupational profile of returnees in three Greek cities. In *The Politics of Return: International Return Migration in Europe*, Daniel Kubat, ed. Staten Island, New York: Center for Migration Studies.

Wilpert, Czarina (1984). Returning and remaining: return among Turkish migrants in Germany. In *The Politics of Return: International Return Migration in Europe*, Daniel Kubat, ed. Staten Island, New York: Center for Migration Studies.

XI. THE NEW SHEILAS: EUROPEAN IMMIGRANT WOMEN IN AUSTRALIA, THEIR STATUS AND ADAPTATION

Helen Ware* and David Lucas**

According to the 1986 census, two out of every three foreign-born persons living in Australia were born in Europe. This paper examines the experience of the female component of that migrant stock. Using census and survey data, the characteristics of female migrants from Europe are compared with those of migrant men, of the Australian-born and of the children of immigrants (i.e., the second generation). In a multicultural society, assimilation is not the aim and, consequently, such comparisons cannot be made under the assumption that homogeneity is desirable. Indeed, official statistics are poor tools for the discussion of cultural differences in status: although they may allow some inferences to be made regarding control over resources, they reveal nothing about respect or esteem and very little about the power to make decisions. One can only guess whether migrants in general have more or less positive attitudes with respect to women's rights than the communities that they have left behind them. However, Australia makes it a requirement for admission that immigrants respect the principle of the equality of men and women.

European immigration to Australia began in the 1790s, when convicts and soldiers settled in the continent, and for decades it remained dominated by men. Australian culture, characterized by its distinctive ethic of "mateship", developed in a context where women formed but a small proportion of the total non-aboriginal population. Inevitably "Australian tradition was always and necessarily one-sided; it left out of account the whole relationship with woman" (Wright, 1965, pp. 133-134). As one of Australia's recent Prime Ministers has written, the present situation is that "we have salved our consciences by eliminating the more obvious discrimi-

nations like unequal rates of pay for work of equal value. But, in fact, we have not eliminated the inheritance ... that women are lesser beings ... which still manifests itself in a whole range of prejudice and other forms of discrimination" (Hawke, 1979, p. 42).

Apart from autobiographies and biographies (Loh, 1980), studies of female migrants to Australia are rare, although not as rare as studies by such women themselves or comparisons with their communities of origin. Only in 1990 the new magazine *Fields, Factories and Feminism*, issued by the Women from Ethnic Minorities and Education (WEMAE, 1990), began to fill that gap by disseminating a large proportion of articles (80 per cent) by women belonging to ethnic minorities. The Victorian Ministry of Education has also launched a series of Rime Books focusing on the experiences of women from ethnic minorities living in Australia. The series was to be published in both English and the minorities' languages in 1991.

Several sections of the encyclopedic *Australian People*, edited by Jupp (1988) make scant reference to women. Authors such as Doczy (1969) deliberately focus on men. Hugo (1986) regards occupation as "one of the most useful indicators of the socio-economic differences between generations" but presents material which does not distinguish between the sexes. In areas such as housing, data are available on women or on migrants but not separately for female migrants (Australian Commission of Inquiry into Poverty, 1976; and Watson, 1988).

A. POST-WAR MIGRATION TO AUSTRALIA

Prior to 1945, immigration to Australia was largely from the British Isles. Because of the increasing variety of immigrant origins in recent decades, the proportion of persons of British or Irish descent

---

**Australian High Commissioner, Lusaka, Zambia.
**Department of Demography, Research School of Social Sciences, Australian National University, Canberra.*

179

declined from 90 per cent in 1947 to 75 per cent in 1988.

During the intercensal period 1933-1947, immigration to Australia virtually came to a halt. After the War, the Government planned to use immigration, mainly from the United Kingdom, to add an extra percentage point to the annual rate of population growth. Since sufficient migrants were not forthcoming from the United Kingdom, other Europeans were encouraged to immigrate to Australia. Soon, immigrants from the United Kingdom were outnumbered by Eastern Europeans (during 1947-1951) and later by Southern Europeans (1951-1961) (Lucas, 1987).

Between 1961 and 1976, 45 per cent of the 1.1 million immigrants admitted were from the United Kingdom or the Republic of Ireland, and 16 per cent from Southern Europe, whereas the numbers from other parts of Europe declined sharply. As a result of the abandonment of the White Australia policy in the 1960s, migrants from Asia became significant. However, the group with British ancestry was reinforced by increased immigration from New Zealand (Borrie, 1988). Throughout the 1970s and 1980s the foreign-born population constituted just over one fifth of the Australian population. Migrants from mainland Europe, the United Kingdom and Ireland comprised 81 per cent of the foreign immigrants arriving before 1976 but only 35 per cent of those admitted between 1976 and 1986 (Australian Bureau of Statistics, 1988).

The massive immigration programme instituted after the Second World War represented a major social experiment, though surprisingly little attention was given to its design. The assumption was essentially that immigrants would gradually merge into the host society making it certainly richer economically and possibly more culturally diverse at the margin but otherwise having little impact on Australian society as a whole. Minimal attention was given to the question of the roles that immigrant women might play aside from their traditional roles as wives and mothers. Until the mid-1970s Government policy rarely took note of women's issues, much less of immigrant women's particular concerns.

Not all immigrants have stayed permanently in Australia and return migration rates have varied significantly over time and across birthplace groups. Between 1947 and 1980, about 22 per cent of persons who had immigrated to Australia had left the country. The equivalent proportion was slightly higher, 24 per cent, among immigrants from the United Kingdom and Ireland, with men being only slightly more likely to leave than women, in contrast to immigrants from Germany, Italy, Malta and Yugoslavia, among whom men were considerably more likely to leave (Price, 1982a).

Some male returnees interviewed by Appleyard (1988) in the United Kingdom justified their return by their wives' failure to adapt. Yet, it is an oversimplification to regard return migration as evidence of failure. Some migrants went to Australia intending to return to their home countries once their economic goals were achieved (Huber, 1977; Thompson, 1980). Other returnees were considering re-emigrating to Australia (Appleyard, 1988). Author Elisabeth Wynhausen was born in the Netherlands, brought up in Australia, and now lives in New York, and, as Giese (1989) says, many clever women of that generation had mixed feelings about staying in Australia.

B. Age at arrival

One very important factor in the integration of immigrant women is their age upon arrival in Australia. Because of the emphasis on family migration in the 1950s and 1960s, there were many children among the immigrants and they are now young adults. For example, among the 160,000 immigrants born in the United Kingdom and the Republic of Ireland and aged 15-24 years in 1981, about 85 per cent had migrated before the age of 15 (Lucas, 1981).

The younger the age at arrival, the easier and more complete is the integration of migrant women likely to be. Indeed, many of those who arrived before their teens have been able to adopt the best from two cultures. That possibility is especially important for women from non-English-speaking countries whose cultural values are very different from those of native Australians, especially with respect to the role and status of women. Australia requires 10 years of compulsory education for all (Australian Bureau of Statistics, 1988) and the longer young women spend in the educational system, the more integrated they usually become. Australia has a wide range of "ethnic" schools teaching the language and culture of countries of origin, but usually such schooling occurs after-hours as an addition rather than a substitute for standard Australian schooling. Some foreign-born parents, however, become so concerned by the impact of Australian schooling that they send their daughters, but not their sons, to relatives in the home country to complete their studies during their later teenage years so that they may be kept from the open mixing between the sexes which is common in all state and most private schools in Australia (Ware, 1981).

C. LANGUAGE

Fluency in English is the key factor affecting the integration of women to Australian society as well as their employment and other opportunities. Currently, among women who immigrate independently, English skills constitute a factor determining admission as an immigrant. In the past, however, Australia was too intent in securing the necessary unskilled labour to be overly concerned about the language capabilities of male immigrants, much less that of their wives (Lynch, 1970).

In 1986, close to one in eight women in Australia had been born in a non-English-speaking country. Census data for that year show that the proportion speaking no English was 6 per cent among women born in Southern Europe, but only 2 per cent among men. Those speaking English, though "not well", were 27 per cent among women born in Southern Europe and 20 per cent among men (DILGEA, 1989c). Canadian census data show similar patterns (Boyd, 1986) and the 1976 census data for Australia showed that the proportions who did not know English approached one half among women born in Southern Europe who were past retirement age (Ware, 1981). Although many had grown old in Australia,

others had probably immigrated to join their grown-up children since it is possible for immigrants to sponsor their parents—generally their widowed mothers. Other groups display similar patterns regarding lack of English skills: women are most disadvantaged in comparison to men among older Italians, Lebanese of all ages and younger Turks (Young, 1989). Predictably, problems regarding English skills among the younger generation are largely confined to the most recently arrived groups, although the data also suggest that women from Muslim countries face special difficulties (presumably cultural rather than linguistic) in learning English.

Despite a range of aids that include interpretation services and multilingual publications provided by the Government (DILGEA, 1988), a woman who does not speak English becomes a virtual non-person outside her own linguistic group. A man will normally pick up some English at work and larger factories sometimes offer English training. Even when employed, women are more likely to be in workplaces or contexts where they have neither the need nor the opportunity to learn English. Many migrant women work at home doing piece-work, such as sewing clothes, or they work in small factories, generally with other women having the same mother tongue. In fact, Southern European husbands have been known to prevent their wives from taking better paid work at ethnically mixed factories where they would learn English (Storer, 1976).

Australia's Report on the Convention on the Elimination of All Forms of Discrimination against Women put special emphasis on female migrants who were unable to speak English, concluding that "... lack of English fluency and an inability to communicate on day-to-day issues in the general community contribute substantially to the difficulties many migrant women experience in adapting to life in Australia" (Office of the Status of Women, 1986, pp. 7-8). The consequences of not knowing English included personal isolation, limited employment opportunities, exploitation in the workforce and vulnerability when widowed. A vivid illustration is provided by the unemployment rates calculated from 1986 census figures: 9 per cent among men and 9.6 among women. Yet, among those in the labour force who spoke their native language at home and were not proficient in English the rates rose to 21.1 per cent for men and 26.5 per cent for women.

Further evidence that a lack of familiarity with Australia has a greater impact upon the employment opportunities of women than of men is provided by the data on the length of residence in Australia. Unemployment was 9.9 per cent for all foreign-born men and 11.2 per cent for foreign-born women, but among those who had been in Australia less than five years unemployment reached 18.6 per cent for men and fully 24.9 per cent for women (Australian Bureau of Statistics, 1988).

The Australian Government now recognizes the crucial importance of learning English, especially for women, and the National Agenda for Multicultural Australia launched in July 1989, focuses on English-language training and on women's needs (Australian Overseas Information Service, 1989). Provisions especially tailored for women include child-care services, home tutors and additional slots for women who were unable to learn English when they were younger because of family responsibilities. There is also a new National Task Force on Non-English Speaking Background Women's Issues.

D. EDUCATION AND QUALIFICATIONS

After the Second World War, Australia set about importing unskilled workmen and took little account of their educational background. Many of the workmen's wives from Southern Europe came to Australia never having attended school or with only limited primary schooling. Consequently, whereas the proportion of Australian and British-born men who had at most primary schooling was less than 3 per cent in 1976, it was 41 per cent among Greek-born men and 55 per cent among Greek-born women. Even in 1986, the proportions of Australian and British-born men and women who had only primary education were less than 2 per cent compared to 35 per cent for Greek-born men and 45 per cent for Greek-born women. Other groups of Southern European origin showed similar, though somewhat less extreme, educational disparities. At the other end of the spectrum, the proportions with university de-

grees were 9 and 8 per cent for Australian and British-born men, 6 and 5 per cent for Australian and British-born women but at most 1 per cent among men and women born in Southern Europe. The absolute numbers of women with Southern European backgrounds who have university degrees have remained small (e.g., in 1986, among the 67,000 Yugoslav-born women aged 15 or over, there were only 618 with university degrees) and, consequently, women are deprived of the services of female professionals from their own backgrounds and of role models to emulate. The very small proportions of highly educated women among migrants of Southern European origin has contributed to reinforce the stereotype according to which Southern Europeans are patriarchal: Australians know little about non-English-speaking feminism (Hellman, 1987).

During the past two generations, the educational attainment of both sexes has improved markedly in Australia and especially that of immigrant women and the daughters of immigrants (Young, 1989). Now only among the Lebanese, Turks and Vietnamese do more than 10 per cent of women still leave school before age 14 (Young, 1989). This finding serves to emphasize the difficulty of making generalizations about female immigrants or even about immigrants from non-English-speaking backgrounds, since the two Muslim groups have little in common with the Vietnamese. Liu Kesha (1989 used data from the 1986 Australian Family Survey to show that women from the second generation were more likely to have completed 12 years of education than other Australian-born respondents. Mistilis (1986) has also shown that in Australia young people with non-English-speaking backgrounds are more likely to go on to tertiary education than those from English-speaking backgrounds. Such advantage among the second generation validates one of the motives for migration: to improve the conditions of life for one's children. The only exceptions are groups that do not consider the prolonged education of women a high priority or even a desirable pursuit. Even groups from the same region vary. Thus, Greek families in Australia place greater emphasis on the education of daughters than do Italians, Lebanese or Turks (Young, 1989). Indeed, the proportion of Greek-born women aged 15-19 who are still in school is 46 per cent as compared with 59 per cent for second-generation Greek women and 47 per cent for second-generation Italian women but only 37 per cent for Australian-born women of Australian parentage (Young, 1989).

A problem faced by both male and female immigrants is that their trade and professional qualifications may not be recognized in Australia. It is estimated that since 1969 about 200,000 immigrants have been unable to use their skills fully. Such obstacles have affected men more than women, since the former are more likely to have relevant skills. In 1989 the Government announced renewed efforts to give such people the chance to demonstrate that they can meet Australian standards, creating the National Advisory Committee on Skills Recognition (Jordan, 1989).

E. MARRIAGE

Marriage to an Australian might be a factor considered to foster the adaptation of immigrants, especially women. Intermarriage has undergone major changes over the years. In 1956-1958, the majority of women from the larger non-English-speaking groups married men from the same origin: 92 per cent of Italian women married Italians and 91 per cent of Greek women married Greeks (the figures for men who had co-national brides were 69 per cent for Italians and 90 per cent for Greeks). By 1981-1983 the proportions marrying spouses from the same birthplace had fallen to 39 per cent among Italian brides, 22 per cent among Italian grooms, 59 per cent for Greek brides and 35 per cent for Greek grooms. In recent years very high proportions of intermarriage have been recorded amongst the more recently arrived Muslim and Vietnamese groups (Young, 1989).

In terms of integration or status, immigrant women who are currently married are clearly in a different situation from those who have no husbands whether because they never married or because of separation, divorce or widowhood. As a result of both cultural differences and differing age structures, the distribution of women by marital status varies greatly across birthplace groups (see table 63). The proportion

TABLE 63. ADULT WOMEN IN AUSTRALIA, BY COUNTRY OF BIRTH AND SELECTED CHARACTERISTICS: 1986

Country of birth	Wtih post-school qualifications	Aged 65 or over	Labour force characteristics			Marital status	
			Labour force participation (percentage)	Adjusted labour force	Unemployment rate	Divorced or separated	Widowed
Australia	23	12	48	56	9	8	10
Other Oceania	28	7	59	64	13	10	6
United Kingdom and Ireland	25	21	46	59	8	9	13
Germany	36	13	46	52	9	12	11
Greece	9	9	46	57	8	4	8
Italy	11	15	36	43	6	3	11
Poland	25	21	36	46	14	10	19
Yugoslavia	11	7	50	53	11	7	8

Source: Australian Bureau of Statistics, *Census 1986*, tables C03, C04, C09 and C11.

NOTE: The adjusted labour force participation rate excludes women aged 65 or over from the denominator. Women aged 65 or over are included in all other statistics presented here.

currently married is as high as four fifths among Greek and Italian-born women but little more than one half among the Australian-born. Widows represent almost one fifth of the Polish-born but about one tenth of the Australian- or Greek-born. Where special services are provided for non-English-speaking women, they are generally focused on young women with children or on older widows. There is very little provision for never-married women, the divorced and the separated unless they have children. To understand the situation of women without spouses one would need to have information on household composition and the availability of informal support networks.

During the 1950s and 1960s, it was relatively common for men from Southern Europe to emigrate in advance, bringing their wives and families to join them in Australia only after they had become established, a process which frequently entailed separations measured in years rather than months (Price and Martin, 1975). Thus, many married women had the experience (rare in their cultures) of becoming sole household decision makers while still in intact marriages.

The completed fertility of migrant women from Europe had tended either to converge with that of the Australian-born or to be already lower than that of the host society (Young, 1989). A general finding of intergenerational comparisons is that the completed family size of second-generation women is generally closer to that of Australian-born women as a whole than was the completed family size of the first-generation of migrants who were their mothers (Price, 1982b). This observation applies whether the first generation had higher fertility (Lebanon, Malta or the Netherlands) or lower fertility (Greece, Italy, the United Kingdom or Yugoslavia) than the native born: convergence is noticeable in both cases.

F. Housing

Data on the housing experience of immigrant women are scarce and what data there are do not distinguish between female and male ownership. Thus Neutze and Kendig (1989) examined the median age at which women first become home-owners

by migration status, but their definition of homeownership includes joint ownership. Data from the 1986 Family Survey show that immigrants achieve homeownership relatively soon after arrival. Women who came to Australia before age 20 became home-owners at slightly younger ages than the native born and those who immigrated between ages 20 and 30 were generally only 2 to 5 years older than their Australian-born peers when they acquired their first home. Even those who arrived after age 30 were not far behind and in most cohorts half of those women had become home-owners by the age of 40. Unfortunately, those data say nothing about the housing situation of female immigrants who do not marry or whose marriages break up. The official *Guide to Living in Australia for New Settlers* (DILGEA, 1988) does, however, consider it necessary to mention women's refuges. The related question of domestic violence is one of the issues dealt with by the women's unit of the Department of Immigration, Local Government and Ethnic Affairs through their network of women's issues coordinators (DILGEA, 1990).

G. Occupation

Being an advanced industrial society where in 1986, 21 per cent of the total population was born abroad, Australia is a particularly interesting society in which to examine how immigrant women adapt to new labour markets. The ethnic diversity of Australia's immigrants makes it possible to separate the consequences of immigration *per se* from those related to the characteristics of immigrants, such as language, culture and the possession of modern work skills (Evans, 1984). According to the 1986 census, 2.6 million women were employed, 1.9 million being Australian-born. Of the remainder, totaling 622,614 women, about one in 3 was born in the United Kingdom or Ireland. As shown in table 64, employed women born in Australia, Germany, New Zealand, the United Kingdom and Ireland display similar distributions by occupation, with about one third of each group working as clerks and one fifth in sales and personal services, so that close to half of all employed women in those immigrant groups are found in those two categories. In contrast, close to one half of the employed women born in Greece and Italy work as plant or machine operators or as

TABLE 64. EMPLOYED WOMEN IN AUSTRALIA, BY OCCUPATION AND SELECTED COUNTRIES OF BIRTH: 1986

	Australia	New Zealand[a]	United Kingdom and Ireland	Germany	Greece	Italy	Yugoslavia	Poland
Occupation								
Managers and administrators	7.8	5.6	6.0	7.5	7.5	9.8	3.5	5.2
Professionals	12.4	10.9	11.4	12.0	3.6	4.2	3.4	12.2
Para-professionals	7.2	8.7	8.3	6.3	.8	1.3	2.7	7.5
Tradespersons	3.6	3.9	3.2	5.0	5.9	7.1	5.4	4.6
Clerks	33.2	32.8	34.5	30.6	9.5	18.0	14.6	16.4
Sales and personal services	20.2	20.5	18.2	14.6	13.4	14.0	9.2	11.8
Plant and machine operators	2.2	3.2	2.6	3.7	21.5	16.0	17.8	9.6
Labourers and related workers	11.0	12.4	13.7	15.1	34.2	25.8	39.9	28.6
Other	2.3	1.7	1.9	2.9	3.5	3.7	3.7	3.9
Employment status								
Wage and salary earner	85.8	89.9	88.4	81.0	74.5	76.7	90.5	85.5
Self-employed	7.6	5.6	6.5	10.6	15.3	13.6	5.6	8.5
Employer	4.8	3.3	3.7	6.4	8.6	7.4	2.9	4.7
Unpaid helper	1.8	1.2	1.3	1.9	1.6	2.3	1.0	1.3
Number (thousands)	1 939	57	226	23	28	41	29	9

Source: Australian Bureau of Statistics, *Census 1986*, tables C11 and C12.

[a]For employment status, New Zealand combined with other areas of Oceania.

labourers and related workers. Indeed women born in Southern Europe (mainly in Greece, Italy and Yugoslavia), who represent only 4 per cent of all employed women, constitute 21 per cent of those who work as machinists and 10 per cent of the labourers. A relatively large proportion of Italian women work as managers and administrators, a category that includes farmers and farm managers, many of whom are Italian women.

Among the Australian-born there are three times as many school teachers as plant and machine operators. Conversely, women born in Southern Europe include 11 times as many plant and machine operators as teachers. Those born in Southern Europe are strongly underrepresented among nurses: while 1 in 20 Australian-born female workers is a registered nurse the proportion among women born in Southern Europe is only 7 per thousand. Such a low proportion of women working as nurses reflects not only differing cultural perceptions regarding the status of the occupation but also lower educational levels.

Among the subgroup of women working as drivers or plant operators, there were virtually no women born in Australia, New Zealand or the United Kingdom. That subgroup, therefore, constitutes an enclave for other immigrant women. The group of labourers and related workers includes cleaners, an occupation favoured by Southern Europeans, which accounts for about 11.5 per cent of both Greek and Yugoslavian employed women. In contrast, less than 2 per cent of the employed Vietnamese women are cleaners. The difference is likely to stem from the fact that cleaning jobs, especially those offered by large institutions, are frequently filled by the friends and relatives of those already holding such jobs, thus providing an advantage to groups that have been established longer.

Length of residence in Australia is positively related to a marked rise in the status of occupations for all non-English-speaking immigrant groups (using a scale of occupational prestige which represents Australian, but not necessarily immigrants' rankings).

Speaking English has an impact equivalent to that of two additional years of formal education in determining the status of the jobs which women are able to obtain (Evans, 1984, p. 1079). Evans (1984) has shown that when educational endowments and length of residence, age, family situation and urban/rural residence are controlled for, most work-related differences among ethnic groups vanish. One clear variation is that women from Southern Europe and from developing countries are more likely to be entrepreneurs than other women—thereby significantly raising their incomes in relation to their qualifications. Evans (1984, p. 1087) concludes that "the Australian labour market appears to be nearly blind to ethnicity, except that Mediterranean women having little education get better jobs than their Australian peers and highly educated Mediterranean women (of whom there are very few) get somewhat worse jobs than their Australian peers".

This finding appears surprising, given a number of studies showing the disadvantages experienced by immigrant women from non-English-speaking backgrounds (Cox and others, 1976; National Women's Advisory Council, 1979; Loh, 1980). However, the question again arises of what constitutes an appropriate comparison since most earlier studies have not controlled for education and qualifications. Work in a chicken-gutting factory or at home sewing 50 pairs of babies underpants an hour is unpleasant, whosoever has to do it, but who gets the raw jobs appears to be determined by education not birthplace. There are, however, two caveats to this conclusion. One is that immigrant women who arrive with no or minimal educational qualifications tend not to have an equivalent group among the Australian-born population. The other is that, as the disadvantages of immigrants decline with increasing years of residence in Australia, informal learning gains importance. A further issue relates to differences in cultural perceptions. To take one example, it is commonly thought that the small number of immigrants among persons employed by the Government may reflect some form of discrimination (Department of Finance, 1989). However, not all immigrant groups are equally likely to apply for government employment. Native-born women and those belonging to certain immigrant groups also differ with respect to how marriage and child-bearing af-

fect their labour force participation. Marriage depresses labour force participation by more than 10 per cent among all groups of women except among those from Eastern and Southern Europe. Similarly, the presence of children, especially pre-school age children, in the household has a different impact on the likelihood of the labour force participation of women from one ethnic group to another. These differences can be interpreted as reflecting the reasons that women have for working outside the home, that is, women who seek employment for self-fulfillment or to increase the standard of living of the family may be more likely to stay at home when their children are young than women who must work to provide their families with the bare essentials. The 1971 Melbourne Survey asked women's reasons for joining the labour force and showed that immigrant women (especially those from non-English-speaking backgrounds) were more likely to be driven by perceived need than career goals, but it also showed that such immigrants placed more emphasis on working to secure home ownership (Ware, 1976).

H. FEMALE/MALE CONTRASTS

The integration experience of migrant women differs from that of migrant men for three main reasons: (a) different educational backgrounds; (b) different familial roles; and (c) different employment experiences. Since immigrant men are better educated than immigrant women from similar backgrounds, they are better prepared to meet a new continent. Their lives are also less bound by family obligations. "Within a supposedly free and independent Australia women are a colonized sex. They are denied freedom of movement, control of their bodies, economic independence and cultural potency. This oppressed state derives from the status of 'the family' in Australia and the responsibilities assigned to women within that institution" (Summers, 1975, p. 29). Men escape to watch and play sports, to their pubs and clubs: women are defined and enclosed by their families. A closely knit family structure has both negative and positive aspects. For immigrant women, especially those from non-English-speaking backgrounds, the extended family (where present, as it surprisingly often is, in the same suburb if not the same household) provides security and emotional support but it also removes the incentive to go out and mix with the broad Australian community. Since immigrant groups who share a common language often prefer to live in the same suburbs, it is frequently possible for a woman to conduct her business with everyone, from the travel agent to the undertaker, in her mother tongue without ever speaking to a native-born Australian (Burnley, 1975; Jupp, 1989). Within her family, the immigrant woman may well be in a more secure position than her neighbour born interstate, but separation, divorce or widowhood can often serve to turn the tables. Some ethnic communities tend to exclude separated and divorced women. Widows are more sympathetically treated but the assimilation by the second generation of Australian norms may mean a reluctance to invite the widowed mother to move in. For the childless widow or divorcee with no second marriage in sight a lack of English can make life bleak. Bertelli (1980a) has described the fate of elderly Italian-born women entering monolingual nursing homes, having forgotten the little English they once knew, as having "entered the tomb before the time of death". Fortunately, such a situation is rare. Data for Sydney show that in 1976 only 70 out of a total 7,181 Italian-born elderly persons were living in nursing homes. In contrast, by the age of 75 some 29 per cent of Italian-born men and fully 57 per cent of Italian-born women had become "ancestors", that is, parents living with their children but not as heads of household. The comparable figures for the Australian-born were 8 per cent for men and 14 per cent for women (Ware, 1981, pp. 97-100).

I. ETHNICITY, RELIGION AND CULTURE

So far we have been using birthplace as a proxy for ethnic affiliation. Although far from ideal, this practice is necessary because of the tools available and has served to show how few significant differences there are between Australian-born women and those born in the United Kingdom and Ireland. Indeed, much public discussion of immigration tends to treat immigrants from English-speaking countries if they were not really immigrants because they are not perceived as being different or as having special problems. Data on religion provide an alternative source of information on some ethnic groups: notably non-Christians and the two large and distinctive Christian groups—the Roman Catholics and the Orthodox. Irish Catholics probably represent the one major English-speaking group which most Australians would perceive as having some claim to being an "ethnic group".

Mol (1971) observed that, in contrast to the United States where conversion is common, in Australia the numerical strength of the various religious denominations reflects original patterns of immigration. Furthermore, religious affiliation has been very closely linked to ethnic and national pride (Mol, 1971, p. 1). Religion can either aid integration to Australian society or be a barrier to it. Catholicism is often an integrating factor uniting immigrant groups with the native-born (26 per cent of the total Australian population are Catholics). Conversely, membership of the mostly Greek-Orthodox community (2.7 per cent of the population) separates Greek immigrants and their descendants from other Australians, especially in the case of groups that require marriage with co-religionists. Perhaps the Islamic faith, comprising 0.7 per cent of the population, is the most devisive because of the particular cultural demands it places on women.

J. INCOME AND WEALTH

In 1981 Eastern European women were the best paid among all employed women (averaging $A7.20 per hour) followed by Australian-born women ($A6.80), immigrant women from developing countries ($A6.80), women from English-speaking countries and from North-western Europe ($A6.60) and, lastly, women from Mediterranean countries (Southern Europe, Western Asia and Northern Africa) who earned $A5.80 an hour, a ranking which was maintained even after standardization by age (Evans, 1984, pp. 1070 and 1082). The average earnings of women from Mediterranean countries would increase by some 90 cents an hour if they had the same educational and skill endowments as the Australian-born. Indeed, among women with limited education, women from Mediterranean countries have somewhat better paid and higher status work because of their greater tendency to be self-employed (Evans, 1984).

The income data from the 1986 Census (Australian Bureau of Statistics, p. 22) show that 23 per cent of men aged 15 or over had annual incomes above $A22,000, compared with only 5 per cent of women and 2 per cent of women born in Greece or Italy. About 6 per cent of men reported having no income. Some 16 per cent of women had no income, but among women born in Greece and Italy the equivalent proportion was 21 per cent. Differences in the proportion in the no-income category by birthplace do not suggest that women from countries without a welfare system are worse off because they are unaware of their welfare entitlements in Australia, but the formulation of the question on income may have been confusing.

In 1987 the *Business Review Weekly* (1987) identified the 200 richest Australians. One in four were immigrants, but only three of the top 200 were women. By 1989 the listing included 11 women, two of whom were immigrants: both Americans who had married Australians (*Business Review Weekly*, 1989).

K. CITIZENSHIP AND POLITICS

Since 1973 immigrants are eligible to obtain Australian citizenship provided that they have lived in Australia for three years, have an adequate knowledge of English and intend to reside permanently in Australia. Marriage to an Australian does not bring automatic citizenship rights to persons of either sex. Until the 1980s, citizens of the United Kingdom had advantages over other immigrants which did not encourage them to seek citizenship (Lucas, 1987, p. 56). Even in 1986 less than half of the immigrants from the United Kingdom and Ireland were Australian citizens, compared with over 90 per cent of those born in Greece and the former USSR (Australian Bureau of Statistics, 1988, p. 22). It is not clear whether an inadequate command of English has deterred any substantial number of immigrant women from seeking citizenship, although Ware (1981, p. 32) has shown that in 1976 Italian-born men aged 35 or over were more likely to be citizens than their female counterparts. Immigrants who had been educated in Australia were more likely to become

citizens than those who were educated abroad (Evans, 1983).

Neither women nor immigrants have had noticeable access to political power in Australian society, where such power remains largely in the hands of men of Anglo-Celtic backgrounds. Higley and others (1979, p. 77) concluded that the higher levels of the Australian political elite are virtually closed to immigrants. Sawer and Simms (1984) show how some women make their political careers by replacing their fathers or husbands in Parliament, a route that is largely barred to immigrant women.

The *Who's Who of Australian Women* (Lofthouse, 1984) includes 35 women who were members of the federal or state legislatures. Only 2 were immigrants: one British, one Italian. German-born Leisha Harvey, the senior immigrant woman politician, became Queensland Health Minister in 1987.

By 1989 about 1 in 8 of Australia's 853 Members of the federal and state parliaments were women (Darby, 1989). Federally, of the 9 women among 224 members of the House of Representatives, 8 were born in Australia and 1 in New Zealand. Women comprised 17 of the 76 senators and 2 were immigrant women, one born in England and the other in Shanghai. Both represented smaller parties (Parliamentary Library, 1988). Overall, the political data show that although women have great difficulty in being nominated as candidates by the major parties, they are not subject to additional bias because of being immigrants (Sawer and Sims, 1984). Studies of the political participation of ethnic minorities in Australia show that it is easier for a man from an obvious ethnic minority to gain political office than for an Australian-born woman, but that women from ethnic minorities can sometimes find that their sex is an advantage, especially in appointed positions, since they can be held to represent two "minority" groups at once (Jupp and others, 1989).

Women also have limited visibility among trade union officials and immigrant women tend to fare even worse both because they work in less heavily unionized occupations and because they have almost no tradition of undertaking public roles. Although women comprise one third of union members, women as union officials are still relatively rare (ESCAP, 1987, pp. 60-61). In recent years, the unions have made a stronger effort to recognize women's special needs by providing, for instance, child-care services for those attending union meetings, but immigrant women still have to overcome cultural barriers to participate actively in the unions. The publication of a multilingual women's trade union newspaper (Tomas, 1987) has not brought about major changes. Despite immigrant women's relative lack of power within the unions, the regulated nature of much of the Australian labour market has worked to the advantage of immigrant women in their move towards wage equality with men (O'Donnell and Hall, 1988). It is in the unregulated, non-unionized areas of "sweat-shop" employment where non-English-speaking women have been at a disadvantage in terms of wages and working conditions.

Australia has a growing battery of federal and state legislation on sex discrimination and affirmative action. From information on controversial cases of sex discrimination and sexual harassment which becomes public (most cases are settled by conciliation), it is clear that some immigrant women, including those from non-English-speaking backgrounds, have been making good use of existing legislation. It is not clear, however, whether they have special need for support. The annual Women's Budget Statement issued by the Office of the Status of Women in the Prime Minister's Department contains an extensive overview of progress in the implementation of the National Agenda for Women, including activities within the portfolio of the Department of Immigration, Local Government and Ethnic Affairs on behalf of Women.

L. Mortality

Although immigrant women may be disadvantaged in other areas, they enjoy clear advantages in terms of survivorship, particularly if they originate in non-English-speaking countries. Such advantages stem in part from the selectivity of migration, since less healthy persons do not even migrate, but are also associated with dietary habits, lower consumption of alcohol, less smoking and use of motor vehicles, all of which increase the chances of surviving (Dasvarma, 1980). One aspect of the lack of integration of immigrant women is the low proportion who have driving licenses. Although their mobility is therefore limited, they are also less exposed to road accidents.

Mortality data show that immigrant women's apparent disadvantages do not always have negative outcomes. Despite the host of true stories of women unable to understand their doctors' instructions, and statistics showing that the children of non-English-speaking migrants are less likely to receive preventive health care (Australian Bureau of Statistics, 1989), such children still have lower mortality levels than the children of the Australian-born. Their lower infant mortality probably reflects a combination of health selection among the parents, higher breast-feeding levels among immigrant groups, and lower levels of births outside marriage which experience relatively high mortality risks. Similarly, if the data can be believed, men from non-English-speaking countries are more likely to commit suicide in Australia than in their country of origin while the reverse is true of women. Young (1989, table 6) has shown that both female and male immigrants (even those with 15 years of residence and more) from Greece, Italy, the Netherlands, England and Wales had significantly lower mortality than the Australian-born. In general, data for 25 birthplace groups show that where male immigrants have an advantage, so do women, often to an even greater extent. The exceptions are immigrants from Muslim countries— Egypt, Lebanon, Malaysia and Turkey—and Canada and the United States, where women have markedly lower survivorship advantages than men.

M. Future migrant entry

The six-member Committee to Advise on Australia's Immigration Policies included two women, both immigrants: a Polish-born professor of economics and an Italian-born scientist. The Committee recommended bonus selection points for the attributes of spouses, that the spouses of temporary migrants be allowed to work and the preparation of information materials to explain the position of women in Australian society (DILGEA, 1989, p. 7; Overseas Information Branch, 1989).

The main categories of Australia's immigrant admissions are still "family", with 71,000 places allocated for 1989-1990, "skilled" with 54,000 places, and "humanitarian" with 14,000 places. Women do not figure very prominently in the skilled category for self-employed business persons. The humanitarian intake includes Indo-Chinese selected from refugee camps in Asia as well as up to 60 "women at risk". The "women at risk" programme represents an innovative approach to provide special resettlement opportunities for unprotected refugee women and their dependants. The scheme uses existing settlement services, such as torture and trauma counselling, child care, English classes, women's health care and the Community Refugee Resettlement Scheme that provide support to refugees during their first two years in Australia (DILGEA, 1989).

The implementation of the 1989 Migration Amendment Act will mean that a significant proportion of women will continue to be admitted as family immigrants or as refugees, many of whom may be poorly educated or unable to speak English. The provisions of the "women at risk" programme indicate that much has been learned about how to help immigrant women to become part of Australian society. Yet, it is still vital to ensure that the tools which should be available are actually accessible to those who have the least knowledge of and ability to enforce their rights (Cox and others, 1976).

As a new generation of women from minority ethnic backgrounds who have been brought up in Australia moves into public life, the old image of women from non-English-speaking backgrounds as being dependent and passive is rapidly dissipating (Women from Ethnic Minorities and Education, 1990). That image was always a caricature of a complex reality in which some women gained a great deal from immigrating to a world of new opportunities, while others were largely cut-off from that world by cultural and linguistic barriers.

———————

REFERENCES

Appleyard, Reginald T. (1988). *The Ten Pound Immigrants*. London: Boxtree.

Australia, Department of Foreign Affairs and Trade, Overseas Information Branch (1989). Immigration policies reformed. Fact sheet No. 38 (October). Canberra: Government Publishing Service.

Australia, Department of Immigration, Local Government and Ethnic Affairs (1988). *Living in Australia: A Guide for New Settlers*. Canberra: Government Publishing Service.

_____ (1989a). *CAAIP Report. Some Questions and Answers*. Canberra: Government Publishing Service.

_____ (1989b). *Procedures Advice Manual: Refugee and Humanitarian Visas*. Canberra: Government Publishing Service.

_____ (1989c). *About Migrant Women: Statistical Profile 1986*. Canberra: Government Publishing Service.

_____ (1990). *Review 1990*. Canberra: Government Publishing Service.

Australian Bureau of Statistics (1988). *Australia in Profile*. Canberra: Government Publishing Service.

Australian Bureau of Statistics (n.d.). *Census 1986: Cross-classified Characteristics of Persons and Dwellings*. Canberra: Government Publishing Service.

Australian Commission of Inquiry into Poverty (1976). *Third Main Report: Medical/Social Aspects of Poverty in Australia*. Canberra: Government Publishing Service.

Australian Overseas Information Service (1989). *National Agenda on Multiculturalism: Fact Sheet*.

Bertelli, L. (1980). *The Italian Aged of Victoria*. Melbourne, Australia: CIRC.

Borrie, W. D. (1988). Changes in immigration patterns since 1972. In *The Australian People*, J. Jupp, ed. North Ryde, Australia: Angus and Robertson.

Boyd, Monica (1986). Immigrant women in Canada. In *International Migration: The Female Experience*, Rita James Simon and Caroline B. Brettell, eds. New Jersey: Rowman and Allenheld.

Burnley, Ian (1975). Ethnic factors in social segregation and residential stratification in Australia's large cities. *Australian and New Zealand Journal of Sociology* (Bundoora, Victoria, Australia), vol. 11, No. 1, pp. 12-20.

Business Review Weekly (1987). Rich 200. August 14.

_____ (1989). Rich 200. May 12.

Cox, Eva, and others (1976). *We Cannot Talk our Rights: Migrant Women*. Sydney, Australia: New South Wales Council of Social Services.

Darby, Andrew (1989). Women MPs get a toehold. *Sydney Morning Herald* (Sydney, Australia), 21 October, p. 7.

Dasvarma, Gour (1980). *Differential mortality in Australia with special reference to the period 1970-1972*. A doctoral thesis. Canberra: Australian National University.

Doczy, A. (1969). The social assimilation of adolescent boys of European parentage in Perth. *British Journal of Educational Psychology*, vol. 39, pp. 193-194.

Evans, M. D. R. (1983). Choosing to be a citizen. *International Labour Review* (Geneva), vol. 22, pp. 243-264.

_____ (1984). Immigrant women in Australia: resources, family and work. *International Migration Review* (Staten Island, New York), vol. 18, No. 4 (Winter), pp. 1063-1090.

Francis, R. (1981). *Migrant Crime in Australia*. St. Lucia: University of Queensland Press.

Giese, Diana (1989). How '60s manly girls became '80s women. *Weekend Australian*, December 9-10, p. 8.

Hawke, Robert (1979). *The Resolution of Conflict*. Sydney, Australia.

Hellman, Judith (1987). *Journeys Among Women: Feminism in Five Italian Cities*. Cambridge: Polity Press.

Huber, Rita (1977). *From Pasta to Pavlova*. St. Lucia: University of Queensland Press.

Hugo, Graeme J. (1986). *Australia's Changing Population*. Melbourne, Australia: Oxford University Press.

Jordan, Beverley (1989). Right to work. *Sydney Morning Herald* (Sydney, Australia), 2 December, section 5.

Jupp, James, ed. (1988). *The Australian People*. North Ryde, Australia: Angus and Robertson.

_____ (1989). *Australian Languages: An Introductory Atlas*. Canberra: Australian National University, Centre for Immigration and Multicultural Studies.

_____, and others (1989). *The Political Participation of Ethnic Minorities in Australia*. Canberra: Government Publishing Service.

Loh, M., ed. (1980). *With Courage in their Cases: The Experiences of Thirty Five Italian Immigrants and their Families in Australia*. Melbourne, Australia: FILEF.

Lofthouse, Andrea (1982). *Who's Who of Australian Women*. Sydney, Australia: Methuen.

Lucas, David (1987). *The Welsh, Irish, Scots and English in Australia*. Canberra: Australian Institute of Multicultural Affairs.

Lynch, P. (1970). *The Woman's Role in Immigration*. Canberra: Government Publishing Service.

Mistilis, N. (1986). *Destroying myths: Second-generation Australians' educational achievement*. Canberra: Australian National University, Department of Political Science.

Mol, Hans (1971). *Religion in Australia*. Melbourne, Australia: Nelson.

National Women's Advisory Council (1979). *Migrant Women Speak*. Canberra: Government Publishing Service.

Neutze, Max, and Hal Kendig (1989). Achievement of home ownership among post-war Australian cohorts. Urban Research Unit Working Paper, No. 16. Canberra: Australian National University.

O'Donnell, Carol, and Philippa Hall (1988). *Getting Equal: Labour Market Regulation and Women's Work*. Sydney, Australia: Allen and Unwin.

Office of the Status of Women (1986). *Convention on the Elimination of all Forms of Discrimination Against Women. Report of Australia*. Canberra: Government Publishing Service.

Parliamentary Library (1988). *Parliamentary Handbook*. Canberra: Government Publishing Service.

Pittarello, A. (1980). *Soup without Salt. The Australian Catholic Church and the Italian Migrant*. Sydney, Australia: Centre for Migration Studies.

Price, Charles (1982a). Appendix. In *Population of Australia*, vol. 2. Bangkok: Economic and Social Commission for Asia and the Pacific.

_____ (1982b). *The Fertility and Marriage Patterns of Australia's Ethnic Groups*. Canberra: Australian National University.

Price, C., and J. Martin (1975). *Australian Immigration, No. 3*. Canberra: Australian National University Press.

Sawer, Marian, and Marian Sims (1984). *A Woman's Place*. Sydney, Australia: Allen and Unwin.

Summers, Anne (1975). *Damned Whores and God's Police*. Melbourne, Australia: Penguin.

Storer, Des (1976). *But I Wouldn't Want my Wife to Work Here: A Study of Migrant Women in Melbourne Industry*. Melbourne, Australia: Centre for Urban Research and Action.

Thompson, L. (1980). *Australia Through Italian Eyes: A Study of Settlers Returning from Australia to Italy*. Melbourne, Australia: Oxford University Press.

Tomas, Natalie (1987). *Women and Trade Unions in Australia: A Bibliographic Guide*. Melbourne, Australia: Victorian Public Service Association.

United Nations, Economic and Social Commission for Asia and the Pacific (1987). *Achievements of the United Nations Decade for Women in Asia and the Pacific*. Bangkok.

Ware, Helen (1976). Fertility and workforce participation: the experience of Melbourne wives. *Population Studies* (London), vol. 30, pp. 413-427.

_____ (1981). *A Profile of the Italian Community in Australia*. Melbourne, Australia: Australian Institute of Multicultural Affairs.

Watson, Sophie (1988). *Accommodating Inequality*. Sydney, Australia: Allen and Unwin.

Women from Ethnic Minorities and Education (1990). *Fields, Factories, and Feminism*. Melbourne, Australia: Women from Ethnic Minorities and Education.

Wright, Judith (1965). *Preoccupations in Australian Poetry*. Melbourne, Australia.

Young, Christabel (1989). Demographic behaviour and intergenerational change among migrants in Australia. Paper presented at the General Conference of the International Union for the Scientific Study of Population, New Delhi, 20-27 September.

XII. MIGRATION OF ASIAN WOMEN TO AUSTRALIA

Graeme J. Hugo*

As in Canada and the United States, immigration to Australia has changed radically in the past two decades. Immigration policy has shifted from being almost exclusively concerned with the recruitment of economically and demographically active European settlers to one in which humanitarian and family reunion elements have become as significant as economic considerations in the selection of potential settlers; and less than half now originate in Europe. In the three months between July and September 1993, 42.9 per cent of the 17,528 immigrants settling in Australia were born in Asia compared to 13.2 per cent born in the United Kingdom and Ireland, and 16 per cent born elsewhere in Europe. As table 65 indicates, the number of Asian-born persons living in Australia increased from 23,293 in 1947, when they represented 0.3 per cent of the total population, to 822,096 in 1991 when they accounted for 4.9 per cent of the total. Many aspects of the migration of Asians to Australia and its impact have been different from those characterizing the earlier postwar immigration experience. One of those differences is that, in contrast to immigrant groups from the other major regions of the world, women outnumber men among immigrants from Asia (table 66).

This paper focuses on the experience of female Asian immigrants in Australia. Because of the general paucity of research focusing especially on female immigrants and of the relative recency of most Asian migration to Australia, it is far from straightforward to assess the effects that migration has had on female Asian immigrants, especially among those who are still at the initial stages of the adaptation process. Furthermore, there is considerable diversity in Asian migration to Australia, especially among women. Thus, the experience of Filipino women migrating to get married in Australia is likely to differ significantly from that of female refugees from

---

*School of Social Sciences, Flinders University of South Australia, Australia.

TABLE 65. CHANGE IN THE COMPOSITION OF THE AUSTRALIAN POPULATION, BY PLACE OF BIRTH: 1947-1991

	1947		1991	
	Number of persons	Per-centage	Number of persons	Per-centage
English-speaking origin	7 438 892	98.1	14 296 358	84.7
Australia	6 835 171	90.2	12 725 164	75.5
United Kingdom ...	543 829	7.2	1 170 986	6.9
New Zealand	43 619	0.6	275 845	1.6
United States and Canada	10 304	0.1	74 757	0.4
South Africa	5 969	0.1	49 606	0.3
Non-English-speaking origin	140 466	1.9	2 553 019	15.2
Other Europe	109 586	1.4	1 125 930	6.7
Asia	23 293	0.3	822 096	4.9
Other Africa	1 531	0.0	38 118	0.2
Other America	1 323	0.0	71 957	0.4
Other Oceania	4 733	0.1	251 178	2.1
TOTAL	7 579 358	100.0	16 849 377	100.0

Source: Australian Bureau of Statistics, *1947 Census; and 1991 Census of Population and Housing: Basic Community Profile, Australia*, tables B01, B08 and B09.

Viet Nam, Cambodia or the Lao People's Democratic Republic, which in turn is expected to be fairly different from the experience of female migrants from Hong Kong admitted in the business category. Nor should national stereotypes be allowed to hide the wide variation in migration motives and settlement experience within the various birthplace groups.

A. EXTENT OF ASIAN FEMALE MIGRATION TO AUSTRALIA

During most of the twentieth century, the Australian population was characterized by a relatively low proportion of women. Thus, in 1901 only 47.6 per cent of the population was female, representing a

TABLE 66. WOMEN AMONG THE FOREIGN-BORN POPULATION IN AUSTRALIA, BY REGION AND PLACE OF BIRTH: 1991

(Percentage)

Region and country or area of birth	Percentage of women
Total population	50.4
Total foreign-born	49.5
Australia	50.7
Africa	49.5
South Africa	51.0
Other countries	48.3
Asia	51.0
China	47.2
Hong Kong	48.9
India	50.0
Lebanon	47.5
Malaysia	51.9
Philippines	65.1
Viet Nam	47.7
Other countries	50.9
Oceania	49.9
New Zealand	49.9
Other countries	49.9
Americas	50.3
United States	48.1
Other countries	51.4
Europe	48.8
Germany	50.9
Greece	48.9
Italy	46.5
Malta	47.2
Netherlands	47.0
Poland	49.1
United Kingdom and Ireland	49.8
USSR (former)	52.3
Yugoslavia (former Republics)	46.7
Other countries	46.5

Source: Australian Bureau of Statistics, *1991 Census of Population and Housing: Basic Community Profile, Australia*, tables B08 and B09.

considerable increase over the proportion recorded in 1861, 42.2 per cent. Although the proportion of women kept increasing steadily during the twentieth century, in 1976 men still outnumbered women slightly in the total population. The relatively slow increase of the proportion female since 1900, which occurred despite the fact that the expectation of life

at birth of women surpassed that of men by wide margins, especially since 1950, can be attributed to the high proportion of men among the immigrants admitted by Australia. Traditionally, immigration to Australia has been male dominated. Indeed, when the first European colony was established in Sydney in 1788, men constituted most of the population. Among the 157,161 convicts that British authorities transported to Australia, only 20,209 were women (Price, 1972, pp. 37-38). Although early in the colonization process, British authorities ordered Governor Phillip, the commander of the First Fleet, to bring in women from the Pacific region, Phillip refused (Price, 1972, p. 40). Consequently, the first major Asian migration to Australia had to wait until after 1840, when employers started importing workers from China after the flow of British convicts was stopped (Lyng, 1935). The number of Chinese workers increased substantially during the gold rushes of the 1850s but, as table 67 shows, very few Chinese women entered the country. The low number of female Chinese immigrants can be attributed to the temporary and circular nature of much of the migration of Chinese male workers to Australia, to traditional Chinese family-lineage rules against female emigration and to restrictions imposed by the Australian authorities (Choi, 1975). Traditional objections became less significant in the early twentieth century, but the restrictive policy of the Government of Australia continued to limit "the entry of wives

TABLE 67. ETHNIC CHINESE POPULATION IN AUSTRALIA, BY SEX: 1861-1966

Census year	Male	Female	Percentage of women
1861	38 247	11	0.0
1871	28 307	44	0.2
1881	38 274	259	0.7
1891	35 523	298	0.8
1901	29 153	474	1.6
1911	21 856	897	3.9
1921	16 011	1 146	6.7
1933	9 311	1 535	14.2
1947	6 594	2 550	27.9
1954	9 150	3 728	28.9
1961	14 237	6 145	30.1
1966	15 406	7 875	33.8

Source: Ching Y. Choi, *Chinese Migration and Settlement in Australia* (Sydney University Press, 1975), pp. 22, 42 and 66.

and dependants, except those of merchants and well-established families" (Choi, 1975, p. 45). Hence, as table 67 indicates, it was only after the Second World War that the proportion of women among the ethnic Chinese population in Australia recorded a substantial increase. However, the numbers of both Chinese men and women in Australia remained low and, even by 1966, women accounted for only one third of the ethnic Chinese population enumerated by the census.[1]

Results from the 1947 census of Australia indicate the limited extent of Asian immigration during the first half of the twentieth century (table 68). The census enumerated only 23,293 Asian-born persons, many of whom were the children of European parents who had served as colonial functionaries in the former Asian colonies. The overwhelming male dominance in those Asian-born groups is clearly in evidence, with men outnumbering women almost two to one. During the early post-war years, despite

the rapid expansion of the overall intake of immigrants, the exclusionary policy towards Asians remained largely in place. Indeed, for a brief period, even the Japanese-origin "war-brides" of returning Australian servicemen were not permitted entry. However, the discriminatory elements of Australia's immigration policy were gradually removed and towards the mid-1970s the exclusionary policy was totally dismantled.

During the 1970s, major changes in the immigration and settlement policy of Australia took place. The most important was the removal of the last vestiges of the "White Australia" policy which had largely prevented the admission of immigrants from developing countries. However, because of the high unemployment levels being experienced at the time, immigration levels were reduced and the admission of persons with needed skills was given priority by making the possession of such skills a major criteria for the selection of immigrants. Family reunification was also a major element of the immigration programme, and a substantial refugee element was added to it after the reunification of Viet Nam in 1975. Such changes led Australia to move from an assimilationist to a multicultural policy in regard to the settlement of immigrants.

The changes in Australian immigration policy interacted with other developments in the South-eastern Asian region and led to a substantial increase in Asian immigration to the country. Developments facilitating such a trend include the growing political, social, economic and cultural ties between Australia and a number of Asian countries; increases in tourism, business travel and the exchange of students between Asia and Australia; the reduction of transport costs within the region; major increases in the two-way flows of information; and the continuation of internal conflict and uncertainty within a number of Asian countries.

TABLE 68. WOMEN IN AUSTRALIA BORN IN ASIA: 1947 CENSUS

Country or area of birth	Number of persons	Percentage of women
Western Asia		
Lebanon and Syrian Arab		
Republic	1 888	45.1
Palestine	1 658	46.3
Turkey	116	33.6
Arabia	33	27.3
Southern Asia		
India and Sri Lanka	8 162	35.7
Afghanistan	22	0.0
South-eastern and Eastern Asia		
China	6 404	19.8
British Malay area	1 768	41.3
Dutch East Indies	1 041	38.4
Hong Kong	762	47.1
Japan	330	43.6
Other British colonies	253	26.9
Philippines	141	34.7
Other Asia	715	31.9
TOTAL	23 293	33.6

Source: Charles A. Price and others, "Birthplaces of the Australian population, 1861-1981", Working Papers in Demography, No. 13 (Canberra, Australian National University, 1984), p. 13.

In terms of Asian migration, the consequences of Australia's new immigration policy have been dramatic. Thus, whereas it had taken the Asian-born population in the country 24 years (from 1947 to 1971) to increase fivefold and reach 112,107, it took only another 15 years for it to register another fivefold increase and thus reach 536,152 in 1986.

The number of Asian immigrants to Australia began growing in 1976/77 and has surpassed all other major immigrant groups since 1983/84.[2] During the 1980s, 8 of the 10 fastest growing groups of foreign-born persons in Australia were Asian and of the 10 foreign-born groups registering the lowest growth were European (table 69).

One of the major changes evident in the Asian-born population is the continued increase of the proportion of women. Thus, whereas even as recently as 1971 women accounted for only 45.8 per cent of the Asian-born population, by 1981 they had reached parity with men and by 1991 they outnumbered men, accounting for 51.8 per cent of the total Asian-born population in Australia (table 70). The increase in the proportion of women among the Asian-born population reflects the maturation of migration flows from the region, the effects of shifts in the categories of immigrants being admitted and shifts in the role and status of women both in the Asian countries of origin and in Australia.

Asian immigration to Australia has been characterized by its heterogeneity, with immigrants from different countries becoming numerous at different times. Thus, the first Asian country to appear among the three major sources of immigrants to Australia was Lebanon in 1977/78, when it accounted for 17.2 per cent of the annual immigration intake. From 1978/79 to 1987/88, Viet Nam consistently accounted for either the second or the third largest contingent of immigrants admitted yearly. In 1988/89 it was replaced by the Philippines. Furthermore, since 1977/78, immigrants originating in a number of other Asian countries, particularly China, Hong Kong and Malaysia, have consistently ranked fourth or fifth with respect to the overall annual intake. In 1992/93, immigrants from Hong Kong and Viet Nam ranked third and fourth respectively among all immigrants to Australia.

An analysis of the size and distribution of the foreign-born population originating in the Asian region but excluding Western Asia, indicates that dur-

TABLE 69. FASTEST- AND SLOWEST-GROWING GROUPS OF FOREIGN-BORN PERSONS IN AUSTRALIA: 1981-1993

Country or area of origin	Number of persons in 1993	Percentage growth during 1981-1993
Fastest growing groups		
Philippines	85 500	15.1
Hong Kong	80 800	14.3
Fiji	35 600	11.6
China	91 500	10.8
Viet Nam	137 300	10.1
Malaysia	84 700	8.3
Sri Lanka	43 600	7.7
Singapore	29 900	7.6
Indonesia	37 200	7.1
South Africa	57 100	6.1
Chile	27 500	5.4
United States	53 100	4.7
Slowest growing groups		
Egypt	38 500	1.5
Poland	68 600	0.8
Former Yugoslav Republics	172 100	0.8
United Kingdom and Ireland	1 224 200	0.3
Germany	119 300	0.3
Netherlands	99 000	-0.1
Greece	145 900	-0.4
Italy	266 900	-0.6
Hungary	26 700	-0.8
Malta	53 300	-1.0
Cyprus	21 900	-1.0
USSR (former)	46 500	-1.1

Source: Australian Bureau of Statistics, *Estimated Resident Population by Country of Birth, Age and Sex: Australia, Preliminary, June 1992 and June 1993*, Catalogue No. 3221.0 (Canberra, 1993), p. 18.

TABLE 70. POPULATION IN AUSTRALIA BORN IN ASIA, BY SEX: ENUMERATED BY THE CENSUSES 1947-1991

Year of census	Enumerated population		Percentage of women
	Male	Female	
1947	13 452	6 167	31.4
1954	23 465	14 472	38.1
1961	35 188	22 796	39.3
1971	65 598	55 421	45.8
1976	77 956	74 175	48.8
1981	132 067	131 977	50.0
1986	202 691	210 467	50.9
1991	331 452	356 398	51.8

Sources: Australian Bureau of Statistics, Population Censuses, various years; ABS, Postwar Census Enumerations.
NOTE: Excluding Western Asia.

ing the 1980s, the Vietnamese became the largest Asian-born group in Australia, replacing the Indians who had occupied first place in 1981 (table 71). The number of Vietnamese in Australia increased three-fold between 1981 and 1991. In relation to its population size, Australia has resettled more Vietnamese refugees than any other country in the world (Hugo, 1990a). The Vietnamese population in Australia has tended to display a very low proportion of women (47.7 per cent in 1991), a feature characteristic of many refugee populations. Similarly, the population born in Cambodia exhibited a low proportion of women in 1981 (47.8 per cent), but its composition by sex became more balanced during the 1980s so that by 1991 women accounted for half of the total. The Cambodian population was one of the fastest growing foreign-born groups during the 1980s.

In 1991, the second largest group of Asian-born migrants was that of persons born in China, whose numbers nearly tripled between 1981 and 1991. The increase in numbers was relatively greater among male Chinese immigrants, since the proportion of women among the population born in China declined from 50 to 47.1 per cent between 1981 and 1991. In contrast, the proportion of women among the third largest group of Asian-born immigrants in Australia, those born in the Philippines, remained very high (at 65 per cent) even as the population born in the Philippines grew considerably, more than quadrupling over the decade. The female dominance in Filipino migration, though also noticeable in the flows directed to other countries of destination, has been particularly strong in the case of Australia because of the immigration of Filipino women to join their Australian-born husbands and fiancés.

TABLE 71. CHANGE IN THE PERCENTAGE OF WOMEN AMONG THE ASIAN-BORN POPULATION IN AUSTRALIA, BY COUNTRY OR AREA OF BIRTH: 1981-1991

Country or area of birth	Population		Percentage growth 1981-1991	Percentage of women	
	1981	1991		1981	1991
Bangladesh	1 008	2 289	127.1	43.8	41.1
Cambodia	3 700	17 555	374.5	47.7	50.1
China	26 800	78 866	194.3	50.0	47.1
Hong Kong and Macau	16 300	58 984	261.9	48.1	50.9
India	43 700	61 606	41.0	49.9	49.9
Indonesia	16 400	33 264	102.8	49.4	49.5
Japan	7 300	25 984	255.9	51.8	59.1
Lao People's Democratic Republic	5 600	9 658	72.5	49.2	49.1
Malaysia	32 500	72 611	123.4	49.4	52.0
Myanmar	7 700	8 260	7.3	51.7	52.1
Pakistan	2 611	5 806	122.4	47.3	40.4
Philippines	15 800	73 660	366.2	64.8	65.2
Republic of Korea	4 400	20 901	377.2	46.7	51.5
Singapore	12 400	24 563	98.1	50.3	53.6
Sri Lanka	17 900	37 283	108.3	50.2	49.8
Taiwan Province of China	..	12 427	..	..	54.5
Thailand	3 492	13 756	293.9	62.8	60.6
Viet Nam	43 400	122 347	181.9	45.8	47.7
Total foreign-born	3 110 900	4 125 370	32.6	48.0	49.4
Total population	14 923 300	16 850 533	12.9	50.1	50.4

Sources: Australian Bureau of Statistics, *Estimated Resident Population by Country of Birth, Age and Sex, Australia, June 1989 and Preliminary 1990*, Catalogue No. 3221.0 (Canberra, 1990); Australian Bureau of Statistics, *1991 Census of Population and Housing, Basic Community Profile: Australia* (Canberra, 1991), expanded format, table E12; Australian Bureau of Statistics, *1991 Census Matrix* (Canberra, 1991), table CSC6258.

NOTE: Two dots (..) indicate that data are not available or are not separately reported.

By 1991, the Malaysian-born population in Australia constituted the fourth largest group of Asian origin, having grown especially rapidly since 1985 when the Malaysian Government adopted a new economic policy (Hugo, Lim and Narayan, 1989). Ethnic Chinese from Malaysia have tended to enter Australia under the business and other economic categories. The proportion of women among the Malaysian-born population has been generally high but, whereas men outnumbered women in 1981, by 1991 the reverse was true (see table 71).

The Indian-born population, which ranked first in terms of size in the early 1980s, failed to keep pace with the fastest growing immigrant groups. It thus ranked fifth among the Asian-born groups in 1991 and its composition by sex remained balanced during the decade, with women accounting for nearly half of all Indian-born persons.

The group of migrants born in Hong Kong and Macau recorded a major increase during the 1980s, partly because of the growing uncertainty associated with the 1997 devolution of the Crown Colony of Hong Kong to China. Persons born in Hong Kong and Macau constituted the sixth largest Asian-born group in Australia in 1991 and had experienced an increase in the proportion of women (table 71). The general tendency for the proportion of women to increase during the 1980s was also noticeable in most of the other Asian-born groups so that by 1991 more groups exhibited a predominance of women than the reverse. However, only the small but rapidly increasing Thai-born population exhibited a dominance of women approaching that among the Filipino-born.

As the stock data suggest, the proportion of women among immigrants from the major source countries in Asia has been increasing, probably as a result of the maturation of migration flows. During fiscal year 1988/89, Asian immigrants constituted a record 38 per cent of the total immigrant intake and, as table 72 shows, the proportion of women among Asian immigrants contrasted markedly with that among immigrants from all other world regions. In fact, the high proportion of women among Asian immigrants was sufficient to ensure that women

TABLE 72. IMMIGRANTS TO AUSTRALIA DURING FISCAL YEAR 1988/89 AND PROPORTION OF WOMEN AMONG THEM, BY COUNTRY OR AREA OF BIRTH

Country or area of birth	Number of immigrants	Percentage of women
Afghanistan	338	47.6
Cambodia	1 480	49.7
China	3 819	51.8
Hong Kong	7 307	50.7
India	3 109	50.8
Indonesia	1 422	52.9
Japan	806	57.8
Lao People's Democratic Republic	426	47.4
Malaysia	7 681	50.8
Pakistan	385	46.5
Philippines	9 204	59.2
Republic of Korea	1 666	53.2
Singapore	1 946	53.1
Sri Lanka	2 937	50.2
Taiwan Province of China	2 100	50.5
Thailand	1 017	60.0
Viet Nam	7 971	51.4
Other Asian countries	987	49.7
SUBTOTAL	54 601	52.7
Oceania	27 999	48.5
Africa	5 040	49.1
United States and Canada	3 055	49.9
Other Americas	4 336	48.5
Western Asia	7 834	47.5
United Kingdom and Ireland	27 978	48.1
Northern Europe	7 692	49.0
Southern Europe	5 767	48.9
TOTAL	144 302	50.2

Source: Bureau of Immigration Research, unpublished data.

outnumbered men in the overall immigrant intake for the year. Among the Asian countries of origin, those in which male immigrants outnumbered female immigrants accounted for only 6.6 per cent of all Asian immigrants. Almost all the Asian countries producing sizeable immigration intakes in Australia exhibited proportions of women above 50 per cent. Even among the Vietnamese, whose stock in 1989 included more men than women, women outnumbered men in the 1988/89 intake. That change is related to a shift in the categories of Vietnamese immigrants, with those admitted for family reunion gaining ground in relative terms. Thus, whereas in 1981/82 virtually all Vietnamese immigrants were admitted as refugees (98 per cent), by 1987/88 refugees accounted for only 63 per cent of Vietnamese settler admissions and persons admitted under the family reunion categories accounted for 35 per cent of the total. By way of contrast, note that among Filipino immigrants, the proportion of women has been decreasing. Thus, whereas in 1982/83, 74.5 per cent of the nearly 3,000 Filipino immigrants admitted were women, by 1988/89 the proportion of women among the 9,200 newly admitted Filipino immigrants was 59 per cent.

Not only has the legal immigration of Asians to Australia been increasing, but there is also evidence suggesting that Asians account for a considerable proportion of persons who enter Australia under a temporary visa (as visitors, students, temporary residents etc.) and overstay the period for which their visa is valid. Because Australia has a good system to register departures, it is possible to match the arrival and departure cards of individuals and hence estimate the number of overstayers. As of 31 January 1984 it was estimated that there were nearly 80,000 overstayers in Australia, at least 43 per cent of whom

were citizens of Asian countries (some of those listed under the "other country of citizenship" category were also Asian). The bulk of overstayers had entered under a visitor visa (74 per cent among all overstayers and 66 per cent among Asians). Among Asian overstayers, those entering under a student visa also accounted for a sizeable proportion (25 per cent). Unfortunately, the Australian Department of Immigration, Local Government and Ethnic Affairs does not routinely produce estimates of overstayers by sex. The only data available relate to students, especially those taking English language courses. As table 73 indicates, the number not stating their sex is high, but it would nevertheless appear that men outnumber women among overstayers on student visas.

B. Processes of Asian female migration to Australia

There are few studies on the causes of immigration to Australia in comparison to the large amount of research devoted to the settlement process. Even less is known about the processes determining the migration of Asian women to Australia. However, as in the case of female international migration in

TABLE 73. OVERSTAYERS, BY SEX, VISA CATEGORY AND COUNTRY OF CITIZENSHIP, AS OF 31 MAY 1989

Visa category and citizenship	Number of overstayers				Percentage by sex		
	Male	Female	Sex not stated	Total	Male	Female	Sex not stated
Chinese	4 190	2 217	2 426	8 833	47.4	25.1	27.5
Students of English	2 636	1 139	685	4 460	59.1	25.5	15.4
Other students	267	177	1 359	1 803	14.8	9.8	75.4
Visitors	1 164	832	297	2 293	50.8	36.3	13.0
Temporary residents	52	15	38	105	49.5	14.3	36.2
Other categories	71	54	47	172	41.3	31.4	27.3
All students of English	4 800	2 226	1 301	8 327	57.6	26.7	15.6
Indonesia	336	131	105	572	58.7	22.9	18.4
Japan	52	76	89	217	24.0	35.0	41.0
Republic of Korea	706	192	124	1 022	69.1	18.8	12.1
Thailand	447	336	132	915	48.9	36.7	14.4
All other students	4 301	3 354	6 363	14 018	30.7	23.9	45.4

Source: Australia, Department of Immigration, Local Government and Ethnic Affairs, unpublished tabulations.

general, institutional factors are likely to play a major role. It is therefore important to consider how Australian immigration policy influences the immigration of Asian women to Australia. Notwithstanding Arnold's (1989, p. 892) dictum that potential migrants have become adept at playing the system and finding innovative ways of being admitted despite the legal restrictions in place, immigration policies and programmes play a crucial role in determining the number and type of women who leave Asian countries to settle in Australia. It must be noted, however, that there is a growing number of other institutions and "gatekeepers" whose influence is not sufficiently understood but who nevertheless act as linkages between the potential immigrant and the ultimate implementation of immigration policy. Such institutions and individuals include: (a) different authorities and officials in the country of origin; (b) Australian officials in charge of implementing

immigration policy; (c) a variety of middlemen, recruiters, lawyers, immigration advisers, marriage brokers, mail-order introduction agencies etc. that facilitate migration; and (d) international agencies, such as the United Nations High Commissioner for Refugees or the International Organization for Migration, that locate immigration opportunities for migrants with special needs.

An examination of Australian immigration policy makes clear that there are substantial differences in the extent to which male and female migrants can fit or use the various eligibility categories that determine admission to the country. Thus, among the immigrants admitted during fiscal year 1992/93, women outnumbered men in almost all the subcategories comprised under family migration (table 74). Women were especially overrepresented among the spouses and fiancés of Australian citizens, who have

TABLE 74. IMMIGRANTS TO AUSTRALIA, BY ADMISSION CATEGORY AND SEX: FISCAL YEAR 1992/93

Admission category	Number of immigrants		Percentage by category		Percentage of women
	Male	Female	Male	Female	
Family migration	13 165	18 937	36.1	47.5	59.0
Spouses and fiancees	5 588	10 925	15.3	27.4	66.2
Parents	1 718	2 445	4.7	6.1	58.7
Children	1 576	1 625	4.3	4.1	50.8
Concessional	4 283	3 942	11.7	9.9	47.9
Economic migration	11 949	10 188	32.7	25.6	46.0
Business migration programme (BMS)	1 805	1 802	4.9	4.5	50.0
Employer nomination scheme (ENS)	1 027	932	2.8	2.3	47.6
Occupational share scheme (OSS)	39	36	0.1	0.1	48.0
Independent skilled migrants	9 078	7 418	24.9	18.6	45.0
Special refugee, humanitarian and special assistance	5 831	5 108	16.0	12.8	46.7
Other categories	5 547	5 605	15.2	14.0	50.3
New Zealanders	4 164	4 191	11.4	10.5	50.2
Special cases	145	159	0.4	0.4	52.3
Others	1 238	1 255	3.4	3.1	50.3
TOTAL	36 492	39 838	100.0	100.0	52.2

Source: Australia, Bureau of Immigration and Population Research, *Immigration Update, June Quarter 1993* (Canberra, Australian Government Publishing Service, 1993), p. 11.

virtually automatic admission to Australia. Similarly, women constituted 59 per cent of immigrants admitted as parents of Australian residents, another subcategory of immigrants where admission is virtually assured. Both the higher expectation of life of women with respect to that of men and the fact that older women are more likely to need the support of their children than older men explains why women outnumber men in the parents category.

The slight female dominance among dependent children joining their parents in 1992/93 is harder to explain and may be due to normal statistical fluctuations. A longer time series would be necessary to ascertain if that caterory also attracts women preferentially. The slight excess of men over women in the concessional category, however, is more likely to be the result of policy implementation. Immigrants admitted under that category must pass a points assessment test in which they gain extra points for being the sibling or the non-dependent child (10 points), the nephew or niece (5 points), the uncle or aunt (5 points) of an Australian citizen (Hugo, 1986a). Given that the general points system favours men and that those sponsoring non-immediate relatives may also favour men over women, the slight excess of males over females in the concessional category is probably to be expected.

The only other immigration category in which women outnumber men is that named "grant of resident status". Persons in that category enter Australia under a temporary visa as visitors, students etc. and are granted resident status because of some change of circumstances, including a political change in their country of origin, marriage to an Australian citizen etc. The slight excess of women in that category probably stems from the possibility of obtaining immigrant status through marriage with an Australian citizen. However, that possibility was eliminated in December 1989 because it was discovered that fraudulent marriages were being systematically to bypass normal immigration procedures.

In most of the other categories, men outnumber women. Of particular importance is that women, though outnumbered by men, constitute nevertheless significant proportions of immigrants admitted in the economic categories (46 per cent overall). It must be pointed out, however, that the numbers admitted in each category include not only principal applicants but also their dependants. Among principal applicants admitted under the employer nomination scheme and the occupational share scheme, men predominate. Women are least well represented among immigrants admitted under the refugee, special humanitarian and special assistance category where they account for only 47 per cent. Interestingly, women who have been traditionally underrepresented among New Zealanders migrating to Australia under the terms of the Trans-Tasman Agreement, which essentially establishes freedom of movement between the two countries, have been outnumbering men in the most recent period (Carmichael, 1993).

Although many of the factors influencing international migration are of equal relevance to both male and female migrants, some have differential impacts by sex. The above discussion suggests that some elements of the Australian immigration policy and its operationalization tilt the balance in favour of women, in the case of the family reunion categories, and against them with respect to categories where selection is based on employment or economic criteria. However, since the data presented in table 74 include, within each category, both principal applicants (that is, persons qualifying for the given category) and their dependants, a firmer conclusion cannot be reached. Indeed, the partial evidence available on the distribution by sex of principal applicants in some of the economic categories and in the concessional category indicate that they are mostly male, while women predominate among their dependants. Yet, the categories of principal applicant and dependant are in many cases only bureaucratic artifacts and they should not be taken either to mean that women are passive followers of men or that they have no economic motive for migration even if admitted under a family category. Indeed, the economic activity of the spouses or partners of principal applicants is high. Thus, a study of immigrants admitted under the occupational share scheme found that 49 per cent had a spouse or partner in the labour force in Australia (Australian Sales Research Bureau, 1986) and a study of immigrants admitted in the concessional category found that 67 per cent of the spouses of principal applicants were in the labour force (Reark Research Pty. Ltd., 1985, p. 33).

Marriage migration: the case of Filipino female immigrants

Thadani and Todaro (1984) have noted that marriage-related motives are an important determinant of female migration, particularly that occurring within countries. In discussing marriage migration, they stress its economic dimensions, noting that for many women marriage is a means of social and economic mobility. Thus, some women may choose to migrate in order to enhance their marriage opportunities both in terms of securing a husband and to achieve upward mobility. Such considerations are particularly relevant in discussing the migration of Asian women to Australia, especially the movement of Filipino women. The dominance of women in the immigrant flows originating in the Philippines has already been noted. Thus, women outnumbered men two to one among all Filipino immigrants admitted by Australia during the 1980s. Accordingly, the Filipino-born population in Australia is constituted predominantly of women, a high proportion of whom are aged 25-44. Many young Filipino women have migrated to Australia as the recently married wives or fiancées of men residing in the country, most of whom are Australian or European-born. Hence, the vast majority of Filipino women have been admitted under the family migration category, as is shown in table 75. Over the period 1982/83-1988/89, 41.4 per cent of all female Filipino immigrants who were admitted to Australia under the family migration category came as the spouses of men residing in Australia and another 31.8 per cent as their fiancées. The equivalent figures for all other birthplace groups entering Australia over the same period were 31.8 per cent and 9.0 per cent, respectively. Clearly, marriage-related migration is a key component of the migration of Filipino women to Australia. Marriage migration also occurs among men. During the period considered, 18.4 per cent of male Filipinos entering Australia under the family migration category were admitted as spouses or fiancés of women residing in Australia, compared with 14.3 per cent among men from all other countries.

The particular nature of some of the Filipino female migration to Australia has been a matter of concern to government officials of both the Philippines and Australia, to the Filipino community in Australia and to women's rights groups (DIEA, 1982a). Given that some of that migration has taken place through the intervention of intermediaries that arrange marriages between Filipino women and Australian men, claims about the legality of such arrangements have been amply discussed in the popular media (DIEA, 1982a). It has been argued that some of the marriages involved are only marriages of convenience used to circumvent Australia's immigration laws; concern has often been expressed about the links between marriage migration arranged by intermediaries and prostitution; some Australian husbands have been deserted by their wives once the latter gain entry to Australia; there have been reports of mistreatment and abuse of Filipino wives by their husbands; and the rate of marital breakdown among those whose marriages have been arranged is high.

There are generally four ways in which Filipino women coming to Australia under the bride or fiancée provisions of the family reunion category met their Australian husbands (DIEA, 1982a). The first is through correspondence initiated through an introduction service, pen-pal club or a friend. Generally, the man visits the Philippines before arranging the marriage. Women using this method of securing a husband are the so-called "mail-order" brides. A second group of women met their future husbands in the Philippines when the latter were on vacation or other type of visit. In some cases men go to the Philippines on a "marriage tour" to seek a bride. Often, tourist agencies and introductory services play an intermediary role. The third group is constituted of women who meet their husbands in more conventional, less institutionalized circumstances, when the men are working or studying in the Philippines. Among these couples, courtship usually takes longer than in the other two groups. The fourth group are women who are introduced to their future husbands through friends or relatives already living in Australia (often, Filipino women married to Australian men).

There are no representative data to indicate the relative significance of each of these ways of arrang-

TABLE 75. IMMIGRANTS BORN IN THE PHILIPPINES, BY SEX AND ADMISSION CATEGORY: 1982/83-1988/89

Sex and admission category	Year of admission							Total	Percentage of women
	1982/83	1983/84	1984/85	1985/86	1986/87	1987/88	1988/89		
Female	2 207	2 327	2 350	2 885	4 243	6 137	5 452	25 601	64.8
Family migration	1 799	1 869	1 823	2 179	2 789	2 674	2 666	15 799	77.7
Economic (OSS and ENS)	257	83	69	97	142	150	149	947	52.2
Business (BMS)	0	12	2	9	25	80	78	206	49.4
Independent	53	1	0	4	1	23	0	82	59.0
Concessional....................	51	302	422	541	1 225	3 150	2 490	8 181	50.9
Refugees and special hardship	23	33	14	18	7	9	5	109	50.2
Special eligibility	0	3	5	3	18	6	18	53	71.6
New Zealand citizens	7	0	2	6	12	21	18	66	78.6
Australian children born overseas	11	14	9	20	17	20	22	113	40.2
Other admissions	6	10	4	8	7	4	6	45	69.2
Male	756	778	932	1 243	2 163	4 290	3 752	13 914	
Family migration	383	412	467	556	835	861	1 032	4 546	
Economic (OSS and ENS)	248	71	72	98	124	131	124	868	
Business (BMS)	0	8	3	9	18	88	85	211	
Independent	36	0	0	1	0	20	0	57	
Concessional....................	44	240	351	519	1 147	3 143	2 453	7 897	
Refugees and special hardship	24	21	14	19	11	10	9	108	
Special eligibility	2	1	0	1	4	2	11	21	
New Zealand citizens	1	1	0	3	3	7	3	18	
Australian children born overseas	16	24	22	32	14	27	33	168	
Other admissions	2	0	3	5	7	1	2	20	
Percentage of women	74.5	74.9	71.6	69.9	66.2	58.9	59.2	64.8	

Source: C. Hagan, "Filipinos in Australia: a statistical profile", Statistical Note (Canberra), No. 41 (1989), p. 27.

ing marriages. Jackson and Flores (1989) conducted a postal survey throughout Australia but only 336 usable questionnaires were obtained from 2,800 sent out, so that its results can hardly be considered representative. The results indicate that both meeting through correspondence and meeting while Australian men are on vacation in the Philippines are the most common occurrences. Introductions through friends also play an important role (see table 76).

Undoubtedly, some exploitation and certain illegal practices are associated with this type of migration. However, it should be remembered that there is a long tradition in Australia of seeking out single women for immigration with a view to providing wives for Australian men. In the early years of European settlement, campaigns promoting the immigration of single women were designed to redress the national imbalance between the sexes. In some respects, contemporary Filipino female migration serves a similar purpose, since a significant number of Filipino women settle in areas where adult men outnumber adult women by relatively wide margins (Hugo and Channell, 1986; Hugo, 1990b and 1990c).

In the State of Queensland, for instance, the 1986 census showed that the index of dissimilarity[3] for the population born in the Philippines and residing in

TABLE 76. FILIPINO WOMEN MARRIED TO AUSTRALIAN MEN,
BY WAY OF MEETING THEIR HUSBANDS

Way of meeting husband	Number of women	Percentage
Introduction or penfriend agency	57	26.6
Husband visited the Philippines	56	26.2
Woman visited Australia	10	4.7
Woman migrated to Australia	19	8.9
Introduced by friends	49	22.9
A combination of the above	12	5.6
Other	11	5.1
Total number of women...............	214	100.0

Source: Richard T. Jackson and E. R. Flores, *No Filipinos in Manila: A Study of Filipino Migrants in Australia* (North Queensland, Australia, James Cook University, 1989), appendix B, table 28.

that state was the lowest of any foreign-born group. At 18.5, the index of dissimilarity indicates only a minor tendency towards concentration. Such an outcome was to be expected because Filipino women usually settle in the house already owned or rented by their new husband (Hugo and Channell, 1986) and because many marriages involving Filipino women are mixed, there is no strong social or cultural reason to expect concentration in ethnic enclaves. Consequently, as the Filipino population in Queensland has increased, it has become less concentrated.

Jackson and Flores (1989) note that the spatial distribution of Filipinos in Australia consists of two distinct patterns: (*a*) Filipino families tend to be highly concentrated in the middle or low-income suburbs of capital cities; and (*b*) mixed Filipino-Australian families tend to be more dispersed, not only within large metropolitan areas but also outside the capital cities. These two types of family having Filipino members cannot be distinguished using census data; however, using their own postal survey data, Jackson and Flores (1989, p. 24) found an index of dissimilarity of 38 for Filipino families and one of only 13 for mixed Filipino-Australian families.

Half of the Filipinos in Queensland live in Brisbane and while there is a slight concentration in the lower and middle-income suburbs of the south-east and inner Brisbane areas, they are well represented throughout the statistical division. Some 1,389 live in the Brisbane City area but there are significant numbers in each of the peripheral local government areas as well. Much of the media attention concerning Filipino immigration to Australia, however, has focused on those settling outside Brisbane. Filipinos are relatively widely spread throughout the state, although, as in the case of other immigrant groups, larger numbers tend to settle in the south-east and in coastal cities. Their spatial distribution dispels some of the prevalent myths regarding Filipino settlement in Queensland. For example, Rodell (1982) claims that half of the Filipinos in Australia have settled in isolated areas of Northern Queensland where the potential for unhappiness is high. Such a statement is not borne out by the facts nor are many of the emotive claims made about Filipino settlement in Australia (especially those related to the so-called "mail-order" brides). Nevertheless, it is apparent that Northern Queensland, especially the cities of Townsville (318 Filipino-born persons in 1991) and Cairns (283), are important foci of Filipino settlement. The community in Mount Isa, with 251 Filipinos in 1991, has attracted particular attention, although again exaggeration of the size of the Filipino community has been common. In a report on Mount Isa, Bailey (1986, p. 7) refers to it as "the Manila of the Scrub. It is home to some 400 Filipinos, mostly women who are the wives of Australian men". Undeniably, North Queensland has a disproportionate concentration of Filipinos in relation to its total population and, as Jackson and Flores (1989, p. 5) point out, the Filipino population is predominantly made up of Filipino women married to Australian-born men. According to their estimates, about 56 per cent of the population born in the Philippines and living outside Brisbane are women married to Australian men, although the popular media tend to exaggerate their numbers. Thus, Lowe (1988, p. 3) is far from the mark in stating that "[a]bout 5,000 mail order brides live in Queensland where they make up 95 per cent of the Filipino migrant community, a much higher proportion than in other States".

Jackson and Flores (1989, p. 2) underscore that almost all the areas of substantial Filipino concentration outside of large urban centres are mining communities with sizeable imbalances in the distribution by sex. In contrast, rural communities where there is no mining tend to have no Filipino migrants. Clearly, in towns like Mount Isa, where adult men outnumber adult women by wide margins, there is a strong pressure to seek brides overseas. As Bailey (1986, p. 7) reports: "Isa men, like others in the remote outposts of Australia, have been forced to look further afield for female company. They answer advertisements in newspapers or magazines and write to introduction agencies in far-away Townsville, Brisbane or Sydney. Many of these agencies specialize in Asian brides and, in particular, Filipino brides".

Although in many ways this pattern of immigrant settlement is unique in Australia's recent immigration history, one must guard against stereotyping the causes and consequences of the phenomenon. As Jackson and Flores (1989) have shown, while exploitation of some Filipino women undoubtedly occurs, that is by no means the norm. Even popular media reports point to the development of cohesive social systems among the Filipinos living in such isolated communities (e.g., Bailey, 1986). Moreover, many of the marriages of Filipino women and Australian men are happy and mutually rewarding.

Clearly, marriage plays a significant role in the process of female immigration to Australia with more than socio-cultural implications. Thadani and Todaro (1984) use the term "mobility marriage" to describe the process whereby upward social mobility through personal attainment can be supplemented or substituted by marrying well and thus acquiring social status through marriage. In the context of female migration they argue that implicit in such explanations of social mobility is an exchange theory of marriage that posits the existence of a marriage market similar to the market in which economic goods and services are exchanged. In such a market, women offer the characteristics that men seek in exchange for the characteristics and status that they desire from men. As the authors stress, another implicit assumption is that rational considerations about changes of status are important determinants of the marital choices of women. However, establishing empirically the extent to which such "mobility marriage" takes place is difficult. Thus, Jackson and Flores (1989, p. 66) note that, for Filipino

women marrying Australian men, the immediate reason for migration was marriage itself and that asking questions about a woman's motivation for choosing an Australian husband was unlikely to elicit truthful answers and might have resulted in a higher level of non-response. Yet, despite such problems, about 16 per cent of the Filipino women who had migrated to marry men residing in Australia reported that they had migrated "to find better opportunities" (Jackson and Flores, 1989, p. 67).

Refugee migration: the case of Vietnamese refugees

Female refugees have constituted another important component of Asian female immigration to Australia. The majority have originated in Indo-China and particularly in Viet Nam, a country that accounted for 79 per cent (85,868 persons) of the total refugee intake registered during 1975-1988 (108,641 persons). Women constituted only 43.5 per cent of the total refugee intake and they were even less well represented among Vietnamese refugees, only 41.9 per cent of whom were women. Cambodian refugees, who constituted 13.4 per cent of the total Indo-Chinese intake, and Lao refugees, who accounted for 7.6 per cent of that total, had higher proportions of women: 49.5 per cent and 48.8 per cent, respectively. The causes of the sex selectivity of refugee migration to Australia have not been investigated, but biases in resettlement programmes cannot be ruled out. Interestingly, women tended to predominate among the Vietnamese admitted by Australian authorities under other immigration categories. Thus, among Vietnamese immigrants admitted under the family reunion category, which has accounted recently for almost as many Vietnamese immigrants as the refugee category (table 77), women constituted 62 per cent during 1988/89. However, due to the predominance of men among Vietnamese refugees, men outnumbered women among the Vietnamese-born population present in Australia in 1991, especially in the young adult ages.

It thus appears that the movement of Vietnamese to Australia occurs in stages, with men moving first, either directly from Viet Nam or from refugee camps in South-eastern Asia, and women moving later to

TABLE 77. VIETNAMESE IMMIGRANTS, BY ADMISSION CATEGORY: 1981/82-1987/88

Year	Refugees	Family reunion	Total
1981/82	10 909	134	11 112
1982/83	6 049	569	8 667
1983/84	7 724	1 732	9 520
1984/85	5 694	2 524	8 494
1985/86	4 468	2 550	7 169
1986/87	3 841	2 635	6 628
1987/88	3 753	2 109	5 981
TOTAL	42 438	12 253	57 571

Source: Australia, Department of Immigration, Local Government and Ethnic Affairs, *Australian Immigration: Consolidated Statistics*, No. 15 (Canberra, Government Publishing Service, 1989).

join their husbands, often by departing directly from Viet Nam under the Orderly Departure Programme. Family reunion has gained importance in relative terms as time has elapsed and information has reached Viet Nam on the opportunities open in Australia. As Viviani (1984, p. 38) suggests, the well-publicized hazards of the journey and the prospects of family reunification have influenced family decisions in Viet Nam regarding who should leave. Consequently, the proportions of young persons among boat arrivals rose and affected the composition of the eventual pool of refugees in camps.

Changes in the composition by sex of the Vietnamese population in Australia were evident in the results of a survey carried out in Sydney and based on a sample of immigrant arrivals. Although in the sampling frame men outnumbered women in the young adult age groups, by the time of the survey the population interviewed showed a fairly balanced composition by sex. Keys-Young (1980, p. 31) attributed this change to the fact that "younger males often serve as the vanguard in a migratory process, being thought most capable of carrying out the initial settlement phase. Once settled other family members follow". A follow-up study (Keys-Young, 1983, p. 31) found that, although 81 per cent of the Vietnamese interviewed were men, 28 per cent still had a spouse or a child in Viet Nam. More than a quarter of the Vietnamese interviewed (27.1 per cent) reported that the most difficult part of leaving Viet Nam was to leave family members behind

(Keys-Young, 1983, p. 77). About 90 per cent of the respondents indicated that they had hopes of bringing other family members to Australia (Keys-Young, 1983, p. 89).

There is some evidence that the refugee selection procedures followed by Australian authorities in the camps of South-eastern Asia and especially in Malaysia, where most of the Vietnamese refugees admitted by Australia had found first asylum, was biased in favour of men, mainly because initially the Government of Australia applied the skills and education criteria used to select immigrants in general to refugees (Hugo, 1986a). As Viviani (1984, p. 121) explains, this policy favoured the selection of young men and married couples without children and reduced the resettlement chances of large families. Furthermore, there was an explicit bias towards the employable, which meant a bias against dependants and those difficult to employ, such as single women, widows, the aged and the illiterate. People without skills were often ineligible to enter under either family reunion or humanitarian criteria.

The inevitable problems caused by this policy led the Department of Immigration to counterbalance the effects of selection based on skills by admitting for resettlement a large number of single women from the camps after 1978. However, whereas until 1978 most young male refugees selected were ethnic Vietnamese, by 1979, when young single women began to be selected, the refugee pool in Malaysian camps had become predominantly ethnic Chinese so that many of the young women admitted as refugees by Australian authorities were Chinese. Because of ethnic differences, there was little communication between the single Chinese women and the single Vietnamese men who had preceded them. Furthermore, although single women were admitted, there was no provision for the admission of their dependent younger siblings who could not qualify for resettlement. Thus, the policy of admitting single women helped convert the children of split families into unaccompanied minors remaining in camps, with major negative consequences for them and their resettled sisters (Viviani, 1984, p. 121-122).

A further recognition that the existing refugee resettlement programme was biased in favour of the selection of men came in 1989 when the Government of Australia initiated a special scheme to resettle refugee women and their dependants if they lacked the traditional male support, were in vulnerable situations or in desperate need of resettlement to ensure the protection of themselves and their families (DILGEA, 1989, p. 11). This scheme includes post-arrival services that help refugees adapt to their new environment, including English classes, women's health-care services, child care, torture and trauma counselling, and other forms of support provided by the Community Refugee Resettlement Scheme (CRSS).

Chain migration

Because Australia's immigration policy favours family migration, that is, the immigration of close relatives of Australian residents, chain migration plays an important role in shaping the immigration of women. Traditionally, immigrants to Australia have benefited from the assistance provided by relatives and friends who had migrated earlier. However, given the economic problems that Australia is experiencing, there is growing debate about the family component of the immigration programme. Understandably, communities of foreign-born persons in Australia have a major concern in this area and they exert considerable pressure to have a more

liberal interpretation of family reunification criteria that includes the extended family (Victorian Ethnic Affairs Commission, 1986, p. 1). Some commentators have argued strongly against any further extension of the family reunification criteria and have even pushed for making them more restrictive, especially as regards the category of siblings and non-dependent children of Australian residents (Birrell, 1984, pp. 43-44).

Both research and relevant data on the size of the multiplier effects of family migration are scarce in Australia. A DIEA (1984) study investigated whether recently arrived immigrants admitted as siblings or non-dependent children of Australian residents intended to sponsor the immigration of other relatives. Over a third (35 per cent) had the intention of sponsoring the immigration of relatives and only 20 per cent had no intention of doing so, but nearly half were undecided. However, this study included only a few immigrants from Asia and the relatively modest multipliers estimated may be different for the more recently arrived contingent of Asian immigrants. Birrell (1984, pp. 41-43) argues that Asian immigrants are more likely to take advantage of family reunification provisions than other immigrant groups. Among Filipinos in Adelaide, for example, Hugo and Channell (1986) found that the multiplier was 2 (table 78). Although over half of the Filipinos interviewed in Adelaide in 1986 had not as yet

TABLE 78. FILIPINOS INTERVIEWED IN ADELAIDE WHO HAD SPONSORED THE IMMIGRATION OF CLOSE RELATIVES, BY TIME SINCE ARRIVAL: 1986

Relationship to those sponsored	Year of arrival in Australia							
	Before 1975		1976-1980		1981-1986		Total	
	Number	Per-centage	Number	Per-centage	Number	Per-centage	Number	Per-centage
Parents	2	8.3	3	9.7	5	9.5	10	9.3
Children	0	0.0	0	0.0	4	7.5	4	3.7
Siblings	6	25.0	10	32.2	6	11.3	22	20.4
Nephews or nieces	3	12.5	1	3.2	2	3.8	6	5.6
Parents or siblings	3	12.5	3	9.7	4	7.5	10	9.3
Have not sponsored anyone ...	10	41.7	14	45.2	32	60.4	56	51.9
TOTAL	24	100.0	31	100.0	53	100.0	108	100.0

Source: Graeme J. Hugo and Kym Channell, "Filipino migrants in Adelaide", paper presented at the Third Conference of the Australian Population Association, Adelaide, Australia, 3-5 December 1986.

sponsored the immigration of relatives, most expected to do so in the future. The bulk of Filipino immigrants in the Adelaide sample were women who had married Australian men and entered the country in the few years preceding 1986. Hence, at the time of the survey many were not yet eligible to sponsor the immigration of close relatives (a two-year residence in Australia is necessary). Yet, over 70 per cent of those interviewed were intending to sponsor the immigration of close relatives, particularly of siblings, and among the 29 per cent of respondents who declared that they did not have any plans to sponsor the immigration of relatives in the future, almost half had already sponsored relatives who had immigrated to Australia or were in the process of doing so.

Among all immigrants present in Australia in March 1987, a third had been admitted on their own, that is, without accompanying family members. Immigrants from Africa and the United Kingdom were the most likely to arrive in family groups. Among Asian immigrants, only a slightly greater proportion arrived in family groups than among all immigrants. One of the few studies of potential chain migration to Australia was based on information from a sample of 1,397 sponsorship applications and on interviews with migration officers (Birrell, 1990). The study concluded that recently arrived immigrants, especially those from developing countries, were more likely to sponsor the immigration of close relatives than immigrants who had arrived earlier (most of whom originated in European countries). It also noted that Filipino women had been among the most active sponsors of the immigration of siblings and parents. In general, the characteristics of close relatives (in terms of education, occupation, language skills etc.) were similar to those of their sponsors.

Birrell (1990) also noted that the tightening of family reunion regulations that took place in December 1988 was likely to reduce chain migration and that the immigration of spouses or fiancées of Australian citizens needed to be subject to closer control to prevent abuses. However, the immigration of close relatives had already generated rapid and unintended changes in immigration levels which had not always been consistent with Australian economic interests.

Some of Birrell's conclusions are open to question, particularly because a longer time horizon is needed to sort out the long-term effects of family reunification. Throughout Australian history, initial immigration waves have been dominated by men, who at a later stage bring in their close family members and thus give rise to immigration flows where women are better represented. When the migration process matures, as is now the case for most European immigrants in Australia, chain migration drops to relatively low levels. Most Asian immigrants to Australia are still in the first phases of the process and Birrell's data, which refer to a single year, cannot give an accurate picture of the overall process.

In the United States, Jasso and Rosenzweig (1986, p. 309) report that immigrants admitted under the occupational categories have a higher multiplier effect in terms of the number of family immigrants that they are likely to sponsor than other immigrants. Such a finding has particular importance for Australia because increasing emphasis is being put on attracting business people and entrepreneurs from Asia. Interestingly, women outnumber men among immigrants from the two Asian countries generating the highest numbers of business immigrants to Australia. While at present men outnumber women in the economic immigration categories (which include both principal immigrants and their dependants), the role of women is significant, especially among Asian immigrants (table 74). Thus, women outnumber men among Filipinos admitted in each of the economic categories (table 75). However, the criteria regarding educational attainment, business experience or employment skills that are used to select economic immigrants to Australia tend to favour men over women, especially among immigrants originating in developing countries where women have less opportunities than men to study or to become entrepreneurs.

In conclusion, although Australian immigration regulations are ostensibly gender-neutral, their application is not always free of biases on the basis of sex. It is important to establish to what extent rules and regulations that do not inherently discriminate by sex or immigrant status produce, in practice or in combination with other rules and regulations, inequitable outcomes which operate to the disadvantage of immigrant women (Boyd, 1987, p. 22).

C. DEMOGRAPHIC CHARACTERISTICS OF ASIAN FEMALE IMMIGRANTS

In Australia, the process of migrant adaptation to the host society has entailed the convergence of the demographic characteristics of immigrants to those of the Australian-born majority as time since immigration increases. Because of the relative recency of Asian immigration to Australia, differences between Asian immigrants and the native population are still substantial. However, examination of some of the demographic characteristics of Asian-born women in Australia can give some insights into the nature of their adjustment to the host society and their relative well-being.

In terms of age distribution, the population born in Asia tends to be concentrated in the age groups between 20 and 44. Such concentration is especially marked among women, who outnumber men among the Asian-born. There is, however, substantial variation among the major foreign-born groups. As would be expected, the groups that have arrived most recently (those born in Hong Kong, Malaysia and Viet Nam) display a younger age distribution and a lower median age (table 79). Yet, Filipino-born women are older on average than the Australian-born, a fact that belies the general image of the "mail-order" bride as being in her teens or early twenties. In fact, survey data indicate that women who migrate to marry Australian-based men are commonly in their thirties at the time of migration (Channell 1986; Jackson and Flores, 1989). Thus, Jackson and Flores (1989, p. 56) found that the median age of their sample of Filipino women married to Australian men was 37.2 years and that of their husbands was 49.5 years. Channell (1986, p. 72) found that 10 per cent of the sample of women that he studied had been either divorcées or widows before marrying their Australian husbands.

The degree of intermarriage is of considerable significance for the adjustment of Asians to Australia. As table 79 shows, there are important variations among the foreign-born groups in the extent to which Asian women marry Australian-born men. The recency of Asian migration is reflected in the low rates of intermarriage, especially among the Vietnamese. Representative data for the Philippines are not available, but the level of intermarriage

TABLE 79. SELECTED DEMOGRAPHIC CHARACTERISTICS OF FOREIGN-BORN GROUPS OF WOMEN, BY COUNTRY OR AREA OF BIRTH: 1986

Country or area of birth	Median age	Percentage marrying Australian-born males	Divorce rate	Total fertility rate	Standardized mortality[a] ratio, 1980-1982
Australia	28.5	82.9	11.9	1.925	104
Overseas	40.4	48.8	10.8	2.039	..
Asia	32.5	29.0	9.6	2.459	..
China	48.5	..	7.7	2.483	79
Hong Kong	28.7	..	9.5	1.756	85
India	41.2	40.3	11.3	1.900	106
Malaysia	28.4	42.4	11.2	1.882	99
Philippines	32.8	..	18.3	3.161	73
Sri Lanka	37.4	..	10.3	1.742	94
Viet Nam	26.6	3.3	6.8	2.195	64

Sources: Australian Bureau of Statistics, *Overseas Born Australians, 1988*, Catalogue No. 4112.0 (Canberra, 1989), pp. 50, 59, 60, 63 and 74; Christabel Young, "Demographic behaviour and intergenerational change among migrants in Australia", invited paper presented at the General Conference of the International Union for the Scientific Study of Population, New Delhi, 20-27 September 1989.

NOTE: Two dots (..) indicate that data are not available or are not separately reported.

[a]Standard mortality ratios (SMRs) are the number of deaths that would be expected to occur if the group experienced the same mortality rates as the standard population.

between Filipino women and Australian men is known to be high. Jackson and Flores (1989, p. 7), for instance, reported that in 62.5 per cent of the households with at least one Filipino-born member, a Filipino-born woman was married to an Australian man. The relatively high proportion of Malaysian women married to Australian-born men is likely to be linked to the fact that many Malaysian women migrate while still single to study in Australia.

With respect to Filipino women, the success of their marriages to Australian-born men is crucial for their well-being and adaptation prospects. Although the matter is not easily amenable to study through a structured survey, some evidence on it has been gathered through detailed interviews. Thus, a study of 40 such marriages by social workers in Melbourne found that only 17 of the women interviewed could be said to have happy or very happy marriages, another 15 were unhappy but persevered in their marriages, and for the remainder the marriage had been irrevocably broken (DIEA, 1982a, p. 29). Interviews carried out in Adelaide, which did not involve the depth of the Melbourne study, suggested that the proportion of happy marriages was higher (Hugo and Channell, 1986). However, in the Adelaide study better adjusted families were more likely to be selected for interview and its results might therefore be biased. According to table 79, data at the national level indicate that Filipino-born women have a higher divorce rate than the Australian-born, the total foreign-born and other major Asian-born female groups. Such data, however, should not be interpreted to mean that the intermarriages of Filipino women and Australian men are more likely to end in divorce. Furthermore, divorce itself cannot be automatically interpreted as failure for the immigrant partner. Thus, Jackson and Flores (1989, p. 33) argue that although divorce and separation indicate that a marriage was not successful, marriages that remain intact are not necessarily devoid of problems and, although they recognize that for a number of years Filipino women have been available "on approval" to Australians and that marriage has sometimes been used to bring Filipino women to Australia for other purposes, abuses have not been only in one direction. The exploitation of marriage by either partner is a universal problem that is not exclusive to inter-ethnic marriage. In the case of Filipino women married to Australian men, marital exploitation occurs in a relatively small number of cases that have, unfortunately, been greatly exaggerated by the media.

Except for Filipino-born women, the proportion of divorced women was lower among all other Asian-born groups listed in table 79 than among Australian-born women. The proportion of divorced women among those born in India and Malaysia was, however, above the average for the foreign-born and close to the Australian average.

With respect to fertility, Australian censuses have indicated the existence of consistent differences between foreign-born groups (Di Iulio and Chung, 1976; Price, 1982; Day, 1983; Hugo, 1986b; Young, 1989). In general, fertility differentials between immigrant groups and the native born decline as the length of residence of immigrants increases and second-generation women tend to display fertility patterns even closer to those of other native women. Thus, the variation of total fertility rates is associated with the average length of residence of the different foreign-born groups in Australia, their migration experience and the prevailing fertility levels in their country of origin. Because of their relatively recent arrival, Asian women in general have a total fertility that is 29 per cent higher than that of Australian-born women. Yet, women born in Hong Kong, India, Malaysia and Sri Lanka had fertility levels below those of Australian-born women. Women born in the Philippines had the highest fertility levels among South-eastern Asians (3.2 children per woman). Contrary to expectations, Vietnamese women recorded relatively low fertility levels (2.2 children per woman which is half the level recorded in Viet Nam), mainly because younger Vietnamese women had fertility similar to or lower than that of Australian-born women (Hugo, 1990a). Only at older ages did fertility differ markedly between the two groups.

The low fertility of Vietnamese immigrant women in Australia is likely to stem from the selectivity of migration, the traumatic circumstances under which many women left Viet Nam, the disruption of their lives brought about by the need to flee, and the wish to conform to the norms of the host society. The disruptive effects of refugee migration are also evident in the relatively high proportion of Vietnamese adults who have never married: in age-standardized terms, 37.7 per cent of Vietnamese men have never married and so have 27 per cent of Vietnamese women, compared to 32.5 per cent and 24.4 per cent, respectively, of men and women in the total population (ABS, 1989a, p. 57). Furthermore, the circumstances surrounding the resettlement of Vietnamese refugees in Australia are likely to have fostered acceptance of Australian norms, particularly because of high housing costs. Lewins and Ly (1985, p. 38) suggest that overcrowding, insecure finances and rapidly growing family size were common among the Vietnamese who were resettled first. They also document the growing assertiveness and independence of Vietnamese women (Lewins and Ly, 1985, p. 63). Families with several children have lacked the support of the extended family and have been faced with a number of problems, especially in view of the pressures for women to work outside the home. Younger women, therefore, have been more likely to postpone child-bearing or to lower their expectations regarding completed family size. To the extent that their future experience in Australia is positive, young Vietnamese immigrant women may eventually make up for the births postponed.

Although there are no data for the entire community, it appears that the fertility of Cambodian immigrants is high (Stevens, 1984). It may be that such high fertility is caused, at least partly, by women's desire to counterbalance the decimation of the Cambodian population during the 1970s which involved the disproportionate death of young persons, especially children (Meng Try, 1981).

With respect to mortality, foreign-born groups have traditionally recorded lower levels than the Australian-born population (Hugo, 1986b). According to table 79, that is also the case for most of the Asian-born groups, especially Vietnamese and Filipino women. Young (1989, p. 7) has argued that the selectivity of migration both through self selection and through the minimum health standards required for immigrants, as well as the distinctive lifestyle of some immigrant groups are the main factors responsible for the low mortality observed among immigrants.

D. SPATIAL DISTRIBUTION OF ASIAN-BORN IMMIGRANTS AND ITS IMPLICATIONS FOR IMMIGRANT ADAPTATION

The Asian-born population in Australia is heavily concentrated in the state of New South Wales, which encompasses the city of Sydney and is home to one third of the total population of Australia, and in Victoria, which is home to one fourth of Australia's population (table 80). Asian immigrants have therefore tended to settle in Australia's two most populous states and, following the trends set by other immigrants, to concentrate in cities with more than 100,000 inhabitants. The cities of Melbourne and Sydney, in particular, comprised 24 per cent and 28 per cent, respectively, of the total foreign-born population enumerated in Australia in 1986. Whereas until the early 1970s Melbourne and Sydney attracted similar proportions of immigrants, the increase of Asian and Pacific immigration tilted the balance in favour of Sydney. Furthermore, because both Melbourne and Sydney have been experiencing net out-migration of Australian-born residents, net immigration constitutes a major component of their growth (Hugo, 1989).

In terms of specific foreign-born groups, the Vietnamese are mostly concentrated in Sydney and

TABLE 80. POPULATION OF AUSTRALIA, BY PLACE OF BIRTH AND STATE OR TERRITORY OF RESIDENCE: 1991

State or territory of residence	Place of birth			
	Australia (percentage)	Overseas (percentage)	Asia Number	Per-centage
New South Wales	33.7	34.8	296 897	43.2
Victoria	24.6	27.2	194 970	28.3
Queensland	18.9	13.5	64 924	9.4
South Australia	8.4	8.3	32 720	4.8
Western Australia	8.6	12.2	73 318	10.7
Tasmania	3.1	1.3	4 238	0.6
Northern territory	1.1	0.9	7 317	1.1
Australian capital territory	1.6	1.8	13 466	2.0
TOTAL	100.0	100.0	687 850	100.0

Source: Australian Bureau of Statistics, *1991 Census of Population and Housing, Basic Community Profile: Various States* (Canberra, 1991), tables B01 and B09.

Melbourne. Indeed, there are indications that Vietnamese who originally settled elsewhere in Australia have subsequently gravitated to Sydney (Burnley, 1989). Large proportions of those born in the Philippines also live in Sydney and Melbourne but they are more widely dispersed than other groups, with significant numbers living in relatively remote communities. As was indicated earlier, women tend to predominate among Filipinos living in those communities. Those born in Malaysia are also concentrated in the two largest cities and a relatively large group resides in Perth. Sizeable groups of people from Myanmar and India have settled in Perth because of its proximity to their region of origin.

It is at the microlevel, within Australia's largest cities, that the greatest degree of spatial concentration is to be observed among Asian-born men and women. The Vietnamese are the most spatially concentrated of any foreign-born group in Australia. It is estimated that in 1981, nearly two thirds of the Vietnamese immigrants would have had to change their local government area of residence to produce a distribution pattern similar to that of the Australian-born population. Such a degree of spatial concentration is unprecedented in post-war Australian cities for any major foreign-born group, and although the spatial segregation of Vietnamese immigrants within the capital cities of four states decreased between 1981 and 1986, that of Vietnamese in Sydney increased. Within Australian cities, the concentrations of Vietnamese are all within the areas of lower socio-economic status. Thus, there is generally a positive association between the proportion of Vietnamese and the prevalence of low incomes, high levels of unemployment, single-parent families and the provision of state government housing.

Burnley (1982, p. 105) points out that ethnic concentrations are "a natural consequence of the need to adjust to a new and strange environment. There is no evidence that they in themselves inhibit the life chances of individuals or create conflict with the wider society. ... The general consensus is that spatial concentration indicates less integration although by no means no learning of the new environment". Desbarats (1985, p. 525) also considers that immigrant clustering "has been found to be beneficial not only to psychological adjustment but also to economic adaptation. Networks organized along ethnic lines have frequently proved decisive in providing newly arrived immigrants with the information and assistance necessary to attain at least basic self sufficiency". Such benefits are especially important for immigrant women, who are more likely to have language difficulties and to need the cultural and kinship links available in their communities of origin. However, Desbarats (1985, p. 525) also differentiates between short- and long-term adaptation and concludes that geographic dispersal is probably of greater value for the long-term adaptation of immigrant groups.

In contrast with Vietnamese immigrants, those born in Malaysia show only moderate degrees of spatial concentration within the large urban centres. They tend to settle in areas with higher socio-economic status that suit their own status as highly skilled or business immigrants. Secondary concentrations of Malaysian immigrants are located around institutions for tertiary education and are associated with the influx of Malaysian students in recent years (Anderssen, 1991). Immigrants from Hong Kong, Macao, Singapore, the Republic of Korea and Taiwan, Province of China exhibit similar patterns of spatial distribution. Because immigrant women belonging to those groups are likely to have greater access to resources, their adaptation experience is probably very different from that of Vietnamese women.

Immigrants born in the Philippines constitute the most dispersed group among Asian immigrants. There are, however, two distinct elements in this immigrant population: family groups that have been admitted to Australia mainly under the economic categories and whose settlement pattern is similar to that of Malaysians; and women who have been admitted as brides or fiancées of Australian men whose pattern of settlement is fairly dispersed both within cities and in non-metropolitan areas.

E. ECONOMIC ADAPTATION

There is considerable debate in Australia concerning the relative social and economic well-being of immigrant groups. The classical view is that each new wave of immigrants to Australia fills the worse paid and lower status jobs in the occupational spectrum and that immigrants, by dint of hard work and entrepreneurial skills, gradually move up the socio-economic ladder. An alternative view is that immigrants are forced into low-paid manual jobs from which it is virtually impossible to escape, so that they are locked into a situation of poverty and deprivation and therefore constitute a disproportionately large section of the exploited proletariat. It is difficult to establish which of these views is most consistent with the experience of Asian immigrants, partly because of the recency of their arrival. Moreover, there is considerable diversity among the Asian-born population. In terms of median weekly income per income unit,[4] for instance, Asian-born immigrants as a group earn somewhat less than the Australian-born (table 81). However, Indian, Malaysian and East Asian immigrants earn more than the Australian-born and South Asian immigrants earn about the same. Only the South-eastern Asian group earns less than the Australian-born, although within that group there are also important differences (Malaysian immigrants, for instance, have a higher median income than their Australian-born counterparts). The Vietnamese stand out as having the lowest income levels, some 23 per cent below the Australian-born and 26.5 per cent below those of all the foreign-born. However, the Gini coefficient indicates that the distribution of income within the Vietnamese community is somewhat less unequal than among other groups.

Income level is an important determinant of the well-being of Asian women in Australia and of the extent and speed to which they are likely to adjust to life in the host country. By participating in the labour force, immigrant women can enhance their income levels. Table 82 shows the level of labour force participation among Asian-born married women in Australia. There are striking differences between the various foreign-born groups. Overall, foreign-born married women have a slightly lower level of labour force participation than their Australian-born counterparts and the Asian-born married women conform to the foreign-born average. However, South-Asian married women have higher levels of labour force participation, largely because of the high participation rates of Indian women. The participation rates for Vietnamese married women are also relatively high, being 10 percentage points greater than the average for the foreign-born. Such high labour force participation rates among Vietnamese married women are particularly striking in light of the traditional values and expectations of Vietnamese. As Lewins and Ly (1985, p. 40) point out, Vietnamese women are expected to stay at home once they have children but in Australia the need for a second income has outweighed such traditional imperatives. Thus, lack of assets in Australia coupled with the high costs of housing and other living essentials in Sydney and Melbourne, which are significantly higher than elsewhere in the country, have contributed to accelerate changes in the roles of Vietnamese women and their position within the family. Furthermore, as table 82 shows, Vietnamese women are especially likely to work full time. In contrast, East Asian and Malaysian-born women display low rates of labour force participation, partly because their spouses are immigrants selected on the basis of their skills or economic assets.

Despite the high employment rates of Vietnamese women, they tend to earn relatively low incomes (table 83): about 22.5 per cent lower than those for their Australian-born counterparts and only about half of the average income earned by Vietnamese-born men. In contrast, women from both South-

TABLE 81. MEDIAN WEEKLY INCOME AND GINI COEFFICIENTS FOR THE INCOME DISTRIBUTION OF INCOME UNITS, BY COUNTRY OR REGION OF BIRTH: SEPTEMBER-DECEMBER 1986

Country or region of birth	Median weekly income (Australian dollars)	Gini coefficient
Australia	325	0.41
Overseas	340	0.40
Asia	303	0.44
Eastern Asia	335	0.44
South-eastern Asia	303	0.40
Malaysia	360	0.42
Viet Nam	250	0.38
Southern Asia	326	0.49
India	387	0.50

Source: Australian Bureau of Statistics, *Overseas Born Australians, 1988*, Catalogue No. 4112.0 (Canberra, 1989), p. 131.

TABLE 82. LABOUR FORCE PARTICIPATION RATES, BY SEX, MARITAL STATUS
OF WOMEN AND COUNTRY OR REGION OF BIRTH: AUGUST 1987
(Percentage)

Country or region of birth	Both sexes	Men	Married women	All women Partici- pation rate	All women Percentage working full time
Australia	63.1	76.4	49.0	50.7	60.0
Overseas	61.1	74.3	48.3	47.2	63.5
Asia	60.3	73.1	48.2	47.8	76.0
Eastern Asia	56.6	67.8	48.9	46.7	63.0
China	51.6	61.5	50.3	41.6	66.6
South-eastern Asia	61.7	73.9	50.6	50.1	79.2
Malaysia	55.1	64.1	44.0	46.5	63.1
Viet Nam	68.6	77.6	58.0	57.4	90.9
Southern Asia	67.9	76.1	62.5	59.7	..
India	71.4	79.4	64.9	64.0	..

Source: Australian Bureau of Statistics, Overseas Born Australians, 1988, Catalogue No. 4112.0 (Canberra, 1989), pp. 100 and 104.

TABLE 83. MEAN GROSS WEEKLY INCOME, BY SEX AND COUNTRY
OR REGION OF BIRTH: SEPTEMBER-DECEMBER 1986

Country or region of birth	Mean gross weekly income (A$) Men	Mean gross weekly income (A$) Women	GINI coefficient Men	GINI coefficient Women
Australia	371	191	0.38	0.46
Overseas	352	191	0.38	0.49
Asia	343	180	0.41	0.51
Eastern Asia	382	180	0.40	0.54
South-eastern Asia	305	204	0.37	0.44
Malaysia	320	175	0.47	0.42
Viet Nam	274	148	0.36	0.47
Southern Asia	484	211	0.41	0.57
India	575	240	0.41	0.57

Source: Australian Bureau of Statistics, Overseas Born Australians, 1988, Catalogue No. 4112.0 (Canberra, 1988), p. 142.

eastern and Southern Asia tend to earn more than Australian-born women though their salaries are still considerably below those of their countrymen.

In 1987 the extent of unemployment among Asian-born women was somewhat higher (14.6 per cent) than either that for Australian-born women (8 per cent) or for all foreign-born women (9.5 per cent). Furthermore, among Vietnamese women the unemployment rate was 23.5 per cent compared to 24.7 per cent among Vietnamese men (table 84). The average

TABLE 84. SELECTED ECONOMIC CHARACTERISTICS OF THE
POPULATION OF AUSTRALIA, BY SEX AND SELECTED
PLACE OF BIRTH: 1987
(Percentage)

Economic characteristic, status and sex	Place of birth Australia	Place of birth Viet Nam	Place of birth Over- seas	Non-English speaking immigrants
Labour force participation rates				
Men	76.4	77.6	74.3	72.1
Married women	49.0	58.0	48.3	45.2
All women	50.3	57.4	47.2	44.1
All persons	63.1	68.6	61.1	58.5
Worker's status (men only)				
Employers or self-employed	18.0	11.3	17.7	20.4
Wage and salary earners	82.0	88.7	82.3	79.6
Average weekly hours worked	42.7	41.7	42.8	43.1
Unemployment rates				
Men	7.3	24.7	8.3	9.6
Women	8.0	23.5	9.5	10.8

Source: Australian Bureau of Statistics, Overseas Born Australians, 1988, Catalogue No. 4112.0 (Canberra, 1989), pp. 100, 106, 117 and 121.

duration of unemployment among Asian-born women was 44.5 weeks compared to 35.2 weeks for Australian-born women (ABS, 1989a). One of the major problems faced by Vietnamese immigrants has been to enter the Australian labour market, partly because their arrival coincided with a period of unprecedentedly high unemployment.

The inability to speak English reduces the employment, occupational and earning opportunities of immigrant workers (Keys-Young, 1980, p. 84; Hugo, 1988). Thus, unemployment is higher among non-English-speaking immigrants (table 84). Lack of English ability is particularly widespread among both the Chinese and the Vietnamese (table 85). Although there has been some improvement since 1981, such improvement has been slow. As table 85 shows, inability to communicate in English is more widespread among foreign-born women than among their male counterparts.

Because of their higher unemployment levels, Asian families tend to rely more on government benefits for their income. Thus, one out of every five Asian-born persons depends on such benefits, mostly obtained because of unemployment. In addi-tion, 17.1 per cent of the persons born in Indo-China were receiving as income some form of government benefit in 1986, a proportion five times higher than that observed among the Australian-born and more than three times that among all foreign-born. When the spouses and dependants of the main recipients are taken into account, 43 per cent of the persons born in Indo-China were dependent on government benefits (table 86). Among that group, 43 per cent had been receiving benefits for more than a year. It appears therefore that persons admitted as refugees face special problems in securing and keeping jobs. This situation is not peculiar to Australia. Desbarats (1985, pp. 523-524) notes that even when economic considerations are not totally absent from a refugee's decision to flee, there is usually a substantial lag between resettlement and participation in the labour force. Most refugees receive some assistance during the initial period following arrival and therefore do not join the ranks of the gainfully employed.

The labour market situation of Asian-born women differs considerably from that of their Australian-born counterparts. Asian-born women are disproportionately concentrated in blue collar jobs (table 87) and they are more vulnerable to exploitation. Exploitation is common when women do "outwork" for the clothing and garment industries, that is, when they work in their own homes, using their own sewing machines, sewing precut garments and being paid by the piece. Using that system, manufacturers

TABLE 85. PERSONS IN AUSTRALIA NOT ABLE TO SPEAK ENGLISH OR NOT ABLE TO SPEAK IT WELL, BY COUNTRY OR AREA OF BIRTH: 1991

Country or area of birth	Unable to speak English well or at all			
	Number		Percentage	
	Men	Women	Men	Women
China	18 499	18 990	47.6	55.5
Germany	1 318	1 950	4.3	5.5
Greece	20 015	27 046	30.6	42.2
Hong Kong	4 743	5 846	18.5	21.9
India	448	1 096	4.3	11.6
Italy	27 615	36 945	23.8	34.0
Lebanon..........	7 617	10 287	22.4	32.9
Malaysia	1 625	2 662	6.9	10.4
Malta	2 201	2 753	11.8	15.2
Netherlands	525	818	2.7	3.9
Philippines	965	1 804	4.7	5.1
Poland	4 827	6 725	17.9	23.2
USSR (former)	3 523	5 156	22.4	27.0
Viet Nam	25 024	29 133	40.7	51.8
Yugoslavia (former)	14 856	19 717	20.2	28.8

Source: Australian Bureau of Statistics, *1991 Census, Expanded Format*, table E12.

TABLE 86. RECIPIENTS OF GOVERNMENT BENEFITS, BY PLACE OF BIRTH: 1986
(Per 1,000 population)

Country or area of birth	Unemployment benefits only	All benefits		
		Main bene-ficiaries	All bene-ficiaries including dependants	
Australia	33.4	37.8	57.5	
Overseas	40.3	48.9	98.3	
Asia	65.0	81.5	207.4	
India	22.7	29.1	53.2	
Indo-China	140.0	170.9	430.2	
Other Asia	28.8	38.4	77.9	

Source: Australian Bureau of Statistics, *Overseas Born Australians, 1988*, Catalogue No. 4112.0 (Canberra, 1989), p. 154.

TABLE 87. POPULATION IN THE LABOUR FORCE, BY OCCUPATION AND PLACE OF BIRTH: 1986
(*Percentage*)

Occupation	Asian-born		Australian-born		Foreign-born	
	Male	*Female*	*Male*	*Female*	*Male*	*Female*
Managers, administrators, professionals, para-professionals ...	26.0	20.1	33.9	28.4	27.7	23.9
Semi-skilled white collar	18.8	37.9	16.7	56.6	13.6	42.2
Blue collar	55.2	42.1	49.4	15.0	58.6	33.6

Source: Australian Bureau of Statistics, *Overseas Born Australians, 1988*, Catalogue No. 4112.0 (Canberra, 1989), p. 150.

save considerably in production and labour costs. A study of Vietnamese women doing outwork in Melbourne's western suburbs noted that the majority had low educational levels and a poor command of English which confined them to jobs in the informal sector that were exploitative (Cuc, Lieu and Cahill, 1989, p. 98). Although most women were happy about being in Australia, they deplored their working conditions. However, they were prepared to endure them because they needed income and the work allowed them to remain at home to take care of their domestic responsibilities. It has been estimated that there are about 30,000 women doing outwork in Sydney alone. Most of them are Asian and earn as little as $A1.50 an hour (Loh, 1988; Scott, 1988; Burnley, 1989).

As already noted, Filipino immigrant women have a distinctive profile. In 1982/83, 90 per cent of all the female Filipino immigrants admitted that year and aged 20-39 were not in the labour force, compared with 56 per cent among other female immigrants. By 1987/88, the equivalent figure was 49 per cent for Filipino women compared to 37 per cent for all other immigrant women, and a smaller proportion of Filipino women had professional or technical skills (Hagan, 1989, p. 16). Women born in the Philippines are overrepresented in blue collar occupations compared to Australian-born women (23.1 per cent versus 12.8 per cent) and only 3 per cent of working Filipino women are in managerial or professional occupations. Filipino women are overrepresented in para-professional occupations. In terms of income, Filipino women display a less equitable distribution than Australian women as a whole.

A study of Filipino women in Adelaide found that 45 per cent were not currently employed, the majority being women who were not seeking work, often because their Australian husbands did not want them to join the labour force (Hugo and Channell, 1986, p. 36). Such restrictions can be a source of intramarital conflict, especially when women need to remit sufficient money to their relatives in the Philippines (DIEA, 1982a, p. 19). Among Filipino women working outside the home, more than one quarter were in technical and professional occupations, and the majority had obtained their qualifications in the Philippines. As other immigrant groups, Filipinos have experienced some downgrading of their occupations in Australia in relation to those they had just before migration (Smith, 1979, p. 122). Thus, only one quarter of those who were employed as professionals in the Philippines prior to migration were able to obtain similar positions in Australia and over 27 per cent were compelled to take unskilled work. However, most of the respondents were aware, prior to leaving the Philippines, that migration could result in a drop in employment status. Thus, only 41.5 per cent of those with professional qualifications thought that they would obtain a similar position in Australia, while over a quarter envisaged that they would be doing clerical work and 3 per cent thought that they would only be able to obtain an unskilled position. The survey also showed that occupational mobility was common so that several qualified immigrants had moved from initial jobs of low status to those in the professional and administrative category.

Lack of recognition of qualifications is a major barrier to the full participation of Asian women in Australia's economy. A 1980 survey of 117 Vietnamese in the Fairfield region of Sydney showed that only 52 per cent were satisfied with their job, 24 per cent were dissatisfied because of language problems, and 18 per cent were dissatisfied because their qualifications were not recognized (Keys-Young, 1980,

p. 92). According to Nguyen (1989, p. 88), among Vietnamese immigrants, many former medical doctors, engineers, lawyers, teachers and pharmacists have had to become blue collar workers because their qualifications have not been recognized. On average, the proportion of Asian-born women with university degrees is higher than that of Australian-born women and a smaller proportion of Asian-born women had left school at a young age (table 88).

The housing situation of immigrants is another indicator of their position in Australia. Over 50 per cent of the Vietnamese live in rented accommodation compared to less than 25 per cent of the Australians (table 89). Since refugees have priority in securing government assistance, over 20 per cent rent accommodation from a government agency, compared to only 7.4 per cent among the Australian-born. In addition, more than one third of the Vietnamese rent accommodation from the private sector where rental costs are rising. Another third live in dwellings that they are in the process of purchasing, a fact indicating their relative success, especially in light of the high mortgage rates prevailing. In 1982 the average size of Vietnamese households was 4.1 persons compared to 2.9 for all households (ABS, 1989b, p. 64).

F. SOCIAL ADJUSTMENT

Although the majority of Asian women who have immigrated to Australia are generally adapting well to the host society, there are indications that certain groups of immigrant women need special assistance

TABLE 88. WOMEN WITH SPECIFIC QUALIFICATIONS, BY COUNTRY OR REGION OF BIRTH: 1986
(*Percentage*)

Country or region of birth	With degree	Other post-secondary qualification	Left school at age 15 or younger
Australia	7.8	33.0	25.0
Overseas	9.9	33.6	26.4
Asia	17.1	12.5	16.0
South-eastern Asia	15.0	17.4	12.7
Other Asia	24.5	12.1	..

Source: Australian Bureau of Statistics, *Overseas Born Australians, 1988*, Catalogue No. 4112.0 (Canberra, 1989), p. 111.
Note: Two dots (..) indicate that data are not available or are not separately reported.

TABLE 89. POPULATION, BY TYPE OF HOUSING AND COUNTRY, AREA OR REGION OF BIRTH: 1986
(*Percentage*)

Country, area or region of birth	Housing			Nature of rental housing	
	Separate house	High rise	Owners, purchasers	Government	Private
Australia	85.2	0.9	72.7	7.4	15.2
Overseas	75.1	2.3	70.3	6.3	19.0
Asia	66.0	4.6	58.5	9.7	26.6
China	66.4	3.7	69.9	5.6	18.5
Hong Kong	61.6	5.0	68.1	3.0	24.3
India	73.9	2.4	71.6	5.3	19.3
Malaysia	65.3	3.5	62.5	4.8	28.8
Philippines	65.9	3.2	60.5	5.5	29.4
Sri Lanka	72.7	1.8	66.3	4.0	26.0
Viet Nam	58.1	8.3	38.7	21.2	35.5

Source: Australian Bureau of Statistics, *Overseas Born Australians, 1988*, Catalogue No. 4112.0 (Canberra, 1989), pp. 157-158.

to adapt. In particular, those who cannot communicate effectively in English have restricted economic prospects and are less likely to develop normal interactions with the rest of society. Immigrant women, who remain in a dependent position because traditional family norms constrain the roles that they may play, also deserve additional support. Furthermore, it is important to combat the prejudice and discrimination that Asian women face in the labour market and to facilitate the official recognition of immigrants' qualification.

Filipino immigrant women, in particular, appear to have special needs. Some studies indicate that they are overrepresented among persons seeking help from organizations such as Women's Refuges (South Australia Department of Community Welfare, 1988). However, few studies are representative of all Filipino female immigrants in Australia and it is hazardous to generalize from unrepresentantive studies focusing only on relatively few migrants. As already noted, studies that have attempted to cover the whole spectrum of Filipino immigrants suggest that the majority of Filipino women assess their migration experience as positive and do not feel subject to exploitation (Hugo and Channell, 1986; Jackson and Flores, 1989). Although such studies may tend to overrepresent the experience of well-adjusted families because they use as sampling frames lists of members of ethnic organizations, they nevertheless indicate that the sensationalist images presented by the media do not apply to the majority of Filipino women in Australia.

Studies of Vietnamese and Filipino women in Australia generally underscore the importance of the extended family and of social networks within each ethnic community in providing economic and emotional support for the women concerned. The possibility of family reunion has therefore critical implications for the well-being of immigrant women and it is a source of concern that changes in immigration regulations may effectively restrict the possibility of reassembling extended families in Australia. Lewins and Ly (1985, p. 28) have shown that as time since arrival elapses, Vietnamese immigrants manage to widen their social networks through the acquisition of friends, group membership and contact with officials.

The ethnic composition of the migrant intake has long been a matter of considerable public debate in Australia. It was not until the early 1970s that the last vestiges of the "White Australia Policy" were removed. This change has not been without its critics and opposition peaked in 1984 when Geoffrey Blainey stated publicly that he considered the Asian component of immigration to be too large and to be straining community tolerance, especially among the poor and disadvantaged. This statement sparked off a resurgence of the debate which unfortunately has too often been conducted in a heated, confrontational, dogmatic and bigoted fashion. As a result, Asian women have often had to adjust to Australia in an unfriendly atmosphere coloured by racism and discrimination (Nguyen, 1989, p. 88). As in virtually all societies in the Asia-Pacific region, racist attitudes are still evident among certain groups in Australia though it is difficult to assess their significance for the adjustment of Asian immigrants to life in Australia. A survey carried out in Sydney (Keys-Young, 1980), which asked Vietnamese settlers what aspects of life they found difficult to adjust to, found that 19.8 per cent cited the unfriendliness or indifference of Australian people, although only 4.3 per cent considered that to be the most serious barrier to adjustment. The barriers most frequently mentioned were the need to know English (81 per cent) and the

lack of suitable employment (45 per cent). These findings are typical of such studies. On the other hand, surveys of national attitudes consistently show a reduction of racist attitudes in Australia (FitzGerald, 1988). However, racism still exists and it affects the daily lives of many Asians, even if, as most surveys show and commentators argue, much of the resentment towards Asian immigrants is caused by a more general opposition to the economic and employment impacts of immigration in a context of high unemployment (Tran, 1983; Viviani, 1984, p. 273; DIEA, 1986; FitzGerald, 1988, p. 26). Nevertheless, a study of the attitudes of Australians living in Adelaide and Sydney, in neighbourhoods where substantial numbers of Asian immigrants have settled (DIEA, 1986, p. 57) found that 23 per cent of the 555 Australian-born persons interviewed agreed strongly with the proposition that immigrants just could not be bothered to learn English; 16 per cent agreed strongly with the view that Asian immigrants were interested only in personal gain and not in building a better Australia; and 23 per cent strongly disagreed with the proposition that the Government of Australia should provide assistance to Asian immigrants to start a new life.

G. Conclusion

This paper has assessed the processes of immigration and adjustment of Asian-born women in Australia. However, the task has been hindered by the tendency of official sources of data to present information only for both sexes combined and by the failure of most immigration research in Australia to recognize that gender has a major significance in shaping the processes of immigration and settlement. A further complicating factor is that most Asian immigrants in Australia are still at the early stages of the adjustment process and that the Asian community encompasses very diverse groups whose experience defies generalization.

With respect to Vietnamese immigrants, for instance, many of the difficulties that they confront are a function of the circumstances in which their immigration took place. Because most were forced to flee their country of origin, their assets in terms of both real and human capital are generally low and, consequently, their adjustment has been more difficult, especially given the high unemployment levels and tight housing market that have prevailed in Australia during most of the 1980s. Women, in particular, are more likely to find themselves in disadvantaged situations, having generally less access to education and employment opportunities.

Among other Asian immigrants in Australia, certain groups have been admitted mostly on the basis of their economic assets or their skills and are, therefore, in a better position to benefit from the opportunities available in the host country. Thus, Malaysian or Indian women tend to do better in terms of socio-economic indicators than those originating in other countries. Among Asian immigrants, those originating in the Philippines have attracted considerable attention because sizeable numbers of Filipino women have been admitted as spouses of Australian-born men. The immigration of brides, although by no means unprecedented in Australian history, has raised concerns about possible abuses of the immigration system and of the women involved. However, the few studies that have tried to obtain representative information about the adaptation experience of those women have shown that it is generally positive. Given the pervasive influence that simplistic stereotypes have on public opinion, it would be important that the results of such studies be more widely disseminated and that more research be geared towards documenting, in an unbiased fashion, the actual adaptation experience of the diverse groups of Asian immigrant women in Australia.

NOTES

[1]The 1966 Census was the last one to include a question on race. The majority of persons included in the full Chinese category were born in Australia.

[2]In Australia, the fiscal year starts on 1 July and ends on 30 June of the subsequent year.

[3]The Index of Dissimilarity measures the evenness of the distribution of two subpopulations. The index can be interpreted as the percentage of a particular subpopulation which would have to change their place of residence if the distribution of that group between subareas of the region under study was to be made exactly the same as that of the other subgroup. An index of 0 would mean that the two subpopulations had exactly the same relative distribution, while an index value of 100 represents a complete "apartheid" situation, with no person of one subgroup living in the same subarea as people of the other subgroup. If the index is less than 20, there is little spatial separation of the two subpopulations; if it exceeds 30, there is some significant separation; and if it exceeds 50, there is a very significant separation (Hugo, 1989).

[4]Income units consist of, at most, two income recipients who are married to each other. Children who are not economically dependent constitute separate income units. Income per income unit is therefore analogous to "family income" (ABS, 1989a, p. 35).

REFERENCES

Anderssen, Curtis (1991). *Malaysian Students in Australia: A Study of Mobility Determinants*. Doctoral thesis. Bedford Park, South Australia: Flinders University of South Australia, School of Social Sciences.

Arnold, Fred (1989). Unanswered questions about the immigration multiplier. *International Migration Review* (Staten Island, New York), vol. 23, No. 4 (Winter), pp. 889-892.

Australia, Bureau of Immigration and Population Research (BIPR) (1993). *Immigration Update, June Quarter 1993*. Canberra: Government Publishing Service.

Australia, Department of Immigration and Ethnic Affairs (DIEA) (1982a). *A Bride for all Reasons: Report on a Pilot Survey of Filipino Brides*. Melbourne, Australia: Department of Immigration and Ethnic Affairs and Philippine Consulate General.

_____ (1982b). *Please Listen to What I'm Not Saying: A Report on the Survey of Settlement Experiences of Indochinese Refugees 1978-80*. Canberra: Government Publishing Service.

_____ (1984). *Profile 81: 1981 Census Data on Persons Born in Vietnam*. Canberra.

_____ (1986). *Migrant Attitudes Survey*. Canberra: Government Publishing Service.

Australia, Department of Immigration, Local Government and Ethnic Affairs (DILGEA) (1971). *Australian Immigration: Consolidated Statistics, No. 5*. Canberra: Government Publishing Service.

_____ (1988a). Indochinese refugees. *Statistical Note*, No. 37. Canberra.

_____ (1988b). *Australian Immigration: Consolidated Statistics, No. 15*. Canberra: Government Publishing Service.

_____ (1989). *Refugee and Humanitarian Visas - Seven Women at Risk (Class 204)*. Canberra: Government Publishing Service.

Australian Bureau of Statistics (1947). *1947 Census of Population and Housing*. Canberra.

_____ (1976). *1976 Census of Population and Housing*. Canberra.

_____ (1986). *1986 Census of Population and Housing*. Canberra.

_____ (1989a). *Year Book Australia 1989*. No. 72. Catalogue No. 1300.0. Canberra.

_____ (1989b). *Overseas Born Australians 1988*. Catalogue No. 4112.0. Canberra.

_____ (1990). *Estimated Resident Population by Country of Birth, Age and Sex: Australia*, June 1989 and Preliminary 1990. Catalogue No. 3221.0. Canberra.

_____ (1991). *1991 Census of Population and Housing. Basic Community Profile: Australia*. Canberra.

_____ (1993). *Estimated Resident Population by Country of Birth, Age and Sex: Australia*, Preliminary June 1992 and June 1993. Catalogue No. 3221.0. Canberra.

Australian Sales Research Bureau (1986). Occupational shares system survey. Report prepared for the Department of Immigration and Ethnic Affairs (17 June).

Bailey, P. (1986). Filipino brides to Mount Isa: with love from Manila. *Good Weekend, Sydney Morning Herald Magazine*, 8 February.

Birrell, Robert (1984). Australia's immigration policy: changes and implications. In *Populate and Perish? The Stresses of Population Growth in Australia*, Robert Birrell, Douglas Hill and Jon Nevill, eds. Fontana, Sydney, Melbourne: Australian Conservation Foundation.

_____ (1990). *The Chains that Bind: Family Reunion Migration to Australia in the 1980s*. Canberra: Government Publishing Service.

Boyd, Monica (1987). Migrant women in Canada: profiles and policies. Report prepared for the Research Division, Immigration Canada, and Status of Women. Toronto, Canada.

Burnley, I. H. (1982). *Population, Society and Environment in Australia*. Melbourne: Shillington House.

_____ (1989). Settlement dimensions of the Vietnam-born population in Sydney. *Australian Geographical Studies* (Australia), vol. 27, No. 2, pp. 129-154.

Carmichael, Gordon A. (1993). *Trans-Tasman Migration: Trends, Causes and Consequences*. Canberra: Government Publishing Service.

Choi, Ching Y. (1975). *Chinese Migration and Settlement in Australia*. Sydney: Sydney University Press.

Channell, Kym (1986). Filipinos in Adelaide: origins and growth of a migrant community. Unpublished Bachelor of Arts thesis. Bedford Park: Flinders University of South Australia.

Cuc, Lam T., Luong T. Lieu and Desmond Cahill (1989). Vietnamese female outworkers in Melbourne's western suburbs. *Asian Migrant* (Manila, Philippines), vol. 2, No. 3, pp. 95-98.

Day, Lincoln H. (1983). *Analysing Population Trends: Differential Fertility in a Pluralist Society*. London: Croom Helm.

Desbarats, Jacqueline (1985). Indochinese resettlement in the United States. *Annals of the Association of American Geographers* (Cambridge, Massachusetts), vol. 75, No. 4, pp. 522-538.

Di Iulio, Orlando B., and Y. C. Chung (1976). *Fertility Data 1966 Census*. National Population Inquiry Research Paper, No. 8. Canberra: Australian National University.

FitzGerald, Stephen (1988). *A Commitment to Australia: Report of the Committee to Inquire into Australia's Immigration Policy*. 3 volumes. Canberra.

Hagan, C. (1989). Filipinos in Australia: a statistical profile. *Statistical Note*, No. 41. Canberra.

Hugo, Graeme J. (1986a). The immigration points system. Report prepared for the Migration Committee of the National Population Council (November).

_____ (1986b). *Australia's Changing Population: Trends and Implications*. Melbourne, Australia: Oxford University Press.

_____ (1988). Outputs and effects of immigration in Australia. In *Immigration: A Commitment to Australia - Consultants' Reports*. Committee to Advise on Australia's Immigration Policies. Canberra: Government Publishing Service.

_____ (1989). Australia: the spatial concentration of the turnaround. In *Counterurbanization: The Changing Pace and Nature of Population Deconcentration*, A. G. Champion, ed. London: Edward Arnold.

_____ (1990a). Adaptation of Vietnamese in Australia: an assessment based on 1986 census results. *Southeast Asian Journal of Social Science* (Singapore), vol. 18, No. 1, pp. 182-210.

_____ (1990b). *Atlas of the Australian People*, vol. III, *Queensland*. Canberra: Government Publishing Service.

_____ (1990c). *Atlas of the Australian People*, vol. IV, *Tasmania*. Canberra: Government Publishing Service.

_____, and Kym Channell (1986). Filipino migrants in Adelaide. Paper presented at the Third Conference of the Australian Population Association, Adelaide, Australia, 3-5 December.

Hugo, Graeme J., Lin Lean Lim and S. Narayan (1989). *Malaysian Human Resources Development Planning Project, Module II: Labour Supply and Processes*. Labour Mobility Final Report, Study No. 4 (January).

Jackson, Richard T., and E. R. Flores (1989). *No Filipinos in Manila: A Study of Filipino Migrants in Australia*. North Queensland, Australia: James Cook University.

Jasso, Guillermina, and Mark Rosenzweig (1986). Family reunification and the immigration multiplier: U.S. immigration law, origin-country conditions and the reproduction of immigrants. *Demography* (Washington, D.C.), vol. 23, pp. 293-311.

Keys-Young, M. S. J. (1980). *The Settlement Process of the Vietnamese, Lao, Kampuchean and Timorese in Sydney*. Canberra: Department of Immigration and Ethnic Affairs.

_____ (1983). *Survey of Vietnamese Refugees*. Canberra: Department of Immigration and Ethnic Affairs.

Lewins, Frank, and Judith Ly (1985). *The First Wave: The Settlement of Australia's First Vietnamese Refugees*. Sydney, Australia: George Allen and Unwin.

Loh, Morag (1988). Vietnamese community life in Australia. In *The Australian People*, James Jupp, ed. Sydney: Angus and Robertson.

Lowe, B. (1988). Mail order misery. *The Weekend Australian* (25-26 June).

Lyng, Jens (1935). *Non-Britishers in Australia: Influence on Population Progress*. Melbourne: Melbourne University Press.

Meng Try, Ea (1981). Kampuchea: a country adrift. *Population and Development Review* (New York), vol. 7, No. 2, pp. 209-228.

Nguyen, Xuan T. (1989). The Vietnamese in Australia. *Asian Migrant* (Manila), vol. 2, pp. 84-88.

Price, Archibald G. (1972). *Island Continent: Aspects of the Historical Geography of Australia and its Territories*. Sydney: Angus and Robertson.

Price, Charles A. (1982). *The Fertility and Marriage Patterns of Australia's Ethnic Groups*. 2 vol. Canberra: Australian National University, Department of Demography, Research School of Social Sciences.

_____, and others (1984). *Birthplaces of the Australian Population, 1861-1981*. Working Papers in Demography, No. 13. Canberra: Australian National University.

Reark Research Pty. Ltd. (1985). *The Category C Migrants in the Workforce. Report on the 1985 Survey*. Canberra: Department of Immigration and Ethnic Affairs.

Rodell, Susanna (1982). The bride's price. *Australian Society* (Australia), vol. 1, No. 2, pp. 13-14.

Scott, B. (1988). Outwork and restructuring in the Australian clothing industry: a geographical perspective. Unpublished Bachelor of Arts thesis. Sydney, Australia: Macquarie University, School of Earth Sciences.

Smith, Rhonda L. (1979). The effects of immigration on the Australian economy. In *Population, Immigration and the Australian Economy*, Peter Brain, Rhonda L. Smith and Gerald P. Schuyer, eds. London: Croom Helm.

South Australia Department for Community Welfare (1988). *Filipina-Australian Marriages and Domestic Violence*. Working Party Report. Bedford Park, South Australia.

Stevens, Christine (1984). The occupational adjustment of Kampuchean refugees in Adelaide. Unpublished Bachelor of Arts thesis. Bedford Park, South Australia: University of Adelaide.

219

Thadani, Veena N., and Michael P. Todaro (1984). Female migration: a conceptual framework. In *Women in the Cities of Asia: Migration and Urban Adaptation*, James T. Fawcett, Siew-Ean Khoo and Peter C. Smith, eds. Boulder, Colorado: Westview Press.

Tran, V. N. (1983). Highs and lows of a new community. *The Advertiser* (29 October), p. 6.

Victorian Ethnic Affairs Commission (1986). Immigration to intake - background issues. Draft notes prepared for use in consultations with Government departments, trade unions and community organizations.

Viviani, Nancy (1984). *The Long Journey: Vietnamese Migration and Settlement in Australia*. Melbourne, Australia: Melbourne University Press.

Young, Christabel (1989). Demographic behaviour and intergenerational change among migrants in Australia. Paper presented at the General Conference of the International Union for the Scientific Study of Population, New Delhi, 20-27 September.

XIII. LABOUR FORCE EXPERIENCE OF MIGRANT WOMEN: FILIPINO AND KOREAN WOMEN IN TRANSITION

*Maruja M. Asis**

The increasing recognition of migrant women as economic actors (Tyree and Donato, 1986) and the growing interest in women's work in general (Sullivan, 1984) have generated considerable research on women as both migrants and workers. In the United States, historical studies reveal that immigrant women were among those who pioneered working outside the home long before American women began entering the labour force in large numbers (Hesse, 1979; Diner, 1983; Ewen, 1985; Glenn, 1986; Weinberg, 1988). Furthermore, immigrant women who were not strictly in the labour force often engaged in home-based productive activities (such as taking in boarders) to help support their families. More recent female immigrants have been no less active in productive activities. Indeed, in the United States, women belonging to some immigrant groups, such as those of Asian origin,[1] are more economically active than the native-born (Gardner, Robey and Smith, 1985; Stier, 1990). For a substantial proportion of immigrant women, working at the place of destination represents their first experience as economic actors (Guendelman and Perez-Itriago, 1987). That is, international migration has the potential of bringing about important changes in the lives of immigrant women. According to Morokvasic (1984), access to salaried employment is perhaps the most important change that can result from migration.

Examining the impact of migration on the work patterns of immigrant women has been hampered by data limitations. Relying mainly on censuses or surveys that produce only cross-sectional data, most studies consider only the occupational adjustment of female immigrants since their time of arrival in the place of destination. The pre-migration experience is reconstructed from the information that immigrants provide upon arrival in the country of destination, and changes since then are measured according to length of residence. As a result, the work transitions that women experience, especially before and after migration, are lost in that "snapshot" perspective. Several questions need to be considered to elucidate the transitional nature of women's work experience. Are the work expectations of female immigrants a reasonable indicator of their actual work experience in the place of destination? Is the process of occupational adjustment similar for those women who have worked prior to immigration and for those who have not worked before immigration? Do female immigrants with work experience fare better than those without that experience, particularly during their first few years in the place of destination? A longitudinal study that follows immigrants over their migration experience, that is, from before departure through their arrival in the place of destination and after some time spent there, is better able to provide some insights into the process of occupational change. Longitudinal data relative to the 1986 cohort of Filipino and Korean immigrants to the United States are used in this paper to examine the occupational experience of migrant women. Although female immigrants are expected to be less economically active than their male counterparts, they in fact join the labour force of the country of destination in significant numbers.

A. FEMALE IMMIGRATION FROM THE PHILIPPINES AND THE REPUBLIC OF KOREA TO THE UNITED STATES

Immigration from the Philippines and the Republic of Korea to the United States dates back to the early part of this century, but it was not until the passage of the 1965 Immigration and Nationality Act that

---

*East-West Center, Population Institute, Honolulu, Hawaii, United States of America. The author wishes to thank Fred Arnold, James T. Fawcett, Robert W. Gardner, Benjamin Cariño and Insook Han Park for granting her permission to use the 1986 Immigrant Pre-Departure Assessment Surveys and the 1988 Immigrant Update Survey. The support provided by the Sloan Foundation through grant No. 85-6-13 and by the East-West Population Institute is also gratefully acknowledged.

levels of immigration from those two countries increased substantially and rapidly (figure VIII). Prior to 1930, immigration from those countries had been dominated by single, young men who were recruited for agricultural work. Those immigrants had mostly low socio-economic origins and were sojourn-oriented. In contrast, among the more recent waves of immigrants from the Philippines and the Republic of Korea, women have constituted a majority.[2] Recent immigrants come from a variety of socio-economic and occupational backgrounds and their aim is to settle permanently in the United States (Asis, 1989). By the 1980s, when Mexico was the largest source of immigrants to the United States, the Philippines and the Republic of Korea occupied second and third places respectively.[3]

Data from the United States Immigration and Naturalization Service for 1972-1985 show that, year after year, more than half of all immigrants from the Philippines and the Republic of Korea have been women. Immigrants admitted as spouses of United States citizens have included the highest proportions of women. Among Filipinos admitted in that category, 8 out of every 10 were women and among

Koreans the equivalent ratio was 9 out of 10 (Asis, 1989). Women migrating as spouses are normally considered to move in association, that is, to accompany or join their husbands. Because most women admitted as spouses are assumed to migrate to the United States for family reasons, they are not expected to display high rates of economic activity. The data, however, suggest otherwise. According to Gardner, Robey and Smith (1985), in 1980, 68 per cent of Filipino-American women and 55 per cent of Korean-American[4] women were in the labour force as compared with 49 per cent of native-born white women. Focusing only on married immigrant women, Stier (1990) notes the high labour force participation rates among those belonging to six groups of Asian origin. Married Filipino women had the highest labour force participation rate (73 per cent) and married Korean women were also highly likely to be in the labour force (52 per cent were).

Immigrant women who are economically active include both women who are working for the first time and those who resume their economic activity after migration. The issue of how work experience affects the work patterns of immigrant women in the

Figure VIII. Immigrants to the United States from the Republic of Korea
and the Philippines: 1950-1990

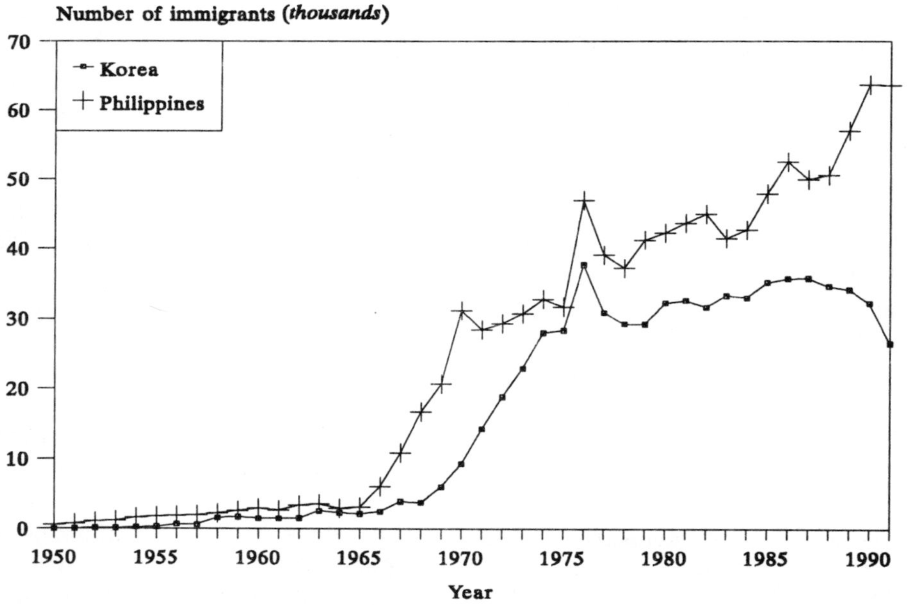

Source: United States, Statistical Yearbook of the Immigration and Naturalization Service, various years.

country of destination will be explored in this paper using longitudinal data on the employment transitions of married women immigrating to the United States. A longitudinal survey of Filipino and Korean immigrants to the United States was carried out by the East-West Population Institute (Hawaii) in collaboration with the University of the Philippines (Philippines) and Hanyang University (the Republic of Korea). The first two phases of the survey took place in 1986 and 1988. In 1986, the Immigrant Pre-Departure Assessment Surveys (IPDA) were carried out in the Philippines and the Republic of Korea among persons intending to migrate to the United States. In 1988, the Immigrant Update Survey (IUS) was carried out in the United States among the immigrants interviewed in the pre-departure surveys with the aim of documenting their experience during their first two years in that country. Respondents to the pre-departure surveys had already received immigrant visas from United States authorities and were therefore getting ready to depart for the United States. Visa holders must enter the United States within 90 days of the visa's date of issue (extensions, however, are possible). At the port of entry, a visa holder is subject to an additional screening by the United States Immigration and Naturalization Service. Those passing that screening are considered to be successfully admitted as immigrants by the United States.

Married women aged 18-64 comprised 28 per cent of the Filipino sample (579 women) and 40 per cent of the Korean sample (734 women) in the 1986 IPDA. Of these, the 1988 IUS was able to reinterview 333 Filipino women and 356 Korean. A preliminary analysis of the characteristics of the respondents successfully traced by the IUS with those who could not be reinterviewed (either because they refused or because they could not be located) suggests that there are no significant differences between the two groups.

B. CHARACTERISTICS OF IMMIGRANT WIVES BEFORE IMMIGRATION

In most societies, men have traditionally been assigned the main economic roles within the family whereas women have been confined mostly to the reproductive and caregiver roles. Cultural norms supporting this division of labour can affect the nature and conditions of women's participation in the labour force. Filipino and Korean societies contrast sharply in terms of the roles assigned to women.

In the Philippines, the public sphere is open to both women and men. Women are the "social equals" of men (Jacobson, 1974), as indicated by their having almost equal access to educational and occupational opportunities as men (Castillo, 1977). Of Filipino women aged 15-64, 48 per cent are employed (ILO, 1987). Married women constitute an important proportion of the working population and the majority work because they need to (Castillo, 1977). Women, just as men, are prone to migrate in order to enhance their employment opportunities. Many women migrate within the Philippines, but a growing number do so internationally. The relatively large numbers of young, single female migrants seeking work in urban areas is considered part of their family's strategy to maximize income (Trager, 1988). However, many migrant women are not single. Thus, the proportion of married women among those migrating to work abroad has been rising (Paganoni and Cruz, 1989), particularly during the late 1980s when women constituted about 47 per cent of all Filipinos migrating as contract workers (Philippine Overseas Employment Administration, 1988).

In the Republic of Korea, the weight of Confucian tradition finds expression in values that define a woman's key role as that of wife and mother. Since the Republic of Korea has a more developed economy than that of the Philippines, one would expect that a greater proportion of Korean women would work outside the home than in the Philippines. However, the labour force participation of Korean women is lower than that of Filipino women (43 per cent versus 48 per cent). Although the rapid industrialization that the Republic of Korea has experienced since the 1970s has broadened industrial employment opportunities for women, the rising share of female employment is mainly due to the increased labour force participation of single women (Jones, 1984; Koo, 1984; Bauer and Shin, 1986). In addition, the labour force participation of Korean women is lower in urban than in rural areas (Koo, 1984).

Cultural norms favouring the family roles of women are partly responsible for the lower than expected increase in the labour force participation of Korean women. Women are expected to work outside the home only when they are single (Koo, 1984). Once married, they are expected to devote their energies entirely to their household and family responsibilities (Cho, 1987; Min, 1987). That expectation is presumably greater among the better-off who are also less likely to be compelled to work because of need. Bauer and Shin (1986) find that, as household income increases, female labour force participation decreases. The labour market further reinforces the ideal of a stay-at-home wife by offering few incentives for women to work. Unfavourable working conditions (low wages and bleak prospects for mobility) discourage highly educated women from entering the labour force (Koo, 1984; Cho, 1987).

Thus, the Filipino and Korean cultures foster divergent views regarding the acceptable roles of women and their participation in the labour force. By allowing a change of environment, international migration can free women from restrictive cultural norms and thus have an important impact on the economic roles that they may play at the place of destination.

The 1986 IPDA data indicate that married immigrant women from the Philippines and the Republic of Korea move to the United States with considerable human capital (table 90). Thus, they have, on average, 10 to 11 years of education, the majority originate in urban areas (especially those from the Republic of Korea) and most report themselves as having a middle-class background. Filipino and Korean immigrant women differ, however, in terms of their ability to use English (Filipino women scored higher than their Korean counterparts) and in terms of other demographic characteristics. Filipino women were older (their mean age was 41 years compared to 34 among Koreans), they had been married longer (17 years versus 10 years on average) and had more children (3.6 versus 1.6) than their Korean counterparts. Most of the immigrant women interviewed were married to men of the same ethnic origin[5] (Filipinos or Koreans, including those with American citizenship). Intermarriage was almost exclusively to American men (defined as excluding Fili-

TABLE 90. SELECTED CHARACTERISTICS OF MARRIED FILIPINO AND KOREAN FEMALE IMMIGRANTS TO THE UNITED STATES: 1986 IPDA
(*Married Filipino women considered = 579; married Korean women = 731*)

	Married Filipino women		Married Korean women	
	Mean (SD)	Percentage	Mean (SD)	Percentage
A. *Human capital characteristics*				
Years of education	10.4 (5.4)	-	11.2 (3.6)	-
Urban residence	-	61.8	-	90.8
English ability[a]	5.4 (2.4)	-	2.1 (1.6)	-
Number of job skills ...	2.2 (1.0)	-	0.5 (0.7)	-
Class[b]	5.4 (1.5)	-	-	-
Upper	-	-	-	4.5
Middle	-	-	-	80.7
Lower	-	-	-	14.9
B. *Demographic characteristics*				
Age	40.7 (11.6)	-	34.1 (13.1)	-
Years married	16.6 (14.8)	-	10.2 (12.7)	-
Number of children	3.6 (3.2)	-	1.6 (1.8)	-
Spouse's origin				
Filipino/Korean	-	84.9	-	71.8
American	-	14.2	-	27.8
Other	-	0.9	-	0.4
Spouse's age	45.5 (15.1)	-	38.0 (12.1)	-
Spouse's years of education	10.6 (3.9)	-	13.2 (3.7)	-

NOTE: SD: Standard deviation; hyphen (-) indicates that the item is not applicable.

[a]Index derived from respondents' self-ratings on range from 1 to 10.

[b]Class was measured differently in the Filipino and Korean surveys (see table 93).

pino-Americans and Korean-Americans). A higher proportion of Korean women had married American men than their Filipino counterparts (28 per cent versus 14 per cent). These characteristics are all likely to influence a woman's decision to participate in the labour force.

C. WORK EXPECTATIONS BEFORE IMMIGRATION

Persons interviewed during the IPDA were asked about their expectations in regard to life in the United States, including those relative to work and employment. Since most studies of the labour force participation of migrants are limited to objective indicators, such as the human resource characteristics of migrants, the role of the subjective component in occupational mobility is not well understood (Segura, 1989). The immigrants' work expectations provide some indication of what their move means in relation to their economic activity and such expectations can therefore provide a useful reference point for comparison with the subsequent work experience of immigrants.

As table 91 indicates, a very high proportion of married immigrant women expected to work in the United States (76 per cent and 83 per cent among Filipino and Korean women, respectively). In fact, the proportions expecting to work were considerably higher than those actually working prior to departure (during the 12 months preceding interview): by 82 per cent in the case of Filipino women and by over 160 per cent among Korean women. Thus, only 42 per cent of married Filipino women reported that they had worked during the 12 months preceding the pre-departure interview and the equivalent proportion was even lower (32 per cent) among married Korean women.

Although most female immigrants had not made any arrangements for employment in the United States, they did not expect serious difficulties in securing a job (Asis, 1989). In general, Filipino women were less likely to expect problems in other areas, such as housing, children's schooling, language or cost of living, than Korean women. The differential between the two groups was greatest in regard to language, where only 17 per cent of Filipinos expected to have some problems compared to 90 per cent of Koreans. On the whole, however, the majority of both Filipino and Korean immigrant women were optimistic about finding work, perhaps because of the types of jobs that they expected to get.

According to table 92, immigrant women expected to get fairly different kinds of jobs in the United States than those they had had in their home countries during the 12-months-preceding interview. Among both Filipino and Korean married women, the proportion expecting to get a job in the service sector was considerably higher than that of women who had actually worked in that sector before departure. A rise in the proportion working in production would also occur if the expectations of migrant women were fulfilled. Furthermore, among Filipino women, the proportion expecting to perform clerical work was also higher than the proportion of those working in that occupation before departure. However, a large part of the gains in services and production were accounted for by a sharp decline in the

TABLE 91. MARRIED FILIPINO AND KOREAN IMMIGRANT WOMEN, BY EMPLOYMENT STATUS BEFORE
IMMIGRATION AND BY EXPECTED STATUS AFTER IMMIGRATION: 1986 IPDA
(Percentage)

Employment status	Married Filipino women			Married Korean women		
	Before	After	Change (percentage)	Before	After	Change (percentage)
Employed	41.7	76.0	82.3	31.8	83.1	161.3
Does not work	58.3	23.9	-59.0	68.1	16.9	-75.2
Student	3.1	0.7	..	2.1	1.1	..
Housekeeper	52.6	20.5	..	65.0	9.5	..
Retiree	1.3	1.0	..	0.5	5.9	..
Searching for work	1.4	0.0	..	0.0	0.0	..
Other	0.0	1.7	..	0.5	0.4	..
Number of respondents	557	576	..	729	727	..

NOTE: Two dots (..) indicate that data are not available or are not separately reported.

225

TABLE 92. MARRIED FILIPINO AND KOREAN WOMEN, BY OCCUPATION BEFORE IMMIGRATION
AND BY EXPECTED OCCUPATION AFTER IMMIGRATION: 1986 IPDA

(Percentage)

Occupation	Married Filipino women			Married Korean women		
	Before	After	Change (percentage	Before	After	Change (percentage)
Professional	40.0	21.7	-45.8	18.5	5.9	-68.1
Managerial...........................	5.9	3.0	-49.2	13.2	3.4	-74.2
Clerical	18.0	23.6	31.1	23.4	20.0	-14.5
Sales	15.6	6.9	-55.8	17.6	14.6	-17.0
Farming, fishing and forestry ...	3.4	2.5	-26.5	4.9	0.5	-89.8
Transport	1.0	0.5	-50.0	1.0	0.0	-100.0
Production	9.8	12.8	30.6	10.2	17.1	67.6
Services	6.3	29.1	361.9	11.2	38.5	243.8
Number of respondents	205	203	..	205	205	..

NOTE: Percentages were based on the responses of those who had worked during the 12 months preceding the interview and those who expected to work after immigration; two dots (..) indicate that data are not available or are not separately reported.

proportion of women expecting to work in professional occupations. Thus, only about half of the Filipino married women working as professionals before departure expected to get similar jobs in the United States. Among Korean married women, the drop was even larger in relative terms, so that only about a third of those working as professionals expected to continue in that occupation once they reached the United States. The fact that a high proportion of women expected to hold service occupations in the United States reflected a rational attitude on their part because, as the United States Bureau of Labour Statistics has noted, the demand for service workers in that country has been rising and is likely to remain high until the year 2000 (Riche, 1988, p. 38).

D. DETERMINANTS OF WORK EXPECTATIONS

As the work expectations of prospective female immigrants suggest, important changes were in store for them when they entered the United States labour market. The question is whether there was any basis for such expectations or, more precisely, to what extent the background of female immigrants influenced their work expectations. To answer this question, it was assumed that the work expectations of female immigrants were determined by their human

capital, their stage in the life cycle and the social resources that they could muster at the place of destination. Human capital factors, measured in terms of educational attainment, ability in using English, previous work experience, number of job skills and social class, are expected to be significant in shaping the work expectations of immigrants who are conscious of the labour-market relevance of such factors. In addition, given that the immigrants considered are women and that the labour force participation of women in general is dependent on certain demographic and social characteristics closely associated with a woman's stage in the life cycle, those factors, measured in terms of age, presence of preschool children in the household and spouse's origin, are also considered relevant in shaping the work expectations of female immigrants. As Nath (1982, p. 14) suggests: "women in their different life phases have different amounts of spare time as well as different degrees of freedom and accessibility". Lastly, immediate family members already established in the place of destination provide women with social resources and information that are likely to influence their expectations. There is considerable evidence indicating that social networks facilitate the occupational adjustment of immigrants (Phizacklea, 1983; Caces, 1985; Ong, 1985; Glenn, 1986; Yamanako, 1986; Cobas, 1987; Portes, 1987; Lee, 1988).

A model relating the variables discussed above to a dependent variable that indicates whether female immigrants expected to work or not in the United States was fitted by using logit regression. A list of the variables used and their definitions can be found in table 93. Table 94 presents the results of fitting the model in terms of adjusted probabilities of expecting to work in the United States for those vari-

TABLE 93. DEFINITION OF VARIABLES USED IN FITTING A MODEL TO PREDICT THE PROBABILITY THAT IMMIGRANT FILIPINO AND KOREAN WOMEN EXPECT TO WORK IN THE UNITED STATES

Variable	Definition or measurement
Dependent:	
Labour force participation	Set to 1 if the woman expected to work in the United States and to 0 otherwise.
Independent:	
Education	Years of completed education measured as an interval variable.
English ability	An index ranging from 1 to 10 was derived from respondents' self-ratings on their ability to read, write and speak English. A score of 10 indicated the highest ability.
Work experience	Set to 1 if the woman had ever worked before migration and to 0 otherwise.
Number of job skills	An interval variable derived from information on the skills that a woman had and that she thought would be helpful in obtaining a job in the United States. For Korean women only skills related to blue-collar occupations or vocational skills were considered.
Class membership	Variable derived from the self-ranking of membership to a social class in the place of origin. Filipino respondents ranked themselves on a ten-point scale, with 10 representing the highest class. Korean respondents ranked themselves as belonging to the upper, middle or lower class. Responses were transformed into dummy variables for the purposes of the multivariate analysis.
Age	Age in years.
Presence of pre-school children	Set to 1 if there were any children under 7 years of age who were in the United States or who would accompany their mothers as immigrants to the United States and to 0 otherwise.
Spouse's origin	Set to 1 if the spouse of a Filipino woman is also Filipino or if the spouse of a Korean woman is Korean and to 0 otherwise.
Spouse's residence	Set to 1 if the husband was already in the United States and to 0 otherwise.
Immediate family in the United States	Set to 1 if a woman had immediate relatives (parents, siblings or children) living in the United States and to 0 otherwise.
Metropolitan residence	Set to 1 if a woman intended to live in a metropolitan area with a Filipino or Korean population of at least 10,000 (as indicated by census data) and to 0 otherwise.
Family-owned business	Set to 1 if a woman's family owned or managed a business in the United States and to 0 otherwise.

227

TABLE 94. ADJUSTED PROBABILITIES THAT MARRIED FILIPINO AND KOREAN IMMIGRANT WOMEN EXPECT TO WORK ONCE THEY REACH THE UNITED STATES: 1986 IPDA

Independent variable	Married Filipino women	Married Korean women
Human capital characteristics		
Work experience in the country of origin		
Yes	ns	.9690**
No	ns	.9322**
Number of job skills		
0	.7881**	a
1	.8786**	a
2	.8887**	a
Demographic characteristics		
Age		
30	.9669**	.9886**
40	.9072**	.9187**
50	.7657**	.7490**
Presence of pre-school children		
Yes	ns	.9167*
No	ns	.9674*
Spouse's origin		
Same as own	.9289**	.9811**
American	.2848**	.7381**
Social resources in the place of destination		
Immediate family in the United States		
Yes	.8768*	ns
No	.9785*	ns
Number of women	(473)	(680)

NOTE: "ns" means "not significant"; * indicates that the variable is significant at the p < .05 level; and ** indicates that the variable is significant at the p < .01 level.

a This variable was not included in the equation because of biases resulting from the way the question was asked.

ables whose coefficients were statistically significant. The results for the variables indicating educational attainment, ability to use English and social class are not shown because they were not statistically significant. The model was fitted separately to each group of female immigrants. Unfortunately, the question used to obtain information on number of job skills among Korean immigrants was not properly phrased and the information could not be used in the analysis. However, the results indicate that at least two of the variables indicating human capital were important determinants of the expectation to work. So were two of the demographic variables, namely, the female immigrant's own age and her spouse's origin. Interestingly, the number of pre-school children in the household was not a significant determinant of work expectations among Filipino immigrant women and it was only a moderately significant factor in the case of Korean women. The presence of immediate family members in the United States was a moderately significant factor affecting work expectations only in the case of Filipino immigrant women.

Most of the variables used to indicate human capital, namely, educational attainment, ability to use English and social class, did not emerge as significant predictors of whether immigrant women expected to work or not. That outcome was probably due to the fact that the dependent variable only indicated a general intention to work. An investigation of the determinants of work expectations in terms of specific occupations did show that educational attainment and language ability were significant predictors of the expectation of getting white-collar occupations (Asis, 1989).

The effects of the other variables indicating human capital cannot be properly compared for the two groups of immigrants considered because of the exclusion of the number of job skills in the model fitted to Koreans. Among Filipino immigrants, only that variable (number of job skills) was significant and it indicated that the more skills a woman had the more likely she was to expect to work.

Among the demographic characteristics, age had the expected effect: younger immigrant women were more likely to expect to work than their older counterparts. The differences by age were considerable. At age 30, almost every woman expected to work: 97 per cent of Filipino immigrant women and 99 per cent of Korean did. For those aged 50, however, that percentage declined to 77 per cent among Filipino immigrant women and 75 per cent among Koreans.

The largest differentials in the work expectations of immigrant women were associated with their husband's origin. Thus, about 93 per cent of Filipino immigrant women married to Filipino men expected to work, compared with 29 per cent of those married to American men. Similarly, whereas 98 per cent of Korean immigrant women married to Korean men expected to work, only 74 per cent of those married to American men did. When both husband and wife had the same origin, they tended to constitute a double-earner household. In contrast, couples in mixed marriages were more likely to conform to the traditional single-earner household. The higher expected labour force participation of Korean immigrant women in mixed marriages compared to that of Filipino women is probably attributable to the fact that the Korean women were more likely to be married to American men connected with the United States Army, whose wages tended to be low. In contrast, Filipino women tended to marry American men who had civilian jobs and better wages.

Having at least one pre-school child reduced the probability of expecting to work among Korean immigrant women but, as noted earlier, that variable had no significant effect in the case of Filipino women. Such outcome may be due to differences in household arrangements, since Filipino immigrants are more likely to live in extended households than Koreans (22 per cent of Filipino immigrants versus 10 per cent of Korean immigrants lived in extended households according to Stier, 1990). Lastly, although having immediate family members in the United States was a significant factor affecting the work expectations of Filipino women, it tended to reduce rather than increase the probability of expecting to work. One possible explanation for that outcome could be that immigrant women with family already in the United States were better off and did not need to find work immediately after migration.

E. Immigrant women in the United States: the first two years

Using the data gathered in the second phase of the longitudinal migration survey, it is possible to consider the actual work experience of married immigrant women during their first two years in the United States. The Immigrant Update Survey (IUS) gathered data through mail questionnaires and telephone interviews. Persons who had been interviewed during the IPDA phase were traced through the addresses and telephone numbers in the United States that they had provided during the pre-immigration survey. Respondents to the IUS were asked about all the jobs that they had had in the United States since arrival. That information allowed the comparison of immigrants' actual occupations in the United States with those that they had had prior to departure from the Philippines or the Republic of Korea and with those that they had expected to have in the place of destination.

F. Occupational changes: group data

The IUS data indicate that, in terms of averages, the employment expectations of the majority of female immigrants were largely realized during their first two years in the United States. Among Filipino women, 67 per cent reported that they had worked during the two years since their arrival but only 58 per cent were still working at the time of interview. The equivalent figures were 72 per cent and 58 per cent among Korean immigrant women. Women who had worked in the country of origin were more likely to be economically active in the United States than women without prior work experience. Furthermore, those with work experience tended to have a more continuous work history than women whose first work experience occurred after immigration. Among Filipino women, 79 per cent of those who had work experience were still working by the time of the IUS interview; in contrast, only 47 per cent of the Filipino women without work experience in the country of origin were working by the end of their second year in the United States. The equivalent figures for Korean immigrant women were 64 per cent and 54 per cent, respectively.

Table 95 indicates the distribution of immigrant women by work-status and occupation at three stages of their employment history: prior to migration, in their first job in the United States and in the job that they had at the time of the IUS interview. Note that the information relative to the period before migration is obtained from the IPDA part of the survey and therefore covers more women. The data indicate that married women of Filipino and Korean origin were more likely to work after migration to the United States than before. Thus, the proportion not

TABLE 95. MARRIED FILIPINO AND KOREAN IMMIGRANT
WOMEN, BY OCCUPATION BEFORE AND
AFTER IMMIGRATION: 1986 IPDA
(*Percentage*)

Immigrant group	Before immigration	After immigration	
		First job	Current job

A. *Filipino women*

Number of women.........	(579)	(333)	(330)
Working	40.0	74.1	58.2
Professional..............	15.0	7.2	8.2
Administrative	2.8	0.0	1.2
Clerical	7.1	16.2	16.7
Sales	6.7	6.0	1.2
Farming, fishing and forestry	1.6	4.5	3.0
Transport	0.3	0.3	0.3
Production	4.1	8.7	11.5
Services	2.4	31.2	16.1
Not working	59.9	25.8	41.8

B. *Korean women*

Number of women.........	(729)	(395)	(396)
Working	31.8	66.1	55.1
Professional..............	5.6	2.3	2.8
Administrative	4.1	0.0	1.0
Clerical	7.4	11.6	7.6
Sales	6.0	13.7	14.4
Farming, fishing and forestry	2.1	0.3	0.2
Transport	0.3	0.3	0.5
Production	2.9	18.2	16.2
Services	3.4	19.7	12.4
Not working	68.2	33.9	44.9

working dropped from 60 per cent to 26 per cent among Filipino women and from 68 per cent to 34 per cent among Korean women as they moved from the Philippines and the Republic of Korea into their first jobs in the United States. However, the data also show that the employment experience of immigrant women is far from stable during the their first two years in the United States. Thus, among both Filipino and Korean immigrant women, the proportion working at the time of interview was considerably lower than that of women who had held a first job.

With respect to occupation, there were sharp changes in the distribution of women by occupation before migration and in their first job in the United States, but subsequent changes were less marked. Thus, before migration, relatively high percentages of both Filipino and Korean women tended to work in the professional, clerical, sales and, to a lesser extent, managerial occupations. After migration, a fairly high proportion of immigrant women worked in services (31 per cent among Filipino women and nearly 20 per cent among Koreans). Filipino immigrant women also tended to cluster in clerical occupations, whereas their Korean counterparts displayed a relatively uniform distribution between clerical, sales and production occupations. After two years in the United States, however, immigrant women tended to be less concentrated in the service occupations (only 16 per cent of Filipino women and 12 per cent of Korean women remained in them). Most of the decline in those occupations appeared to be accounted for by the increase of the percentage of non-working immigrant women. That is, the relatively high turn-over rates characteristic of many service occupations seemed to be responsible for the increasing proportion of non-working immigrant women as time since their arrival in the United States elapsed.

G. WORK EXPERIENCE BEFORE AND AFTER MIGRATION

So far, changes in occupation have been discussed in terms of general distributions of groups of women, without taking account of the employment histories of individual women. This section focuses on the latter. Thus, table 96 presents data linking the occupation of women prior to migration to the one they had in their first and current jobs in the United States. Only those occupational categories with at least 20 cases are presented.

The data available permit an exploration of how an immigrant woman's occupation in the country of origin is related to the one she managed to secure in the United States. Among Filipino women, three groups of immigrants are considered: those who worked as professionals or clerical staff while in the Philippines and those who did not work prior to departure. As table 96 indicates, those in clerical occupations were fairly successful in finding similar occupations in the United States: for 57 per cent the first job was in clerical occupations and 54 per cent still held a job in that occupation at the time of the IUS interview. Professionals were less successful in finding professional jobs after immigration. Thus, only 28 per cent of the immigrant women who had been professionals in the Philippines managed to remain as professionals in the first job that they obtained in the United States. That percentage, however, tended to rise as time elapsed, reaching 34 per cent by the time of the IUS interview. Former professional women were the least likely to stop working after migration and those who could not get a professional job tended to cluster in clerical or service occupations and, to a lesser extent, in production. Former clerical workers were more likely than professionals to remain in the non-working category and they tended to move mostly into sales or services when clerical work could not be found. Women who had not held a job before migration were the most likely to remain without a job after migration (56 per cent were not working at the time of the IUS). Yet, over half had the opportunity to work after they moved to the United States, mostly in service, production and, to a lesser extent, clerical occupations.

Among Korean women, four occupational categories could be considered, namely, professional, clerical, sales and that of women who had not worked prior to migration. In contrast with Filipino immigrants, no category of Korean women who worked prior to departure had a large chance of remaining in that category. Only slightly over a quarter of clerical workers and about a tenth of professional and sales workers were likely to remain in those occupations when they secured their first job in the United States. Furthermore, neither clerical nor sales workers saw their chances of remaining in their original occupations improve as time elapsed. Only Korean professional women were considerably more likely to be in professional occupations two years after arrival than when they secured their first job. However, professional women were also the group exhibiting the largest percentage in the non-working category after two years in the United States (50 per cent). Their experience thus contrasted with that of their Filipino counterparts. Former sales workers also exhibited a relatively high percentage of women in the non-working category and they experienced major occu-

pational changes after immigration, being concentrated mainly in services and production when they secured their first job. Former clerical workers had the lowest percentage in the non-working category and tended to move into sales or service occupations when they could not secure a first job in the clerical occupations. Korean women who had not worked prior to migration were far more likely than their Filipino counterparts to secure a job after migration (62 per cent did) and they tended to be fairly evenly distributed among service, production, sales and clerical occupations. As time elapsed, their concentration in the first three categories increased somewhat.

H. Work expectations compared with work experience in the United States

The data available permit us to link work expectations with actual work experience after migration. Table 97 presents the data for Filipino and Korean immigrant women in terms of expected occupational groups with at least 20 respondents. At the individual level, the relation between expectations and actual work experience varies considerably by occupational category.

Among Filipino women, the best match between expectations and actual occupations is found among those expecting to work as clerical workers, 43 per cent of whom found a first job in that occupation and 54 per cent of whom were in that occupation two years after they had arrived in the United States. Those expecting to work as professionals also were fairly successful in realizing their expectations. Thus, 38 per cent secured professional occupations in their first job after migration and 55 per cent were working as professionals after two years in the United States. Relatively low proportions of those expecting to work in services and production fulfilled their expectations: after two years in the United States only about one fifth of those expecting to work in services were in that occupation and only a fourth of those expecting to work in production held production jobs. In addition, both groups of women, but particularly those expecting to work in service occupations, had relatively high proportions in the non-working category. Thus, after two years in the

TABLE 96. MARRIED FILIPINO AND KOREAN IMMIGRANT WOMEN IN DIFFERENT OCCUPATIONAL GROUPS, BY WORK EXPERIENCE PRIOR TO MIGRATION AND BY OCCUPATION IN THEIR FIRST AND CURRENT JOB AFTER MIGRATION: 1986 IPDA AND 1988 IUS
(*Percentage*)

Occupation before migration	Occupation in the United States			
	First		Current	
A. Filipino female immigrants				
Professional	Professional	28.0	Professional	34.0
	Clerical	22.0	Clerical	22.0
	Services	18.0	Services	14.0
	Production	10.0	Production	6.0
	Sales	4.0	Farming	2.0
	Farming	2.0	Transport	2.0
	None	16.0	None	20.0
	Number of women	(50)	Number of women	(50)
Clerical	Clerical	57.1	Clerical	53.6
	Sales	10.7	Services	10.7
	Professional	3.6	Professional	3.6
	Services	3.6	None	32.1
	None	25.0		
	Number of women	(28)	Number of women	(28)
None	Services	19.1	Services	13.9
	Production	13.9	Production	12.9
	Clerical	8.2	Clerical	9.3
	Farming	5.7	Farming	4.1
	Sales	3.6	Sales	2.1
	Professional	1.5	Professional	1.0
	None	47.9	Managerial	1.0
			None	55.7
	Number of women	(194)	Number of women	(194)
B. Korean female immigrants				
Professional	Services	25.0	Professional	17.9
	Sales	14.3	Clerical	10.7
	Professional	10.7	Sales	7.1
	Clerical	10.7	Services	7.1
	Production	10.7	Managerial	3.6
	None	28.6	Production	3.6
			None	50.0
	Number of women	(28)	Number of women	(28)
Clerical	Clerical	28.2	Clerical	25.6
	Sales	25.6	Sales	20.5
	Services	15.4	Services	10.3
	Production	5.1	Professional	2.6
	Transport	2.6	Transport	2.6
	None	23.1	Production	2.6
			None	35.9
	Number of women	(39)	Number of women	(39)

TABLE 96 (continued)

Occupation before migration	Occupation in the United States			
	First		Current	
Sales	Services	26.1	Services	17.4
	Production	17.4	Production	13.0
	Sales	8.7	Clerical	8.7
	Clerical	4.3	Sales	8.7
	None	43.5	Managerial	4.3
			Professional	4.3
			None	43.5
	Number of women ...	(23)	Number of women	(23)
None	Services	18.0	Sales	15.9
	Production	17.6	Production	15.9
	Sales	13.6	Services	12.7
	Clerical	10.8	Clerical	4.4
	Professional	2.0	Professional	1.6
	Farming	0.4	Managerial	0.8
	None	37.6	Farming	0.4
			None	48.4
	Number of women ...	(250)	Number of women	(250)

NOTE: Occupational categories which have less than 20 cases were excluded. Percentages do not add to 100 because of rounding.

United States, 47 per cent of the women expecting to work in services and a third of those expecting to work in production were not working. Those numbers contrasted markedly with the 14 per cent and 20 per cent of non-working women recorded after two years in the United States among Filipino immigrants who intended to work as professionals or clerical workers. The proportion of non-working women was also relatively low among those intending to work in sales (23 per cent after two years) although most of them had difficulty in securing the jobs they expected: after two years in the United States scarcely 4.5 per cent were working in sales. Lastly, women who did not intend to work remained largely out of the labour force. Nevertheless, about 29 per cent did secure a first job after immigration and two years after arrival 24 per cent were still working. It is worth noting that, almost irrespective of a woman's work intentions or expectations, most groups of women displayed relatively high proportions actually working in service or clerical occupations. The traditional segregation of women into those occupations and the demand for such workers in the United States thus played a role in determining the types of jobs that immigrant women could secure, irrespective of their expectations.

Among Korean women, only three categories of occupational expectations could be considered: clerical, sales and not working (see table 97). In contrast with the experience of Filipino immigrant women, Koreans expecting to work in clerical occupations were not very successful in realizing their expectations. Only 29 per cent secured a first job in that occupation and after two years in the United States only 14 per cent were clerical workers. Again, in contrast with the Filipino experience, Korean immigrant women who expected to work in sales were more successful in fulfilling their expectations: after two years in the United States 28 per cent were working in that occupation. At that time, sales had also become the major occupation of those intending to work in clerical occupations. Just as in the case of Filipino women, most Korean immigrant women who did not intend to work remained unemployed. However, a slightly higher proportion secured a first job (33 per cent), though after two years in the United States only 27 per cent were working. The

233

TABLE 97. MARRIED FILIPINO AND KOREAN IMMIGRANT WOMEN IN DIFFERENT OCCUPATIONAL GROUPS, BY THEIR WORK EXPECTATIONS PRIOR TO MIGRATION AND BY OCCUPATION IN THEIR FIRST AND CURRENT JOB AFTER MIGRATION: 1986 IPDA AND 1988 IUS

(Percentage)

Expected occupation in the United States	Actual occupation in the United States			
	First		*Current*	
	A. *Filipino immigrant women*			
Professional	Professional	37.9	Professional	55.2
	Clerical	20.7	Clerical	10.3
	Services	17.2	Production	6.9
	Production	13.8	Services	6.9
	Sales	3.4	Managerial	3.4
	None	6.9	Transport	3.4
			None	13.8
	Number of women ...	(29)	Number of women	(29)
Clerical	Clerical	42.9	Clerical	53.6
	Production	14.3	Services	10.7
	Services	14.3	Production	8.9
	Sales	8.9	Managerial	3.6
	Professional	7.1	Professional	1.8
	None	12.5	Sales	1.8
			None	19.6
	Number of women ...	(56)	Number of women	(56)
Sales	Services	31.8	Clerical	27.3
	Clerical	27.3	Services	18.2
	Professional	9.1	Production	13.6
	Sales	9.1	Professional	9.1
	Production	9.1	Sales	4.5
	None	13.6	Farming	4.5
			None	22.7
	Number of women ...	(22)	Number of women	(22)
Production	Services	29.6	Production	25.9
	Production	18.5	Clerical	14.8
	Clerical	11.1	Services	14.8
	Sales	7.4	Professional	3.7
	Farming	3.7	Managerial	3.7
	None	29.6	Farming	3.7
			None	33.3
	Number of women ...	(27)	Number of women	(27)
Services	Services	25.3	Services	22.0
	Production	15.4	Production	16.5
	Clerical	7.7	Clerical	8.8
	Farming	4.4	Professional	4.4
	Professional	3.3	Sales	1.1
	Sales	3.3	Farming	1.1
	None	40.7	None	46.2
	Number of women ...	(91)	Number of women	(91)

234

TABLE 97 (continued)

Expected occupation in the United States	Actual occupation in the United States			
	First		Current	
None	Services	13.0	Services	16.7
	Clerical	6.5	Clerical	3.8
	Production	6.5	Production	2.6
	Sales	1.3	Professional	1.3
	Farming	1.3	None	75.6
	None	71.4		
	Number of women ...	(77)	Number of women	(77)

B. Korean immigrant women

Expected occupation in the United States	First		Current	
Clerical	Clerical	29.0	Sales	15.9
	Sales	16.1	Clerical	14.3
	Services	11.3	Services	9.5
	Production	9.7	Production	6.3
	Professional	3.2	Professional	1.6
	Farming	1.6	Farming	1.6
	None	29.0	Transport	1.6
			None	49.2
	Number of women ...	(62)	Number of women	(62)
Sales	Sales	26.7	Sales	27.9
	Services	21.7	Production	18.0
	Production	18.3	Clerical	9.8
	Clerical	11.7	Services	9.8
	None	21.7	Managerial	4.9
			None	29.5
	Number of women ...	(60)	Number of women	(60)
None	Services	9.4	Production	7.8
	Production	9.4	Services	6.3
	Sales	7.8	Clerical	4.7
	Clerical	4.7	Professional	3.1
	Professional	1.6	Sales	3.1
	None	67.2	None	75.0
	Number of women ...	(64)	Number of women	(64)

NOTE: Occupational categories with less than 20 cases were excluded. Service occupations were omitted in the case of Korean women because of data problems. Percentages do not add to 100 because of rounding.

proportion of Korean immigrant women who were not working after two years in the United States also tended to be high in other occupational groups: 30 per cent among those intending to work in sales and 49 per cent among those expecting to work in clerical occupations. On the whole, therefore, Korean immigrant women appeared to be less successful than their Filipino counterparts in securing the jobs that they expected, keeping those jobs or even keeping the alternative jobs that they secured when they entered the labour market in the United States for the first time.

The differences detected suggest that the work experiences of Filipino and Korean married immigrant women in the United States vary considerably for reasons that have little to do with their work expectations. It is likely that differences in their human capital characteristics, particularly in terms of their ability to use English, may influence their employment experience. The norms and values shaping women's roles in the societies of origin are also likely to play a part.

I. CONCLUSION

The use of longitudinal data to document the employment transitions of immigrant women has permitted an analysis of the relations between their work experience and expectations prior to migration with actual employment outcomes after migration. Among both Filipino and Korean married women who had decided to become immigrants to the United States, a high proportion expected to join the labour force at the place of destination even though considerably smaller proportions had been economically active before departure. That finding alone suggests that, even among married women migrating with their families, the economic motivations for migration are not absent. Indeed, the data indicate that during their first two years in the United States, immigrant married women were about twice as likely to work than they had been in their countries of origin.

However, the information on the employment and occupational expectations of female immigrants also reveals that many women had difficulty realizing their expectations, particularly in terms of the types of jobs that they expected to secure in the United States. Although their expectations seemed modest and realistic, only in rare cases did even half of the number of women expecting to work in a certain occupation manage to secure and keep a job in that occupation. Filipino women were somewhat more successful in fulfilling their expectations, particularly when they intended to work in the clerical occupations or as professionals.

A variety of factors are likely to influence the occupational experience of female immigrants. Starting with their work expectations, this study showed that they were influenced by certain human capital characteristics (such as the number of job skills or the previous work experience of women) as well as by the age of the woman concerned and the origin of her husband. Interestingly, women married to men of the same origin than themselves were more likely to expect to work after migration than those married to American men. Having had previous work experience not only made it more likely for women to expect to work after migration but also enhanced their chances of securing a job and keeping it once migration had taken place.

The data available showed that there were considerable differences between the occupational experience of Korean female immigrants and that of their Filipino counterparts. Some of those differences may arise because of the different cultural backgrounds of the migrants. For Filipino women, who come from a society that values the economic roles of women, entry into the United States labour market may be more a function of greater job opportunities than of changing values. In contrast, Korean women, whose society of origin generally restricts their economic roles, may undergo a more complex process of adaptation when they opt to join the United States labour market. That is, when Korean women become economic actors at the place of destination they start a process of normative change designed to relax the barriers against their exercising an economic activity outside the home. Economic need or the need to accumulate savings may be the immediate reasons allowing Korean women to effect such change.

Information on the expectations of immigrants is useful not only to assess their relative success after immigration but also to define appropriate reference groups. Most studies of occupational mobility compare groups defined by the researcher, so that the extent to which those reference groups are meaningful from the standpoint of the group under study may be questionable. In the case of recent immigrants it would be important to establish which group serves as model in the sense that immigrants compare their experiences to those of that group and interpret their experiences accordingly. In the case of the Filipino and Korean immigrant women studied here, their work experience in the United States, for instance, can only be described as intermittent rather than continuous or stable. However, one cannot conclude from such evidence that the commitment of immigrant women to the workplace is weak. Morgan and Taylorson (1985, p. 5) suggest that the nature of "women's work", which is routine, sometimes physically demanding, of low status and poorly paid, may be a more significant reason for the discontinuous character of the work experience of migrant women than conflicts between their family responsibilities and their commitment to work. As Morokvasic (1983) notes, subjective assessments by the migrant women themselves about their occupational experience would help clarify whether and to what extent their disadvantaged position stems from their own feelings of inadequacy or from objective barriers.

This paper has been limited to occupational changes experienced by immigrant women. It has not examined other issues that are central to the occupational mobility of female migrants, such as wage differentials and working conditions. It has been noted, for instance, that despite their high levels of educational attainment, Asian-Americans in general (with the exception of Japanese-Americans) receive lower wages than the native born and that the differential is particularly strong among women (Barringer, Takeuchi and Xenos, 1990). In that respect, it would be useful to know how Asian immigrants reconcile their failure to achieve wage parity with other groups despite their relatively high educational levels or how immigrants who work in ethnic enclaves assess their experience. The exploration of these dimensions of occupational mobility requires further information on the perspective of the immigrants themselves.

Notes

[1] In the report by Gardner, Robey and Smith (1985), Asia includes "Pakistan and the countries lying east of it in South Asia, Southeast Asia, and East Asia, but not Soviet Asia or the Pacific Islands" (p. 5). Asian Americans include "immigrants and refugees from these countries and the United States-born descendants of earlier arrivals living in the United States, plus students, businessmen, and their families from those countries whose 'usual' residence is the United States at the time of the census (which is conducted on a de facto basis). Excluded are visitors and others from Asia who are temporarily in the United States".

[2] Female predominance among immigrants of Filipino and Korean origin was evident even before the passage of the 1965 Immigration and Nationality Act, which eliminated the national origins quota system on which immigrant admissions were based until then. The earliest data available on immigrant admissions by sex indicate that already in 1951 Filipino women outnumbered Filipino men among immigrants and that by 1952 the same was true among Korean immigrants.

[3] In 1988, the Republic of Korea ranked fourth after Mexico, the Philippines and Haiti. The increase in the number of Haitians granted permanent resident status (from nearly 15,000 in 1987 to 35,000 in 1988) resulted from the large number of refugee adjustments made possible under the Cuban/Haitian entrant provision of the 1986 Immigration Reform and Control Act (INS, 1989).

[4] See note 1 for a definition of "Asian-American".

[5] The questions used to determine the ethnic origin of a woman's husband or fiancé were: if your husband or fiancé was not born in Korea (or the Philippines), is he Korean (or Filipino)? If not, what is he?

References

Asis, Maruja M. (1989). Immigrant women and occupational changes: a comparison of Filipino and Korean women in transition. Unpublished Ph.D. dissertation. Bowling Green State University, Ohio, Department of Sociology.

Bauer, J., and Y. S. Shin (1986). *Female Labor Force Participation and Wages in the Republic of Korea*. Working Paper No. 54. Honolulu: East-West Population Institute.

Caces, Maria Fe (1985). Personal networks and the material adaptation of recent Filipino immigrants. Unpublished Ph.D. dissertation. University of Hawaii, Department of Sociology.

Castillo, Gelia (1977). *Beyond Manila: Philippine Rural Problems in Perspective* (3 vols.). College, Laguna, Philippines: University of the Philippines at Los Baños.

Cho, Haejong (1987). Korean women in the professions. In *Korean Women in Transition*, Eui-Young Yu and Earl H. Phillips, eds. Los Angeles: California State University.

Cobas, Jose (1987). On the study of ethnic enterprises: unresolved issues. *Sociological Perspectives* (Greenwich, Connecticut), vol. 30, No. 4, pp. 467-472.

Diner, Hasia (1983). *Erin's Daughters in America: Irish Immigrant Women in the Nineteenth Century*. Baltimore: The Johns Hopkins University Press.

Ewen, E. (1985). *Immigrant Women in the Land of Dollars: Life and Culture on the Lower East Side, 1890-1925*. New York: Monthly Review Press.

Gardner, Robert W., B. Robey and Peter C. Smith (1985). *Asian Americans: Growth, Change and Diversity*. Population Bulletin, vol. 40, No. 4. Washington, D.C.: Population Reference Bureau.

Glenn, Evelyn Nakano (1986). *Issei, Nissei, War Bride: Three Generations of Japanese American Women in Domestic Service*. Philadelphia: Temple University.

Guendelman, Sylvia, and Auristela Perez-Itriago (1987). Double lives: the changing role of women in seasonal migration. *Women's Studies* (New York), vol. 13, No. 3, pp. 249-271.

Hesse, S. (1979). Women working: historical trends. In *Working Women and Families*, Karen Wolf Feinstein, ed. Sage Yearbook in Women's Policy Studies. Beverly Hills and London: Sage Publications.

International Labour Office (1987). *1987 Yearbook of Labour Statistics*. Geneva.

Jones, Gavin W. (1984). Economic growth and changing female employment structure in the cities of Southeast and East Asia. In *Women in the Industrial Workforce: Southeast and East Asia*, Gavin W. Jones, ed. Canberra: Australian National University.

Koo, Sung Yeal (1984). Trends in female labour force participation in urban Korea. In *Women in the Industrial Workforce: Southeast and East Asia*. Gavin W. Jones, ed. Canberra: Australian National University.

Lee, Hye-Kyung (1988). Socioeconomic attainment of recent Korean and Filipino immigrant men and women in Los Angeles Metropolitan area, 1980. Unpublished Ph.D. dissertation. University of California at Los Angeles, Department of Sociology.

Min, Pyong Gap (1987). Korean immigrant entrepreneurship: A comprehensive explanation. Paper prepared for the Annual Conference of Korean-American University Professors Association, Atlanta, Georgia, 2-4 October.

Morgan, David H. J. and Daphne E. Taylorson (1985). Introduction. Class and work: Bringing women back in. In *Gender, Class and Work*, Eva Gamarnikow, David H. J. Morgan, June Purvis, and Daphne E. Taylorson, eds. Hants, England: Gower Publishing Company Limited.

Morokvasic, Mirjana (1983). Women in migration: beyond the reductionist outlook. In *One Way Ticket: Migration and Female Labour*, Annie Phizacklea, ed. London: Routledge and Kegan Paul.

_____ (1984). Birds of passage are also women... *International Migration Review* (Staten Island, New York), vol. 18, No. 4 (Winter), pp. 886-907.

Ong, Paul (1985). Does assimilation matter? Labor participation among Chinese immigrant wives. Unpublished manuscript. University of California at Los Angeles.

Paganoni, Anthony, and V. P. Cruz (1989). *Filipinas in Migration: Big Bills and Small Change*. Quezón City, Philippines: Scalabrini Migration Center.

Philippine Overseas Employment Administration (1988). *Annual Report*. Metro Manila.

Phizacklea, Annie (1983). In the front line. In *One Way Ticket: Migration and Female Labour*, Annie Phizacklea, ed. London: Routledge and Kegan Paul.

Portes, Alejandro (1987). The social origins of the Cuban enclave economy of Miami. *Sociological Perspectives* (Greenwich, Connecticut), vol. 30, No. 4, pp. 340-372.

Prieto, Yolanda (1986). Cuban women and work in the United States: a New Jersey case study. In *International Migration: The Female Experience*, Rita James Simon and Caroline B. Brettell, eds. New Jersey: Rowman and Allanheld.

Riche, Martha Farnsworth (1988). America's new workers. *American Demographics* (Ithaca, New York), pp. 34-38.

Segura, D. A. (1989). Chicana and Mexicana immigrant women at work: the impact of class, race and gender on occupational mobility. *Gender and Society* (Newbury Park, California), vol. 3, No. 1, pp. 37-52.

Stier, Haya (1990). Immigrant women go to work: analysis of immigrant wives labor supply in six Asian immigrant groups. Paper presented at the 84th Annual Meeting of the American Sociological Association, San Francisco, 9-13 August.

Sullivan, Teresa (1984). The occupational prestige of women immigrants: a comparison of Cubans and Mexicans. *International Migration Review* (Staten Island, New York), vol. 18, No. 4 (Winter), pp. 1045-1062.

Trager, Lillian (1988). *The City Connection: Migration and Family Interdependence in the Philippines*. Ann Arbor: University of Michigan Press.

Tyree, Andrea, and Katharine M. Donato (1986). A demographic overview of the international migration of women. In *International Migration: The Female Experience*, Rita James Simon and Caroline B. Brettell, eds. New Jersey: Rowman and Allanheld.

United States, Immigration and Naturalization Service (1989). *1988 Annual Report*. Washington, D.C.: Government Printing Office.

Weinberg, Sydney S. (1988). *The World of our Mothers: The Lives of Jewish Immigrant Women*. Chapel Hill: University of North Carolina Press.

Yamanako, Keiko (1986). Labor force participation of Asian-American women: ethnicity, work and family. Unpublished Ph.D. dissertation. Ithaca, New York: Cornell University, Department of Sociology.

Part Four

FEMALE MIGRANTS IN DEVELOPING COUNTRIES

XIV. SEX SELECTIVITY OF MIGRATION REGULATIONS GOVERNING INTERNATIONAL MIGRATION IN SOUTHERN AND SOUTH-EASTERN ASIA

Manolo I. Abella*

It is estimated that while in 1976 women constituted less than 15 per cent of the 146,400 Asian workers reported to have left their countries to work overseas, by 1987 they comprised some 27 per cent of the million or so Asian workers who left that year to work temporarily abroad. Although these estimates probably understate the true extent of female participation in temporary labour migration in the Asian region, they indicate that the number of female migrant workers originating in Asia has been significant and is growing. Concentrated in a small set of low-paid unskilled occupations in the service sector, Asian women migrating as temporary workers constitute a large pool of cheap labour for countries other than their own.

During the 1960s most female migrant workers originated in India, especially in Kerala and Goa. Diversification of sources took hold during the late 1970s. In 1987 alone some 180,500 female migrants left the Philippines for employment abroad. According to Indian authorities, 10 per cent of the 125,000 workers who left the country in 1987 were women, though many more were probably not counted. The same year, some 50,000 Indonesian women and another 20,000 from Sri Lanka were recruited to work as housemaids in the oil-rich countries of Western Asia. In contrast, Pakistan appears to have been the source of a tiny number of female migrant workers with only 463 nurses and 131 housemaids reported to have left the country between 1984 and 1989.

The migration policies of the countries of employment probably explain most of the growth of female labour migration during the recent past. Guest-worker programmes in the newly-industrializing countries of Eastern and South-eastern Asia as well as in the oil-rich States of Western Asia have largely determined the volume and composition of labour migration and, during the 1980s, have provided greater scope for women's participation. The contribution of the migration policies adopted by the countries of origin to the shaping of these flows is probably more subtle and, given the inconsistencies that have characterized such policies, their role is likely to have been marginal.

This paper considers the exit rules and regulations adopted by the main countries of origin in Southern and South-eastern Asia to examine the extent to which they have contributed to the sex selectivity of migration. Exit regulations are that subset of migration policies which specify the conditions under which nationals are permitted to leave their country and take up residence in another. They normally involve conditions to obtain a passport (citizenship, absence of a criminal record), the required exit permits (possession of a work contract or a work visa, a pre-departure briefing etc.), the payment of travel taxes, registration with emigration authorities, or compliance with a compulsory national service in the case of certain occupations, especially those in the medical field. Because the point of departure is the last stage at which would-be emigrants can be identified and "controlled", exit regulations tend to be viewed as the cornerstone of policies on emigration. Other factors, such as education and training policies, wage policies, income taxes or foreign exchange policies, are considered to be too remote and indirect to influence migration outcomes.

One problem in examining the effect of regulations on sex selectivity is the hypothetical nature of any exploration into the supply side of the migration equation. One would need to know, for instance,

---

*Regional Adviser on Migrant Workers, International Labour Organisation, Regional Office for Asia and the Pacific, Bangkok, Thailand.

how many women would have attempted to migrate had there been no restrictions on their departure or whether more women would have gone abroad if exit policies had been more favourable. Although actual migration outcomes can give clues to the "potential" participation of women in migration, the effects of policy on that potential is more difficult to establish. Educational attainment, social attitudes regarding the economic roles of women and structural changes in the economy would generally be stronger determinants of such potential, and migration policy would tend to reflect them.

The increase in female labour migration is associated with a growing demand in a few highly "femininized" occupations, such as domestic service and nursing. Such expansion occurred despite the restrictions imposed by many Asian countries on the employment of young unskilled women abroad. Thus, while restrictions determined which countries responded to existing demand and which did not, the evidence available suggests that it was the pattern of overseas demand rather than the supply of potential migrants that shaped actual migration flows.

National sensitivities regarding the plight of women working abroad have given rise to regulations restricting women's access to attractive remunerative employment abroad. The practice of changing frequently the rules and regulations governing overseas female employment has led to a confusing picture of where Governments really stand. In many instances, however, the apparent contradictions characterizing public policy in this area have been resolved through the actual implementation of policy. Thus, in countries where women already constitute a significant proportion of the labour force, restrictions on the overseas employment of certain categories of female workers have been more symbolic than real. Authorities in the Philippines and Thailand, for example, have found ways of exempting many categories of women from official prohibitions against their employment abroad. On the other hand, in countries such as Bangladesh and Pakistan where the labour force participation of women has been constrained by social norms and values, formal restrictions have merely strengthened society's tendency to keep women at home.

A. LAWS AND REGULATIONS TO CONTROL EMIGRATION

In Southern Asia, emigration control was first instituted by the Indian Emigration Act of 1922 which prohibited the emigration of unskilled Indians except to countries specified by the Governor-General (Appleyard, 1988). After independence, the Southern Asian States generally maintained such prohibition together with the regulatory machineries and systems to enforce it. However, starting in the late 1970s, the Act was replaced in one country after another: by the Emigration Ordinance of 1979 in Pakistan, the Foreign Employment Agency Act No. 32 of 1980 and the Foreign Employment Act No. 21 of 1985 in Sri Lanka, the Emigration Ordinance of 1982 in Bangladesh, and the Emigration Act of 1983 in India.

Such new legislation formally repealed the prohibition set by the Emigration Act of 1922 which was, in any case, no longer effective in preventing the emigration of workers from the Southern Asian countries. Thus, much of the massive flow of construction workers to Western Asia that started in the mid-1970s was not even recorded by the responsible administrative authorities. The new laws established statutory powers that the Government considered necessary both to maximize the number of nationals employed abroad and to minimize the fraud and abuses connected with their recruitment. Under those laws Governments retained the power to regulate migration for employment, being able to prohibit the emigration of any person or "class of persons" to any country if such emigration was not deemed to be in the "public interest" (Bangladesh and Pakistan), if the nature of work involved was unlawful or if the terms and conditions of employment were exploitative or discriminatory. Governments used their regulatory powers to set procedures and standards regarding emigration and the granting of licences to recruit workers, as well as to impose stiffer and more realistic sanctions against violations of recruitment procedures.

In South-eastern Asia legal restrictions on emigration did not exist until, during the 1970s, fraud and abuses in recruitment grew and forced Governments to exercise some control. In Indonesia, for instance, only Ministerial Regulation No. 4 of 1970, requiring a "written permit" from the Minister of Manpower for anyone engaging in recruitment, established some constraints on recruitment practices. Such constraints were later elaborated further through a series of decrees which were consolidated in the Department of Manpower Ministerial Decree of 1986. Similarly, in the Philippines there had virtually been no legal restrictions on emigration until 1987 when administrative measures restricting the migration of female domestic workers were put into effect. However, the Labour Code of 1974 did prohibit foreign employers from hiring Filipino nationals directly and provided for the eventual take-over of all recruitment services by the Government. The latter provision was repealed in 1978. In Thailand, prior to 1980, the licensing of recruitment agents fell under the jurisdiction of the provincial Governments. In 1980 a new law transferred such responsibility to the Labour Department. In Myanmar, after Newin assumed power in the 1960s, control of emigration was exercised through the issuance of passports and the prohibition of recruitment through agencies other than the Department of Transport (for seafarers) or the Department of Labour (for other workers).

Restrictions on the emigration of female workers

Current regulations regarding female labour migration have taken the form of bans on the emigration of women below a certain age, of those intending to work in certain countries or of those having certain occupations. Table 98 lists the restrictions currently in force in 10 Asian countries of origin.

TABLE 98. RESTRICTIONS ON FEMALE WORKER MIGRATION IN SOUTHERN AND SOUTH-EASTERN ASIAN COUNTRIES OF ORIGIN AS OF JANUARY 1990

Country	Restrictions
Bangladesh	Women are allowed to work in Western Asian countries as domestic workers only if accompanied by husband
Burma	Ban on recruitment of female workers except in the case of professionals
India	Women under age 30 are not allowed to work as domestic workers in Western Asia or Northern Africa, with exceptions made on a case by case basis;
Indonesia	Women must be at least 22 years of age; restrictions regarding place of employment for household workers and male/female ratio recruited by authorized agents may be lifted under certain conditions
Nepal	None
Malaysia	None
Pakistan	Women intending to work as domestic workers must be 35 years or older; nurses cannot migrate
Philippines	Selective ban on the employment of female domestic workers according to country of employment; women intending to work as entertainers must be certified by Professional Entertainers Certification Center
Sri Lanka	Ban on the migration of nurses for employment
Thailand	Ban on recruitment of women except in the case of selected countries of employment

Source: Ministries or Departments of Labour responding to the author's enquiry.

Most restrictions relate to women intending to work as domestic workers in Western Asia. Among the major suppliers of domestic workers, only Sri Lanka did not resort to restrictions on the emigration of women. The major country of origin, the Philippines, since 1982 has adopted various restrictions, relaxed them and then imposed them again.

According to the Emigration Rules of Pakistan, women intending to migrate and work as domestic workers (ayahs and governesses) must be at least 45 years old and the Federal Government may, from time to time, fix other age limits for different categories of female migrants. The Rules also prohibit recruiters from accepting requests for younger female workers. The Federal Government may, however, in special cases and for reasons to be recorded in writing, relax the minimum age limit by five years. Although such age limits apply only to certain occupations, in practice the Bureau of Emigration and Overseas Employment applies them to all female migrants. Thus, the administration has generally tended to discourage the emigration of female workers, although the 1989 decision to lower the minimum age limit to 35 may be an indication of changing attitudes.

In India, even as early as 1961, executive orders banning the migration of Indian women to work as domestic workers in Western Asia had been issued. Despite the ban, however, the migration of female domestic workers continued clandestinely on a large scale (Gopinathan-Nair, 1986). Thus, protests from Goanese and Malayalee families led Indian officials to permit quietly the continuation of those flows (Weiner, 1982).

In Bangladesh, as in India and Pakistan, the general attitude of public authorities has been to discourage women from migrating to work overseas, though no official restrictions on migration existed prior to 1978. However, the growing number of reports of abuses among Bangladeshi women in Western Asia prompted the Cabinet to ban the emigration of female domestic workers to that region as of 1978. Since then the ban has not been relaxed, except in cases where women migrate together with their husbands to work abroad in the same household.

In Thailand the emigration of female workers was banned by law as of 1980 (Sumalee, 1986), though exceptions were made regarding certain countries of destination (e.g., Japan, Macau or Singapore). In Indonesia, the Minister of Manpower issued a similar ban on the deployment of women to Western Asia as of 1980 (Cremer, 1988). In 1982, however, the ban was lifted and substituted by certain restrictions, including a minimum age standard.

Some of the restrictions adopted by the countries of origin are a direct response to those imposed by the countries of employment. Thus, Indonesia sets a minimum age limit of 22 years for domestic workers but a higher one for those going to Saudi Arabia because the Saudi Government adopted the latter. Similarly, the Philippines bars the emigration of domestic workers to Italy because the latter enacted an immigration law banning the further inflow of those workers. Without such restrictions, potential migrant workers can be easily duped by unscrupulous recruiters.

Restrictions related to countries of employment are usually part of the unwritten policy of the countries of origin since such restrictions can cause adverse reactions from the countries singled out. Thus, the Philippines had to relax a ban it imposed in 1982 on the emigration of Filipino domestic workers to Saudi Arabia when the Saudi Government threatened to freeze all labour recruitment from the Philippines. To avoid a similar incident, the Aquino Government decided in 1987 to impose instead a general ban on the emigration of domestic workers and make it subject to relaxation for countries of employment that agreed to enter into special bilateral agreements ensuring the protection of female Filipino workers.

When restrictions are based on occupation, they may affect women selectively if the occupations singled out are characterized by sex segregation. Such is the case of nurses, whose emigration has been banned in Pakistan and Sri Lanka. Similarly, the massive exodus of nurses from the Philippines to Canada and the United States prompted the Government of the Philippines to impose a mandatory period of service at home for all nursing graduates before migration could be allowed.

Procedural restrictions

Restrictions may take the form of administrative requirements or procedures applied more stringently in the case of women than of men. As a safeguard against exploitation most countries of origin now require that recruitment agents present job offers to be attested to or authenticated by the country's diplomatic mission in the country of employment or by the latter's local diplomatic mission. The labour attaché usually requires that employers confirm in person the job offer and ascertain their willingness and capability to comply with the terms of the employment contract. Such a procedure provides an opportunity for the authorities of the country of origin to "screen" prospective employers and make them aware of the minimum standards that they must abide by.

Such attestation or authentication procedures are being used by Governments for various purposes, including barring nationals from working in certain countries without formal clearance to do so. Thus, when the Indian Embassy in Kuwait stopped attesting visas for female domestic workers it effectively made it impossible for Indian women to accept job offers in that country legally. Since 1987 the Sri Lankan Government has likewise used authentication as a means of "screening" foreign employers. In addition, when the Singapore Government refused to impose minimum wages for foreign workers, the Government of the Philippines sought to enforce its minimum standards by making their observance a condition for the authentication of job offers. Consequently, the Embassy of the Philippines in Singapore only authenticated job offers which provided for a monthly salary of at least US$200 and where the employer put up a bond for US$1,000 to guarantee full compliance with the terms of the contract.

The conditions set by the Indonesian Government in 1985 on the recruitment of female workers provide interesting examples of how Governments have tried to resolve policy contradictions, though with little apparent success. The Government declared that female workers could migrate to Saudi Arabia only if they were to be employed in the households of the royal family, of high-ranking civil servants, military officers or other families recommended by the Indonesian Embassy. Then, probably to offset existing policy biases that made it more profitable to recruit women, the Government established that agents had to recruit two men for every three women. Lastly, it required that women sign an agreement stating that they would themselves bear the risks related to working in Saudi Arabia.

In 1978, in order to stop the migration of women who might engage in prostitution, the Government of the Philippines established a certification requirement for all those wishing to work overseas as entertainers. An Entertainment Certification Center was established to test applicants and issue the so-called "blue-card" to those deemed qualified. In 1988 the Philippines and Japan concluded an agreement whereby only those certified by the Center would be issued visas by the Japanese Embassy in Manila.

Some policies, however, may favour the recruitment of women rather than that of men. In Indonesia, for instance, the Department of Manpower allows private recruiters to charge at most US$870 for each man recruited, while it allows a fee of up to US$1,350 to be charged from foreign employers for each domestic worker placed abroad. Consequently, private recruiters often specialize in hiring female domestic workers (Juridico, 1987; Cremer, 1988). In cases where the recruitment costs are ultimately borne by the worker, this policy would be unfavourable to women, but there is no evidence to indicate that the employers of Indonesian workers eventually shift the burden of such fees on them. In fact, in Western Asia, Indonesian domestic workers are reported to receive slightly better wages than their counterparts from other countries, possibly because of the premium attached to their Muslim background.

In contrast to the case of women, no restrictions applying to male migrant workers are related specifically to their sex. In the few cases where limits are set on the emigration of persons having certain skills, men are likely to be differentially affected because of their predominance among those having such skills. The Philippines, for example, at one time tried to stop aircraft mechanics from leaving the country because the operation of the national airline was being adversely affected by shortages of qualified personnel. However, the measure proved impossible to enforce and was quietly set aside. Indeed, most Governments encourage men to seek employment abroad by offering subsidized training in sex-segregated occupations.

Figure IX contains a schematic display indicating where different Asian countries stand in a continuum representing the degree of sex-selectivity of their emigration policies. At one end of the continuum one finds countries having no exit regulations specific to female migrants, such as Malaysia and Sri Lanka. At the other, one finds countries, such as Pakistan, having strict controls specific to female migration. In locating a country within that continuum, account was taken not only of the declared policy of each State but also of the overall system of formal and informal controls on the employment of women abroad. Thus, while the Philippines may have banned Filipino women from accepting jobs as domestic workers abroad it still falls to the left of centre because exceptions to the strict enforcement of existing regulations often apply. Pakistan, on the other hand, not only has adopted stringent restrictions but the authorities apply them strictly.

While most Asian countries have adopted similar restrictions on the emigration of women, there is considerable variation on how they are administered. The enforcement of regulations depends on whether they are compatible with the prevailing socio-cultural milieu, with labour market realities and with the political system in place. In Indonesia, for example, the largest Muslim organization (Muhammadiyah) strongly opposed the "export" of female workers but the Government stood firm on its policy of allowing women to take up jobs in Western Asia. In Thailand few people are even aware of the existence of a law prohibiting women from migrating to work in certain countries. In Pakistan, however, it is doubtful whether many women would migrate for employment even in the absence of sex-selective regulations.

There are other dimensions of migration policy that are not reflected in figure IX, although their inclusion would not change the relative position of the countries considered. One is the degree to which Governments get involved in actively finding jobs for female migrants. The Philippines and the Republic of Korea appear to be the best organized and most successful in developing "markets" for the services of their skilled and educated manpower, whether male or female. The Government of India, on the other hand, has been careful not to be seen as promoting the emigration of its nationals, especially women.

B. ASIAN FEMALE LABOUR MIGRATION FLOWS

If restrictions on the migration of women had any effects, they were not reflected in the overall growth of female migration (see table 99). In 1988 alone, over a quarter of a million Asian women were

**Figure IX. Degree to which rules and regulations regarding exit are
selective by sex for selected countries of Southern and
South-eastern Asia: schematic display**

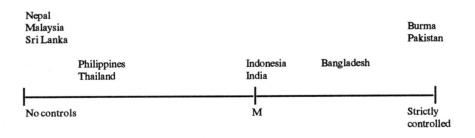

TABLE 99. ANNUAL NUMBER OF MIGRANT WORKERS AND PERCENTAGE FEMALE, BY SELECTED
COUNTRIES OF ORIGIN IN SOUTHERN AND SOUTH-EASTERN ASIA: 1978-1988
(*Thousands*)

Country of origin	1978	1979	1980	1981	1982	1983	1984	1985	1986	1987	1988
Southern Asia											
Bangladesh											
Total	22.8	24.5	30.6	55.8	62.8	59.2	56.8	77.7	68.7	74.0	68.1
Percentage female					n e g l i g i b l e						
India											
Total	69.0	171.8	236.2	276.0	239.5	225.0	206.0	163.0	113.6	125.4	..
Percentage female					estimated at 10 per cent a year						
Pakistan											
Total	130.5	125.5	129.8	168.4	142.9	128.2	100.4	88.5	62.6	..	84.8
Percentage female					n e g l i g i b l e						
Sri Lanka											
Total	17.7	25.9	28.6	57.4	22.5	18.1	15.7	12.4	16.4	16.1	19.0
Percentage female	..	47.3	50.8	52.5	24.0	43.2	36.7	95.1	31.4	34.0	48.4
South..eastern Asia											
Indonesia											
Total	8.2	10.4	16.2	17.9	21.1	29.0	37.9	56.7	65.5	59.4	64.0
Percentage female	..	..	..	..	..	41.5	53.9	70.5	59.6	74.6	77.4
Philippines											
Total	88.2	137.3	214.6	266.2	314.3	434.2	425.1	389.2	414.5	496.9	477.8
Percentage female	15.0	..	18.0	..	..	..	..	..	..	36.3	..
Thailand											
Total	14.7	10.6	21.5	26.7	108.5	68.5	75.0	69.7	112.4	106.0	118.6
Percentage female	..	..	..	..	..	..	..	..	6.4	9.2	12.7

Source: Compiled by the International Labour Office from reports received from: Bureau of Manpower Employment and Training (Bangladesh); Protector-General of Emigrants (India); Bureau of Emigration (Pakistan); Sri Lanka Bureau of Foreign Employment; Department of Manpower (Indonesia); Philippine Overseas Employment Administration; Department of Labour (Thailand).

NOTE: Two dots (..) indicate that data are not available or are not separately reported.

reported to have migrated to work abroad. Women dominated the flows from Indonesia even though that country ostensibly imposed stringent conditions on their recruitment. Women also predominated among labour migrants from Sri Lanka, a country that had espoused a laissez-faire policy regarding female labour migration. In the Philippines and Thailand, where women have achieved high levels of education and of labour force participation, women also constituted a high proportion of departing migrant workers. India, which has traditionally been a major source of female workers, lacks adequate data relative to female migration. The Protector of Emigrants in Trivandrum claims that during most of the 1980s some 10 per cent of all the clearances issued were granted to women, but the actual number of female migrants must be considerably higher since many of them belong to categories that are not required to get emigration clearance (e.g., women who have previously been employed abroad, women having college degrees or women who pay income taxes) and labour migration often takes place clandestinely. Malaysia, lacking administrative controls on the emigration of labour, also lacks a statistical system to monitor flows.

In Bangladesh and Pakistan, where deep-rooted social and religious values limit the participation of women in employment outside the home, their emigration appears to be negligible. Among the half a million Pakistani workers who were reported to have left during 1984-1989, only a couple of hundred were women, mostly nurses and domestic workers. The number of women originating in Bangladesh has probably been higher, but is still insignificant compared to the number of male migrants from that country. Only in Sri Lanka did official records show a dramatic increase in female labour migration between 1979 and 1981, a trend that probably continued over subsequent years although it is not accurately reflected by official statistics. The Bureau of Foreign Employment has acknowledged that actual flows have probably been double the number registered.

To understand the different modalities of female labour migration it is useful to identify various migration subsystems operating in the Southern and South-eastern Asian regions (Kritz and others, 1992). Five subsystems, each distinguished by geographic characteristics and by the policy issues characterizing the countries involved, are considered.

Subsystem 1. This migration subsystem operates between the countries of Southern and South-eastern Asia and the oil-rich countries of Western Asia. It involves the migration of unskilled women originating mainly in India, Indonesia, the Philippines and Sri Lanka, who tend to work abroad as domestic workers. They account for the bulk of female migration originating in the region. Kuwait and Saudi Arabia have been their main countries of destination. Saudi Arabia alone received some 192,200 Indonesian female workers during 1983-1988, plus some 8,000 annually from the Philippines and about 2,000 from Sri Lanka. Such flows, having become the concern of policy makers in the countries of origin, have given rise to the regulations and restrictions currently in force. Especially in South-eastern Asia and Sri Lanka, private recruitment agents have played key roles in maintaining these flows and fraudulent practices have been common. On average, some 95,000 women have migrated annually through legal channels and an additional 50,000 to 60,000 have done so through clandestine means.

The numbers of Asian women working in the oil-rich countries of Western Asia are probably higher than the numbers reported by their respective Governments. It was estimated that in 1983, 70,000 of the 800,000 Indian migrant workers present in Western Asia were living with their families (Gulati, 1986). More recently, the large presence of Asian female migrants (both workers and non-workers) in Saudi Arabia has been confirmed by the proportion of women among persons granted new residence permits (see table 100). Since only foreign professionals are allowed by the Government of Saudi Arabia to enter the Kingdom with their families and professionals account for at most 15 per cent of the worker inflows to the Kingdom, there are relatively few Asian families settled there. Consequently, the proportion of women among persons granted new residence permits can be taken as indicative of the level of female worker migration to Saudi Arabia. Assuming that those proportions represent the sex distribution of all workers from Asia, the number of Asian female workers in the country towards the end of 1986 would have been of about 219,000.

Subsystem 2. This subsystem encompasses the flows of women from Asian developing countries—mostly Indonesia, the Philippines and Thailand—to the newly industrializing countries of South-eastern Asia (i.e., Brunei, Hong Kong, Singapore and, more recently, Malaysia). Such flows generally involve women intending to work as domestic workers or as hotel and restaurant personnel. During the late 1980s, the annual flow of women in this subsystem amounted to some 62,000, although those moving from Indonesia to Western Malaysia and from the southern Philippines to Sabah[1] are not reflected by that number (Lim, 1988). Clandestine migration is estimated to be small, amounting to some 3,000 to

TABLE 100. PERCENTAGE OF WOMEN AMONG PERSONS RECEIVING NEW RESIDENCE PERMITS IN SAUDI ARABIA: 1980-1986

(Percentage)

Country of origin	1980	1982	1984	1986
Southern Asia				
Bangladesh	25.9	19.4	20.0	14.5
India	27.0	20.0	32.0	36.3
Pakistan..............	28.6	24.2	29.1	18.7
Sri Lanka	76.3	90.1	88.1	52.6
South-eastern Asia				
Indonesia	63.1	77.8	93.0	94.1
Philippines	..	..	47.9	59.3
Republic of Korea .	15.3	7.4	17.4	16.0
Thailand	32.0	33.3	42.9	33.8

Source: Saudi Arabia, Ministry of Interior, *Annual Statistical Yearbook*, various issues, cited in ILO/ARTEP, *Recent Trends and Prospects of Asian Workers in Selected Middle East Countries* (Bangkok, 1988).

NOTE: Two dots (..) indicate that data are not available or are not separately reported.

5,000 women a year. Migration is generally arranged by recruitment agents, though the proportion of women finding employment abroad through friends or relations is higher than among those migrating to Western Asia. Strong cultural and linguistic affinities within the region facilitate the adjustment of migrants to the host society and periods of stay abroad tend to be longer than among women going to Western Asia.

Subsystem 3. This subsystem comprises the flows of female workers from the Philippines and Thailand to Japan, most of whom are entertainers recruited by private booking agents. It is a fast-track, highly organized subsystem, characterized by rapid turnover. Women are generally recruited for Japan's growing service or leisure industry. Before the 1990 amendment of the Japanese immigration law, visas issued to this type of foreign workers were limited to six months at a time, without extension. During the six-month period, booking agents, many of whom are closely associated with the notorious underworld organization, Yakuza, would arrange the employment of women with various employers all over the country. Both the possibility of high earnings and the need to pay the high fees charged by recruiting agents have induced women to overstay their visas. The Japanese Ministry of Justice estimated that there were some 50,000 illegal foreign workers in the country by the end of 1987. Apprehensions of illegal workers that year numbered 14,129 of whom 60 per cent, or 8,493, were women, mostly from South-eastern Asia and working in the entertainment industry. Assuming that those who were caught were representative of the total illegal population in Japan, in 1987 there would have been about 30,000 illegal female migrants in the country. It is further estimated that the flow of legal entrants has amounted to some 35,000 women annually during the late 1980s.

Subsystem 4. This subsystem comprises the flows of skilled female workers, mainly from India, the Republic of Korea and the Philippines, to the oil-producing countries of Western Asia. Statistical evidence suggests that some 28,000 skilled women migrate every year from the Philippines. Data for India are not available. Clandestine migration within this subsystem is estimated to be practically nil.

Most women with needed skills are recruited to work in the formal sector. They often work for government institutions such as hospitals and public schools, or in managerial and administrative jobs in the private sector. Migration is generally arranged on a Government-to-Government basis and periods of stay tend to be long. These types of flows are the least problematic from the perspective of countries of origin, except in cases where the skills involved are in short supply.

Subsystem 5. This subsystem encompasses the flows of female migrant workers originating in Southern and South-eastern Asia and going to Canada, the United States and Europe. According to existing statistics, some 8,000 to 10,000 women (mostly nurses admitted as temporary workers) migrate annually to Northern America, whereas the flow to Europe amounts to some 6,000 to 8,000 a year. In both regions of destination, clandestine migration surpasses legal flows, amounting to some 20,000 to 30,000 women who move annually to North American countries and 15,000 to 20,000 heading for Europe. Whereas flows of Asians to Canada or the United States are relatively well documented, those to European countries have only begun to be noted, particularly in countries like France or Italy. Often migration does not take place directly from Asia to a developed country. Thus, many of the nurses taking the American FCGMS exam in Amman are Asians employed in Western Asia.

Prior to 1982 it was easy for Asian domestic workers to work in Italy legally. The Italian Government then restricted the issuance of work permits, thus forcing many women into clandestine migration. According to the Government of the Philippines, at most 2,600 contract workers of both sexes went to Italy during 1975-1982 and only 7,621 during 1983-1988, yet the size of the Filipino community in Italy is currently estimated at roughly 60,000, around 70 per cent of whom are female workers. Clearly, either most of those workers left the Philippines without securing exit permits or they originated in third countries. In 1987, an Amnesty Law adopted by the Italian Government allowed the regularization of 9,121 illegal migrants from the Philippines and of 9,393 from Sri Lanka (Campani, 1989).

C. Sex selective regulations and clandestine migration

Although the estimates of both legal and clandestine flows presented thus far are based on different pieces of evidence having varying reliability, it is nevertheless apparent that large numbers of Asian women are migrating for employment. It is not clear, however, whether considerably greater numbers are being prevented from leaving by sex-selective restrictions imposed by their respective Governments. Our impression is that Governments, even when intending earnestly to do so, are not controlling exit so effectively. Control is mainly being exercised by the countries of employment.

Figure X presents in schematic form the relationship between sex-selective restrictions and the estimated rate of clandestine emigration of female workers. Since a positive correlation would be expected, countries should be arrayed diagonally across the graph. Instead, hardly any relationship emerges. Sri Lanka, despite being low on restrictions, is high with respect to clandestine emigration. Pakistan, on the other hand, is high on restrictions but low with respect to clandestine departures.

Sri Lanka is special in that its emigration laws and exit regulations are quite liberal compared to those of other Asian countries of origin and, consequently, one would expect little clandestine emigration. Every citizen, except those with criminal records, can secure a passport and no emigration clearance is required. There is ample evidence, however, pointing to the existence of large numbers of clandestine departures from Sri Lanka. During 1979-1988, the Bureau of Foreign Employment registered 87,743 women as departing domestic workers and among them some 30,000 were supposed to have gone to Kuwait. Yet, in early 1990 the immigration authorities in Kuwait reported that there were 60,300 Sri Lankan domestic workers with valid work visas in the country. The difference is even more significant when one considers that Sri Lankan women working in Western Asia have shown a marked tendency to return to their home country after relatively short periods of stay abroad (Eelens, 1988).

Such high levels of clandestine departures appear to be related to the policy that sets limits on the fees that licensed private recruiters can charge prospective migrants and that requires them to pay the Bureau of Foreign Employment a fee for every person recruited. The paperwork and red tape which characterize the issuance of passports is probably also a contributing factor. Consequently, there are many unlicensed recruitment agents operating in the country and even the licensed ones underreport the number of workers recruited so as to reduce the fees that they must pay to the Government.

A survey of migrants returning to Sri Lanka (MARGA Institute, 1986) revealed that more than a third accepted employment abroad through informal arrangements and not on the basis of a formal contract. Usually a friend, a relative or a sponsor

Figure X. Relationship between the degree of restrictiveness of emigration policy, by sex and the level of clandestine female emigration: schematic display

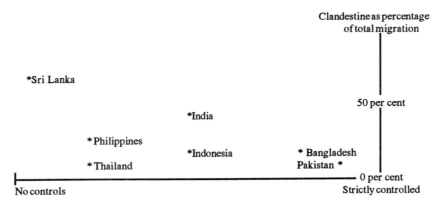

250

abroad would secure a work visa and the migrant would leave Sri Lanka without having received a contract. In such cases, Sri Lankan authorities would not have any record of their departure. Among the returning migrants interviewed, some 77 per cent were women, 45 per cent of whom reported using informal arrangements to secure a job abroad, a proportion that compares with only 22 per cent among men. The study also noted that most of the migrants with contracts did not have a chance to study them prior to departure, and less than a quarter (most of them men) attempted to bargain for better wages.

D. Sex segregation in migration

As already noted, most Asian female migrants, whether working in Western Asia, in South-eastern Asia or in European countries are in feminized occupations: domestic services, entertainment (including prostitution) and nursing. This pattern evidently reflects the sex-segregation by occupation typical of both countries of origin and countries of employment. Male migrants, on the other hand, are concentrated in construction and transport, occupations that are traditionally male-dominated at both ends of the migration chain. However, the influence of supply-side conditions—educational attainment of

women relative to men, relative wages, public policy promoting emigration and the like—is significant. For instance, the fact that 43 per cent of all professionals (excluding entertainers) who left the Philippines in 1987 were women reflects the influence of supply-side conditions on the sex distribution of migrants. Indeed, the Philippines is the main Asian source of women migrating as contract workers and they are found in a relatively wide range of occupations. Thus, among the 180,000 female migrant workers who left the country in 1987, 44 per cent were domestic workers, 17 per cent were entertainers, another 17 per cent were professionals such as doctors and nurses, and the rest were production workers and clerks.

Table 101 compares the proportion of women among the total employed workforce in the Philippines with that among workers leaving the country in 1987. Women account for a large proportion of all employed professionals and of persons employed in sales and service occupations. A similar pattern is observed among the migrant workforce. Among the latter, females outnumbered males in sales and service occupations (even if the 82,300 domestic workers recorded were excluded from the latter category) and would have outnumbered men also among professionals if entertainers were included. Persons working in entertainment activities, who are likely to

TABLE 101. Sex composition of the domestic and overseas workforce of the Philippines,
by occupational group

Occupational group	Total domestic workforce, 1985	Overseas workers deployed in 1987		
	Percentage female	Male	Female	Percentage female
Professional, technical and related workers	64.8	40 393	31 221	43.6
Entertainers	..	2 345	31 579	93.1
Managerial, executive and administrative workers	21.9	1 372	131	8.7
Clerical workers	51.9	9 888	3 806	27.8
Sales workers	68.8	1 773	1 946	52.3
Service workers	59.7	21 904	106 800	83.0
Agricultural, forestry and fishery workers	27.5	2 902	13	0.4
Production and transport workers, equipment operators and labourers...	23.1	121 911	4 942	3.9
All occupations	..	202 488	180 438	47.2

Sources: Philippines, *Statistical Yearbook 1985* (Manila); Philippines, *Statistical Compendium 1975-1987* (Philippine Overseas Employment Administration, Manila).

Note: Two dots (..) indicate that data are not available or are not separately reported.

be legitimate entertainers because they were certified by the Entertainment Certification Board, clearly dominated the professional occupation group.

Several factors are likely to be responsible for the greater participation of Filipino women in migration, most of which also determine the relatively high levels of female participation in professional, administrative, clerical, sales and service occupations in that country. Literacy among Filipino women is among the highest in Asia. It stood at 83 per cent in 1980, compared to only 13 per cent in Pakistan and 25 per cent in India. In addition, over a quarter of all Filipino women had completed high school or a higher educational level. While considerable sex segregation by occupation is still noticeable, no cultural or religious mores comparable to the Islamic purdah or the Hindu laws of Manu inhibit greater participation of women in economic activities outside the home (Nayyar and Sen, 1987).

E. Conclusion

Policies relative to the migration of labour in Asian countries of origin have generally contained, to a greater or a lesser extent, elements that would lead to the sex selectivity of migration. Yet the evidence available suggests that they have played a relatively small role in shaping the participation of women in international labour flows. The typical segregation of women in occupations that are greatly in demand by the countries of employment explains much of the sex selectivity characterizing recent migration flows. However, factors related to the supply side of migration do influence the capacity that different countries of origin have shown in responding to existing demand. Prevailing social norms and values, religious beliefs and practices, language and ethnic propinquities, political and economic conditions, population pressure and geography all influence to some extent migration potential and outcomes by sex. Institutional factors, such as laws and regulations, often reflect the sum total of such influences and have an impact to the extent that they are consistent with the larger forces at play. Laws and regulations that run counter to economic realities are bound to be unenforceable unless existing socio-cultural norms and values reinforce them.

NOTE

[1] Of the 250,000 Filipinos in Sabah, only about 100,000 are considered as refugees by Malaysia. All the rest are considered economic migrants. The flows of Filipinos to Sabah are reported to have declined during the 1980s.

REFERENCES

Appleyard, Reginald T. (1988). International migration in Asia and the Pacific. In *International Migration Today*. Vol. 1: *Trends and Prospects*, Reginald T. Appleyard, ed. Paris: United Nations Educational, Scientific and Cultural Organization.

Campani, Giovanna (1989). Du tiers-monde à l'Italie: une nouvelle immigration féminine. *Revue Européenne des Migrations Internationales* (Poitiers, France), vol. 5, No. 2, pp. 29-50.

Cremer, G. (1988). Indonesia's overseas employment policy, present state, and prospects. Discussion paper, Research and Documentation Centre, Yayasan Tenaga Kerja, Indonesia.

Eelens, Frank (1988). Early return of Sri Lankan migrants in the Middle East. *International Migration* (Geneva), vol. 26, No. 4 (December), pp. 401-416.

Gopinathan-Nair, P. R. (1986). India. In *Migration of Asian Workers to the Arab World*, G. Gunatilleke, ed. Tokyo: United Nations University.

Gulati, L. (1986). The impact on the family of male migration to the Middle East: some evidence from Kerala, India. In *Asian Labor Migration Pipeline to the Middle East*, Fred Arnold and Nasra M. Shah, eds. Boulder, Colorado: Westview Press.

International Labour Organisation (1988). Recent trends and prospects of Asian workers in selected Middle East countries. Working Paper. Bangkok: Asian Regional Programme on International Labour Migration.

Juridico, E. (1987). A systematic approach to overseas employment administration: analysis of Pusat Akan. Discussion paper, INS/82/013. Jakarta: International Labour Office.

Kritz, Mary M., Lin Lean Lim and Hania Zlotnik, eds. (1992). *International Migration Systems: A Global Approach*. Oxford, United Kingdom: Clarendon Press.

Lim, Lin Lean (1988). International labour migration in the ASEAN region: The main perspectives. In *Current Issues in Labour Migration in Malaysia: A Collection of Seminar Papers*. Kuala Lumpur: University of Malaya, Population Studies Unit.

MARGA Institute (1986). Migrant workers to the Arab world. Colombo: Sri Lanka Centre for Development Studies. Mimeographed.

Nayyar, R., and S. Sen (1987). The employment of women in Bangladesh, India and Pakistan. In *Women's Economic Participation in Asia and the Pacific*. Bangkok: United Nations Economic and Social Commission for Asia and the Pacific.

Philippine Overseas Employment Administration (POEA) (1988). Statistical compendium 1975-1987. Manila. Mimeographed.

Sumalee, P. (1986). Thailand. In *Middle East Interlude: Asian Workers Abroad*, Manolo I. Abella and Y. Atal, eds. Bangkok: United Nations Educational, Scientific and Cultural Organization (UNESCO).

Weiner, Myron (1982). International migration and development: Indians in the Persian Gulf. *Population and Development Review* (New York), vol. 8, No. 1 (March), p. 1-36.

XV. POLICY DIMENSIONS OF FEMALE MIGRATION TO THE ARAB COUNTRIES OF WESTERN ASIA

Sharon Stanton Russell*

Migration has been a major and longstanding phenomenon throughout Western Asia. Over the past 40 years and, particularly, over the past 15 years the proportionate significance of international migration has been especially notable in the Arab oil-producing countries of the region. Many factors have contributed to the volume, direction and composition of population movements in the region: patterns of commerce since ancient times, the spread of Islam, regional and imperial conflicts, economic differentiation, the establishment of nation States and government policies.

This paper will focus on the implications of one of these factors—government policies—for the sex selectivity of migration and the status of female migrants. Because of the salience of international migration in the oil-producing States of Western Asia, the paper will further focus on those States, placing special emphasis on the case of Kuwait.

A. GENERAL CONDITIONS SURROUNDING MIGRATION

The implications of policies for female migrants are grounded in the general economic, demographic and political context of migration within Western Asia and especially to the member States of the Gulf Cooperation Council (GCC), namely, Bahrain, Kuwait, Oman, Qatar, Saudi Arabia and the United Arab Emirates. Arguably the most significant economic factor shaping migration in the region has been the exploitation of oil reserves. The role of the 1973 oil price rise in fuelling migration during the subsequent decade is well known. However, oil-related migration began as early as the 1930s, drawing workers from Arab countries in Western Asia

and Northern Africa and from the Indian subcontinent to staff both the oil sector itself and the growing service sector.

Government strategies to develop physical and social infrastructure during the 1950s and 1960s, and to extend social and industrial development in the 1970s, expanded demand for labour well beyond local sources of supply. Indigenous populations of the GCC member States were (and remain) small in absolute terms and their contribution to labour supply was and is further constrained by low levels of labour force participation, linked in turn to very low levels of female labour force participation, high proportions of population under working age and, more recently, expansion of enrolment in secondary and higher education.

Political factors have also shaped the timing, volume, direction and composition of migration flows. Regional conflicts have been a major cause of population displacement. The war of 1947-1948, culminating in the establishment of the State of Israel, internal violence in the Syrian Arab Republic, surrounding the coups of 1963 and 1966, the Arab-Israeli wars of 1967 and 1973, and the onset of civil war in Lebanon in the early 1970s are some of the major events that have triggered population movement, often by whole families and even entire communities.

Changes in political boundaries, also, have had a fundamental effect on migration policies. Jordan's annexation of the West Bank in 1950 was the backdrop for adoption of that country's liberal naturalization law in 1954. During the 1960s and early 1970s, the withdrawal of European powers from the Persian Gulf and the related emergence of independent sovereign States created the need for the formulation of national laws that are the bedrock of current migration policy.

*Research Scholar, Center for International Studies, Massachusetts Institute of Technology, Cambridge, Massachusetts, United States of America.

Migration to Western Asia has also been affected by political factors outside the region. Economic recession in Western Europe during the early 1970s was closely followed by dramatic changes in migration policies in that region, to which Northern African countries, in particular, responded by redirecting migration toward Western Asian destinations.

B. General patterns of migration in Western Asia

Estimates of the volume and direction of migration flows to Western Asia have generally pertained to migrant workers and are widely recognized to be only rough approximations. In addition, data on regional worker migration are of limited use for the analysis of female migration because they are generally not disaggregated by sex and, by definition, they do not refer to total migration flows, thus precluding the estimation of secondary or associational female migration. Nevertheless, data on migrant workers serve to illustrate three major trends: the significant increase of migration as of the early 1970s, the major attraction exerted by the six States of the GCC, and the shift from Arab to Asian countries of origin.

As of 1970, there were approximately 884,000 migrant workers in the region (Choucri, 1983, table 3-1). Of the total, 77 per cent were concentrated in GCC countries and the remainder were in the Libyan Arab Jamahiriya and Lebanon. All but 12 per cent of those workers originated in Arab countries, mainly the former Yemen Arab Republic, Egypt and the Syrian Arab Republic in rank order, with the fourth largest group being migrants of Palestinian origin. By 1975, the total number of migrant workers is estimated to have reached 1,884,200 (Choucri, 1983, table 3-2(b)), with 74 per cent in the GCC States, and the rest in the Libyan Arab Jamahiriya, Iraq, the Islamic Republic of Iran and Algeria (also in rank order). As a result of the 1973 "open door policy" (*infitah*) adopted by Egypt and its 1974 abolition of exit visas, that country became the main labour exporter to Western Asia. Workers from the former Yemen Arab Republic and those of Jordanian and Palestinian origin occupied second and third place, respectively. In addition, the proportion of non-

Arabs (mostly Asians) had increased substantially to reach 41 per cent of all migrants. By the early 1980s, there were an estimated 4 million migrant workers in Western Asia, 60 per cent of whom were in the GCC States (Choucri, 1983, table 3-7).[1]

The data available for 1985 cover only the six GCC States, where migrant workers were estimated to number 5.1 million, constituting 72 per cent of the total labour force in those countries (Birks, Seccombe and Sinclair, 1987, p. 2). Altogether, 63 per cent of the migrant worker stock originated in Asia: 43 per cent in Southern Asia and 20 in South-eastern Asia. These numbers alone do not convey adequately the relative importance of foreign nationals in the GCC States. By the early 1980s, migrants in Bahrain constituted one third of the total population and 60 per cent of the labour force; in Oman, they accounted for about half of the labour force; in the United Arab Emirates and Qatar, almost 90 per cent of the workforce was foreign, and in Kuwait migrants constituted about 60 per cent of the total population and nearly 80 per cent of the labour force (Choucri, 1986, p. 260).

C. General trends in migration policies

The migration policies of the receiving countries in Western Asia and, particularly, those of the GCC States have undergone considerable changes during the past 30 years. To determine how those changes may have affected the sex selectivity of migration and the status of female migrants, it is necessary to examine country-level data. The case of Kuwait is illustrative. As table 102 indicates, seven phases can be identified in the evolution of that country's migration policies.

The foundations of Kuwait's migration policy were laid during the period immediately preceding and following independence in 1961 (Russell, 1987 and 1989). The original Aliens Residence Law, the Labour Law for the Private Sector and the Nationality Law were all promulgated in 1959. In 1960, the Government adopted the Law of Commercial Companies regulating foreigners in business, and a new Private Sector Labour Law was passed in 1964. Taken together, these laws had the effect of allowing

TABLE 102. PHASES IN THE EVOLUTION OF MIGRATION
POLICIES IN KUWAIT

Period	Policy stance
1959-1965	Relatively free migration
1965-1966	Adoption of instruments introducing restrictions for the first time
1967-1973	Restrictions for political security
1974-1977	Liberalization
1978-1979	Consolidation and regulation
1980-1983	Restrictions to maintain cultural homogeneity
1984-1985	Restrictions to achieve population balance

the relatively free inflow of foreign labour, while they maintained strong Government controls over the entry, residence, departure, rights and employment of migrants. They also established special prerogatives for nationals, requiring foreigners to have Kuwaiti partners in any business enterprise, guaranteeing Kuwaitis majority ownership and limiting aliens' participation in lucrative sectors of the economy.

The years 1965-1966 marked a notable transition in migration policy motivated, at least in part, by a decline in the Government's budget surplus, by evidence from the 1965 census that non-Kuwaitis had become more than 50 per cent of the total population and by growing internal political opposition from Kuwaiti Arab nationalists who enjoyed broad-based support among resident Arab migrants. Accordingly, in 1965, the Aliens Residence Law was amended and regulations for its enforcement issued, transferring control over migration from the Ministry of Social Affairs and Labour (traditionally concerned with employment) to the Ministry of the Interior (whose principal concern was security). Although these changes did not reduce migration inflows, they did establish new measures for tightening control over entry, exit and conditions of employment.

A more significant shift was discernible between 1967 and 1973, the dates of the two Arab-Israeli wars, when regional tensions and internal political dissent increased. During that period the Ministry of the Interior took more direct measures to limit migration. In March 1969 Decree No. 3 relating to the

Aliens Residence Law introduced penalties for those who entered the country illegally and revoked earlier provisions that had waived visa requirements for Arabs and for citizens of countries that had offered similar waivers to Kuwaitis.

As the data presented in table 103 indicate, the growth of the non-Kuwaiti population slowed significantly between 1965-1970 and 1970-1975, passing from an annual average growth rate of 9.2 per cent to a little under 5.8 per cent during the second period. The 1973 increase in the price of oil, however, made more apparent the manpower constraints that were beginning to be felt in 1972, so that from 1974 to 1977 migration policies were considerably liberal-

TABLE 103. AVERAGE ANNUAL GROWTH RATES OF THE
POPULATION OF KUWAIT, BY CITIZENSHIP,
FOR DIFFERENT INTERCENSAL PERIODS
(Percentage)

Intercensal period	Kuwaiti	Citizenship		
		Foreign		
		Total	Arab	Asian
Both sexes				
1957-1961	8.39	12.85	..	..
1961-1965	7.81	11.12	..	..
1965-1970	9.17	9.21	..	..
1970-1975	6.12	5.78	..	..
1975-1980	3.61	8.32	..	..
1980-1985	3.72	4.97	..	..
Male				
1957-1961	8.44	11.06	..	..
1961-1965	7.31	10.23	..	..
1965-1970	8.92	6.85	7.62	4.57
1970-1975	5.96	4.57	5.01	3.44
1975-1980	3.41	9.58	7.19	15.99
1980-1985	3.77	4.67	2.14	9.50
Female				
1957-1961	8.34	18.46	..	..
1961-1965	8.34	13.38	..	..
1965-1970	9.43	13.89	14.72	9.45
1970-1975	6.28	7.66	6.98	13.49
1975-1980	3.81	6.36	5.08	11.76
1980-1985	3.68	5.47	2.40	14.86

Sources: Kuwait, Ministry of Information, *Kuwait Facts and Figures*, 1987; Kuwait, Central Statistical Office, *Annual Statistical Abstract*, 1987, p. 25, table 9.

NOTE: Two dots (..) indicate that data are not available or are not separately reported.

ized. In April 1974, the Council of Ministers transferred control of migrant employment from the Ministry of the Interior back to the Ministry of Social Affairs and Labour. New regulations reintroduced earlier provisions allowing the waiver of entry visas for nationals of States with which Kuwait had reciprocal agreements and allowed the issuance of transit and temporary visas at points of entry without the previously required prior evidence of security clearance. Aliens with valid residence permits were permitted to reenter Kuwait without "return visas" and were allowed to change the type and purpose of their residence permit (from accompaniment to employment, for instance). New entrants could remain in the country without residence permits for up to one month.

Between 1976 and 1977, the number of new work permits issued more than doubled (Kuwait, 1978). There was, however, a noticeable shift in the origin of migrants. The proportion of new labour permits issued to Jordanians and Syrians dropped, while those to Egyptians rose (Kuwait, 1977b, p. 129). Most striking was the inflow of new Asian groups, primarily from Bangladesh, the Philippines and the Republic of Korea.

The years 1978 and 1979 marked a period of consolidation and regulation in Kuwait's migration policies. Following several years of rapid growth in migrant inflows and foreign employment, the need to achieve greater stability and continuity of the labour force was felt. Measures to reduce labour turnover were adopted, including the requirement that workers remain with an employer at least one year before transferring to another job and the extension of residence permits from two to five years. There was simultaneously a growing concern over migrant settlement. Various measures introduced during 1978 to restrict the entry of dependants were followed in January 1979 with explicit restrictions on their employment: only those dependants with residence permits issued before 1979 were permitted to work and then only with the approval of the migrant's Kuwaiti sponsor or "kafeel" (Kuwait, 1979c).

Issues of migrant settlement and growing cultural heterogeneity assumed new prominence between 1980 and 1983. The 1980 census showed that nearly one third of all non-Kuwaitis had been resident in the country for at least 10 years and that nearly 16 per cent had been resident for at least 15 years (Kuwait, 1985, p. 51). Furthermore, not only had the proportion of Asians risen, so had the proportion of non-Muslims: the number of Christians had nearly doubled between 1975 and 1980 (from 44,718 to 87,080), while the number of other non-Muslims had increased more than fivefold (from 5,338 to 28,161) (Kuwait, 1984c, p. 26). At the same time, the results of the 1981 elections demonstrated the growing political strength of Kuwait's religious conservatives.

Several changes in migration policy ensued. As will be seen below, the 1980 amendment to the Nationality Law included changes affecting the citizenship of women, and in 1982 the law was further amended to restrict the acquisition of citizenship to Muslims; that is, non-Muslims cannot be naturalized. The Aliens Residence Law was also amended in 1982 (July) and measures were introduced that affected domestic workers specifically. In addition, explicit restrictions were placed on visits by the relatives of migrants and the issuance of family visas was restricted to workers with a minimum monthly salary of 400 Kuwaiti dinars (KD) (approximately US$1,400). With an average monthly salary of KD 115 (Shah and Al-Qudsi, 1989, table 7), most non-Kuwaiti female workers were clearly prevented from being joined by family members.

By 1984-1985, negative reactions to migrant inflows were exacerbated by declining oil revenues, security concerns linked to the war between Iran and Iraq, and increasing awareness of the social costs of migration. The implications of subsequent policy changes were mixed for migrants. New regulations associated with the Private Sector Labour Law (Kuwait, 1984a) asserted the Government's right to deny the renewal of work permits, even as they removed the 1979 restrictions on the employment of related dependants and explicitly permitted "non-related dependants" (such as nannies or household servants) to join the general labour force. In 1985, the Ministry of the Interior eased restrictions on the return of children of expatriates.

In 1985, however, the census revealed that Kuwaitis had dropped to 40 per cent of the total population and that over 300,000 aliens—nearly 30 per cent of the non-Kuwaiti population—had been born in Kuwait. As an initial response, the Ministry of the Interior proposed to limit the number of migrants in Kuwait (*Al-Ra'i al-Am*, 1985), a measure that was subsequently vetoed by parliamentary committee. In more considered responses, the minimum salary required to bring in dependants was raised to KD 450 and the draft national development plan unveiled in April 1985 called for the attainment of a "50-50" balance between Kuwaitis and non-Kuwaitis in the total population by the year 2000.

D. IMPLICATIONS OF ADMISSION AND RESIDENCE POLICIES FOR FEMALE MIGRATION

Just as Kuwait's admission policies have changed over time, so too have the implications of those policies for female migrants, although the effects of admission policies have differed also by nationality. Broadly speaking, female migration to Kuwait consists of two distinct streams, Arab and Asian (well over 90 per cent of all female migrants belong to one of those groups). Two further and somewhat cross-cutting streams can be distinguished: a group whose ties to Kuwait date back to the early 1960s and whose inflow is probably linked to family migration or reunification; and a group comprising those women for whom Kuwait is a relatively new destination and whose migration is linked more directly to the growth of labour market opportunities during the 1970s. Early Asian migrants and all Arabs except Egyptians fall into the first category. For the Arabs in particular, migration to Kuwait has often been associated with flight from political conflict. Egyptian Arabs and more recent Asian migrants (i.e., those arriving after 1974) belong to the second group.

In 1957, Kuwait's first census showed that non-Kuwaitis already constituted nearly 45 per cent of the total population but, as a result of the predominantly male composition of earlier migration inflows, women accounted for only 21 per cent of all foreigners (see table 104). The relatively liberal migration policies that prevailed until the late 1960s permitted the admission of substantial numbers of foreign women. As table 103 shows, the average annual growth of the female foreign population was 18.5 per cent between 1957 and 1961, and ranged between 13 per cent to 14 per cent between 1961 and 1970. By comparison, the average annual growth of the male foreign population declined from just over 11 per cent to about 7 per cent over the same periods. By 1970, women of all ages accounted already for almost 38 per cent of all non-Kuwaitis in the country (see table 104).

The vast majority (83 per cent) of the foreign women enumerated in 1965 were Arab, with Jordanians and Palestinians taken together, Iraquis and Lebanese constituting the three largest groups. Egyptians accounted for only 8 per cent of foreign Arab women (Russell, 1987, p. 69). Asians (primarily Pakistanis, Indians and Iranians in rank order) constituted only 13 per cent of all foreign women. As table 103 shows, over the following five years the foreign Arab female population grew at an average annual rate of 14.7 per cent, while that of Asian origin increased by less than 9.5 per cent per annum. A comparison of the 1965 and 1970 census results suggests that a large part of the increase of the foreign Arab female population was associated with the 1967 Arab-Israeli war: the number of Jordanian and Palestinian women increased by more than 142 per cent (Russell, 1987, pp. 69-70).

The effects of the tightening of admission policies during the late 1960s and early 1970s are evident during the 1970-1975 intercensal period, when the overall average annual growth rate of the foreign female population declined to 7.7 per cent from 13.9 during the preceding five-year period. However, the slowdown affected Asian and Arab women differently. The average annual population growth of foreign Arab women dropped to just 7 per cent, while that of Asians jumped to over 13.5 per cent. There were some notable differences even within those two major groups. Whereas most foreign Arab groups registered only modest gains in size, the number of Egyptian women increased by 90 per cent, so that by 1975 they constituted 14 per cent of the Arab total. Kuwait's revocation of visa waivers in 1969 together with the liberalization of Egypt's exit policies in 1973-1974 are the most likely explanation for this outcome. Among Asians, the largest increase occurred in the Indian female population, whereas "other Asians" (i.e., those from origins

TABLE 104. EVOLUTION OF THE POPULATION OF KUWAIT ACCORDING TO SUCCESSIVE CENSUSES: 1957-1985

Census year	Citizenship	Male (thousands)	Female (thousands)	Percentage female	Percentage non-Kuwaiti
1957	Kuwaiti	59.2	54.5	47.9	
	Non-Kuwaiti	72.9	19.9	21.5	
	TOTAL	132.1	74.4	36.0	45.0
1961	Kuwaiti	84.5	77.4	47.8	
	Non-Kuwaiti	116.2	43.5	27.2	
	TOTAL	200.7	120.9	37.6	49.7
1965	Kuwaiti	112.6	107.5	48.8	
	Non-Kuwaiti	173.7	73.5	29.7	
	TOTAL	286.3	181.0	38.7	52.9
1970	Kuwaiti	175.5	171.9	49.5	
	Non-Kuwaiti	244.4	146.9	37.5	
	TOTAL	419.9	318.8	43.2	53.0
1975	Kuwaiti	236.6	235.5	49.9	
	Non-Kuwaiti	307.2	215.6	41.2	
	TOTAL	543.8	451.1	45.3	52.5
1980	Kuwaiti	280.6	285.0	50.4	
	Non-Kuwaiti	496.0	296.3	37.4	
	TOTAL	776.6	581.3	42.8	58.3
1985	Kuwaiti	338.8	342.5	50.3	
	Non-Kuwaiti	626.5	389.5	38.3	
	TOTAL	965.3	732.0	43.1	59.9

Sources: *1957-1980*: Population figures from Ministry of Information, *Kuwait: Facts and Figures, 1984*; *1985*: Kuwait, Central Statistical Office, *Annual Statistical Abstract, 1987*, p. 25, table 9.

other than India, the Islamic Republic of Iran or Pakistan) accounted for barely 1 per cent of the Asian female total.

The assertion that Arab and some Asian female migration during the 1960s and early 1970s was largely associated with family migration or reunification is supported by data on labour force participation and reasons for residence (see tables 105 and 106). The labour force participation rate for Arab women hovered around 10 per cent between 1965 and 1975, and in the 1975 census only 10 per cent reported employment as their primary reason for residence. The picture was somewhat different for Asian women. In 1965 their labour force participation rate was comparable to that of Arab women (10 per cent), but it rose to 16 per cent in 1970 and reached 30 per cent in 1975, mostly as a result of the religious and cultural acceptability of female employment among Asian women and the arrival of

new female migration streams from Southern Asia consisting mainly of domestic workers.

The liberalization of Kuwait's migration policies in 1974 did little to halt the decline in the growth rates of the foreign female population. Indeed, during 1975-1980 the average annual growth rate of the male foreign population exceeded that of foreign females for the first time (9.6 per cent versus 6.4 per cent). Once more, the growth rates of the foreign Arab and Asian female populations differed significantly. The former grew by 5.1 per cent annually, while the latter grew by 11.8 per cent. Such fast growth of the Asian female population is associated with the increase in low-paying employment opportunities in the service sector, the willingness of Asians to accept lower wages than foreign Arab workers and the tight supply from the traditional Arab source countries. In addition, there are indications that Kuwait and other GCC states were inter-

TABLE 105. NON-KUWAITI WOMEN, BY CITIZENSHIP AND LABOUR FORCE PARTICIPATION, AND LABOUR FORCE
PARTICIPATION RATES: 1965-1985

Year	Arab	Asian	African	American and European	Not stated	Total foreign
Total number of women						
1965	61 559	9 908	67	1 991	12	73 537
1970	128 120	15 863	188	2 703	24	146 898
1975	181 762	31 179	123	2 433	84	215 581
1980	234 289	56 148	702	5 210	—	296 349
1985	264 110	118 035	976	6 327	64	389 512
Women in the labour force						
1965	6 461	1 005	3	199	8	7 676
1970	11 650	2 557	19	311	4	14 541
1975	17 972	9 204	30	319	—	27 525
1980	27 073	19 920	439	842	—	48 274
1985	32 989	72 505	627	1 204	—	107 325
Female labour force participation rates (percentage)						
1965	10	10	4	10	67	10
1970	9	16	10	12	17	10
1975	10	30	24	13	—	13
1980	12	35	63	16	—	16
1985	12	61	64	19	—	28

Sources: For total female population, *1965-1975*: Kuwait, *Statistical Abstract, 1977*, p. 25; *1980*: Kuwait, *Statistical Abstract, 1982*, p. 47, table 33; 1985: Kuwait, *Statistical Abstract, 1987*, p. 56, table 43. For total female labour force, *1965-1975*: Kuwait, *Statistical Abstract, 1981*, table 112; *1980*: Kuwait, *Statistical Abstract, 1982*, p. 96, table 79; *1985*: Kuwait, *Statistical Abstract, 1987*, p. 124, table 112.
NOTE: Female population over age 15 is not available by groups of countries, thus only the labour force participation rates with respect to the total population can be calculated; em dash (—) indicates that the amount is nil or negligible.

ested in admitting less politically active migrant groups (Russell, 1989, p. 36).

The rising concern over migrant settlement that emerged during the late 1970s and early 1980s was reflected most directly in policies to reduce the admission and residence of dependants. Their effects are seen in the proportion of non-Kuwaitis living in family groups, which declined from 82 per cent in 1975 to less than 74 per cent in 1980 (United Nations, 1988, p. 37). In addition, the dependency ratio among non-Kuwaitis dropped from 53.9 per 100 persons aged 15-59 in 1980 to 43.3 per 100 in 1985 (Kuwait, 1987, p. 34).

These policies had a strong impact on the foreign Arab population. Thus, whereas the average annual growth rate of the Asian female population was 14.9 per cent during 1980-1985, that of the Arab female population dropped to 2.4 per cent. The data in table 105 suggest that most of the increase among Asian women was associated with the admission of female migrant workers: the labour force participation rate of Asian women jumped from 35 per cent in 1980 to 61 per cent in 1985, while that for non-Kuwaiti Arab women remained unchanged at 12 per cent.

E. POLICIES RELATED TO EMPLOYMENT AND THEIR IMPACT ON MIGRANT WOMEN

Early Kuwaiti law was implicitly liberal on the issue of female employment. The 1964 Private Sector Labour Law established that any unemployed worker (Kuwaiti or non-Kuwaiti) was eligible to

TABLE 106. NON-KUWAITI FEMALE POPULATION, BY REASON OF RESIDENCE AND CITIZENSHIP: 1975 AND 1980

| Year and citizenship | Employment | | | Accompaniment | Other | Total | Percentage for employment |
	Diplomatic	Private	Government				
1975							
Arab	37	8 524	9 559	161 602	2 040	181 762	10
Asian	12	8 002	1 189	21 862	180	31 245	29
African	2	25	3	79	14	123	24
American and European	15	240	59	1 983	48	2 345	13
Other	—	5	—	99	2	106	5
Total foreign	66	16 796	10 810	185 625	2 284	215 581	13
1980							
Arab	36	9 670	16 977	206 229	1 377	234 289	11
Asian	16	16 689	3 108	36 152	183	56 148	35
African	—	409	26	224	43	702	62
American and European	21	577	212	4 270	68	5 148	15
Other	1	5	4	52	—	62	15
Total foreign	74	27 350	20 327	246 927	1 671	296 349	16

Sources: Kuwait, Central Staistical Office, *Statistical Abstract, 1987,* p. 53, table 38.

NOTE: Slight discrepancies in total female population figures from those in table 3 are found in the original data; em dash (—) indicates that the amount is nil or negligible.

register with the Ministry of Social Affairs and Labour for assistance in finding a job. Regulations issued in 1965 by the Ministry of the Interior to implement the Aliens Residence Law stipulated that aliens on non-working residence permits (largely female) and students would be eligible to work after being granted a "No Objection Certificate" by the Ministry of Social Affairs and Labour (Dib, 1978, p. 58). Such provisions may account in part for the observed increase in the labour force participation rate of Asian migrant women between 1965 and 1970, although there was no comparable effect for Arab migrant women.

The generally favourable labour market conditions that prevailed from 1974 through 1979 appeared to have a modest positive effect on the employment of foreign women. The activity rate of non-Kuwaiti women aged 15 and over increased from just over 24 per cent in 1975 to 29 per cent in 1980 (Kuwait, 1987, pp. 48 and 124).

A marked change in policy occurred in 1979, when the employment of dependants was restricted to those who had entered Kuwait prior to January

1979, a restriction that remained in force until February 1984. This measure, intended to reduce the incentives for family reunification and prevent the settling of foreigners in Kuwait, also affected employment trends by ensuring that the inflows of female migrants were increasingly constituted by women admitted as contract workers in their own right. Consequently, the activity rate for non-Kuwaiti women aged 15 and over increased to nearly 44 per cent. Data shown in table 105 suggest that much of that increase resulted from the inflow of Asian female workers: the labour force participation rate of Asian women rose from 35 per cent to 61 per cent during 1980-1985 whereas, as already noted above, that of foreign Arab women remained virtually unchanged at 12 per cent. In addition, between 1980 and 1985, the absolute increase in the Asian female population (of about 62,000) was considerably greater than that of the foreign Arab female population (only 30,000). Altogether, 66 per cent of the Asian women present in Kuwait in 1985 had entered the country within the preceding four years, compared with only 25.5 per cent of foreign Arab women (Kuwait, 1987, p. 56). Between 1985 and mid-1989, the total number of non-Kuwaiti women in the labour force increased by nearly 48 per cent to reach 158,655, largely as a result of the growing numbers of Asians, whose share of the female labour force rose from 68 per cent to 75 per cent (International Labour Organisation, 1989).

The growth in Asian female employment paralleled that of Kuwaiti female employment, spurred in turn not only by the rapidly rising levels of educational attainment among Kuwaiti women, but also by explicit policies to encourage the "Kuwaitization" of the labour force. Between 1970 and 1975, the proportion of Kuwaiti women aged 15 and over in the labour force increased from 2.1 per cent to 6.2 per cent. By 1985, the proportion of Kuwaiti women in the labour force had more than doubled to 13.8 per cent (Russell, 1987, p. 67). Given that Government policy had encouraged both child-bearing and employment among Kuwaiti women (United Nations, 1988, p. 4), one effect of the increase in their employment was to stimulate demand for domestic workers, large numbers of whom were Asian women from Bangladesh, India, the Philippines and Sri Lanka. It is estimated that, in 1975, there were 11,921 foreign female domestic workers in Kuwait, comprising 43 per cent of the foreign female labour force. By 1985, the 63,250 foreign domestic workers present in the country accounted for 60 per cent of all foreign female workers (Shah and Al-Qudsi, 1989, p. 32).

Indeed, the inflow of female domestic workers was sufficiently sizeable to prompt a number of policy directives explicitly on the issue. The regulation of domestic workers was covered under the Aliens Residence Law of 1959 and thus fell under the Ministry of the Interior's purview. In 1975 new regulations were issued under that law providing for the relatively liberal admission of domestic workers and hardly restricting their internal mobility. Entry visas were given on the strength of a "No Objection Certificate", issued at the request of the employer. The type and purpose of the residence permit could be changed, regardless of the type of visa under which an alien was admitted.[2]

Ministry of the Interior Order No. 84 of 1977 (Kuwait, 1977a), which permitted residence permits valid for two to five years to be granted to domestic workers, sought to limit their labour market mobility by increasing the employers' control over them.[3] The employer's name and address were recorded on the residence permit stamped on the worker's passport, and any domestic worker resigning before the expiration of his or her contract would have the permit cancelled and be subject to deportation. Under those circumstances, domestic workers could not be granted a new permit (i.e., they were not allowed to change employment) without the consent of the previous employer unless the worker had been out of Kuwait for two years.

In 1982, those regulations were codified into law as revisions to the Aliens Residence Law, and a further provision was added stipulating that employers had to notify the Ministry of the Interior within two weeks of the resignation of a domestic worker and that the worker had to leave the country within three months unless a new residence permit were granted. Notes accompanying the Law refer explicitly to the problem of domestic workers who leave their original employers to take up new jobs, "which may result in serious social and security problems" (Kuwait, 1982).

By 1984, attitudes toward the labour mobility of domestic workers changed. New labour regulations issued that year specifically permitted "non-related dependants" (such as nannies and other domestic workers) to move into the general labour force. The factors motivating this change in policy are not entirely clear. The economic difficulties associated with the drop in oil prices after 1982 may have put pressure on Kuwaiti households to make do with fewer domestic workers and it may well have been less costly for private sector employers to recruit workers already present in the country than to hire them abroad. It has also been suggested that some women arriving in Kuwait as domestic workers were actually the spouses of male migrants already present in Kuwait (United Nations, 1988, p. 38). If so, the desire to keep male turnover down may have prompted the change in policy.

In general, non-Kuwaitis have limited employment-related benefits. They are excluded from the social insurance scheme established for Kuwaitis in 1976, although private sector workers (estimated to include about 13 per cent of foreign female workers)[4] may be eligible for a lump sum compensation upon termination of service, provided they have worked at least five years. Government workers may qualify for end-of-service compensation, depending upon the terms of their employment contracts (International Labour Organisation, 1988, p. 57). That provision could affect the nearly 26 per cent of foreign female workers who are employed by the Government (United Nations, 1988, p. 50).

The 60 per cent of foreign female workers engaged in domestic service are not covered by either social insurance or the end-of-service compensation provisions of the Labour Law.[5] The ILO has noted that the special problems of female domestic workers are a source of concern in Asian sending countries, given the difficulties of enforcing labour standards for this category of workers. There have been reports of physical mistreatment by employers, of workers leaving before the expiration of their contracts, and of abandonment by recruitment agents even before the workers reach their countries of employment (International Labour Organisation, 1988, p. 30).

The earnings of foreign female workers differ significantly from those of both Kuwaiti women and foreign men, although it is difficult to establish how much of the differential results from policy and how much from market forces. Certainly, foreign women have little choice but to be employed in "culturally acceptable" occupations. According to a 1983 survey, female workers (Kuwaiti and foreign alike) earned about half of what males earned, despite the fact that their average educational levels were somewhat higher than those of males and that they worked longer hours than men (Shah and Al-Qudsi, 1989, p. 46). The monthly salaries of Kuwaiti females, 54 per cent of whom worked in professional occupations and had an average educational attainment of 12.1 years, were 46 per cent higher than those of Jordanian and Palestinian women, whose concentration in professional occupations was comparable and whose educational attainment (13.0 years) was slightly higher. In addition, Jordanian and Palestinian men in professional occupations had salaries that were 50 per cent higher than those of their professional countrywomen, despite the fact that only 28 per cent of males were in that category and their average educational attainment was only 10.2 years (Shah and Al-Qudsi, 1989, tables 2, 3, 7 and 8).

The salary differentials between Kuwaiti and foreign women are most clearly attributable to policy factors, since Kuwaitis of both sexes receive specific allowances as citizens. Yet, those between foreign men and women suggest that wage discrimination by sex is at work, though age and length of professional experience would also need to be taken into consideration to prove this case beyond any reasonable doubt.

F. SOCIAL DIMENSIONS OF FEMALE MIGRATION

As of 1974, Kuwait was committed to providing free education and other social services to both Kuwaitis and foreigners in its territory (United Nations, 1980, pp. 7-22). However, in the late 1970s and early 1980s, as concerns over the social costs of migration mounted, this situation began to change. While efforts begun in 1982 to impose fees for medical services to foreigners were not successful (Russell, 1987, p. 218), efforts to shift the costs of education to migrants met with somewhat greater success.

As part of those efforts, access to free education in government schools was limited to dependants of non-Kuwaitis employed by Government. Simultaneously, the expansion of private schools was permitted and the Government decided to subsidize 50 per cent of the tuition in Arab schools, but provided no financial assistance to non-Arabic private schools (United Nations, 1988, p. 38). The move in 1982 to restrict the admission of dependants only to foreigners earning monthly salaries over KD 400 was, in part, a recognition that only middle and high income migrants could afford the costs of private education. As a result of these measures, the proportion of foreign students in kindergarten through grade 12 enrolled in private schools grew from 30.5 per cent in 1980/81 to 38.1 per cent in 1986/87 (Kuwait, 1981, pp. 352 and 366; 1987, pp. 374 and 381).

The combined changes in education and admission policies had two implications for female migrants.

First, given that over 70 per cent of both male and female migrants were employed in the private sector, most no longer had access to free education for their children. Even if migrant women themselves were eligible to remain in Kuwait by virtue of their own or their spouse's income level, it became increasingly likely that they would be separated from their school-age children. Indeed, the proportion of the foreign population under age 15 dropped from nearly 40 per cent in 1975 to under 29 per cent in 1985, with the decline in the 10-14 age group resulting from the emigration of adolescents (especially Asians) to pursue their education in the home countries (United Nations, 1988, p. 24).

Second, the growing number of private schools (which are staffed totally by non-Kuwaitis) changed the structure of demand for foreign female teachers. The number teaching in private schools nearly doubled from 2,331 in 1980/81 to 4,131 in 1986/87. During the same period, the absolute number of foreign female teachers in government schools declined slightly, from 7,873 to 7,419. As a proportion of all female teachers in government schools, foreigners dropped from 64 per cent to 48 per cent (Kuwait, 1984c, p. 298; 1987, pp. 374 and 381).

For most foreign Arab women and the older cohorts of Asian female migrants from India, the Islamic Republic of Iran or Pakistan, social integration in Kuwait has been facilitated through professional, cultural, civic and religious associations organized by their own national groups. The General Union of Palestinian Women plays an important role in identifying and meeting the needs of that community (Russell, 1988, p. 202) and Asians from the Indian subcontinent have established their own schools, hospitals, social welfare organizations and clubs (United Nations, 1988, p. 36). The Overseas Pakistanis Foundation supports such activities as educational and religious institutions, community centres and associations for Pakistani workers abroad (International Labour Organisation, 1988, p. 35).

The situation may be less favourable, however, for Asian women from new source countries (the Philippines, Sri Lanka and Thailand) and for young single migrants from traditional source countries. These women work an average of 64 hours per week, mainly in domestic service (Shah and Al-Qudsi, 1989, table 7), and have therefore little time for other activities. Their relatively recent presence in Kuwait coupled with their generally low socio-economic status and varied cultural backgrounds limit their opportunities for social integration. Ironically, their social marginalization may be exacerbated by the degree of influence that they are perceived to have on the Kuwaiti social fabric as a result of their roles in the Kuwaiti household. During the early 1980s, the Ministry of Planning conducted a study on the influence of foreign domestic workers on families and society in Kuwait (Kuwait, 1983, p. 125). At about the same time the Arab Planning Institute and the Center for Arab Unity Studies held a symposium that included papers on "The social influence of foreign nannies" and "The consequences of foreign labour on social integration" (Fergany, 1983). Both in those studies and in the popular media, the social influence of Asian domestic workers was viewed in generally unfavourable terms.

G. NATURALIZATION

Throughout the countries of the Gulf Cooperation Council, citizenship requirements are notably restrictive. For most migrants, the period of uninterrupted residence required before an application for naturalization can be made is typically long, ranging from 10 years for Arabs in the United Arab Emirates to 30 years in Kuwait, and knowledge of Arabic is a prerequisite. In Kuwait, nationals of Bahrain, Oman and Qatar are eligible for naturalization after only three years of uninterrupted residence.

Furthermore, the rights of naturalized citizens are different from those of "original" citizens in several instances. Naturalized citizens are not eligible to vote in the United Arab Emirates, and they must wait 10 years in Bahrain and 20 years in Kuwait to do so. The latter restriction has little relevance for women since even "original" female Kuwaiti citizens are not eligible to vote. In Egypt, Iraq, Jordan, Lebanon and the Syrian Arab Republic, the conditions for naturalization are more liberal, with required lengths of residence ranging from four years in Jordan to

10 years in Iraq, and in the case of Jordan the residence requirement may be waived for Arabs (Russell, 1988, table 8-1).

In a review of naturalization laws in eight Arab countries (Russell, 1988), the sex of the applicant was not found to be mentioned explicitly among the conditions for acquiring citizenship. However, implicit sex selectivity may be at work and the citizenship of an applicant's father or mother has different bearings in certain circumstances. For instance, anyone born in Egypt of a foreign father who was also born in Egypt has a right to Egyptian citizenship.

In Kuwait, the wife and children of a man who becomes Kuwaiti by naturalization have the option to take Kuwaiti citizenship or to retain their own (Dib, 1979, p. 8). Recent changes in Kuwaiti law have not altered the options available to non-Kuwaiti women, but have affected those of Kuwaiti women. Under the original Nationality Law, a Kuwaiti woman who married a foreigner was required to take her husband's nationality if the law of his country permitted it. In contrast, Law 100 of 1980 not only allows a Kuwaiti woman married to a foreigner to keep her citizenship, but provides that a woman who lost her citizenship through marriage is eligible to have it restored if she lives in Kuwait.

Law 100 also changed the rules regarding the citizenship of children from mixed marriages. Previously, children of a Kuwaiti mother married to a foreigner were eligible for Kuwaiti citizenship if they maintained residence in Kuwait until their majority, and if the father had abandoned or divorced the mother, or died. The new law eliminates abandonment as a condition, but allows such children to be considered as Kuwaitis only until they reach "the age of reason" (State of Kuwait, 1980; Russell, 1987, p. 204).

H. CONCLUSION

Comparably detailed data on female migration to countries of the Gulf Cooperation Council other than Kuwait are sparse and one can hardly generalize from this single case. Sabagh (1988, p. 169) points

out that in 1985 the ratio of males to females in Kuwait (1.61) was notably lower than that in Bahrain (3.03) or in the United Arab Emirates (2.92), suggesting that migration for family reunification (as was observed until the early 1970s) and demographic settling have been more common in Kuwait than elsewhere in the GCC States. The fact that, by 1985, nearly 30 per cent of the non-Kuwaiti population had been born in Kuwait (Russell, 1988, p. 186) certainly raises the issue of their possible integration or the likelihood of repatriation.

On the other hand, the increase of female worker migration, especially that of Asians starting in the late 1970s, is not unique to Kuwait. Data on the proportion of foreign women in the labour force of receiving countries other than Kuwait are not published for the 1980s, but data for selected labour-sending countries suggest the importance of such migration (Abella, chapter XIV in this volume). Sri Lanka and Indonesia stand out as countries where women predominate in the migrant flows directed to Western Asia. In a survey of migrants from Sri Lanka, Eelens and Speckmann (1990, p. 301) found that some 77 per cent were women, that about one third had gone to Kuwait, a further third to Saudi Arabia and another 16 per cent to the United Arab Emirates. In the late 1980s, Indonesia reported that 87 per cent of migrants going to Kuwait, Saudi Arabia, and the United Arab Emirates were women, with the vast majority going to Saudi Arabia (International Labour Organisation, 1989).

Even among countries that send mostly men as migrant workers, such as the Philippines, female migration to Western Asia is far from insignificant. As of 1987, Filipino women working in GCC countries numbered nearly 45,000 or 15 per cent of the estimated total of Filipino migrant workers abroad that year (International Labour Organisation, 1989).

Given the restrictions on naturalization prevalent in the GCC States and their policies favouring the repatriation of migrant workers upon termination of employment, it is likely that women belonging to the earlier migration cohorts who moved originally for family reunification might find themselves migrating again—this time for retirement in their home countries. While many (if not most) have maintained close ties with their communities of origin, such moves inevitably will entail significant adjustments for both women and their families.

Women who have migrated for short-term employment face common problems in Kuwait and elsewhere in the GCC States. Those engaged in domestic service, in particular, are not entitled to any form of social insurance, are dependent upon their employers for access to medical care and even for personal mobility, and have limited recourse options when they are physically or sexually abused or subject to harsh working conditions.

It is important to note that not all migrant female workers in the GCC States are domestic workers. Nearly 60 per cent of Filipino women in the GCC are employed as nurses in Saudi Arabia and women comprise 57 per cent of the expatriate physicians and veterinarians in Kuwait. The former group is subject to the restrictions on personal mobility that affect all women in Saudi Arabia. Although, except in Kuwait, those in occupations other than domestic service are not necessarily excluded from social insurance, they are subject to the differential treatment accorded to any foreign worker, including exclusion from pension schemes.

The in-depth analysis of the sex selectivity of migration and the status of female migrants in Western Asia remains constrained by the lack of comparative data on both migration flows and migrant stocks by sex as well as by the dearth of information on migration policies. As the case of Kuwait suggests, future studies on this subject need to take into consideration not only trends in flows and policies, but also the changing origins of migrants, since policies are likely to have differential effects on the various national groups involved.

_____

Notes

[1]The apparent decline in the proportion of migrant workers in the GCC countries over the period 1970-1980 is attributable largely to a substantial increase in migration to Iraq where, according to Choucri's data, the number of migrant workers rose from 8,400 in 1975 to approximately one million in the early 1980s. In addition, there were smaller flows to Jordan where the stock of foreign workers amounted to some 120,000 and to the Libyan Arab Jamahiriya which was a major importer of foreign labour throughout the period under discussion.

[2]Visas, "No Objection Certificates", residence permits and work permits are among the various types of documentation used to regulate the admission, stay and mobility within the labour market of migrant workers and their dependants. Visas are issued by the Ministry of the Interior to aliens seeking to enter Kuwait. There are various types of visas: entry visas for work, visit visas, transit visas, temporary visas and, during certain periods, return visas. A "No Objection Certificate" (NOC) may be required by the Ministry of the Interior prior to issuance of a visa or work permit to a prospective migrant seeking entry for employment. When in use, the NOC is issued by the Ministry of Social Affairs and Labour after consideration of labour regulations and manpower requirements. Residence permits with varying lengths of validity are issued by the Ministry of the Interior and are generally required of all aliens who wish to stay in Kuwait. Those permits are a means of controlling the transition between a migrant's admission and the subsequent period of stay, especially since they stipulate the place of residence of an alien residing in Kuwait. Since the mid-1970s, the Ministry of Social Affairs and Labour has been responsible for issuing work permits of different types: "entry permits for work", "first-time work permits", "renewals" (i.e., permits to work in the same job and for the same employer), "cancellation and transfer" (i.e., permits to change jobs or employers), and "cancellation and departure" (permits required by workers who are discontinuing employment in Kuwait and leaving the country).

[3]The mobility of foreign workers engaged by the private sector and by the Government has also been restricted. Ministry of the Interior Order No. 22 of 1975 (Kuwait, 1975) required the approval of the Ministry of Social Affairs and Labour before the residence permit of a foreign worker engaged by the private sector could be changed from one employer's sponsorship to another, and Ministerial Order No. 37 of 1979 (Kuwait, 1979b) stipulated that such a transfer required the agreement of the previous employer and fulfilment of at least one year of service with the latter. As of 1982, non-Kuwaitis in government service were also required to have their employer's consent before being granted a permit to change jobs.

[4]According to 1985 census data (United Nations, 1988, p. 50), 73.3 per cent of non-Kuwaiti women worked in the private sector, as distinct from the government and mixed sectors. If, as Shah and Al-Qudsi (1989, p. 32) reported, 60 per cent of non-Kuwaiti women worked in domestic service in 1985, then 13.3 per cent of them would be working in private establishments covered by the Labour Law.

[5]A recent study of Asian migration (International Labour Organisation, 1988, pp. 50-58) noted that, throughout Western Asia, domestic workers were usually not covered by either employer's liability or social insurance schemes. The situation varies in the case of foreign workers engaged by the private sector or the Government. In Iraq, Jordan and the Libyan Arab Jamahiriya, aliens are insured on the same basis as nationals. In Bahrain and Saudi Arabia, aliens are entitled to the same type of coverage as nationals for work-related injuries but not for pensions.

_____

References

Al-Ra'i al-Am (Kuwait) (1985). 1 April.

Abella, Manolo I. (1995). Sex selectivity of migration regulations governing international migration in Southern or South-eastern Asia. Chapter XIV in the present volume.

Birks, J. S., I. J. Seccombe and C. A. Sinclair (1987). Labour migration in the Arab Gulf States: patterns, trends and prospects.

Paper presented at the Round Table on International Labour Migration in the Philippines and South-East Asia, Manila, 8-11 December 1987.

Choucri, Nazli (1986). Asians in the Arab world: labor migration and public policy. *Middle Eastern Studies* (United Kingdom), vol. 22, No. 2 (April), pp. 252-273.

_____ (1983). *Migration in The Middle East: Transformations, Policies, and Processes*, Vol. I. Technology Adaptation Program, Report 83-8. Cambridge, Massachusetts: Massachusetts Institute of Technology.

Dib, George (1978). Migration and naturalization laws in Egypt, Lebanon, Syria, Jordan, Kuwait, and the United Arab Emirates. In *Population Bulletin of the U.N. Commission for Western Asia*, Part One: "Migration Laws", No. 15 (December), pp. 33-62.

_____ (1979). Migration and Naturalization Laws in Egypt, Lebanon, Syria, Jordan, Kuwait, and the United Arab Emirates. In *Population Bulletin of the U.N. Commission for Western Asia*, Part Two: "Naturalization Laws", No. 16 (June), pp. 3-18.

Eelens, Frank, and J. D. Speckmann (1990). Recruitment of labour migrants for the Middle East: the Sri Lankan case. *International Migration Review* (Staten Island, New York), vol. 24, No. 2, (Summer), pp. 297-322.

Fergany, Nader (1983). *Foreign Manpower in the Arab Gulf States: Research and Proceedings of the Symposium*. Beirut: Center for Arab Unity Studies, August.

International Labour Organisation and United Nations Development Programme (1988). *Agenda For Policy: Asian Migration Project*. Bangkok: International Labour Organisation Regional Office for Asia and the Pacific.

_____ (1989). *Statistical Report 1989. International Labour Migration from Asian Labour-Sending Countries*. Bangkok: International Labour Organisation Regional Office for Asia and the Pacific.

Kuwait (1964). Law No. 38 Concerning Labour in the Private Sector (issued 1 August). Ministry of Social Affairs and Labour.

_____ (1969). Minister of Interior Order No. 3 Enforcing the Aliens Residence Law. Ministry of the Interior.

_____ (1975). Minister of Interior Order No. 22 Promulgating the Implementing Regulations of the Aliens Residence Law and Repealing the Order of the Minister of Interior No. 3 of 1969. Ministry of the Interior.

_____ (1977a). Ministerial Order No. 84 Duly Regulating the Condition and Formalities of Private Servants Ordinary Residence (issued 12 September). Ministry of the Interior.

_____ (1977b). *Statistical Abstract*. Central Statistical Office, Ministry of Planning.

_____ (1978). *Annual Report on Employment and Essential Characteristics of Immigrant Manpower*. Ministry of Social Affairs and Labour, Manpower Organization Office, Employment Control.

_____ (1979a). *Review of Employment Activity and the Basic Features of Expatriate Manpower During the Year 1978*. Ministry of Social Affairs and Labour, Manpower Organization Department, Employment Control Division, Statistical Section (January).

_____ (1979b). Ministerial Order No. 54 Adding a New Article to the Implementing Regulations of the Aliens Residence Law. Ministry of the Interior.

_____ (1979c). Decrees No. 37 and 39, Enforcement of the Private Sector Labour Law. Ministry of Social Affairs and Labour.

_____ (1980). Law 100, Amiri Decree Amending the Nationality Law. Office of the Amir.

_____ (1981). *Statistical Abstract*. Central Statistical Office, Ministry of Planning.

_____ (1982). Law No. 55 Amending some Provisions of the Aliens Residence Law (issued 5 July). Office of the Amir.

_____ (1983). *Yearbook*. Ministry of Information.

_____ (1984a). Ministerial Order No. 77 Concerning Work Permits for Non-Kuwaitis in the Private Sector. Ministry of Social Affairs and Labour.

_____ (1984b). Ministerial Order No. 78 Concerning the Issue of Work Permits for Non-Kuwaitis in Special Sectors. Ministry of Social Affairs and Labour.

_____ (1984c). *Statistical Abstract*. Central Statistical Office, Ministry of Planning.

_____ (1985). *Statistical Abstract*. Central Statistical Office, Ministry of Planning.

_____ (1987). *Statistical Abstract*. Central Statistical Office, Ministry of Planning.

Russell, Sharon Stanton (1987). Uneasy welcome: the political economy of migration policy in Kuwait. Cambridge, Massachusetts: Massachusetts Institute of Technology, Department of Political Science. Unpublished doctoral dissertation.

_____ (1988). Migration and political integration in the Arab world. In *The Politics of Arab Integration*, Giacomo Luciani and Ghassan Salame, eds. London: Croom Helm, pp. 183-210.

_____ (1989). Politics and ideology in migration policy formulation: the case of Kuwait. *International Migration Review* (Staten Island, New York), vol. 23, No. 1 (Spring), pp. 24-47.

Sabagh, Georges (1988). Immigrants - the Arab Gulf countries: "sojourners" or "settlers"? In *The Politics of Arab Integration*, Giacomo Luciani and Ghassan Salame, eds. London: Croom Helm, pp. 159-182.

Shah, Nasra M. (1986). Foreign workers in Kuwait: implications for the Kuwaiti labor force. *International Migration Review* (Staten Island, New York), vol. 20, No. 4 (Winter), pp. 815-832.

_____, and Sulayman S. Al-Qudsi (1989). The changing characteristics of migrant workers in Kuwait. *International Journal of Middle East Studies*, vol. 21, No. 1 (February), pp. 31-55.

United Nations (1980). *The Population Situation in the ECWA Region: Kuwait*. Beirut: Economic Commission for Western Asia.

_____ (1988). *Case Studies in Population Policy: Kuwait*. Population Policy Paper No. 15, ST/ESA/SER.R/82. Sales No. E.90.XIII.30. New York: United Nations.

XVI. MIGRATION OF SRI LANKAN WOMEN TO WESTERN ASIA

*Frank Eelens**

Since 1980, considerable numbers of Sri Lankan citizens have engaged in temporary worker migration to the oil-rich countries of Western Asia. Estimates of the stock of Sri Lankan workers in those countries compiled from a number of sources are presented in table 107. According to those estimates, the stock of Sri Lankan workers in Western Asia is likely to have increased from some 40,000 to 50,000 in the early 1980s to somewhere in the vicinity of 200,000 towards the second half of the decade. Flow statistics indicate that in 1980, 51 per cent of the migrant workers leaving Sri Lanka were women (Rodrigo and Jayatissa, 1989). Most women worked abroad for only a few years. Consequently, they constituted sizeable proportions of the return flows experienced by the country. According to a survey on returning migrants carried out in 1986, about 70 per cent were women, among whom over 60 per cent were married. Out of the returning married women, 67 per cent had left at least one child behind. Almost all Sri Lankan female migrants had been employed as domestic workers while abroad.

During the 1980s, Sri Lankan women were more likely to find a job in the oil-rich countries of Western Asia than their male counterparts because, as oil revenues declined after 1982, the economic slowdown that ensued reduced the demand for male workers, especially those in the construction sector. However, the demand for domestic workers was not greatly affected by the economic slowdown and may even have increased as new lifestyles were adopted. In some oil-rich countries, even lower-income families can afford to hire domestic workers from abroad, whose salaries tend to be low. Furthermore, the availability of domestic workers may free local women from having to devote their time to household chores. Another development militating against the rise of male worker migration has been the constant increase of the recruitment fees charged to male work-

TABLE 107. ESTIMATED NUMBER OF SRI LANKAN MIGRANTS IN THE OIL-RICH COUNTRIES OF WESTERN ASIA
(*Thousands*)

Source	Reference year	Migrants
World Bank	1980	40
Demery (1983)	1981	50
Fernando (1983)	1981	40
Fernando (1983)	1982	50
MARGA (1985).............	1982	132
Korale (1983) ...:..........	1983	150
Korale (1984)	1984	185-215
ARTEP (1985)	1985	200-212[a]
	1988	182-238[a]

Source: Rodrigo and Jayatissa (1989), p. 256.
[a]Projected.

ers, fees that can no longer be afforded by poor households in countries like Sri Lanka. In contrast, the recruitment fees charged directly to domestic workers have tended to be considerably lower, mostly because agents also charge a fee to the prospective employer. Consequently, it is more likely that poor families can afford the expenses involved in female labour migration.

In Sri Lanka, the migration of women to work in the oil-rich countries of Western Asia has become an issue of public debate, especially because various groups in Sri Lankan society strongly disapprove of such migration. They denounce the living and working conditions of women abroad and stress the harmful consequences of the long-term separation of spouses on the well-being of families. The press often reports cases of children who engage in crime because of the absence of their mother, of husbands who squander the remittances sent by their wives, or of marriages that break up because of prolonged separation. There are also numerous reports about women who have been duped by bogus recruitment agents, who have been left stranded on the way to the country of employment, or who have been harassed by their employers. Yet, despite such negative publicity, the Government of Sri Lanka has consis-

---

*Netherlands Interdisciplinary Demographic Institute, The Hague, The Netherlands.

tently promoted the migration of workers to Western Asia. In contrast with the Governments of other labour-exporting countries, including Bangladesh, India, Pakistan and the Philippines, the Government of Sri Lanka has not taken any measures to restrict the migration of women to work abroad. Economic considerations underlie such policies. During the early 1980s, remittances from migrants working abroad were second only to tea exports as a source of foreign exchange for the country (Korale, 1986). Such foreign exchange is needed to pursue social and economic development plans, especially given the deteriorating political situation in Sri Lanka.

This paper reports on the results of a project whose purpose was to document the social and economic context in which labour migration from Sri Lanka to Western Asia took place and to assess the consequences of labour migration for Sri Lankan society. The study focused on the labour migration of persons belonging to the lower socio-economic rungs of society. Consequently, highly educated migrants who left to work as professionals in Western Asian countries were not included in the study. Their numbers, however, were small in comparison with the number of unskilled migrants. The study included a survey carried out in the districts of Colombo and Gampala between December 1985 and July 1986. The survey covered a random sample that included 899 returning migrants, 858 close relatives of current migrants, and 409 non-migrants. In addition, an anthropological study of the consequences of labour migration at the individual, family and community level was carried out in four communities: the towns of Colombo and Matale, and two villages of southern Sri Lanka.

A. MIGRATION AS A MEANS TO ENSURE HOUSEHOLD SURVIVAL

As Lim (chapter III in this volume) suggests, the societal restrictions to which female migration is normally subject can change because of economic necessity. The labour migration of women from Sri Lanka is a case in point, since it occurs despite the strong moral objections that Sri Lankan society has against the migration of women on their own. One major reason for the continued participation of women

in labour migration is financial need. Indeed, most of the women leaving to work abroad belong to the poorer groups of society. Thus, households from which female migrants originate, tend to have practically no other adult member with a stable income (Brochmann, 1986). The migration of women therefore becomes a necessity to ensure household survival.

There is no doubt that the remittances sent by migrant workers from abroad contribute to resolve the economic problems faced by the families left behind. Most Sri Lankan women who engage in labour migration do so to provide the basic necessities for their families back home and to work towards the improvement of their lives in the long run. Thus, 42 per cent of the informants interviewed indicated that providing an income for their family was the main motive for their migration (Eelens and Schampers, 1989, p. 71). Returning migrants were asked whether they thought that migration could ameliorate their lives in the long run. The views on that point expressed by women who had been domestic workers abroad did not differ significantly from those of skilled and unskilled male migrants. Thus, 84.3 per cent of the 899 returning migrants interviewed thought that migration could lead to long-term improvements. The same view was expressed by 86.1 per cent of the women who had been domestic workers abroad. However, when asked whether they had expected greater financial benefits prior to migration, 74.9 per cent of all returning migrants and 74.7 per cent of the women who had been domestic workers stated that the outcome of migration had been disappointing.

Most of the female domestic workers who had close family members in Sri Lanka reported that they had sent their full salary to their family every month or every other month. Most of the remittances received were spent on daily consumption and, consequently, savings were generally small. Indeed, 64.5 per cent of the women who had been domestic workers reported having no savings when they returned home and very few had made any investments. As would be expected, households with a larger number of dependants were less likely to save. The migrants themselves were more likely to save while abroad than relatives back home. However, relatives and neighbours who were in charge of spending remittances did so rationally, especially given the lower consumption standards prevalent in rural areas. Nevertheless, households tended to become dependent on the migrant's remittances and the family was often confronted with serious economic difficulties when the migrant returned. Consequently, many women tended to engage in repeat migration (Brochmann, 1986). Among the 699 returning female migrants who had been domestic workers and who were included in the survey, 64 per cent were trying to obtain a new contract to work abroad.

B. RECRUITMENT

To be successful, labour migration depends on a reliable recruitment procedure. The recruitment of Sri Lankan women to work in domestic service abroad generally takes place through private recruitment agencies or through personal and social contacts established by the prospective migrant herself. Significantly and in contrast with the recruitment of male labour, the recruitment of women as domestic workers is left almost completely in the hands of the private sector. The Bureau of Foreign Employment makes few efforts to place domestic workers abroad, probably because the Government wishes to promote the more lucrative migration of male workers and because the migration of men employed by established commercial enterprises abroad is easier to monitor than that of women working for private individuals.

Although most Sri Lankan female migrants are placed abroad by private recruitment agencies (68 per cent of the domestic workers interviewed got their jobs through those agencies), they tend to make far greater use of informal channels than their male counterparts (32 per cent of the female domestic workers used informal channels compared to 16.5 per cent of male workers). The social contacts inherent to the work of domestic workers are the likely cause of such outcome. Prospective female migrants attach great value to the mediation of a migrant whom they know. The expected trustworthiness of the potential employer as well as the possibility of receiving help and advice from an experienced migrant play an important role in facilitating migration. The

prospective employer is also likely to view the friend or relative of a good domestic worker as a more desirable candidate than a complete stranger (Mook, 1989).

Throughout Asia high costs are involved in securing a job in the oil-rich countries of Western Asia through private recruitment agencies. In Thailand and the Philippines, for instance, the average cost of obtaining a job abroad has been estimated at about US$900 (Arnold and Shah, 1984, p. 299). Migrants have to work for months to repay the debts they incur while securing a job abroad. The cost of job placement has a direct impact on the level and composition of contract migration. In Sri Lanka, the fees charged by private recruitment agencies are considerably higher than the costs involved in migration arranged by friends or relatives. However, it is becoming increasingly difficult for Sri Lankan workers to find jobs in Western Asia through informal and less costly arrangements. In 1980, 64 per cent of the migrants interviewed were able to find a job abroad without having to pay a placement fee, but by 1985 only 45 per cent were able to do so. An analysis of trends and differentials in the recruitment fees paid by migrants who secured a job through commercial recruitment agencies indicates that, with the exception of professionals, placement fees have risen markedly since the beginning of the 1980s (Eelens and Speckmann, 1990). Between 1980 and 1986, the fees paid by skilled male workers increased more than fivefold and those paid by female domestic workers rose from approximately Rs. 826 to 4,314.[1] The high fees charged to male workers result from the declining labour demand in the main receiving countries and the virtually inexhaustible supply in sending countries. Consequently, poor households can no longer afford to send their men to work in Western Asia and even the fees involved in placing women abroad are beyond the means of many poor households. Thus, some 60 per cent of female migrants who obtain a job in Western Asia through recruitment agents have to borrow money to pay the fee and about a quarter of them (25.5 per cent) obtain loans from private money lenders or by pawning jewellery and other valuables. Because interest rates in the streets of Colombo are usually above 15 per cent per month and can even be as high as 30 per cent monthly, women must devote considerable proportions of their earnings while abroad to repay such loans.

To reduce recruitment costs, the prospective migrant can try to obtain employment through the mediation of relatives or friends already working in Western Asia. However, that placement method is not without cost, since mediators often request some financial compensation for their services (Mook, 1989). Because the migrant would usually have to pay such compensation only after having worked for a few months abroad, there are still advantages in that means of placement.

A major source of concern regarding female labour migration is the high incidence of problems stemming from the activities of illegal or bogus recruitment agents. Almost weekly, Sri Lankan newspapers publish articles about agents who charge high recruitment fees from prospective female migrants, only to disappear subsequently. There are also reports of women who are left stranded on the way to the country of employment. Since none of the oil-rich countries of Western Asia has an embassy in Sri Lanka, visas have to be obtained abroad, usually in Bahrain, India or Pakistan. In most cases, visas are obtained by the recruitment agent or the prospective employer, but illegal agents send migrants through Manama, Bombay or Karachi, presumably to obtain the necessary documents, but in fact to leave them stranded without money.

C. Living and working conditions in Western Asia

The living and working conditions of domestic workers the world over are generally poor. Among the female migrants interviewed, 65 per cent reported that they worked more than 12 hours daily and over one third (35 per cent) reported that they worked more than 15 hours per day. Only 13 per cent reported that they had one day off per week and 71 per cent did not get any paid holidays during their contract period. The average salary of Sri Lankan domestic workers is low. Although the Sri Lankan Bureau of Foreign Employment had established that the minimum acceptable salary for migrant women engaged in domestic service in Western Asia should be US$100 per month, only 29 per cent of the domestic workers interviewed earned at least that amount per month. The policies of countries of origin seem therefore to be ineffective in safeguarding the rights of female migrant workers while abroad.

Since nearly all domestic workers (99.4 per cent) reported that they lived in their employer's home, it is likely that their living conditions represented a considerable improvement compared with those prevailing in their own homes in Sri Lanka. Table 108 presents information on the types of facilities that migrants had in their living quarters while abroad (Spaan, 1988). It indicates that the living quarters of migrant women tended to have somewhat better facilities than those of male migrants, most of whom lived in work camps or had to find their own cheap accommodation. However, female migrants were more likely to work in environments that limited their social contacts either with friends or family (see table 109). Contacts included both meeting people or calling someone by telephone. Although 27 per cent of the migrant women interviewed reported that they had daily contacts with friends or relatives, 31 per cent reported no such contacts whatsoever. In comparison, only 20 per cent of the migrant men reported no contacts and a full 72 per cent reported daily contacts. Clearly, migrant women, especially those engaged in domestic service, have fewer opportunities for meeting friends or relatives, since their mobility outside their employer's home is restricted and they have no access to the telephone.

TABLE 108. Sri Lankan migrants reporting specific types of housing facilities in the living quarters occupied while working in Western Asia
(*Percentage*)

	Male	Female
Air conditioning	80	86
Fan	60	78
Electricity	92	96
Running water	36	36
Bath/shower	24	28
Television	32	48
Radio	20	52

Source: E. Spaan, *Labour Migration from Sri Lanka to the Middle East* (Instituut Culturele Antropologie Leiden, No. 83, 1988), p. 157.

TABLE 109. SRI LANKAN MIGRANTS REPORTING VARIOUS
FREQUENCIES OF CONTACT WITH RELATIVES OR FRIENDS
WHILE WORKING IN WESTERN ASIAN COUNTRIES
(*Percentage*)

	Male	Female
Daily contact	72	27
Every few days	—	8
Weekly	8	10
Few times a months	—	6
Once monthly	—	8
Every few months	—	4
Once yearly or less	—	3
No contact	20	31

Source: E. Spaan, *Labour Migration from Sri Lanka to the Middle East* (Instituut Culturele Antropologie Leiden, No. 83, 1988), p. 160.
NOTE: Em dash (—) indicates that the amount is nil or negligible.

Spaan (1988) documents the isolation in which domestic workers live by noting that migrant women reported that their only means of communication with friends was by throwing letters over the wall to the domestic worker in the neighbouring house or by giving letters and cassettes to street cleaners who acted as messengers. Such tapes had become a popular means of communication.

The first few months in a Western Asian country are probably the most stressful for domestic workers because of the great differences in living conditions, environment, culture, climate, attire and language. The worker must adapt to the new culture largely on her own, given her relative isolation. Since Sri Lankan domestic workers know neither English nor Arabic, they must learn by a process of trial and error, and the inability to communicate and express their feelings, to get their doubts and fears cleared up produces stress with which the migrant must cope largely without outside help (Camaratunge, 1985).

Sri Lankan domestic workers in Western Asia find themselves in an overly dependent position and are liable to exploitation. Domestic workers are dependent on their employers with regard to almost all aspects of life. Because they normally live in their employer's house and are restricted from leaving it, they are entirely dependent on the employer for food and clothing. Often, their dependence is reinforced when the employer takes possession of the domestic

worker's passport upon her arrival. Domestic workers generally depend on the employer's family for social contacts and information. They usually accompany the family in outings or visits and are thus able to meet other domestic workers. In some cases, the employer mediates the communication between the domestic worker and her own family in Sri Lanka by mailing letters or allowing the use of the telephone. According to some domestic workers, employers often control such communication in order to prevent them from becoming homesick and leaving prematurely.

For some domestic workers, the only way of getting some time for themselves is to go to church on Fridays. In Kuwait, for instance, the Catholic Church is known to be a popular meeting place. Many employers do not permit their personnel to go there because attendance at church involves the free intermingling of the sexes. Since Buddhists and Hindus are not able to practice freely their religion in Kuwait, domestic workers tend to misinform their employers about their true religion. Among the domestic workers studied by Spaan (1988), one in five had told her employer that she was Catholic, while she was, in fact, Buddhist or Hindu.

Domestic workers in Western Asian countries are prone to exploitation because labour laws do not protect them. Consequently, employer malpractices, such as the non-payment or the late payment of salaries, breaches of contract, lack of payment for overtime etc., cannot be dealt with in the local courts. Only in the case of serious criminal offenses can legal action be taken (Shadid, Spaan and Speckmann, 1989). Because of the lack of legal protection regarding working conditions and salaries, domestic workers are frequently duped by employers. Exploitation is facilitated by the fact that a large number of female migrants leave Sri Lanka without a signed contract. Thus, 35.5 per cent of the domestic workers interviewed were not in possession of a contract upon their departure from Sri Lanka and 9.9 per cent of them had to sign a contract drawn up in Arabic upon their arrival in the country of employment. Yet, only 20 per cent of the female migrants interviewed reported not to have been satisfied with the living and working conditions in the countries of employment.

The most common types of irregularities in the treatment of domestic workers are withholding or delaying the payment of salaries, refusal to grant periods of rest, withholding of the worker's passport, refusal to provide a return ticket at the end of the contract period, physical violence, sexual abuse and docked wages. Only a few domestic workers protest against the mistreatment they undergo. Among the migrants interviewed, only 3.7 per cent of those working in domestic service reported to have submitted a complaint to the recruitment agent in the country of employment; 3.1 per cent reported that they had gone to the police, and 1.2 per cent had asked the Sri Lankan Embassy for assistance. A further 10.1 per cent had openly complained to their employer or "madam" but had not sought official redress. The nature of the complaints lodged is provided in table 110. The main cause of complaint was too heavy a workload. Physical violence was the cause of complaint of 13.3 per cent of all those lodging a complaint and 8.3 per cent of all respondents reported that they were beaten at least once a week. Among the 699 domestic workers interviewed, 16 reported that they had been raped.

Given the unfavourable working conditions that domestic workers often find abroad and the difficulties in adaptation to a confined and alien environment, a high proportion of female domestic workers return to Sri Lanka before the end of their contracts. Women are more likely than men to return prematurely to their home country. Thus, about 12 per cent of the domestic workers return home within the

first year of employment in Western Asia; 20.6 per cent do so before having completed 18 months abroad, and another 6 per cent return home between 19 and 22 months after their arrival in the country of employment.[2] In the case of male migrants, the equivalent proportions are 8.3, 14.6 and 5 per cent, respectively. The average duration of stay abroad was found to be 24.4 months for female migrants and 37.9 months for male migrants (Eelens, 1988, p. 402). These data indicate that, despite their vulnerability to exploitation and the hardships of work abroad, many women find that the benefits of labour migration outweigh the risks involved. Indeed, some women are treated well by their employers and become almost part of the family.

D. MIGRATION AND THE FAMILY LEFT BEHIND

The migration of an unmarried son or daughter generally has a small effect on a family's daily routine, whereas the long-term departure of a parent or spouse has more important consequences. Apart from the emotional toll of separation, domestic tasks have to be reassigned, especially if the migrant is the mother of young children. In a nuclear family the problem of finding someone who will take care of the children left behind is likely to be more difficult to solve than in an extended family where other adult women may undertake the tasks of the absent mother. Among the migrants interviewed, 69 per cent were living in nuclear families before their departure. Generally, close relatives of the migrant woman were engaged to take over such activities as cooking, washing or caring for children. Otherwise, there was severe neglect of essential household tasks. Neglect of the children left behind was frequent in poor slum environments (de Bruijn and others, 1989).

The separation of spouses because of migration has important impacts on marital stability. Table 111 presents data on the incidence of marital disruption (divorce or separation) among ever-married migrants returning from abroad. The marital status of returning migrants was recorded at two points in time, before departure and at the time of the survey. For comparison purposes, the percentage of divorced or separated persons is also presented for the population of Colombo as a whole (de Bruijn and others,

TABLE 110. SRI LANKAN FEMALE MIGRANTS REPORTING COMPLAINTS, BY REASON OF COMPLAINT

Reason	Percentage
Reduction of wage	5.5
Facilities retrieved	1.6
Unsatisfactory living conditions	6.3
Breach of contract	5.5
Too heavy a workload	47.2
Sexual harassment	7.1
Physical assault	13.3
Non-payment of salary	3.2
Other complaint	10.3

Source: Survey on Social, Economic and Demographic Consequences of Labour Migration from Sri Lanka to the Middle East.

TABLE 111. DIVORCED OR SEPARATED PERSONS AMONG THOSE
EVER MARRIED, BY MIGRATION STATUS AND SEX

| | Urban Colombo | Returning migrants separated or divorced | |
		Before migration	At the time of interview
Men..................	0.7	1.6	1.6
Women..............	1.0	8.4	16.5
Number of cases ..	..	671	671

Source: de Bruijn and others (1989).

NOTE: Two dots (..) indicate that data are not available or are not separately reported.

1989). The data for Colombo indicate that divorce or separation is rare: only 0.7 per cent of ever-married men and 1 per cent of women were divorced or separated. The percentage of separated and divorced men among returning male migrants, whether before or after migration, does not differ markedly from that of the population of Colombo. Among returning female migrants, however, the proportions of divorced or separated women were several times greater than those among the female population of Colombo, amounting to 8.4 per cent before and 16.5 per cent after migration. As in other contexts, divorced and separated women are more likely to migrate because of financial need than their married counterparts. For those women, there is often no possibility of gainful employment in Sri Lanka, especially of employment providing a salary sufficient to support dependent children. The fact that almost twice as many women were separated or divorced some time after migration than before, suggests that migration may have negative effects on the stability of marriage. Yet, since migration seems to have virtually no effect on the stability of the marriages of migrant men, there is the possibility that migrant women may be selected among those whose marriages were unstable to start with. Indeed, there is evidence indicating that the incidence of separation among prospective female migrants increases during the year preceding migration. Such increase may be related to marital tensions stemming from the decision to migrate (women may insist to do so against the wishes of the husband) and to those rooted in previous marital discord. Moreover, as already noted, separation itself can lead to migration, as separated or divorced women are forced to support themselves and their children.

Assuming that in 1985 there were 200,000 Sri Lankan workers in Western Asia, that they had the age and sex distribution proposed by Korale (1985) as well as the number of children per migrant reported by that author, the number of children in Sri Lanka who had at least one parent working abroad was estimated (Schampers and Eelens, 1986). The estimates obtained for 1985 were 100,000 children whose father was working in Western Asia and 260,000 children whose mother was working abroad, 200,000 of whom were under the age of 10. Furthermore, an estimated 19,000 children were less than a year old when their mother or father left to work abroad for an extended period.

Interviews with 45 teachers in Colombo about the effects of labour migration on the well-being of children elicited their views on its positive and negative consequences on education. Their opinions are presented below. The figures in brackets indicate the number of times a certain topic was mentioned as important by the teachers interviewed. On the positive side, all those topics scoring high are related to the direct financial and material benefits of labour migration. Almost half the teachers indicated that the children of migrants had better access to needed supplies (books, pens, pencils etc.). It was thought that migrant parents spent more money on education than non-migrants (14), that they sent their children to more expensive schools (17), that they paid the fees for facilities and services regularly (8), and that their children were better dressed.

However, teachers remarked that a lack of love and affection had a negative effect on the school performance of the children of migrants (20) and that caretakers were not seriously interested in the mental and educational well-being of the children left behind (18). Studies of the urban poor indicate that the negative effects of the mother's migration on the education of the children left behind were worse than those associated with the father's absence. Among the teachers interviewed, 26 considered that the migration of the mother was harmful to the education and general well-being of her children, and 10 stated that the absence of the father is not harmful and may even be beneficial. Children in the lower grades seem to be especially affected by the absence of the mother. Several female teachers said that many young children whose mothers had migrated were in need of affection and were likely to place the teacher in the role of the mother-figure. One small boy even wanted to leave his father to go and live with his female teacher. Teachers suggested that the psychological stress produced by parental absence resulted in more playfulness (14), stubbornness (7), unruly behaviour (6), a lack of discipline (4), and high absenteeism (2).

Teachers complained that neither the migrant parents nor the caretakers were interested in the education of the children left behind (18) and that encouragement in learning was lacking (4). Consequently, the children of migrants lacked proper supervision after schoolhours (14), were less punctual with their homework and tended not to study after school (4). It is possible, however, that the effect of the migration of parents on the education of children left behind may be quite different in rural areas than in the slums and shanties of Colombo, especially because the social control system in rural areas is more strict and encompassing: strict in the sense that the behaviour of children is more controlled than in urban areas and encompassing in the sense that, within the extended family, the absence of a parent does not deprive the child of effective care.

An important consequence of the migration of mothers is its impact on the prospects for older children, especially female children who are often compelled to drop out of school to undertake the household and child-care tasks that the mother used to perform. Young girls who thus adopt the mother's role at an early age are prone to experience significant psychological stress. Furthermore, when teenage girls lack a mother's supervision, they are more likely to enter into love affairs at young ages.

E. LABOUR MIGRATION AND THE STATUS OF WOMEN

Many researchers have argued that the migration of women can be liberating by initiating a process of change from tradition to modernity (Kosack, 1976; Abadan-Unat, 1977; Whiteford, 1978). Thus, Abadan-Unat (1977) argues that migration contributes to the emancipation of women by weakening extended family relations; promoting the adoption of nuclear family patterns; contributing to the fragmentation of family structure; facilitating the participation of women in the labour force and their access to information; promoting a decline of religious practices and a stronger belief in equal opportunities for girls and boys, especially in terms of education; and leading to the adoption of consumption-oriented behaviour and norms.

However, in most of those studies, moulded in the mainstream idiom of the modernization theory of the 1970s, naively complacent and ethnocentric assumptions prevail. Not only do they implicitly assume that the poles of attraction of female migration are identical to the centres of modernization, but they also equate modernization with a Western style of life. Differences in the economic, social and political conditions in the regions of origin and destination are usually neglected or minimized. Furthermore, the heterogeneity of the position of women prior to and during migration as well as the type of work migrant women engage in are ignored. Does migration from Sri Lanka to Western Asia create new opportunities for the emancipation of female contract workers? If by female emancipation one means the process leading towards a fuller realization of a woman's own potentials by removing man-made barriers, in our opinion, for the majority of Sri Lanka women, labour migration to Western Asia hinders or even reverses that process.

There are several reasons for that conclusion. First, women in most Western Asian countries are in an earlier stage of emancipation than in Sri Lanka. Women in Sri Lanka have better access to education than their counterparts in many Western Asian countries; the labour force participation of Sri Lankan women is far higher and more diversified than that of Arab women in Western Asia; in Sri Lanka, women have similar political and legal rights as men, and greater freedom of movement and expression than their female counterparts in Western Asia. The difference in status between Sri Lankan women and those in the oil-producing countries of Western Asia is illustrated by the female literacy rates for Sri

Lanka and Kuwait. Whereas in 1986, 93 per cent of the women in Sri Lanka could read and write, only 50.3 per cent of those in Kuwait could do so (UNESCWA, 1987). There are, indeed, considerable differences in the degree of emancipation enjoyed by women belonging to the various social classes and ethnic groups in Sri Lankan society. However, even Muslim women in Sri Lanka, who are considered to be the least emancipated, are less constrained than women in general in the countries of employment.

When a Sri Lankan woman migrates to Western Asia to become a domestic worker within an Arab household, working conditions are such that the migrant is exposed to and socialized into the typical Arab norms and values regarding appropriate behaviour for women. Because of her dependent position, the domestic worker cannot question, much less challenge, the prevailing norms and values. Given that communication with her peers is restricted, there are few opportunities to question the status quo. Furthermore, domestic workers know that their stay abroad will be easier and more remunerative if they accept their subordinate position. Consequently, their experience in Western Asia is unlikely to be emancipating.

Most Sri Lankan female migrants are the sole or most important source of income for the families that they have left behind. Their increased financial contribution to the household could, under normal circumstances, lead to new opportunities for emancipation and a gain in status. However, that is not the case for women engaging in domestic service abroad. Having been separated during prolonged periods from their immediate relatives and living within a constricting environment, they are ill-equipped to take up new challenges. Furthermore, since upon their return, most of the money that they have remitted has already been spent, they have few means to exert power. Because of the poor financial situation of their families, women are often compelled to migrate in order to ensure family survival, but such migration is hardly beneficial for the women themselves. In our opinion, the process of women's emancipation is hardly enhanced when women put themselves at the service of their families, sacrificing their own interests and even renouncing direct control over family decisions or over the use of

remittances. Furthermore, the emancipation of returning female migrants can hardly be enhanced by the lack of respect accorded to women who migrate to engage in domestic service abroad. Allegations about the misconduct of Sri Lankan women while abroad are common, and it is considered a sign of need and poverty to engage in such migration.

F. GOVERNMENT POLICY ON LABOUR MIGRATION IN SRI LANKA

In general, the Government of Sri Lanka imposes no serious restrictions on citizens, whether male or female, wishing to migrate. On the contrary, Sri Lankan policy has actively promoted labour migration by, among other things, the establishment of foreign missions in Western Asian countries to help solve the problems of Sri Lankan citizens working in them, the granting of two years of leave for government employees wishing to work abroad, and the granting of subsidized air fares to migrant workers going to Western Asia.

During the 1980s, some measures were taken to protect the interests of migrants. They concentrated mostly on recruitment procedures. An important step forward was the establishment, through Act No. 21 of 1985, of the Sri Lanka Bureau of Foreign Employment (BFE). The BFE thus became a unit independent from the Department of Labour and took over all tasks related to the placement of workers abroad. The 1985 Act also contained a number of radical modifications concerning the activities of private recruitment agents. For instance, an agent was henceforth obliged to pay Rs. 10,000 (about US$370) a year for a license. Moreover, each agent had to post a bank guarantee amounting to Rs. 100,000, to be used in covering the repatriation expenses of any migrants who might be left stranded. The Act also established that the commission which the recruiter could legally charge the migrant should not exceed Rs. 2,700 (about US$100).

It must be recognized, however, that the Government of Sri Lanka has limited possibilities to intervene in improving the living and working conditions of domestic workers in Western Asian countries. It has already been mentioned that few domestic workers obtain salaries that meet the minimum standards set by the Government. Moreover, the Sri Lankan missions in Western Asian countries have few means of intervention in solving problems related to employer malpractices because of the lack of labour laws protecting the rights of household workers in the countries of employment. Lastly, domestic workers may be prevented by their employers or by recruiters from contacting their representatives abroad.

G. Conclusion

Despite the strong moral objections prevalent in Sri Lankan society to the migration of women on their own, considerable numbers of women engage in labour migration as a result of the economic difficulties faced by their families. Most spend several years employed as domestic workers by Arab families in Western Asian countries. Their migration is mostly prompted by the survival needs of their families and generally does not result in the long-term improvement of the family's economic situation. There is no denying, however, that the remittances of domestic workers make possible a temporary improvement in the living conditions of their families left behind.

The evidence on the situation of Sri Lankan migrant women in Western Asian countries indicates that their position is weak throughout the migration process. Once in the country of employment, they receive low wages for long working hours and are prone to exploitation because of their dependent position and lack of widely recognized rights. Many domestic workers return to Sri Lanka before the end of their contracts because they are not able to cope with the stringent living and working conditions that they find abroad. Given the high recruitment costs that many women have to bear and the high dependence of their families on remittances, a premature return may have serious negative consequences for the family.

During the 1980s, the Government of Sri Lanka developed various initiatives designed to improve the protection of Sri Lankan migrants abroad. One of its most important measures was to establish the Sri Lanka Bureau of Foreign Employment and to strengthen the Fraud Bureau's efforts to curb the practices of illegal recruitment agents. However, given the magnitude of labour migration, those organizations are not suitably equipped to deal with existing problems and have therefore been unable to protect female migrants adequately during the recruitment process. Furthermore, the possibilities of protecting female migrants while abroad are even more restricted. Although some female migrants lodge complaints with the Sri Lankan Embassies in Western Asia, legal action usually cannot be pursued unless a specific criminal offence has taken place. Even then, because of the domestic nature of most offences, cases normally hinge on the word of the employer against that of the domestic worker, and tend to be resolved in favour of the former.

Sri Lankan female migrants in Western Asia are in an unfavourable situation for a number of reasons, including that they are foreigners and do not have the same rights as the women who are citizens; that women in general are second class citizens in the oil-rich countries of Western Asia; that, not being Muslims, many have difficulty adapting to the local culture; and that most of them come from lower socio-economic classes that command little respect in the country of employment.

Despite the multitude of problems encountered by Sri Lankan migrant women both with respect to their work abroad and to the family left behind, migration is often the only means of securing a viable wage. If the possibility of female migration were no longer there, thousands of Sri Lankan families would suffer increased deprivation. Consequently, it is not surprising that, despite the negative aspects of migrating to work abroad, women continue to engage in labour migration since it provides the only hope of a half-decent livelihood for their families at home.

Notes

[1] At the time of the study, 27 rupees were equivalent to one United States dollar.

[2] The cut-off point was taken to be 22 months instead of 24 because some migrants are allowed to spend their paid holidays in Sri Lanka at the end of their two year contract. They thus return home two months earlier.

Abadan-Unat, Nermin (1977). Implications of migration on emancipation and pseudo-emancipation of Turkish women. *International Migration Review* (Staten Island, New York), vol. 6, No. 1 (Spring), pp. 31-57.

Amjad, Rashid, ed. (1989). *To the Gulf and Back: Studies on the Economic Impact of Asian Labour Migration*. New Delhi: International Labour Organisation-Asian Employment Programme (ILO-ARTEP).

Arnold, Fred, and Nasra Shah (1984). Asian labor migration to the Middle East. *International Migration Review* (Staten Island, New York), vol. 18, No. 2 (Summer), pp. 294-319.

de Bruijn, B., and others (1989). Labour migration, household structure and their impact on the well-being of children. Paper presented at the General Conference of the International Union for the Scientific Study of Population, held in New Delhi, 20-27 September 1989.

Brochmann, Grete (1986). Female migration from Sri Lanka to the Middle East. Mimeographed.

Camaratunge, L. K. (1985). *Coping with the Unknown: Sri Lankan Domestic Aides in West Asia*. Colombo: International Centre for Ethnic Studies.

Eelens, Frank (1988). Early return of Sri Lankan migrants in the Middle East. *International Migration* (Geneva, Switzerland), vol. 26, No. 4, pp. 401-415.

_____, and T. Schampers (1989). Survival migration: the Sri Lankan case. In *Women, Migrants and Tribals*, G. Lieten, O. Nieuwenhuys and L. Schenk-Sandbergen, eds. Manohar.

Eelens Frank, and J. D. Speckmann (1990). Recruitment of labor migrants for the Middle East: the Sri Lankan case. *International Migration Review* (Staten Island, New York), vol. 24, No. 2 (Summer), pp. 297-322.

Korale, R. B. M. (1986). Migration for employment in the Middle East: its demographic and socio-economic effects on Sri Lanka.

In *Asian Labor Migration. Pipeline to the Middle East*, Fred Arnold and Nasra Shah, eds. Boulder, Colorado and London: Westview Press.

_____, and others (1985). *Foreign Employment. Sri Lanka Experience*. Colombo: Employment and Manpower Planning Division, Ministry of Plan Implementation.

Kosack, G. (1976). The move to western Europe. On step towards emancipation. *Race and Class* (London, United Kingdom), vol. 17, No. 4, pp. 369-379.

Lim, Lin Lean (1995). The status of women and international migration. Chapter III in the present volume.

Mook, T. (1989). Middle East migration at the micro-level: a village case-study. Mimeographed.

Rodrigo, Chandra, and R. A. Jayatissa (1989). Maximising benefits from labour migration: Sri Lanka. In *To the Gulf and Back*, Rashid Ajmad, ed. New Delhi: International Labour Organisation-Asian Employment Programme (ILO-ARTEP).

Schampers, T., and Frank Eelens (1986). The effect of migration on the well-being of Sri Lankan children left behind. Paper presented at the Workshop on Foreign Employment held at the MARGA Institute, Colombo, December 1986.

Shadid, W. A., E. J. Spaan and J. D. Speckmann (1989). Labour migration and the policy of the Gulf States. Mimeographed.

Spaan, E. J. (1988). Labour migration from Sri Lanka to the Middle East. Instituut Culturele Antropologie Leiden, No. 83.

United Nations Economic and Social Commission for Western Asia (UNESCWA) (1987). *Demographic and Related Socio-Economic Data Sheets for Countries of the Economic and Social Commission for Western Asia as Assessed in 1986*. Amman.

Whiteford, M. B. (1978). Women, migration and social change. A Colombian case study. *International Migration Review* (Staten Island, New York), vol. 12, No. 2 (Summer), pp. 236-247.

XVII. HOUSEHOLD ECONOMY AND GENDER IN INTERNATIONAL MIGRATION: THE CASE OF BOLIVIANS IN ARGENTINA

*Jorge Balán**

This paper explores the role of gender in international migration by focusing on Bolivian migration to Argentina. Gender has been recognized as an important variable in migration ever since Ravenstein proposed his famous "laws of migration" about a century ago (Ravenstein, 1885). Gender has been used as an independent variable to study the process of selectivity involved, that is, to understand in what circumstances more men than women migrate. Thus, Ravenstein explained the fact that the proportion of women among international migrants was lower than among those moving within a country by suggesting that women were more mobile over shorter distances than men. The assumption underlying such observations is that gender makes a difference because it is associated with specific roles in the society of origin.

Bolivian migration to Argentina has a long history, whose various stages have been characterized by different levels of female participation in migration flows. This paper will review the changes that Bolivian migration to Argentina has undergone during the past 50 years. It will then focus on the changing roles of men and women in the Bolivian family by considering kinship systems and the role of women in the household economy of villages and rural areas in Cochabamba, the area of origin of many migrants to Buenos Aires. An understanding of the different roles and status of men and women at origin is crucial to understand the processes leading to migration and the differential participation of women in the ensuing flows. By analysing the contrasting migration experience of men and women both at the place of origin (a village in Cochabamba) and at the place of destination (the city of Buenos Aires), the paper will highlight the ways in which migration interacts with the status of women and its likely long-term impact on that status.

*Centro de Estudios de Estado y Sociedad (CEDES), Buenos Aires, Argentina.

A. BOLIVIAN MIGRATION TO ARGENTINA

The 1930s marked a turning point in migration to Argentina. European immigration, which had played a crucial role in the economic and demographic growth of the country since 1860, lost impetus, while migration from neighbouring countries increased. Flows from Bolivia, Chile, Paraguay and, to a lesser extent, Brazil and Uruguay were initially a response to regional labour scarcity in the primary sector of Argentina's border areas. Workers from neighbouring countries were attracted by the jobs available in the North-western (Salta and Jujuy), Southern (Patagonia) and North-eastern (Misiones and Corrientes) regions of the country. Although most of the foreign workers recruited were men, women and children often followed and helped in harvesting or provided services to male workers. Temporary jobs for men could be supplemented by the jobs open to women, so that an increasing number of families could settle in the border areas. Settlement in towns, rather than villages or rural areas, was favoured since urban areas offered a better mix of employment opportunities for both men and women. In the long run, technological change and economic crises led to a decline in rural employment, further stimulating the urbanization of migrants from neighbouring countries. Ever since the 1950s, migrants have been increasingly attracted by the largest industrial centre, the metropolitan area of Buenos Aires, where jobs in construction, industry and services paid better wages than those available either in the countries of origin or in the border provinces.

Bolivian migration to Argentina became sizeable when the sugar plantations in Salta and Jujuy replaced domestic seasonal workers with those hired across the border. Long-standing wage differentials, reinforced by changes in Bolivian society arising from the 1932-1935 war, political upheaval and

278

agrarian reform, made Bolivian labour a viable alternative for the sugar plantations. During the 1940s and 1950s this system of labour migration, which recruited mostly male workers, expanded both in terms of the numbers involved and of its geographical scope. Thus, plantations and farms throughout the region and in the Western province of Mendoza proceeded to hire Bolivian harvest workers. Different harvest seasons for the various crops gave rise to an almost year-round labour demand with urban demand filling the gaps left. Consequently, many foreign workers settled in villages or towns from which they could maximize their job opportunities by moving around the country (Whiteford, 1981). Foreign women, who tended to follow men during the harvest, entered the country in greater numbers and long-term settlement in urban areas became common.

Starting in the 1960s, the mechanization of sugar-cane production and a decline in its processing eroded the demand for migrant labour in the North-west. Concomitantly, Bolivian nationals were attracted by job opportunities in Buenos Aires, especially those in construction. The urban labour market in Argentina was characterized by a chronic scarcity of unskilled labour to fill unstable and physically demanding jobs, jobs that Bolivian, Chilean and Paraguayan men found attractive. Many went to Argentina as temporary migrants leaving their families behind. Paraguayan women also became part of the flow of migrant workers, moving as autonomous migrants. Bolivian and Chilean women, in contrast, usually migrated to accompany their male relatives (Balán, 1988).

By 1970 over a third of all Bolivian migrants living in Argentina were residents of the Buenos Aires metropolitan area, whereas the proportion living in the North-west had declined from 77 per cent to 46 per cent between 1947 and 1970. By 1980, a greater proportion of Bolivian migrants was living in Buenos Aires than in the North-west. The distribution of the foreign-born population by place of residence indicates, with some lag, the changing destinations of migrants. However, the increasing concentration of Bolivian migrants in Buenos Aires was associated with only slight changes in their distribution by sex. By 1980, the Bolivian-born population in Argentina

still displayed relatively low proportions of women, especially in comparison with the population born in Paraguay (see table 112).

Important differences existed between the various arrival cohorts originating in the three countries neighbouring Argentina (see table 113). As expected, for all countries of origin, earlier cohorts displayed lower proportions of women. Among the more recent arrivals, the proportion of women was higher but there were still important differences according to country of birth, with the lowest proportion of women present among Bolivian-born migrants. Of course, census data reflect only persons who were resident in Argentina in 1980 and the proportion of women may not be representative of that in the actual flow of migrants because of differential return migration or mortality by sex. However, the trends displayed by census data are congruent with what is known about the decline in agricultural work, which attracted more men than women, and the increasing importance of family reunification. Furthermore, the difference between Bolivian and Paraguayan migrants is unlikely to arise solely because of differences in return migration or mortality by sex.

The generally low labour-force participation rates of Bolivian female migrants are revealing (see table 112). For most age groups, the proportion of women who are economically active is lower among those born in Bolivia than among those born in Chile or Paraguay. Bolivian women, who tend to move in associational migration, are also more likely to earn an income through self-employment, an attitude that echoes that prevalent in Bolivia. Since work in the informal sector is probably not reflected properly by census data, it is likely that the many Bolivian women engaging in petty trade or domestic crafts, which are major female occupations in Bolivia, go unrecorded. That may be one of the causes of the differences noted between Bolivian women and other female migrants from neighbouring countries. For the same reason, the differences between the various groups of economically active migrant women by branch of activity shown in table 112 are suspect. According to those data, in 1980 both male and female Bolivian migrants were still more heavily involved in agricultural work than other Latin Ameri-

TABLE 112. POPULATION ENUMERATED IN ARGENTINA AND BORN IN BOLIVIA, CHILE AND PARAGUAY,
BY SELECTED CHARACTERISTICS: 1980 CENSUS
(Percentage)

	Country of birth					
	Male			Female		
	Bolivia	Chile	Paraguay	Bolivia	Chile	Paraguay
Total population .... (thousands)	64	108	120	52	99	140
Percentage female	55.2	52.3	46.1	44.8	47.7	53.9
A. Total population, by age group						
20-19	11.9	16.6	11.3	13.5	18.5	11.7
20-49	65.4	59.5	60.4	64.4	60.7	61.5
50 + ...	22.7	23.8	28.4	22.0	20.8	26.8
B. Economically active, by age group						
20-29	91.4	95.2	94.3	30.8	30.5	40.0
30-39	96.6	97.7	97.1	24.7	30.0	33.3
40-49	96.0	96.7	95.8	25.7	30.1	32.9
50-59	89.2	92.3	88.1	19.6	23.2	24.8
60 + ...	46.8	57.2	48.8	7.2	8.2	8.0
C. Economically active population, by branch of activity						
Agriculture	25.1	16.2	13.9	13.0	3.5	1.7
Manufacturing	19.3	18.1	25.5	16.2	13.0	21.3
Construction..............................	34.0	35.5	33.2	1.1	1.6	0.8
Commerce	6.8	9.2	9.2	20.7	19.2	13.1
Personal services	7.1	8.2	8.2	42.5	53.3	54.4
Other	7.7	12.8	10.0	6.5	9.4	8.7

Source: Argentina, *Censo Nacional de Población 1980* as reported in CELADE, "Investigación de la migración internacional en Latinoamérica", *Boletín Demográfico*, vol. XXII, No. 43 (January 1989).

can migrants. Among females, the Bolivian-born showed a smaller though still fairly high proportion working in personal services (mainly but not only of a domestic nature) and, in contrast to Paraguayan women, a higher proportion engaged in commerce.

Data on border crossings and temporary migration to Argentina are very poor. Estimates vary widely and are seldom based on actual counts. There is little doubt that many Bolivian men and some women enter Argentina on a temporary basis, often with improper documentation, looking for jobs that will allow them to remit money home. However, an unknown proportion manage to obtain legal resident

status and settle in Argentina, while others enjoy the benefits of dual residence (Balán, 1992).

B. KINSHIP, GENDER AND HOUSEHOLD ECONOMY IN COCHABAMBA

Bolivia is a large and heterogeneous country, twice the size of France, with only about seven million people. Despite the rapid urbanization of recent decades, the population is still largely rural and more than half is engaged in agriculture. Most Bolivians live in the valleys, the highlands and in the high plateau (the Altiplano). Intensive agriculture, often

TABLE 113. PERCENTAGE OF WOMEN AMONG THE POPULATION
BORN IN BOLIVIA, CHILE AND PARAGUAY, BY YEAR OF
ENTRY TO ARGENTINA: 1980 CENSUS

Period of arrival	Country of birth		
	Bolivia	Chile	Paraguay
Before 1960	42.6	43.6	52.4
1960-1964	43.8	47.3	51.3
1965-1969	43.4	48.9	51.8
1970-1974	48.8	48.2	56.7
1975-1980	48.0	52.1	59.2
TOTAL	44.8	47.7	53.9

Source: Argentina, *Censo Nacional de Población 1980*, as reported in CELADE, "Investigación de la migración internacional en Latinoamérica", *Boletín Demográfico*, vol. XXII, No. 43 (January 1989).

in terraced high altitude mountain slopes, is still practised on the basis of cropping techniques that predate the Inca period. Peasant households have gained access to land through the massive redistribution that took place after the 1952 revolution. The tropical lowlands constitute an agricultural frontier that covers over half of the national territory.

Bolivia is also the most Indian of the American republics, with only a minority consisting of monolingual Spanish speakers. Bilingualism has become the rule only in recent years, although one of the two major Indian languages has always been used by the majority of the population in the domestic sphere. Indian monolingualism is considerably more marked among women, a high proportion of whom are illiterate. Only the younger female cohorts have had access to schooling on an almost equal basis to men. Monolingual persons are more common in the Altiplano and the highlands, less so in the irrigated valleys and along the southern border and almost non-existent in the tropical frontier.

International migration is highly selective by place of origin. Within the same country one finds regions, towns and villages that specialize in migration, while others do not. Such differences are often explained by the operation of social networks: people learn about opportunities abroad and gain access to them through family and friends originating in the

same locality. Thus, once some persons emigrate from a particular village, others will eventually follow. Yet, the initial impulse to migrate must be there and the conditions sustaining migration must continue for such a process to operate. The analytical debate has therefore centred on the set of conditions stimulating or inhibiting migration.

Starting in the 1950s, the irrigated valleys near the city of Cochabamba became a major area of emigration to Argentina. The region, located midway between the capital city of La Paz, the major mining centres and the core areas of Indian settlement on the one hand, and the agricultural frontier of Santa Cruz on the other, was ethnically and culturally mixed. The densely populated rural areas and villages along the valleys are largely bilingual, while the neighbouring mountain regions ("la Sierra") is monolingual Indian. Agrarian reform and highway construction during the 1950s and 1960s provided an impulse for the already commercialized and highly diversified peasant economy. Agricultural activities were combined with a variety of crafts and interregional trade activities. Although the local population, urbanized along the major highways, has not abandoned agriculture, it is no longer the major source of income. The migration of male labour to Argentina and to the tropical lowlands has become the major source of cash income. Trade in the regional markets, located in all major towns and villages, is very active and largely dominated by women. Agricultural products from the valleys, mountains and tropical lowlands, together with cattle and local domestic crafts (like textiles, hats and the local beer, "chicha"), are the main items traded in a complex marketing system operating in the valley villages. Trade in coca leaves and, more recently, in coca paste, both produced in the adjoining lowlands, is a major source of income. Migrant men often stay away for extended periods, while marketing activities demand a high mobility of women for shorter periods.

The Andean kinship system is bilateral, giving equal importance to men and women (Bolton and Mayer, 1977). Neolocal residence prevails, with adult children establishing their own independent households after marriage, normally after a short period of residence in the house of the groom's parents. Inheritance, often anticipatory to facilitate household formation, is of the partible, bilateral type, with all children, male and female, receiving a share of the family property. The nuclear family household is embedded in a wider organizational framework based upon kin on both sides. However, there is no corporate group normally associated with lineages or descent groups. The different nuclear families of parents and married children often live in a cluster of houses and engage in a series of exchanges of labour and products, but each nuclear family controls its own productive resources, storing and marketing its crops separately, and processing and cooking its own food.

Among Andean families, patriarchal elements in social relations are not primarily placed within the domestic unit (Harris, 1985). Rather, one tends to find complementary gender roles and unity between the couple, both at a symbolic level and in the actual operation of the domestic economy. Rituals usually involve the presence of the couple; single people must be accompanied by somebody from the other sex. The two parts are unequal, but both are needed for reproduction and also to ensure the fertility of land and animals. Men and women are expected to work together in agriculture and animal husbandry. The product of labour belongs to the household, rather than to one of its members. Each couple has a unique set of kin relations with other units, making use of bilateral kinship ties. Differentiation between siblings and affinal kin within the same generation is minimal.

Most historical and ethnographic studies of peasant households in the Andes have insisted on the contribution of female labour to the family economy, recognizing that the position of women is not markedly inferior to that of men. These gender roles were fully entrenched before the Spanish conquest. The long colonial exploitation of Indian labour did weaken the status of women, but it did not exclude them from production (Larson, 1983). Although women were not officially involved in the colonial systems of forced labour (for instance, in the mines), they were an important part of the productive process. "Mitayos" or workers that the communities were forced to send as tribute were accompanied by their wives. Women organized the small-scale marketing of minerals and monopolized market activities through which inhabitants of the mining towns were clothed, fed and entertained. Hence, although the complementary gender roles and relatively high female status in the Andes is of pre-Columbian origin, it has probably undergone a number of changes since then.

The rural society in the Cochabamba valleys was heavily commercialized and subject to acculturation during the colonial period and just after independence (Larson, 1988). The category of independent peasants, which grew in the first decades of this century, tended to diversify activities in response to increasing pressures on the land. Both married and single women participated in local and regional markets, being involved in crafts, trade and agriculture. Agrarian reform and the improvement of roads that took place during the 1950s further pushed tertiarization and urbanization of the regional economy, reinforcing the pattern of female participation in the rural economy and creating conditions favourable to male involvement in seasonal labour migration.

C. Gender in the peasant economy and its implications for migration

A study of migration and household formation in an upper-valley town (Ucureña) and a smaller village in the Sierra (Ayopaya) as well as in migrant settlements in the agricultural frontier of Chapare and in the urban neighbourhoods of the city of Cochabamba was carried out (Balán and Dandler, 1986). Since migration to Argentina is a practice of upper-valley peasants but not of the Sierra population, the data used in this paper were obtained from a census conducted in the town of Ucureña supplemented by a survey of upper-valley Bolivian migrants in Buenos Aires.

The upper valley of Cochabamba is characterized by extreme land fragmentation. The urbanization of rural areas and the development of a highly commercialized economy were fostered by the proximity of the capital city and by the construction of a road leading to the booming tropical area of Chapare. Most farming occurs on unirrigated land and only one yearly crop is possible. Agriculture has declined as a source of income and absorbs a decreasing proportion of available household labour, although in most households all adult family members devote some time to agriculture or animal husbandry throughout the year. The land market is very tight, being characterized by high prices and few transactions. A small plot is used for residence and as a platform for a variety of economic activities including growing crops and raising livestock on a small scale. Above all, land is the basis for the establishment and continuity of a household.

Campesinos (peasants) are distinguished from the *gente de pueblo* (town people) living in the county capital. The distinction entails a set of distinctive cultural traits, including language, dress and rituals. Peasant women rely more on *Quechua* than on Spanish and wear the typical Indian skirt rather than an urban dress which is uncomfortable for heavy manual work. Elopement and other rituals, common in rural areas, are looked down as *campesino* ways by town people.

Among peasant families, everyone—male or female, young or old—is involved at one time or another in agriculture and animal husbandry. Children start helping with those activities at an early age and take on increasing responsibilities as they grow older. Schooling has become more prevalent in recent decades, taking children away from the land. Girls, however, tend to stay fewer years in school than boys. In Ucureña, only one third of all women aged 14 and over had completed at least primary school whereas, among men in the same age group, two thirds had done so (see table 114). Although at present families expect considerably more schooling for their children than in the past, differences by sex are still noticeable, reflecting deep-seated values and expectations for the future.

Girls are expected to start contributing to family income very soon, taking up craft or trade activities under the supervision of older women, whereas boys have few chances of earning an income until they have gone through military service at age 18. Most

TABLE 114. EVER-MIGRANT AND NON-MIGRANT POPULATION AGED 14 OR OVER IN UCUREÑA (BOLIVIA),
BY LEVEL OF EDUCATION AND TYPE OF OCCUPATION
(Percentage)

	Migration status					
	Male			Female		
	Ever-migrant	Non-migrant	Total	Ever-migrant	Non-migrant	Total
Education						
None	1.9	11.8	8.7	9.5	30.0	28.9
Primary (incomplete)	36.1	24.6	28.1	54.8	34.6	35.5
Primary (complete)	30.5	18.7	22.3	26.2	17.6	18.0
Secondary	20.3	22.5	21.8	8.3	11.2	11.0
Higher	11.2	22.4	19.0	1.2	6.7	6.5
Occupation						
Self-employed: crafts	35.2	20.2	24.8	28.4	20.8	21.2
Self-employed: trade	6.5	6.5	6.5	37.0	43.2	42.9
Wage earners	23.7	10.7	14.6	0.0	0.7	0.7
Salaried or professional	9.0	16.7	14.4	1.2	4.4	4.2
Students or in military service	1.0	22.1	15.7	3.7	8.6	8.4
Agriculture only or no occupation[a]	24.5	23.8	24.0	29.6	22.3	22.6

Source: Special census of the Ucureña population conducted in 1984-1985 (Balán and Dandler, 1986).
[a] Since most adults report work in agriculture, this category includes only those who do not report other occupations and the few with no occupation.

adult women take care of domestic activities, including the management of the family farm, and earn an income in one way or another: they produce and sell beer (*chicha*), make hats, engage in trade in local markets, butcher animals and sell meat. Only 23 per cent of adult women reported being engaged only in farm activities (see table 114). Almost two thirds were engaged in crafts or trade, although very few were wage earners. Even if women travelled often and spent one or more nights away from home, trade and craft activities were conducted as an extension of household work and without losing touch with it. Younger women, who start working under the supervision of older ones, take over autonomous activities only after marriage. Women's cash income, often considerable, is managed by themselves, at least once their work becomes autonomous. Wage work, however, is uncommon: only educated women, who work as teachers, nurses or in other semi-professional activities, earn a salary. Paid domestic work is very rare in rural areas and the market for domestic service in urban areas is not attractive for young women from the valley. Women from the Sierra or other areas often identified as Indian do engage in domestic service in the towns and cities.

Male employment opportunities are restricted by the household division of labour, land shortages and the requirements of military service. Families do not expect boys to help in household activities and they rarely work in the family farm before adulthood. The most lucrative craft and trade activities are considered to be female activities, with only a few exceptions (e.g., tailors or barbers). Trade, which occupies over 43 per cent of women, is reported as an activity by only 6.5 per cent of adult men (see table 114). Agriculture has traditionally been the major activity of men, but shortages have delayed their access to land and reduced the amount of labour that agriculture may eventually absorb. For men, wage labour is available only after the military service is completed and local labour demand is low. Consequently, temporary work in the Bolivian lowlands or in Argentina is today a major source of employment for men, while women engage in considerable local and regional mobility but seldom travel in search of paid employment.

About half of all men aged 30-49 and living in Ucureña had migrated at least once to Argentina by 1984 (see table 115). Among those aged 20-29, that proportion reached only 27 per cent, partly because those who had left had not returned yet and many others had not yet become migrants. It bears stressing that the data presented refer to men who, having migrated to Argentina at least once, were residing in Ucureña at the time of interview (1984), thus excluding all those who were abroad at the time. The latter may be estimated by considering that slightly over 10 per cent of the adult population of Ucureña was reported as "currently in Argentina". The low proportions of men aged 50 and over who had ever migrated to Argentina reflects, at least in part, the

TABLE 115. EVER-MIGRANTS AMONG THE MALE AND FEMALE POPULATION OF UCUREÑA (BOLIVIA), BY AGE, LEVEL OF EDUCATION AND OCCUPATION
(*Percentage*)

	Male	Female
Age group		
0-19	0.8	1.1
20-29	27.4	5.3
30-39	49.7	8.0
40-49	46.4	5.5
50-59	27.1	5.1
60+	8.6	0.0
TOTAL	21.3	3.6
Education		
None	6.6	1.6
Primary (incomplete)	39.4	7.5
Primary (complete)	41.9	7.1
Secondary	28.6	3.7
Higher	18.1	0.9
Occupation		
Craft	43.3	6.3
Trade	30.4	4.1
Wage earners	49.3	0.0
Salaried or professional	19.1	1.4
Students	2.0	2.1
Agriculture only or no occupation*	31.1	6.2

Source: Special census of the Ucureña population conducted in 1984-1985 (Balán and Dandler, 1986).

*Since most adults report work in agriculture, this category includes only those who do not report other occupations and the few with no occupation.

fact that emigration from the village became established only towards the 1960s.

The proportion of ever-migrants among women is considerably lower than among men for all age groups (see table 115) and is almost zero for women aged 60 and over. Among women aged 30-39, only 8 per cent had ever migrated to Argentina. The pattern of multiple migration involving several stays abroad, which was common among men, was not so among women, suggesting that permanent migration might be more common among the latter, especially since the censuses of Argentina indicate that the proportion of women among the Bolivian-born population was considerably higher than that found among ever-migrants in Ucureña. Among the women in Ucureña who had migrated to Argentina, about half reported that they had not worked while in that country, whereas all men said that they had worked, mostly in construction. Even if women's exercise of an economic activity while in Argentina was underreported, it seems clear that female migration, in contrast to that of men, is not a response to labour market opportunities.

The educational selectivity of migrants to Argentina is evident among both men and women (see table 115). In Ucureña, the percentage of persons who had ever migrated to Argentina was highest among adults who had either some primary education or had completed primary school. Higher educational attainment was associated with a lower proportion of ever-migrants among both men and women. Low proportions of ever-migrants were also recorded among persons with no schooling, illiteracy being an important barrier to mobility.

The proportion of ever-migrants tended to be higher in certain occupational categories, especially among men (see table 115). Thus, ever-migrants were proportionately more numerous among men working for wages and among independent craftsmen. Yet, it is difficult to establish the direction of causality in this instance since the data in table 115 refer to occupations at the time of interview and not to those pursued by ever-migrants before migrating. It may be that, upon return, migrants are more prone to engage in non-agricultural activities.

Other features of male temporary migration are relevant in the analysis of migration and gender. Only 60 per cent of male migrants were single the first time they emigrated to Argentina. Not only was the proportion married high at first migration but it was even higher among migrants leaving for the second or third time. The median age at marriage in the valley is relatively low and there is only a two-year difference between men and women. Labour migration, marriage and household formation are often closely linked processes in the case of men, since economic autonomy is required to establish a new household and men can seldom achieve such autonomy locally (Dandler and Medeiros, 1988).

The situation for women is almost the reverse. Because women contribute to family income from a quite young age, they are usually an asset to their families. By age 20 most women are already experienced traders or craftsmen. Parents are normally opposed to their daughters marrying "too early", since they fear losing an important asset (Balán and Dandler, 1986). Furthermore, according to local marriage norms the age difference between bride and groom should be fairly small and men in their early twenties are hardly able to support a household unless they emigrate. Valley norms call for strong and often strenuous opposition from parents to the marriage of young women, and elopement is common both among peasants from the valley and among those from the Sierra, where the household economy is almost entirely based upon agriculture, land is more abundant and the female contribution to family income more limited.

Since women find many ways of earning an income locally, there is no good reason for them to look for temporary work abroad. Yet women are by no means sedentary. On the contrary, the organization of regional markets involves considerable mobility among female traders. Traditional markets are scheduled for different days of the week in the various towns and villages of the valley, and the city of Cochabamba, about two hours away from Ucureña, offers daily possibilities for trading. Short trips by women offer, in fact, many possibilities for dating and elopement. Mobility is not circumscribed to daily trips; single and married women may be absent for several days or even weeks, especially when travelling to the lowlands or the mining towns.

When married men leave to work in Argentina and their families remain behind, they normally rely on male relatives to take care of the few tasks that are supposed to be too hard for their wives (Dandler and Medeiros, 1988). Otherwise, women take care of all household subsistence needs. Only very poor families would face untenable strains from the absence of adult men and therefore prevent their emigration. Men seldom send money back while abroad but try instead to save all they can and bring it back personally, either in cash or as presents. There are no formal mechanisms to transfer money and informal means are not reliable. The temporary absence of men both reflects and reinforces female autonomy within the household.

Trips to Argentina vary in length but, on average, last a year or so. The urban labour market offers possibilities all year round. Thus, men tend to stay abroad until they have saved "enough" money, a sum that is highly subjective. All other things being equal, that sum will be saved faster when the exchange rate is favourable to migrants, that is, when the Argentine currency is over rather than undervalued. Thus, the exchange rate is as relevant as real wages in Argentina in attracting migrants.

D. Bolivian women as migrants and workers in Buenos Aires

This section focuses on female Bolivian migrants in Argentina, bearing in mind that, according to the data on Ucureña, few women from the Cochabamba region engage in temporary labour migration. In 1984-1985, a non-random sample of 100 women aged 15 to 60 who had been born in Bolivia—a majority of whom originated in Cochabamba—was interviewed in Buenos Aires. The women interviewed were located using a snowball technique with different starting points to insure some variability. The sample included both legal and illegal migrants in Buenos Aires.

Migrant women can be classified according to the age and marital status that they had when they first arrived in Argentina. Four groups are considered:

(a) school-age children who migrated with relatives; (b) single women who were no longer at school and who normally migrated on their own; (c) marrying women, that is, those for whom marriage and migration were related, either because marriage (or elopement) immediately preceded migration or because they migrated in order to get married in Argentina; and (d) married women (including those widowed or divorced) who generally migrated with their children. There were approximately the same number of women in each category. However, some women had migrated more than once and belonged to different categories at various points in their life histories. For that reason and also because of the non-random nature of the sample, it seems advisable not to give too much weight in the discussion that follows to the percentages of women belonging to each category.

The women who migrated as children were usually accompanied by one or both parents. In many cases, the father migrated first and was later followed by his wife and children. Several women in that group had initially lived in the Northern provinces of Argentina, Salta and Jujuy, and then moved to Buenos Aires. That migration pattern was common among women arriving in Argentina during the 1960s, a group that was well represented in this category of migrants.

Women who migrated to Buenos Aires while still single tended not to have a job in mind, although several had been informed of well-paying job opportunities by friends or relatives. Others expected to continue their studies in Argentina, but few remained in school for an extended period. The most striking characteristic of this group was the large number of women who reported having lost one or both parents before migrating. As orphans, they had an uncertain status in Bolivia and had to deal with changes in family structure, including the presence of a step-father or a step-mother. A large number reported living initially with siblings in Buenos Aires, generally brothers who had already established a family abroad. Thus, a typical case was that of an orphan migrating to join an older brother in Argentina, having hopes of better prospects and expecting to help in raising her brother's children. The prospects of finding a job were seldom given priority in making the decision to migrate, but most single women who did not have heavy family responsibilities did look for work outside the household, either as domestic servants or in the garment industry.

Another important event determining the decision to migrate is marriage. Women who had just married or expected to get married constitute the third category in the sample. Migration of this type is common because of the unbalanced sex distribution of the Bolivian community in Argentina and because migrant men from Bolivia rarely marry women from other countries. In addition, given that elopement is common in Bolivia, a couple facing strong disapproval from either the bride's or the groom's relatives may choose to emigrate in order to avoid an unpleasant situation. Generally, the prospective groom in such cases had already been living in Argentina and either went back to get married or brought his fiancée to Argentina. There were also a few cases in which the bride and groom decided to migrate soon after contracting a normal marriage in Bolivia. In general, however, the most salient causal links between female migration and marriage were the previous migration of men or elopement brought about by strong family opposition to the marriage.

Married women, normally accompanied by their children, constituted the fourth category of migrants in the sample. The typical case was that of families where the husband, who had migrated first and either remained in Buenos Aires for long periods or engaged in circulation, was joined by wife and children. In a few cases, however, both husband and wife migrated at the same time accompanied by their children. Yet rarely did the husband lack any previous migration experience.

Separation because of migration always entails some strains within the family, especially because the women remaining behind must assume greater responsibilities. Although Bolivian women are probably in a better position than most to cope with those responsibilities, they would probably like to share them with their spouses. In addition, long separations increase the likelihood of marital disruption. Either husbands abroad or wives at home may start new relationships during long periods of separation. For that reason, the most likely outcomes of the recurrent or prolonged absences of husbands are either family reunification or divorce.

A key question regarding the migration of married Bolivian women to Argentina is to what extent it is an alternative to their husbands' return to Bolivia and under what circumstances the former is preferred to the latter. The evidence available indicates that the two possibilities function indeed as alternatives and are often explicitly confronted with the third option, namely, separation or divorce. Such an assessment is linked to the nature of the labour market in Buenos Aires where, in contrast with agricultural work in the Northern provinces of Argentina, work is available all year round. When men work abroad only during the harvest season, the household economy and the family can be organized accordingly: the absence of men is short and, upon their return, they can resume their normal roles within the family aided by the savings made abroad. The need for further migration is predictable and the cycle can be repeated. In the city, however, demand is not cyclical. If the economic conditions are favourable, men may find well-paid jobs in construction for the full year. Consequently, the decision to return depends on the target amount of savings expected, a figure that is likely to be revised as expectations change and the advantages of remaining abroad longer become clearer.

The data therefore suggest that wives join their husbands when the latter have been relatively successful, being able to pay for the family's transfer and resettlement without counting on the wives' possibility of earning an income in the short-term. There were no cases in which wives had taken a truly autonomous decision to join their husbands or migrate with them, it was at best a family decision. However, it may well be that the decision not to migrate was the wife's prerogative resulting from her increased autonomy at home when the husband was absent.

Although labour-market considerations are not the major determinant for the migration of Bolivian women to Argentina, it is appropriate to discuss what women do once they are in Buenos Aires. In particular, it is important to consider the continuities and discontinuities in their work experience brought about by migration. In contrast with their situation in Cochabamba, family status keeps many Bolivian women out of the labour market in Buenos Aires. Given the characteristics of Bolivian migration to

Argentina, at any particular time there are relatively few single migrant women in Buenos Aires and those married generally have children. Since the presence of children generally does not prevent married women in Cochabamba from working, it is important to understand how that is a constraining factor for their labour force participation in Buenos Aires.

The informal sector in Cochabamba includes a variety of economic activities for women that have been subsumed under the terms "crafts" and "trade". Similar activities are more limited in Buenos Aires and, when they exist, they involve the acquisition of local knowledge that is not without cost. In addition, certain traditional crafts, such as weaving, knitting, making hats or butchering small animals, find no market in the city. Trade in the informal sector is also limited, though it is an important source of income for Bolivian women in Buenos Aires, since they are often engaged in street vending, normally selling fruits and vegetables. However, as is often the case with persons working in the informal sector, their work has very low status and they are often subject to harassment by police, municipal inspectors or other bureaucrats. Thus, street vending is an option only for those migrant women who are less integrated into Argentine society.

Domestic service is one of the main employment outlets for migrant women in Buenos Aires, although it is not as extensive as in other Latin American cities. Both internal and international female migrants have traditionally engaged in domestic work to earn an income in the city. Bolivian women are no exception, though their involvement in domestic service is less than among other migrants, especially Paraguayan women. Marriage limits participation in certain types of domestic service and Bolivian women are seldom single. Furthermore, domestic service is an occupation of very low status in the society of origin, especially in Cochabamba. Bolivian women are more sensitive to their original prestige scales than to local ones and may therefore prefer street vending to cleaning homes for a wage. The former offers at least greater freedom and some prospects of improvement (by setting a small shop, for instance).

A third employment alternative open both to married and single women is work in the garment indus-try. Many small and medium-sized manufacturers hire women to do piece-work at home. Women are paid by the piece and employment is informal. During the last decade or two the industry has changed considerably, with Korean immigrants opening new shops that tend to rely on out-work. Bolivian women have become a preferred source of labour. Two of the migrants interviewed mentioned that they worked for Koreans whose shops were visited by the interviewers. The shops were not registered and workers did not receive any of the social security or health benefits typical of formal employment.

Migrant women engaging in formal employment as wage or salary earners are generally young and have some education. Such employment is common among the "second generation", that is, migrant women who arrived in Buenos Aires as children and grew up in the city. Their situation contrasts markedly with that of migrant women of similar age who are recent arrivals.

E. Conclusion

The case of Bolivian migration to Argentina is characterized by marked differences between men and women in the way migration is organized. Most men engage in temporary labour migration, though some of them tend to settle abroad as their work is prolonged. The latter tend to be joined by their families or to go back to Bolivia to get married and bring their wives with them. Although most Bolivian women are seldom autonomous migrants, tending instead to follow male relatives, some migrate all by themselves while still single. Yet, Bolivian female migrants seldom acknowledge that their migration is prompted by the search of better economic opportunities abroad. Family considerations play a more important role in initiating migration. Although family considerations are also relevant in determining male migration, they are usually viewed from an economic perspective deriving from the need to support the families left behind. Clearly, the interrelations between gender and family status are complex and they affect the migration of men and women in significantly different ways.

When female migration is not driven mainly by labour market opportunities at destination, it is better understood by considering gender roles and the household division of labour in the society of origin. The clear economic value of women, even at early ages, and their autonomy in Bolivia together with the egalitarian kinship system prevailing in that country, are key in understanding how Bolivian female migration to Argentina is organized. Single women seldom migrate alone and the exceptions indicate that they only do so when their family status is precarious, as in the case of orphans. Married women may wait a long time before joining their husbands abroad and may never do so, preferring rather to wait for their return. Women enjoy a more secure and autonomous position in Bolivia than in Argentina, where the typical skills of Bolivian women are not easily marketable. The return of men depends not only on economic considerations, such as accumulated savings or work opportunities in Bolivia, but also on the need to assure marriage stability by avoiding prolonged separation, especially when wives are unwilling or unable to go abroad.

Understanding the role of gender in international migration within a specific context should be helpful in clarifying some policy issues. In the case of Bolivian migration to Argentina, there are relatively few bases for concern about the women left behind when men leave, since those women appear able to cope with added household responsibilities despite obvious strains. Two other sources of concern are, however, evident. One is the changing status of Bolivian women arising from their migration to Buenos Aires and the other is their limited labour force participation in Argentina.

This study has indicated that Bolivian female migrants experience negative changes in their status when they migrate to Buenos Aires, since they lose autonomy in the economic sphere. While in Bolivia, women are part of the cash economy, handling all their household needs and often participating in trade. They have considerable freedom to travel and to find mechanisms that allow them to combine work with household duties. The availability of a family network that provides support probably reinforces their status in relation to their husbands. By constraining their economic independence and weakening their links to the community of origin, migration probably entails changes in the relations between husband and wife that may not necessarily be positive for the latter.

Bolivian women in Buenos Aires are handicapped to find work in the formal sector, since most of their work experience relates to the informal sector in a rural environment and their levels of education are generally low. Their only option then is to vie for low-status, low-paid jobs that leave them vulnerable to exploitation. Thus, Bolivian women working in the informal sector in general and those doing piecework at home, in particular, lack every type of social security or health benefit. Furthermore, they are subject to the economic vagaries of the industrial world. Their position in Argentina seems therefore more precarious than the one they had in Bolivia. There is hope, however, in that the prospects for the second generation seem to be better.

REFERENCES

Balán, Jorge (1988). International migration in Latin America: trends and consequences. In *International Migration Today*, R. T. Appleyard, ed., vol. I. Paris and Nedlands: United Nations Educational, Scientific and Cultural Organization and University of Western Australia.

_____ (1992). The role of migration policies and social networks in the development of a migration system in the Southern Cone. In *International Migration Systems*, Mary M. Kritz, Lin Lean Lim and Hania Zlotnik, eds. Oxford: Clarendon Press.

_____ and J. Dandler (1986). *Marriage Process and Household Formation: the Impact of Migration in a Peasant Society*. Report submitted to the Population Council.

Bolton, R., and E. Mayer, eds. (1977). *Andean Kinship and Marriage*. Washington, D.C.: American Anthropological Association.

Dandler, J., and C. Medeiros (1988). Temporary migration from Cochabamba, Bolivia to Argentina: patterns and impact in sending areas. In *When Borders Don't Divide: Labour Migration and Refugee Movements in the Americas*, Patricia R. Pessar, ed. New York: Center for Migration Studies.

Harris, O. (1985). Complementaridad y conflicto: una versión andina del hombre y la mujer. *Allpanchis* (Cusco), vol. XXI, No. 25, pp. 17-42.

Larson, B. (1983). Producción doméstica y trabajo femenino indígena en la formación de una economía mercantil colonial. *Historia Boliviana* (La Paz), vol. 3, No. 2, pp. 173-188.

_____ (1988). *Colonial and Agrarian Transformation in Bolivia: Cochabamba 1550-1900*. Princeton: Princeton University Press.

Ravenstein, E. G. (1885). The laws of migration. *Journal of the Royal Statistical Society* (London), vol. 48, No. 2, pp. 167-227.

Whiteford, S. (1981). *Workers from the North: Plantations, Bolivian Labour, and the City in Northwest Argentina*. Austin, Texas: University of Texas Press.

XVIII. FEMALE MIGRATION IN SUB-SAHARAN AFRICA: THE CASE OF NIGERIA

Folasade Iyun* and United Nations Secretariat**

Perhaps more than in other world regions, in Africa there is a dearth of information on the participation of women in international migration and even less on their status with respect to international male migrants or to female non-migrants. Lack of attention to female migration is common in most of the world. In the African context, it has been further accentuated by colonial policies that discouraged or even prevented women from migrating with their husbands and by the marginalization of women's economic activities.

Population mobility within sub-Saharan Africa has always been part of the life of the different groups of people living in the region. Prior to the colonial period, migration flows entailed the movements of nomads, traders and ethnic groups fleeing conquest (Abumere, 1988). Since most of those movements were a group phenomenon, they necessarily involved the participation of women (Surdarkassa, 1977). Under colonial rule, distinctive patterns of international migration, largely of an economic nature, developed. Thus, French authorities instituted forced labour recruitment while their British counterparts relied on agricultural development and other economic policies to ensure labour mobility (Abumere, 1988).

After independence, international migration in sub-Saharan Africa has been driven mostly by economic and political factors. Ecological variations within the region are associated with differences in agricultural productivity and socio-economic development between countries that often lead to the migration of people from poorer areas to those in which better employment opportunities are thought to exist. In Western Africa, in particular, the lengthy dry season

in the interior of the region (which usually runs from December to March) has fostered a system of seasonal labour migration to coastal plantations, where "development pockets" had been established during the colonial period in countries like Côte d'Ivoire and Ghana.

In Eastern and Southern Africa, official arrangements were made between areas or countries having excess labour, such as Botswana, Burundi, Lesotho, Malawi, Mozambique, Rwanda or Swaziland, and those requiring workers to pursue large-scale agricultural activities or mining, particularly in the former Rhodesia, in Uganda or in the Republic of South Africa. During the past two decades, however, only the Republic of South Africa has been a major receiver of migrant workers and its increasing reliance on local labour has meant that labour migration flows directed to the country have been declining. In most cases, the participation of women in labour migration flows, especially those highly regulated by the receiving countries, has been low. The practice of preventing women from migrating with their husbands which, as noted above, was common during the colonial period, has not changed markedly in a number of countries, especially since labour shortages exist in sectors that are not considered "suitable" for women. However, women have not been entirely absent from international migration in Africa, even if their economic roles are not always recognized.

Evidence on the participation of women in international migration can be derived from census data on the distribution by sex of the foreign-born population. As table 116 indicates, data from the 1970 and the 1980 rounds of censuses are available for 32 of the 50 countries constituting sub-Saharan Africa. Although in the majority of countries data on place of birth were available, in 10, only information on country of citizenship could be obtained. Consequently, the data on the foreign population were used

---
*Department of Geography, University of Ibadan, Ibadan, Nigeria.

**Population Division of the Department for Economic and Social Information and Policy Analysis.

TABLE 116. FOREIGN-BORN POPULATION IN SELECTED AFRICAN COUNTRIES, BY SEX, AND PERCENTAGE OF WOMEN

| Country | Year | Foreign-born population | | | Foreign-born as percentage of total population | |
		Male	Female	Percentage of women	Male	Female
Western Africa						
Benin[a]	1979	21 268	20 016	48.5	1.3	1.2
Burkina Faso	1975	52 854	57 827	52.2	1.9	2.1
Côte d'Ivoire[a]	1988	1 696 037	1 343 000	44.2	30.7	25.4
Gambia	1973	33 334	21 220	38.9	0.3	0.2
Ghana	1970	210 846	139 028	39.7	5.0	3.2
Guinea Bissau	1978	6 471	6 460	50.0	1.7	1.6
Liberia	1974	35 759	23 699	39.9	4.7	3.2
Mali	1976	73 458	72 631	49.7	2.4	2.2
Mauritania[a]	1977	16 488	11 680	41.5	2.5	1.7
Senegal	1976	50 109	33 725	40.2	2.7	2.0
Sierra Leone[a]	1974	48 336	31 078	39.1	3.6	2.3
Togo	1970	69 294	74 326	51.8	7.4	7.3
Central Africa						
Cameroon	1976	120 442	97 627	44.8	3.4	2.7
Central African Republic	1975	21 844	22 739	51.0	2.5	2.5
Congo	1984	47 797	48 842	50.5	5.1	5.0
Sao Tome and Principe[a]	1981	3 518	3 102	46.9	7.3	6.4
Eastern Africa						
Burundi	1979	42 147	40 704	49.1	2.2	2.0
Comoros	1980	8 301	9 191	52.5	5.0	5.5
Kenya	1979	82 298	75 073	47.7	1.1	1.0
Madagascar	1975	13 371	8 248	38.2	0.4	0.2
Malawi	1977	140 421	148 323	51.4	5.3	5.2
Mauritius[a]	1983	2 522	2 449	49.3	0.5	0.5
Mozambique[a]	1980	19 759	19 383	49.5	0.3	0.3
Réunion	1982	19 440	16 141	45.4	7.7	6.1
Rwanda[a]	1978	21 411	20 500	48.9	0.9	0.8
Sudan	1973	156 519	151 244	49.1	1.5	1.5
United Republic of Tanzania	1978	219 188	196 496	47.3	2.6	2.2
Zambia	1980	113 470	101 434	47.2	4.1	3.5
Zimbabwe[a]	1982	301 490	226 950	42.9	8.2	5.9
Southern Africa						
Botswana[a]	1981	8 788	6 831	43.7	2.0	1.4
South Africa	1985	1 206 287	648 273	35.0	10.5	5.5
Swaziland	1986	17 049	14 694	46.3	5.3	4.1

Source: United Nations, International Migrant Stock: Africa.
[a]Data refer to foreign population.

as indicators of international migration, even though foreigners need not be migrants, especially in countries where citizenship is granted on the basis of *jus sanguinis*.

According to table 116, women tend to be underrepresented among the foreign-born or the foreign population in most of the countries with data available. Thus, only in 9 of the 32 countries considered did women account for 50 per cent or more of the migrant stock enumerated by the census. Nevertheless, women were not as strongly underrepresented among international migrants in Africa as is generally believed. Thus, the median value of the proportion of women among the migrant stock was 47 per cent, and in slightly over half of the

countries considered women represented between 42 and 50 per cent of all migrants. Indeed, the lowest proportion of women among the foreign-born was recorded in the Republic of South Africa in 1985, where women accounted for 35 per cent of all lifetime migrants. That is, even in the country imposing the most stringent restrictions on the admission of female migrants, women constituted over a third of the migrant stock.

There were significant differences in the participation of women in international migration depending on their region of origin. Women tended to be better represented among African migrants than among those originating in other regions (see table 117). Thus, in half of the 27 countries having data on the

TABLE 117. FOREIGN-BORN POPULATION BY AFRICAN AND NON-AFRICAN REGION OF ORIGIN, IN SELECTED AFRICAN COUNTRIES AND PERCENTAGE OF WOMEN AMONG THEM

| Country | Year | African migrants | | Non-African migrants | | Difference in the percentage of women |
		Total	Percentage of women	Total	Percentage of women	
South Africa	1985	1 404 975	30.7	496 910	48.1	-17.4
Senegal	1976	70 922	38.6	12 912	49.3	-10.7
Gambia	1973	53 300	38.9	1 254	40.0	-1.2
Liberia	1974	47 654	39.4	11 804	41.8	-2.4
Ghana	1970	333 918	39.6	15 956	42.2	-2.6
Côte d'Ivoire[a]	1975	1 437 319	40.6	37 150	47.0	-6.5
Madagascar[a]	1975	1 078	41.1	49 305	45.9	-4.8
Botswana[a]	1981	8 733	42.7	6 886	45.1	-2.4
Cameroon	1976	203 513	44.6	501	43.3	1.3
Kenya	1969	84 286	45.7	74 460	45.1	0.6
United Republic of Tanzania	1967	409 552	46.4	42 193	40.9	5.5
Swaziland	1986	25 089	46.5	6 654	45.7	0.8
Sao Tome and Principe[a]	1981	6 432	46.9	188	45.2	1.7
Zambia	1980	184 742	47.3	30 162	46.6	0.7
Mali[a]	1976	72 365	48.7	4 549	40.0	8.7
Sudan	1983	294 831	49.2	12 932	47.1	2.1
Burundi	1979	79 902	49.3	2 820	45.0	4.3
Rwanda[a]	1978	36 789	49.3	5 122	45.9	3.4
Seychelles	1971	1 337	49.4	1 410	34.3	15.1
Réunion	1974	7 762	49.7	14 766	44.7	5.0
Congo[a]	1984	80 127	50.2	8 263	45.3	4.9
Central African Republic	1975	41 362	51.4	14 556	46.8	4.5
Malawi	1977	281 806	51.5	6 938	46.1	5.4
Burkina Faso	1975	107 517	52.3	3 164	49.7	2.6
Mauritius[a]	1983	772	53.5	4 137	48.4	5.1
Comoros	1980	13 377	53.7	4 616	48.4	5.3
Mozambique[a]	1980	14 841	57.1	24 301	44.9	12.3

Source: United Nations, International Migrant Stock: Africa.

[a]Data refer to foreign population.

292

foreign-born or the foreign population classified by region of origin, the proportion of women among the migrant stock varied between 41 per cent and 50 per cent (the interquartile range). Their median value was 47 per cent, and the extremes of the distribution were 31 per cent recorded in South Africa in 1985, and 57 per cent recorded in Mozambique in 1980. Indeed, in about a quarter of the countries considered, women outnumbered men among migrants originating in Africa. In contrast, women were consistently outnumbered by men among migrants from other regions. Thus, the extremes of the distribution of the proportion of women among non-African migrants were 34.3 and 49.7 per cent, the latter recorded in Burkina Faso in 1975. The median value was 45 per cent, lower by two percentage points than that of the equivalent distribution among African migrants, and the interquartile range went from 43 per cent to 47 per cent, meaning that half of the countries considered displayed proportions of women among non-African migrants within that range.

These data indicate that there is greater variability in the participation of women in international migration within the African region than with respect to migration originating outside the region. Furthermore, as table 117 illustrates, whereas in most countries the proportion of women among African migrants exceeds that among non-African migrants, the reverse is true for countries having relatively low proportions of women among African migrants (below 43 per cent). Indeed, some of the largest negative differences between the proportions of women among African and non-African migrants are found in the Republic of South Africa and Senegal, the two countries displaying the lowest proportions of women among African migrants. In 1885, Ravenstein formulated several "laws" of migration, one of which refers to women and states that women tend to be more mobile over short than over long distances (Ravenstein, 1885). To the extent that international migration within Africa involves shorter distances than that originating outside the region, one would expect that the proportion of women among African migrants would be higher than among their non-African counterparts. Since that is indeed the case in about three quarters of the countries

considered, the rest appear to be exceptional. Their existence suggests that the relatively low proportion of women among African migrants in those countries may be the result of specific measures that prevent the inflow of female migrants rather than a reflection of the lower migration propensities of African women in general. The fact that major migrant receiving countries, such as Côte d'Ivoire and the Republic of South Africa, are among those where women are strongly underrepresented among African migrants further validates that point, since it is well-known that both countries have favoured the migration of male workers from neighbouring countries while discouraging that of women. However, more detailed information and in-depth research are needed to establish the extent to which women are being prevented or dissuaded from migrating in search of better economic opportunities.

Although very few African countries have data allowing an assessment of changes in the international migrant stock, those that have the required information have tended to record increases in the number of foreign-born women (see table 118). However, only in half of the 10 countries considered did those increases surpass the ones recorded among male migrants and therefore lead to a rise in the proportion of women among the migrant stock. Significantly, Côte d'Ivoire and the Republic of South Africa, the countries having the largest numbers of migrants, did record an increase in the proportion of women among the migrant stock. Yet, despite such increase, South Africa remained among the African countries having the lowest proportions of women among the foreign-born population.

Information on the age distribution of migrants and its changes through time is also scarce (see table 119). However, in the seven countries having comparable data from two censuses, the age distribution of the female foreign-born population indicates that migrant women have tended to become more concentrated in the middle of the age range, that is, in the working ages. Since there have also been increases in the proportion of female migrants at older ages, reductions, sometimes of a sizeable magnitude, have been recorded in the proportion of female migrants in the younger age groups.

TABLE 118. CHANGES IN THE FOREIGN-BORN POPULATION OF SELECTED AFRICAN COUNTRIES, BY SEX: COMPARISON OF TWO CONSECUTIVE CENSUSES

Country	Year	Foreign-born population			Year	Foreign-born population		
		Female	Male	Percentage female		Female	Male	Percentage female
Botswana[a]	1971	4 747	6 114	43.7	1981	6 831	8 788	43.7
Congo	1974	27 670	26 553	51.0	1984	48 842	47 797	50.5
Côte d'Ivoire[a]	1975	600 396	874 073	40.7	1988	1 343 000	1 696 037	44.2
Kenya	1969	72 138	86 554	45.5	1979	75 073	82 298	47.7
Liberia	1962	12 042	19 591	38.1	1974	23 699	35 759	39.9
Réunion	1974	10 595	12 205	46.5	1982	16 414	19 440	45.8
Seychelles	1971	1 143	1 604	41.6	1977	748	1 185	38.7
South Africa	1980	328 113	635 119	34.1	1985	648 273	1 206 287	35.0
Swaziland	1976	13 906	12 554	52.6	1986	14 694	17 049	46.3
United Republic of Tanzania	1967	207 202	244 543	45.9	1978	196 496	219 188	47.3

Source: United Nations, International Migrant Stock: Africa.
[a]Data refer to foreign population.

TABLE 119. FOREIGN-BORN WOMEN IN SELECTED AFRICAN COUNTRIES, BY AGE
(Percentage)

		0-14	15-54	55+
Botswana[a]	1971	34.8	55.8	9.4
	1981	32.8	59.4	7.8
Congo	1974	24.7	70.1	5.2
	1984	21.4	73.8	4.9
Seychelles	1971	41.6	49.6	8.7
	1977	27.7	60.9	11.4
		0-19	20-59	60+
Réunion	1967	40.0	54.4	5.6
	1974	36.9	57.8	5.3
	1982	35.1	59.3	5.6
Swaziland	1976	32.3	60.0	7.6
	1986	31.3	60.7	8.0
		0-19	20-54	55+
South Africa	1980	18.5	56.1	25.3
	1985	21.6	60.2	18.2
		0-14	15-64	65+
Zambia	1969	41.1	57.7	1.2
	1980	22.3	73.5	4.2

Source: United Nations, International Migrant Stock: Africa.
[a]Data refer to foreign population.

The greater concentration of migrant women in the central age group has been more than matched by a similar trend among migrant men and, consequently, the proportion of women among migrants in the working ages has tended to decline in most of the countries considered (table 120). The main exceptions are the Republic of South Africa and Zambia, where the proportion of women in age groups 20-54 and 15-64, respectively, increased from one census to the next. In South Africa, however, the proportion of women in the working ages remained at a very low level. Significantly, in South Africa as in most other countries, the proportion of women among migrants in the younger age group has been and remains relatively high. It appears therefore that the sex selectivity of migration is less pronounced among younger migrants, particularly among children.

This brief review of the data available on the participation of women in international migration within sub-Saharan Africa indicates that women have tended to be underrepresented among international migrants, especially in the main African countries of destination. Although data on labour migration per se are not available, it seems safe to conclude that policies favouring the admission of men as migrant workers have contributed to reduce the migration opportunities for women and are at the root of their relative underrepresentation among migrant stocks.

TABLE 120. PERCENTAGE OF WOMEN AMONG THE
FOREIGN-BORN POPULATION, BY AGE GROUP

		0-14	15-54	55+
Botswana[a]	1971	48.7	43.0	35.1
	1981	50.8	41.4	41.6
Congo	1974	52.8	51.5	40.2
	1984	52.6	50.4	45.4
Seychelles	1971	50.7	38.0	31.8
	1977	45.7	37.0	34.0
		0-19	*20-59*	*60+*
Réunion	1967	55.5	45.3	34.0
	1974	51.4	46.6	37.7
	1982	49.0	44.9	42.2
Swaziland	1976	51.2	54.3	46.0
	1986	46.8	46.0	46.7
		0-19	*20-54*	*55+*
South Africa	1980	47.8	28.3	44.6
	1985	48.0	30.1	44.2
		0-14	*15-64*	*65+*
Zambia	1969	50.1	44.2	41.8
	1980	50.2	47.8	40.5

Source: United Nations, International Migrant Stock: Africa.
[a]Data refer to foreign population.

Yet, even if subject to greater constraints than migrant men, women constitute significant proportions of all migrants and the number of women migrating between African countries is growing. Indeed, the data analysed so far generally fail to reflect the other type of migration that has been common in Africa during the post-colonial period, namely, the movement of refugees. As of early 1993 there were 5.4 million refugees in Africa and although little is known about their distribution by sex, it is generally acknowledged that women constitute a major component of refugee flows within the continent (UNHCR, 1993). Clearly, better documentation of women's participation in all types of international migration flows would go a long way in calling attention to the major role that women play in the migration process.

A. MIGRATION TO AND FROM NIGERIA

Although Nigeria is the most populous country in Western Africa, until 1970 it had not figured prominently as a destination for citizens from other countries in the region. However, the lack of reliable demographic data that has characterized Nigeria during most of this century precludes the possibility of assessing the true extent of migration to that country. Migration originating in Nigeria is somewhat better documented. Thus, it is estimated that around 1975 there were some 116,000 Nigerians living in other Western African countries (Zachariah and Condé, 1981). Most Nigerian migrants were concentrated in what were then the main attraction poles of migration within the region, namely, Ghana and Côte d'Ivoire, which hosted, respectively, 56,000 and 50,000 Nigerians. Given its population size, Nigeria was the source of relatively few migrants, especially when compared with countries like Burkina Faso, which accounted for 956,000 international migrants in Western Africa around 1975, Mali with 396,000 or even Togo with 260,000 (Zachariah and Condé, 1981).

During the 1960s, developments in one of the main receiving countries of Nigerian migrants, Ghana, further contributed to reduce enticements for the migration of Nigerians. Like other newly independent African States, Ghana began to require residence and work permits from foreigners living and working in its territory. In November 1969 the Government issued an Aliens Compliance Order authorizing expulsion from Ghana of all foreigners who had not obtained the required permits. It has been estimated that at least 200,000 foreigners left Ghana within six months of the Order's issuance (United Nations, 1979). Nigerians were one of the most severely affected groups. Thus, the Nigerian population enumerated by the censuses of Ghana declined from 191,800 in 1960 to only 55,500 in 1970. Although it is likely that foreigners may have evaded enumeration in 1970 and that the figures yielded by the census may understate the true size of the foreign population left in Ghana, sizeable return flows undoubtedly occurred.

As table 121 indicates, women constituted an important part of the return flows that took place.

TABLE 121. NIGERIANS ENUMERATED BY TWO CENSUSES OF
GHANA, BY SEX AND PLACE OF BIRTH

	1960	1970	Difference
Nigerian men	107 507	33 114	74 393
Born in Ghana	39 603	12 757	26 846
Born abroad	67 904	20 357	47 547
Nigerian women	84 295	22 425	61 870
Born in Ghana	37 760	11 214	26 546
Born abroad	46 535	11 211	35 324
Percentage of women			
Nigerian population .	43.9	40.4	45.4
Born in Ghana	48.8	46.8	49.7
Born abroad	40.7	35.5	42.6

Sources: Ghana, Census Office, *1960 Population Census of Ghana*, vol. III: *Demographic Characteristics of Local Authorities, Regions and Total Country* (Accra, 1964), table 11; Ghana, Census Office, *1970 Population Census of Ghana*, vol. III: *Demographic Characteristics of Local Authorities, Regions and Total Country* (Accra, 1975), table C13.

Thus, the female population of Nigerian origin in Ghana declined by nearly 62,000 between 1960 and 1970. Some 57 per cent of that decline was accounted for by a reduction of the population of Nigerian origin born outside Ghana (presumably in Nigeria itself), and the rest corresponded to reductions in the number of Nigerian women born in Ghana. In general, women tended to be better represented among the latter group, and because women tended to be somewhat overrepresented in the return flow of Nigerians, the proportion of women among Nigerian migrants who were still in Ghana by 1970 tended to be lower than had been the case a decade earlier.

During the 1970s, major economic changes within Western Africa and at the global level had important implications for international migration in the region. One such change was the rise of oil prices that took place in 1973 and which contributed to fuel an economic boom in Nigeria, an oil-rich country. As a result, the country became an important attraction pole for international migrants from the region, most of whom entered Nigeria under the terms of a protocol of the Economic Community of West African States, which allows the free movement of nationals of member States within the region but at that time

did not allow long-term residence of migrants nor their exercise of an economic activity in countries other than their own. During the boom years, the presence of such undocumented migrants was tacitly allowed by Nigerian authorities but, during the early 1980s, as oil prices went into decline, undocumented migrants were increasingly seen as a burden. In January 1983, the Government of Nigeria decided to expel all illegal aliens then in its territory. According to press reports, over one million migrants, mostly Ghanaian, left Nigeria within a couple of months (United Nations, 1985). Press sources noted that most were "young men". There is reason to doubt the accuracy of the figures cited and, given the lack of reliable statistics on migrant flows in the region, the true number of migrants expelled will never be known. However, for our purposes, it is important to note that by the early 1980s Nigeria had become an important country of destination, particularly for Ghanaian migrants whose country was experiencing economic difficulties.

B. A SURVEY OF WOMEN WHO MIGRATED FROM GHANA TO NIGERIA

Given the general paucity of information on female international migration in Western Africa in general and that directed to Nigeria in particular, a purposive survey was carried out in 1989 among a group of migrant women in Nigeria. A total of 102 migrant women were interviewed, all but 2 living in Ogbomoso. Because the sample used was not drawn on the basis of probabilistic principles, it is not representative of international female migrants in Nigeria. However, the information obtained is useful in furthering an understanding of the migration process from the female perspective and in suggesting hypotheses to be tested in future research on the subject.

Among the 102 women interviewed, 68 were Nigerians who had returned from Ghana and, consequently, will be henceforth identified as returnees. The rest (34) were Ghanaian women who had migrated to Nigeria. Because the characteristics and experiences of each group differ significantly, they will be discussed separately below.

Nigerian female returnees

Among the female returnees interviewed, slightly over half (52 per cent) had returned because of Ghana's Aliens Compliance Order of 1969; 38 per cent had returned for family or domestic reasons; and the remaining 10 per cent were compelled to return to Nigeria by Ghana's worsening economic situation. Most had returned to Nigeria during the 1960s (91 per cent), and the rest had done so during the 1970s. That is, both their original emigration from Nigeria and the return had occurred, in most cases, at least 20 years before the interview, so that the likelihood of recall errors or rationalization in providing information was high.

As table 122 shows, most returnees had spent lengthy periods in Ghana. Indeed, 25 per cent reported having spent at least 20 years abroad, 27 per cent had been abroad between 10 and 19 years, and the largest group (47 per cent) had spent between 5 and 9 years in Ghana. Given that 92 per cent of the returnees were under age 30 at the time of return, most were very young women or even children when they left Nigeria to settle in Ghana. Their relatively young age distribution when they returned to the home country implied that a high proportion were still single at the time of return (24 per cent). Their life in Ghana seemed to have opened relatively few opportunities for self-improvement, since upon return a full 67 per cent declared that they had had no schooling and only 12 per cent had gone beyond primary school. The range of occupations in which returnees engaged in was narrow, both while they were in Ghana and in Nigeria. Most returnees were engaged in petty trade, working on their own account as part of the informal sector (see table 122). Only 5 of the 68 returnees interviewed had white collar jobs in Ghana and, upon return, in Nigeria (though it need not be the same 5 women in both cases).

With respect to the immediate reason for returning to Nigeria, practically all the female returnees who were married at the time of return reported that they wished to accompany or join their husbands. The remaining women were equally divided among those who returned accompanying relatives (13 per cent) and those who went back because of job opportuni-

TABLE 122. NIGERIAN FEMALE RETURNEES: SELECTED CHARACTERISTICS

	Female returnees	
	Number	Per-centage
Year of arrival in Nigeria		
1960-1969	62	91
1970-1979	6	9
TOTAL	68	100
Years spent away from Nigeria		
1-4	1	2
5-9	28	47
10-14	7	12
15-19	9	15
20+	15	25
TOTAL	60	100
Age at the time of return		
15-19	13	22
20-24	13	22
25-29	29	48
30-44	5	8
TOTAL	60	100
Marital status at the time of return		
Single	16	24
Married	51	76
TOTAL	67	100
Educational attainment just before return		
No schooling	46	67
Primary schooling	15	22
Post-primary	8	12
TOTAL	69	100
Occupation before return		
Farming.................................	2	3
Petty trading	40	60
Crafts, sewing, hairdressing etc. ...	12	18
Teaching, office work	5	7
Housewife	6	9
Student..................................	2	3
TOTAL	67	100
Occupation after return		
Petty trading	44	76
Crafts, sewing, hairdressing etc. ...	8	14
Teaching, office work	5	9
Housewife	1	2
TOTAL	58	100

ties available in Nigeria (13 per cent). Regarding the decision to work and the type of work female returnees engaged in, the majority (67 per cent) reported that they had made decisions by themselves and 28 per cent said that it was a joint decision with their husband. Interestingly, all returnees said that they had sole control of their income and resources.

Returnees cited few benefits obtained from migration. Over half of the female returnees said that their time abroad had allowed them to master a language different from that of their home community (53 per cent), 28 per cent said that the lifestyle they had had while in Ghana was better, and 19 per cent commented that migration had allowed them to know other places. Virtually all female returnees (96 per cent) reported that their status at the time of interview was worse than it had been in Ghana. When asked to list important items that they had brought back from Ghana, 87 per cent mentioned clothes; 76 per cent, jewellery; 65 per cent mentioned cash, and only 35 per cent referred to household items. These responses suggest that a good deal of rationalization is taking place among returnees. Since most of them were young women with very low levels of educational attainment when they returned to Nigeria, it is unlikely that they would have accumulated sufficient savings or that they would have had the income necessary to buy anything but common consumer goods. Furthermore, their view that their position was better prior to return does not take into account the changes that have taken place in both Ghana and Nigeria during the past 20 years. Given the economic problems that both countries have faced, it is not certain that Nigerian women would have been much better off if they had stayed in Ghana.

Ghanaian female migrants in Nigeria

Most of the 34 Ghanaian female migrants interviewed in Nigeria had migrated to that country since 1970 (91 per cent), and by the time of interview all but 3 per cent had spent at least 5 years in Nigeria (see table 123). Indeed, 81 per cent had been in Nigeria between 5 and 14 years already. Although none of the Ghanaian women interviewed had migrated above age 40, the age distribution of Ghanaian female migrants at the time of migration was skewed towards older ages, with the modal age group being 30-34, and 54 per cent of all migrants being concentrated in age group 25-34. Given their

TABLE 123. GHANAIAN FEMALE MIGRANTS IN NIGERIA: SELECTED CHARACTERISTICS

	Ghanaian female migrants	
	Number	Per-centage
Year of arrival in Nigeria		
1960-1969	3	9
1970-1979	15	44
1980-1989	16	47
TOTAL	34	100
Years spent in Nigeria		
1-4	1	3
5-9	13	39
10-14	14	42
15+	5	15
TOTAL	33	100
Age at the time of migration		
15-19	3	9
20-24	6	18
25-29	7	21
30-34	11	33
35-39	6	18
TOTAL	33	100
Age at the time of interview		
15-29	3	9
30-34	4	12
35-39	9	26
40-44	13	38
45+	5	15
TOTAL	34	100
Marital status at the time of return		
Single	3	9
Married	30	88
Other	1	3
TOTAL	34	100
Educational attainment just before return		
No schooling	2	6
Primary schooling	7	21
Post-primary	25	74
TOTAL	34	100
Occupation before return		
Petty trading	5	15
Crafts, sewing, hairdressing etc.	8	24
Teaching, office work	13	38
Housewife	6	18
Student	2	6
TOTAL	34	100
Occupation after return		
Petty trading	10	29
Crafts, sewing, hairdressing etc.	9	26
Teaching, office work	11	32
Housewife	4	12
TOTAL	34	100

lengthy periods of residence in Nigeria and their relatively high ages at the time of migration, Ghanaian female migrants were relatively old at the time of interview, with 80 per cent being over age 35.

Because they were older at the time of migration, Ghanaian migrants were generally married by then (91 per cent) and some were already divorced, separated or widowed (3 per cent). In contrast with female Nigerian returnees, Ghanaian female migrants showed higher levels of educational attainment. Thus, only 6 per cent had had no schooling before migration and a full 74 per cent had gone beyond primary school. Their intermediate levels of educational attainment resulted in a relatively favourable occupational distribution, both before and after migration. Thus, 32 per cent worked in white-collar jobs in Nigeria, and 46 per cent worked in occupations typical of the informal sector. Although the latter percentage was slightly higher than that before migration, the numbers are too small to attach much importance to such differences.

When asked about the reason for migrating, about three of every four Ghanaian women reported that they did so to accompany or join their husband, but the quarter remaining declared that they had migrated in search of better job opportunities. About half of the Ghanaian women interviewed said that they had taken the decision to work on their own and 44 per cent said that it was a joint decision with their husbands. Although a large number of the migrant women interviewed did not report whether they had sole control over their income or not, 87 per cent of those who did said that they exercised such control. Only 13 per cent said that they shared control with their husbands. In fact, 72 per cent of the Ghanaian women interviewed reported that they kept separate accounts from those of their husbands.

Regarding the perceived benefits of migration, about 40 per cent of the Ghanaian female migrants reported "comfort and happiness", 27 per cent reported that they valued the opportunity to learn Yoruba, and another 27 per cent said that they had gained greater freedom to do what they wanted. The other responses put forward had few adherents. On the whole, Ghanaian women were satisfied with the results of migration, with 77 per cent declaring that

their status at the time of interview was better than before migration.

Although Ghanaian female migrants had remained away from their home country for a number of years, they still sent remittances to their families. Thus, 97 per cent of the Ghanaian women interviewed said that they sent remittances, though 82 per cent said that they sent them only occasionally and only 6 per cent sent them regularly. Furthermore, 85 per cent declared that they sent "just a little" of their income, and 9 per cent reported that they sent nothing. Some 55 per cent had at some point discussed with their husbands the sending of remittances, 23 per cent had always done so, and the rest had never done so. Most of the women sent remittances to their parents (87 per cent) or to relatives (10 per cent). Remittances were generally used to care for parents (59 per cent) or children (7 per cent), but in 35 per cent of the cases, they were put into savings.

C. CONCLUSION

Female migration in sub-Saharan Africa has many facets. The general review of women's participation in international migration within the continent suggests that African women have continued to be constrained from becoming migrants even after the end of colonial rule. Thus, the proportion of women among African migrants present in the major receiving countries of the region has tended to be relatively low, even though increases have been recorded in recent periods. Although there is little evidence relating the status of African women to their participation in international migration, factors that increase women's dependency on their male kin are likely to reduce their capacity to migrate internationally, especially in contexts where the migration of dependants is discouraged or even banned.

Although the survey undertaken is not representative of female migrants in Nigeria, it nevertheless shows that women have agency. Thus, most Nigerian returnees, as well as most Ghanaian migrants, engaged in some sort of economic activity and well over half of them reported that they had made the decision to work on their own. It is also noteworthy that most of the women interviewed, whether return-ees or migrants, reported that they had control over the income that they earned. Yet, despite those signs of relative independence, women still tended to re-port that their migration had primarily been prompted by the need to accompany or join their husbands or families. That is, female migrants saw themselves as "followers" of men and probably accorded less im-portance to their own economic activities than to those of their male kin. Indeed, despite their high level of economic activity, female migrants probably earned fairly low incomes; at least, the Ghanaian migrants interviewed seemed to have difficulty in setting aside enough money to send back home.

The contrasting experience of female returnees and Ghanaian migrants in Nigeria serves to illustrate both the heterogeneity of migration and the selectiv-ity that it entails. The returnees, who were mostly very young women at the time of return, were generally compelled to return to Nigeria because of Ghanaian policies and the deteriorating economic situation in that country. Ghanaian migrants, in contrast, opted for migration without official com-pulsion and were more likely to be responsive to the opportunities available in the country of destination. Consequently, they tended to be more selected in terms of skills or educational background. Among the small group of women interviewed, the human capital characteristics of Ghanaian female migrants were better than those of Nigerian returnees. The former were therefore more likely to reap the ben-efits of migration than their Nigerian counterparts, as was reflected by their higher degree of satisfaction with the outcome of migration.

Although tentative in nature, the survey results discussed above suggest that women are likely to benefit from international migration provided they and their families can make informed decisions and the host society provides opportunities for migrants to use their skills. There remains, however, much that needs to be known about female migration in Africa. As the case of the Nigerian returnees illus-trates, migration has a long history in the continent, and it has likely marked the lives of considerably more people than those being recorded by censuses as being born abroad. In depth studies of interna-tional migration in Africa and its impact on women, men and the families they belong to are sorely needed.

REFERENCES

Abumere, S. I. (1988). Changing patterns of population movements and economic development in the ECOWAS region. African Population Conference, Dakar, pp. 4.1.1-4.1.15.
Ravenstein, E. G. (1885). The laws of migration. *Journal of the Royal Statistical Society* (London), vol. 48, No. 2 (June), pp. 167-235.
Sudarkassa, N. (1977). Women and migration in contemporary West Africa. In *Women and National Development: The Complexities of Change*, Wellesley Editorial Committee, ed. Chicago: Univer-sity of Chicago Press.
United Nations (1979). *Trends and Characteristics of International Migration since 1950.* Sales No. E.78.XIII.5.
_____ (1985). *World Population Trends, Population and Development Interrelations and Population Policies: 1983 Moni-toring Report*, vol. 1. Sales No. E.84.XIII.10.
_____ (1993). International Migrant Stock: Africa.
United Nations High Commissioner for Refugees (UNCHR) (1993). *The State of the World's Refugees*. New York: Penguin Books.
Zachariah, K. C., and Julien Condé (1981). *Migration in West Africa: Demographic Aspects*. New York: Oxford University Press.

Litho in United Nations, New York
03497—February 1995—4,850
ISBN 92-1-151281-6

United Nations publication
Sales No. E.95.XIII.10
ST/ESA/SER.R/126